Pushing the Envelope:
a life of love and adventure

ALDINE von ISSER

Pushing the Envelope: Attempting to extend the limits of an aircraft's performance—or to go beyond commonly accepted boundaries.

MY STORIES

Alex, Tana, Aldine & Max - 2017

This memoir is a reflection of my life which I will tell as stories. My primary purpose in writing it was to provide my grandchildren with memories of their Nana and to tell them about the extraordinary life I led for a woman of those times. A secondary gain was the enormous pleasure I found in recalling significant moments of my life and in rekindling memories of people I loved.

Dedicated to my grandchildren

Tana Jay von Isser
William Maxwell von Isser
Josef Alexander von Isser

If I had to choose between loving you and breathing, I would use my last breath to tell you I love you.

Nana

Table of Contents

Part One – My Life

Part Two – My Travels

PART ONE

MY LIFE

1

❦

MY CHILDHOOD

The Sinclair Family: Murray Sr., Aldine Jr., Aldine Sr., Carol & Murray Jr.

Too often it is in retrospect that we come to appreciate our parents and our childhoods. This has been the case with me. In writing this memoir I have renewed my deep gratitude for the parents who brought me up and the manner in which I was raised. As children we are typically oblivious to the love bestowed upon us and the sacrifices made for us. I have been blessed through writing these episodes of my life to have the opportunity not only to review my life but also to restore my bond with my incredible parents, Aldine and Murray Sinclair.

Carol, Murray & Aldine with dog Peppy - 1942

Both my parents were born in Toronto, Ontario, Canada — as were I, my older brother Murray and my younger sister Carol. As a young man, my father was a member of the Argonaut Rowing Club in Toronto when rowing was a very popular sport worldwide. It demanded his absolute commitment to his team. They once vied in the Olympics. When the coach heard that Dad was courting a young lady, he issued an ultimatum. Either my father was to give up rowing or give up his girlfriend. He opted for the former and married my mother on July 27, 1929.

I came into the world at Toronto General Hospital on May 29, 1933. For most of my early years we lived on Anderson Avenue in Toronto, near Eglinton and Avenue Roads. I went to Oriole Park School and faithfully attended Timothy Eaton Memorial Church. I come from Scottish ancestry the influence of which was a pervasive part of my upbringing. As children we knew our limits, stayed within them, and lived peacefully and happily.

My parents were not demonstrative but we children learned that a loving look can be as much a caress as any physical touching. A look from them could also signal significant disapproval and was to be assiduously avoided. They were firm in applying discipline, but the parameters of appropriate behavior were clearly delineated. If we stepped outside those boundaries it was at our own risk.

My mother was born Margery Aldine Eagen on February 7, 1908 and died in Tucson from colon

Aldine & Murray - 1938

cancer on October 22, 1994. She was of Irish heritage—a grounded woman, unflappable and totally devoted to her family. During the time my siblings and I were youngsters, our mother stayed home. In those days, children typically went home from school for lunch and mothers were expected to be there. Later in life she became one of Tucson's finest real estate brokers, certainly the most highly respected. You will learn in reading these stories what a truly remarkable woman she was. She has always been my role model.

Mother - 1935

My father was born in Cabbagetown in Toronto on September 23, 1904. He died in Tucson of emphysema and related health issues on June 1, 1984. Dad was from a Scottish family of limited means. He had only a high school education but was a man of broad knowledge with an impeccable memory—a great asset for a newspaper reporter, which was to be his life's work. Dad could conduct an interview taking only a few notes, return to his office and write the story with accurate quotations.

Dad - 1929

He was my hero, as is so often the case for girls. I adored him. I remember that as a child a daily highlight for me was waiting at the bus stop for my father at the end of the day. I would walk with him the two blocks to our home. I was allowed this ritual even in the dead of the cold Canadian winters. Some days I almost froze but I would wait sometimes as long as an hour as bus after bus arrived, knowing that eventually my father would step off one of them.

Aldine - 1939 age 6

There is little question that my father was on his way to becoming an important reporter on the *Toronto Daily Star* when he became very ill in 1938. He developed pneumonia that quickly became life-threatening asthma. He was told by doctors that he would not survive another winter in Toronto and to start looking for a warmer climate in which to live with the hope that his health would improve. This was encouraged by his superiors at the newspaper, Harry Hindmarsh and Joe Atkinson. They were incredibly kind and supported our family throughout this quest.

During his search, my father was away from home a great deal of the time which was very hard on me. I missed him terribly. Wanting to remain in Canada, he first tried

the Okanogan Valley in British Columbia. That was not effective. Then he went to Pinehurst, North Carolina followed by Biloxi, Mississippi. None helped. He remained very ill.

Finally in 1943 my father came to Tucson, Arizona—a town of about 25,000 inhabitants and very far from home. He found a little inn called Christopher Square at 1035 E. Mabel Street. Its purpose was to provide a home for "gentle" people who were without their families and needed a place to stay. This philanthropy was one of many by a remarkable woman whom we came to know well—Helen D'Autremont. She also donated the land for the Desert Sanitarium which is now Tucson Medical Center.

Dad in Pinehurst, NC-1943

My father lived at The Square for two years and made friends with fascinating people there—for example, scholars, authors, artists and musicians. Over time, Dad's health improved and he was able to accept a job as the Associated Press correspondent for southern Arizona. It was 1945 and time to have his family with him.

My mother was a heroine. Our move to Tucson required her to leave the only home she had ever known, Toronto, as well as her family with whom she was very close. In preparation for our arrival, Dad had rented a beautiful house located in the Sam Hughes district, a

Christmas in Toronto - 1943

historic neighborhood near the University of Arizona. We all loved it immediately. My parents tried but failed to buy it from its reluctant owner. We lived there for five years, at which time my parents built a house in another historic neighborhood—San Clemente—that was further east in Tucson. We moved into it in the late summer of 1950 and it was there we had my wedding reception 2 ½ years later.

My father was never well but rarely complained and worked in journalism until shortly before his death. My mother devoted her life to his well-being. At age 56 my father was diagnosed with colon cancer. Both of my parents suffered this fate. Dad had to have a colostomy which was the bane of his existence ever after.

After many years with the Associated Press, Dad transitioned to becoming a reporter for the *Arizona Daily Star* where he worked for the remainder of his life. He loved to write, as you will see in the chapters ahead, and spent hours every day at his typewriter. He used only three fingers for typing but was as fast on the keyboard as anyone I have ever seen.

My father was well known in Tucson for a column that was published three times a week on the front page of the second section of the *Star*. For many years this column touched the hearts of its many readers drawing laughter as well as tears. He was a fine journalist with a unique style. He was a member

Aldine - Toronto Age 11

of the Session at St. Mark's Presbyterian Church. His primary passion, however, was his family for whom he sacrificed so much. One could never ask for a finer or more moral father. He was a gentleman of great substance.

Our first house in Tucson - 1945
Carol, Murray, Aldine in front, Mom on the porch

In spite of limited means, we always lived in beautiful houses in Tucson. My brother and I were enrolled in Mansfeld Junior High School and my sister attended the well-known Sam Hughes School. I continued my education at Tucson Senior High, graduating in 1951. That September I began my freshman year at the University of Arizona (UA) where I joined the sorority of my choice, Kappa Kappa Gamma. I mentioned parental sacrifice at the beginning of this chapter. At the time I pledged Kappa, my parents could ill afford that extra expense. Without a word, they simply accepted that this was important to me and to my life. It was unspoken love.

My father received many accolades during his lifetime. One was an invitation to membership in the Literary Club, a small group of intellectual gentlemen who met once a month for dinner and to hear a colleague present his essay—a different member at each meeting. It was considered so private a group that there was a tacit understanding that it would not be mentioned even in one's obituary. (My husband Tony was a member as well.)

After my father died, The Little Chapel of All Nations was established on the University of Arizona campus at 1052 N. Highland Avenue. It was founded by a prominent Tucsonan, Ada Peirce McCormick, and since 1937 has hosted deep thinkers and soul searchers. It had been housed in many settings over the years. Now it had a permanent home, intended to draw people from all walks of life to a place for meditation and for study. Ada had been a friend of my parents as well as Tony's parents. What an honor my father received when the library there was named the Murray Sinclair Library. On its walls are portraits of my mother and of my father. I have served on the board there for many years and each time I enter the library for our meetings I never fail to reflect on what wonderful parents I had.

I'd like to add a bit more about my father's family. (My mother's life will emerge throughout the chapters ahead.) Dad was the middle child of three boys. Gordon, four years older than my father, was the eldest. Although he never completed his first year of high school, he became a very famous Canadian about whom people still talk today. He was an outspoken, opinionated newsman who went on to become the most renowned radio broadcaster Canada has ever known. People timed their days so that they could listen to Gordon Sinclair on CFRB Toronto at "ten to twelve" and again at "ten to six." He was on national television in Canada as well.

My father and Uncle Gordon worked at the *Toronto Star* at the same time as Ernest Hemingway. They did not like him, nor did Hemingway like the *Star*. It was from Toronto that he went to Paris and started writing in earnest.

I worked for Uncle Gordon at the *Star* during the summer of 1952 when I was 19 years old. What a fascinating experience! As my uncle was both revered and abhorred, the items sent to him by listeners as tokens of their feeling ran the gamut. One of my jobs was to open these gifts. One box might contain freshly baked banana bread wrapped in a tea towel. Many held dog poop. As I say, some loved him and others hated him.

He was the author of a well-known article called *"The Americans"* that had broad popularity in the United States at one point. It was widely revived following the September 11, 2001 attacks and again in 2005 in the devastating aftermath of Hurricane Katrina. (See Appendix 1) He was a recipient of the Order of Canada.

Uncle Gordon died on May 17, 1984 at age 83, three weeks before my father, having just signed another five-year contract with CFRB. He had just given his broadcast and then fell dead. On May 22nd there was a memorial service at Toronto's city hall and, as my brother said, there will never be another event in Canada to compare with it.

While my father was a gentle man, Uncle Gordon was bombastic. The third son was cut from a   different bolt of cloth entirely. George Sinclair came along when my father was 12 years old. They always had a very formal relationship. They did not dislike each other but they were reluctant to show emotion. I remember being with my father in a restaurant one summer when, quite by chance, we passed Uncle George. Dad said "George," and he said "Murray," as way of greeting. Each went on his way without another word. They hadn't seen each other for two years! Talk about Scottish understatement!

I was old enough during WWII to remember Uncle George as a dashing pilot with the RCAF. He flew 56 missions over Europe in a Lancaster bomber—an unheard of number of missions. The Lancaster was the most famous and the most successful of the WWII bombers but it was unheated and unpressurized. The crew wore oxygen masks that were attached to oxygen lines in the aircraft. Frequently these malfunctioned, froze, or were damaged in battle leaving the airmen without oxygen. Many died due to oxygen deprivation. It was the cause, also, of my uncle losing the sight in his right eye.

As Canada joined the war in 1939, I was involved in the spin-off from it from the time I was six until I was 12 years old. We had blackout curtains and regular air raid drills. Rationing was in force, but we took it as a matter of course that there was limited sugar and "butter" was white. Packets of color were available if we wanted to stir them in to make it yellow, but we didn't bother.

When I was old enough to go to Saturday afternoon matinees, I was subjected to seeing newsreels presented by Pathé News. They held nothing back in their effort to inform us about the atrocities taking place in Europe. Piles of bodies were shown at the crematoria in the concentration camps with smoking chimneys in the background. It was frightening for children to see these images but they brought home with clarity the reality of the world situation.

A tradition at movie theaters at that time in Toronto was to play "*The King*" at the end of each film. Everyone would stand with hand on heart to sing *God Save the King*. Elizabeth had not yet come to power. Often people were willing to miss the end of a movie to avoid this ritual. It should be added that movie theaters, stores and gas stations were not open on Sunday. In each region of Toronto, there was an assigned pharmacy and gas station available on an emergency basis. In my family, playing cards and the like was off limits.

In spite of setbacks, as they grew into men the three Sinclair boys were indomitable. They certainly came from strong Scottish blood. Uncle George, with limited education, went on to become President and then Chairman of the largest advertising firm in the

British Empire—McLaren Advertising. Advertising is a cut-throat business but Uncle George did it with finesse and charm. He grew to be a very wealthy man.

George had married his beautiful and gracious wife, Jane. It was the custom during WWII in Canada for young women to live with the parents of their husbands while they were away on duty even if their own parents lived in the same city. Jane dutifully

The brothers - Gordon, George & Murray - 1976

moved into the attic at the home of her parents-in-law, Bessie and Alexander (George) Sinclair—my grandparents—who were as dour a couple as you could ever meet. Jane was a saint!

The Sinclair men of all ages donned their kilts for all appropriate occasions—marriages as well as wakes and family reunions. No, they did not wear underwear beneath their kilts. There are three Sinclair tartans; my sister and I used a strip of the ancient tartan as ribbon for our bouquets at our weddings. Bagpipes continue to accompany all significant events.

There are many ways of saying the surname Sinclair. I grew up being Aldine Sinclair pronounced "sink-ler." In my determination to find out the definitive pronunciation, I dropped into a post office in the town of Wick in the far north of Scotland. Surely the postmaster there would have the answer as the Sinclair clan hailed from Wick. He affirmed that it was indeed "sink-ler" and when I asked if he were sure he said, "I should be. It's my name." Most of our family use a variation that is more easily understood. I stick with "sink-ler."

I am a product of the Sinclair clan with all its eccentricities and determination. As a result, mine has been an interesting and challenging life and for this I am grateful. (The Sinclair family tree is provided in Appendix 2.)

2

C3&80

MY EARLY EDUCATION

Even as a child I seemed to sense that "life is a journey and not a destination." (Ralph Waldo Emerson)

Through these writings, I have examined just what circumstances directed the paths I took in life. Although the "middle child syndrome" is not universally accepted, I know that I had to work a great deal harder to garner the attention of my parents than did my charismatic older brother or my adorable, curly haired blonde younger sister.

It was Beryl Markham who said, "I've sometimes thought that being loved a little less than others can actually make a person, rather than ruin them." That may have been true in my case.

Hence, I strove in my early years to please my parents by bringing home excellent report cards, spelling all the words correctly on the Friday spelling tests, and so forth. This seemed to delight them, and excellence in academic performance became a way of life for me.

I began kindergarten in 1938 and completed my Ph.D. in 1974. That constitutes a great many years of academic pursuit!

My years in elementary school in Canada went smoothly but our move to Arizona came when I was ready to enter junior high school and the path became rather rocky. In Canada there were rigid standards that established comfortable boundaries. Even in public school, we wore uniforms—navy blue pinafores with white blouses. The girls formed one line to enter school through the girls' entrance, while the boys lined up at their entrance.

Suddenly I was at Mansfeld Junior High in Tucson, and I simply did not fit in. I was the recipient of a great deal of taunting because I looked different and I spoke differently. Such comments as, "Did you live in an igloo?" reverberated against the walls in the stairwells as we changed classes. It wasn't a happy time for me.

Tucson Senior High was a different matter entirely. I could pour myself into studying Latin, which I took from the two Miss Butts (as did Tony in his years there before me), Spanish, chemistry and botany. I loved it. And to be sure that I fit in, I joined every club of interest to me which included:

Science Club (Bi-Chem-Phi)
Allied Youth (against alcohol)
El Cervantes (Spanish Club)
Sophomore Tennis Club
Tennis Squad
Honor Service Society
National Honor Society
Junior Guard
Senior Follies Committee
Tucson Hi (Tucson High Y.W.C.A. group)
G.A.A. (Girls Athletic Association)
T-Club (for girls earning major letters in sports)
Decoration Committee (for all big dances)
Spring Dance Program
Tucsonian Staff (Tucson High School Year Book)

Graduation - 1951

I am sure there were more but I write them here more as a reminder to myself of how very hard I tried to be accepted and to feel myself valued. Achieving became my default mode and has stayed with me throughout life.

My diaries remind me that I had quite a few boyfriends and even experimented with kissing. My parents were rigid about whom I could see and who was off limits. When the time came, I was ready for university and the next adventure.

It had been my dream to pledge Kappa Kappa Gamma sorority and I did. I soon met and married the love of my life, Anthony Kent von Isser.

3

⚮

MEETING ANTHONY KENT von ISSER

Bedazzled is the word that comes to mind when I think of my first meeting with my husband-to-be, Anthony Kent von Isser. It was for me love at first sight.

My freshman year at the University of Arizona began in September, 1951 and I met Tony on November 2nd. It was his last semester at UA. He majored in History.

Proper introductions were important back in those days. As it happens, a very lovely lady, Elaine Drury, was a friend both of Tony's father and of my parents. She felt the young people—Tony and I— should meet. Mrs. Drury was a widow and the daughter of the former Governor General of Newfoundland, Canada—Sir Richard Squires and his wife Lady Helen Squires. You can already infer that the dinner party for the introduction would be a formal affair. And it was.

Tony as a boy - 1940

In drawing us together, I think Mrs. Drury failed to take into account that Tony at 25 was seven years my senior, and a very sophisticated gentleman of the world. Tony had elegance, was a veteran of WWII, a world traveler, and had flown professionally for two airlines.

I was 18 and a high school graduate.

11

As planned, Tony picked me up at my home. As he came through our front door, I was instantly smitten. Here was this tall, handsome, charismatic gentleman with a smile that melted my heart.

It was an evening that will be forever etched in my mind. Another couple was there, Persis and Stephen Congdon, who later were in our wedding party. Steve was Tony's best friend. I was in awe of all these sophisticated people.

I didn't hear from Tony for quite some time afterward, but I really hadn't expected that I would. I was dating other young men at the university, and life was wonderful. Eventually Tony phoned and invited me out. That time it took! I later asked him why he ever phoned at all and he replied that "his upbringing demanded it." I was to hear that often over the years ahead.

We had the most interesting courtship a girl could want. We went spelunking (cave exploring), flying (about which you'll hear later), mountain climbing, motorcycling, panning for gold, camping and traveling. Many of our trips were to San Carlos, Mexico. Let me hasten to add that <u>every</u> time we went away together, on a trip or camping, we <u>always</u> had a chaperone or two. Yes, that is true. A good friend of Tony's father, Mary Lewis, was often our companion. She was a much older and very staid lady so these events were often rather stilted. Nonetheless, this arrangement insured that Tony and I would remain chaste until marriage, and we did. That would be practically unheard of nowadays, but that was the way it was back then—even for my worldly fiancée who was 26 years old when we were wed.

Tony on our camping trip to
Southern Belle Mine - 1953

Tony had left high school with his parents' permission at age 17. He joined the U.S. Navy and served in the Pacific for several years on an escort carrier called the *Tulagi*. He was a radioman—yes, in a radio shack. He also flew on strafing missions in aircraft sent off from the carriers. He did not like this part of the job.

Tony in the Navy - 1943

12

He developed a lifelong friendship with a buddy in the radio shack, Ed Vineyard. He and Tony were the same age. Ed had simple beginnings in Oklahoma but went on to become the president of Oklahoma University. He cared deeply for Tony, especially when Tony saw him through the grief of losing his only brother in the war. When word came to the *Tulagi* to advise Ed of this loss, Tony never left his side. When Tony was dying, Ed and his wife came all the way from Oklahoma to say goodbye.

Sadly, Tony was not in Tucson when his mother died suddenly in 1946. He arrived home two hours too late. When he was discharged from the Navy, he moved home to Tucson to live with his father. He delayed his education in order to travel to Europe for several months with his friend, William R. Mathews, Jr. You'll hear about that trip later.

He was a pilot for the Grand Canyon Airlines. He looked like a kid, which is what he was, and many people who had bought tickets for a scenic flight over the canyon looked first at Tony and then at the aircraft—a Travelair 6000—and turned in their tickets. Tony looked much too young to fly a plane, and the plane was so old it had wooden windows that could be raised and lowered!

In the summer, between semesters, he was a pilot with the Wien Alaska Airline and fell in love with Alaska. It was his intention to complete his university degree and move to Alaska permanently where there was a job waiting for him. Meeting me scotched that plan.

As I say, Tony was in his last semester at UA planning to complete his degree in December. He was to leave for Alaska in January. He tarried. Our courtship continued. He decided to get a job in Tucson and thought that Hughes Aircraft Company sounded like a good place to start. When filling out his application to become Personnel Director, he was embarrassed to have to ask the secretary how to spell "personnel." Georgia Lewis helped him out and they became the best of friends in the years to come. He got the job.

In April, only five months after we had met, he proposed. This momentous occasion happened on Mt. Lemmon under the General Hitchcock tree. I truly was not prepared for it but handled the situation with more finesse than I imagined I had. Tony said, "I wonder what you'd say if I asked you to marry me." "Well," said I, "I guess you'll never know if you don't ask." Gathering his courage, he formally proposed. Many another young woman had only dreamt of this opportunity as Tony was quite a catch.

I hedged somewhat, pointing out that I was only 18 and we hadn't known each other for long. I did agree to being "promised" and not engaged with the understanding that if, on November 2nd when we had known each other for a year, we still wanted to marry that I would accept with all my heart. He waited. My mother thought I was taking a terrible chance.

I received a beautiful engagement ring on November 2nd and married Tony on March 28, 1953 when I was 19 years old. That was the best decision I have ever made and I loved that precious man with all my heart until he died in 1989.

Understandably, my parents were initially reluctant to approve our courtship as I was so young. I think the turning point came one day while I was helping my father with an outdoor project. Our front doorbell rang. I need to step back and explain that I had been seeing other young men, too, one of whom was a dashing man named Gene Hamilton. Once when Tony was visiting, a florist had arrived with a delivery for me—a dozen long stemmed red roses from Gene. Tony was abashed but I reassured him that I would rather receive two dandelions from someone who mattered to me than a dozen

Count Josef Caspar Maximillian Isser von Gaudententhurm

red roses from anyone. Back to the doorbell. My father went to the door to find a florist holding a very elaborately decorated and beribboned box. He watched while I opened it and there inside were—yes—two dandelions. The note that came with it read, "I'd rather receive two dandelions from someone who cares than one dozen long stem roses from someone who doesn't. (Above quote from statement made by Aldine Sinclair) Love, Tony." Dad was won over.

I have to admit to being intimidated by Tony's father, the Count Josef Maximillian Caspar Isser von Gaudententhurm. He had a heavy German accent and was slow to smile. A graduate of Baliol College at Oxford, he was a scholar. His entire life was spent in reading and studying. He spoke seven languages fluently and read and wrote Latin. Additionally, he was a heel clicking and hand kissing nobleman which made my mother ill

Josef in front of his casita - 1954

at ease. Finally she said, "Joe, now that we are going to be seeing a great deal of each other could we just shake hands when we meet?"

When we became engaged, Tony's father very kindly turned over to us his charming little house on San Francisco Boulevard in Tucson to renovate and improve as we wanted. He moved next door to a pink casita that was more to his liking as he grew older. Tony's parents had met in Europe and were married in Ajaccio, Corsica when they were both forty years of age. Neither had been married previously and I wonder if Tony didn't come as a bit of a surprise. Hence, Tony grew up as an only child with much older parents than would be typical.

The days flew by for us with many parties being given in our honor. It was amazing how many friends Tony's father and my parents had in common given their disparate backgrounds and ages. One couple who had significant importance in Tony's life was Helen and Hubert D'Autremont. As Tony's mother was ill for many years and his father was fully engaged in caring for her, Tony, at age 11, had moved to Canelo, Arizona to live on a ranch with a childless couple. He had a great deal of responsibility for a boy his age, but managed to go on horseback every day to a one-room schoolhouse a few miles away. When the time came for high school, it was necessary for Tony to move to Tucson. As his parents were unable to care for him, he became the ward of the D'Autremont family. They lived only two miles from the home of Tony's parents so he saw a good deal of them.

Mr. D'Autremont was the founder of the Southern Arizona Bank and Trust Company which now bears the name Chase Bank. They owned the property at the intersection of Grant and Craycroft Roads which they donated so The Desert Sanitarium could be built. It now is called Tucson Medical Center.

They were definitely of the old school and I knew that Mrs. D'Autremont would be "calling" soon after we were married so I was prepared to receive her calling card on the essential silver salver which was placed on a table near the front door. Brides were expected to "receive" at four o'clock each day and to serve tea to guests. And indeed Mrs. D'Autremont was my first caller. Young ladies are not burdened with these kinds of traditions in today's society but I had to follow the rules back then.

The D'Autremonts had a lovely party for us as did several other couples I'll mention. Dickson and Sue Potter were a charming Southern couple who had moved to Tucson for the health of their son Clifford who became Tony's close friend. They also had a daughter, Suzanne, for whom they could not find an appropriate school. There were many boys' schools here, many of them residential, but none for girls. So the Potters decided to start one. It was called The Potter School and was built close to their beautiful home. It drew young ladies from across the country who were in need of living in Tucson for their health. One of these was my dearest friend, Katherine Worth Altaffer, who came to Tucson without her family because of severe asthma.

Tony became involved with the school for many reasons, not the least of which was that he was needed for the Potter School dances and recruited to be an appropriate escort. He became very close to the Potter family. He flew in his own plane to Santa Barbara to be Cliff's best man when he married his lovely bride Sylvie. He sat beside

Walter Pidgeon at the reception dinner. On returning to Tucson late at night, he ran very low on fuel somewhere over rural California and knew he was going to be in serious trouble if he didn't get help. So he repeatedly buzzed a small town with hopes they had a landing strip. This was a recognized procedure indicating that a pilot was very much in need of fuel. The man in charge of the strip dutifully rose from his bed, dressed and went out to the airport to light the airstrip so Tony could land and refuel his aircraft. He made it back to Tucson safely.

The Potters had a beautiful reception for Tony and me. The Potters are gone now and their lovely estate is now known as Potter Place across from the Arizona Inn on Elm Street.

Another very special couple who feted us was Ada Peirce McCormick and her husband Fred. They both held special places in the hearts of both Tony's family and mine. Tony was honored to be a pallbearer for them both. Ada's lovely old estate is now known as McCormick Place. She was the founder of The Little Chapel of All Nations which is situated on the university campus and on whose board I have served for many years. It houses the "Murray Sinclair Library" in which hangs a handsome painting of my father as well as a lovely photograph of my mother taken by our son Kent. It is nondenominational and houses a chapel that can be entered at any time of the day or night for quiet contemplation or prayer. It is operated by a philanthropic group that supports projects that fit within the parameters of Ada's wishes.

Ada was eccentric. She talked to herself. People driving past her in their cars would see a woman involved in an animated conversation—with herself. She always wore sneakers. There is a wonderful story concerning her brother. He had set sail on a large liner from New York Harbor on his way to Europe. When he was two miles out to sea he realized he was leaving behind the woman he truly loved. It occurred to him that he couldn't live without her and so he dived from the ship into the ocean and swam the two miles back to shore. They were married shortly thereafter.

Tony & Aldine - 1953

My parents' friends had showers for the bride and I was well supplied with lingerie items and kitchen utensils. And, of course, our friends had parties for us too, so we were well-celebrated as an engaged couple.

As I have said, my father was a strict Scot and I was quite unprepared for a little talk he had with me prior to the wedding. He advised me that when I was married he and my mother would never lend me money, never give

16

me advice, and never could I come home again to live. I stayed within the confines of those rules always. It became clear to me over time that this edict was never laid on my brother and sister.

Our wedding day - March 28, 1953

Tony and I were married at St. Mark's Presbyterian Church in Tucson by our beloved minister, Dr. Paul David Sholin on March 28, 1953. My bridesmaid was my precious sister Carol who was then all of 14 years old. The maids of honor were Persis Congdon, Susan White, and Teta Martyn. Tony's best man was Stephen Congdon and his ushers were William H. Woodin, William R. Mathews, Jr., Benjamin Hawkes, John P. Adams, and Thacher Loring. Sadly, of all in our wedding party, only Bill Woodin, Carol and I, are still living.

Our wedding reception was held in the patio of my parents' home. We went from there to our little home on the desert where we spent our first night together.

Wedding reception - with our parents

Two days later we left on our honeymoon. Our first destination was Mexico City but there were no non-stop flights in those days. We flew in a DC3 with seven stops en route. People even brought their chickens (in coops) on board and we seemed never to be without screaming children. It was a long, exhausting journey.

We loved exploring Mexico City and went from there to Acapulco. It truly was a sleepy little fishing village in those days. I remember being

Honeymoon in Acapulco - 1953

horrified at seeing what must have been dozens of big turtles on a wharf lying on their backs with their little legs flailing in the air. They were left there to die after which they would be made into green turtle soup. I must admit that soup was a delicacy and the bits of turtle meat were scrumptious, but I could never eradicate the vision of those suffering turtles.

There is a beach near Acapulco called Pie de la Cuesta. It is very, very dangerous. Of course, Tony and I were unaware of this and certainly there were no warning signs. The undertow there was the strongest I have ever known. I could not stand up in the water even to my ankles without being pulled out by the current. Tony, however, was undaunted and sure he could deal with the situation. We noticed Mexicans approaching and sitting on the dune above us—watching. I am sure they were expecting to see the death of a gringo that day. It came close. Tony was swept out almost immediately upon stepping into the water and only his cool mind and strong swimming stroke saved his life. I almost became a widow on my honeymoon!

We returned to Tucson—I to finish the semester at UA (we were married during spring break) and Tony to return to Hughes. Our normal married life began, and we were blissfully happy. Prior to approving Tony's request for my hand in marriage, my father had one caveat. I must finish my university education. That was my goal.

I resumed my studies at UA continuing with my chosen major—journalism. During my brief stint in this field, I was Associate Editor of the *Kitty Kat*, UA's student humor magazine, and was a reporter for the *Arizona Daily Wildcat*, UA's newspaper that was founded in 1899. However, I was unable to continue in journalism as it was not possible to fulfill the schedule that program imposed on its students and still hope to lead a normal married life. In those years, young women typically chose a conventional path toward a profession limited primarily to teaching, nursing, or becoming a secretary. I had no interest in any of these but selected teaching as it seemed a way I could make a living, if it were ever to become necessary, and have time in the summer with the children I hoped to have.

It had been our intention that the year following my graduation from UA would be spent traveling throughout Europe. Nature intervened, however, and I became pregnant. It was decided that pregnant or not, we would fulfill this dream. So I discontinued my studies at the university. Tony left his job, and with medical approval we set out for Europe when I was three   months along. The next chapter will tell the story of our remarkable experiences abroad. We returned to Tucson in time for the birth of our beloved son, Josef Kent, in the spring.

Tony had told me early in our relationship that he wanted two sons, heirs to the von Isser legacy and the future Count von Isser. Tony had assumed the title of Count after his father passed away. Our son Tony is the current Count. Tony also said he would like the birth of his first son to take place on our second wedding anniversary. My greatest joy in life was pleasing my husband and so it came to pass that our firstborn,

Proud mother (age 21)
and newborn Kent

Aldine holding Kent after
university graduation (B.A.) - 1956

Josef Kent von Isser came into the world on—yes—our second wedding anniversary, March 28, 1955. Two and a half years later our darling son Tony—Anthony K. von Isser—was born. I had fulfilled this obligation and had two sons whom I absolutely adored and who have been the light of my life.

Let me hasten to explain that women didn't typically plan to go to work. We attended university, met our husbands, married and stayed home to raise children. That is what I anticipated my life would be. To fill in the spaces, we would join the Junior League and serve our community. I did my part in the latter by founding the Childbirth Education Association of Tucson.

I fulfilled my father's wish to complete my education and eventually graduated for the last time in 1974 with a Ph.D. in education and psychology. He was so delighted that he decided a celebration was in order. Hence, he took the whole family to Tahiti about which you will read elsewhere.

4

ADVENTURES IN EUROPE WITH TONY

As I mentioned, life as Tony and I had planned it changed considerably when I learned I was pregnant in the summer of 1954. Tony had yearned to take me to Europe for an extended trip following the completion of my bachelor's degree. I thought that clearly was not to be, but Tony decided to simply move the plan forward, notwithstanding my "delicate condition."

We took stock of our finances, consulted the obstetrician and, finding no impediments to this plan, left for our trip to Europe on September 21st. After a big family dinner prepared by Tony's father, we went to the movies to fill in time. Friends took us to the train station and at 1:00 a.m., having been seated in the chair car, we departed Tucson. Without taking you through the whole excruciating journey, suffice that we slept poorly, ate badly, felt dirty, and I wondered why I had ever left home. With the exception of our honeymoon, I had never been away from home.

TORONTO—NEW YORK

Our first destination was Toronto for Tony to meet my family and see the sights of the city. There had been a subway added since I had lived there which impressed me greatly. Then it was on to New York for a visit with Katharine Merritt, Tony's godmother. That is when my morning sickness set in! The humidity was 98%, the hotel room was $10.00 per night, and I wanted to go home.

While Tony meandered through New York City drawing a great deal of attention wearing his Stetson hat, I remained in the awful hotel with morning sickness. Finally that night, our last in NYC, we met Katharine. She took us to her club, the Cosmopolitan Club. It was very formal and I found her manner austere. Since Katharine played a big part in our lives forever after, it is important for me to tell you more about her.

Katharine was one of two daughters, neither of whom had children, of the famous Schuyler Merritt after whom the Merritt Parkway was named. It was the first throughway—actually a National Scenic Byway— of its kind built in the U.S. and connected New York City and Connecticut. Schuyler Merritt had attended Yale and Columbia Law Schools and was a Republican Member of the U.S. House of Representatives from 1917 to 1931 and again from 1933 to 1937. The Merritt family lived in Stamford, Connecticut.

Katharine Krom Merritt - 1954

Katharine, born in 1884, attended Vassar College and was the roommate of Tony's mother, Dorothea Buhl King, also born in 1884.

When Katharine went off to school, her father extracted a promise from her—that she would not make any friends from "the West." He considered that pagan territory. As it happens, Dorothea was from Rochester, Michigan, definitely "the West." Katharine didn't keep her promise. They became the closest of friends.

Following their graduation in 1908, Dorothea struck out for Europe and a Bohemian lifestyle in France. Katharine, on the other hand, continued her education at Johns Hopkins where she went to medical school and became a pediatrician. Her father was dismayed that one of his daughters had gone into a "profession." In fact, she took a position at Columbia Presbyterian Hospital and was a part of the team that discovered the connection between German measles and birth defects.

Katharine was very wealthy and while in NYC lived in an impressive apartment at 439 East 51st Street—between First Avenue and the East River. She had a full-time staff including Delia Cahill, her maid, and Ralph Brio, her driver. Delia had come from Ireland when she was but 16 years old to work for Katharine, and died in that same apartment when she was a very old lady. Other than the Roman Catholic Church, Delia had no friends or social contact her entire adult life. She died on June 25, 1977. Katharine also maintained a full-time staff in Stamford, Connecticut, her principal home. It was on Shippan Point, on the shore of Long Island Sound.

AT SEA

After bidding Katharine goodbye, we left New York on October 1st from Pier 92 where we boarded an old but elegant Cunard ship, the *Parthia*. I missed the "gala dinner" and welcoming activities due to—morning sickness. We were, however, well cared for as Tony had a butler, Mr. Foley, and I a maid. There were only 98 passengers aboard.

I was sick again the next day, but the very solicitous Mr. Foley took me under his wing. He said, "But, madam, how can you be seasick. We haven't even left New York Harbor?" This didn't bode well. But I couldn't have imagined what was to come.

In the history books is the story of a terrific hurricane in October of 1954 in the Atlantic with Force 12 winds, apparently maximum for that range. We found ourselves in the middle of it. The winds were over 100 mph. I will quote from my diary. "The hurricane came up all day and was treacherous in the afternoon. The waves were enormous—some 50 feet high. They looked higher than the ship. The ocean was green and the air white with spray. It was like being in a valley with mountains of waves." Tony was one of two young men permitted to don the yellow outdoor gear and go out into the storm. He was in his element. Inside, the intrepid British continued with their afternoon tea which was, of course, a disaster with broken china and desperate waiters.

Ironically, I was neither morning sick nor seasick during that episode! That year there were a significant number of serious hurricanes in the Atlantic in October. I believe this one was named Hurricane Dolly.

THE BRITISH ISLES

On October 9th we arrived in Liverpool. We spent the day sightseeing, but I think we were the main attraction there. It was, after all, 1954 and the people of Liverpool weren't used to seeing a cowboy in a Stetson hat. We sailed for Belfast that night. I noted in my diary that I continued to be sick. We loved Belfast and its people. Again my diary notes that I was sick on the bus. It must have been awful for Tony!

On October 11th, Tony succumbed to one of my whims. We traveled by train from Belfast to Londonderry. Now why it was so important for me to see Londonderry I am not quite sure. Certainly I loved the music— *Londonderry Air*. The tune is played as the victory anthem of Northern Ireland at the Commonwealth Games and is well-known throughout the world. The song "Danny Boy" uses the tune, with a set of lyrics written in the early 20th century.

Londonderry was quite a depressed region at that time and, unable to stand the stares of the local people any longer, Tony ditched his Stetson. It was a fascinating city with so much history partially enclosed by a stone wall built in 1622. That night we sailed for Glasgow.

Glasgow as it was then is a far cry from the city it has become. It was dark, dingy and depressed. Having traveled there recently, I can assure you it has become a bustling, clean and productive city. We didn't stay there long as there was no compelling reason to do so. On we went to Edinburgh which is a city steeped in history and of great interest to me because of my Scottish roots. Tony bought a "very British cap and a scarf" for immediate use. It was cold and windy.

We spent a wonderful day in Edinburgh visiting museums and art galleries. I was so impressed with the artists whose works we saw that I listed them all in my diary. This was a whole new world for a girl who had no travel experience whatever. We went by bus to the Firth of Forth. (Need I add that I was "morning" sick!)

We took an overnight train to London arriving at 6:30 a.m. It was difficult to locate an acceptable place to stay given that we were on a very tight budget. We found a room at the home of a Mrs. Morris ($3.55 a night) and went off to see London. I was particularly taken with Madame Tussaud's Gallery and I noted that the Horror Chamber was really horrible.

Now, I have mentioned frequently that I had been sick, really sick in my stomach every day. It wouldn't be noteworthy except for the following story. My Auntie Elma in Toronto had given me the name of a Harley Street doctor in case I should need one. I did. I was sure my unborn child was starving to death as I had kept very little on my stomach since leaving New York.

Tony in St. James's Park - London

Harley Street surgeons are so exclusive that they don't even use the title doctor. So I saw a Mr. G. F. Gibberd at his offices that looked nothing whatever like what one would see in America. There were Persian rugs and antique furniture and patients were examined behind a Japanese silk screen. He was not gentle with me. He told me in a brusque manner that there was not a thing wrong with me and that I would stop this business of being sick immediately. I whimpered that I feared that my child was not being adequately nourished and he told me he had seen mothers deliver babies in concentration camps who had practically no food and the infants were perfectly healthy. He let me know that he would brook no more of this nonsense on my part. And I wasn't sick even once for the rest of our long trip!

Tony & Aldine visiting my
pen pal

On October 17th we took a train trip to Colchester to visit my pen pal of many years, Margaret Cock. There is a special chapter herein devoted to her and to our unique relationship. It was a wonderful experience.

We continued to leave no stone unturned in London. I am glad we were young and energetic because, in order to save money, we walked everywhere—and I mean great distances. We went to Stratford-on-Avon and I've never forgotten the exquisite hotel in which we stayed—The Haytor. What an impression it made on me!

On we went to Oxford where Tony's father had graduated with a Ph.D. from Baliol College. On returning to London we checked into a perfectly dreadful boarding house in Paddington—the kind where you put shillings in a little heater in your room to stay warm. Typically guests congregate in a main room primarily, I think, to stay warm.

Here I must tell a story. Tony and I had some rather impressive connections in London. One was a couple, Marguerite and Dwight Ross, whom we knew well at our cottage in Canada that is near the town of Dwight. It had been named after his grandfather.

I have always held Dwight Ross in the highest esteem. He was an Air Commodore in the RCAF in WWII. As Base Commander in Yorkshire, England, he took a keen interest in those under his command and waited outside every time his men were returning from a mission. One time an RCAF Halifax returning from Northern France was delayed and barely struggled back to the airfield on three engines. On landing, the pilot lost control and veered his aircraft into a parked Halifax which was fully loaded with fuel and bombs. The aircraft broke into three parts. Air Commodore Ross ran out to save the pilot who was severely injured. He returned to the plane to help others. He was just removing the bombardier at the very moment that ten 500 lb. bombs on the second aircraft exploded. Dwight's right arm was almost completely severed. He walked calmly to an ambulance, was taken to the nearest surgery tent, and had his arm amputated. He was awarded the George Cross in 1944.

I had known Dwight for many years and never, ever did I hear him mention the incident or complain about the horrendous inconvenience of having lost his right arm. He loved to sail and often took my sons with him as a crew. One time Tony Jr. was with him when he got into trouble with the main sheet and had Tony not subtly remedied the situation I am sure Dwight Ross would have drowned. He had an elegant mustache, a swagger and was a magnificent gentleman.

In any case, Marguerite and Dwight had invited us to dinner at their home in a part of London called Roedean. We were waiting in the boarding house "parlor" when Dwight's batman* arrived. He opened the door to the "parlor" and formally announced that he was seeking Mr. and Mrs. von Isser. There were a good many surprised faces as we were led out to Dwight's staff car.

The next day it happened again, only this time it was Lady Astor who was having us picked up. Into the parlor came her uniformed driver announcing he was there to pick up Lady Astor's guests. It really was quite funny to see the faces of the disbelieving guests.

Lady Nancy Astor (Viscountess Astor) is a famous name in history as she was the first female member of Parliament. Here I will go into the story of Tony's close association with Lady Astor. As I mentioned in the story about Tony, he had taken time off from university to travel with a close friend to Europe in 1948. His friend was William R. Mathews Jr. whose father was the well-known owner and publisher of the *Arizona Daily Star*. Mr. Mathews was a formidable figure with an impressive background. He had witnessed and documented unique historical events such as the signing of the Japanese surrender and the Bikini bomb test. He was special advisor to James B. Forrestal who was the first U.S. Secretary of Defense having been appointed by President Harry S. Truman. Hence, he was close friends with many Washington politicians as well as other notable individuals such as Margaret Sanger Slee and Isabella Greenway King. It should be noted that Margaret Sanger Slee opened the first birth control clinic in the United States, having popularized the term "birth control." That clinic eventually evolved into the Planned Parenthood Federation of America. She spent a great deal of time in Tucson, a good friend being Isabella Greenway King, longtime owner of the Arizona Inn with many historical connections of her own.

One of William R. Mathews' close friends was Lady Astor and so it was that Bill and Tony were invited to her infamous estate, Cliveden. Again I must step aside from the story to tell you about Cliveden, an Italianate mansion and estate in Buckinghamshire, England. The site has been home to an earl, three countesses, two dukes, a Prince of Wales, and, of course, the Viscounts Astor.

As the home of Nancy Astor, the house was the meeting place of the Cliveden set of political intellectuals. Later, during the 1960s, it became the setting for key events of the notorious Profumo Affair.

Tony and Bill were delighted to accept an invitation from Lady Astor for an extended visit to Cliveden. Her own sons would come and go on weekends. They, by the way, had attended the best private schools in England. I mentioned earlier that both Tony and I had four years in Tucson High School studying Latin. Well, one day Lady Astor suggested to her sons, and to Tony and Bill, that they take a walk around the premises. Surrounding Cliveden, etched high up on its walls, were words written in Latin. Lady Astor asked her sons to translate some of it for her. They could not. Tony volunteered. He was able to do a credible job of reading the Latin, to the delight of Lady Astor and the chagrin of her sons.

Bill continued his trip leaving Tony behind at Cliveden. Tony's greatest delight while there was attending afternoon tea with people who left him with a lasting impression. One of these, with whom he shared tea frequently, was George Bernard Shaw—or GBS as Lady Astor called him. Those were energetic exchanges of thought that Tony talked about for years to come.

Tony had spent several weeks at Cliveden and I was confident that an invitation to visit Cliveden would be forthcoming when we visited Lady Astor in London. She was there staying in her "town house" that week but suggested that we come to Cliveden for the weekend. I was quite terrified at the idea as I felt utterly unprepared to engage in this lifestyle. Fortunately, Tony interpreted my kick under the table correctly and politely refused the invitation on the basis that other unalterable plans had already been made. Sometimes I kick myself for passing up that rare opportunity.

PARIS, France

We arrived in Paris on October 23rd. Our first hotel was far too expensive at $5.60 per night. Thus, our first task was to find reasonable lodgings which turned out to be the Hotel de Pantheon in the Latin Quarter at $2.00 per night. As they say, you get what you pay for! We had to walk up a stairway for four floors and then found that the room had no soap nor toilet paper which would have been of little use anyway as we didn't have a bathroom. Finally we located one on a different floor entirely. It was filthy.

Bathrooms were something of a problem for me in Paris. The old "pissoir" was evident on almost every main street corner. These were screened urinals (put there to decrease the frequency of men urinating in the streets) and I was shocked to see men inside while still holding hands with their lady friends outside. The pissoir has been phased out over time and no longer exists. I really had led a sheltered life and I had difficulty in using public bathrooms in Paris as they were shared by men and women together. However, no matter how inexpensive our lodgings, there was always a bidet. (I had never seen one before and couldn't believe their purpose!)

We loved Paris and I doubt there was an inch we didn't explore. The first day, of course, had to include a trip up the Eiffel Tower. I was nervous about heights and thought this phobia might give me a little trouble. Instead, the terror I felt emanated from two elevator attendants who, on the ascent, got into fisticuffs—literally. There they were punching away at each other for what seemed a very long time and nobody was "minding the store." As I remember, Tony was holding me up as I was about to pass out. Eventually we reached the top safely and the swaying of the tower in the wind

seemed a minor horror compared to what I had just experienced.

As it was Sunday, we went to a service in Notre Dame. The next day we walked through the Louvre and the Tuileries Gardens to Place du Concord— among other sightseeing events. I didn't think the day could hold any more drama, but I was wrong. That night Tony took me to the Folies Bergère. My innocence did not prepare

Versailles

me for what I saw—naked women being lowered in birdcages to almost audience level. I think Tony had as much fun watching me as he did the performance. And this was only my second day in Paris!

I have failed to mention that instead of studying Spanish at university as I should have, I had taken two years of French. This did help us somewhat. I will spare you a travelogue of Paris; we all see the same amazing places. I will now move on to Switzerland.

LUCERNE, Switzerland

We arrived in Lucerne on October 30th. I will not tarry here for, although it is a beautiful city, our pleasure was dampened by very wet and foggy weather. We did, however, see all the places on our list and walked for miles and miles in the rain. After four days, we left.

INNSBRUCK, Austria

Our next stop was Innsbruck, Tony's family's home for centuries. We could afford only one night at our first hotel, the Goldener Adler ($3.50 per night with baths extra, as usual) so we embarked on a quest for cheaper lodgings. That turned out to be the Goldener Stern at $2.90 a night. It should be noted that the price included all meals.

Tony's family home - Hall, Austria

Later in the day we sought and found Tony's grandmother's home with its von Isser coat of arms on the door. When Tony had been there in 1948 he had met many of his family; now all were gone. He remembered having given bicycles to all the young people in his family for whom such luxuries were not readily available so soon after the war. A highlight for me in Innsbruck was taking a one-cable cable car for an hour's ride to the top of the Alps to a magnificent place called Seegrube. It was just above zero F. but we climbed to the very highest peak. There is a photo of me standing on the top of the Alps in the hall at our cottage.

Later in the week we located Tony's cousin, Waltraud Rauch, who had two teenage daughters who spoke a bit of English. It was lovely to catch up on family news.

Aldine on Seegrube

Tony near Igls, Austria

THE TYROL, Italy

On November 7th we traveled by train through the magnificent Brenner Pass to Meran. Being in this area was a significant reason for the trip as in a nearby town in the Alps, Partschins, was the ancient von Isser schloss (castle) known as the Gaudententhurm. We wanted very much to connect with an old woman—Tony's father's sister Berta von Sölder— to find out how we might visit the castle. How were we to find her? We had neither her address nor phone number.

We reasoned that if we wandered around the central area of Meran, we might spot someone of her approximate age who might know of her. I need to mention that we spoke no German. So we put our sights on a very frail old lady and approached her. She was brusque. She was Austrian after all, as were most who lived there. That part of what is now Italy was taken over by the Italians from Austria after WWI.

Tony spoke to the old lady in his best German accent saying the name of his aunt. "Berta von Sölder?" "Ja, ja," she replied. We repeated it. Impatiently she said, "Ja, ja. Berta von Sölder." Unbelievable as this is, the first person we approached was indeed Berta von Sölder. Now, what are the chances! She was very excited when she learned that Tony was her nephew from the United States.

The most wonderful things happened as a result of connecting with her. She took us to her son, Dr. Peter von Sölder and his wife Dr. Edith von Sölder. With sign language and determination we were able to communicate. We let them know we wanted to visit the Gaudententhurm. You will learn much more about this amazing place when you read of my visit there when I took my sons Kent and Tony and my parents to see it. Tony wanted very much to see the estate that had been in his family for hundreds and hundreds of years and to which, as the legitimate Count von Isser, he had ownership. Word was sent to the Gaudententhurm that we would be visiting the next day so that we could be permitted entrance.

The next question was how to get there. It was a very basic road and not frequently traversed. There were no buses. Taxi? Not on our budget! And so began a scary episode for me.

We rented a motorcycle—a 125cc Benelli, little more than a dirt bike. Tony was an experienced motorcycle driver. Money was paid, papers signed, and maps provided. Off we went with me on the back. I wondered what this bumpy road might do to my poor unborn child. (Throughout his life he loved motorcycles!)

We reached the charming village of Partschins high in the Alps on a beautiful, sunny day. I will now quote my diary. "It is a town untouched by modern times and the streets, sewers, and houses are just as they were in the middle ages. It dates back to before the 1200s. We easily found the Gaudententhurm. The first recorded date of the original tower, five feet thick, was AD 1357. The woman renting one floor from Berta von Sölder took us through the whole place including the cellar and attic. It was indeed fascinating and full of von Isser history and belongings. We were taken through the private churchyard where a myriad of Tony's ancestors lie."

Aldine at entrance to the Gaudententhurm

The Gaudententhurm was all we imagined it to be—fortified, ancient, and daunting. I do recall asking to use the ladies room and was ushered to a room—cavernous with stone walls and very cold—that had naught but a hole in the center of a sloped floor. The indignity of it all was almost too much for me, but what choice did I have!

At dusk we decided to make use of the daylight left us to return to Meran. But—the motorcycle had a flat tire, and we had no spare. Big trouble! We weighed our options. The only choice available to us was to **walk** back to Meran. I am not a complainer, but this did test me. As we approached Meran I begged Tony to just walk away from the whole thing. They knew where we were going and they could find their motorcycle in the morning. It just wasn't worth the hassle to try to get a refund and I wasn't at all sure we would anyway.

You may have determined by now that Tony was tight with a penny. There was no way on earth he wasn't going to go back, give the motorcycle renter hell, and demand a refund. Well, it didn't work that way. It was now late at night. I was exhausted and wanted to be anywhere but where I was. Into the shop marched a very indignant and angry Tony only to be greeted by irate and near violent agents. They had to stay open until our return and when we didn't have their motorcycle with us they were out for blood. They wanted their motorcycle back, and they wanted

Tony on "the motorcycle"

it **now**. Tony had gone in thinking he'd be in control. Now the situation was totally out of control.

We suddenly realized we were in serious trouble. The rental agency called the police to report that Tony had stolen their motorcycle. The police came and took me hostage—yes **hostage**. When the motorcycle was returned, Tony could have me back. So off Tony went in the middle of the night up that long road on the back of a motorcycle driven by one of their mechanics with a new tire to retrieve the stolen property. It took hours and hours but they did return—on two motorcycles. I was saved!

The remainder of our time in Meran was quite pleasant. We managed to find another of Tony's relatives—Franz von Sölder. Having connected with the von Sölder family in 1954, we have been in touch ever since. Although Peter died, Edith is very much alive and full of energy although she is quite old now. She hikes up and down the Alps as if she were a teenager. Through photographs, we watched their sons, Philipp and Christoph, grow up. Now we are in touch with their children through written word, e-mail and Facebook. Philipp and Elisabeth's children are Anna, Otto, and Maximilian, all of which names I find charming. Christoph's wife, Christine, lives in the Gaudententhurm. She has two children, Sylvia and Felix. In 2008, I took my entire family on a trip to Europe and the Mediterranean which included a very meaningful and touching visit with the family in Meran and Partschins. The group returned saying it was one of the most magical experiences of their lives.

VENICE, Italy

As our train did not arrive in Venice until quite late, we were pleased when a nice young boy approached us in the station to ask if we needed a place to stay. We did and were taken to his "uncle's place." That lad must have thought we were poverty stricken, but as it was a good price, we stayed. It was beyond awful. There was cold water only and I was afraid to drink it. I dropped iodine—yes, the old fashioned iodine—into the water hoping it would purify it!

We ate in the kitchen with the family—typically spaghetti. In the morning we had breakfast with them during which time the "uncle", clad in undershirt and pants, shaved at the only mirror in the place—in the kitchen. I must have been a very docile wife to have condescended to accepting this level of living.

We loved Venice and found it great fun to take a steamer instead of a taxi as cars weren't used in Venice. We did the usual sight-seeing—St. Mark's Square, the Palace of the Doges, the Basilica of St. Mark and the astronomical clock tower. Of course we took a steamer through the Grand Canal and I noted in my diary that Venice is virtually falling apart.

FLORENCE, Italy

Having survived Venice, we headed for a place I had been so eager to see—Florence. We checked into the Hotel Fenice ($2.75) and I note in my diary that it was definitely third class.

I think even Tony could not stand the conditions at our hotel, so our second day in Florence we found an acceptable pensione—Pensione Aprile—and began our enchanting visit to this

Basilica of San Marco - Venice

beautiful city. A quick travelogue here. We walked through the church Santa Maria Maggiore, the Baptistry of San Giovanni, saw Giotto's clock tower, Palazzo Vecchio, the Palace of the Uffizi, the Ponte Vecchio, the Palazzo Pitti with its Boboli Gardens, the Basilica di Santa Croce, the Piazza San Marco and the church Maria Novelle. We walked many miles and saw magnificent statues everywhere.

While passing a shop, I fell in love with a pair of shoes—Ferragamo—($20). Tony's father had given me money to buy myself a Christmas present, and I had found it. The weather in Florence was beautiful. We spent the next morning in the Museum of Uffizi where we saw sculpture and paintings that left us breathless. We particularly liked Botticelli's Birth of Venus and Leonardo's Annunciation.

Aldine & Neptune - Florence

In the afternoon we took a bus to a town that will be etched in my memory forever—Fiesole. It is on a hilltop not far from Florence.

PISA, Italy

We couldn't miss seeing the Leaning Tower of Pisa, and I was determined to climb it in spite of my fear of heights. It was a strange sensation to be climbing stairs on an angle and provided me with considerable angst, but we made it to the top. What happened next will be memorable forever. I needed to sit down, and did so right under the big bell. But, I hit my head on the bell. It was all too much and I simply sat and sobbed. What we hadn't taken into consideration was the hour. It was noon. Suddenly the bell was ringing and ringing and ringing and

Teary Aldine beside the bell at the Leaning Tower of Pisa

Tony at the Leaning Tower of Pisa

what little composure was left in me vanished entirely. Enough of Pisa, thought I, and we left for Rome.

ROME, Italy

We arrived in the lovely railroad station in Rome and soon found a hotel—Pensione Quisisana— with a fountain. That was a step up! Or so I thought until one morning when I was using the communal bathroom, as was always the case, and became aware that I had visitors. It seems that bathrooms were a problem for me throughout this trip. Above the bathroom door was an open transom window through which three men were ogling me and thoroughly enjoying themselves. Being a private person, I was humiliated and frightened. Certainly the initial good impression made by the fountain outside was cancelled and it became just another awful hotel.

We were impressed, however, with the many fountains throughout Rome. We managed to fit in a great deal of sightseeing our first day and I was particularly pleased when we visited the Colosseum to find that we were the only tourists there! I was able to take a picture of Tony in this huge and impressive space all by himself. That photograph now hangs in the hall at the cottage. You have to really search to find Tony in that picture.

We, of course, visited all the highlights of Rome but for me the most impressive was the Sistine Chapel. It was magnificent. It was very cold in Rome while we were there which did slow us down somewhat. Another site that impressed us was the cemetery of Cappuccini which is in the cellar of a chapel. Here there were the remains of thousands of monks of a particular order all arranged neatly in stacks and designs. We visited St. Paul's and the awe inspiring St. Peter's.

After several days in Rome, we took an extremely bumpy bus trip to Tivoli with its lovely water cascade. Villa d'Este with its 500 fountains and beautiful gardens was another highlight for us.

Tony in the Colosseum - Rome (beside arrow)

NICE, France

Le Jardin - Cagnes sur Mar

After a week in Rome, we took an exhausting 13 hour train trip to Nice. We required a couple of days to recover and then set out for Cagne-sur-Mer, a town Tony had heard about all his life. It was a very quaint village clinging to a hillside overlooking the Mediterranean Sea. With the help of a 25-year-old photograph we located the charming home that Tony's mother had lived in with her friend Helen (Mickey) Wilson around 1920. We had tea and accepted her invitation to spend a few days there with her later in our trip. We dropped in next door to see Doll Watley, another old friend of Tony's mother. Back to Nice.

The following day we traveled the magnificent Grand Corniche with its charming towns including Ville Franche. We were in the clouds sometimes. We passed through Monaco to Monte Carlo and in the evening visited the casino there. Because of the way Tony was dressed, we were not allowed to enter. He scouted around and found a dreadful jacket to rent, thus making our apparel acceptable. In fact, we found the casino small and disappointing.

We took a train to Cannes the next day to sit on the beach and watch the marine activity. It was Thanksgiving, our feast was meager and I was terribly homesick. We had been away a long time and I was ready to take the active child in my tummy and me back to Tucson.

It was exciting to return to Cagne-sur-Mer for our visit with Mickey Wilson. She had tea ready for us and we chatted for ages. Afterwards, we took a long walk through the town and she showed us Tony's parents' old house where Tony had his beginning! On one of our frequent dinners out, we had chicken that had been cooked on an interesting 200 year old spit. One evening Mickey cooked dinner and it smelled so delicious that I peeked into the cooking pot only to see the huge head with black eyes and the claws of a chicken boiling away. It was ghastly to look upon, but delicious to eat.

Tony & Aldine-Cagnes sur Mer

Mickey was an artist, as Tony's mother had been, so we had great fun watching Mickey work and in viewing her art. Her good friend, Doll Watley, was an artist as well and had us to dinner at her home with her brother Brian Ross.

On December 1st, after six days with Mickey, it was time to head for Cannes and our departure for home. We boarded our ship, the *Independence*, that evening and set sail. While we had been in first class accommodations for our trip to Europe, that was not the case on our return voyage. Whatever the lowest class was, that was where we were. We had small metal bunk beds in a tiny room and communal eating. The main problem was our neighbors. I am choosing my words carefully to say that it is doubtful they had any training in good manners while being raised. They rarely closed their doors and wandered the halls in their underwear yelling at one another at full volume. The bathrooms were a disgrace. The primary language was Italian. It was a truly horrible experience for me.

We had no amenities whatever and the library that we were allowed to use was limited in its selection. Tony decided he would make good use of his time aboard to study Nostradamus, the daunting psychic who was born in 1503. He did indeed become well informed on his many predictions and prophesies. We spent a lot of time sleeping on this trip often not bothering to go to dinner. I was always on the verge of being seasick. I will say there were festivities the last evening, perhaps in an effort to leave one memory of the journey that was pleasant. Now, you know I am not a complainer, so this had to have been bad, bad, bad.

On December 9th we arrived back in New York City and were met by Katharine Merritt who took us to her lovely apartment. It was good to be in familiar territory again and we spent several lovely days enjoying Katharine's company and kindness before returning, at last, to Tucson.

We had set out to see the splendors of Europe, and we achieved our goal. While not always a comfortable trip, it provided us with memories to last a lifetime.

*A batman was a soldier or airman assigned to a commissioned officer as his chauffeur, valet and personal servant.

5

CRWD

MY FIRST TEACHING JOB

As I have mentioned previously, my first son was born in the spring of 1955 and I returned to UA in the fall. My wonderful parents were babysitters while I attended classes. My parents always lived next door to us, in several locations, until their deaths. When I graduated with a B.A. in Education in 1956 (a year late) it was with cap and gown and Kent on my arm.

I entered my "Junior League years" and life was bliss. Unexpectedly, Tony was offered an excellent job in Los Angeles, that of Assistant Labor Relations Director for the entire Hughes Aircraft Corporation. This required our moving to Los Angeles, exciting for Tony but devastating for me. I had never been away from my family and friends.

My first assignment was to find a home for us that did not exceed a commute of more than 30 minutes for Tony. I found beautiful places but Tony considered one that I loved in Sycamore Canyon to be a potential fire trap. A second was on a cliff above the beach and Tony nixed it on the grounds that it could fall into the ocean. He was right on both counts.

Palos Verdes Estates fitted the bill and over the next three years we lived in three lovely houses. We rented the first two and finally bought our own home on Via Acalones. However, soon after moving to California I found myself at loose ends. Both my sons were in school and I had neither family nor friends nearby. I found myself sitting in front of the television set eating Honey Buns. This wouldn't do at all! Hence, I decided—yes— to go back to school.

It seemed reasonable to me that the coursework I should pursue would lead to a teaching certificate in California. So, in December I headed for the Palos Verdes Unified School District Office and met with their personnel director. I requested assistance in determining what courses I should take to augment my Arizona teaching credential.

After a few minutes of conversation, he said, "I think we have a teaching position for you." I replied emphatically that I was not seeking employment. That was not a role I envisioned for myself at all. He went on to tell me that the position was in a third grade classroom in Silver Spur School. No, I repeated, I just want to take coursework and, in any case, I wouldn't qualify for an appointment. I was not certified in California. He saw that as no impediment at all—they would simply grant me emergency certification. "But you see," I told him, "I can't take a teaching position because I am not even a U.S. citizen. I am Canadian." This stopped him for a moment but then, with victory so close, he assured me that they would expedite my naturalization. I was sunk. Saying "no" has never been easy for me and as a result I unexpectedly found myself employed. Alas.

I was told the specifics of my new job. The teacher I was replacing, Jennie Webb, had been fired and would leave at the time of Christmas vacation. The children had not been told and would not be expecting a new teacher in January. Apparently the students in the class were remarkably bright as most of their parents were in the space industry that surrounded the area, or in medicine. In any case, it was probable that the children were from upper income families to be able to live in that school district.

Then he hit me with a disheartening disclosure. "There is one problem," he told me. That problem was a little boy named Brian M. He was a severely disturbed, unpredictable and often violent child. However, I was reassured that he was on a waiting list for a full psychiatric residential care facility and that I would have him for only a few weeks.

Trust me, in no way was I prepared to be a teacher. I never expected to be a teacher nor had I really given my full attention to coursework during my university education. But January came and my classroom of almost 30 students immediately bombarded me with reasonable questions. "Where is Mrs. Webb?" "When will she be back?" Parents were phoning the school to express their concern. Oh, woe!

As is my nature, I poured my heart and soul into my new role. I was honored one day when the principal, John Lewis, called me into his office and told me I had received an award. It was from the janitors naming me as having "the most untidy, messy classroom they had ever seen." I was crushed. The explanation was simple. I had turned my classroom into a living learning experience. When the curriculum called for a study of the Los Angeles Harbor, my husband Tony jig sawed a big piece of plywood outlining the harbor. We placed it on a child's size swimming pool and outfitted it with all the appropriate boats—tugs, ferry boats, etc.—to float on the harbor. Yes, a little water got spilled but—it was a classroom.

Annually we incubated and hatched chickens in the classroom. What a wonderful learning experience! Of course I taught the terminology that was germane to gestation and as the days went by we would open an egg to see the progress of the growing embryo. When the chicks became viable, we left them to hatch on their own. The children loved it. When the chicks finally hatched there was great excitement. Of course, chickens and their droppings were all over the classroom.

I had a measuring center, an art center and a communication center. Children were allowed to leave their seats to work in one of these areas if they became antsy and needed to move around. This resulted in the classroom being even messier!

I was called into Mr. Lewis's office again. This time it was the other third grade teachers complaining that their students and their parents wanted more "hands on" learning such as I was providing. They balked and were unwilling to change their routines. So I was told to "tone it down."

Another complaint that came my way was that I appeared to be a Communist. This was really out of left field. Rather than having the children memorize poetry, I decided we would learn all the verses of the major U.S. patriotic songs. You have no idea how long some of them are. And so my children knew all the verses of "Oh, beautiful for spacious skies..." etc. Now, I ask you, how could that impugn my loyalty?

Children are very sensitive to the mood of their teacher. During a parent-teacher conference, I was taken aback by a comment from the parents of my student, Joey Sterrett. He had told them that I was always nice except when I wore my orange dress. I thought about this for a moment, and then had a secret chuckle. That was my "default" outfit for days I had PMS and could not fit comfortably into anything else! I never wore the orange dress in the classroom again.

I found that I loved, absolutely loved, teaching. And the students loved me. (Eventually, their parents did, too.) We had student-created rules and a schedule they assisted in developing. And, I made sure there was a moment of joy in the life of every child every day—a reason for them to come to school whether they had wanted to or not. It was a hiatus of joy for me during the three years we lived in California.

But, what of Brian? This is such an emotional story it is difficult for me to tell. I loved that little boy with all my heart. It was, as I had been forewarned, almost impossible to have him in the classroom. He was the unhappiest child I have ever known and deeply troubled. I could not let him out of my sight or he would go into destruction mode—

knocking everyone's books off their desks, tearing down their art work and so forth. He was intelligent and ingenious in his ways of creating havoc.

In my mind's eye Brian had <u>black</u> all around him. He wore black, his eyes were black and at his desk he pulled his black jacket over his head of black hair. When he took a spelling test he would write every word backwards (but correctly) with a black pencil and <u>all the circles (a, b, d, p etc. were heavily blacked in.</u>

I tried everything to alter his behavior but my arsenal of strategies was limited. I tried loving him and reinforcing all his appropriate behaviors. He deteriorated. I tried ignoring him. No effect. Finally, against everything in my code of ethics, I went to the principal and told him I was failing miserably with Brian and could I please hit him. He instantly acquiesced. He knew I cared deeply about Brian and he trusted me. Besides, the child was soon to leave for long term psychiatric hospital care and what harm could one last-ditch intervention do. He checked with Brian's parents who were so grateful for my efforts that they approved even this "therapy."

And so it began. On the next occasion of Brian's deviant behavior I swatted him on his behind. All the students were, quite naturally, shocked. Teachers didn't hit children! Brian tested the system and—yes—his next misbehavior resulted in a punch to his arm. He smiled. It was the first time I had <u>ever</u> seen him smile. On other occasions I would pick him up by his black jacket, shove him against a wall, and give him a good shaking. Brian was thriving. I was practically ill from the experience. The more I punished him, the happier he became and the more miserable I was. Well, this couldn't continue. Again parents were calling the principal. I was a pariah.

Time went on. The hospital placement was delayed deliberately as Brian was doing so well. Suffice that over time I ameliorated my behavior in cadence with Brian's improvement. It worked. I decided that teaching was definitely my calling.

Brian's story was sad and tragic and is the reason I do not mention his last name. Brian's parents were Roman Catholic. They went every Wednesday night to bingo games. They hired a baby sitter for the three children—a daughter two years older than Brian and a son who was two years younger. The young man who was the sitter had been recommended by friends and appeared trustworthy. The children were told weekly by their parents to behave themselves and do what they were told. They didn't want any bad reports on their return.

And every week Brian lay in his bed and listened to his sister Carrie crying in the next bedroom while she was being raped by the babysitter. Brian felt helpless and pulled his blankets over his head to try to block out the sounds. He hated himself. He couldn't tell his parents and badly wanted the punishment he thought he deserved. And he had found it in my classroom. His behavior had been an attempt to elicit punishment to alleviate his self-loathing. During this time, Carrie developed asthma which ultimately crippled her life. Their parents had been oblivious to what was causing all the havoc in their home until… One day Mrs. M. (Brian's mother) received a phone call from a friend to whom she had recommended the babysitter. Screaming at Mrs. M. she said, "Do you know what that babysitter tried to do to our daughter last night?" Suddenly, Mrs. M. knew.

Mr. and Mrs. M. came to my classroom to tell me this story. They were confident that these events probably precipitated Brian's deviant behavior. They were full of gratitude for all I had done to help Brian. I know in my heart I saved that little boy's life and somehow I feel that out there somewhere is a productive, happy middle-aged man.

Brian was in fifth grade when Tony and I returned to Tucson to live. He was class president! The end of this story touches me more than any other accolade in my teaching career. Shortly before we departed California, Brian's father phoned that they would like to drop by to say goodbye. Brian had with him a gift (a ceramic chicken that I still have) and a note. Let me share the note with you. Notice that all the letters are now filled with happy faces!

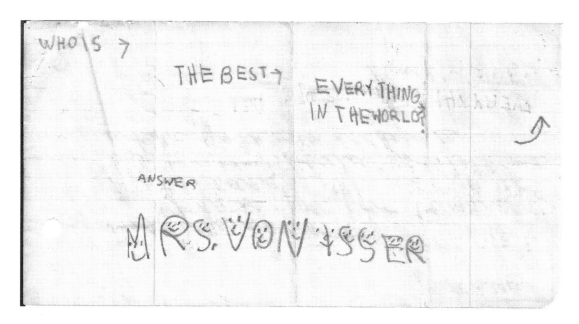

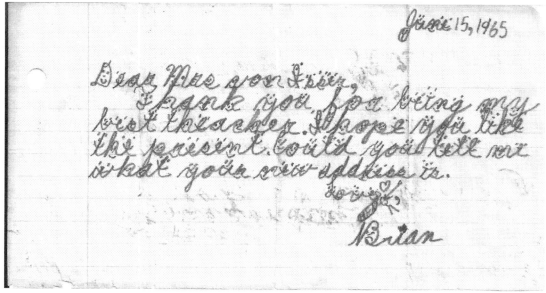

A new world had opened for me.

6

✂ᑭᔕ✂

MY GRADUATE DEGREES

After three years in California it was not difficult to make the decision to return to Tucson to take up our lives there once again. Tony had recently been offered the position of Director of Labor Relations for the entire Hughes Corporation, an excellent job that most would not turn down. Tony did. His position already required his being away from home for days on end, dropping by only to shower and shave and then returning to the negotiating table once again. The job also required a great deal of drinking. He seriously believed that in ten years time he would either be an alcoholic or dead. No job was worth that sacrifice.

Returning to Hughes Aircraft Company in Tucson inevitably meant a demotion in status as well as in pay, but we accepted both conditions willingly. Kent and Tony Jr. had not been happy in California; they missed their grandparents and their friends. So in 1965, we slipped back comfortably into our previous lives. My parents had been living in our house while they built one next door to us, so that transition went easily as well.

Back into the Junior League I went but somehow I felt unfulfilled. I had tasted success in the classroom and I was hungry for more. When I was 33, I returned to UA, started my Master of Arts degree in Special Education, and took coursework that certified me as a Psychoeducational Diagnostician. I worked well with troubled children and this gave me the opportunity to test them, diagnose their problems, and establish remedial programs for them with their teachers and parents. I loved it.

The principal at the one of the schools to which I was assigned as the psychologist—Mary Meredith, after whom an elementary school was later named—arrived at work very excited one day. She told us that the famous Dr. Samuel A. Kirk was coming to Tucson and would be teaching a   course at UA the following semester. While in California I had heard of Dr. Kirk, a pioneer in the field of learning disabilities. He even coined the term "learning disabilities" and was the author of the seminal test entitled The Illinois Test of Psycholinguistic Abilities (ITPA). This test diagnosed learning disabilities in young children.

Dr. Kirk was a professor at the University of Illinois and was happy in his work there. However, when John F. Kennedy established the Bureau of Education for the Handicapped in 1967, he spoke to Dr. Kirk directly asking him to head the new bureau. Sam couldn't turn him down even though it meant a drop in salary and becoming a government employee. Sam eventually left the bureau and returned to his work at the University of Illinois. Ultimately he was ready to retire, and he and his wife Winifred were looking at Tucson as a potential location.

Dr. Samuel Alexander Kirk

My friend Bette Layton and I enrolled in the upcoming course which was taught in the evening once a week and drew educators from across the State of Arizona. Bette and I sat in the front row every week showing far too much leg and occasionally talking to one another—albeit quietly.

One night at the end of Dr. Kirk's class, he pointed to Bette and me and told us to stay. We were quite sure we were going to be expelled. On the contrary, he inquired as to who we were and asked whether we knew of a good real estate agent. As you will read later in this memoir, I was a real estate agent for quite some years. Dr. Kirk invited us to his rental home in the foothills for a drink that night. Winifred was not there as she was still in the East selling their home and getting ready to move. And, it has to be said, Dr. Kirk liked a pretty girl. We became very close friends with them both until their deaths.

Dr. Kirk joined the faculty of the Department of Special Education in the College of Education at UA and soon became a member of my master's committee. It was made up of five men. I suspect that Dr. Kirk arrived with the intention of showing our college how a real university should be run, but he was subtle in making strides to that end. I was a victim in the process.

It wasn't easy for me to be working on a master's degree while raising a family, selling real estate, accruing flying hours, teaching, and working on an Indian project,. My habit was to go to bed at the same time as my family, and get up in the morning with them. But, every night my alarm went off at midnight at which point I slipped into our library and worked for three hours. The alarm then reminded me it was time to go back to bed. With this arrangement, I caused as little disturbance to our family routine as possible and I still could get my university work accomplished. This went on for at least a year while I wrote my master's degree thesis.

I was overly ambitious in selecting the topic of my thesis—*Perceptual Disorders: Their Identification and Remediation.* I poured my heart into it and, when complete, it numbered 240 pages. I was incredibly proud of my accomplishment and when May came I had completed my coursework and had only to defend my thesis before my committee before receiving my master's degree. Then I would be off to Canada for the summer and I had a good job awaiting me in the fall.

The day of the defense of my thesis was indeed a red letter day for my parents as, not only was I the first university graduate in our family but certainly the first to receive a graduate degree. My parents and Tony had a big party planned that evening—balloons, champagne—the whole thing. I was, after all, a shoo-in.

Dr. Kirk chose this moment to flex his muscles. I had hand-delivered my thesis to each member of my committee some three weeks earlier to give them ample time to make criticisms or recommend changes to it. I had heard back from none of them. All was well. On the day of the meeting everyone was all smiles. I was their star pupil. Most master's degrees awarded at UA in that college were Master of Education (M.Ed.). Mine was unique in that it was a Master of Arts (M.A.). The director of my committee, Dr. Gerald Holmberg, introduced Dr. Kirk to those who did not know him and indicated that the meeting should not take long as everything appeared to be in order.

It was then that Dr. Kirk tossed my thesis on the desk in front of him and said he was not accepting it. Mouths fell open. Dr. Holmberg asked him why he was denying it and he responded, "Because I haven't read it and I don't intend to." Dr. Holmberg pointed out that he had had sufficient time to alter the thesis if he thought there was a need to do so. Dr. Kirk went on to say that my thesis consisted of 240 pages and that no academic paper needed to be that long. He considered it unacceptable. I was crushed—heartbroken.

Dr. Kirk offered to work with me over the summer to revise it to an appropriate length. Not even for a master's degree would I give up the summer in Canada with my family and I told him I was unavailable over the summer. He offered to do it in the fall.

I accepted. Downhearted, I went home to my family with the news that I had not passed. A pall fell upon the assembly. We didn't feel very lighthearted that night.

Gone was the euphoria of a happy, carefree summer ahead with just the job I had wanted awaiting me in the fall. But, Dr. Kirk had made his point that the Department of Special Education was now on notice that he would brook no mediocrity. No one would have dared to take the famous Dr. Kirk to task.

I returned to UA in the fall to complete my M.A. degree. I worked under Dr. Kirk's tutelage while he assessed what needed to be done. Believe it or not, the thesis remained at 240 pages. He agreed that it was necessary for it to be that long for me to accomplish an assessment and consolidation of the research. We changed some of the wording in a few paragraphs, but there was no major revision required.

I did substitute teaching for the remainder of the fall semester, which I thoroughly enjoyed. And then, with Dr. Kirk's encouragement, I embarked on my Ph.D. Knowing this was a major commitment not only on my part but also that of my family he took Tony aside and explained the demands that would be made on me. He needed assurance from Tony that he would support me through the next few years even though there would be a cost to our family of my available time for them. Tony understood and agreed.

In order to finance my degree, I continued to sell real estate and taught at Green Fields School in Tucson. (I was Acting Headmaster at the school for one year.) Kent and Tony Jr. both attended Green Fields, a highly regarded day and residential school. They were day students. I taught English to the seniors and found it necessary to use university textbooks to challenge them. They were incredibly bright lads.

Dr. Kirk and a host of other well-known professionals worked with me throughout my doctoral program. I am name dropping when I mention that Dr. Herbert C. Quay, Head of Psychology at Temple University and later at the University of Miami, and Dr. Frank M. Hewitt, Chair of Special Education at UCLA assisted with both content and statistical issues. And both became very close friends. I made frequent trips to Miami and Malibu for their help. Later, when I had my own graduate program at UA, they also visited Tucson as, in those times, there was sufficient federal funding to support visiting professors as consultants and speakers.

Here I must throw in a little trivia. One summer Herb came to visit our cottage in Canada. At the time Herb came we were still in the old three-story white wooden building, definitely a firetrap. Herb took a look at it, weighed his options and took his chances. There were frequently as many as 22 in the cottage on weekends and it was often a zoo. The oldest resident was my Auntie Irene who died at 102. The youngest was whichever grandchild had most recently been born.

I remember one Sunday morning after we had been to church that Herb decided he needed to do some laundry. He was dressed in formal wear, even a tie as I recall. I have a photograph to record the incident. You see, the washing machine was an old wringer washer that sat on an uneven cement pedestal outside. We had old tin washtubs filled with clean water to receive the laundry as it was wrung through. Then, of course, the swishing around and the returning of the laundry to clean water in the machine through which it was wrung yet again. Then, the clothes line. As Dr. Quay was a fastidious and staid gentleman, I doubt any of his students or colleagues would believe he would ever stoop to this level of domesticity. That he tackled this antiquated method for getting his clothes clean sent him up several notches in my esteem.

My brother Murray was fascinated with Herb's credentials and intellect and was eager to garner his opinion on the personalities he had encountered in our family. He invited Herb to lunch in Toronto on the day of his departure with a burning question. Who was the most normal person at the cottage? Murray intended the response to include only family members so was surprised with Herb's quick retort—the babysitter, Joanne Reid! (Joanne was also Tony Jr.'s girlfriend and one of three babysitters we had for the summer.)

I want to return to the subject of my doctoral dissertation. Its title was *Psycholinguistic Abilities in Children with Epilepsy.* It was a unique study in that it required combining the disciplines of both medicine and education. Hence, the assistance I received from many quarters was essential to its completion.

I must give special mention of Dr. Joseph C. White, Chief of the Department of Neurology at the Barrow Neurological Institute in Phoenix, Arizona, who was responsible for locating a great many of the subjects in my study. He not only took time out from his many obligations in order to counsel and advise me, but also made available the professional resources of the EEG clinic and its staff. In addition, he reviewed each case used in this study to assure that the established criteria were met.

I also want to recognize Dr. Richard G. Curless, Professor of Pediatrics and Neurology at the University of Arizona College of Medicine as well as Dr. Derek Harwood-Nash, Professor of Radiology at the Hospital for Sick Children in Toronto, Ontario. This multi-disciplinary study took a good deal of coordination from many sources.

Basically, the purpose of the investigation was to study the linguistic, cognitive, memory and perceptual functions of a group of petit mal epileptic children and a group of children evidencing mixed epileptic seizures to determine whether any differences existed when these two groups were compared with each other or with a comparable group of non-epileptic children of average intelligence. Amazingly, I was able to evaluate fifty epileptic children. Finding this many subjects in Arizona was very difficult as it meant meeting with them individually wherever in the state I could find them, often in rather unusual places. I remember testing one child (with his parents nearby) on the dusty altar of a rural church with a desiccated lizard off to the side.

As I say, these children were compared to a contrast group of 50 children equivalent with respect to age and intelligence. I was delighted to conclude that no cognitive impairment as a result of epilepsy per se could be demonstrated in the epileptic cases studied suggesting no need for special education intervention.

This was a very ambitious study for me to undertake given the difficulty in locating appropriate subjects. But I did it, and the results were enthusiastically accepted and published in appropriate peer reviewed journals.

Becoming used to being called Dr. von Isser was another hurdle to overcome. It isn't a title one adjusts to overnight, and I don't think I fit the picture in people's minds of what a Dr. von Isser would look like. One time I was in the Los Angeles airport when the loud speaker asked for Dr. von Isser to come to the desk to take a phone call. When I arrived I told them I was there to receive a phone call and they responded that no, there was no such call. I told them I had heard my name on the loud speaker. They said, "**You** are Dr. von Isser?" I am not sure they believed me.

I always asked my students to call me Aldine. They were all adults in graduate school. Some never could bring themselves to do so. I thought such formality created a schism between people not so disparate in age.

I earned my Ph. D. on December 12, 1974 at age 41. I was ecstatic. It had been a long and demanding road. That night Winifred and Sam Kirk had a big party to celebrate. In attendance were my parents, my sons, all the members of my doctoral committee and their wives and, of course, Tony who had been my support all those years. Bette Layton and her sons—Rick and Randy, good friends of my boys—were there as well.

The following night Tony had a party in my honor with 35 people in attendance. It was a great success as indicated by the fact that our guests didn't leave until well after midnight. I felt thoroughly feted and very loved.

My parents were exceptionally proud of my accomplishment and decided to take the whole family to Tahiti in recognition of my accomplishment.

7

ଔଈଠ

THE PRESCHOOL INDIAN PROJECT

An interesting interlude in my life was my involvement in a project with Arizona Indians. It was entitled The Model Preschool for Handicapped Indian Children and was funded by the Bureau of Education for the Handicapped and implemented through the Department of Special Education where I was completing my doctoral degree. My role was that of project psychologist.

There are 22 sovereign American Indian reservations in Arizona. Our project visited all of them with the exception of the Navajo who had their own Head Start training program.

In Arizona, reservation land covers over a quarter of the state. Some tribes descend from Arizona's very first inhabitants. An estimated five to six percent of Arizona's total population is of American Indian ancestry. In fact, our state has the second largest American Indian population in the entire United States.

The project ran from 1970 to 1974 under the leadership of the Program Director, Elizabeth (Bette) Sharp, Ph.D., Assistant Professor of Special Education at UA. Bette ran a tight ship. She and I have been close friends for many years.

The project also had the support of Gordon Krutz who was the Coordinator of Indian Programs at UA and Emory Sekaquaptewa. Emory, a Hopi elder, was hired by Gordon to be the Assistant Coordinator of Indian Programs at the university in 1970. It was then that he became involved with our project.

Emory, now deceased, had a fascinating history. He was believed to be the first Arizona Native American to attend West Point. Later he attended law school at the University of Arizona. He held various leadership positions within his own village of Kykotsmovi on the Hopi Reservation as well as positions on the Hopi Tribal Council and the appellate division of the Hopi Tribal Court.

Emory is best known, however, for his role in compiling the first dictionary of the Hopi language. I remember the disapproval he suffered from the older members of his tribe who did not sanction a dictionary at all. In fact, the dictionary is credited with playing an important role in revitalizing the Hopi language.

In April of 1973 while doing a special workshop on the Hopi Reservation, Emory took us to meet his family and see his home in Old Oraibi, one of the four original Hopi villages. Old Oraibi is the oldest village on the continent having been lived in since AD 1150. In the 1540s the village was recorded as having up to 3000 residents.

Visitors were not encouraged there. Posted at the entrance to the Old Oraibi mesa was a sign saying "White men are not welcome here. You do not respect our laws. You do not even respect your own." I was honored to be part of a team that was welcome there and I learned a great deal of Hopi lore.

This project started with two model classrooms—one for Papago (Tohono O'Odham) children on the Papago Reservation and one for Yaqui children in the Pascua Yaqui area. Our students were all in Head Start Programs and we worked with the teachers and the parents of these children as their cooperation was an essential component in the success of the project. I had wonderful colleagues one of whom—Dr. Gail Harris—has held a significant place in my heart and my life. We continue to maintain a close relationship.

Establishing trust and friendship with the Indians was critical. It took me a while to "break the ice." Our director had urged me to "dress conservatively," which was a challenge for me. But, I toned down the color and looked as pedestrian as I could. Later, she had to admonish me to try harder as one of our Tohono O'Odham team members, Mario Flores who was a member of the Yaqui tribe, referred to me as the project's "satellite." He meant to use the word socialite.

I have many memories of my experiences with the project, one of which still sends chills up my spine. In the Yaqui classroom there was a darling three-year-old girl with the abundant glossy black hair so typical of her people. However, she was cursed, so I thought, with one long white hair that was a daily distraction to me. At that stage in my own life, I pulled every such offender that I found on my head and I was quite sure I would be doing this child a favor if I were to surreptitiously pluck hers. I waited for the right moment. Fortunately, it never came. The spirits must have been looking after me as

I learned a short time later that this child, by virtue of having one white hair, was blessed by the angels and therefore special in her tribe! I had a lot to learn.

Another incident that might have caused me to be run off the reservation occurred during a workshop I was presenting to the tribal teachers in Sells, Arizona. In an effort to explain the difference between neurotic behavior and psychopathological behavior I offered an analogy I thought would be helpful. I compared sociopathic behavior and its remediation to the difference between an onion and an apple. Like an onion, with sociopathic children you could work and work, and peel and peel, and in the end you would find no core. There was little hope that one could change the behaviors of these types of children. On the other hand, in the classroom we are typically working with behaviors easily remediable. As with an apple, you peel away that thin red skin and on the inside is the healthy white fruit.

Suffice that I was oblivious to the habit of Native Americans of referring to their brothers who had "turned coat" and moved into the white culture as, yes, apples—red on the outside but white on the inside! I didn't get much applause after that presentation.

Ultimately I think I did win the respect of most of the teachers with whom I worked. They knew my heart was in the right place.

The classroom phase of the project was completed in two years. Then began our outreach component requiring us to travel to the 22 reservations I have mentioned. As I say, I was the project psychologist and was faced with a great many problems that were new territory for me. I will cite one example so that you will understand the conundrums I often faced. At one Head Start program on a reservation that I will not identify, was a little boy who was out of control. His behaviors were bizarre and often dangerous. I was asked to assist the teachers in developing methods for ameliorating his outbursts.

This was his history. In his tribe the birth of twins is a tragedy. The father will claim the first one born, but not the second. That child was the spawn of someone else. The child of whom I speak was a second born twin and was taken immediately after his birth by his mother and hung in a swaddle from a tree, abandoned and left to die. By chance, a Bureau of Indian Affairs nurse happened to hear of the situation and rescued the baby. But, what could be done? His natural mother would have nothing to do with the child. It was under duress that the sister of the mother said she would take him into her home. This did not include accepting him into her family. The little boy lived in a dark closet at night—no bed. When the family went to the mercantile all the other children were given a treat, but not this little boy. He didn't belong to them. Is it any wonder that a sad, neglected, unloved little boy would have emotional problems? I had my work cut out for me. I can only hope that my recommendations for intervention were followed and that life became better for that neglected and abandoned child.

On one trip, on our departing day from the White River Apache reservation, I was presented with a beautifully made beaded necklace that the mother of a child with whom I had worked closely all week had stayed up all night to make for me. As you can imagine, I treasure it and wear it frequently.

During this outreach phase of the project, we often traveled to the reservations every other week, occasionally enduring rather uncomfortable accommodations and situations. Indians were often treated badly in Arizona at that time. We quickly learned which restaurants would accept Indians and which would not allow them to eat there. Rather than a dialogue of where we went and the conditions we encountered, I picked at random two entries from my diary.

Tuesday, April 9, 1974
"We went to the Yuma Head Start Program (Fort Quechan Indians) to have a workshop all day. It was very windy and dusty and we worried about driving through the dust storm. We left there about 3:00 p.m. and I drove Mario to our next stop in Parker (Arizona) arriving about 5:00 p.m. The place was crammed and we couldn't believe the number of tents along the river (Colorado). We stayed in an awful motel—The Kahok."

Wednesday, April 10, 1974
"I slept well in a dreadful smelling little motel with eight Hell's Angels in a room down the hall with their revving motorcycles. They were stuck in Parker because of dreadful dust. Went to Head Start to consult re: behavior disorders all day. It is cold here! Went to lunch with two Indian ladies to discuss their problems. At the end of the day I drove back to Tucson."

Because of the uniqueness of the project, we often had professors who would intern with us for a few months. I well remember Paul Moffitt, a psychology professor from Australia who had worked with Aboriginal tribes there. As I was the project psychologist, he was assigned to work with me. You will read more about Paul elsewhere in these writings.

As I mentioned, we did not visit the Navajo Reservation. I did, however, teach there for one semester—every Thursday evening during the spring semester of 1979. Because of the great distance, it was necessary that I be flown there and UA required that their professors fly in twin-engine aircraft only. The type used for my transportation was a Navajo Piper Seminole—an apt name for the aircraft—and the pilot allowed me to sit left seat. I logged four hours of flying time every week.

I have maintained an emotional connection with the Tohono O'Odham tribe by annually attending the Christmas concert at Mission San Xavier del Bac on the reservation. San Xavier, founded by Padre Eusebio Kino in 1692, is about 10 miles south of Tucson in the middle of the Tohono O'Odham Reservation. It is one of over twenty missions Father Kino founded in the Pimeria Alta area which extends from the Mexican state of Sonora into Arizona.

As difficult as it was to fit the preschool Indian project into my schedule at that time, I have never regretted taking this opportunity to learn more about the rich heritage of our Indian population and, in a small way, to contribute to the improvement of the lives of many children.

THE HOPI SNAKE DANCE

Writing about the remarkable experience I had with the preschool Indian project reminds me of an   adventure I had with my family on August 25, 1946 when I was 13 years old. My parents were taking my sister, my brother, my old grandmother and me on an extensive tour of Indian monuments which I shall list later. As a reporter, my father was eager to write a story about the mystical Hopi Snake Dance and was able to arrange for us to attend it. It is held every other year. I wrote in my diary that it was one of the most "interesting days of my life."

We traveled on a primitive road to reach the base of the Hopi mesas which we had to climb to reach the plaza where the dance rite was conducted. The kiva, a holy structure, housed the snakes that were to be used. There were few tourists and we were basically ignored by the Hopis.

To provide some background, the Hopi Tribe believes that their ancestors originated in the underworld. Their gods and spirits live there. They consider snakes their brothers who have the ability to carry their prayers beneath the earth to beseech their gods to send rain, so critical to their lives.

For four days the Snake Clan hunts for snakes in the desert. The majority of them are rattlesnakes. They are taken to the Kiva and washed—seemingly hundreds of them. On the day of the ceremony, the men of the tribe gather snakes in their arms and carry them in their mouths to impart prayers to them.

After the dancers have made a circuit around the plaza four times, a priest draws a circle on the ground. All the snakes are thrown in. It is then that the snake priests grab handfuls of them, run into the desert and turn them loose to carry their prayers to their gods.

As soon as the ceremony ended, my father hurried us all down the mesa anticipating the rain that would inevitably arrive. And did it ever! No sooner did we get to the car than the deluge started and I tell you the absolute truth when I say that ours was the last vehicle that got out. All the cars behind us were bogged down and had to wait out the storm.

What an exciting experience it was! Not knowing how long my family would continue to live in Arizona, my father wanted us to see all the Southwestern sites possible. On that trip we also visited:

Bandelier National Monument
El Morro National Monument
The Painted Desert
The Petrified Forest
Sunset Crater
Grand Canyon
The Navajo Reservation
Montezuma's Castle

That extensive trip exploring ancient Indian dwellings and geological anomalies left me with indelible memories.

8

⚜

MY UNIVERSITY CAREER

As mentioned, I now had a Ph.D. and was unsure of how I would put it to use. The problem was solved quickly enough.

One afternoon in the summer of 1975 the phone rang at the old cottage in Dwight, Ontario. The call was for Dr. von Isser. What a surprise I had when a professor in the College of Education at the University of Arizona (UA) in Tucson, Arizona asked me what textbooks he should order for the courses I would be teaching in the fall. I had not been contacted about a position there and thought he had made a mistake.

The request soon came from the Department Head that they hoped very much that I would accept a temporary position as Head of the Division in the Graduate Studies Program in Behavior Disorders. Let me explain the "temporary." It is very unusual for a university to hire its own graduates. The only route around that was to take a position at another university after graduation and later submit an application for a faculty position at UA. I, therefore, was not eligible for a permanent assignment.

In fact, the man who preceded me in that position had been one of my professors and the department had an active search committee whose duty it was to replace him. The search had thus far been fruitless; they were very discerning, after all. I was asked to cover the position while they continued their search. I felt completely unprepared for this assignment having had no forewarning and the new semester was bearing down upon me. Still, it was a challenge, and I loved a challenge.

I returned to Tucson and, in the blink of an eye, transitioned from student to faculty. I fell completely in love with the job and the students and told the department head that I felt that I should be paying them instead of the other way around. Well, the second semester came and I was still there and the search committee was abandoned. With special permission from the Provost of the university, I was assigned that position permanently as an Assistant Professor.

The Department of Special Education was made up of individual programs, each addressing a specific handicapping condition, i.e. mental retardation, physical disabilities, vision and hearing disabilities, learning disabilities and emotional disturbance. All programs were at the graduate level only.

I was a one-person program which meant that I taught all the coursework associated with the disability as well as supervised all the interns. That was a huge assignment and some years I had two Graduate Assistants to assist with the burden.

Other graduate students than just my own could take the coursework which meant I often had large classes. Seminars and colloquia were for my full-time students only. I taught Master's Degree and Doctoral Degree students. As each doctoral committee required five professors, I was on a great many doctoral committees for students studying other disciplines as well.

Some years I had as many as 16 full-time master's students which therefore required 16 internship sites. This was another challenge as each placement had to be in a special class for emotionally disturbed, behaviorally disordered, or delinquent students up to 18 years of age. My students had the option of selecting the type of placement they wanted and to interview the cooperating teacher and school or institution in which they would be working. It was a year-long assignment for them.

The opportunities for placement were legion, including day-care facilities, public school special classes, residential treatment centers, psychiatric hospital classrooms, jail facilities and correctional institutions. Also, we had classrooms for autistic children only. It was fascinating to watch my students work with such a variety of youngsters.

One could scarcely believe some of the diagnoses of these children. One year at the Arizona Children's Home, a state subsidized residential treatment center, there were two boys named Robert. Both were adorable little guys who would crawl on my lap or hug me. One, at age 5, had killed his little sister. The other was systematically pulling out his hair as well as pulling all his teeth. He was a very disturbed little boy and ultimately ended up in Phoenix at the State Mental Institution.

Before my students ever went into their assigned practicum classroom, I had a lengthy seminar with them about what constituted appropriate behavior for *them*. One young woman, Molly White, arrived wearing a sequined tee shirt on the front of which was written, "In case of rape, this side up." That was a good place for me to begin! I advised them not to wear hanging earrings; they would be pulled from their ears. I warned them that a good many of them, male and female, would be propositioned or "required for extracurricular activity" by their mentors. It never failed to happen, at least once a semester.

One year my intern, Mark Roleski, married his cooperating teacher before the end of the second semester!

I always prepared them for the likelihood that this demanding work would suck their wells dry and that they absolutely needed to find ways to take care of themselves and to refill their wells. We made sure that as a group we shared many times of great fun.

Annually my husband would ask why these fine people would go into a field that demanded so much of them. I can only say that when one has a breakthrough with a young person the feeling is so rewarding and ego-boosting that it makes all the hassles worthwhile.

My students were taught to maintain a position in the classroom from which they could see every child at all times. This was particularly true in classrooms for autistic youngsters whose behaviors were unpredictable. Mary Bacon, a thirty year veteran in classrooms for the autistic, allowed that rudimentary rule to slip past her just once. While working one-on-one with a student, she failed to notice a child coming up behind her. He whacked her on the head with a chair. She suffered brain damage and was never able to teach again. These youngsters can be dangerous and each of my students was trained to protect not only the safety of their students but of themselves as well.

Of fascination to us all is the savant quality of autistic students. One day while visiting a junior high school special class for the autistic, I noticed one lad deeply involved in a writing project. When I saw that he was writing a page from the book *Cosmos* by Carl Sagan I asked his teacher about it. She told me that he happened to have glanced at that page in the book at his home the night before and today he had total recall of everything on that page including the punctuation. He could neither read nor understand it, but he could duplicate it. There were students who could reproduce the entire solar system, the metro system in Paris, and on and on. Many could be told the date of my birth and respond immediately that I was born on a Wednesday. The mind is a mystery and trying to make strides into normalizing it can be a tricky and discouraging process.

In detention facilities we had to be particularly cautious to avoid allowing our emotions to become involved with the students. Sometimes a young person would be on the edge of making a breakthrough but not withstanding that was ejected from the program the day he turned 18 years of age. It was heartbreaking to see students so close to "getting it" only to be turned out into their harsh, real world because of a date on the calendar.

Some students remain part of your life forever. Such is the case for me with a beautiful woman named Magda Urban (Misty) who was a doctoral student early in my career. She continues to be a beloved friend and an outstanding professional lo! these forty years later. I am godmother to her two children.

Many of my doctoral students came from abroad—England, Canada, France, Korea, Turkey—and I have been fortunate to stay in touch with some of them.

Kwang Sun Blair stands out. She came to UA to work with me for her doctoral degree. I have never known a more dedicated or competent student. She was married in the U.S.—to a man named Kym Blair—and after she completed her Ph.D. they returned to Korea for her to work at the university level. When her parents died, she came back to the U.S. and now teaches at the University of Southern Florida. We exchange Christmas cards and family news annually.

Another doctoral student from Korea was Eunhee Sue Pak. The completion of her degree was nip and tuck. As a member of her doctoral committee, I had received a copy of her dissertation well in advance of the date she was to defend it before her doctoral committee which was made up of four male professors and me. I read it, saw no red flags, and assumed that she would have no difficulty with the oral exam.

I still get upset when I remember that occasion. Eunhee Sue did not speak English clearly, but she had been a stellar student throughout her program. Well, during this exam I could see that the male members were deliberately giving her a hard time. She was becoming flustered and anxious. Under this kind of stress her facility with English deteriorated. I was absolutely furious. They were setting her up for failure. When the committee chair called for a brief recess I could see the writing on the wall. They did indeed plan to reject her dissertation—to fail her. I would have no part of that. It simply was not fair.

I brought to their attention that Eunhee had fulfilled every requirement toward her degree adequately or with excellence and that if there was a problem with her dissertation it should have been brought to her attention long ago. I pointed out that she had a job awaiting her in Korea and that she was leaving immediately after the exam. I am not usually so assertive, but this was a critical juncture in this woman's life. I fought—and won. Eunhee passed. She will never know how close she came to having all her dreams dashed. (And she'll never know the part I played in it.)

As you will see in the section "Summary of my Life," I held many highly responsible positions at the university level as well as at my college level—The College of Education. I was elated on August 22, 1979 to be assigned to a two-year position on the department's executive advisory committee—a great honor.

In August of 1984 I was asked to chair the Peer Evaluation Committee. I was quite overwhelmed as this meant reviewing biannually each faculty member for his or her contribution to the department and to the field. I held this position for many years.

I was quite surprised on August 22, 1984 to be asked to take on the role of Assistant Department Head. All these accolades and recognitions were coming to me all at once, it seemed.

Another honor came when the Vice-President of UA invited 11 professors to a luncheon—one from each of the colleges at the university. He asked me to represent the College of Education. It should be noted that of the 11 professors in attendance, I was the only woman!

In 1988, the year before Tony died, I was asked, even begged, to take on the leadership role of my department for one year. I would be Department Head for the Department of Special Education and Rehabilitation, although the title would be as Assistant Coordinator of the Division as it was a temporary assignment. The faculty knew, of course, that Tony was very ill, but they prevailed upon me and I ultimately capitulated. My own program was taken over by two Graduate Assistants but remained my responsibility as were all the administrative issues within the department. I made it through the year and was rewarded with the letter which I have added on the next page. The following year I took a full leave of absence and was with Tony every minute until his death eight months later in January, 1989.

I look back on my career in special education with a sense of great gratitude and satisfaction. I am confident that the many individuals I trained made a significant positive impact on the lives of troubled youngsters and their families. The time had come, however, for me to make room for new blood and innovative approaches. I retired in 1997 at the age of 64 and received the title Professor Emerita. I loved every moment of my career at UA.

THE UNIVERSITY OF ARIZONA
TUCSON, ARIZONA 85721

COLLEGE OF EDUCATION
DIVISION OF SPECIAL EDUCATION AND REHABILITATION
(602) 621-3214
(602) 621-3248
(602) 621-7822

May 9, 1988

Aldine von Isser, Ph.D.
Division of Special Education and Rehabilitation
College of Education
University of Arizona
Tucson, Arizona 85721

Dear Aldine:

We send you our fondest congratulations on your achievements as our Assistant
Coordinator of the Division. You took to the role of administrator with the
same gusto as the best of the female mud-wrestlers -- jumped in, took hold, and
came out on top, looking good.

We have watched you stand tall to the call, bemoan the mess of bedlam, pour out
the piles of paper, gallop grandly through the administrative garrison, suffer
the pain of unfair fate, and do it all with a "joie de vivre" that was
infectious for faculty and staff.

Now that your tenure in the role is to terminate, at least for awhile, we are
thanking you for having the heft when needed but demonstrating it always with
the purest and sweetest intent. Some of your accomplishments are visible to
all, and many will be known only to you and the individual(s) affected. In any
case, you left a legacy of good humor balanced with serious consideration,
prompt response tempered with appropriate deliberation, and intellectualism
coupled with common sense.

We wish for you the best of all that is possible during your leave, and lay a
perpetual welcome mat inviting your return.

You are appreciated.

Sincerely,

Faculty and Staff

9

☙

WORKING IN SOUTH AMERICA - 1976

I should never have gone. It was far too dangerous. It was 1976 and South America was a hotbed of violence and atrocities. It certainly was no place for a 43 year old woman to be traveling alone for almost two months. I knew nobody in any of the places I was going so if I got into trouble there was no "fail-safe"— no plan B.

But indeed there were adventures. I was able to obtain visas for all the countries I needed to visit for my work with the exception of Argentina. The State Department wisely denied it. That very year, on March 24th, a coup d'etat overthrew Isabel Peron and a military junta was installed. An official estimate is that between 1976 and 1983 up to 30,000 had been killed or had "disappeared."

I was well aware of the danger but was willing to take the risk because I knew such an opportunity would never come my way again. In retrospect, it was worth it. Educators were anathema and reports were that as punishment for their "subversive activities," many were tied to bed springs and electric shocked. Some disappeared completely. So, what was I doing in that part of the world?

It all came about because Dr. Samuel A. Kirk, "the father of special education," asked me to write the first test to assess learning disabilities in monolingual Spanish-speaking children. I loved a challenge and this was the granddaddy of challenges.

This was to be an adaptation of a test developed by the University of Illinois—The Illinois Test of Psycholinguistic Abilities (ITPA) published in 1961. It was the seminal instrument in learning disabilities written by my mentor, Dr. Samuel A. Kirk and his wife Winifred. Dr. Kirk actually coined the term "learning disabilities."

As mentioned earlier, Dr. and Mrs. Kirk moved from the East to Tucson. I was his protégé. The University of Illinois asked him to develop a test similar to the ITPA to be used throughout the Spanish-speaking world. I was recruited. I had the background and the enthusiasm, and I was proficient in Spanish. It would be necessary for me to become fluent, and I did.

Since I was on faculty at UA at that time, it was complicated to take care of my responsibilities there as well as to work half time for the University of Illinois. Winifred and I toiled for three years writing the test with frequent visits to a linguistics specialist in Mexico City to confirm and correct our usage of Spanish. Finally, the test was written—La Prueba Illinois de Habilidades Psicolingüísticas (SITPA).

It was ready now to be standardized and I was the only one who could do it. Linguistically speaking there were three basic regions in South America and we selected representative cities in each for me to do the work. These regions represented distinctive approaches to the Spanish language. The standardization had to take all of these variations into consideration. For example, the word fence could be a different word entirely in each of these regions (barda, verja, cerca) and each of these needed to be included in the manual of instructions as an option for the person administering the test. Each distinctive culture and its idioms had to be recognized.

In retrospect, I realize that there were many dimensions to the experience I was about to undertake. Foremost was my involvement as a professional. Training psychologists to administer the test in order to amass the statistical data was my primary responsibility.

The second dimension would evolve quite naturally—that of being a tourist. I was eager to see all the sights and absorb the various cultures to the greatest extent possible.

The third dimension came as a surprise to me. I was warmly accepted into the lives and the homes not only of the people with whom I worked but also with people who had been contacted and told by friends that I would be in their cities. This opportunity to experience the customs of South Americans was precious to me.

The fourth dimension was the profound effect my exposure to the people and to their unique ways of living had on me personally. Since this experience in South America, I have never again been quite the same person who left on this journey quite unprepared for what I would encounter.

Each of these dimensions will become evident as this chapter unfolds.

We will begin with the first dimension—my responsibilities as a professional. In each city, I was to work with a group of approximately five psychologists to whom I would teach the techniques for administrating the test. It was a complex instrument and would require considerable focus on the part of the psychologists with whom I was working. I met with them Monday, Tuesday and Wednesday in the training phase. On Thursday they would be on their own to perfect their skills and I would embark on my second dimension—that of an enthusiastic tourist. On Friday we would gather together again to address any difficulties they had encountered. It was also the day for their final examinations as each had to administer the test to me until they had it down pat. After I departed their cities, they would test appropriate children in their communities and send the results to the University of Illinois to be statistically evaluated and the norms established.

I had assumed that educated Mexican and South American psychologists would have at least a working knowledge of English. I was wrong. None spoke even a word. Prior to the trip, I had been diligent in developing my fluency with Spanish, thank goodness. Eventually I even dreamed and talked to myself in Spanish! It wasn't until the third city that the "students" had the courage to tell me that one word I was saying was definitely not appropriate. I'll explain.

One of the tests assesses manual expression. I would ask "the child" to show me what we do with—and proceed to show them a picture of perhaps a hammer and a nail. They were to physically enact the motions and I would evaluate them on the actions they produced. One such picture was of a comb and mirror. I said, "Enséñame lo que hacemos con un peine y un espejo." Show me what we do with a comb and mirror. Except—I was pronouncing peine as pene which has a very, very different meaning. What private giggles my students must have had before the error was brought to my attention!

MEXICO CITY, Mexico

I left Tucson on Sunday, October 30th, 1976 and made my first stop in Hermosillo, Sonora to deliver testing materials. I also delivered materials to Ciudad Obregon, Culiacan and Guadalajara prior to reaching Mexico City. It must be explained that transporting the testing materials was a major difficulty for me. They were heavy, packed in many boxes, and had to be carefully guarded at each stop. They cost thousands of dollars in excess baggage charges.

On Monday I began the training of seven people at El Instituto Mexicano de La Audición y El Lenguage (IMAL). That night the Kirks phoned me. They were very upset that they had let me leave on this trip. Apparently the moment my plane took off they had serious regrets. It had been a terrible mistake—far too dangerous. Thank goodness they made that decision after I had left.

CARACAS, Venezuela

On November 6th I flew to Caracas, Venezuela arriving at a hotel at 2:00 a.m. Although I was exhausted having started the trip 20 hours previously, it was clear I could not stay at this place. It wasn't a hotel at all but rather some hostel for young people who were still actively partying at 3:00 a.m. I knew I had to leave. There was not even a lock on my door.

Fortunately I was able to find a taxi, hauled all my material out, and checked into the Caracas Hilton at 5:00 in the morning. Sunday I had time for laundry and my weekly phone call to my husband Tony in Tucson. We had arranged that I would phone him every Sunday night to assure him I was fine. But, what on earth would he have done if I hadn't called? He didn't know where I was for the most part and if I had disappeared he wouldn't know where to begin to look for me. As a "fail-safe" it was totally inadequate but it was all we had.

It was now Monday and the beginning of my training at the Instituto de Psicología. I found that it was difficult for me to speak Spanish in Venezuela as they speak very, very quickly. It felt as if their words were coming at me from a machine gun—quickly and forcefully. I overcame the problem and the training went well.

I spent the weekend at the Macuto Sheraton seeing sights I had hoped to be able to add to my itinerary including a cable car ride to Mt. Avila which took me above the clouds. It was beautiful. There was also some time for walking on the beach and swimming.

BOGOTA, Colombia

On to Bogotá, Colombia where the elevation was 8500 feet. I had my weekly chat with Tony. On Monday I started the training with four women who, as was typical, spoke not a word of English and unfortunately knew very little about the concept of learning disabilities. I had my work cut out for me. Two were from Bogotá, one from Medellín, and the fourth from Barranquilla. People came substantial distances to receive the training.

Bogotá was a very, very dangerous city. I was warned about wearing my wedding rings outside the hotel. "Oh," said I, "I'll be careful to keep them on my finger at all times." I was told they would simply take my finger, too. Women in Bogotá not only have their purses snatched, but their children as well. I was careful and survived without incident.

While in Bogotá I found sufficient time for sightseeing. One place I had yearned to visit was the Salt Cathedral located about an hour's drive outside the city. It was a huge cathedral built (of salt, naturally) deep in a salt mine. It had been constructed almost entirely by the miners who needed a place to pray to God beseeching Him to prevent accidents which occurred frequently and were often deadly. Because of the deterioration of the infrastructure—the shoring was breaking down—it was considered too dangerous for tourists to enter. Thus, it had been closed the year previous to my visit. Wasn't I fortunate that it had been reopened briefly during the time I was in Bogotá? The following year it was closed permanently. I'll admit to having had an almost overwhelming case of claustrophobia inside the mine.

And now evidence of the third dimension of my experience in South America. Wednesday evening, after a full day of work, I spent a gracious evening in the home of a delightful couple who had been told of my visit to Bogotá. My host was a gentleman who was the head of the Bank of London in Colombia and his wife was an elegant and beautiful Colombian. Dinner was served early—9:30 p.m.—as they were expecting friends to drop in afterwards! As frequently was the case in my evenings out, I did not leave until 2:00 a.m.

Although suffering from insufficient sleep, it was nonetheless necessary for me to continue the training all day Thursday as well as we were unable to meet on Friday. I worked without stopping from 9:30 a.m. to 6:30 p.m. The termination of our work together at the end of the week was very emotional. We had formed a close bond and each had a gift and a hug for me when we parted.

At 7:30 that evening I was picked up and taken to a beautiful home for a dinner party in my honor. Again, friends had written the hosts of my visit in Bogotá. I was exhausted from working in Spanish for nine hours straight only to discover that the entire evening, until after 1:00 a.m., was conversed in Spanish only!!! The couple hosting the party was most interesting, as were their guests. He was a brain surgeon (Tomás Posada, a Colombian) and she an absolutely stunning French woman named Mira. As they were wealthy and targets for skullduggery, they had to take special precautions with their home and their children. An armed guard was posted on the roof 24 hours a day. Their children were driven to and from school each day by a chauffeur and an armed guard. As I say, Bogotá was a dangerous city and I was very fortunate to have no unpleasant incidents.

In typical fashion, dinner was not served until 10:30 p.m. and when I was returned to the hotel I was a rag. Still, I then had to pack everything before going to bed about 2:30 a.m. in order to get up at 5:00 a.m. to check out!! It was time to go to Ecuador.

QUITO, Ecuador

No sooner did I arrive in Quito than I was contacted by the son of dear friends of mine with whom I went on many of the trips to Greece I have written about in another chapter. Their names were Prudie and Peter Mennell. He had been British Ambassador in Quito until the previous year when he had been transferred to Bermuda. Their son Simon remained in Quito.

I was unable to accept their invitation to a party that night as I was truly exhausted. The following evening, however, revived and excited, I was picked up at my hotel by

Aldine in Quito, Ecuador

Simon and his wife who took me to their home for dinner—again a very late affair.

I was invited to other delightful parties in Quito, a city of great beauty that I grew to love. Another lovely young couple with whom I had dinner was to leave Ecuador permanently two weeks hence to live in England. Economic conditions there had literally pushed them out.

I had read a considerable amount about Ecuador and knew of places I wanted very much to see. Early one morning I hired a taxi for the day to ferry me to my destinations. Being a typical tourist, I asked that our first stop be the equator. Of course I had the driver take my photograph with one of my feet in the northern hemisphere and the other in the southern hemisphere. I did this again in Africa when I traveled there with my mother.

I had heard of a very infrequently visited area quite a distance from Quito to which I asked the dubious driver to take me. We drove to the top of a mountain along a little used road—ultimately a path— where it simply stopped. Stepping out of the car, I saw a sight that I'll never forget. I was looking down thousands of feet into a huge crater and below were thatched houses and Indians working their fields as they have for centuries.

Clouds hung low on the mountains surrounding the crater, and I simply couldn't believe people could live in such isolation. There was a trail to the valley below and climbing slowly to the top was an old Indian - 66. Only Indians inhabited this crater. I waited quite some time for him to reach the top as I very much wanted to know more about life below. I hoped he spoke Spanish. He did. For the next almost two hours I was spellbound by his stories.

Aldine with old man, his valley in the volcano in background

He had departed his village in the crater at 5:00 a.m. to begin his annual pilgrimage to visit to La Virgen del Cinche, many, many miles away. His shoes had holes in the sides and bottoms and he was poor and filthy but the warmth in his eyes enchanted me. After a lengthy conversation—fortunately he spoke Spanish instead of a dialect— I asked the driver to drive him back to Quito with me. He could continue his pilgrimage from there. No sooner were we in the car than he tugged a bottle out of his filthy sack. It contained what was known as "trago," pure alcohol from cane. I felt ashamed to refuse his offer but somehow the thought of swigging from the same bottle as those two convinced me I'd contract a gastrointestinal disorder from which I would never recover.

En route to Quito the old man continued his stories and even the taxi driver couldn't believe all he heard. He told of his faith and of "El Señor del Arbol." I was thrilled when I was invited to go to the church to learn for myself about the miracles of which the man spoke. El Señor is a natural piece of wood with arms outstretched and a knob that could be construed as Christ's head. The church had been built in preparation for the placement of El Señor del Arbol above the altar. A face had been carved into it, and a silver crown and long hair added. I was taken to see the walls on which were paintings with stories beneath each telling of the miracle depicted in that particular picture. Each miracle had occurred as a result of people invoking the mercy of "El Señor del Arbol" in times of distress.

So, this dear man continued with his own stories of miracles he had known. These were some of his tales. A friend of his had accidentally chopped into his leg with a hatchet so that it was barely hanging on to his body. He wrapped the leg in leaves and invoked La Virgen del Cinche to heal him. Then he slept. Two hours later he removed the leaves to check the leg and it was completely healed!! <u>True.</u> Only a scar.

He told of a mother who had been tending her baby in the woods and left briefly to take care of another child. When she returned, the baby had been eaten by a bear and only the bones remained. She ran in grief to her husband to tell him of the tragedy. He was so distraught that he killed her with his machete. In despair he took the bones of his child and laid them at the feet of the Virgin. He invoked her mercy. Within a few minutes his child was whole and it was as if nothing had happened. He never mentioned whether the wife was restored to life.

I had become confused about what Virgin or Señor was responsible for which miracle but the important thing is that my aged friend was at peace with both his faith and his stories. And so was I.

It was time to move on to Chile.

SANTIAGO, Chile

When I arrived in Santiago de Chile at 8:00 p.m., I was scared. I disembarked the aircraft and saw armed guards everywhere. I finally "got" that I probably shouldn't be there. I looked back at the aircraft and thought seriously about getting right back on. But retreat was not my style.

It must be noted that the bombing of La Moneda in Santiago had taken place only three years earlier, on September 11th, 1973. This came after a period of unrest during which Salvador Allende was overthrown by the armed forces and the national police.

As a parting gift, Tony had given me a handsome leather briefcase. At customs a grim looking security agent looked at it, and then me, and murmured some words I did not understand. I panicked. I told him if he wanted to keep it he could—that I was hiding nothing—that I would get back on the plane if he preferred. I felt threatened and unwelcome, and this was just the beginning. As it happens, he was complimenting me on the good looking briefcase. I was shaking too hard to appreciate the irony.

Then a strange thing happened. In each city I had been met by someone arranged for before my departure from Tucson. This gave me the security of knowing I was with the correct person. Here I was met by a man, Alamíno Alvardo, about whom I knew nothing. I said that I was expecting to meet Sylvia Gallardo and was told by him that he had been sent in her place. I was wary but allowed him to take me to the Carrera Sheraton where I was spending the week.

The hotel was on the square at La Moneda and the bullet holes and damage were clearly evident even then. The entire city was under curfew and armed military were on every corner. I knew that educators were regarded as subversive.

Alamíno claimed to know no English and told me that he had difficulty understanding my Spanish. By now I spoke Spanish well and I couldn't understand his problem. I will tell you, however, that you would never hear a Chilean say that he spoke Spanish. The name of their language is Castellano and has a very different pronunciation. For example, the street on which I live in Tucson is Calle del Caballo (Street of the Horse). In Chile they would pronounce it Cajhe del Cavajho. Also, they dropped their "s" sound so that the term "mas o menos" (more or less) would be "ma o meno." I had to accustom my ear to a new way of speaking and I found it charming.

Alamíno invited me to have a drink with him at the hotel. I accepted. Time passed and he advised me he could no longer leave the hotel—that curfew was in place. He suggested he would have to share my room. I let him know that wasn't happening and that he could sleep on the stairway as far as I was concerned. In fact, I don't know where he slept but he picked me up at 8:45 in the morning to take me to his institute where I worked with his group until evening. They even had lunch brought in, I think to keep me out of sight. I kept wondering what had happened to the cadre of people I was supposed to be training.

The next day we worked until 5:00 p.m. at which time I was taken to the home of Gladys, one of my students, for tea with her family. Afterwards her father took us on a tour of the city which included a visit to a hill in the center of the city—San Cristobál. That night Alamíno took me for a lovely dinner to a restaurant called Canta Galle situated at the edge of the city for a special dish called parrillada. Then the truth came out.

Alamíno admitted that he did indeed speak some English but it was important for him to keep me confused when I first arrived. He had usurped the place of the group at the university with whom I was supposed to work and instead had me working at his private institute. It was rather frightening to realize I had been hijacked and working with "strangers" all week! A letter of apology was eventually sent by the University of Illinois to the university group with whom I had been scheduled to work that week. I will always wonder how I managed to be totally "hoodwinked."

But that is as nothing compared to what I did at the airport the next day before my flight to Lima, Perú. While sitting in the departure lounge, I was approached rather furtively by a nice looking man who sat down beside me. He asked if I were taking the flight to Lima and I confirmed that I was. He told me his story. His niece was to be married in Lima and he had a wedding present for her that he was afraid to send through the mail system as he thought it unreliable. Would I be good enough to take it to Lima. "Of course," said I obligingly, "but how will I find your niece?" He asked where I was staying and assured me his brother would pick it up at my hotel. And so I slipped the package into my carry-on luggage and boarded my flight.

LIMA, Perú

Unfortunately, en route to Lima I ate a sandwich with chicken. It must have been very, very tainted chicken as by the time I arrived in Lima in the wee hours of the morning I was sick and exhausted. Of course, the militia was out in full force on every street corner. It was way past curfew. Apparently certain airport taxis are allowed to pass through the streets to get their passengers to hotels. There was no problem. This was another country under military rule.

In Perú that year, 1976, the Revolutionary Socialist Party was formed by a group of radical army officers. Sendero Luminoso adopted an armed struggle as the only means to achieve its "anti-feudal, anti-revolution" goals.

I checked into the Lima Sheratón desperate to get to bed. No sooner did I get settled in my room than there was a knock on my door—at 3:30 a.m.! Of course it was the "brother" who had arrived to pick up the "wedding present." And then it hit me. I had been a mule. I was sure I had been carrying drugs. Had I been caught I doubt if I ever would have seen my family again. To this day my hands shake when I think of what a very foolish thing I did.

I was very sick the next day and cancelled work. Instead I dressed, found a taxi and went to a farmacia. Antibiotics can be purchased over the counter there so back to the hotel I went fortified with "kaomycin."

I was far too ill to leave my room and was fortunate that the head psychologist, Leonor de Cotler, was willing to come to the hotel to work. Somehow we got the job done. I trained her well enough that she could train her colleagues. Finally, I had to have the hotel doctor come. It is not nice to be alone and sick and know no one in a big foreign city. I wanted only to go home. Therefore, my next move will be difficult to understand. I felt so ill that it was simply too much effort to try to rearrange my schedule so I decided to go forward. I am so glad I did. The most exciting experiences were yet to come.

CUZCO, Perú

In planning this trip to South America, the greatest thrill of all was to be a week of sightseeing in the highlands of Perú. This area of the world had long held a fascination for me, and this was my opportunity to see it thoroughly, albeit by myself. I knew I would be truly on my own during this adventure with no contacts anywhere, but I forged ahead.

Although I still was not up to par, I flew the Faucet Line to Cuzco. Having mentioned to the pilot before takeoff that I myself was a pilot, I was invited to sit in the cockpit for the landing. Cuzco was magnificent. At an elevation of 13,000 feet, it didn't take long for me to get the ubiquitous headache associated with altitude. Nonetheless, I toured the city with a delightful couple from Austin, Texas with whom I am in touch to this day—Audrey and Dick Cooper. Of particular interest to me was a fortification located on a steep hill overlooking the city, a place called Saksaywaman. Although people had lived there since AD 900, the first sections were actually started in AD 1100. Huge stones were fitted together without mortar. It was amazing. Homesickness had really set in as my diary noted daily now.

Aldine at Machu Picchu

The following day I traveled through the Urubamba Valley to the famed Machu Picchu. En route the train's engine broke down and we were left sitting on the tracks for six hours. Panic had set in that we might miss the experience entirely, and there was no food on the train. Although I had left Cuzco at 7:00 a.m., the train did not reach Machu Picchu until 5:00 in the afternoon. I wrote in my diary that "It is more incredible than I ever would have believed—one of life's treats." Fortunately there was ample daylight for me to take excellent photographs and there were so few tourists that day that I have one without a single person visible in it.

PUNO, Perú (Lake Titicaca)

After departing Cuzco at 7:00 a.m., I took an exhausting train trip to Juliaca arriving at 6:00 p.m. The train had made 34, yes 34, stops en route and took me to an elevation of 14,430 feet. I could barely breathe and remember sticking my head out the window with my mouth wide open trying to get more oxygen. Of course, that was ridiculous because there was no more oxygen outside the window than inside!

I traveled from Juliaca to Puno by bus where I was met by a van and driver that I had prearranged. And then began a scary night for me. It was late by now and I was taken to an "inn." I never saw any sign of an inn and began to doubt that there even was one. The van driver walked me along a long and dusty path, in the dark, to a hut. I was in the middle of nowhere in the middle of nowhere. It was cold. The first thing I did was to fill my hot water bottle—with cold water of course, as there was no running hot water—so that I could sleep with it and have warmish water in the morning for washing and shampooing. Then I decided that before unpacking I would slip under the blankets to write a few postcards until I warmed up. Big mistake! Suddenly the one light bulb in the room went off. My driver had failed to mention to me that the electricity was turned off at night.

I hadn't even opened my suitcase so I did not have a flashlight. It was pitch black, and cold, and I came close to panicking. I crawled out of bed, found my suitcase, was able to open it and located my little flashlight. I knew that even if I had wanted to find the "inn," I had no idea which path to take or what direction to go. There I was with no phone and no contact whatever to the outside world. I asked God to please not let me get appendicitis that night. I survived but will never forget that night of cold and terror.

In the morning, the van driver reappeared at the appointed time. We drove to Lake Titicaca where the two of us climbed into a small boat with an outboard motor. We set out on a trip I had long anticipated—a visit to the Uros Indians on Lake Titicaca. This is the largest lake in South America with an elevation of 12,057 feet and is considered the highest navigable lake in the world. After about an hour, we approached the first of the Uros' "islands." The Uros live on about 30 or so floating islands made of reeds. Initially, this way of life enabled them to escape their enemies quickly by simply moving from island to island.

Typically these people live their lives naked and in very primitive circumstances. Due to our arrival, they had made a semblance of covering themselves—failing miserably I might add. They live in open shelters and have no bathroom facilities whatever. When an island gets too smelly, they simply shove it off into the lake and replace it with another they have at the ready. After visiting several of the "islands," we made the return trip to Puno. It was an experience as fascinating as I had expected it to be.

Later in the day I walked for about two hours to visit a trout hatchery. I found climbing hills at 14,000 feet a difficult task. I walked through the little town of Chucuito satisfying myself that I was seeing Peruvian life at its most basic. My next stop was a pre-Inca burial ground ruin called   Sillustani. I was quite used to making these little side trips on my own.

Enduring another bus trip, I made the return trip to Juliaca.

JULIACA, Perú

I remember Juliaca for its great poverty. There are many stories of mothers with bedraggled children pleading for help at railroad stops. I had friends who saw an indigenous woman begging and then simply drop dead in front of them, presumably from starvation. She was merely shoved to the side to get her out of the way. My heart went out to these people, and I bought whatever wares they were selling. These Indians often lived below ground, digging out a room for their family with a tunnel to the surface. I could barely endure seeing it—starving children and desperate parents—but I understand circumstances there now are not as onerous. I so hope that is the case.

From my civilized perspective, many of the places I stayed were very primitive. I rarely had hot water and I became used to washing and shampooing in cold water. After seeing Juliaca I knew I had nothing to complain about. And now it was time to go to the train station for the nine hour trip to Arequipa.

AREQUIPA, Perú

Although Arequipa is the second most industrialized city in Perú, it has a unique charm. I was delighted to visit this beautiful place after noting in my diary that the trip to get there was long and with scenery that was "<u>dull</u>, and <u>dry</u> and unchanging and <u>dusty</u>." I went through passes with an elevation of 15,000 feet. I wish I could say that I became used to oxygen deprivation, but I did not. When I fly, I try to stay at 10,000 feet or below for the comfort of my passengers (and myself). In planes supplied with oxygen, I start using it at about ten or twelve thousand feet.

It was all worth it as I loved this charming town and the lovely hotel in which I stayed. It is a place to which I would like to return someday, but for now it was time to go back to Lima to fly home to the U.S.A.

MIAMI, Florida

I had been alone and lonely far too long. I was hankering to get back to Tony. My sons, Kent and Tony Jr., were attending a military academy prep school that Tony Jr. had enrolled in following his graduation from high school. Kent decided to go as well in order to hone his academic skills before entering university. The school, Millard, was in Bandon, Oregon and they were not expected home until December 22nd. I would have to wait a while before I could see them again.

A strange thing happened when I returned to the United States. I had been speaking, thinking and dreaming in Spanish for weeks and weeks. However, the minute I started using English again my fluency with Spanish fled. I have never spoken it well since.

It was an incredibly successful trip—a magical time in my life. I met fascinating people, saw remarkable sights, and accomplished the task assigned to me by the University of Illinois. I remember the trip clearly—a treasured time in my life. I arrived in Tucson on December 6th. It was so very good to get back to Tony and my wonderful life with him.

10

⊗⊗

WORKING IN SPAIN - 1984

The Spanish adaptation of the Illinois Test of Psycholinguistic Abilities (SITPA) had been an enormous success in Latin America and had attracted the attention of educators and psychologists in Spain. With so many cultural and linguistic differences between Latin America and Spain, it was necessary to develop an entirely new adaptation of the test. Winifred and Sam Kirk and I were invited to Spain to assist them in this endeavor.

The term "Latin America" denotes the Western Hemisphere nations south of the United States, with most of those countries using Spanish as their primary language. In Spain the Castilian language and culture dominate, and Spaniards would <u>never</u> say they speak Spanish; they speak Castellano. They consider Spanish a crude language and I know I often offended them with some of the terminology I used.

On November 19, 1984 I flew to Madrid with the Kirks, the authors of the original ITPA. We arrived at 8:00 a.m. with an eight-hour time change and gritty eyes. We stayed in my favorite hotel in Madrid, the Plaza, and settled in for a little rest. Time is scheduled much differently in Spain so we had to adapt to doing everything later than we would have in the U.S.

The afternoon we arrived, we met with our colleague Soledad Ballesteros who acted as translator throughout our trip. She took us on a walk around the Plaza España—we needed to stretch our legs—before driving us to the principal education building in Madrid. Our meeting there—at 7:00 p.m.—was with Dr. Marchessi, the assistant director for special education in Spain. Afterwards we went for dinner to the home of Soledad and her husband José. The meal was served at 10:00 p.m., the typical time for the evening meal in Spain. When we finally returned to our hotel we were quite exhausted having had so little sleep and so much activity.

The next day was equally busy. Soledad picked us up at 9:30 a.m. to take us to la Universidad Nacional de Educación a Distancia (UNED) where we did a radio broadcast—my portion being entirely in Spanish. On to la Universidad Complutense de Madrid where Sam and I lectured to about 200 people. I had been unaware that I would have these responsibilities and felt ill prepared. Had I only been warned!

I remained vigilant in my attempt to maintain my recent weight loss—a difficult feat in Spain with its very delicious food. And with a face lift looming the following month I was even more motivated. I carried a tiny scale with me and checked it daily. Additionally, I exercised. The easiest exercise equipment I could take with me was a gadget with ropes and pulleys that was popular at that time. One hangs a loop over the handle of a door, secures it, lies on the floor and inserts one's hands and feet into loops in ropes attached to pulleys. Pulling on the ropes raises and lowers one's arms and legs and it is a technique successful in toning all the muscles of the body.

In our hotel each bedroom had an anteroom that the butler and maids could enter to take and leave laundry without disturbing the occupant. Not wanting to dirty any of my clothes I decided to do my workout naked on the bedspread on the floor of my anteroom. There I was—starkers—and ready to go. I gave a big pull on the ropes and— the door to the hall flew open. The door did not have a round handle but a lever that unlocked when moved from the inside. Can you imagine what the guests of the hotel thought as they walked past my room and saw a woman struggling—naked—on the floor trying to extricate herself from a mass of ropes, loops and pulleys! Of course, in my distress I became completely entangled and it seemed to take an eternity before I could rise, walk with as much dignity as I could muster to the door, and close it. I sat down and wept. I was away from home with dreadful jet lag, expected to present lectures for which I was unprepared, and humiliated in the most grotesque manner.

Later that day, Soledad whisked us off for more speeches! Again we spoke on the radio in the afternoon but eventually made our escape and headed for the Prado, my favorite museum in the world. We stayed until closing time and later met friends at Casa Botín for dinner.

The following day we were picked up by Dr. Cordero, director of the company— TEA Ediciones—that was to publish the Spanish adaptation of the ITPA, and given a tour of the facility. Lo! these many years later I am still in touch with TEA annually as I continue to receive royalties. He was our gracious host at lunch. We continued the day with consultations and in the early evening made a presentation to about 60 psychologists. In spite of being exhausted, we were picked up at 10:00 p.m. by Soledad and José who took us to their country club for dinner.

Another of those "why did I do it?" moments occurred the next day after Soledad and José picked us up for a "day off." We drove to Toledo, always a very special place for me, where I found a gift shop selling the most beautiful handmade and hand-painted plates I had ever seen. I could not envision our home without them. They were local art—and very heavy. Sam made it clear I was on my own if I bought them—he had no intention of carrying them even one step for me. Emotion outweighed logic and I bought 24 of them! The boxes in which they were packed were extremely awkward to manage but, without a complaint, I carried them throughout the trip and back to Tucson where they encircle the walls of my kitchen.

As I usually do in Toledo, I visited the cathedral, the house of El Greco, and saw once again the painting of the Interment of Count Orgaz. I had always been deeply moved by the ambience of Toledo. We returned to Madrid and at 10:00 p.m. that night had dinner accompanied by a flamenco show at the Corral de la Moreria considered the most spectacular flamenco show in Madrid as well as the most famous in the world.

Never having been to Valencia, I was excited the next day when we took a train to that elegant city where we were met by education dignitaries—Francisco Alcantud and José Maria Peiró. They took us to an institute—Fundación Valenciana de Estudios Avanzados— where important visitors are housed. It was most unusual and very uncomfortable—but we were honored to have merited their special housing. My room was beside the classroom and I do not know who was in the room next to mine on the other side but I did not like the fact that we were sharing a bathroom and there was no lock on the door!

The day was spent in being toured around Valencia—a fascinating city. We had paella for lunch—always a treat. The conference, which I had dreaded for months, began at 6:00 p.m. Looming ahead the following day was a lecture I had to present in Spanish to perhaps 200 erudite psychologists of Spain. That evening I was just a spectator. We were the honored guests at a fantastic Basque meal at Eguzki Restaurant. We didn't return to our rooms until after 1:00 a.m. and I was exhausted.

The following day I was a featured speaker at the conference that was held at La Universidad de Valencia Department of Psychology. While Sam had the benefit of a translator during his lectures, I did not. Until the day I die I will not forget the mortification I experienced that day. I had ample time to prepare my lecture knowing before I left Tucson that this presentation would occur. I was ready. My notes in Spanish had been checked and rechecked.

I stood on the dais, microphone in front of me and a sea of faces facing me—and I froze. It had never happened to me before, nor has it since. My mouth opened, but nothing came out. I was paralyzed. After an agonizing few moments, Sam saw my plight and took over for me. He graciously never referred to this debacle again.

We had a late lunch at Les Graelles and left at 5:00 p.m. for a five-hour train ride to Barcelona where we stayed at the Hotel Colón. It had a lock on the door! The Kirks, well into their 60s or early 70s, seemed never to run out of energy. We visited amazing landmarks in the city the following two days—Barrio Gótico, Gaudí's church of La Familia Sagrada, the Picasso Museum and a trip to the top of Tibidabo which overlooks Barcelona and is the highest mountain in the region. In addition, I walked the length of La Ramba, a street with *al fresco* shopping. We ate at wonderful restaurants, my favorite of which was Quo Vadis with its outstanding flamenco show.

On November 30th, we flew from Barcelona to Palma de Mallorca. It was a fascinating old city that catered to tourists. As we were off-season this was not a problem, although it was cold. We awakened to rain the next day and I will quote my diary to provide an "on the spot" record of the day's event. "As you know, dear diary, I am terrified of driving with Sam. My nightmares were realized. It was awful. I was navigator and got completely lost in Palma which is all circles. Dispositions disintegrated." We had traveled in tranquility until that day which was rather a miracle as Sam had quite an explosive personality. Fortunately the next day was the last of the our trip. We spent it visiting Monaco.

We returned to Tucson on December 3rd after traveling for almost 26 hours. These had been a memorable 15 days with many high moments and some very low moments. It was a never-to-be-forgotten experience. My first hug at the airport in Tucson with Tony was memorable, too.

11

ೞೲ

SABBATICAL LEAVE IN NEW ZEALAND - 1993

My sabbatical leave was approaching—the academic year 1993-1994. I had spurned previous opportunities in favor of remaining in Tucson as I loved my job. This would be my last chance as it was required that we fulfill at least one more year at the university following our sabbatical leave. I factored that into my plan to retire two years hence in order to spend more time with my family at our summer cottage in Canada.

The term sabbatical is derived from the word Sabbath—the seventh day of the week—a day for rest. These years of "rest" were available to tenured professors every seventh year. In actual fact, the university did not grant these leaves without caveats. If one took a semester off, one would receive full pay and not have to produce research. A full-year sabbatical reduced one's salary and required documentation both before and after an approved project.

I selected the latter. The fall semester I was not professionally productive but I had a wonderful time at our cottage where I stayed from May 31st to October 14th.

There was only one place in the world where I wanted to be for the academic portion of my sabbatical year—New Zealand. I was very fortunate to have met Dr. John Werry at a GAP (Group for the Advancement of Psychiatry) conference in Chicago which I was attending as a guest of Dr. Joseph Green, a close friend and colleague. Our meeting had been brief and I doubted he would remember me. Nonetheless, I phoned him in Auckland where he was a distinguished professor in the Department of Psychiatry at the University of Auckland. His wife told me he was out sailing at that moment and suggested a time I might call again. I had little hope that he could help me, but nothing ventured, nothing gained!

When Dr. Werry and I finally talked on the phone I introduced myself and his first words were, "Ah, the merry widow!" I guess I had made an impression! He assured me he remembered me and that he would be delighted to be in touch with the University of Canterbury in Christchurch on the South Island. He was sure they would be very happy to have me join them for a semester. I couldn't believe my good luck.

Dr. Kathleen Liberty from Christchurch phoned me and arrangements were made. I would join their faculty for two months. Having now received blessings from all quarters I embarked on one of the very precious adventures of my life.

The night before my departure, December 29, 1993, my amazing mother at age 85 had a big family bon voyage party in my honor. She had wanted to go with me to New Zealand, but I felt it was too long trip for her and I wouldn't have a great deal of time to spend with her there. Mother died ten months later at age 86.

My good friend Howard Shenk was eager to be my companion for a month and, as we traveled well together, it sounded like a good idea. On December 30th, we flew from Tucson to Honolulu where Howard had lived for 13 years. We visited with his friends there and then embarked on December 31st for the second leg of our journey which would take us to Auckland.

I noted in my diary that I missed New Year's Day entirely that year as we did not arrive in Auckland until January 2, 1994. The International Date Line has always confused me!

Jet lag has always been my nemesis but we rented a car and bravely set out on January 3rd to drive to the Bay of Islands on the North Island. We took turns terrifying ourselves and each other as we learned to navigate on "the wrong side of the road." We headed for Paihia as my beloved student/friend, Misty, and her family were on an *Island Princess* cruise that was moored there. How we wangled our way onto the tender and got aboard still boggles my mind. Misty was not on board as she was on a land tour so Howard and I decided to have a drink and await her return. When I signed Misty's name on her bar tab the jig was up. (One can't pay in cash on these ships.) Misty would have been well known on the ship within 24 hours. She is beautiful, effervescent and loud to the max! I certainly was not Misty. We disembarked with our tails between our legs and headed for shore. And whom did we find there but Misty with her family. All was not lost.

Fortunately the next day was gorgeous, and hot, so Howard and I took a beautiful five-hour cruise through the Bay of Islands. We were not so fortunate the next day as it was raining heavily and there was dense fog. We reached Auckland grateful to be alive after driving in those conditions.

Rotorua was our destination the next day and its beauty made the four-hour drive worthwhile. We were guests that night at a Maori hangi. The Maori are the indigenous Polynesian people of New Zealand who arrived in the country sometime between AD 1250 and 1300. The hangi is a Maori technique for cooking food using heated rocks buried in a pit. This was accompanied by a colorful floorshow. It was magical. The following day we explored the region and absorbed its glorious scenery and history.

We were so pleased to be able to take the incredible boat trip through the caves at Waitomo with its awesome glowworms. After lunch there, we drove a tortuous mountain road to Wanganui—a lovely little city where we spent the night.

The next day we drove to Wellington, took the city tour, and boarded the ferry for a very rough trip from the North to the South Island. We checked into the Koromiko Spa on the outskirts of Picton.

In a driving wind and rain, we set out the next day for Greymouth on the west coast of South Island. Because of torrential rain, the Milford Sound area was being evacuated thus requiring us to cancel our Milford Trek, a disappointment as it is world renowned for its incredible beauty.

Franz Josef Glacier was our next destination and I can tell you it was an experience I will never forget. The rain had washed out the trail to the glacier and a path had been carved which, in many places, hung on the edge of drop-offs into the river. Cold and miserable, I was incapable of actually climbing the glacier, a disappointment after the five-hour hike.

Howard on difficult hike to Franz Josef Glacier

The Wizard of Christchurch

On to Christchurch after a spectacular drive over Arthur's Pass. The roads were in bad shape as a result of the flooding. I couldn't wait to see the University of Canterbury campus and I was not disappointed. The following day I met with several professors at the university and we established some plans for my tenure there. However, I was not due to move into my quarters or start my work until later in the month. Howard and I checked out Christchurch and even listened to the rantings of the famous "Wizard" for a while. The Wizard was a Christchurch celebrity and icon who regularly addressed crowds in Cathedral Square. In the evening we took Ann Sinclair, my brother's first wife, out for dinner. She was spending a few days on the South Island.

The following day Howard and I started our tour of the South Island. I will not go into detail except to point out

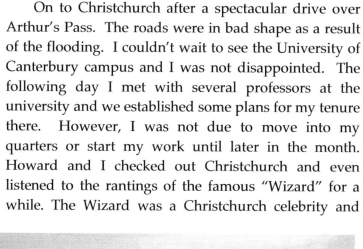

Howard & Aldine

Aldine on Hooker Trail at Mt. Cook

that we visited Dunedin, Invercargill, and then Bluff, which fascinated me. It is the southern-most extremity of the country and it is my understanding that it is the closest piece of land to Antarctica. From there you could even see Stewart Island which is nineteen miles south of Bluff and has a population of 381 people. Every day of this entire trip we took rigorous hikes both to stay in shape and to see what was out in the countryside. In Bluff we took the difficult Glory Trail.

On to Wanaka and a beautiful drive to Lake Hawea. Queenstown was our next stop; I have mentioned some of our adventures there in another chapter. Our hope of seeing Milford Sound was dashed once again when we learned that it had rained 22 inches in the previous 24 hours—the worst rainfall in its history. Lake Wakatipu was running into the streets so our river trip there was cancelled.

Regrettably, we were able to take one trip—the Dart River Jet Boat Safari—a five-hour nightmare from which we didn't think we would ever recover. This jet boat went very, very fast and the rain was torrential. Hence, without any protection we were being pelted with rain hitting us at about 75 miles an hour. It was truly painful—excruciating in fact. Well, my trip selection had been the Franz Josef Trail while the Dart River was Howard's. So, it was a draw. We felt even-steven with respect to punishing the other.

Howard on our rigorous climb up Mt. Iron near Lake Wanaka

The next day, Monday, Queenstown was completely flooded and we saw people being ferried to shops and to work by boat! Nonetheless, we set out for Mt. Cook in the rain and sadly we were in a cloud as we approached it. We stayed there overnight and were lucky that the next day was sunny with clear skies, puffy clouds and spectacular views. This was a day to remember before we set off for our return to Christchurch.

Before the Dart River Jet Boat Safari trip

Howard and I spent several wonderful days exploring Christchurch, the region and the university campus. On his last day in New Zealand, we took a punt down the picturesque Avon River. I drove Howard to the airport that evening, January 29th for his return to Tucson. I was on my own. Now that Howard was gone I changed to a smaller rental car. I then drove to my new home in Christchurch and settled in.

Aldine cruising the Avon
River - Christchurch

While walking on campus on the weekend I noticed that there was no sign whatever of activity. At the University of Arizona there are usually professors working in every building every day of the week so I asked a security guard on a bicycle why there was no one in sight. "Oh," said he, "You're not meant to be working on the weekend. That is the time to be with your family and in the out of doors. If you can't get your job done in five days, then you oughtn't to have the job at all." I foolishly asked another question. "There doesn't seem to be a television set in my little house. Was that an oversight?" He was genuinely shocked at the very idea of my even thinking of spending time watching TV. I did, however, rent one as I envisioned spending many evenings alone. That was not to be.

The house provided by the university was more than adequate but rather unusual. The downstairs had a garage and a kitchen with a bathroom off it. "Oh," thought I, "how convenient to have this tiny bathroom downstairs." Upstairs there were two bedrooms and a large living room over the garage that had windows on three sides. However, no bathroom.

Another unusual feature was that there was not one wall hanging—not one—anywhere in the house, not even a calendar. The only item on a wall was a tiny mirror in the tiny bathroom which was of no use to me as it was hung so high. It was, of course, intended for a man.

Further, the color selection astounded me. Everything from rugs to furniture, from curtains to bedspreads and towels was brown, or a shade thereof. Boring!

I admit to a degree of angst as I left for my first day as temporary faculty at the University of Canterbury. I met with Kathleen Liberty at 9:30; she showed me to my office, introduced me to the staff, and took me to tea. Every day all work at the university stops at ten o'clock for the ritual teatime. Being a bit nervous, I tended to babble to the people I met. My first social gaffe cost me dearly.

In talking to one rather formidable lady I commented on my housing and noted that all the decorations were in shades of brown. I suggested it was wise of the university to keep towels, bedspreads etc. interchangeable with other faculty houses. What I did not know was that all New Zealanders have the same color scheme in their houses—brown. She was not impressed with my observation. News of my rudeness spread. Soon thereafter I simply stopped going to tea. I seemed a bit of a pariah, and I earned the reputation. I guess I did everything I could to forward the legend of the ugly American.

New Zealanders are the ultimate in egalitarianism. Everybody is equal. I had learned before departing the U.S. about "the tall poppy syndrome." A tall poppy in a field of level poppies is quickly cut off. I had been warned not to expect applause when I gave a lecture or speech, and not to expect the audience to ask questions. That would make them "tall poppies." They were true to form.

Another gross error on my part was in my selection of clothing for the trip. Wanting to appear professional but chic, I took tailored but **very** colorful outfits. I looked like a peacock surrounded by wrens. I learned too late that, like home décor, all women dressed in the same colors—white, navy blue and beige. They alternated their skirts and blouses to add variety but the colors were always the same. I am sure I was a source of fascination for them but I suspect that my outfits did not win their approval.

I spent time in my office every day working on the many projects that had been planned for me. Kathleen Liberty, a faculty member in charge of watching over me,

Joe Green, Kathleen Liberty & Doug Neil, and Aldine

and her husband Doug Neil had several dinner parties at their home in my honor. In fact, I was included in a great many parties many of which were to introduce me to curious professionals. I was something of an anomaly—a woman professor alone in New Zealand who was actually there to work. Apparently a great many professors plan a sabbatical in this beautiful country but do little more than give a lecture. I worked very, very hard.

It was a shock to me on Thursday when I received a phone call from my friend Joe Green in Tucson that he was arriving two days hence. He had hinted that he might like to join me but nothing specific had ever been planned. I had thought that no news was good news and that I was off the hook. As fond as I was of Joe, he and I tended not to get along well together. This visit was true to form. We fought like cats and dogs. In another chapter I mention *his* social gaffes that pulled the good old U.S.A. down yet another notch.

I managed to talk with people in Tucson frequently and with great ease as, although there was a one-day difference in time, the hour of the day differed by only three hours. Therefore, I could call my mother on Monday at 9:00 a.m. when she was just getting home from church on Sunday. It was good to stay in touch with my "real" life.

I was managing very well with driving although I never conquered the tendency to walk to the wrong side of the car when I left a building such as a bank or the dry cleaners. Inevitably I did a double-take when I saw that I had approached the passenger's side. It never failed to embarrass me. Another concern was looking right instead of left when pulling out into traffic.

Joe arrived on Saturday, his luggage lost and a tooth broken. This, of course, required my taking him to a dentist. He accepted with good grace that he had the much smaller bedroom in my little house and never, but never, did he enter mine. Ours was always a platonic relationship. Maybe that is why we argued so much.

When we took trains in New Zealand, he had to be facing forward. It made him nauseated to sit looking back. He absolutely would not drive as it made him nervous to drive on the left hand side of the road and he could not cope with the "roundabouts" that take the place of traffic signals and stop signs in New Zealand. Another unique feature of driving in New Zealand was the crossing of bridges. Outside the cities, bridges were typically one-way only. Whoever planned to cross first flashed his lights and then it was every man for himself. Road rage would be a disaster there, but then, another quality of New Zealanders is that they are incredibly polite and absolute rule-followers.

Their egalitarianism extended even to their gardening habits. I heard of no one there who did not have a vegetable garden; even the mayor had one. An endearing trait of these people is their accent. Vegetable would sound like "veegeetable." All their "e's" are long. I worked with a man, Bob Best (pronounced Beast) who seemed oblivious to my American pronunciation of his name.

On Joe's first day, I left him to attend a gathering that had been previously planned. It was at the home of Dr. John Church and his wife Doris. A friend, Pat Pilkington, was there as well and the three of us women sat in the spa and talked. That was when I met their charming daughter Annabelle and her best friend Fiona.

It is my belief that John did not like me. It was into his department that I was placed for my tenure there. He was not happy that an "expert" and a woman, for goodness sake, was in his domain. Add to that our philosophies which were 180 degrees apart. Each of our attitudes about punishment was repugnant to the other. He believed in "spare the rod and spoil the child." I mean this literally. He supported beating children. I was a proponent of positive reinforcement as a means of altering behavior. We avoided each other, although they were very gracious hosts to me several times.

Doris Church was a remarkable woman. She had a previous marriage and was a battered woman. She still had teeth missing when I met her. You see, wife beating was legal in New Zealand and men took advantage of it. It was Doris Church who decided enough was enough. After she married John, she started a movement dedicated to creating legislation to protect women from violent husbands. It was a dangerous undertaking as men "ruled" and liked things just the way they were.

Doris developed an enormous following of women who would risk their husbands' ire as well as police intervention when they staged protests such as "lie downs" in the middle of busy streets. Many a time they were beaten away with batons. They persevered. John would receive phone calls in the middle of the night telling him to stop his wife's pursuit or there would be serious repercussions to his family. Doris would not stop.

Eventually, due to Doris's persistence, a law was enacted making illegal the mistreatment of women, thus changing the lives of so many battered wives. Doris had won.

I mention this because it was during my time in New Zealand that Prince Charles came to visit. After an unfortunate day in Auckland where he was sprayed with shaving cream by a dissident citizen, he arrived in Christchurch. His purpose there was to represent his mother, Queen Elizabeth, in bestowing The Order of the British Empire on Doris Church accompanied by the appropriate medals—large and ornate for evening use and smaller for the daytime. The Queen was granting her this honor for her work toward women's rights. As if any New Zealander would ever wear a medal!

Annabel, John & Doris Church

I had no idea that this ceremony was to happen at City Hall one evening. Doris, of course, never mentioned it. My secretary at work "let it slip" to me. The following night I was at the Church residence for dinner. I asked Doris if indeed she had met Prince Charles. "Oh, yees," she said. I asked her to tell me about it. She suggested that maybe her daughter Annabelle might tell me and called for her.

I told Annabelle that I had heard that she had met Prince Charles the previous night. "Oh, yees," she said. I asked her what they had discussed. She was highly embarrassed to be talking about it but mentioned that Prince Charles had asked her about her school and her life. I commented that it must have been exciting to share with her friends at school that day. "Oh," she said, "I didn't mention it." When I suggested that surely she had told her best friend Fiona she confessed that she hadn't spoken of it to anyone. Now that truly is egalitarianism! Annabelle did bring out the medals for me to see. I, an American, wouldn't be offended!

Aldine at Greymouth

While I was working, Joe took day trips around the South Island. On weekends we traveled together. One weekend we took the train to Greymouth stopping in Arthur Pass. As New Zealand is only 80 miles wide, it is easy to cross from one coast to the other in a day. There we found no telephone and no taxi but thumbed a ride to The Bealey Hotel, six miles away. It was barren there and the hotel was cold and barren as well. Joe was taciturn, so it was a pretty barren experience altogether.

The next day we walked the six miles back to Arthur Pass and continued on by train to Greymouth, my second visit there. We shopped, explored and returned to Christchurch later in the afternoon—in the rain.

One particularly colorful weekend was spent in Christchurch. We attended the Festival of Flowers with its lovely parade of floats festooned with flowers, as were the cathedral and other significant buildings. Thousands of children participated wearing hats bedecked with flowers. Christchurch was known for its magnificent gardens. Joe and I walked through the botanical gardens that afternoon.

Joe Green at Victoria Park - Christchurch

On another occasion we took a three-hour drive along winding roads to Kaikoura for a whale watching expedition. We left early in the morning anticipating a delightful day. It was not. Joe was carsick and miserable. He insisted, however, that I take the three-hour boat trip to look for whales. I saw the same whale twice, a rather disappointing outcome. And, on the very rough water I became seasick.

We met at the appointed time and I felt anger in the air. He could see that I was unwell but asked if I might be patient while he took a stroll along the water's edge. He was gone two hours! I think there was a little passive-aggressive behavior being exhibited. He had to wait for me—so I would have to wait for him. We still had the three-hour return drive to Christchurch and we know who was driving! There was hostile silence throughout. I would hesitate writing what my diary had to say about the experience and about Joe.

Joe accompanied me to many social events held in my honor. One was dramatic and memorable. We drove to Diamond Harbour across from Lyttelton to go to the "bach" of my colleague Karen France and her husband Steve. A bach in New Zealand is a modest holiday home or beach house. Theirs was high on a cliff with magnificent views

Joe Green

that seemed to go on forever. There were only six of us and I enjoyed every minute of that special evening.

Finally it was time for Joe to leave Christchurch. It was none too soon! I took him to the train station for his trip to Dunedin. He was then going to wend his way around the south of the island and end up at Milford Sound. He was fortunate enough to have good weather and to be able to take the Milford Trek, which I had missed. It is a backpacking trip requiring several days under the aegis of a guide but Joe, an inveterate hiker, found it tough going. Weeks later when I had returned to Tucson he showed me his black toenails—the result of his downhill trekking. Later the nails dropped off entirely. Perhaps I was fortunate that bad weather saved me from that outcome.

Now, having mentioned that I had worked very hard in New Zealand, it is incumbent upon me to cite some of the more interesting professional events for which I was responsible. Much of my work was meeting with a great many small groups.

Many professionals there thought that I was an expert in all areas of psychology and special education including its administration, and a great deal was expected of me.

Every Monday there was an agenda of activities scheduled for my week but there were many surprises tossed in. During my first week on the job I saw that I was expected to be at the Shirley child abuse center. I assumed that I would be meeting with personnel there to discuss their problems. Instead, I walked in only to discover that the auditorium was filled with more than 20 psychologists who had come from all over South Island and were expecting me to present a lecture on child abuse from 9:00 a.m. until noon.

I was not psychologically prepared for this task nor did I have the appropriate materials with me. I was so upset I didn't think I could drive so Bob Best drove me home where I collected the necessary papers. I valiantly pulled myself together and did a credible job although I think I would have done better if I had known what was coming. The New Zealanders are certainly parsimonious in their communication!

The following day I was a nervous wreck once again as I had a major eight-hour presentation to deliver to the entire Department of Education at the University of Christchurch. This was an audience who would inevitably take exception to some of my precepts as many of us came from different disciplines and divergent schools of thought. After such a lecture in the United States I would have been set upon by lingering participants who would want to chat further about one issue or another. Not so there. It ended with a smattering of applause and the audience leaving en masse. I attributed this more to the reticence of New Zealanders than to my failure to perform. Still, a little enthusiasm would have been reassuring.

The following day I had a delightful surprise. I was to meet with Miles Ellery, the Principal of the Thomas Seager School, and his staff for the morning. I was delighted to receive a traditional Maori greeting with my being seated while everyone else stood. It was very impressive.

At noon, the Adolescent Psychology Unit, the staff and the students had a Maori barbecue for me. I was expected to stay all afternoon but fatigue set in and I needed to go home and rest for a while. I was very touched by the thoughtfulness shown me that day.

Two days later I met with a cadre of colleagues at the College of Education for an intense discussion of critical issues in special education, after which they had a luncheon for me. This was followed in the afternoon by my presentation of a lecture to an audience of 30 teachers.

Then on to hear a lecture presented by University of Arizona colleagues who were in Christchurch briefly, thus qualifying them for their time away from the University of Arizona. I questioned my sanity for having accepted so demanding a job for my sabbatical.

Later I drove them to Kathleen Liberty's home in Sumner and was their hostess for the evening at a charming restaurant, The Beachcomber. Every night I fell into bed exhausted.

Frequently I visited the McKenzie Residential Home for seriously disturbed children. There were only two such institutional settings in New Zealand.

I met often, also, with the principal and counselors at Burnside High School, the largest in New Zealand with 2000 students. Another frequent destination was Opawa where I met with the SES support group for hours at a time. These facilities always wanted me to spend the day, but I found I became tired after two to three hours of being the center of attention. They all were so hungry to draw every bit of knowledge they could from me.

Saturday, February 19 arrived, the day I had worried about for seven months! I presented an eight-hour workshop on behalf of the Department of Continuing Education at the University of Canterbury to an audience of 44 people—all of them at the top tier of education in the country. They came from as far away as Invercargill, Dunedin and Hamilton. I had worked on this project for many weeks and felt at the end that it had gone very well. That night Doris and John Church had a party at their home in my honor. There were 17 in attendance.

I was honored to be invited to speak at the second residential treatment center for delinquents in Kingslea.

On another evening I delivered a lecture at the Disabled Persons Centre addressing issues associated with Attention Deficit Disorders to over one hundred parents. Prior to the presentation I was invited to dinner at the home of Sally Seguran, the mayor's sister.

And so it went, day after day. Somehow I managed a daily visit to my office where I received mail, prepared presentations and was given my upcoming assignments.

I remember with warmth the great kindness of the people. I was invited to meals in a great many homes and treasured this opportunity to learn about the New Zealand people and their culture.

On my last day, I took Doris and John Church, and their daughter Annabelle, to a posh restaurant in the Park Royal Hotel. Their friendship had meant a lot to me in this land so far from home. I never had a moment's loneliness in New Zealand, although I did indeed miss my family.

My return trip to Tucson was a 24-hour journey. I traveled from Christchurch to Auckland to Papeete to Los Angeles to Phoenix and finally to Tucson. My incredible mother was ready with a family party for me on my arrival.

My experience in New Zealand fulfilled—no, exceeded—all my expectations. However, I doubt I ever would have acquiesced to this assignment had I known the demands it would place on me personally and professionally. I fell short of meeting all their needs in New Zealand, I am sure, but I know I made a difference in the lives of many families. This was enough to count my sabbatical leave as more than worthwhile.

12

∽⃝

MY UNUSUAL MARRIAGE

My marriage to Tony was unique. Until we started living together, I had been unaware of his strong independent nature and his need for time alone. Nor was I prepared for his long absences, such as his sailing trips, in his quest for solitude. I had expected my marriage to be like that of my parents—one of spending as much time as possible with each other and of dependence on the other. Such was not to be for me.

Early in the marriage I made a plea for more attention. I wrote Tony a note and left it on his pillow. I will quote part of it.

"I love you, Tony. You are as necessary to me as the sun is to the flowers, or as the air is to animals that breathe. Just like the sun you give me warmth and like the air you are around me and in me constantly. But, Tony, like a rich ore mine that has just been scratched on the surface is my love for you. To get the full wealth of the mine requires thought, patience and earnest effort. It won't just be handed to the prospector. Nor will my love for you, my darling, come naturally. It must be sought. But, unlike a mine, the source is inexhaustible. Few men have ever enjoyed the riches within your grasp—the complete love and respect of a woman. But I must explain the word complete. Of course I love you completely now, because you have all the love in me that could go to one man. But after all, a complete seed blooms into a complete plant which blossoms into a complete flower. In other words, my darling, I need watering.

Now, tuck this little message into your heart and don't do a thing until the spirit moves you. This message is not from a dying love but from one that wants to grow. I ask God every night for our marriage to become more beautiful with every passing day."

Tony never commented on my letter.

His love never waned over our 36 years together before his death, and certainly mine did not. Perhaps to assuage his guilt over denying me the intimacy I craved with him, or perhaps to generate time on his own, he encouraged me to travel—to seek adventures.

It was with considerable trepidation that I embarked on this new chapter—his life, my life, our life. I would not have chosen it to be thus although it provided me the opportunity for my "audacious adventures." He himself initiated and encouraged my new independence. He counted on my absences from home; he thrived on them. Interestingly, when we reunited after these times apart we were blissfully happy together—the perfect couple.

I know that marriage and fatherhood were difficult for Tony; he told me so. It gave him a sense of being trapped. My omnipresence was suffocating him and denying him what he wanted most—peace and privacy. Strangely, in what appeared to be selfishness on my part in pursuing my own dreams, I was gifting him with what he needed most—solitude. In my traveling, I was strengthening my marriage—not jeopardizing it.

I never, ever started a project or embarked on a trip without Tony knowing where I was going or with whom. So, gentle reader, if dates within this memoir make you scratch your head, be assured that the behavior on both our parts was always above board. Ours was a love uniquely expressed. Our marriage thrived not in spite of our time away from each other, but because of it.

After Tony died, I went to see the therapist whom he had depended upon to help him make his life and death decisions. Her name is Kathy Norgard and she is wonderful. Tony said she reminded him of his mother whom he considered to be his guardian angel. We both appreciated Kathy's help in easing Tony's angst as he approached his final day.

My purpose in visiting Kathy was to tie up some loose ends—to clarify some issues that had confused me. Before we could start, however, she interrupted me with a question. She asked, "What was it like being married to a hermit?" That question gave me a sense of peace. It confirmed the need for the lifestyle we had chosen. It affirmed my value and my choices.

While many would not choose it for themselves, I think back on my marriage with appreciation, gratitude and love beyond bounds. I was a lucky woman to be married to the man I adored and to experience without guilt the many opportunities that came my way.

13

∽⁑∾

MY FLYING CAREER

MY FIRST FLIGHT

Perhaps the best way for me to introduce my life in aviation would be to quote from a newspaper article written on December 17, 2003. It was on the front page of the *Arizona Daily Star* to commemorate the 100th anniversary of the Wright Brothers' inaugural flight. The article, which included photographs of me bedecked in helmet and goggles, chronicled my first flight of my many years of flying.

Aldine's first flight - 1951

I will quote the article as it does a good job of reporting what happened to me.

Flight Fright Held Her Until "The Bug" Pried it Loose

When Aldine von Isser took her first flight, she felt quite sure it would also be her last. In fact, for a brief moment von Isser believed that she was facing her last moment on Earth. That was only due to the "wonderful sense of humor" of her fiancé, she said.

"As a young woman of 18 years in 1951, I approached in terror my first flight," von Isser, now 70, recalled. Her husband-to-be was an avid pilot and member of the Air Force Reserves, and a few years earlier he had bought a military training aircraft at a Navy surplus sale.

Though Aldine was scared to fly, Tony, her fiancé, insisted they go up one afternoon. Tony warned her that he would perform a few aerobatic maneuvers, but he neglected to mention he had installed a special modification to give his passengers a rare treat.

She never saw the cable that was rigged to her seat. She had no idea that Tony would pull it—with the open-cockpit plane flying upside down at 5,000 feet—causing her to fall a few inches before being caught by the seat belt.

"At the end of the flight, I was furious and vowed I would never fly again," she said. As it turned out, Tony had pulled the joke on many others before.

"He had a wonderful sense of humor, but I didn't think so at the time," von Isser said of her late husband. "He wanted to give his passengers a thrill, something they would never forget.

"He did it to some friends and they never forgave him. Obviously, I did."

Eventually von Isser was able to fly with her husband again—they traveled extensively by air—but she remained terrified. Tony thought that if she learned about flight and understood the principles behind it, she would no longer be afraid, so she started taking flying lessons in 1966.

As soon as she climbed into the cockpit as a pilot, Aldine von Isser had found her new love. "I just got the bug," she said. After only a few hours' instruction, she was begging to do her first solo flight. And in a few years' time, she had earned her commercial license—surpassing her husband's pilot rating.

Von Isser describes her passion for flight in this way: "When you get into a cockpit, you leave the world behind you and you're in a different sphere entirely," she said. "When you're flying, you're completely absorbed in that activity, and precision and excellence are necessary."

For a short time, von Isser worked as a "bush pilot," making runs into and out of Baja California for a remote hotel. She ferried sick people and delivering mothers to the hospital, carried much-needed supplies from Mexico and the United States and even brought in contraband.

Von Isser eventually moved on to a less-adventurous career—she worked for the University of Arizona's College of Education for 30 years—but flying was always a major part of her life. She is a proud member of the international organization of women pilots known as the 99s.

"I think when you get the flying bug, it's incurable," she said.

Written by Kevin P. Thé

As mentioned in the article, Tony was eager for me to take a few flying lessons to assuage my fear of flying. He assigned his good friend Al Marshick to the task of being my first instructor. The next chapter tells that story!

MY ADVENTURES FLYING WITH AL MARSHICK

I called them "The Three Musketeers." They were three dashingly handsome young men who met and bonded at an airfield on the outskirts of Tucson called Gilpin Airport. They had very disparate backgrounds but one common passion—flying! And they were definitely "chick magnets." I married two of them, for goodness sake, and gave serious consideration to the third.

Hal Grieve with Tony beside his Ryan PT-22

Tony was the eldest, followed by Al Marshick and a much younger Hal Grieve. Upon returning to Tucson from serving in the Navy in the Pacific, Tony immediately took up flying. Interestingly, his flight instructor was a woman named Bobbie Kroll, who was also Hal's instructor. Sadly, she committed suicide in 1948 as a result of her husband's infidelities with which she could no longer cope.

Tony with his Ryan PT-22 - 1947

Tony bought a government surplus Ryan PT-22 that had been a Navy training plane in WWII. He paid $500 for it, and it came with a spare engine! The same airplane restored is now worth millions and is the type of aircraft that Harrison Ford recently crashed in California. I mention much more about Tony and this airplane in my chapter "Meeting Tony."

Hal, five years Tony's junior, had long been interested in learning to fly. As he was only 15 years old, he didn't have a driver's license so he rode his bike about 15 miles to get to the airfield. This was still his only mode of transportation when he soloed in an aircraft at age 16. While Tony and Hal had been buddies even before Tony went into the Navy, Al Marshick was the new member of the trio at Gilpin. They did all manner of jobs there, often in trade for flying time.

At one point Hal, who was homeless at the time, lived in the airport tower there sleeping on an old army cot. His job was to service aircraft that came in after dark. The pilot would buzz the field announcing his arrival and Hal would go out, turn on the runway lights, and assist with refueling or whatever their needs were upon their landing. Hal and Al worked as line-boys directing incoming traffic, chocking wheels and refueling as necessary. Tony's job was taking care of the office.

Tony had to watch his pennies so every minute in the air was precious. In an effort to get on the ground as quickly as possible, his landings were often dangerous. The type of aircraft he frequently flew was an old Waco UPF7, the proud possession of the owner of the airfield, Walter Douglas, Jr. (An elementary school was later named after him as was a school for Hal's stepfather, Ted DeGrazia.) A serious idiosyncrasy of that old Waco was its tendency to go into a "flat spin," without doubt one of the most dangerous situations in which a pilot could find himself. Nowadays, aircraft are designed to recover from a flat spin. In those days that wasn't necessarily so. Well, the fastest way to lose altitude is a spin so Tony, in his effort toward economy, would spin an aircraft as low as he could before pulling out to prepare for landing. Foolishly, Tony used this maneuver with Mr. Douglas's favorite aircraft, the Waco, on a day when Mr. Douglas was present. He looked up and saw Tony in a flat spin and cursed. He was sure that both Tony and his Waco were going to buy the farm that day. Tony knew what he was doing, or so we think, and managed to get the aircraft under control. He made a perfect three-point landing. Mr. Douglas was <u>furious</u>. Tony didn't pull that shenanigan again, at least while Mr. Douglas was at the airport. I want to mention that part of my flight training was recovering from a spin—an uncontrolled stall—and I absolutely hated that procedure. It terrified me.

When Walter Douglas sold the airport, it was renamed Freeway Airport. I did a great number of take-offs and landings from it. Often I would take off from Tucson International Airport (TIA), fly over to Freeway, pick up Tony with engine running, and off we'd go for some fun. I had to hide Tony as my logbook recorded this as solo flight, a certain number of hours of which I had to accrue to apply for my license.

Now, about Al Marshick. He was a short, cocky stud who claimed that what God denied him in height he had made up for more than generously elsewhere. He had five wives, all of whom were very attractive. Over the years, several of my friends were quite enamored of him as well but were smart enough not to make matrimony the end game. Frankly, I was enamored of all three of these young pilots.

Al was extremely intelligent and graduated from the College of Engineering at UA. While I was working on my psychology certification, I had to give several tests of

Al Marshick

performance and intelligence (IQ) to at least ten people per test after having been carefully trained in their administration. Each final test occurred on campus with a trained specialist behind a mirrored window so that my every move could be observed. The examiner also had a microphone to check my wording and timing.

I had asked Al to be my subject for my "final exam" on the Wechsler Adult Intelligence Scale (WAIS). I was nervous about it and wanted it to go perfectly. I should have known Al would play games with me, but I bit. First he required that I take him to lunch at his favorite restaurant. Okay with me. When we arrived he immediately ordered a margarita. "Oh, no", said I. "No drinking. You need to be sharp for the test." Well, one didn't say no to Al. Just to upset me further, he drank a second, and a third and then he was willing to head for campus and the test.

If I had been nervous before, I was a wreck now and to further exacerbate my anxiety we found that the "observer" was unable to procure the proper facility for observation and we were forced to be a threesome in a classroom. Cocky as ever, Al aced every test but we still had the most difficult test ahead—that of digit recall which required the repetition of digits first forward and then in reverse—difficult for anybody. To my thinking, there was no way he could pull that off while drunk. But, we're talking about Al. And so I said, "Listen, repeat after me the following …" We started with four digits, worked up to six, and then eight. He didn't miss one! Now he had the same task, but repeating the digits backwards. No one I have ever tested, and there have been hundreds, has ever repeated, from memory, eight digits backwards repeatedly, but Al did. He didn't miss one. Naturally, he ended up with a very high I.Q. and I passed "my test."

When Tony was courting me, our adventures often included flying. His friend, Ben Hawkes (one of his ushers in our wedding) had his own slick plane and I would sit, miserable, in the rear seat sure that the bottom was going to fall off the plane or that we were in imminent danger of crashing. Tony wisely decided that I should take a five-hour "pinch hitter" course to learn the basics of flight and thus become more comfortable in the air. He felt strongly that it should be someone other than he who would train me, and picked—yes, Al Marshick.

In those days, $100 would easily cover five hours of flying in a two-place Cessna 150. My first flight with Al was scheduled. As you know, I study. So when the time came for take-off I told Al I wanted to do it by myself with as little interference as possible. I knew all the airspeed recommendations for take-off, climbing etc. and was oozing confidence. And I did just fine. We headed for a practice area west of Tucson to begin instruction in climbing, recovering from stalls, making perfect 360s and 720s and the like. All was going well until I felt a new tension in the cockpit. I looked over at Al who had asked to take the controls for a while. He was rigid with concentration. This did not look good to me.

Suddenly we were making a loop. I was horror stricken. The Cessna 150 is <u>not</u> certified for aerobatic maneuvers. This had to be executed <u>absolutely</u> perfectly or we would surely die. First, it could have stalled out at the top of the loop due to insufficient airspeed that would cause loss of control. Or, on the backside of the loop we could exceed airspeed limitations and thus risk losing our wings when pulling out at the bottom of the loop. Obviously we survived but I think even Al was a little pale at the end. He knew he shouldn't have done it, and it was only the first of many times that I was furious with him. But it has to be noted that Al was an F102 fighter pilot with the Arizona Air National Guard, thus he was God.

You will read about the most dangerous flying that I, and all of my flying family, have ever seen in air shows or anywhere else, in my section about our adventures in Cañon del Oro. Al did indeed prove that he was immortal in the escapades that took place there.

Al declared me ready for solo at the end of our five hours together in flight but he was not a CFI—certified flight instructor. Hence, he had to turn me over to a legitimate flight instructor at Tucson International Airport, Roger Cutter, with whom I am still in touch on Facebook. Roger wanted three hours of flight with me before he would discuss solo flight. One does not know when the solo will occur until one's flight instructor tells you to pull over to the edge of

The day Aldine soloed with her family to cheer her on 1968

the runway and he gets out! I had eight hours of flight time when I soloed.

The first time you fly a plane without a second person in it there is a whole new dimension of flight. Suddenly, in an aircraft that weighs only 1500 pounds anyway, you have just reduced the weight by about 175 pounds. Everything feels different. You have lifted off before you know it. And landings seemed quite different. Eventually one grows to love it and solo time in an aircraft becomes almost a spiritual experience.

I earned my private pilot's license in 1968 and immediately joined the 99s—an international group of women pilots. It was on November 2, 1929 that women pilots met at an airfield on Long Island to create the organization. The name of the group was decided upon then since 99 of the 117 licensed women pilots at that time signed on as charter members. Amelia Earhart was one of them. By the way, the first woman pilot was named Blanche Scott. In 1910 she was permitted to taxi an aircraft and somehow it became airborne!

I went on to receive my commercial pilot's license in 1972. This is described in more detail in my chapter on Flying Adventures in Baja. This was another example in my life of having to "prove myself."

My final membership in a flying organization is one of which I am very proud. I am a UFO—United Flying Octogenarian. To qualify for membership, one must be pilot in command of an aircraft on or after one's 80th birthday. Hal and I did it! I am the only female UFO in Tucson, and I believe in Arizona. While I may never fly again, I can look back on 48 years filled with moments of elation, satisfaction and abject terror.

But, back to Al. He was always very much a part of our lives. (He was Kent's godfather.) Still, there were times in my life that I didn't speak to him for months on end. Some of his flying behavior was unforgiveable.

Take, for example, the time that we were in separate airplanes, with passengers, flying back to Tucson from Guaymas, Mexico. Al and I talked back and forth on the radio checking on location and so forth. Suddenly he said, "Take up a heading and an altitude and stay there. Don't deviate at all!" Not wanting to query why he was asking this of me, I complied. Thank goodness I did. He came on the radio and said, "Look to your right." And there he was, tucked into my wing in a flight formation attitude. He seemed only inches away. I was shocked and scared. He was a veteran in flying in formation and I knew nothing whatever about it. And my passengers were in danger as well, a cardinal sin to me. Eventually he rolled off and the remaining flight was uneventful, until we landed. I let him know then and there that I never wanted to see him again, and I meant it.

Obviously I ultimately relented, leading to my next story. One never, ever touches the controls of an aircraft being flown by someone else unless the pilot in command loses consciousness, dies or is risking lives. I was none of these when, on landing in Tucson with Al in right seat, he suddenly grabbed the controls and took over our landing. I was aghast. He had no right nor need to do that and when I asked for an explanation after landing he told me that I was in imminent danger of damaging the aircraft on touchdown. That was utterly untrue and I told him I never wanted to see him again, and I meant it.

Then there was the time four of us had gone in a Cessna 172 for lunch in Tubac where there was a landing strip. After lunch with Al's inevitable margaritas he took left seat in the airplane. There is a reason for the requirement of "eight hours from bottle to throttle." Pilots have an inflated opinion of their flying prowess with a few drinks under their belts that can lead to big trouble, and in this case it did. It was a hot day, thus decreasing the ability of the plane to take off. It needed a lot of runway and we didn't have it. Also, we were overloaded for that aircraft on a hot day so this was a potentially disastrous situation. Tony was in right seat and his secretary, Cass Cardona, and I were in the back.

We started our take-off. Al ran out of runway so lifted off with the stall warning horn sounding. This alarm strikes fear in the heart of any pilot. Instead of getting his nose down as soon as possible to pick up airspeed, he proceeded to do a tight turn over the resort where we had eaten lunch—with the stall warning sounding all the way. Only a miracle was going to save us from stalling out. I saw my life flash in front of my eyes. But, oh, I forgot, God (Al) was at the controls. The miracle occurred. When we landed safely at TIA I told Al I never wanted to see him again, and I meant it. I am shaking as I recall these stories. They were very upsetting.

Another incident with Al occurred during the period when I was doing data collection for my doctoral dissertation. Subjects for the study, epileptic children, were very difficult to find, but Barrow Neurological Institute in Phoenix offered to assist.

As I would spend every other week in Phoenix, Tony towed our fifth-wheel to a trailer park on Thomas Road there. It was a luxurious trailer—36 feet long— and it felt so good to have a comfortable place to come home to each evening. One night I was particularly tired and eager for a peaceful evening. I entered the trailer, turned on the air-conditioning, closed all the curtains, lit 18 candles (for atmosphere), and put soothing music on the stereo. I drew a bubble bath and slipped into it with a glass of chilled white wine. Ah, the bliss of feeling the tension leave my body. Heaven! Suddenly everything stopped. No air-conditioning, no music—nothing. My adrenalin level soared as I immediately wondered what had happened and how I was ever going to fix it. I exited the bathtub, dried myself, grabbed a robe and went in search of the problem. The mood was broken! I pulled back the curtain on the sliding glass door to step outside to analyze the problem and who was smiling up at me but, yes, Al Marshick. He was in Phoenix and thought he'd drop by for a visit. (He had been married for the fifth time the previous Saturday!) He knew the best way to get my attention was to turn off the power. It worked. He certainly got my attention; I was furious. However, being furious with Al was my default position. What a cheeky devil he was!

Tony and I often had rather formal dinner parties. We had invited Al to one of these. Knowing he was highly unorthodox in his choice of clothing, we felt it advisable to tell him the dress code for the evening – necktie required. Al arrived on the appointed evening having complied with my request. He was indeed wearing a necktie – no shirt – just an elegant necktie!

One last story about Al. I mention in my section on my graduate degree education that my friend Bette Layton and I sat in the front row during Dr. Samuel A. Kirk's weekly lectures one semester. We were the cause of yet another disturbance that plagued him, one that I failed to mention. Every week Al, knowing where the lecture was taking place and that Bette and I were there, flew his F102 overhead and just at the right moment let off the afterburner. One could see Dr. Kirk's lips moving but hear not a word he said for quite some minutes. He never learned the source of those interruptions.

Al died of cancer in 2012. It is a miracle that he died of natural causes rather than in a flying disaster. At a 99's Christmas party I sat with Lorraine Newhouse and her boyfriend who had been in the Arizona Air National Guard with Al. He couldn't stand Al and loudly declared that he had thoroughly disliked being in the same squadron with Al. He added, "Hell, I didn't even like being in the same airspace with Al!"

As I said earlier, the Three Musketeers had totally different backgrounds and personalities. Although Hal admired and liked Al, early on he adopted the policy of staying clear of Al as much as possible because he considered him dangerous. He referred to him as "the crown prince of macho bullshit" and his pugnacious, competitive lifestyle was offensive to Hal. Hal did not choose to be any part of Al's ongoing arm wrestling and push-up contests modus operandi.

To me Al had a unique, never-to-be-duplicated spirit and was a man with whom I had a love-hate relationship. I think, however, that it leaned toward love. There will be a special place in my heart for him forever.

MY FIRST PASSENGER

For everyone there are significant "firsts" in life. An important one for me was my first passenger after receiving my private pilot's license. As I adored my father and knew he loved an adventure, I thought he might be thrilled with the idea of being my guinea pig. Dad was a highly respected journalist in Tucson and so this event would not go unnoticed. In fact, there was a two page article with seven photographs devoted to covering this story in the *Tucson Daily Citizen* newspaper. I shall let my father tell you of his experience of flying with me for the first time.

No Fright Like First Flight
By Murray Sinclair
Tucson AP Writer

When your daughter asks you to be her first passenger after she gets her pilot's license, you don't say no, even if you have reservations about small planes.

For a moment, of course, I thought of the first time she steered the outboard motor boat. In three minutes she had glanced off a dock, narrowly missed hitting two other boats, then managed to stall it.

On pilot graduation day her instructor, Roger Cutter, said she was good. The Federal Aviation examiner, Lum Edwards, apparently agreed. Mrs. Anthony K. (Aldine) von Isser was now a pilot.

When I reached Tucson International Airport for the maiden flight, the March winds were blowing. We couldn't go up. The next day was worse. The third time we tried there was both wind and rain. I wondered if fate were trying to tell me something.

Last Saturday there wasn't enough wind to make it dangerous,. Bumpy, yes. Dangerous, no.

When I arrived she was in the middle of her check list. I counted the items. There were 95. "Does that mean there are 95 things that can go wrong?" I wanted to know.

"More than that," she said. "Some things you can't check." That was reassuring.

Grandsons Kent and Tony, fascinated with the small opening for the small engine, measured the hole and reported it 9 by 14 inches. Recently they had put together a model plane engine that seemed not a great deal smaller—to me anyway.

"How many horsepower?" I asked. "One hundred. This one has lots of power." "But the outboard motor has more power than that." "I know. But all this motor has to do is drive the propeller."

"That's all the outboard has to do—and if it stops, you don't sink." I had to admit it couldn't take much power to drive the dinky propeller. It looked five feet long at the most. "Sixty nine inches," Aldine said.

Just then an Air National Guard single seater F102 landed. "How many horsepower has that?' I asked my son-in-law Tony. "15,000," he said. "It goes faster."

The check list completed, we taxied toward the runway. The inside of the plane—like the whole plane—was smaller than I had expected. I measured the inside. From door to door it was 36 inches—for two people.

Checking checklist in the cockpit

"I don't talk much because I have too many things to do," she said. "If you see another airplane when we get up, be sure to tell me." When she turned the wheel, the dual wheel on my side hit my knees. "You'll have to move back a little" "I can't. I'm back as far as the seat will go." When I twisted my leg to get it out of the way of the wheel, I got a cramp.

There was a decided squeak coming from somewhere. "What," said I, "is that?" "Nothing to worry about, Pop, it's the nose." I didn't see why the nose would squeak but I didn't say anything.

The takeoff was great. As we climbed, she said again, "If you see another plane, for goodness sake tell me." There were a couple of other planes in the air, but nothing close. "I always stay away from Davis-Monthan," Aldine said. "The traffic out there is terrible. Don't forget," she said for the third time. "If you see another plane, tell me. They can be hard to see."

I didn't see as much of Tucson as I should; I was too busy watching for planes. We circled our houses on East Glenn Street. (I hadn't realized how much empty space was around them.) Then we headed back to the field.

Aldine picked up the microphone. "Tucson tower," she said. "This is seven two niner three Sierra (that's airplane talk for 7293) 8 miles north, inbound. "That tells the tower who I am, where I am and what I'm going to do," she explained. The tower came back, "Niner three Sierra, runway one two left. Advise when over river."

"What river do you think he's talking about?" Aldine asked. "It HAS to be either the Santa Cruz or the Rillito, " I said. "I know, but I can't find either. Can you?" I couldn't. She picked up the mike again. "This is seven two niner three Sierra at "A" mountain. May I have a straight in for one one two left."

"Niner three Sierra. Possible straight in. Advise over river." "Tucson tower. This is niner three Sierra. I can't find the river." "Three miles northwest." "I think I'm closer than that now." The tower came on again. "Niner three Sierra. Change to one two right due to jet traffic." "Roger."

"Niner three Sierra. Expedite clearing for final one two left." "That," said Aldine, "means he wants me to get out of the way as fast as I can. But I can't go any faster." I looked at the speedometer. It showed 70 miles per hour.

In a few seconds the towers crackled to life again. There was no question he wanted action, and quickly. "Niner three Sierra, do you see the jet on your left wing now? Clear to land runway one two right."

We saw the jet all right and there was no question in my mind—it needed the runway more than we did. My landing couldn't have been smoother. Perfect!

The tower again: "Niner three Sierra, can you stop short of first intersection? There is a Lear jet passing in front of you." Aldine veered the plane off the runway and came back on when the Lear had passed. Ground control came on the air: "Niner three Sierra, thank you for holding short of the runway." "Wasn't that nice of him?" Aldine asked.

As we started down the taxi strip again, a jet—a big jet—was coming toward us. "Isn't he coming pretty quickly?" I said, not wanting to appear nervous. "Oh, we'll be out of his way in plenty of time." We were, of course.

As we taxied up to the greeting squad of my wife, son-in-law Tony, and two grandchildren, Aldine said, "Next time you can take the controls for a few minutes." I made no comment.

Aldine's father exiting aircraft

My wife went up for a quick ride. Driving home, she was quiet for a few moments. Then she asked, "What do you think of my taking flying lessons?" I didn't volunteer to be HER first passenger.

My parents were frequent passengers on flights into Mexico during the following years. Thank goodness it was always smooth flying.

FLYING IN MEXICO

Among our many flying adventures together, Tony and I had dozens of flights into Mexico. Our principal destinations were Alamos and Guaymas. I will recount several of these trips, some of which still leave me trembling.

Once I received my pilot's license in 1968, Tony moved over to right seat and left me to be pilot in command. I want to attest that while I was a good pilot, Tony was a great pilot. He had an extra twenty years of flying under his belt before I ever started. I flew by the book. He flew by instinct. I read the manual and obeyed the manufacturer's flight limitations. He figured out what would work and did it.

One weekend we were flying to Guaymas with our friends Jane and Bob Ward, an older couple but game for anything. We were in a Cessna 182 and excited about the days ahead staying at the beautiful Playa de Cortes Hotel in Guaymas, Sonora.

As we approached Guaymas, I could see that weather conditions had deteriorated considerably from the information we had been given in Hermosillo where we had landed to go through customs. It was evident to me that the windsocks and the tetrahedron indicated a very, very strong crosswind to the runway. I was sure it exceeded the capability of the aircraft to land safely. I also didn't think my flying skills were up to the challenge. That wind was very gusty and blowing like billy-be-damned. As pilot in command, my decision was to return to Hermosillo, which had multiple runways, and wait it out. "No way," said Tony and with my enthusiastic endorsement he took over from right seat—not an easy transition in my opinion. Everything typically done with the right hand is now done with the left. Our passengers were probably wondering what they had gotten themselves into!

Tony established an extreme crab (putting the nose of the plane into the wind and thus approaching the runway with the aircraft sideways.) At the very last second he straightened the plane lining it up with the runway and made a landing as smooth as silk. He applied full aileron and we taxied to the terminal with Tony smiling like a Cheshire cat all the way. I repeat, he was a superb pilot.

My son Tony has the same natural instinct for flying. Kent also was a pilot and soloed on his sixteenth birthday! One day, before leaving work at the university, I asked the professor in the office next to mine, Dr. Richard Morris, a well-known child psychologist, if he'd like to go flying for an hour or two. I suggested we fly over his house and do a little sight-seeing over Tucson. He thought it was a great idea so I phoned young Tony, who worked at Hughes Aircraft Company near the airport, to ask if he'd like to join us. The three of us met at Tucson International Airport where I assumed left seat—pilot in command. About a half hour later I asked Tony if he'd like to take the controls. To this day, Tony is an <u>avid</u> enthusiast of anything aeronautical and he quickly accepted. I thought I'd been doing a fairly creditable job of flying, but the moment Tony took over he cranked in a little rudder control here and a little elevator control there and that plane was practically flying itself. He, like his father before him, is a natural.

I'll add an aside here. Rick Morris, whom I have just mentioned, was asked by the Prentice Hall Publishing Company to write a textbook on child psychology. He asked me to be co-author. I was flattered and knew it would be a great boon to me professionally. I accepted his offer. After signing the contract and receiving an advance I had second thoughts. I realized that this commitment would significantly reduce the time I could spend at our cottage in Canada. This was not a sacrifice I was willing to make as my time with my family each summer was and remains the most important activity of my year. As no progress had been made with the book, I was still able to graciously extricate myself from the contract with no harm done. I have never regretted that decision.

As I say, we often flew to Guaymas where the beautiful hotel at which we typically stayed was situated on a magnificent beach with waving palm trees and poolside sun bathers enjoying the serenity it offered. Well, Tony never let a visit go by without one <u>very</u> low buzz job over the hotel on our last day— just one—that barely topped the trees. Tony knew a second pass might get him identified, arrested and jailed. It was an impressive spectacle that I am sure many guests talked about for years.

Another destination was Alamos, Sonora—an enchanting colonial town. It was founded in the late 17th century following discoveries of silver in the area. Through the years it has managed to retain the charm and pace of earlier times. Alamos is known as "La Ciudad de los Portales." Portales are tall, arched, covered verandas or walkways fronting many of the cobblestone streets or "calles." This town represents a fine example of classical architecture from Mexico's colonial period.

There one sees haciendas that otherwise would be seen only in movies. It is the home of a good many American ex-pats who find the gracious lifestyle and inexpensive household help worth leaving behind the conveniences one has in living in the U.S.

One lovely trip to Alamos was with Katharine Merritt and Guy Meek in January of 1972. Guy Meek was a rather stuffy British friend of Katharine whom we met on cruises on the Aegean. I was quite surprised that they would submit themselves to the discomforts of a small plane. We did, in fact, have a lovely weekend together.

On another trip in May of 1973 we were with our friends Polly and Dick Knight. There we were hosted by her friends Bill and Dolly Walsh in their old and magnificent hacienda with its gorgeous gardens and multiple servants.

Typically we stayed at a magnificent hotel, Casa de los Tesoros, an 18th century restored Spanish colonial landmark in Alamos. During our visits it was owned and operated by a delightful woman, Dolly Gordon, who always made us feel like her favorite guests. One time we had taken my sister Carol who was recovering from a divorce and in need of some special attention. Did she ever receive it! At 2:00 a.m. she heard outside her window a small mariachi group led by a handsome young Mexican gentleman who was wooing her with the most romantic Latin songs you could imagine. Her trip was a success.

An interesting note is the story of a man—a very old man known as "El Baron"—who lived at the airport in Alamos sleeping under the wings of parked aircraft. He never left his post. Food was brought to him. He was the self-proclaimed on-site guardian of the airport and he took the job seriously. While it was only a tacit understanding that he would be paid, pilots always tipped him for his good service and the safety of their aircraft. He was not

Carol in Alamos with "El Baron" - 1982

employed by the airfield, which was really nothing but a dirt strip, but I think he made a decent living and felt he fulfilled an important role. He was sufficiently interesting that there was an article about him in the *Arizona Daily Star*!

Another time I had flown to Alamos with my parents. My father, a syndicated feature writer, was doing an article on Mexican prisons. There was one in Alamos. He allowed me to go with him for his interview with the "warden" and I came away with a unique necklace made by an inmate who had braided horsehair in an intricate manner. Making such items was a way for prisoners to earn money. The Mexican prison system is quite different from ours. No food is provided. Hence, the families of the inmates must climb the hill to the prison three times a day to provide meals. I wondered what the arrangement would be for an inmate with nobody nearby. Presumably they make a deal with the family of another inmate. (As they have conjugal visits on a frequent basis, I wonder if other families take care of this need, too!) There are no luxuries for these prisoners but they have ample freedom to walk around as an escape would be futile. There is no place to hide and they would be quickly found.

On another trip I was returning alone to Tucson from Alamos and gave myself a little scare. Pilots calculate fuel consumption carefully when flying to Alamos but I was always confident that I could get back to Guaymas, or even Hermosillo, before I had to refuel. Well, on this flight I got lost. It was a frightening feeling as there were no radio navigational systems in Mexico at that time and it was necessary to fly using visual flight rules (VFR) only. The problem was that the terrain looked all the same with no unique visual reference points. One had to depend on one's compass only. I knew I was heading west but there was a lot of nothing to the west and I knew I had to find a community with an airstrip and fuel.

When in Mexico, I tended to monitor the emergency radio frequency—121.5. I held little hope that anyone would be flying within radio range but optimistically I picked up the mike and advised my aircraft numbers and requested assistance. Finally, I made contact. Just hearing other voices gave me comfort. Apparently two U.S. Forest Rangers were monitoring that frequency and picked up my call. They knew the region well and asked me to identify visual references. They then told me I was directly over a railroad and to take up a certain heading. They led me along via radio until eventually I could determine where I was and set up a heading that took me to Guaymas and <u>fuel</u>.

But that tiny scare couldn't begin to compare with one of the worst flying incidents I have ever experienced and, again, I learned a life lesson the hard way.

Tony and I had planned a trip to Alamos with good friends, Nancy and Bill Masland and Ginny and Juan Fonseca, in a Cessna 206 which was big enough for all of us. At that time Tucson had few neurologists and I believe both Bill and Juan were neurosurgeons, a profession which I had assumed required great equanimity and self-confidence. One evening we all went out for dinner in Tucson to plan the trip. I was surprised when Juan said he wouldn't be able to go with us—that he was terrified of flying. This put a damper on things so I encouraged Juan by saying that I was certain I could get him past this problem. I suggested that the two of us meet at the airport after work, take a little flight and have a drink together afterwards. I think the latter part of the plan appealed to him and that he would try to get through the former. We took off and I flew him over his house (standard procedure for me when I am taking a passenger out for a joyride) and over the foothills. Then I made a suggestion that almost cost me my life. I told Juan he might feel even more comfortable while flying if he had a better understanding of the dynamics of flight. I offered him the opportunity to take the controls and feel how the plane moves with ascent and descent. He accepted.

Suddenly I knew I was in great trouble—Juan had frozen at the wheel. His face was deadly white and set like a mask. He was paralyzed and I don't know if he could even hear me when I spoke. Fortunately we were flying straight and level but I knew I HAD to get the controls back. His hands were rigidly stuck to the wheel. I can't tell you the terror I felt at being helpless in the cockpit. Over the next several minutes I spoke gently to him, I stroked his arm, all in an attempt to get him to relax. It seemed like hours before I finally convinced him to release his death hold and I could take back my life and my plane and get us back to the airport.

We did not have that drink. The Fonsecas did not go to Alamos. I learned later from my flight instructor, Lum Edwards, that a situation such as this is not uncommon but often people don't live to tell about it. He said that many, many fatal small aircraft accidents are the result of suicide often perpetrated by either the pilot or a passenger who want to end it all. Lum was also known as "the professor" as he was a tall, strikingly handsome and gallant gentleman who knew all there was to know about flying. In 2008 he was inducted into the Arizona Aviation Hall of Fame which is located at the Pima Air and Space Museum in Tucson, Arizona. Tony and I attended the ceremony.

As I look back on my active flying days, I think I carried only one fear with me during every flight — the possibility of fire. Ever cautious, I always had fire extinguishers with me. It is interesting that during flight training a student is taught that in case of an engine fire the pilot is always to slip the airplane so that the fire is away from the passenger. Now I ask you, how is a passenger helped if the pilot is on fire!

MY ADVENTURES AS A BUSH PILOT IN MEXICO

Probably one of the most dangerous of my flying experiences happened in Baja California. For two months in 1971 I was basically a "bush pilot" in compromising situations of all kinds.

Pilots love to hang out at the coffee shop at the base of the Tucson International Airport (TIA) tower. I was no exception. After flying, I would drop in for a cup of coffee and eavesdrop. Pilots enjoy telling their stories and I was fascinated by listening in on them. One Saturday I overheard a tall, lanky man mention that his pilot had a family emergency and was not going to be available for a couple of months. He needed a replacement quickly.

As it happens, it was the end of the spring semester, both my sons were off to various locations for the summer, and I had some time. Kent had gone to work at the Three Rivers Ranch in Jackson Hole, Wyoming where Katharine Merritt had a ranch. He was a ranch hand there for several years. Tony Jr. was in Nantucket with the Hyde family learning to sail and play tennis. We always finished the last month of the summer at the cottage in Canada.

Typically I was the only woman pilot in the coffee shop during those "bull" sessions so when I approached the tall man he was not prepared for what I said. I told him I was a pilot and that I would be interested in hearing more about the job he needed to fill. It didn't take long for us to consummate a deal.

Although I had my private pilot's license I still needed an additional two hundred hours of flying time to qualify for a commercial license. Flying was expensive and I hadn't determined a way of accumulating the necessary hours. This appeared to be a good opportunity to chalk up some valuable flying time.

The man's name was Cleve Crudgington. He and his wife Mimi owned and operated a hotel on the eastern coast of Baja California at a place called Punta Chivato. At that time the 1000 mile highway down the Baja had not been constructed. The only way to get to this hotel was by air or sea. Typically the hotel guests flew their own planes to get there. Many came from California. Often, however, the hotel had to provide the ferrying. This was but one of the pilot's many responsibilities. The hotel was very beautiful and elegantly appointed and drew guests from far and wide.

The plane owned by the hotel was a Cessna 210—a magnificent single engine aircraft that was turbo-charged and had its own oxygen supply. It also had retractable landing gear, a new experience for me. Thus, I would have a lot to learn to prepare for a job such as this.

Cleve was delighted to find a replacement so quickly and offered to pay for the instruction I would require to acquaint myself with this aircraft. Lum Edwards, the highly respected Certified Flight Instructor (CFI) at TIA, took me under his wing. Not only did I have to learn the systems and controls, but I also needed instruction in other areas unfamiliar to me such as emergency landings at sea.

The plane was hangered at TIA while in Tucson. En route to Baja, there was a required stop in Hermosillo, Sonora to pass through customs and immigration. From there one flew across the Sea of Cortez to reach Punta Chivato. It was about an 80 mile stretch of ocean. I flew across at 18,000 feet, which is where flight levels begin. Even at this altitude if I were to have engine failure there were eleven minutes when I could neither glide back to mainland Mexico nor could I reach land on the Baja side. This required my learning how to land at sea, exit the aircraft and inflate the life raft. While we didn't make any practice landings on the ocean, I did learn that one puts down in the trough of a wave! Fortunately, I never had any such incident.

I made that crossing dozens of times but I swear that on every one of those flights the engine went into "automatic rough" during that period of time with a point of no return.

Lum eventually signed off on my log book. I was a qualified Cessna 210 pilot and the adventure began. I have to admit to having butterflies in my stomach the first time I took off to fly alone to a basically uninhabited part of Baja, Mexico. I had been warned that there was only one runway—a dirt strip—at Punta Chivato and it could be landed on going only one direction—toward a mountain. Hence, one had to make an approach to land with that obstacle taken into consideration. If one ran out of runway, well, just too bad. It also meant that take-offs were downwind when flying out of the airport which usually required all the runway available. There were a considerable number of fatalities in aircraft there but in most cases alcohol was involved.

I was told the story of four men who had taken off on a joy ride two weeks before my arrival who were three sheets to the wind. They ran out of fuel and had to ditch in the bay in front of the hotel. While everyone looked on in horror there was nothing anyone could do to save them. The plane sank and they all drowned.

As I mentioned, the plane was hangered in Tucson part of the time to pick up supplies. I was phoned when it was time for me to go to the airport for my flight south. The aircraft was always   fully loaded when I arrived and I had no idea what the plane held. All the seats in the aircraft, except that of the pilot, had been removed to make more room for cargo with no thought to the essential components of weight and balance. I had always been a stickler for staying within the envelope but I soon capitulated to their style of stowing and said an extra prayer.

My first stop was, of necessity, the Hermosillo Airport which I have always found to be the most difficult airfield in the world to locate. I think the customs officials were surprised to find that the pilot was a woman, and one who spoke Spanish. Both these attributes put me in good stead with them immediately. That is just as well as I quickly learned that a good many times the contents of the plane were contraband. On my first few trips the items were not severely illegal so they granted me the courtesy of turning a blind eye. One wonders why shoes and dog food would be considered contraband, but they were. And of course the hotel needed birth control pills so that their maids would not get pregnant. Help was hard to find in that remote region of Baja. And why would sanitary pads be illegal, and they were. It seemed to me that I took enough of them down to have taken care of every woman in Mexico!

Later, the officiales took a more austere assessment of my load—diesel and air conditioning parts and ammunition of one kind or another. You see, anything the hotel needed had to be flown in and was more easily available in the United States. I knew I was pressing my luck but I smiled my nicest smile and never once did they stop me. Now, mind you, they did start to look only at what was on the top layer of cargo and I thank goodness they didn't dig deeper. I think I'd have ended up in jail. I was beginning to wonder if the hours of flying time I was accruing were worth the risk I was taking.

When I arrived at Punta Chivato I would buzz the hotel and a car would be sent out to pick me up. I did not like the fact that Cleve took the airplane's keys from me when I got there. It really made me feel like a prisoner and, in fact, I was. There was no fail safe for me here; I was on my own.

Flying this route as frequently as I did ultimately came to be what a bus driver must feel. It was familiar and repetitive.

When I had no other responsibilities at the hotel I enjoyed spending time with Cleve's two young daughters. They had no opportunity to go to school so I took on the role of tutor. In exchange, as they were bilingual, they helped me with my Spanish.

Punta Chivato is situated between Mulegé and Santa Rosalia, large towns for that area. If anyone in our region became seriously ill or needed access to more sophisticated medical treatment I flew them to mainland Mexico. In that respect, I guess I was a flying ambulance as well. Once I flew an expectant mother to the mainland for an emergency caesarian birth.

A very dangerous part of the job was flying to the mainland to pick up food supplies, a weekly requirement. Few comestibles were available in the dry region surrounding the hotel, so I did our "grocery shopping" in Guaymas, Sonora on the mainland. When loaded, the aircraft was a disaster waiting to happen. Those loading the plane had no knowledge of—or concern for— weights and balances. They threw the melons and heavy stuff in the tail of the aircraft while the more delicate and lighter items would be saved for last to be put on top. Not good!

One time Tony had flown down with me to spend a weekend and kindly did the grocery run to the mainland in my stead. He was not at all pleased with the loading technique there. In spite of his concern he climbed aboard for the return flight to Baja. However, when he was ready to taxi for take-off the tail was too heavy for him to move forward. It required two men to hold up the tail of the aircraft before he could start his taxi roll. The plane was so overweight that he barely had enough airstrip for take-off. Then he had to contend with the climb-out which was very, very slow indeed. He was barely above water when he reached the ocean and he never could climb to a safe altitude before it was time for him to start his landing procedure. He did that once, and once only. Tony had a lot of flying experience but he never sweated a flight as much as he did that one.

On one of those runs to Guaymas I had my only experience with vertigo. It was quite terrifying. The sea and the sky were the same color—gray—and there was no horizon visible to me. The vista was monochromatic. Although I was not instrument rated, I had no choice but to depend upon the gauges in front of me. Vertigo makes you feel as if the instruments are wrong because your brain is giving you different information. Depending upon an artificial horizon gauge that you don't trust is tough. It takes a great deal of courage to fly by instruments rather than by instinct. Of course, in order to get a pilot's license it is necessary to have time "under the hood." That means that the student pilot has to put on a helmet that obliterates all visual reference except the instruments. The instructor then puts you in unusual attitudes and it is up to the pilot to recover as quickly as possible.

I was getting cold feet about this job. One weekend, when Cleve had promised that I would be free to return to Tucson for a class reunion he told me he was unable to make the aircraft available. Other unwanted requirements were put on my roster of duties. I was expected to be available at night to function as a hostess to the single gentlemen who had flown in. I realized one night that I was truly in over my head and I didn't know how to extricate myself. I felt trapped. I noticed that Cleve had put a man in the bedroom next to mine, with a connecting bathroom. My bedroom did not have a lock on the door. Mimi, Cleve's wife, turned a blind eye to everything so I had no one to turn to for help.

I went to bed that night knowing I would have a visitor and I was quite sure that Cleve had told him I would receive him willingly. I was shaking with fear when I heard the door open. The man climbed into my bed and I turned to the only arsenal a woman has in a situation such as that—I burst into tears. I just sobbed and sobbed and it didn't take long for this man to realize I was not going to be a willing participant after all. He left.

I picked up my blanket and a pillow and wandered the hotel until I found a door that locked. The following morning I passed Cleve as he drank his coffee and not a word was said between us.

The next time I was sent to Tucson for a pick-up I simply left the key in the ignition and walked away. I earned every one of those flying hours!

I continued adding hours to my log book. After weeks of intensive air-work with my instructors—Lum Edwards and Roger Cutter—I was ready for my final check ride on May 15, 1972. I passed it with flying colors! At long last I was a commercial pilot. The following Saturday night Tony had a huge party for me—50 guests—to celebrate. Most of them were people involved in flying.

In the 1960s a pilot had a certificate number; mine is 1917522. Soon thereafter social security numbers were used instead. I am very proud of my old original number.

14

∞

ADVENTURES IN SAILING

SAILING WITH TONY

Possibly Tony's greatest passion in life was sailing—superseding even his love of flying.

His concept of heaven on earth was blue water sailing—sailing in the deep water far from shore as compared to coastal sailing. He loved being off on the ocean for weeks at a time all by himself. He became an internationally recognized single-handed sailor and had articles published in sailing magazines in several languages.

This hobby was not without its dangers and as a young father he took this into consideration and bought life insurance for the periods of time he would be gone. Still, I never had a moment's peace when he was on these voyages. Often when he left he would say, "We'll see who wins this time—she or I." He was referring to the ocean.

These voyages were the highlights of his life and provided the challenges that he needed. I always made him promise to wear a life-line in case he was swept overboard. I don't think he really listened to me but admitted gratefully that he did heed my advice on one occasion when he was indeed washed into the sea during a hurricane on the Sea of Cortez. At the time he was battening down his tender—named *Tender Behind*. As Tony would say, no cry is more mournful that that of a single-handed sailor who shouts "man overboard." I think that incident gave him pause for thought and thereafter he trailed a line with plastic containers that he could grab onto if he was "man overboard."

An inlet on an island called Sal Si Puedes was his port in the storm when he knew a big blow was coming. That translates literally to "leave if you can." He was the charter member of a one person organization called the Joshua Humphrey Society. Its tenet was as follows: if you know of a beautiful place that is little known, either stigmatize it as being horrible—or never mention it at all.

Such a place for him was Bahia San Juanico, a bay on the eastern coast of Baja California. He would sail there, put down anchor and stay for days. Of course he'd never see another living being. It was his goal to have me sail there with him. We had talked about it for years but I was reluctant to try it as I get terribly seasick. However, eventually I capitulated and we planned the impending trip with great care. We stowed appropriate medications as well as plenty of food.

We left from San Carlos, Sonora on April 21, 1985 under the impressive and distinctive mountain peaks called Tetas de Cabra (teats of the goat) with strong winds and a high sea. It wasn't long before the inevitable occurred—I was desperately seasick. I was vomiting so badly that Tony had to tie me in the boat. I looked back at the Tetas as they grew more and more distant and finally they were only a blip on the horizon and I was sure my life was coming to an end. And I welcomed the thought! I think if I had been Tony I would have just let me heave myself into the sea so that he could carry on in tranquility. After four hours of torture for us both, he realized there was no way we were going to be able to sail across the gulf to the utopian destination he so greatly wanted to share with me.

Going about to return to land was a defeat that neither of us ever forgot. As I watched the Tetas grow larger and larger in the distance, I had ambivalent feelings. I knew I had disappointed Tony terribly, but I was so glad to be approaching terra firma. Perhaps it was God's will as, when we returned to shore, I phoned Tucson to learn that my father was very ill in hospital and had asked that my brother Murray and his brother Gordon be called. I took the next flight back to Tucson. Tony continued to sail on the Sea of Cortez for three weeks longer.

Tony had many sailboats over the years and the one he owned when he died was his dream come true—a 26-foot San Juan that he bought on January 3, 1982 and named *Aldine*. This required his selling *Aldine Baby*. He had modified the new sailboat to the smallest detail and even had an interior decorator

Tony leaving Tucson with "Aldine" for the Sea of Cortez - November 1982

come to insure beauty, quality and comfort throughout the cabin. He did insist on keeping one pin-rail that was historical to him. During one heavy storm he had been tossed across the cabin and hit his forehead on this pin-rail leaving a serious gash and a permanent scar. He wore it with pride.

Tony was a member of the Tucson Sailing Club presiding as its commodore for several years. At the annual Change of Command banquet in 1971, Tony was awarded the trophy for Sailor of the Year. In his article about this event in the *Arizona Daily Star*, Pete Cowgill, a highly respected reporter, wrote "It takes a special breed of man (or woman) to head out into the wilderness solo. I'll tackle a lot of places on land all by myself. But the sea is something else."

Tony receiving the trophy for
Sailor of the Year - 1971

Annually, for many years, we attended the Columbus Day sailboat races in Guaymas, Sonora, Mexico. Tony typically placed and occasionally won.

For many years he sold sailboats through his own little company called Desert Boat Sales, and he did very well. Interestingly, Arizona has more boats per capita than any state in the union, according to Encyclopedia Britannica and other reliable sources. His own boats always had *Aldine* as part of the name. First there was *Aldine Baby* and later *Aldine 1* and *Aldine 2*.

Aldine & Tony sailing in Mexico

An incident in *Aldine Baby* caught the interest of sailing magazines in many countries. On one voyage, Tony's boat caught the fancy of a very, very large whale. Many yachts are lost at sea by the harmless cavorting of whales. Tony came close to being one of these. I will let Tony tell you this exciting story in his own words in Appendix 3. The article was published not only in U.S. publications such as *Boating* (April, 1974) and *Sea* (January, 1976) but also several European sailing magazines, complete with photographs.

Tony had no radio communication whatever. When he set sail, he was on his own. That is the way he wanted it—to be totally self-sufficient and self-dependent. He, of course, had to sleep while sailing and had three self-steering devices. They were critical to his survival. One night in December of 1982 he failed to set the correct heading and in the wee hours of the morning was jolted awake; he had gone aground.

This was a potentially deadly situation. The boat had been going at quite a clip and was buried in the sand of the beach he hit. If he could not get himself out of this situation, he would die. There was neither civilization nor help for perhaps hundreds of miles. Maybe it was the adrenalin generated by this frightening experience that energized him, but somehow over the next few hours, and with the help of the tides, he got his boat back in the water. He didn't talk about that episode often. I think it was far too scary for him to think about.

When our sons were young, he wanted them to have the ocean wilderness experience. As I have written elsewhere, he wanted his lads to be able to take care of themselves in any situation. So it was that in 1966, Tony, Kent (11), Tony Jr.(9), and I set sail in a 21-foot sailboat and headed south down the western coast of Mexico. Each night we would moor the boat out, swim in with all our gear, and sleep on the beach. We cooked over campfires and slept in sleeping bags. I remember that I always made the boys wear pajamas and say their prayers. I couldn't let go of some of my ingrained habits. One of the beaches toward the end was made famous in the movie *Catch 22*. This was before the movie was made and the runway constructed for it. It was indeed a pristine and spectacular beach.

It was a wonderful trip with memories for us all. I knew that we were very fortunate to make such a trip without incident. Friends of ours, who were members of the Tucson Sailing Club, were not so lucky. Nonie and Fred were passionate about sailing. Their spouses were not. The two couples were close friends and, with the blessings of their loved ones, they set out on a sailing trip down the west coast of Mexico. As we had done, they moored off shore and swam their supplies onto the beach.

Tragically, they awakened one morning to find their sailboat gone. It was nowhere in sight. It had floated off during the night. They knew, of course, that they were as good as dead. There was no one to help them. Their supplies were limited. Fred chose to set out on foot to see if—-hope beyond hope—he could find help. There was no hope. Nonie was eventually found dead on the beach and Fred's body was never found. The sea is an unforgiving force.

We had quite an adventure on the Sea of Cortez in November, 1972. With *Aldine Baby* in tow, Tony, Tony Jr. and I left for Kino Bay. As always, it took hours to go through the border. We didn't get to Old Kino until 8:00 p.m. Karl Pattison and his son John were already there and joined us for drinks. That night we slept in the boat on the trailer.

The following day, November 23rd, it was very cold. While I swam, Tony and Tony Jr. who was 15 at the time, rigged the sailboat. We launched *Aldine Baby* and sailed to Pelican Island to have breakfast. We bought lots of shrimp and flounder from a Mexican fishing boat. I cooked the shrimp in a coffee pot and Tony Jr. shelled them.

We left Pelican Island and rendezvoused at noon at New Kino with 24 sailboats and set sail for Dog Bay on Tiburon (shark) Island 22 miles away. Suddenly a <u>very</u> heavy wind came up requiring us to sail at hull speed—7 knots—most of the way. I admit that Tony Jr. and I were terrified. We finally reached the island, moored the boat and had flounder for dinner. Karl Pattison joined us.

From 4:00 a.m. on the boat rocked violently; the wind had abated but the swells were huge. Karl swam out and joined us for breakfast. Most wives had not accompanied their sailor husbands on this trip. Tony Jr. and I took our tender, *Tender Behind*, to shore and spent an hour or two exploring Tiburon Island—inhabited only by Seri Indians. That afternoon we all met on the beach and Tony and I provided gallons of Ramjet Punch, Al Marshick's recipe, that left a lot of drunken sailors lying around.

The following day all three of us went ashore and hiked around Tiburon. On our return to our boat via tender, Tony and Tony Jr. went skin diving and were thrilled with all the fish they saw. Later the life-boats and tenders rafted together for cocktail hour. Great fun!

The next day, Sunday, was a sail neither Tony Jr. nor I will ever forget. As my diary says, "It was a horrible, terrifying day." We left Dog Bay and sailed to the mainland in a chubasco—a Mexican Hurricane or very heavy wind. It was blowing about 30 knots with six-foot waves. I had never experienced wind such as this and the boat was heeling significantly. I was sure we would capsize.

For the first time ever Tony ordered us to "batten down the hatches," and he did not mean it as a cliché. He meant us to close the hatch and tie down securely everything in sight, including ourselves. I knew we were in for a terrifying and very wet trip. Sailing never had been a peaceful experience for me, and this was a nightmare. Tony Jr. and I just hung on for dear life. As I have said, Tony was a skilled sailor and we made it to shore safely after what must have been for a sailor one of life's all-time thrilling sails. I am sure it gave a feeling of accomplishment for Tony to have managed that sail so well. For Tony Jr. and me, success was in having survived it.

Another adventure also occurred on the Sea of Cortez. A large group of us with sailboats in tow, drove to Kino Bay in Sonora, Mexico. The plan was for us all to sleep on the beach that night. In the morning the men would launch their sailboats while we wives drove the trucks and trailers to San Carlos, Sonora. A huge storm was approaching. All the men except Tony opted to wait until morning to put their boats in the water. Tony chose to sail out about 50 yards from shore and moor his boat there.

In the morning the wind was ferocious and the waves enormous. Tony, Kent and Tony Jr. had to swim out to our boat to climb aboard. It was a nightmare for me to watch my three beloved ones swim out in huge waves and try to board a boat that was rising and falling about ten feet. It had a ladder on the transom which they would try to grab on the downward slope, but it kept eluding them. My great fear was that the boat would come smashing down and crush them. Eventually they were aboard with no choice but to sail on to that night's destination, Bahía San Pedro. They were there alone.

As Tony set off, the sailors on the beach were attempting to launch their boats, an impossible task in that wild surf. Our close friend, Karl Pattison—an indomitable sailor—attempted to get his Sabot in the water but it soon capsized and broke the mast. No one launched that day. Finally they all had to drive to the ultimate destination, San Carlos. I, of course, drove our rig.

Meanwhile, my three men were out on the turbulent sea and Tony Jr. remembers being desperately seasick for hours. What a miserable experience for them all, and dangerous. Ultimately, we all met up and had happy days together on the beach in San Carlos.

We had many little sailing adventures in our tiny Montgomery 6 when we were staying at our fifth-wheel trailer on the beach in Mexico. I have referred to Tony's tender— *Tender Behind*. In fact, this six-foot boat is a sailboat! We spent a good deal of time in it in Mexico, Canada, and on Arivaca Lake in southern Arizona. It is presently stored in Arivaca.

An example of the fun we had with it took place on November 8, 1973. One beautiful morning while we were at our trailer, Tony, Tony Jr. and I decided to take the Montgomery across the bay to have breakfast at La Posada Inn. What we hadn't counted on was the sudden emergence of big waves. You would have to picture three full-grown adults in this tiny six-foot boat to appreciate that this was a risky business. It was a distance of about two to three miles. We approached the shore with many onlookers urging us on and there to help us when we beached the boat. What a sight we must have been! We waited until the waves abated before our return trip.

As Tony was sometimes gone for three weeks at a time on his single-handed blue water trips, it meant that he had used up most of his vacation time from work for the year. Hence, he missed a lot of summers at the cottage. This may have been yet another reason I was never enthusiastic about his long sailing trips.

With hopes of wooing him to the cottage, each year I transported an incentive. I always drove with Kent and Tony Jr. and whatever dogs we had at the time to Canada every summer. Sometimes I would drive our camper as Tony only enjoyed the big old cottage when he could escape the inevitable throngs of people staying in it to slip quietly out to his own domain. The privacy he could find in his own little Shangri-La made life there endurable for him. Sometimes the lure worked and he made time to join us there.

Other trips I would tow a sailboat to provide him the getaway that he needed. One year I towed a sailboat that I knew he would be very tempted by as he had put hours of work into refining its design. He didn't go to Canada that summer so, of course, I towed it back to Tucson. The boys and I were pulling out of the parking lot of our motel in New Mexico for our last day of driving home when a disaster occurred. I got the hull of the boat caught on the fin of a Cadillac. I was heartbroken. After five thousand miles of towing it, I destroyed it on the last day. I was sure Tony would be furious. In fact, he accepted it with great equanimity and set about doing the extensive repair job.

One summer he was scheduled to attend his annual Air Force Reserve Training Camp at Chanute AFB in Illinois. I took a sailboat to Canada anyway with hopes he might find a reason to cancel the camp. Time went on and I had not heard from him about what his plans were. I phoned him in Tucson. No answer. I grew worried. Where was he? Finally I phoned Chanute to see if he was there. I asked to speak to Lieutenant von Isser and was told there was nobody there by that name.

This meant, I thought, that he was going to come to the cottage and hadn't been in touch because he was going to surprise us. Still no word. My worrying increased so I phoned Chanute once again and asked to speak to a commanding officer. I insisted that Tony must be there. He investigated and advised me that Lt. von Isser was in hospital in Tucson, Arizona having been bitten by a rattlesnake. This, I thought, was a very creative excuse for Tony to use to cancel camp and again my excitement level rose.

Still no word. I became increasingly concerned and started phoning Tucson hospitals. I found out that he was in Tucson Medical Center and had been for several days. This is what had happened. In preparation for leaving Tucson, he had installed a tonneau cover on his Porsche. A black widow spider fell out of it and into his gaping sock. It bit him five times. Each bite, by the way, left a scar. I had always told my sons that if something were to bite or sting them, they should try to put it in a jar to take to the doctor if necessary. Tony heeded this suggestion, put the spider in a jar, and headed for the hospital.

He was very, very ill from these bites, and I am quite sure that without the medical intervention he received he most certainly would have died. When he was able to speak to me on the phone, we agreed that he should come to the cottage to recover. Eventually he flew to Toronto where I met him at the airport. He took the wheel to drive north and was soon weaving all over the road. I quickly took over and we drove safely to the cottage.

There was no fun for Tony that summer. His central nervous system was badly compromised and he could not handle having even a sheet over him at night. Loud noises were anathema as was touch of any kind. It took him months to fully recover.

Although Tony Jr. had a beautiful sailboat at the cottage—a Fireball—and the boys

Tony sailing on the Oxtongue River

shared a Venture catamaran, I thought Tony should have his own sailboat there. Hence, for Christmas of 1979 I gave him a Banshee—a hot little sailboat about 12 feet long. He towed it to the cottage, launched it, christened it *Wet Dream* and had many happy hours sailing our beautiful Lake of Bays. Still, it was a far cry from the type of sailing he truly loved.

In spite of my reluctance to sail on the ocean, I was a reasonably good lake sailor and even won our "Daiquiri Dinghies" sailing competition one year at our regatta on Dwight Bay in Canada.

My husband Tony was indeed a swashbuckler and much of his charisma derived from his independent nature and willingness to take on a challenge. He was quite a guy!

SAILING WITH FRIENDS

Tony and I spent considerable time sailing with our good friends Laura and Mike Finch.* Most of it had occurred in Mexico on the Sea of Cortez (Gulf of California). For many years an annual event was competing in the Columbus Day Race in San Carlos, Sonora with them. We also visited them at their home in Coronado, California frequently and sailed with them in Mike's sailboat there. One such time was in September of 1971.

On that visit we decided to expand our horizon for 1972 and arranged for a bare-boat charter in Greece. (This means the boat comes with neither crew nor provisions.) We met in Athens after Tony and I had completed our cruise on the *Dorita*—the yacht Katharine Merritt chartered biennially. Off we went to find our own yacht—a beautiful 30′ French Arpege named *Marija*. After appropriately outfitting her, we motored from Piraeus to Aegina, our first port of call. We anticipated smooth and peaceful sailing. Neither was meant to be.

At Aegina we swam, went out for dinner, and called it a night. This was when we discovered that Mike was a snorer—I mean big-time. Laura, who was petite and adorable, warned us of this potential sleep hazard. At bedtime (we were all in the main cabin) she calmed him with a hug and some lovey-dovey words. The snoring began. She moved on to scathing warnings for him to **shut up.** An hour later she was punching him and screaming obscenities that left even my husband agog. That these unseemly words could come from those cute little lips shocked me to the core. Nothing worked. The snoring worsened. We were in for it for the duration. To underline how really dreadful it was, I mention that Tony once had his good buddy Mike visit him at our place in Canada. (I was in Tucson working.) Although Mike's bedroom was upstairs at one end of the cottage, and Tony's downstairs at the other end, he later reported that Mike's snoring was so severe that the walls of the cottage were literally shaking. True story.

Another problem we encountered was the "head." It was small but should have been adequate. However, every time I was using the head, Mike had an urgent need. He would stand above the open hatch, look down and ask, "How much longer are you going to **be?**" My response was always that it would be a lot longer if he continued staring down at me. And Tony was denied one of his God given rights—lingering on the john with a cigar. We simply didn't see how this was going to work with <u>four</u> of us.

Sleep deprived and constipated, we thought we only imagined the dark clouds roiling up on the horizon. No, it was a full-fledged melteme (a Greek hurricane) approaching. Clearly we had to find the nearest port to find safe-haven and it happened to be on the island of Hydra. We knew that we might well be tied up there for several days. This was the 3rd of July. We settled in to wait out the storm.

Fast on our heels that day was—of all things—another Arpege approaching port racing ahead of the storm to seek shelter. Of course, Tony and Mike were there to meet and assist them on the dock and came back with exciting news. There were seven young French people aboard, all in their twenties, and none was married. My first thought was, "Oh, my gosh, how do they handle the head?" Further, we learned that none spoke English—French only.

Let me step back. Laura, whose maiden name had hinted toward French ancestry— Fernald— had always implied that she had gone to French-speaking schools and was bilingual. What a relief to know that we would have a translator for these new arrivals. Not! When three of the young French women enthusiastically approached our vessel, Laura went below deck, and did not emerge until the storm had dissipated and the other Arpege long gone. The girls were there to invite us to a party on their boat the following day—the 4th of July. They had even found an American flag to hoist in our honor. Somehow with my two years of university French we were able to communicate and, of course, you know what I needed to find out immediately. How did seven of them make do with one head! A smiling mademoiselle with a twinkle in her eye took me below to show me. She opened the head door and—*voilá*—a wine cellar. My mouth dropped open and I asked the obvious. She demonstrated by hanging her *derriere* over the taff rail which was their official head. Ah, the intrepid French.

Our cruise continued on to Poros. Tony and I were badly in need of some private time by then so we checked into a hotel for the night. The next day we continued sailing and our cruise took us along the coast of the Peloponnese and around the peninsula of Methanon en route to our destination, the old port of Epidaurus. The following day we hired a taxi and visited Epidaurus, which fascinated and charmed us. Finally, we sailed back to Aegina for our last night on our yacht before returning to Athens to say goodbye to the vessel that had served us well.

Tony sailing out of Hydra

Tony did a splendid job of summing up this unique sailing experience. He wrote, "Byron's 'wine deep purple sea' describes the Aegean. It is a beautiful sea with an aura all its own. Even the sunlight has a different sort of golden tint. The island villages are spotlessly clean, the life simple but often austere.

"Unlike the Sea of Cortez where history for the most part is still to come, there is a different kind of satisfaction in sailing the Aegean. Out there a feeling of the past is ever present and is heightened by the thought of your own wake blending into that of ten thousand ancient ships gone before. Those were the ships which made possible the glory that was Greece and the grandeur that was Rome. They were the means through which the birth of our own western culture was conceived. It was a delightful sailing experience and an adventure well worth repeating."

After a brief stay in Athens, Tony and Mike returned to the U.S. leaving Laura and me behind to enjoy the city for a while and then continue on with yet another cruise.

While there, I reconnected with a colleague, John Paraskevopoulos, a professor at the University of Athens and a former professor at the University of Illinois. We spent a day swimming at a beautiful beach and later joined Laura at the Astir Palace clubhouse for lunch.

On July 11th we returned once again to Piraeus, this time to board our cruise ship, the *Stella Oceanis*. Our ports of call were Crete, Rhodes, Ephesus, and Istanbul—all of which were familiar to me.

As always, the eyes of the men on board followed Laura as I tagged along in her wake. She really was quite a beauty. One member of the crew—a handsome man named Georgio—was smitten. He asked me Laura's age. I responded that I neither knew nor cared. "Ah," said he, "but you will know by the end of the cruise." I could not have anticipated what this implied.

Our final day on board we were told to claim our passports at reception before breakfast. I dutifully collected mine and received a big wink from Georgio who was manning the desk that day. My heart sank. Suddenly I just knew that I had Laura's passport, and she had mine. Indeed it was so, and I approached the breakfast table, where Laura was already seated, with my heart racing a hundred miles an hour. She'd know that I had the information she had protected covetously for so many years. I had to tell her that a mistake had been made. We traded passports and not a word was said.

Until—we were taking a taxi together to the airport and Laura, dripping guilt, admitted she had been traveling with a passport with false information and she hoped I would protect her when we reached immigration. She asserted that her passport, with an inaccurate birth date, had arrived mere days before their departure. There was no time to have it corrected. Mike insisted she go on the trip anyway and that it was unlikely the error would be noticed. I never alluded to this discussion again, nor did I ever tell anyone her age—but she was certainly older than she looked.

I guess every "memoir" must have its *ménage a trois*. I can't let the reader down. Sometime after our trip to Greece, Laura met Retired Brigadier General Brad Lorrimer and Mike became history. In fact, the only thing I can think that those two lovely men had in common was that each had close to 25,000 flying hours. That is a lot! Brad was handsome, ramrod straight, and charming. He had more distinguished service medals than you could count. He was, as they say, a chick magnet, and Laura is the one who stuck. Brad was with the aerospace division of Hughes Aircraft Company in Tucson.

When Laura and Brad were to be married in California in December, 1973, I was the only guest from Tucson invited to the wedding. Laura and I flew to Los Angeles together and shared a room in the Hotel Bel-Air while Brad was in another. This did seem a little strange to me. A friend and colleague of mine who lived in Malibu, UCLA professor Dr. Frank Hewett, joined us for dinner. Eventually—bedtime. About 2:00 a.m., Laura awakened me—she was cute remember—and suggested that we pay a surprise visit to Brad. Her idea was to pull our sheets over us and pretend we were little lost lambs seeking shelter. Well, this was not my cup of tea, but hey, it was her wedding. So off we went, across the magnificent courtyards in the dark, and knocked on Brad's door. In retrospect, I don't think he looked as surprised as he should have when he saw us. All too quickly I realized that I was intended to be the third actor in a three-way play and in two shakes of that lamb's tail I was out the door and back to the room where I threw up. I phoned Frank and told him this little lamb really did need to be rescued.

I attended the wedding, returned home to Tucson, and have said nary a word about that scenario until this moment. I am not sure if it would have diminished or enhanced the good general's reputation. Although I think I was in their bad book for letting them down, we never mentioned the incident again. Both are now deceased. However, Laura's obituary let the cat out of the bag. She was born in 1921 and died at 95 in 2016!

*With the exception of Frank Hewitt, I have used fictitious names.

15

∽⧓∾

ADVENTURES IN CAÑON DEL ORO

Cañon del Oro. Canyon of Gold. The years we spent camping there as a family were indeed golden and imprinted on our minds forever.

Located on the north side of the Catalina Mountains near Tucson, it was a magnet for us most weekends when our boys were growing up.

Tony and I loved to camp and for some time we had been exploring roads at the back of the Catalinas hoping to locate the perfect camping spot. We had dreamed of finding a pristine and isolated area with big cottonwood trees and a creek running through it. It seemed unlikely that such a location existed. It did.

Disobeying the *DO NOT ENTER* and *PRIVATE PROPERTY* signs we headed up an unlikely, unmaintained road and *eureka*, we had found it. It was part of the Little Hill Gold Mine property belonging to a couple named Lila and Bob Burney. We had been told he was a tough person to deal with, but we took our chances.

The creek is called Cañada del Oro, also meaning Canyon of Gold. It originates in the remote Cañon del Oro and is fed by rainfall and melted snow from the northern face of Mount Lemmon. It flows northward toward the town of Oracle. At the higher elevations it is a perennial creek. We camped at about 4500 feet in elevation and it ran year round. Where we camped it was wide and fast running in the winter but with less water in the summer. The creek ultimately feeds into the Santa Cruz River, the principal watershed channel in the Tucson valley. The water was always cold. It was shallow in many parts—making it possible for us to drive across—but had plenty of deep swimming holes.

To watch over and protect the sanctity of his property Bob Burney had hired a year-round caretaker—Doyle Bartt. He was to become part of the fabric of our lives. Doyle was a real mountain man. Except for an annual visit to Nogales to take care of his carnal needs, Doyle never left the mountain. Food was brought to him weekly. His appearance would shock the faint of heart. He was long-haired, had rotten teeth and the wore dirtiest hat I have ever seen. He was slow moving and slow talking.

Doyle knew when we were coming into the canyon; he could feel the rumble of our truck on the road. He was always there to meet us every time we went camping. His intention the first time we arrived was to boot us off the property fast. However, he and Tony started talking, shared a beer, and we "were in."

Doyle Bartt

We still had Bob Burney to deal with but he turned out to be a taciturn and decent guy and eventually he and his wife became friends. However, we didn't see them often. In our two decades of going there, Doyle never allowed anybody else to stay in the canyon. We became family to him.

Doyle rarely saw a woman and I think he was pleased to have me around. However, there was a problem. In the morning, when he would have no reason to stop by, I could feel his presence. I knew he was out there watching us. Of necessity, we had to go off in the woods to take care of bathroom needs.

Our road - with overhang

We carried a collapsible toilet seat and a roll of toilet paper and off we would go. I typically looked forward to these moments with nature but something was wrong. I felt exposed and uncomfortable. I could sense Doyle's eyes on me. I was sure he was sitting on the side of the mountain relishing this intimate moment. He got his kicks in strange ways!

Our campsite was heaven on earth and all we'd ever hoped to find. Getting there was the trick. The road was narrow and bumpy. Where it had been cut through the mountainside, there were low overhangs and precipitous drop-offs. The rickety old wooden-plank bridge we had to cross was high over the creek and considerably past its "use by" date. I felt we took our lives in our hands with every crossing. It was about 40 feet long with no side rails. As the bridge was only nine or ten feet wide, we could look out the truck windows straight down 30 feet to the creek below. I never failed to close my eyes for that minute and a half, except when I was doing the driving.

From an early age, our sons took great pleasure in crossing the bridge on their motorcycles. They had fun lying in wait under the bridge hoping for trucks to cross over at which time they poked sticks up through the planks to get the full effect of their passing overhead. They never lacked for adventures there.

Also, to get to our campsite it was necessary to ford the creek. Tony did a great deal of work moving rocks so that we had something of a roadway for getting across. I always held my breath on this stretch of our journey as well. One time when I had six lads in tow—Tony was joining us later after work—the transfer case on our 4-wheel drive truck broke down while I was half-way across the creek. I was mighty glad Tony would be following so that he could cope with the situation. The boys, however, were thrilled and loved playing in the creek while we waited.

In due time the Burneys realized how much we loved their canyon and were kind enough to sell us a portion—the Pretty Fair Mine claim.

When Kent came along, Tony and I continued camping on the ground by a campfire. However, now we brought with us all the paraphernalia for a baby including a crib that was screened in on all sides. When Tony Jr. joined our family we realized it was time to arrange for something more substantial so we bought a camper—the slide in type that sits on the bed of a pick-up truck. Campers were a new concept back then. I

Tony Jr. & Kent above dam

felt we were living in luxury with its little kitchen, its cab-over bed and a kitchen table and banquette that converted to a bed for the boys at night in the winter.

A focus early on in our years there with our sons was the building of a dam. It was worth all the man hours that went into it as it created deeper swimming holes. The boys didn't mind that work at all.

Ordinarily we slept outside in sleeping bags on the ground. Tony Jr. fondly remembers those nights of looking up at the sky and seeing shooting stars.

We did our cooking over a campfire. Tony had a favorite rock that he used as a footstool and a shelf for frying pans. From time to time we would change the location of our campsite. Each time, Tony would take "his" rock with us to be the basis for the new fire pit. Over the years it collected grease stains and dirt but was a familiar talisman for us.

No matter where we set up camp, we were found by two wild burros. They became our friends and our pets. The first time we met them, however, we were not prepared for their visit. I had left a big basket of apricots on our tailgate. When we returned from a hike one day there was nary an apricot in sight but nearby were two satisfied looking burros. They seemed to take to our boys and soon they were riding them. What fun they had!

Tony frequently brought his motorcycle to ride into the canyon while I drove the truck. As the boys grew older they brought their own motorcycles with them. They were probably nine and seven years old when that

Tony cooking at his rock

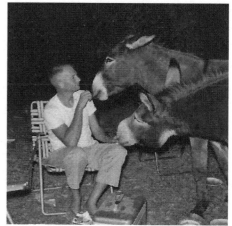

Tony with our wild burros

tradition began. We would drop them off with their bikes at the turn-in from the highway and they would ride the eight miles to the campsite. What an adventure that was for them. They were proficient motorcyclists by then. Eventually, they rode their motorcycles throughout Cañon del Oro.

Tony Jr. & Kent with Fang

We had occasional visitors to the Pretty Fair. One family that came was Hal and Bette Grieve and their three children—Scott, Greg and Linda. Another frequent guest was Al Marshick. Children always had fun as there were ropes hanging from trees to swing into the river. As well, there was exciting exploring to be done. We knew that Doyle had a close eye on all the happenings.

Tony Jr. on 1970 CZ motorcycle

Kent and Tony Jr. frequently had friends come with them. That kept Tony and me on our toes as one, Mike Ramsay, was a hyperactive trouble maker. One day Tony and I took a group of young people on a hike. Inadvertently we happened to trek into a box canyon—a canyon with no exit. To our dismay, at the end of the canyon we came upon one lone bull—and he looked angry. He was trapped. Tony was genuinely worried that he might attack. He halted the group and in a low and urgent voice admonished the boys to be very, very quiet and to back up slowly. All but Mike obeyed. Instead, Mike let out a whoop and charged the bull that was now pawing the ground and looking at us menacingly. Somehow with Tony's calm guidance we got out of there unharmed, but we were very lucky to have escaped serious injuries.

A birthday Tony Jr. will never forget was in 1969 when he turned 12. A gang of his friends had come for the weekend to celebrate the occasion. Unfortunately, it was alternately raining and snowing even though it was only October. The boys had decided that they were going to sleep in a mine shaft that night—an exciting adventure for them. Off they went with their sleeping bags and climbed deep into a shaft and set up camp by flashlight. They built a fire and thought it would be a cozy night. Well, it was not! The lads choked all night on the smoke from the fire and almost froze to death it was so brutally cold in the mine. They came stumbling back to camp in the morning saying it was an awful night and they were so, so cold. It was,

Mike Ramsay with arm raised

however, a memorable adventure. Sometimes we wondered how our boys survived childhood and often questioned what *were* their parents thinking.

Target practice was another highlight for our lads. Tony did an excellent job of training them in the safe and appropriate use of guns and they became excellent marksmen.

Heavy rain would often make the road into our camp very muddy. In December, 1976 we took my brother Murray and his children who were visiting from Toronto, as well as other friends, into the canyon for a picnic. We almost rolled the truck three times!

In April of that year Kent took his whole class on a picnic there. It was always an adventure for young people.

As I look back, I am amazed at the degree of freedom we gave our boys in that isolated area. They were often gone for hours and returned with exciting stories of their discoveries and their adventures. They loved exploring old mines. Their dogs always went with them whether they went by foot or by motorcycle.

Kent was gifted at catching live rattlesnakes which he continued to do for the rest of his life. He would often bring them back to our camp for us to see. The particularly large ones we skinned and slid over long sticks to use as conversation pieces.

Tony Jr. & Kent at a mine

One time a rattlesnake that Kent had caught almost caused a disaster. It was a nightmare I never want to repeat. He returned to camp shouting, "Dad, Dad, help." He had picked up a rattlesnake behind the head as he always did. However, while bringing it back to show us, the snake had coiled around his arm and was pulling its head back through Kent's hand. Another inch and it could strike. He was in grave danger. Tony took control of the situation while I looked on in terror. He told Kent that he was going to uncoil the snake from Kent's arm and when he shouted "toss it" Kent was to immediately throw it as hard and fast as he could before it could strike. Kent followed instructions and the rattlesnake arched into the air landing hard and slithering away. Kent, as I say, continued to catch snakes, but he never gave another one the chance to coil around his arm.

As our lads grew older, we allowed them to go with their friends alone to Cañon del Oro. On September 3, 1971 Kent was 16 and Tony 13 years old when they and their friend Larry Kotz went off in jeeps. Kent had his own four-wheel drive jeep by then and was legal to drive. The following day Tony and I were invited to be their guests in the canyon. They met us along the road and chauffeured us the remainder of the way to our campsite in their jeeps. The cottonwoods were in full leaf, the foliage was very green and the creek was running high. It was beautiful. After a picnic Kent drove us back to our truck and we returned to Tucson. We were finding it difficult to adjust to our boys' new level of independence!

We returned the following weekend—the boys in Kent's jeep and we in the camper. Of course Doyle dropped by as did the Burneys. It was getting altogether too popular up there. Tony and I decided to hike up to the Pretty Fair Mine accompanied by our dogs Fido and Joey— a rugged six-mile walk. We swam in the creek many times along the way.

When we returned to the campsite Kent's friends Larry Kotz and Randy Sharp were there. The older boys decided to return to Tucson. It was the first time we had ever let Kent be at home alone. The next day Tony Jr. was bored and we all missed Kent. So back to Tucson we went.

An exciting adventure for our lads happened in October of 1972. They were 17 and 15 years old. Tony and I dropped them off with their Montessa motorcycles at Charleau Gap, a canyon northeast of Catalina, Arizona. It is on the west side of the Catalina Mountains. There was a trail of sorts but it was rugged terrain and tricky to navigate. It had once been a road but hadn't been maintained for decades. They reached our campsite on the other side of a mountain in just one hour and 45 minutes. A record!

Over the years Al Marshick had his own method of advising us of his intention to come and visit us later that day. Al was in the Air National Guard and flew F-102s every Saturday morning with his squadron. When their flying maneuvers were finished, Al would peel off from the rest and fly over our campsite in the mountains. At just the right moment he would hit the afterburner making an incredible noise that shook the hillsides. JP-4, the fuel used in jets at that time, filtered down from above and its cinders inevitably dropped into our scrambled eggs! A couple of hours later Al would arrive.

One weekend was unique and unforgettable. It is believable only

Al's jet

Al approaching for a "fly over"

because we caught it on video. One of the boys was having a birthday party up there with his friends. Al said he would be putting on a special show for them—so get ready! At the appointed time, we piled into jeeps and drove to the top of the highest peak in the vicinity. I am shaking recalling the "show." We could not hear Al's jet approach because the noise was behind him but we saw it coming up the canyon barely above tree level. Then he flew over us at 300 mph coming so close that we had to duck as we were sure we were going to be hit. It was insanity and there was nothing we could do to stop it. He made pass after pass. Each time as his jet grew larger and larger as he approached us coming up the canyon we grew more and more frightened. I was sure he was going to kill us all. After one pass Kent saw his jeep antenna wobbling; he was sure Al had touched it. Of course the lightweight chairs we had taken with us were blown all over. Tony Jr. took refuge behind a big rock, well aware that it would provide no protection at all.

Then came the finale. Just as Al was about to fly over us he inverted his jet. He was doing this pass upside down! I swear I could have reached up and touched his canopy. We estimate that he was flying about 20 feet over the ground. We could see Al's helmet but not the grin that we were sure he had under his oxygen mask. When he arrived at our campsite later in the day he was proud as a peacock but we let him know we were not pleased that he had put our family and their friends at serious risk. It never happened again, but we still play that footage from time to time to convince ourselves it really did happen!

After having years enjoying our idyllic spot in the Catalina Mountains, we knew the end of the era was looming. This came about for two reasons. First, our sons were teenagers and wanted to spend time with their friends—not camping with their parents in the boonies.

The second impetus for change occurred on New Year's morning, 1973. Two of the boys' friends were sleeping in the camper with us—Nicky and Curtis Simmons. We awoke to heavy snow on the ground and an exterior temperature of about 12 degrees F. This was our last family weekend in the canyon. The time had come. The boys wanted freedom and I wanted comfort. We soon bought a 36-foot fifth-wheel trailer and parked it on a lovely beach in Mexico.

We continued to enjoy many picnics there over the years and the boys often took friends for the weekend in their jeeps. On New Year's Day in 1976 Kent and Tony Jr. had gone in Kent's Bronco to Cañon del Oro and almost got trapped in a snowstorm. They continued to have many adventures there in the years ahead.

On December 30, 1982 we had a family picnic at our campsite. Little did we know we were going to get into a snow storm—38 inches—so the picnic was rushed. We had been told at the gate (one needed authorization to enter the canyon now) that Doyle was very ill and not expected to live. We were so glad that we were there and able to visit him to say our goodbyes. He had kept an eye on our boys for so many years and had treated them as if they were his own sons. For the first time ever, we went to his little home up the canyon. I noted that there was little visible that could tell us anything about his life—just a single photograph of a woman. It was difficult for all of us to see this hardened mountain man in his frail condition. It was obvious he was dying. We all shook his hand warmly and with love, thanked him for his friendship for so many years and left. We never saw Doyle again. (Bob Burney had died in 1975 and Lila followed him soon thereafter.)

When Tony died in 1989, the boys and I talked about the interment we planned for him in July at our little cemetery in Dwight, Ontario near our cottage. Tony Jr. had arranged for a plaque but I was concerned about finding an appropriate gravestone for Tony. Without hesitation Kent said, "There is only one rock in the world that Dad would appreciate—his rock at the campfire in Cañon del Oro." He found it easily and brought it to me in Tucson. That summer it took all my wiles to have the airline agent accept it as baggage due to its great weight. You will read about Tony's wonderful burial in another chapter.

The golden years in the canyon of gold were behind us, but the stories of those days will continue to be told and the memories will linger forever.

16

 C880

ADVENTURES IN ARIVACA

The halcyon days in our trailer on the beach of San Carlos, Mexico as a weekend retreat came to an abrupt halt with Kent's devastating accident in January of 1975. That event changed his life forever as well as the lives of everyone who loved him. He never fully recovered from his injuries. That story will be recorded elsewhere but accounts for our decision to bring the trailer (fifth-wheel) home to Tucson. We knew that our lives would now center around visiting Kent in Toronto as often as possible. He was in St. Michael's Hospital there for almost a year. I traveled to see him at least twice a month, sometimes staying for extended periods—especially at the times of his surgeries.

Tony, however, needed a place of solitude and silence to substitute for his escapes to Mexico and launched a search of available land in Southern Arizona that could provide him with—aloneness. On August 28, 1977, he bought a twenty acre lot about 70 miles southwest of Tucson—barely five miles from the Mexican border. It is located three miles outside a little town called Arivaca where life is simple and harks back to the days of cowboys and Indians. It is populated primarily by hippies and society dropouts who are escaping the constraints of civilization. Arivaca is situated at an elevation of close to 4000 feet and thus is a good deal cooler than Tucson. We even have snow in the winter!

To reach Arivaca, one leaves the highway at the town of Amado and drives west for 23 miles. For me, turning onto this road has always marked the beginning of a special time—and the scenery is spectacular. As well, the road has a rich history. It was a

Hohokam trading route for early native peoples who had lived here along the spring fed cienegas and creeks since AD 1400. Pima and Papago Indians continued to inhabit the lands they called "Arivaca"— variously meaning "little reeds" or "little springs"—long after the Hohokam had disappeared.

The Spanish colonials were the first to define the trail as a road. In their conquest of the native souls and mineral-rich lands, they drove their horses, cattle and wagons laden with ores from the rich Cerro Colorado and many other of the nation's earliest mines, over this stretch, paving the way for their dominance of the earth and the minds of the inhabitants.

Arivaca boasts the oldest post office in Arizona (1878) as well as its first library. Electricity made a somewhat belated appearance in 1956 uplifting Arivaca from the dark ages into modern times with electric lights, appliances and TV.

Annually we make a drive from Arivaca to Nogales, Sonora that never fails to delight me. The scenery is magnificent and changes with the altitude through which we are passing. Some years the road is in such poor condition that it takes a canny driver to wend a way through the rivers and ruts. The time to make this drive varies from between 2 ½ to 3 ½ hours.

A place of great interest along this road is Ruby, one of the two best preserved ghost towns in the state. It is loaded with history that includes lawlessness, murder and mayhem and is about half an hour's drive from our cabin. Mining was Ruby's reason for being and the first miners were the Spaniards in the 1700s. They soon moved on to richer prospects.

Not until 1854 were the rich veins of gold and silver discovered that drew prospectors and investors from all over the country. With the inevitable greed, and its proximity to Mexico, the region was considered highly dangerous. Arivaca is still thought to be so. Between 1920 and 1922, Ruby was the scene of three gruesome double homicides committed by Mexican rebels or bandits. The Ruby mine closed in 1940 and by the end of 1941 the town was abandoned.

Our property near Arivaca is ringed by the San Luis and Las Guijas Mountains with a majestic view of the sacred Baboquivari Peak rising to salute the heavens while the "Sleeping Princess" continues her mountainous slumber undisturbed. In the center of our land is a mesquite forest (bosque) and that is where Tony relocated the trailer. The distance was not so far that he couldn't commute easily from Arivaca to work in Tucson. It was ideal for his needs.

He settled the trailer in, built a rustic porch in front, outfitted it with his needs (minimal) and felt that he had found heaven. His first task was to erect a barb-wire fence around its perimeter to keep out stray cows and roaming horses—as well as all forms of human life. When the utility companies approached him, he accepted electricity but all else was abjured, including telephone service. This was highly inconvenient for me as I had no way of reaching him from Tucson where I continued to live and work. I entreated him to at least allow the telephone company to lay the line across the desert—just in case he might change his mind someday. Absolutely not. Kent later had to do that job on his own, quite an undertaking.

In November of 1977 while Tony and I were spending a weekend at our place in Arivaca, we were visited by Kent and his girlfriend Janice. We could feel that love was in the air and it wasn't long before their hearts were lost to one another. The romance blossomed into a strong and enduring marriage.

I was in search of a new home in Tucson as our hacienda had grown altogether too large for us now that the boys were launched. When I found a place that would suit us, I would have to drive to Arivaca to ask Tony to come home to check it out. You understand, these were the days before there were such things as cell phones.

Frequently I was invited for weekends when Tony took over the role of host. It was bucolic and relaxing. I grew to love it there as much as Tony did.

When Tony died, I didn't think I could ever be there again. I wept my heart out every time I tried. So Kent, Tony and I set out to find another location to build a cabin, but we found ourselves pulled by some invisible force back to Arivaca. We sold the trailer and built a lovely new cabin which could accommodate our growing family. I now had grandchildren coming along and we had definitely outgrown the trailer. We moved into it on August 17, 1996 during a monsoon! The weather there is never dependable. In October of the same year it snowed for hours and hours. It was very beautiful, but cold.

Our cabin - Rancho Escondido - looking east

Our place is perfect for us. We named it Rancho Escondido (Hidden Ranch). On the exterior it looks very ordinary (but still a great deal sounder than most other structures in the Arivaca area). This is to discourage illegal immigrants or drug runners who may think there are things of value inside. However, upon entering the front door one is transported into a different world. The cabin is lined with rough pine that Tony Jr. ordered from New Mexico. The huge rock fireplace extends to the top of the 16′ ceiling. It is carpeted throughout. There are three bedrooms and a loft that has held untold numbers of young people. There are four beds and countless sleeping bags aloft.

The kitchen is modern; we even have a washer and dryer. We now have wireless and have access to the world. (Tony would roll over in his grave.)

And, we have danger. There are many who question our sanity for exposing ourselves to this area so rife with crime. There have been home invasions, murders and inevitably an incredible number of migrants passing through. A group of about fifty men was seen crossing our property one time. Kent regularly found abandoned campsites on our property. It was clear to him that they had been used multiple times, probably known to followers as a potential campsite. Hal always had a gun nearby and even carried a Derringer in his robe pocket when he went at night to shower in our outdoor shower.

One year I invited my book group, Kindred Spirits, to come to Rancho Escondido for our book discussion and lunch. Given that our book for that month was about Arivaca and the history of the area, I thought it a perfect place to hold the meeting. The book was titled *A Beautiful, Cruel Country* by Eva Antonia Wilbur-Cruce, a story that captures the essence of that region and of its people.

Several in my book group wouldn't even think of going to Arivaca—far too dangerous—and claimed their husbands wouldn't allow it. Those that did attend were clearly nervous and seemed relieved to get in their cars for the journey back to Tucson.

One cannot tell the story of Arivaca without including an incident or two in its infamous bar, La Gitana (The Gypsy). This bar, lauded by Esquire Magazine in 2011 as one of the best bars in the country, was built in 1880. La Gitana has a past that reads like a passage straight from an Arizona history book. It began as a dance hall, drawing area miners and ranchers who were looking to kick up their heels. Next door stood a brothel, so dancing wasn't the only attraction.

To this day, the bar causes the heartbeat to elevate upon entering its swinging doors. You just never know what you might find going on inside. And so it was with some trepidation that my sister Carol and I took our good friend Margaret Ruscica there one evening to enjoy some local color on her first visit to Arivaca. No matter how hard we had tried to look like native Arivacans, it just couldn't be done. We were far too conventional looking. We climbed up on our stools at the bar and did a little visual reconnaissance. Margaret was seated next to a man with long white hair and an impressive beard. He clearly was with the woman on his right but the intrepid Margaret tried to draw him into conversation—by taking hold of his beard and turning his face toward her.

The lady on his right yanked him back and continued with a heated conversation they had been having. I overheard her say several times, "Do you want to take this out in the alley and settle it there?" Margaret continued to tug his beard and told him he didn't need to listen to his unpleasant companion. Suddenly a large woman loomed up behind Margaret and spun <u>her</u> around.

Then the trouble began.

Standing in a threatening position she said to Margaret, "Do you know who that woman is? Well, that there's Miss Vicky and no one messes with Miss Vicky. She's a lady and even knows what fork to use. And she's been known to fist fight with Bandidos (the motorcycle group) and win. Why, one time she saw one of the bikers beatin' up on his girlfriend and she decked him good. Didn't work out too well for her as they came lookin' for her. If she'd been a guy they probably would have kilt her. Instead, because they respected her, they just stripped her naked and shaved off every hair on her body. She got off lucky. So—**don't mess with Miss Vicky.**"

Margaret was undaunted by this threat—but Carol and I were. We had to bodily pull her out of the bar to take her back to the cabin. It wasn't easy as Margaret is a dog lover and any dog that appears to be unattached or unloved becomes her reason for living. Well, there on the floor as we were leaving was, to me, a perfectly happy looking dog. Margaret got down on the floor, took the dog in her arms, and announced that she was taking it home. She was adamant and it took several of us to haul her up and move her along to our car, without the dog.

While all of Margaret's shenanigans were taking place, Carol and I had been regaled with local lore by a good looking cowboy who was fascinated with three respectable looking women in that bar at night. One story he told was of Miss Vicky's illness. She apparently developed a sizable tumor and "wouldn't go see no doctor about it." When she was convinced that her death was imminent, she decided to deal with it on her own terms. So she took her horse, headed out to a steep mountain, and climbed pretty much straight up. She knew that at a point the horse would lose his footing and they'd both tumble down hundreds of feet to their deaths. This, of course, was her intent. And stumble they did. On the bumpy trip down the mountain, Miss Vicky noticed that the tumor "had busted and was spewing pus all over the place." When her fall finally came to a stop, she was shaken but could still walk. And the tumor—it was gone, never to return. An instant, but painful, cure.

On our way back to the cabin, Carol drove a circuitous route to be sure we weren't being tailed. Three ladies alone out on that lonely desert at night were fodder for mischief. Additionally, Margaret was freaked out by a neighbor's "landscaping" which includes three rather substantial graves, all with crosses, at the front of his property. It is probably intended to discourage illegals, but in Arivaca who can be sure! The neighbor, Marcelo Dominguez, does not have a sense of humor when it comes to illegals crossing his property, so anything is possible.

Over the years we had successfully remained anonymous and unnoticed. When we built the cabin we did not use local workers. We brought them all down from Tucson. We knew we were vulnerable as our place, simple as it is, verges on elegance when compared to most of the homes in that area.

One time four of us went for a weekend to Arivaca—two couples. Joe Green was my "date." Ben Storek, who is mentioned elsewhere in these writings, drove down in his Rolls Royce—shiny clean and deep maroon—and the lady with him was my dear friend Joee Teplitsky.

As part of a tour of the area, we drove in Ben's car to the famous federally funded National Wildlife Refuge which includes a bird sanctuary. It is a mere three miles from our cabin and attracts people from across the country and around the world. There is a two-mile boardwalk with bridges that ford streams and has lookouts complete with big telescopes.

Some birds in that area are rarely sighted and bird watchers come in droves. We once passed a young man who was glued to his binoculars and I couldn't refrain from interrupting his reverie to ask what bird he had sighted. It was a vermillion flycatcher and he told us he had come all the way from New Jersey to see it. We are fortunate that we merely have to sit on our cabin's screened-in front porch to

Alex, Max & Tana on front porch - 2003

see all manner of bird life, another great plus for our area.

Another pleasure for us on our front porch is the screeching and moaning of our magnificent windmill. No ranchito is complete without a noisy windmill!

Our windmill

As our group exited the bird sanctuary, I said, "If we go left we'll go into the little town of Arivaca. If we go right we'll return to the cabin." Ben turned left. A big mistake. I hadn't taken into account that this type of vehicle would be a rare phenomenon in this wilderness town and thus make us a big attraction. What a scene! Folks were running home to get their cameras to have their pictures taken in front of this awesome car. Everyone wanted to know who we were—celebrities of course! I felt our long protected anonymity slipping away and lamented my foolishness. I had to admit this folly to my boys and ask them to keep an especially close eye on our place for about a year afterwards. Lo! these many years later, no one seems to know who we are or that our place is even there—just as we want it. By the way, we are, to my knowledge, the only "weekenders" in the entire valley. Everyone else lives there full time.

A few years ago I wrote of one experience Hal and I had that left a profound impact on us. I am going to tell the story. Hal recalled it as the most emotional day of his life.

It was necessary for me to write this article in third person. Aiding or abetting an illegal is a federal offense with heavy punishment including prison time. Also, one is forevermore recorded as a felon. Having it read by the wrong person was a chance I could not take. My son Tony had the highest security rating at Raytheon and his job depended on it. He was Senior Principal Engineer and responsible for the integration and testing of the SM3 missile. For his mother to be a federal felon would have done him no good. As you will see, we risked a lot in saving the life of an illegal, but there was no alternative for us.

This is our story. The "friends" of whom I speak are indeed Hal and I.

FROM RHETORIC TO REALITY

Why, when we help another human in need, must we fear for our own safety? This was a question asked by friends recently when a pleasant morning of kayaking on Arivaca Lake, a few miles from the Mexican border, turned into a nightmare.

As the couple, who have a residence near Arivaca, were returning home through a very remote and rural countryside, they noticed a person standing near the roadside leaning against the trunk of a mesquite tree. As they passed, a very tentative "thumb" was displayed. Since it was not unusual to see illegal Mexican border crossers in this area, they thought little of it. The previous weekend they had seen 55 to 60 of them either in custody or walking along the roadways. Here, however, it was clear that this was a different matter entirely since this person was alone and a woman. They pulled to the side of the road and the woman limped over to them. They recognized the danger of helping such a person, so they asked as few questions as possible. She was confused, disoriented and discouraged. She was surprised to learn that she was in the United States and seemed oblivious to the fact that she was in danger— and here the couple was about to put themselves in danger as well. The legal repercussions imposed by the Federal Government for those transporting and helping an illegal crosser could certainly lead to arrest, possibly jail, and even financial devastation.

They offered to take her to Arivaca, a distance of about eight miles. During the drive they learned that she was 29 years old and had left her two children in the care of her mother in Chiapas, Mexico on November 18, 2005, two and a half months earlier. She had been traveling during most of that time, having stopped in Ciudad Juarez to work while she awaited the group with whom she would cross into the U.S. In this group, in addition to the coyote (hired guide), there were some of her cousins and brothers.

When my friends found her, she had been alone on the desert for quite some time where the temperatures at night dip into the 20s at that time of year. She had been abandoned by the group after she had fallen and injured herself and could no longer keep up with them. They had told her to look for roads and follow the arrows—whatever that meant. The poor woman had no idea where on earth she was. Clearly she was very ill and it was obvious to my friends that without help she might wander back into an arroyo, curl up and die. Suddenly their own safety became irrelevant.

When they arrived in Arivaca, she asked to be taken to a bus that would take her to Phoenix, her final destination. They explained that there was no bus and no possibility of taking any public transportation to Phoenix. Not knowing what to do to help this vulnerable woman, they drove to the local church to see if there was compassionate help available. No one was there. Then they went to the Post Office, the hub of the small village. The people there were unable to provide any assistance. My friends were surprised when they found that there were no Border Patrol vehicles in town. At Arivaca Lake there had been a Border Patrol van and a pickup truck with a large horse trailer. Additionally, the omnipresent helicopters had been circling the area. Usually there are at least 8 to 10 Border Patrol cars, vans and trucks in that area. That the woman had not been spotted was a miracle.

Not knowing of any humane alternative, my friends took the woman, Graciela, to their home. She was in bad shape. First they made sure she was hydrated and provided her with a shower and clean clothes. Then the nightmare began. Graciela needed immediate medical attention. They were afraid the Border Patrol might not recognize the severity of her condition. They needed help badly. Graciela had lists of telephone numbers in her wallet and they went to work. Finally, they made contact with the wife of the coyote who had abandoned her. Fortunately, my friend spoke Spanish and was able to elicit from the coyote's wife the promise that she would come to Arivaca to pick up Graciela. Later, after many phone calls from this woman, my friends were asked what they would charge to drive Graciela to Phoenix. They explained that this was impossible. Finally, the Phoenix woman agreed to come for the sum of $13,000. Again, not possible.

Friends in Arivaca were phoned for suggestions. None was forthcoming. Then my friends called people in Tucson who might have some ideas. It was Saturday afternoon and few could be reached. Finally, a contact was made with a caring, kind and courageous man. He said he would make a call and be back in touch with them. He did so and provided the name and number of someone who might help. This person was contacted and said she would call back.

My friends were desperate. Since it was now late in the day, they thought it likely they would have to keep Graciela overnight, and they were scared for her and for themselves. Issues in the security of their families were in the forefront of their minds and increased the terror of their being found out. Add to that, their neighbors in Arivaca have a hatred for illegal crossers and would certainly have turned Graciela and my friends over to the authorities had they known she was there.

They tucked an exhausted Graciela in bed and waited. Soon the call came. Would that these incredible, caring people called Samaritans could be identified and lauded for what they do. They explained that they were able to pick up illegal crossers only if they were children or a woman alone who was injured. Graciela qualified. They took the directions to the Arivaca house and said they would be there late in the evening.

Apparently the Samaritans have an implicit understanding with the Border Patrol that they will pick up only these abandoned people. They do not attempt to disguise their mission to the extent that their name is on the side of their vehicle and, although there is no guarantee, they are usually allowed past the Border Patrol checkpoints.

The stress of the day's events was just too much for my friend and she went into an attack of atrial fibrillation. The situation was desperate. My friend could not have driven herself to the hospital in Tucson, and with Graciela asleep and the volunteers on their way, the man could not leave their home. A man in Tucson was called to come and pick up my friend. Before his arrival, the volunteer angels were at the front door. They were briefed on Graciela's story and condition before they awakened her.

No one can ever know the relief of seeing that dear young woman being checked over by the volunteer, a registered nurse, and knowing that she would get the medical attention she so desperately needed. When she left my friends to be taken to Tucson, there were many tears and hugs. Graciela wanted so much to give a gift of thanks to my friends who had rescued her from the desert, and more than likely, from death. All she had to give was the well-worn photo of her family that she had carried with her throughout her travels. Although my friends protested, they finally accepted this touching offer. The love that passed between them when the gift was given and received will stay with my friends forever.

Graciela's photo with her sons

And so the volunteers left for Tucson with Graciela, to whom my friends had given sufficient money to provide a measure of security once she continued on her way. The volunteers suggested that my friends call in three days to see how the situation had resolved.

Epilogue: Graciela had been taken to a compassionate doctor at a Tucson hospital where she was diagnosed with a torn ligament and a brace was put on her knee. Further, she was treated for an upper respiratory infection. The volunteers had made contact by telephone with her family in Arriaga, Chiapas who provided the name and phone number of her brother-in-law in Phoenix. After being told of Graciela's plight, he went to Tucson in the early hours of the morning and took her home with him to Phoenix. She reached her destination. But, what of her comrades who had abandoned her in the desert? All had been rounded up by the Border Patrol and sent back to Mexico!

My friend endured three days in a Tucson hospital getting her heart stabilized. But if you were to ask her if she would do it again she would say, "In the wink of an eye."

What has happened in our nation that opening one's heart and home to someone in desperate need can generate this kind of fear? The United States and Mexico must find a solution to the flood of illegal immigrants who cross our borders. In the region of Southern Arizona south of Tucson, 282 illegal entrants died in the previous year alone due to dehydration, starvation, freezing temperatures or extreme heat, as well as criminal predators.

There are approximately 12 to 15 million illegal immigrants in the U.S. today accounting for about one in every 20 workers. In Arizona, the illegal immigrant population is estimated at 500,000. Our borders must be secured, but we must not give up our moral obligation as Samaritans to the abandoned men, women and children who have been lured to a better life in the United States and fallen prey to severe conditions they could not have anticipated.

My friends don't have an answer, but they now have a personal perspective much different from the rhetoric they had experienced before this event.

The author of this story is a Professor Emerita from the University of Arizona who has had a residence in Arivaca for forty years.

We were told by a Tucson journalist that our story would quickly be syndicated if we released it. That was not possible. But now I want to tell you the full story which is much more interesting.

My family keeps boats in Arivaca. One is a six-foot sailboat that Tony had used as a tender on his ocean sailing. It is called *Tender Behind* and has seen a lot of use on the sea, in Canada, and on Arivaca Lake. We have an electric motor to propel it. We also kept kayaks there.

Well, in fact, Hal and I had been kayaking on a lake near Arivaca the day we found Graciela—

Aldine in kayak on Arivaca Lake

Arivaca Lake, also held as Arizona's best kept secret. It is a very beautiful lake surrounded by mountains. When there has been a lot of rain, the water level is high and thus the lake wends its way deep into many canyons making the experience all the more spectacular.

One day Hal and I were making a particularly long day of kayaking when, suddenly, I absolutely had to get to land and take care of a call of nature. Ever gallant, Hal extricated himself from his kayak at the shoreline in order to help me get out of mine. Regrettably, he slipped and got soaked from the waist down. We took care of the situation and headed back to the landing. Now, as I said in the story about Graciela, this was a cold season in Arivaca and, although the day was sunny and beautiful, Hal was frozen when we disembarked. With a lot of coaxing, I got him to remove his wet levis and put on my silky green jogging pants. I reassured him that no one was going to see us so his dignity would remain intact. And I was comfortable with just my very long sweat shirt.

Certainly we didn't expect to encounter anybody on our return to the cabin so we confidently started home in our rather unusual ensembles. When we first encountered Graciela, we didn't want her to see how we were dressed so we asked her to sit on the tailgate between the kayaks. Also, Hal's pickup truck had only two seats with the gear shift between them. We tried leaving Graciela about ¼ of a mile outside of Arivaca to avoid any complications in our lives and gave her all the U.S. dollars we had with us. When it became evident that Graciela simply couldn't walk, we knew that we would have to seat her in the front with us and drive her into town. I lamented to Hal, "Well, if I am going to be arrested and put in prison it isn't going to be with no pants on." So Hal and I got out of the truck; he put on his wet jeans, and I put my pants back on. I am sure Graciela must have thought Americans were indeed strange.

I also want to add that it was our good friend Howard Shenk who drove all the way from Tucson to Arivaca to pick me up to take me to hospital in Tucson. My attacks of atrial fibrillation were unpredictable, frequent, and severe. Ultimately I had surgery that eliminated the problem entirely, at some risk, and about which I will write elsewhere in these chapters.

And then there was the visit by the drug dealer. It was clear when he approached the cabin that he was of a different ilk given his clean clothes and cool-dude manner. He asked to use our phone. I told him he could not come into the cabin and summoned Hal to lend him his cell phone. He made contact; we noticed later that the person he called was in California. He said he needed to get to Tucson and that he had friends waiting out in the bosque. We refused, of course, to help him. He was obviously taking the lay of the land—two pick-up trucks, two old people and isolation. I was nervous but offered to give him food and water to take to his friends. I put it all in a canvas bag as it was heavy, and off he went. An hour later he was back, ostensibly to return the canvas bag. Hmmm. He told Hal that he had to get to Tucson and offered $2000 to Hal if he would take him and his compadres there. Hal said in no uncertain terms that if he tried to help them, they all would definitely be caught at the Border Patrol check point along the road, and that they would go back to Mexico and he would go to prison. In other words, no way, José.

We carefully considered the precarious position we were in. It would be no problem for him and his buddies to return, put us in grave danger, and steal a pick-up truck. So, we decided that night to leave a pick-up out with keys in it and a bright light above it and hope they would simply steal the truck and leave "the old folks" alone. We had a sleepless night, Hal with gun in hand. To our surprise, the next day we found the truck still there. Disaster averted.

There have been adventures in Arivaca too numerous to mention. Rattlesnake encounters are frequent. Kent once found three in the outhouse that fortunately gave ample warning they were there before Kent got in serious trouble.

When the children were young and intrigued with pirates and buried treasure, Elizabeth and Tony conspired to give them a thrill they would never forget. Tony created a treasure chest from old material and it did indeed look like a pirate's chest. He took two months to make it as he had to do it in secret when his boys were asleep. He found about 5000 old pesos at various coin shops around Tucson. They were old and out of circulation so he was able to buy them by the bucketful. Elizabeth found a lot of costume jewelry and some old brass plates and mugs as well. When

The opening of the treasure chest - 1998

ready, Tony secretly buried the chest on the property and there it remained for six months while the grass regrew. Elizabeth created a very convincing map made from leather that identified the location of the buried treasure. Conveniently, the boys "happened" to find it. What fun they had following the map from point to point and ending up at "the spot." Their eyes were as big as saucers as they unearthed it, opened it and found the treasure trove. What excitement for my grandchildren!

Tony beside his "balancing guy"

Tony, who is a world-class metal worker, has created and erected many beautiful and unusual sculptures and weather vanes that provide endless pleasure as we watch them move gracefully with the wind. They dot our landscape, each with its own distinct personality. One, I am quite sure, is a memorial to Kent. He also has a "balancing guy," a sculpture about twelve feet tall which, when given some momentum, will swing around in circles for quite a long while. Children love playing with it.

We have many happy family times there, our favorite being our annual Thanksgiving celebration when recently 40 friends and family (and 8 dogs) gathered to spend the day. Tony always has new activities for us—pumpkin catapulting, potato gun shooting, as well as two cannons. The larger cannon is for shooting footballs and the like while the smaller is for shooting golf balls. There are knife throwing contests, as well as hatchet throwing, and often archery competitions.

Kent readying a pumpkin for the "trebuchet"

Carolyn Friedl shooting potato gun - Thanksgiving 2014

Tony has lots of farm equipment—five tractors, two ATVs, a number of jeeps, and a go-cart. He maintains the property mowing by hand at least an acre of grass surrounding our dwelling and keeping the place neat and tidy. None of this could happen without him.

We have a pet cemetery on the property with wooden crosses to remind us of all our animal friends who brought such joy to our lives. On each cross hangs the collar of the dog, cat or other pet who is buried there.

My grandchildren often take their friends to Arivaca, and it brings me enormous pleasure to know that for over forty years this remote area has been the source of so much adventure, peace and happiness for my family and a multitude of friends.

Tony with Tana, Max & Alex on tractor swing - 1998

Max & Kent playing Twister in the cabin

Nana helping Alex with his
Easter basket - 1994

Our family - 1998

Family campfire - a nightly ritual

Tana with Tony using blow gun-Easter 2003

Alex with Sparky in the golf cart -
Thanksgiving 2003

Kent in his Jeep - 1991

Hammock time - Easter 2000 with Aldine, Tori, Stephanie,
Harper, Aldine Meister, Aldine Chandler

Kent with Tana on the quad - 1992

Elizabeth, Janice, Tony & Kent - 2002

Tana riding go-cart - 2004

Hal with Buddy - Thanksgiving 2014

17

ೞೲ

ADVENTURES AT OUR COTTAGE IN CANADA

1945—1953 MY TEENAGE YEARS

As I entered my teenage years, my family left behind the old Cobble Cottage and Beacon Lodge near Dwight, Ontario, Canada in which we had spent summers since I was one-month old. This period of my life is recorded in Appendix 4—The History of Charlie Thompson Road. We were ready to embark on new adventures at Lake of Bays, halcyon summers spent at the old white cottage on Charlie Thompson Road at the end of Dwight Bay—Birch Spring. (Appendix 5 provides a map of the area.)

Having been unable to have children, my aunt and uncle, Ella Mae (Elma) and Alan Walker, had adopted my siblings and me as their surrogates. They bought a three-story run-down old summer home near Dwight in order to provide a place for my family to come each year. My parents had moved our family to Tucson the previous year—1945—a place that met my father's need for a dry climate as he had severe asthma. My mother and Elma were very close sisters and were going to miss each other terribly. My aunt knew this cottage

The family at the old white cottage, Birch Spring
Murray, Mom, Carol, Elma, Dad, Aldine & Al

would be an irresistible lure, and indeed it was. It came with the name Birch Spring and always remained its original color—white.

My aunt and uncle had worked hard all year getting the place habitable after its having been empty and neglected for decades. My diary indicates that it was June 29, 1946 that we spent our first night there as a family noting that "Al and Elma's cottage is super." It was the first of 33 summers I spent there. Al was a tall man—6'4"—and very handsome. Elma was a raven-haired beauty who had the temperamental characteristics typically attributed to red-heads. They doted on us and we adored them.

Al & Elma Walker

Mother had taken us by train to Tucson in August of 1945. My father had been living there for two years and was desperately lonely without his family. His health was greatly improved and he was

Aldine - 1945

ready to have his family join him. He had met us at the train station and took us to our new home which my diary described as "lovely." That was high praise from a 12-year-old! Ensuing summers we returned to Toronto and the cottage by car with my intrepid mother doing all the driving as Dad had to remain in Tucson both for his health as well as his job as the Associated Press correspondent for southern Arizona. It was a long hot drive in those times but typically we completed the trip in five days.

Having spent so many years on Charlie Thompson Road, my brother and I already had a cadre of friends at the cottage and we resumed our happy days immediately upon settling in at our "new" home there. As I reflect on these years, I recognize my parents' wisdom in balancing our responsibilities with our recreation. My diary reminds me that I washed floors and painted them, did laundry for the family and ironed it, and cleaned the cottage and cooked. My sister Carol, more than five years my junior, was excused from this type of drudgery.

Aldine wearing Mexican sombrero

Aldine sailing

What I remember most vividly, however, were the wonderful times we had. We sailed, swam, had water fights and went on picnics. We took boat rides up the Oxtongue River and climbed the rocks at Marsh's Falls. We attended the little white church down the hill faithfully on Sunday. We went "surf boarding," played tennis and dove off high rocks. We went paddling and rowing and occasionally for a ride in someone's power boat. Trips to the local dump in the evening where we inevitably found scavenging bears were a big treat. We regularly drove to Algonquin Park, only 12 miles away, and invariably would encounter a moose or two. We rode bicycles for miles—our only available transportation on land.

We went to friends' cottages for parties but the best of these were always held in the old boathouse down near the dock that my uncle had made into a clubhouse for us. We ate wieners, played music on a Victrola, and danced. It all seemed so romantic to two hormone-driven teenagers—my brother Murray and me.

Dancing at Birch Spring - 1945
John Burgar with Aldine, Murray with Mary Burgar, Bob Munns
with Beth Burgar

165

Birch Spring boathouse party - 1946
Beth, Mary & John Burgar, Carolyn & Alastair Souter, Aldine, Eileen Baggs & Murray

In spite of being only 12 years old, a day that had a profound effect on me was August 14, 1945—VJ Day. Canadians celebrated this victory with great enthusiasm. We had been in WWII since 1939—six long years. My Uncle George had just returned from having been a bomber pilot for many years in the RCAF.

Frequently we visited my Uncle Gordon, a famous Canadian newscaster, at his cottage—Wit's End on Lake Muskoka. Even at that age, I was invigorated by the repartee and became fascinated with the news media. There always seemed to be strife between my father and Uncle Gordon but time ultimately healed the rifts. At one time they didn't speak for seven years! We saw very little of my Uncle George but my diary notes that we did meet him once in Huntsville for lunch on July 21, 1947.

Also in 1947, Al built a diving tower down at the shoreline. What a hit this was with all the

Diving tower with boathouse in background

energetic teenagers in the area! It was almost seven feet tall and the water below was five feet deep. We spent countless hours enjoying the thrills it provided.

My fondest memories, however, were the square dances held every Friday night at the little community center in Dwight. These brought the old and the young alike from far and wide, and it didn't take long for that room to be rife with the odors of beer, cigarettes and bodies. I loved it. It was there each year that I met my beau for the summer—all of whom became lifelong friends. These attractive young men—Robert Prittie, Doug Mochrie, Dave McBride and others—came to our cottage to see me and an interesting phenomenon occurred. In almost every case, they became good friends with my brother as well. As life went along they became business associates and they all were in attendance at the memorial service for my brother in 2014.

Aldine with Bob Munns 1947   Aldine with Doug Mochrie 1948

I often incurred my parents' disapproval for staying out too late at night with these boys. In 1949 my boyfriend was Robert Prittie. One night, July 25th, we had rowed up the Boyne River to the point where it met the Boyne Falls. We jumped out on the shore, climbed the falls, and then sat on the beach where we talked and shared one chaste kiss. (I was 16 then.) When it was time to leave it was dark and we couldn't find the rowboat. As my diary said, "When we tried to find our way back we were surrounded by swamp. We were lost. We had to walk home in our bare feet." Eventually we found our way out and the greeting that we received upon our return to the cottage was cool at best. The rowboat was retrieved the following day.

Aldine with beau - 1948

My grandmother whom I adored—Ella Gertrude Eagen—continued to come to the cottage into very old age. She died at age 98. As I shared a room with her I was familiar with her habits. In spite of her very advanced years, she always knelt to pray at night. How she ever got up again, I don't know but I watched her from the corner of my eye to be sure she made it.

Imagine, that big cottage with seven bedrooms had only one bathroom! Often on weekends over the years we would have as many as 17 to 22 in residence. That bathroom served yeoman's duty and was no end of trouble with its recurring plumbing problems. Fortunately the outhouse was a "two seater" so there were few crises.

My diary noted that we finally had hydro in 1949 and on July 5th the electricians came to connect a stove. It had only three little burners, but after 17 years at the cottages cooking on wood stoves, you can be sure we thought it was luxurious. My mother's pies, however, were never quite as good as they had been from the wood stoves which had to be monitored and fed wood to maintain a proper baking temperature. She seemed to take all these inconveniences in stride.

Toward the end of summer my father would typically come by train from Tucson and join us at the cottage. He helped my mother with the driving on the return trip to Tucson and never failed to make it an educational experience for us children. We traveled a different route every year visiting museums and national parks along the way. Could any young girl have asked for more caring parents? Yet I was oblivious to their sacrifices until many years later.

In 1950 our summers changed. This was initiated by a devastating accident my brother experienced. Several days before departing Tucson, Murray had been swimming at a local pool. As he entered the water after a high dive, he saw that his head was going to hit bottom and so he snapped it back. Later he had a horrible headache but a doctor whom he saw assured my parents it was nothing serious and that they should continue with their travel plans for going to Canada.

With my mother at the wheel as usual, we departed Tucson on June 5, 1950 and it wasn't until the night of June 6th that Murray developed an incapacitating headache that kept Mother awake all night caring for him. She knew we were in trouble but had no alternative except to put her foot on the accelerator and head for Toronto. As my old grandmother was with us, she knew it was imperative to reach home as fast as possible and get Murray under medical care. She drove non-stop arriving at Toronto General Hospital very late at night.

Murray was diagnosed as having had a subarachnoid hemorrhage and doctors were not optimistic about his survival. He was placed in a position wherein he could not move and had sandbags on either side of his head so that he was immobilized. He wasn't even allowed to talk. And there he remained for eight weeks.

When he finally was released to go to the cottage, he was frail indeed and my mother was admonished to keep noise, movement and excitement to a minimum. It must have been very difficult for my athletic and energetic brother to have had these restraints imposed upon him. And then came August 9th. I will quote from my diary. "While Al and I were out sailing, we heard a terrific explosion which shook the cottage. Carol came running to the dock to tell us Murray had his hand splattered and there was blood all over him. I went up and looked and he was white as a sheet and faint. His hand was bloody, purple pulp and his face also cut. The explosion blew his thumbnail…right off in one piece and other nails shattered." Apparently he had touched a very old sulfur candle that exploded, parts of which were found out in the hallway. Smoke was thick.

Groups were sent out to find doctors whom we knew on the lake. Three came. There was little they could do except render first aid. Over time, Murray recovered but he was never the same again. The brother whom I knew as fun and thoughtful had become a different person. I think he felt that since he probably wasn't going to live a long life that he would take whatever he could from it while it lasted. In time, he became a ruthless business man and, in many ways, a mean brother. He never lost his charm or charisma but part of this came from taking chances with his own life as well as that of others. My sons were not allowed to go in a boat or a car with Uncle Murray.

That summer continued as usual for the rest of us, but Murray missed out on all the fun. We departed for Tucson on September 5th.

The next summer—1951—I graduated from high school in Tucson on May 25th. We left for Toronto on May 31st—bursting at the seams. There were seven of us in the car as Dad was with us on this trip, as well as his parents, Bessie and George Sinclair. Nonetheless, Dad drove us all to the Grand Canyon where we stayed at the Bright Angel Lodge. He wanted my grandparents to see the Petrified Forest and the Painted Desert, so we stopped there as well. We reached Toronto on June 6th.

By June 10th we realized there was a serious problem with my Uncle Alan—Al—who was experiencing severe pain and a high fever. He entered hospital on June 15th and it was clear that we'd be spending a lot of time in Toronto that summer to support him and Elma who was distraught.

The family decided, however, to spend a weekend at the cottage. Thus, on June 29th, Carol and I were dispatched to drive north with a family friend to open the cottage—untouched since last year. We cleaned and scrubbed and were ready when they arrived—my mother, grandmother, Aunt Sue and Irene (Grandma's sisters), Murray and Dave McBride, one of my boyfriends that summer and my guest for the weekend.

Thereafter, I spent most of the summer in Toronto. I had a job at the jewelry counter at the T. Eaton Company. I did manage to find a ride to the cottage on weekends and even learned to water ski that summer.

Al's health continued to decline—he had lost over 50 pounds since our arrival in June. My father arrived from Tucson on August 3rd. I wrote in my diary on August 18th, "I was very sad and cried most of the day. Our family is in such a mess. Al is dying and Mom isn't coming back to Tucson with us, and I have to start university soon without her help." We started our trip back to Tucson on August 27th. The very day we left, Al died from cancer at age 47. He had been a chain smoker.

We reached Tucson on August 31st and Mother came home by train on September 8th. My new life was about to begin. On September 16th Carol turned 13 and I pledged Kappa Kappa Gamma sorority. My dream had come true! But the best was yet to come. Later that semester I met my beloved husband-to-be, Anthony Kent von Isser. There is much more about that subject in another chapter.

After a magical year as a university student and now "promised" to the man I loved, summer rolled around and it was time to make our annual trip to the cottage. Murray and I drove on our own that year. Murray was not a good driver and, after an unpleasant trip during which I lamented in my diary that I was lonely and missed Tony terribly, we arrived in Toronto on June 2, 1952.

Now that Murray was 21 and I was 19 years old, it was time we had proper summer jobs. My fascination with radio and the media had only grown over the years and I had dreamed of working in the largest radio station in Toronto—CFRB. Imagine my euphoria when I was offered a position to work as secretary to the newsroom working with famous Canadian newscasters such as my uncle—Gordon Sinclair—and Jack Dennett and Wally Crouter, all of whose names remain in older people's memories today. I was covering for a woman, Kay Bennett, who was off for the summer.

I started the job—9:00 a.m. until 5:00 p.m.—on June 11, 1952 and was able to commute to the cottage on weekends. More about this job is written elsewhere in this memoir.

Murray had taken a job with the *Toronto Daily Star* newspaper working from 5:00 p.m. until 1:30 a.m. We were very fortunate to have been given the use of my grandparents' garden apartment in downtown Toronto while they were away. It had one bedroom with twin beds and I rarely, if ever, saw Murray as he had left for work when I returned home and he was sound asleep when I tiptoed off in the morning. We had weekends at Dwight and the magic of our summer connections and activities continued. Our last night at the cottage that year was August 23rd and all our friends joined together for a wiener roast in Algonquin Park—25 of us. What a wonderful send-off. We headed back to Tucson the next day.

Tony was practically on our doorstep when we arrived. My diary said, "I love him <u>so</u> and I have missed him <u>so</u> much. I'll never leave him so long again." We became officially engaged on November 2nd and married on March 28, 1953. I was 19 years old.

And so began a new era. My next visit to the cottage would be as a married woman. What a magical adolescence I had at the old white cottage in Dwight!

1953—1980   LIFE AT THE COTTAGE WITH MY SONS

Having married Tony at age 19 and having become a mother at age 21, I transitioned very quickly from being a carefree youth at the cottage into being a mother with considerable concerns about the safety of her first-born surrounded with what I perceived as being threats to his very life. Birch Spring had always been a place that attracted people of all ages, some of whom had a bent toward unusual and perhaps dangerous activities.

An example of the latter was the type of party my brother often had there with friends–many of whom I considered debauched. Consider the time he brought a goat to the cottage for such nefarious purposes as we can only guess. In the wee hours of the morning there was a good deal of ribaldry going on downstairs. I sadly report that the poor goat was found in the morning, tethered to the flag post outside and dead. My parents cast a jaundiced eye at this sort of activity but had long before accepted that "Murray was Murray."

Sanitation was another worry as I admit to having been obsessive-compulsive about cleanliness when it came to my babies. Carol, a nurse, used to express considerable concern for my methods in preparing my son Kent's formula. I completely closed off the kitchen so that no one could enter during my bottle-preparation time. I would boil those bottles until no germ could possibly survive before I would pour in the sterilized milk. One could barely see in the kitchen through the steam I created in the process and Carol insisted I had created the world's biggest petri dish. I literally would break into tears if anyone infiltrated my "sterile field."

Safety was a serious issue. The old cottage was a tinderbox. It would have taken little to start a fire that would have incinerated the place in mere minutes. In his early years there, Tony had not recognized the frailty of the old building and on one cold morning started a huge fire in the fireplace that would dry us out and heat us up. The chimney was not used to that sort of punishment and soon hot cinders were leaping out the top. One landed on the roof that was very, very old and certainly not fireproof.

A minor blaze began. We had one short hose trailed through a window from the kitchen, unattached except when needed for laundry. That wasn't going to help. Tony's solution to the problem was to grab an extension ladder and, tied at the waist with a rope and brandishing a rum bottle full of water, mounted the three stories of the cottage to douse the blaze. I was tied at the other end of the rope in case he fell over the roof.

Now really! Having dumped the first rum bottle, he sent for another. It must have been Tony's lucky day as he neither incinerated the cottage nor did he kill himself!

Great Grandmother Ella Eagen with Tony, Kent, Scott & Murray

My aged grandmother, Ella Eagen had her routines from which she would not stray. One was putting on her corset in the morning. That was a life-long habit and nothing, but nothing, would prevent her from performing it. On the morning of the "fire" there was near panic and Grandma was admonished in no uncertain terms to get out of the cottage immediately. "I will, after I put on my corset," was her reply. And she meant it. It was some few minutes before the deed was accomplished and she exited the cottage, her dignity intact and her waist cinched, in her own good time and on her own terms. Grandma was born in 1870 and died at age 96 in 1966. What a woman!

In the early years, there was no such thing as baby furniture. We made do. My babies slept in drawers in dressers built into the old walls. They survived. Baby baths were in the kitchen sink which had an idiosyncrasy that made it a difficult task. The base of the sink slanted the wrong direction—away from the drain rather than toward it. There was no end of cursing over the years as people always had to deal with the sludge collected at the "wrong end."

There was to be a birthday party one night for which Mother had gone to considerable effort by baking a birthday cake. She had placed it on the wood stove which was then used primarily as a side table for the dining room. An incident occurred that day after one of these baby baths. Mother had assisted me and when we were finished took Kent in hand while I cleaned up at the sink. On passing the wood stove, still naked, Kent (age 4 months) let fly! His aim was perfect—right in the middle of the cake. Mother handled the situation with her usual calm, scooped out what urine she could and smoothed the icing over beautifully. She commented that her cake would be moister than usual. And no one was the wiser. It was a successful birthday party and everyone raved about the cake!

Adults took their baths by whatever means they chose—in the lake or with a wash cloth—but not in a bathtub. There was, indeed, a huge bathtub in the bathroom but no hot water to it. Many of us used the washtub approach. We would spread newspaper on the floor in the kitchen, place an old dented galvanized washtub on it and heat sufficient water on the stove to fill it. What a luxury to climb into a hot bath, although one had to contort one's body to make it work.

Aldine bathing in a washtub

Diapers were a problem, too. I was a purist about sterilized cloth diapers held together by huge safety pins. Actually, in those days there wasn't an alternative. As we now had hydro, we were able to install a wringer-washer outside on a slab of cement near the cottage. The wash water was, of course, cold but we were usually satisfied with the result. One would squeeze the washed items through the wringer and into a tub of cold water on the ground. This was repeated until an acceptably clean piece of clothing, or diaper, would emerge. On good days there was no problem in drying clothes on the clothes line. Since good weather could not always be counted on, many were the days that diapers were strewn throughout the cottage with prayers that they would dry "in time."

Kent was the first of 10 grandchildren who would come along and he was everybody's darling. Hence, sickness was another worry for me. With so many people in the cottage arriving from all directions on the weekends, I was quite sure he would contract a dreadful illness from someone as he was passed from person to person. It never happened!

Kent sailing in *Too Tired* - 1956

My father, who loved to build things, made a sailboat for Kent. It was very small—an inner-tube in a frame with a little mast and sail. It was christened *Too Tired*. Our upstairs bathroom in Dwight has dozens of photographs hanging in it, and the one of Kent in his little sailboat drifting out into the lake by himself always causes a great stir. While no adult is visible in the picture, we were right behind the camera ready to save him. This, however, does little to convince our friends that it wasn't a downright dangerous thing to do.

As Kent began to develop language, he learned the easy words quickly. However, Grandma and Grandpa eluded him and segued into Mia and Bumpa. And these were my parents' names ever after not only to all successive grandchildren but to most of their friends, and ours, as well. Tony Jr. was the second grandchild and the adoration from my family doubled.

Getting to Canada was another dilemma for me. At first, my mother would cross the country with me, the boys and our dog by train. I was exhausted by the time we arrived as keeping two active little guys occupied and happy for 2 ½ days on a train was a challenge. I kept them on leashes. Clearly this did not meet with the approval of strangers. In Chicago during a layover we visited Marshall Fields, a department store. One onlooker saw the leashes and said she would call the police if we did not untether those boys immediately. She considered my technique to be "child abuse." Well, they never got lost, in any case.

Kent & Tony on rocks at
Dwight Bay

Kent & Tony overlooking
Dwight Bay from Charlie
Thompson Road - 1962

Tony on rail fence with
Dwight Bay in background

When Al bought the cottage, there were hundreds—perhaps thousands—of bats in residence. They hung everywhere and were not pleased when the cottage was opened and air and light allowed in. Annually, upon his arrival, my father would have a little talk with the bats. Standing on the landing of the second floor, he would reason with them that they had the use of the place all winter long and we were only asking for a couple of months. He entreated them to find another home for the summer and allow us a bat-free environment. While he never succeeded in completely eradicating them from the premises, he did reduce the population considerably. Occasionally a rebel would taunt us by swooping through the cottage and setting off a cacophony of shrieks.

Kent sailing Sunfish - 1963

Tony the fisherman - 1964

Kent exiting Tony's rowboat - Tony on oars

At a young age Tony Jr. became an avid fisherman. The cottage is full of photos of him holding strings of big fish; some seemed almost as big as he was. To expand his fishing horizon, which had been restricted to our dock, he bought a rowboat when he was seven years old. He paid $5 for it and invested another $5 in its repair. Oh, the feeling of ownership and independence it gave him, although he was always accompanied by an adult when he went far from home.

Among Kent and Tony Jr.'s favorite destinations on the lake were two places that became focal points of their summers. The first was a spot on a nearby bay— Ruggles Bay—where they could dive directly from the beach into very deep water. They called it the "drop off" place and my grandchildren continue to enjoy this beautiful and isolated spot.

Tony in his precious rowboat - 1964

Tony - 1963

However, the owners have cordoned off part of the area with a net and buoys and placed "no trespassing" signs liberally throughout their property. Not very Canadian, although they do have a raft there with a Canadian flag mounted on it.

176

Jumping from White Rock

The second location was "white rock," a cliff that rises at least 40 feet to a place from which the boys could jump into deep water below. There were intermediary rocks for beginners, but the leap from the top was the goal of all young people. My grandchildren continued to challenge themselves year after year until the owners of the property decided it was a safety hazard and fenced it off completely. What a disappointment for the children in this area. A rite of passage was being denied them. To my knowledge, no one was ever injured there.

While my boys always took their dogs to the cottage, they seemed to acquire a new menagerie of pets each year. One summer they doted on two white geese. Actually geese make very poor pets, hissing and nipping you on the leg at the most unexpected times. Naturally they were not housebroken! This didn't prevent my boys from bringing them into the cottage. My parents were, as I say, saints!

Kent & Tony with their ducks - 1964

One night, we had a number of guests, one of whom decided to catch a goose and determine whether it was male or female. The geese panicked. Wings flapped and feathers flew and chaos reigned. One ran into the open burning fireplace and caught its tail feathers on fire. Then it scampered around the room, scattering sparks on very burnable floor matting. Half the adults extinguished the sparks while the rest joined the children in chasing the geese through an open door, which wasn't easy. The smell of burning feathers lasted well into the next day! The singed goose recovered nicely. Before leaving the cottage, we always found appropriate homes for the pets of the season.

Kent and Tony Jr.'s favorite duck ever was named Peepers. They were adamant that he could not be left behind in Canada. The boys wanted him in California where we were living at the time. Feeling indomitable, I conjured a way to make this happen. The duck was put in a handbag that we placed beneath our feet on the airplane. When the hostess passed by, we all made sounds with a quacking overtone to obliterate the real sounds made by the duck. It remained unnoticed throughout our flights. I had thought it might garner some attention in the ladies room at O'Hare Airport where I filled a basin with water to give Peepers a little swim. Again, no one seemed to take notice. It appeared that it took a lot to startle seasoned travelers.

Peepers remained our pet to the end of his life. What fun my sons had taking baths with him!

Kent - age 8 - water skiing in front of old white cottage - 1963

Kent slalom skiing

Tony on slalom ski in Dwight Bay

A telephone at the cottage was a luxury back then. Long distance was all but forbidden due to the high charges incurred, but if we absolutely had to make a call, it was permitted only after 11:00 p.m. when lower rates went into effect. Also, we were fortunate to have only one person on our party line—Mrs. Van Cleef. (She was the mother of my beloved friend Jacquie Hatkoski.) She was not always gracious when she had to put up with children listening in on her conversations and answering her personal ring.

Although it was difficult to make the trip to Canada each summer, somehow I managed. As I have mentioned in other parts of the memoir, some of the trips were very difficult for me. I will feature one of these as an indication of the troubles I often encountered. We were living in California at the time—1964. Kent was nine years old and Tony Jr.

was six. We were in our camper—hoping that by having it in Canada Tony would be tempted to join us for a week or two. Our dog was with us. Seat belts were not required at the time so I allowed the boys to spend part of our driving day in the camper, which was a separate unit mounted on the bed of our truck. That gave them the freedom to move around, snack and play games. Rules were established about behaviors that would not be permitted—including going near the door at the rear of the camper.

On a busy highway I noticed that drivers in passing cars were frantically waving at me and pointing to the rear of the camper. I realized there had to be a problem so pulled over as soon as possible. I discovered that not only had Kent opened the camper door, but he was standing on the little tailgate waving at passers-by. How easily he could have fallen and what an inadequate mother I felt I was! Obviously, I made it impossible for this to happen again.

As we continued on, we entered the Turner Turnpike in Oklahoma. Suddenly, I was almost deafened by a horrible grinding sound that shook the truck. I couldn't believe we had broken down in such an isolated area. There were no cell phones in those days so I had no choice but to stand at the edge of the highway to thumb a ride. I was scared but desperate. Finally a driver stopped and I explained my plight. He looked abashed when I told him that I had two boys and a dog in the camper. Graciously, however, he accepted us all and drove us to the nearest garage in the town of Bristow, Oklahoma.

We waited there while our truck was towed off the highway and into Bristow. It was a Friday afternoon. It was quickly determined that the transfer case on our four-wheel drive had broken. It would be Monday before they could order a new part and several days of work to install it. I was devastated and asked them to please tow us to a park for the weekend so that my boys would have a place to play. They squelched this idea in a hurry indicating that we would not be safe. I assured them I would lock the camper carefully at night but I was told, "Oh, they'll get you out. They'll set a fire under the camper and—you'll come out."

One of the managers—Grady Davenport—came to my "rescue." He suggested I borrow his truck and check into a motel. There was, of course, a caveat—I had to advise him of where we were staying and that he'd be "checking in" on us. I knew his intentions, and they were not honorable. But desperate times require desperate measures, so I accepted his offer. I drove to a town many miles away and checked into a motel with a swimming pool. I did not advise Grady of our whereabouts. Days later, when I was sure our truck had been repaired, I phoned and made arrangements to return his truck and pick up our rig. Grady was beyond irate and had thought seriously of advising the police that his truck had been stolen. I was saved that disgrace but was duly contrite for not keeping my part of the deal.

While retrieving our truck, I had left Kent in the motel with the dog intending to pick him up later. Upon our return, I could not get Kent's attention either by banging on the door or knocking on the windows. Finally, I had the motel manager open the door only to find Kent unconscious. I rushed him to the nearest hospital to learn that he had heat stroke and was severely dehydrated. First aid was administered and Kent revived quickly. When given the OK for Kent to leave, we set off down the highway once again. Soon we were on the Will Rogers Turnpike—and the truck broke down again. This breakdown was not as serious but I had reached the end of my rope. I simply couldn't go on and phoned Tony to come and get us.

After a little pep talk, he convinced me to continue to Chicago where he would meet us at the airport and drive us the rest of the way to the cottage. And he did. Year after year I subjected myself to the harrowing trip which was never without complications, but I was determined that my sons would spend every summer with their family at the cottage in Canada. And they did!

There were a lot of chores expected to be done by my lads at the cottage. One particularly onerous one fell to Tony Jr. when he was only 12 years old. A ditch needed to be dug to facilitate the laying of new electrical line. It was extremely difficult work as the ditch was to start at a power pole in the woods and reach the cottage 50 feet away. Tony was given this assignment—much too big a task for such a young boy—and he remembers it as being incredibly difficult as he had to dig through roots and clay, and it was very muddy. It took him a couple of days but there was never a word of complaint on his part.

Until their cousins came along, the boys had only themselves to play with but that changed with the arrival of my brother's sons—Murray, Scott and Craig—whom he had with his first wife Ann. Carol, in the meantime, produced Stephanie, Ted and Aldine. What fun those young people had throughout their young years and how much love there was among them. To this day they adore each other and, although

The four Aldines - 1986

they live thousands of miles apart, they arrange to get together regularly.

Each was unique in personality. Let's start with Stephanie. She was a lovely child and, being the first girl, garnered a lot of attention. While an obedient little girl, she had a bit of the devil in her as well. Once, after dinner, she went out in the motor boat to taunt Sam and Eve who fished every night in front of our cottage. They were a couple who worked for our neighbors, the Hickoks. Well, Stephanie made circles—tighter and tighter circles—around Sam and Eve's boat. The waves she created grew huge until finally Sam and Eve were close to being swamped. You may be sure Stephanie got the dickens for that little caper.

At age 12, she fell madly in love with Corky Chandler—a close friend of Kent and Tony Jr.—who was several years older than she and visiting my boys at the cottage. Hers was a teenage crush on steroids and when she found a disgusting, sweaty old tee-shirt of Corky's lying around she thought she had died and gone to heaven. She wore that shirt morning, noon and night. How mean were her older cousins when they cornered her at the lake one day and threw her in—tee-shirt and all! She was inconsolable that some of the patina had been washed away and she didn't speak to them for days. More shirts became available to her when she married Corky seven years later! (She is now married to Tyler Meigs.) Stephanie has become a beautiful woman beloved by all. I am proud indeed to be her aunt and her godmother.

There was a big wood box in the kitchen of the old white cottage that had always been kept full of firewood for use in either the wood stove or the fireplace. It took on a different purpose during Ted's childhood. Ted was often a complete little brat and there seemed only one place to get him under control—the wood box. It had been emptied and was just the right height to incarcerate him. Unfortunately it was right beside the "dining room" table and often conversation was impossible during his temper tantrums. He is now a highly successful executive with CBS and charming to the core.

And my sister's youngest child—Aldine. She is and always has been a blithe spirit. What an enchanting and innocent looking child she was with her blonde hair and blue eyes, but who knew the fire that lay beneath! Pity my sister who took Aldine to the supermarket, ensconced her in the shopping basket and launched forward to do her marketing. Carol knew what was to come; it always did. Some kindly stranger would remark, "What a beautiful child," to which Aldine would respond, "F_ck off!" The worst part was that she slid the words out the side of her mouth with malice. Carol would apologize, admonish Aldine to behave, and carry on.

This behavior continued for months. On my arrival at the cottage, Carol, seeing me as the wise older sister and a certified psychologist, begged me to help her solve this problem. Piece of cake, thought I! As it happened, my father never swore but when pushed to his limit he used the word "macadamia" with great feeling. The children knew his mood was to be respected when that oath was uttered.

Well, suggested I, it is a simple matter. Aldine and Dad will trade words. She can have his word and he can have "f_ck off." Both were in accord with this solution. Henceforth, by father owned "f_ck off" and Aldine, and only Aldine, could use "macadamia." It worked like a charm—for a while. Dad, however, was not using his words often enough and Aldine's word didn't seem to claim the power it had held for her grandfather. So she slipped back into her old ways—to the chagrin of the whole embarrassed family. "Now what?" said Carol. "No problem," said I. Dad simply has to use "f_ck off" more often and remind Aldine that those are his words now—not hers. This was not easy for my father who had never used "his" words in his life.

His opportunity arose on a day all the family and a multitude of our friends climbed on my brother's houseboat and went to our favorite place down the lake for a picnic—Breakfast Rock. After lunch, my father left the group to return to the houseboat for a little siesta. There he was lying, eyes closed, when Aldine skipped gaily back to the boat and shouted, "Bumpa, will you help me get on the boat?" My father's loud response was, "F_CK OFF, Aldine!" What he didn't know was that behind Aldine were several of our friends who were also returning to the boat. Now, how could a grandfather possibly explain his behavior to people whom he barely knew. Aldine, however, was all smiles and delighted that Bumpa had used his words. Aldine continues to be a spirited and very beautiful woman and I wouldn't be a bit surprised if she steals Bumpa's words for her own use from time to time!

My parents deserve to be acknowledged for their incredible patience and loving acceptance of their children, their grandchildren and all their many friends. They subjected themselves to noise, confusion, squabbling, temper tantrums, sandy feet and wet bathing suits with never a complaint. Mother would lie on the living room sofa to read and have a little nap in the afternoon and seemed oblivious to the din surrounding her. My father's default position was at his typewriter in a corner of the living room. How he could block out the confusion around him is beyond my ken! As I have said, often there were 21 in residence in the cottage with our children, grandchildren and an aged grandmother and her sisters. We also had at least two babysitters in the throng each year.

As can be imagined, meal times were difficult with an antiquated kitchen to work from and so many mouths to feed. One summer Mother put her foot down and said we were going to bring in a cook from the local area. We did indeed have some good cooks, Mrs. Robitaille, Wally—a Chinese man who had a way with herbs—and finally Eddie

Gouldie. Eddie was a drunk but a good cook. He had to be picked up each day as he had long since lost his driver's license permanently due to DUIs. Each day he had delivered to the cottage by taxi a case—24 count—of beer. None would be left when he went home! Well, it was the going home that caused the problem and was finally the reason for Eddie's dismissal. Eddie was gay and fell in love with my husband Tony. He would practically stamp his feet if he could not have Tony drive him home. Tony finally rebelled—enough was enough—and while Eddie grew petulant, his meals simultaneously went downhill. He lasted longer than most of our cooks, however, who rarely made it through a season. They simply couldn't stand the job.

Tony towing Kent - 1965

My father brought from Tucson each year a suitcase full of treasures for children— candy, little toys, games and so forth. He had one big drawer in a bureau in the living room that was known as "Bumpa's Store." What a treat it was for children to be given permission to visit this revered location.

Murray, Scott and Craig were spirited lads and constant companions to my boys as they all grew up at the cottage. They particularly enjoyed joining their older cousins in nighttime bear hunting! They all would don their bear-fighting uniforms and, borne by their parents by car to the garbage dump, would brandish their "sabers," emit loud yells and, of course, frighten the bears. At least, that is what they hoped. Often there were six or more bears there for them to terrify. A technique for capturing the bears was devised—a bicycle inner tube tied to a rope with which they intended to lasso them. Somehow, the bears eluded that fate!

Kent walking with Murray at his side and Scott on his shoulders

They were very excited when Kent and Tony Jr., as teenagers, were allowed to have their own cabins. They could become a part of the activities of the older kids and they thrived. These small cabins had been purchased during the winter and hauled into place over the snow. One had been a little library and the other—one room only—had been the home of an entire family. For that one I had to pay $85. As the years passed, more names and hearts and messages were carved into the walls and beams of the structures immortalizing those moments in time.

Aldine with teenagers Tony & Kent

When we moved to our new place in 1980, one of the cabins was towed over and became a part of our new complex. There is considerable history recorded on its walls that continues to be added to year by year.

Mary and Murray's children came along much later and were therefore never able to be a part of the original gang of cousins. Christopher was born in 1980 and has delighted everyone with his charm and spontaneous laughter ever since. It must be added that he is also very handsome and charismatic. Candice came along three years later—Murray's only daughter from his five children. He adored her, as do we all. She is very beautiful and has a loving soul and beguiling manner.

As my sons grew older, we varied their summer activities. Kent, for several years, was a ranch hand on Katharine Merritt's Three Rivers Ranch in Moran, Wyoming, near Jackson Hole. Tony Jr. was there for a year as well. He also went for a couple of years to visit the Hyde family on Nantucket—their son Ted was his good friend—where he learned to sail and play tennis. He became a superb tennis player. One summer he was his Aunt Ann's "baby-sitter" at the cottage for Murray, Scott and Craig.

We always, however, ended the summer at the cottage together. Both boys were there under the watchful eye of their grandparents when I returned from a trip to Greece in 1972. While they had their cabins, I was relegated to the third floor of the old cottage—definitely not a safe place to be. The cottage was in danger of collapsing and the threat of a fire was real. The boys worked hard around the cottage doing the majority of the maintenance. But the work was interspersed with wonderful, happy times.

Kent owned the first jet ski on Lake of Bays—probably the first jet ski in Canada. He had purchased it as soon as they became available in Tucson. It was a bit tricky to transport it to the cottage. First he test drove it in our swimming pool in Tucson. Then, in order to mount it on the roof of his Sirocco car, he had to create a pulley apparatus with ropes and chains over one of our big trees there. Safely ensconced, he drove it north to our lake which has well over 100 miles of shoreline and no end of destinations for a jet skier. Everyone was intrigued by this unusual marine apparatus and they had hours of pleasure riding it.

Family at Breakfast Rock - 1980
Tony, Kent, Scott, Craig, Ted, Dad,
Stephanie, Carol, Mom & Aldine

Both my boys were superb water skiers and on July 28, 1972, Tony Jr. watered skied all the way back from Breakfast Rock where we had gone for a picnic—a distance of perhaps six miles. This might not have been difficult behind a fast power boat, but being towed by a slow houseboat full of passengers really taxed his muscles.

Breakfast Rock is a rocky peninsula that rarely has visitors so typically we have it all to ourselves. It has huge trees and magnificent views. We go there frequently for picnics and swimming. In order to preserve its unique privacy and incredible beauty, my brother and a group of his friends bought that shoreline for use by anyone who wanted to enjoy it. They donated it to the Province and there is a plaque posted there in their honor.

The year 1972 was also the first summer we had a hot water heater. Suddenly the lonely old bathtub in the cottage bathroom had more use than it could handle. What bliss to climb into a big hot tub of water and relax!

Popular bathtub - Tony, Stephanie
& Corky Chandler with little Aldine
looking on

As I have written elsewhere, in 1973 I took my sons and my parents to Europe so we all were a little later than typical in getting to the cottage. It was that summer — on August 8th — that I met Mary Johnston who would become my brother's second wife. I continue to love and admire her to this day.

An annual event has always been a swim across Dwight Bay—a distance of about a mile. The number of participants varied from year to year but my boys and I always participated—that is, until I hit 50 years of age. Janice is still doing it in her upper 50s.

Aldine's lovely sister in law
Mary Johnston Sinclair

Aldine & Murray Sinclair at
Camp Lake

Another tradition was visiting Ann Sinclair's cabin on Camp Lake. On August 25, 1973, 16 of us traveled in two cars to the landing, launched canoes and carefully paddled our way over to the landlocked cabin on a big lake with only two other cabins—neither of which was ever occupied. It was beautiful Ontario at its best. We spent the day taking boat rides, swimming, and sharing treasured companionship. Mary made wonderful spaghetti. While the rest of us returned to the cottage, Kent, Tony Jr., Murray and Scott remained there for the night. Kent was then 18 and able to be responsible for the younger boys who loved this new-found independence.

In 1974, I had been on an extended trip abroad and didn't reach the cottage until July 28th. When I stepped off the bus I had taken from the Toronto airport to Huntsville, I was overwhelmed to find a huge reception awaiting me—Kent, Tony Jr., Carol, Terry, Stephanie, Aldine, Ted, Murray, Scott, Craig and Mary. They honked horns and blew whistles and made me feel not only very welcome but also a little less guilty for having been away so long. My parents, who had remained at the cottage, had waited up for my arrival and the camaraderie continued. I went to bed at 3:00 a.m. that morning!

As a result of Kent's accident which is chronicled in detail elsewhere in these writings, the summer of 1975 was a blur of doctor visits, seeing Kent in the hospital, and watching over him carefully when he was given a furlough to go to the cottage.

Tony Jr.'s summer remained unaffected except for the distress of Kent's plight. Once again Tony Jr. water skied home behind the power boat from a picnic on Breakfast Rock—a long ski indeed! He also worked hard at the cottage that year painting all the outdoor furniture, the kitchen and the entire living room. There was no chore that Tony disliked more than painting—and he used up 12 gallons of paint! He played a good deal of tennis that year, as well. That is the summer he discovered the joy of reading and could barely be pried from his books.

Family photo - 1975

Kent passed his time at the cottage that summer largely in the company of his adoring cousins who followed him everywhere he went. It was good for him to feel he was contributing and keeping his active young cousins busy and happy. It was very much appreciated by all the family.

My aunt, Ella Mae Walker, who had died in 1970 at age 65, had left the cottage to my mother. That year, 1975, Mother decided to split the property in three parts—one for each of her children. Carol was going to build her own cottage on the property which she did in July of 1976. As Murray already had a lovely cabin on another portion of the property, it was decided that I would inherit the old white cottage. I was ecstatic. Tony arrived earlier than usual that summer—on July 9th—in order to assist with the planning of the separation of the Birch Spring property into three sections. We both were thrilled with the plan.

On August 6th it was time for Kent to leave the cottage to return to St. Michael's Hospital in Toronto. He was in good spirits and ready for what lay ahead. As he had lost 50 pounds over the previous months as a result of his accident and hospitalizations, it was necessary for him to have a new wardrobe. After his surgery and recovery in hospital, I was able to take Kent to a hotel—the Four Seasons Sheraton—for a period of recuperation and follow-up visits with his doctors. Mercifully, the Canadian Immigration came there to provide Kent with his student status papers. Keeping him legally in Canada for so long had become a dicey project but I was conjuring as many strategies as possible to make it work.

Finally on August 15th Kent was permitted to make the trip back to the cottage and his spirits perked up right away. I stayed there for a week to be sure he was settled before I returned to Tucson on August 23rd. I left Kent behind with my loving family who would take good care of him. I was home for the first day of Tony Jr.'s senior year in high school on August 25th and for Tony's 49th birthday on August 26th. And for me it was another year on faculty at the University of Arizona.

I made an early trip to Canada in 1976 as we needed to consult with Kent's physicians. I arrived in Toronto on May 14th and the following day we visited with Dr. John McCullough—Kent's surgeon. He had decided to perform no more surgeries in the foreseeable future. Kent heaved a big sigh of relief! Our first outing was a shopping trip to find the perfect gift for Dr. McCullough—the book *The Himalayas*.

Kent and I proceeded to Montreal on May 18th to meet with lawyers and government officials to deal with the many legal issues concerning workmen's compensation and immigration that had arisen as a result of his accident that had occurred in the Province of Quebec. We conducted our business in mere hours and flew together to Tucson where Tony met us. Shortly thereafter, Tony and I flew to Greece to join Katharine Merritt for the biennial cruise on the Aegean.

I arrived back in Canada on July 5th having had a very unnerving experience. I had flown from Greece to New York City where I was the first passenger to deplane to facilitate my getting through customs as quickly as possible. I was first in line and was asked if I had anything to declare. "No," said I, "not a thing." I had planned this carefully and had mailed the gifts I bought for people. I was asked to open my suitcase. Of course, nothing was found. Finally I was told to open my overnight bag. I kept insisting that there was nothing to declare. They proceeded to go through my bag item by item. People behind me were becoming irate due to the delay. Eventually, after digging through all my possessions, they looked in a container housing my toothbrush. And there, wrapped in a piece of Kleenex, was a little gold cross about which I had completely forgotten. "Ah," said the customs office, "Everybody has <u>something</u> to declare." Lesson learned.

I raced to the departure gate for my flight to Toronto and was told at the ticket counter that I didn't have a seat. They had overbooked the flight. I insisted I had a confirmed ticket but they rejected my pleas. Taking matters into my own hands, I found the plane, entered it, and took my assigned seat. There was not a soul in sight—neither airline hostess nor agent.

Finally the passengers started boarding. Eventually there was only one man walking up and down the aisle, obviously not finding a seat. After he consulted with the hostess, I was approached and told that I was in this man's seat and it was necessary for me to deplane immediately. I stayed my ground. I said I had a confirmed ticket with this seat assignment and I wasn't going to budge. Soon an agent came to reinforce the need for me to get off the plane—now! I refused to leave. Then two burly policemen with batons arrived and said that if I didn't leave of my own accord they were going to have to forcibly remove me.

Forgetting that I was now in the U.S., I told them that if they laid a finger on me I would call the American Embassy. By now, other passengers were aware there was a major problem on-board and were angry that their flight was being delayed. An irate man behind me took my ticket, reviewed it, and loudly announced to everyone within hearing that, "This woman has a confirmed ticket for this seat so let's get the show on the road." The police left. I remained. The other passengers applauded. After take-off, a hostess came to me praising me for having stood my ground. She said that people had been bumped all summer because of flights having been overbooked. She was so proud of me that she brought me a glass of champagne. Quite truthfully, I was shaking like a leaf but knew I was within my rights. When my Uncle Gordon, the newscaster, heard the story he aired it on the radio. He, too, was impressed that I hadn't given in.

The family was there to greet me at the cottage including Kent. He and his friend, Corky Chandler, had driven to the cottage together in my old Ford Galaxy having had four false starts. First the battery died—so they returned to Tucson. Next the transmission went—so they returned to Tucson. Then the alternator broke—so they returned to Tucson. On the fourth try they decided not to stop even for meals and made the trip, with stops for gas only, in 50 hours—surely a world record. They discovered on their arrival that the car tires were shredded! Kent had towed a trailer that contained a new sailboat, a compressor, a bicycle, rugs and chairs. It had also held two other very important items—Tony Jr.s' 6-wheel drive amphibious vehicle and a green 3-wheeler Honda, the first ATV that Honda had ever made. You can imagine the amount of use these received! Another important vehicle at the cottage was Kent's special racing go-cart that went very, very fast. He was somehow able to use it even with his leg propped-up in a cast.

Tony Jr. arrived a day later having missed his plane in Chicago where he had to spend the night. But at last we were all together and ready to enjoy a wonderful summer surrounded by our precious family.

We wasted no time and went for a picnic to Breakfast Rock the next day. It was an emotional experience for me as Kent actually water skied on his new ski. We thought he would never water ski again but he did a magnificent job and was thrilled with his success.

Uncle Murray had a boat—a Chrysler jet V8—abhorred by all on Dwight Bay as it was exceptionally noisy. Not only that, but he terrified unsuspecting passengers with one of his "tricks." He would take the boat to maximum speed, about 60 mph, and head for the cliffs at the entrance to Dwight Bay. Hurtling closer and closer to the cliffs, I am sure his passengers saw their lives flashing in front of them as they anticipated certain death. Mere feet before impact—perhaps 20 feet—Murray would throw the gear into reverse and the boat would stop after a few feet. This was supposed to be a thrill for his passengers but I think the victims of this prank viewed it more as an impending execution. Their anger didn't faze Murray one bit and he kept at this dangerous antic for years to come. I often wondered if Murray ever took into consideration the possibility that the gears might jam at the critical moment.

While I wouldn't allow my sons to be in that boat with Murray, he often lent it to Kent. One day Kent took me on a private ride and pulled Uncle Murray's stunt. It left me shuddering but Kent was excellent with boats having been raised with them, as was his brother Tony Jr.

That year Kent had brought a new catamaran sailboat to the cottage. He loaded it on the roof of the Galaxy in Tucson, still in its original boxes. What he hadn't banked on was rain that would soak the boxes. A good part of that trip was made with wet cardboard hanging down and obscuring the windows! The catamaran provided many years of sailing pleasure. The days were golden.

Tony Jr. sailing, with Murray Jr. on windsurfer

My father was always interested in the weather at the cottage and had his own system for rating each day—from a one to a ten. Tens were few and far between as they required just the right puffiness in the clouds and just the right gentleness to the breeze. Temperature was also a consideration. One such "10" occurred on July 22nd of that year—1976. It was fun to ask my father every day how he had rated it. To this day I still

Sinclair Family Reunion at Caledon, Ontario 1976

The brothers and their wives

record a "10" in my diary, although it doesn't happen often in Ontario!

Another tradition was the biennial Sinclair family reunion. For many years these were held at the homes of the three senior Sinclair brothers and were memorable occasions complete with bagpipes and Scottish fare. The men wore kilts and, no, they did not wear underwear underneath! One of these events was held in Caledon at the home of my Uncle George and his wife Jane on July 17, 1976. My diary records all 33 who were in attendance.

As the brothers grew old and died, the next generation took over and we continued to enjoy each event. I actually hosted the reunion in 1993—the first woman to do so—and the next and last one was shared by my sister and me two years later.

Kent and I had scheduled more meetings with lawyers in Montreal. We drove there on August 10th and spent several days in a hotel. While Kent drove back to the cottage, I flew to Tucson on August 13th where I was enthusiastically met by Tony bearing a dozen red roses. I had been away from Tucson since May 27th! I was back at work at UA on August 16th. It had been a busy summer.

The summer of 1977 started on a high note—a cruise with my parents and sons to visit countries on the Baltic Sea. However, it deteriorated into one of the most traumatic years ever spent at the cottage. There was serious illness and unforgivable betrayal.

While Tony Jr. and I proceeded to the cottage after our return from Europe to Toronto, Kent went back to Tucson to tow his new jet ski north. Having been told that the old white cottage was to be mine, I had spent the winter amassing items that would make the aged dwelling a more attractive and comfortable place—new curtains, rugs, bedspreads and even a new vacuum. I was chomping at the bit to get started on settling "our" new home.

Over the winter I had a big screened-in front porch built and when Tony Jr. and I first saw it we were thrilled. It was just what I had dreamed of—a meeting place big enough to handle a throng of people. In spite of my having ownership of it, the cottage would continue on as it had been—a gathering place for all the family.

Having done battle with a bat my first night there—it even landed on me—I was weary but excited to get started the next morning. We

The old white cottage after Aldine's additions - 1978

happened, however, to arrive during a cold snap and both Tony Jr. and I could even see our breath at breakfast time, and that was with the wood stove going beside us!

Family arrived day after day and soon we were a full house. One unexpected visitor was my beloved minister, Dave Sholin, who had been in New York and decided to visit us. He arrived on June 29th.

I was incredibly excited when I bought my first canoe on June 30th. I named it *Wee Tipsy*. It was indeed a very tippy vessel. I put a 1 ½ hsp motor on it and Dave and I took a happy trip through the sunny, sparkling water of the lake. Tony Jr. took Dave and me sailing later that day.

Aldine at the helm of *Wee Tipsy* with Tony, Carol, Terry & Ted

Our days were full of very difficult work on the cottage— scraping and painting and cleaning out dirty kitchen cupboards. But all of that faded into the background when we suddenly received news that would change our lives forever. My sister Carol had been diagnosed with lung cancer. She was only 39 and had three young children. I was shattered by this news, as was all the family. What serendipity that our pastor for so many years, Dave Sholin, was visiting at the time and could help us through those shattering days. Carol had adored Dave since she was a young girl.

Carol was brave indeed while waiting for the day of her surgery. On July 3rd, 15 of us went on a picnic to Breakfast Rock and she enjoyed herself thoroughly.

My father was having a difficult time dealing with Carol's illness. Suddenly he himself became very ill. On Sunday, July 10th, Kent drove my parents to the hospital in Toronto and my father was taken for immediate emergency surgery. He had a gallbladder removed that was the size of a football and ready to burst. He came through it well, but was in and out of hospital with associated complications for the rest of the summer.

The surgery to remove Carol's right lung was performed two days later in the same hospital—North York. Kent had remained in Toronto to support my mother who remained strong for her husband and daughter. The entire family was devastated by these catastrophic events. We were filled with fear and concern. I was worried about

Kent, too, because, as I wrote in my diary "he feels things deeply but doesn't let them out."

Tony Sr. & Aldine sailing on
Dwight Bay with Terry Belsham

My job was to take care of Carol's children and keep the home fires burning. The boys and I continued to rework the plumbing, install a new toilet, and upgrade the electrical systems. They even made flower boxes to hang on the new front porch. I painted the porch and continued to scrub and clean and cook for the whole family. I was enormously relieved when my husband Tony arrived on July 14th. I needed him there, and so did his sons.

July 23rd was a red letter day. Carol had been released from hospital and came immediately to the cottage. She looked drawn but was upbeat. I was so proud of her. Also, that was the day we raised the new 50-foot flagpole Tony Jr. had built. It was a beauty and very tall. In honor of Carol's return, we had a little ceremony and hoisted the Canadian and the Scottish flags.

Dad, however, was still in hospital and very depressed. He was not healing well.

On July 25th I finished painting the bathroom—yellow—and was exhausted when I received shocking news that would forever change the summers ahead. The legal papers naming me as the new owner of the cottage had never been filed. It was not mine at all. The signed papers had been given to Murray to deliver to a lawyer in Toronto. He chose not to do so. He wanted the cottage for himself. I was bereft.

After three weeks in hospital, Mother brought Dad home on July 30th. Both Carol and he were incredibly pale and weak but the Sinclair spirit carried them through, and they both made full recoveries. As my diary reported, "They have spunk."

By now, my husband Tony had had it! He wanted to return to Tucson as quickly as possible. He had poured blood, sweat and tears into "our" new cottage, and suddenly the rug had been pulled out from under him. He was fed-up with my family. We flew together to Tucson on August 1st, leaving Kent and Tony Jr. behind. At ages 22 and 19 we knew they would be a great help at the cottage taking care of their grandparents and Carol's children.

Dad & Carol recovering from
surgery - 1977

I, too, must have had spunk. Over the winter, it was decided that Murray and I would share in the ownership of the old white cottage. I concluded that something was better than nothing, and, not wanting to deny my sons a summer with their extended family, I flew to Toronto with Kent and Janice on July 13, 1978. This was only one day ahead of the arrival of my German friend, Peter Marquardt. Tony Jr. had been at the cottage for several weeks.

I noted in my diary that my brother Murray was in residence at his cabin "but I hope never to see him again." Kent was thrilled that Janice's reaction to the cottage was so positive and they had a wonderful summer together. It was the first time both my friend Peter and Janice had ever water skied! The annual swimming of Dwight Bay took place on July 18th with Tony Jr. coming in first while I came in last!

I was sad that summer as evidenced by the notation in my diary that "I feel I do not belong here at the cottage and if it weren't for the boys I'd leave immediately. I have no guns to fight with so I must surrender."

The Sinclair family reunion was held at our cottage—Birch Spring—that year, 1978. There were 36 in attendance as well as a bagpiper and even a newspaper reporter. This event was getting coverage!

Ray Hickok was a bright spot in my life that summer. He was charming and attentive and we spent a great deal of time playing tennis together. But for me the summer couldn't end soon enough. I returned to Tucson on August 8th leaving Kent, Janice and Tony Jr. at the cottage to be of help to the family. I had an enjoyable flight sitting beside a man—Bunny—who was the world's yo-yo champion. He impressed the passengers with a performance using me as his assistant! Tony met me in Tucson and it was a great relief to be home with him.

I returned to work at UA on August 24th with 14 full-time master's degree students—each of whom I would have to supervise in an internship. Fortunately, I was assigned a tack-sharp graduate assistant, Mary Von Seggern Davis. I dove into my work and put behind me the sharp edges of life at the cottage.

In 1979 I started the summer by going to Denmark alone, about which I write in another chapter. To celebrate my parents' 50th wedding anniversary, I later joined them, Mary and Murray, and Carol and Terry for a North Cape cruise. We returned to Toronto on June 22nd to honor my parents at a huge party with all their friends from years ago. Without having gone to the cottage, I returned to Tucson on June 28th. Kent and Tony Jr. left for the cottage on July 2nd. My mother, Janice, her brother—Sam Angevine—and I flew to Toronto and drove to the cottage on July 12th.

This was the beginning of our last summer at Birch Spring. The animosity between my brother and me was palpable. Murray had become hostile toward me, and even toward Kent and Tony Jr. whom he had always adored. When Uncle Murray started cutting down trees that they had used and loved since childhood—one from which they hung a rope ladder and another where they always had a "tire" swing—they knew they were no longer welcome. They told me they wanted to go home. We looked for other cottages in the area that we might consider buying. Nothing in our price range was available.

On August 18th, Kent, Janice, Tony Jr., Sam Angevine and I returned to Tucson never to live at Birch Spring again. As my diary noted, "What a lack of balance there is in this family." That was putting it mildly.

My parents concluded that Murray should inherit the cottage and suggested he give me $40,000 in lieu of any claim I had on Birch Spring. It took months before I received it but it enabled me to consider buying another cottage. On September 28th, Tony and I flew to Toronto where Carol and Terry met us and drove us to their cottage in Dwight. We had several days to search for a new place but we were unsuccessful. There was nothing for sale in that area.

Another idea germinated; we thought perhaps we could build a modular home on the hill behind the old white cottage. We met with the ministry of environment and had their approval to build a septic tank there. Granted, the "cottage" would be way up on a hillside across the road from Birch Spring and we would have no water rights, but we would have our own place and be near the family in the summer. We were excited about this possibility and presented it to my father. He scotched it immediately saying there would be no modular home built on the property.

We returned to Tucson somewhat discouraged and were taken quite by surprise when we received a phone call from my old friend, Alastair Souter. He had bought a third of Charlie Thompson's island, built a permanent home there for his wife, Monta, and their four children and then found that he could not afford it. He had heard that I was in the market for a cottage on Lake of Bays and his was for sale. We struck a bargain on the phone and by the summer of 1980 we were the happy new owners of a cottage of our own. We all were ecstatic. Our new life on Rat Bay—one bay west of Dwight Bay—was soon to begin and we were about to embark on our happiest summers of all on Lake of Bays.

1980—2000   OUR YEARS AT PELICAN POINT

We were ecstatic about having our own cottage. We had bought it sight unseen in January of 1980 and were anticipating with great enthusiasm our arrival there on May 19th.   Having envisioned a beautiful country cabin ready and waiting for my family, we were sadly disappointed with the reality. What we found was

Kent, Tony, Aldine & Tony Jr. - 1980

merely the shell of a cottage. The living room and kitchen were complete—albeit with bulbs hanging from the ceilings rather than fixtures and with brown carpet stained green from years of dogs having lived there.

The upstairs bedrooms had only insulation in the walls, and the downstairs was nothing more than an enormous concrete wasteland with two jacks that supported the floor above. My heart sank.

It has to be said, however, that it was a beautiful piece of property, a third of an island on which there was only our cottage. The island was connected by a causeway to the mainland. Ultimately the other two cottages were built but they were quite isolated one from the other. And, we had the luxury of 555 feet of shoreline.

Kent and Tony Jr., with the help of their friend Sam Angevine put their noses to the grindstone and by summer's end we had a gracious and comfortable cottage on "our" island that continues to bring us joy summer after summer. It is still a work in progress and gets lovelier year by year.

Upstairs the boys put paneling on the walls and doors on the closets.   They stained and painted. Downstairs they chalked potential walls on the concrete floor for me to approve. The walls went up, the ceiling housed over 500 feet of conduit for electricity, and the carpet was laid.   The boys had worked their hearts out. Tony put a fireplace in our

Mother & Tony Jr. at our new cottage - Pelican Point 1980

downstairs bedroom and surrounded it with a rock wall built with rocks he found on our property.

Kent, Janice, Sarah Winkler & Tony Jr.
Pelican Point - 1980

There was still time for fun. Janice arrived to visit Kent and a lovely girlfriend of Tony Jr.—Sarah Winkler—came from Tucson to spend time with him. We had jet skis, water skis, a paddle boat, sailboats and our faithful tin boat—*Fare Thee Well*. We also had a power boat. We had a rope tied to a birch tree on our hill and a favorite activity was swinging way out into the lake and letting go. There was another rope swing as well that wasn't quite as challenging. And always there was the hammock which drew all ages for moments of solitude. We all played tennis and volleyball and spent hours on the dock, on our beach and in the lake.

Janice continued our ongoing tradition— swimming across Dwight Bay. The event started at my brother's dock and ended on a beach over a mile away. As the years went by, all ages participated; I discontinued my participation when I was in my late 40s. My nephew Scott was an incredible athlete. One year as we were diving into the water for the long swim, he sauntered down from his dad's cottage to ask us what we were doing. Now it has to be mentioned that Scott was pretty drunk at the time. Nonetheless a few minutes later

The rope swing - 1995

he had dived in the lake to join us, caught up with us, and was waiting at the finishing point long before any of us reached it!

My parents spent their summers in the old white cottage at Dwight Bay until my father's death in 1984 after which my mother managed being there on her own. She spent her last summer there in 1994, only months before she died.

There were parties galore that often went on until four and five o'clock in the morning. Tony Jr. played a lot of tennis with Ray Hickok that summer and all of us indulged in "daiquiri doubles" tennis games as well as "daiquiri dinghies" sailboat races.

Murray hosted the family reunion that year—1980—at the old cottage and had arranged for a steamboat to take everyone on rides. All three of the old brothers—Murray, Gordon and George—were there and got along remarkably well, which had not always been the case.

We noticed that summer that Janice and Kent spent a great deal of time at Ann Sinclair's isolated cabin on Camp Lake. Romance was in the air. On August 4th, Ray Hickok introduced Tony Jr. to one of his great heroes—Al Rockwell, who was the owner of Rockwell International that built the space shuttle. What a thrill for Tony Jr.

Kent, Tony, Aldine & Tony Jr. - 1980

<u>1981</u> It wasn't until the following year that we were ready to give our cottage a name—a tradition in Canada. Tony Jr. had dumped loads of soil into the lake until our shoreline

Aerial view of Pelican Point

met with an old oak stump in the lake. He then put flagstones down creating a lovely point from which we can see down our bay—Rat Bay—and out to the main channel of Lake of Bays. And into this big oak stump at the end of the new point he placed a post in which he inserted a metal sculpture of a pelican! There is nary a pelican for hundreds of miles from our cottage, but this whimsical pelican weathervane that Tony had welded was simply perfect for the spot and resulted in our naming our cottage Pelican Point. We had a little ceremony to christen the point on May 20th.

On July 5th, our dear friends Misty and Gary Grynkewich and their baby Julia came for a visit. They entered into the activities with genuine enthusiasm.

I did a great deal of sailing that year and entered a sailing competition on Dwight Bay with eight boats registered. To my amazement, I won. There was a proper awards ceremony, much of it tongue in cheek, and I received a gold medal!

Tony & Aldine on a "booze cruise" in
Tender Behind - 1982

1982 Tony Jr. and I arrived at the cottage on May 17th to find that the entire deck around our upper level had collapsed. Our handyman, Percy Clark, had shoveled snow off the roof during the winter as we had asked him to do. However, he had pitched it onto the deck below and, over time, the deck could not sustain the weight and simply disconnected from the building and slid down the hill.

Prior to leaving the cottage the previous fall, we had thought that beneath the deck would be an excellent place to store the boats as we did not have a boathouse at that time. What a mistake that had been! The carnage was devastating, but ultimately all the boats were restored. We made sure the next deck was well anchored!

We took our first swim that summer on May 27th. The lake temperature was 61 degrees. Brrrr.

Tony Jr. & Sarah Finley playing
tennis at the Ruscica's

In 1982, Sarah Finley, a delightful young lady, came to visit Tony Jr. A neighbor from Tucson whom we adored—Lilli Brandt—came for a week and Tony Jr. led us all to Lost Lake. Since my childhood, a trek to find Lost Lake has been an annual event. Some years we find it; some we do not. Tony Jr. has a knack for locating it. Everyone was thrilled. It is beautifully situated atop high cliffs and one can find pitcher plants there that actually trap flies and devour them.

The following day Kent, Janice and Sam arrived. We sadly said goodbye to Tony Jr. and Sarah on June 15th as Tony Jr. was soon to begin his job at Hughes Aircraft Company and had to get back to Tucson to pack and move to Los Angeles. His first day on the job was June 29th.

Kent left soon thereafter to resume his studies at Brooks Institute of Photography in Santa Barbara.

Tony and I were on our own now. One evening we had an out-of-this-world experience. We had

Kent & Janice - 1982

gone to Huntsville to see the much touted film *ET*. It was dark when we returned to the cottage and we decided to take a last swim before bed. Suddenly the sky around us was on fire flashing red, orange, green—every color of the rainbow. It was visually overwhelming and actually quite frightening. Having just seen the science fiction movie, we felt somehow that we had entered a new realm. In fact, it was the Aurora Borealis as we had never seen it. These northern lights are rarely seen from our cottage but on this evening it was as if we were enmeshed in a firestorm.

Another of our adventures was a trip to Camp Lake, about which I have written elsewhere, for a several day visit. We took our canoe *Wee Tipsy* with a 1.2 horsepower Neptune Mighty Mite gas-powered engine on it. What an idyllic little getaway!

The summer was marred by the dreadful car accident of my nephew, Scott Sinclair. How he survived remains a mystery. He had been partying with friends at a nearby resort, decided to leave and en route home lost control of his car. It was literally wrapped around a tree and he was stretched out between the front and backseat mushed up against the car's roof. His recovery took a long time but somehow he overcame all his injuries and is now the happy father of two young boys. Prayer must have been a major part of the miracle of his survival.

Tender Behind under sail

1983 Each summer was similar in activities but had its own special excitement. As I was on the faculty at UA, I had only 2 ½ months at the cottage but made the most of every moment. We raised a magnificent flagpole with a cross staff from which flew the Canadian and U.S. flags as well as the Ontario and Arizona flags.

Another tradition was tea with a delightful British couple across our bay—Marge and Geoff Alexander, sister and brother. Weekly we would get together, alternating cottages. On our first visit to their place we noticed they had enormous floor-mounted binoculars—trained right on our property. Suddenly we guessed that our nude swims were not as private as we had thought! They were an older couple, and very proper. I think the names of our boats shocked them—*Wet Dream* and *Tender Behind*—but secretly I think they enjoyed all the "scurrilous" activities at Pelican Point.

On one occasion, rather raucous friends of ours dropped by for a visit. We knew that the Alexanders' binoculars would be trained on our beach for their four o'clock tea time. Hence, when our friends asked if they could go down to the beach for a swim they were forewarned that they had to wear bathing suits and behave themselves. As they appeared to have had a snootful, Tony and I decided to walk down to the lake, with our puppy—Stacy—to check on the demeanor of our guests. Well, as we approached the beach we could see that they were not only naked but *mooning* our staid friends across the bay. Tony turned to our pup and said, "Well, Stacy, you have just seen your first beaver."

Another weekly tradition was attending Stewart Memorial Church every Sunday. It has been a part of our cottage life since I was a small child.

The cottage is also a repository for photographs—some taken over a hundred years ago. They chronicle our family history and I have counted over 300 framed pictures on the walls. They are a priceless record.

Tony Jr. with his model
sailboat - 1987

Tony and Tony Jr. had built radio-controlled sailboats in Tucson that were four feet long with six foot masts. They were very beautiful, sleek crafts scaled down from 12 meter sailboats that would have been 36 to 38 feet. The 15 pounds of lead in the keel kept them well balanced. Tony Jr. remembers well when he took his to the cottage. First it had to go on the airplane. Then, along with his other baggage, he had to get it on a bus to take to the subway in Toronto to get to the train going north to Huntsville. The mast was proving to be almost impossible to deal with. He was truly challenged to get the loading and unloading coordinated. When he finally arrived at the cottage with it, unscathed, he breathed an enormous sigh of relief.

On August 6th my parents hosted the Sinclair family reunion at the old white cottage. It was, according to my diary, a "tremendous" success and well attended. In addition to water skiing and other lake sports, Tony and Tony Jr. had sailboat races with their radio-controlled vessels. The betting stakes were high and great excitement was generated by these events.

<u>1984</u> Tony left for the cottage the day following Janice and Kent's wedding at St. Mark's Presbyterian Church On May 19th. As he had retired, he could make his own schedule. I, however, could not and would not leave Tucson as my father was dying and my heart was breaking.

As he was in Tucson Medical Center (TMC), Dad could not attend the church ceremony but very much wanted to be a part of the wedding festivities. Janice and Kent arranged for the wedding party and all the visiting relatives to gather at TMC to have a photograph taken with my father. As sick as he was, he dressed for the occasion and was ready in a wheelchair in the garden at TMC when all the wedding party arrived. It included many of his grandchildren who had come from far and wide. Those were the last photographs we have of my father as he died shortly thereafter on June 1st at age 79. Uncle Gordon had died three weeks before.

As Dad neared death, I slept in the waiting room at TMC night after night to be sure there was someone close by for my father. The chairs were incredibly uncomfortable but I must have fallen asleep as in the morning I would find that the staff had covered me with a blanket. My mother took the day shifts.

Our grief at his passing was palpable. We all had adored—even worshipped—my father. His marriage to my mother had truly been a love affair and she was inconsolable. I never left her side and we departed together for the cottage on June 21st—the two puppies we had purchased after Dad's death in tow. Mom had decided she did not want to stay at the old cottage as she would not be able to handle the memories. She stayed with Tony and me.

On July 6th, my father was buried at Mount Pleasant Cemetery in Toronto with our Tucson minister—Dr. Paul David Sholin (Dave)—officiating. According to my diary, "It is a rainy, foggy Scottish day. Not ideal for those in attendance—but appropriate for saying farewell to Dad. How I've loved him and how I'll miss him."

Dave returned to the cottage with us and Mother decided it was time she moved into her own place. In no time, Carol and I had it shipshape for her and helped her move into her old white cottage. On July 17th mother had all the family for dinner, including friends of hers who were visiting, and the meal she produced was delicious. As my diary noted, "Never have I known anyone like my mother—her acceptance, her courage, her dignity."

Tony Jr. had only one week at the cottage that year but he made the most of it. He sailed the radio-controlled boats with his father and sailed in his two sailboats. On July 28th he, his father and I took rides in an ultralight that was parked on Dwight Beach and available for hire. What a different experience it was to see Lake of Bays from 1500 feet above the water.

The following day we had a rare treat—attending a dinner party on a steamboat that belonged to a neighbor—Sandy Thompson—on Rat Bay. His hobby was restoring the old vessel to its original splendor. He could rarely take it out on the lake as it required a licensed captain to sail it, and Sandy did not qualify. That night, the *Wanda III*, was outfitted to perfection with lace tablecloths, Waterford glasses and subtle lighting.

<u>1985</u> Mother had returned to her old cottage and people continued to drop by to see her every day as she was such an appealing person to talk to. I had several visitors at Pelican Point one of whom was Joe Green with whom I always had a love-hate relationship. What a week we had!

Joe had flown from Madison, Wisconsin to Toronto and had taken the bus north to Huntsville where I met him in my old Oldsmobile. There was a heavy rainfall and the passenger's side windshield wiper did not work. Mine did, fortunately. There was Joe on his first visit to this region totally disoriented by the driving rain and no visibility. He was a little undone by the time we reached the cottage.

Eventually, the rain stopped and I suggested that we go for a boat ride in *Fare Thee Well*, an aluminum boat. It sounded all right to Joe so off we went to explore our end of the lake. But what was that black cloud pursuing us? Rain! Suddenly the heavens opened, thunder boomed and lightning struck—very close to us. And here we were out on the water in a metal boat just asking to be incinerated. I opened the throttle wide and headed for home. We learned later that people in their cottages looking out on the lake were saying, "Go, Aldine, go!" All were relieved we made it home safely but no one more than Joe who was shaken to the core.

Mother was staying with me and after drinks and dinner our dogs, Jock and Angus, took an evening walk as they usually did. They always came home, only this night they both had porcupine quills in their mouths and on their lips. They were frantic. So was I. Reminding Joe that he was a doctor, I said we could handle it. What a nightmare! I held each dog down while Joe used pliers to extract the quills, one by one. I am sure by now Joe was quite ready to go home. But this was just the beginning.

After breakfast the next morning, Mother moved back to the old white cottage but invited Joe and me for drinks that night. When Joe and I prepared to leave for the evening we found that my car wouldn't start. The battery was dead! Not a problem, said I. I have a spare battery down in the workshop. Now Joe was no mechanic but he was confident he could replace a battery. And he did. What neither of us knew was that this was a marine battery with connection posts on top. We managed to make it to Charlie Thompson Road before the engine caught fire. The positive post was touching the hood of the car causing a short circuit which resulted in a fire. Smoke was spewing out and Joe and I, again in terror that we were about to be incinerated, leapt from the car. Somehow I raised the hood and used a fire extinguisher to put out the flames. Now, this was before the advent of cell phones, so there we were.

We returned to the cottage by foot and phoned my mother who came to our rescue. Leaving my car there, off we went to Mom's and I am sure we got properly smashed that evening. The car was ultimately repaired and returned to me by Slim's Garage.

Nothing else could go wrong, could it? Oh, yes! It rained and thundered again the next day and Joe and I were perfectly prepared for a peaceful afternoon reading when we discovered the septic tank had backed up. Not pleasant! We called a plumber who dug a huge hole in the ground finally discovering the location of the tank. That is when he stopped to think things over and said he'd return the next day.

That night mother and I made a wonderful dinner at the old white cottage and included Mary and Murray and their five wonderful children.

It continued to rain and the septic tank area was a muddy mess. I wrote in my diary, "A truly frustrating day. Almost made me sick of cottage life. No plumbing! Joe and I had to use the woods!" We had invited people for drinks and I made sensational Ramos Gin fizzes and had to send our guests outside for potty purposes.

Joe was very nervous about the huge and very deep hole outside and took it upon himself to string rope around it for safety. Days later it was repaired; it had been a clogged baffle. Joe was ready to leave. It was years before he came for another visit!

Both Tonys arrived on July 13th that year—1985. Five days later Tony Jr.'s "guest of the summer"—Molly Thomas—arrived for a visit. She was another lovely young lady.

There was an unexpected family reunion at the celebration of life for Jane Sinclair, George's wife, who had died of cancer on July 19th. It was held in Caledon at the home of my charming Uncle George who carried it off to perfection.

The scheduled family reunion that year was held on the weekend of August 3rd by my cousin Gordon and his lovely wife Linda at their home on the Lake of Two Mountains in Quebec.

1986   In the spring of 1986, Tony's cancer—mesothelioma—had been discovered. Nonetheless, we headed for the cottage on May 1st. Although he was in constant pain, we spent a delightful month there by ourselves before he had to return to Tucson to check in with his job—one that he loved at UA—and with his doctors.

Tony Jr. arrived on July 19th for his two-week vacation. It was good to have him to myself before the arrival of Kent, Janice and Sam on the 22nd followed by Tony on the 26th. I had my whole family together at last. Tony's medical reports had been good and he was ready for a happy time.

The founders of RBYC - Treacy, Tony, Aldine and Bob
with Bruce and Linda below

Tony and I were founding members of the Rat Bay Yacht Club (RBYC). Initially there were only three couples—Linda and Bruce Davey, Treacy and Bob Canavan and ourselves. What crazy times we had. At one of our early meetings we had decided to have a "murder" night—a game where everyone is assigned ahead of time a part in a mystery evening where each acted his role from beginning to end. We all took it quite seriously, especially Tony who was determined to play his part as the "roué" to perfection. He was clad in white with a cap and scarf and looked dapper indeed, but he felt something was missing. In order to complete the picture he took a sock to the beach, filled it with sand and hung it down his leg on the inside of his pants. It truly was impressive and was the finishing touch to his convincing costume.

We hadn't taken into account that none of us knew each other very well so that when we arrived at the Canavan's for the party all eyes descended to Tony's groin area. Mouths dropped open. Seeing their disbelieving eyes, he quickly assured them it was part of his costume. I think they were disappointed!

RBYC grew to include family members—and Dorothy Thompson as an honorary member. We had serious nautical competitions such as a parade of all our boats decorated to the max. It was quite amazing; each was colorful and unique. Where we amassed so many boats I can't imagine! One year, 1994, we had our minister, Susan Manning, in full regalia stand at the end

Aldine in *Wee Tipsy* at RBYC "float parade" Tony
in *Wet Dream* - 1994

of the Canavans' dock for the "blessing of the fleet." Each boat was floated by for her to anoint.

Our uniform was required at meetings—Eddie Bauer tee shirts, red and white striped, and white pants or shorts. We had our own burgee and stationery and were legitimate members of the Ontario Sailing Club and the Canadian Yachting Association which gave us international privileges! Annually we had a change of command dinner with the passing of the emblem to the new commodore. In 1986 the meeting was held at the Davey cottage with just the six of us plus Kent and Tony Jr.

One story that is hardly believable took place in 1989, the summer following Tony's death. The annual dinner was at our cottage and Kent had taken over as commodore. He began the meeting on our deck outside with the request that all heads bow as we remembered our fallen leader—Tony. Now this was back when there was neither a road nor cottages across the bay—only woods. Suddenly, at the moment our heads were bowed, we heard *Taps* being played on a bugle. It was played hauntingly once only and came from across the bay. No one had set this up. It was a miracle that happened. My sons were there to witness that amazing inexplicable moment.

As the original members of RBYC died off, the group disintegrated until only Linda Davey and I remained. But the memories that we accrued will live on.

And memories abound as we recall the Ruscica family parties each year at their magnificent cottage at Dwight Bay. They were always lively and frequently raucous in the extreme. All ages were represented and each participated enthusiastically. One always needed to have a "party piece" at the ready as many of their gatherings required guests to sing a song, recite a ditty or play a musical instrument. The dancing afterwards went on into the wee hours of the morning.

That year, 1986, is also notable as it was on August 5th that Katharine Merritt died at age 100 and ½ years old. We knew that ½ year was important to her as it meant she had outlived her father by several months, a goal she had often mentioned.

Tony and I returned to Tucson on August 14th in time for me to be at the doctoral defense of one of my favorite students, Beth Lasky, with whom I remain in touch. She passed with flying colors and became Dr. Lasky.

<u>1987</u> Still able to travel, Tony left for the cottage early and I joined him in mid-May. He had never been to the Canadian Maritime provinces, a trip that had been on his bucket list. On June 1st we left the cottage to spend a beautiful week together motoring through Quebec, New Brunswick and by ferry to Prince Edward Island. Years later, a bridge was built to access the island. We visited Johanna Plaut's sister—Gertrude Partridge—at her bed and breakfast there. On we went to Nova Scotia where we thoroughly enjoyed the Fisherman's Museum in Lunenburg.

The following day we took a ferry from Yarmouth to Bar Harbor, Maine and wended our way back to the cottage traveling through Vermont, Quebec and eastern Ontario. It was a lovely trip with Tony doing all the driving.

Aldine windsurfing - 1987

That summer we took up wind surfing. It was a short-lived hobby.

Tony left on July 12th to return to his job in Tucson and to see his doctors. Tony Jr. arrived on July 25th and used his vacation well. He jet skied, water skied and did a tremendous number of jobs around the cottage—painted 10 outdoor chairs, cut down trees and moved rocks in preparation for a boat house that would be built over the winter.

On July 19th, we all were waiting for a phone call from Tony who had had a CT scan. When the results came we were devastated. The cancer was back. I was beside myself with grief. On July 31st my diary said, "I was practically non-functional today waiting for Tony's call. He saw the oncologist and it is mesothelioma and he will start chemotherapy a week from Monday. He is in good spirits. I am in shock."

Tony insisted that we continue with our summer plans. Tony Jr. handled his sadness by moving 15,000 pounds of rocks to strengthen the shoreline. The following day he drove to Toronto to meet a delightful young lady at the airport—Liz McIntire, soon to become Elizabeth von Isser. Over the years, his father had been highly impressed with each of Tony's lady friends who visited. In spite of his father's urging each time that "she was ideal for him," Tony Jr. held out for perfection. This time he found it!

Al Marshick was visiting us at the time as well. Our relationship was another one of those love/hate situations and I must say I was feeling the latter rather strongly when Al took off one day in our boat, *Fare thee Well*, for four hours. I was frantically worried about him but he was just off seeing the lake. Now I was as furious as only Al could make me!

Leaving Tony Jr. and Liz behind at the cottage, a young friend drove my mother, Al and me, along with three dogs, to Toronto for the return trip to Tucson on August 7th. It fell to me each year to assemble and disassemble the dog cages at the airport and I was practically apoplectic when I finally achieved this task in the crowded Toronto airport. Tony and Kent met us in Tucson with two vehicles and we managed to get everything and everyone safely home. Liz and Tony Jr. returned two days later.

The next day was the first of three days of Tony's chemotherapy—vinzolodine which made him feel crummy. He didn't sleep well, was hot and sweaty, weak and bled easily. My diary described it as "hell." A new and heartbreaking chapter of our lives began.

<u>1988</u> at the cottage was both agony and ecstasy— a year of endings and beginnings. It would be Tony's last summer at the cottage. It was the summer of Tony and Elizabeth's wedding and the visit of our first grandchild, Tana Jay von Isser, the daughter of Janice and Kent, born on May 2nd.

The von Isser family with dogs Gus and Stacy - 1988

The summer began with my illness. I seemed unable to handle the enormous stress of the past year, which included being department head at UA, as well as Tony's terminal illness. Within a week of our arrival on May 13th, I had a devastating attack of atrial fibrillation which required hospitalization in Huntsville and electro-cardioversion. I was warned that the next such episode could kill me. Tony was now in a position of having to take care of me, and he did it thoughtfully and graciously.

But there was a full summer ahead and I knew I had to rally quickly. A delightful surprise occurred on my 55th birthday—May 29th. Linda and Bruce Davey picked us up in their car on which there was a huge placard—"Aldine Baby's Limo Service." They took us to my favorite restaurant for dinner—The Norsemen.

The cottage was a hive of activity. The new boathouse was being completed. The cottage was being painted. I was, after all, preparing for a wedding! And then I found that I was covered with a dreadful rash. Several trips to doctors in Huntsville determined that it was a reaction to my new heart medication.

And then Tony became very ill. In the middle of the night he was in great pain and could barely breathe. The symptoms frightened both of us. When he inhaled, he had pain and pressure in his ears, jaw and left shoulder. We called doctors in both Tucson and Huntsville and with a great deal of pain medication the symptoms abated.

On July 11th Tony Jr. and my mother arrived. I was delirious with joy. Tony Jr. had come for only one week in order to take care of cottage projects that he wanted to finish before his wedding. He went right to work wiring the boathouse and the bunkie–the little cabin where he and Elizabeth would spend their honeymoon! Another big project was taking apart our old dock which no longer served any purpose. After totally reorganizing our workshop, he packed and returned to Tucson.

The emotional strain of Tony's illness, our busy social life, and preparing for the wedding caused another serious bout of atrial fibrillation. I was put in intensive care in the hospital in Huntsville. More heart medication plus a tranquilizer. Eventually, I converted to a normal rhythm and was allowed to go home.

Elizabeth & Tony with their Sikula relatives

Two days later Elizabeth and Tony Jr. arrived. What excitement! As Tony was too ill to attend a wedding elsewhere, they had brought their wedding to us. How very kind of them both. We had been planning it for months and every detail had been addressed. On July 21st people started arriving. We were thrilled to see Janice, Kent and adorable Tana who

was only 2 ½ months old. The same day friends of Elizabeth and Tony's from Tucson arrived and the following day Elizabeth's parents and her siblings— three sisters (her one brother was unable to attend)—and their children arrived as well as other family members. Everyone was staying either at our place or at the old white cottage.

That night we had a big rehearsal dinner at our cottage with about 30 in attendance. I did all the cooking!

The wedding day arrived—July 23, 1988—and it was, quite literally, a dream come true. Elizabeth

Elizabeth & Tony on their wedding day - Stewart Memorial Church - July 23, 1988

and Tony Jr. were married in the little Dwight church and, as they wanted, the reception was held under a canopy at the old white cottage. We all walked to the church, and back—even Tony. The weather was perfect, and there were the traditional bagpipes.

About 75 people were in attendance and my brother put on a fireworks display worthy of the event.

Off on their "honeymoon" on Tony's 1966 Trail 90 motorbike

The bride and groom departed the reception on Tony Jr.'s old motorbike trailing tin cans and a "just married" sign. Their "honeymoon suite" was our bunkie, which still had bunk beds in it!

The next day was rainy and all of Elizabeth's family departed. Elizabeth and Tony Jr.'s friends stayed on for a few days.

On July 27th there was a dreadful accident on Dwight Bay. Four young men, drunk from having been at a party, raced across the bay in the dark of night heading for the bay's exit at the end of some cliffs. At full speed, they hit the rocks and three of the young men died. The driver survived and spent a good deal of time in prison. The imprint of the boat was visible on the cliffs for many years.

Kent had to return to work in Tucson after just a week at the cottage, but Janice and Tana stayed on. What a joy for me! On July 30th Mary had an incredible party for herself at the Hickok camp with 110 guests for dinner to celebrate her 40th birthday.

The following day Elizabeth and Tony left to return to Tucson and their jobs but they indeed had a memorable wedding.

With the big push of the wedding behind him, Tony's health started to deteriorate rapidly. His tumors were getting huge—he could no longer button his shirts—and he was in terrible pain and couldn't breathe well. Everyone had left by August 5th and Tony was so relieved to have the cottage to ourselves.

While we continued to see friends and get out as much as possible, Tony was no longer able to eat and grew thinner each day. I thought it would be his choice to die at the cottage and was surprised one day when he said it was time to go home. I knew he meant to go home to die. We left the cottage on October 12th having been at Pelican Point for five months. I was so glad I was able to be with Tony every day of that time.

Tony loved his job as Employee Relations Director at UA and continued to go to work sporadically throughout the fall. We had our last Christmas as a family and he died on January 8, 1989.

<u>1989</u> A widow at age 55! I knew life would never be the same for me without my Tony. As I was on leave of absence from UA I was able to depart for the cottage on May 11th. I was lonely there but I had hundreds of letters to write to thank people for their thoughtfulness at the time of Tony's death.

Mary decided I needed a reprieve from my isolation and invited me to Toronto to see *Les Miserables* and to spend the night with them. It seemed like a lot of effort but I did it. First, my dog had to be taken to friends to "dog sit" for me. I phoned a restaurant in Huntsville to ask if I might park my car there for the days I was away since it was close enough to the train station for me to walk to it. Mary met me at the impressive Union Station in Toronto. Following a lovely dinner, Mary, Murray, Margaret Ruscica and I went to the theater. We were seated front row center—a perfect location. I was eye to eye with the actors and felt as if I was right on stage with them. It was magical. Suddenly Margaret gave me a nudge and whispered that we had to leave. I was incredulous. Another poke and I knew she meant it. The four of us had to file out, with the inevitable disruption to the actors and the audience, to return to the lobby. What was going on?

It seems that Mary had grabbed tickets that she had purchased for a fall performance they were to attend instead of the tickets for that night. Alas. There were no extra seats. So home we went and I reversed my procedure returning to the cottage—terribly disappointed to have gone to all that trouble for naught. The dog was glad to see me!

Cabin fever had set in by June 9th and I took the opportunity to visit Dr. Robert Blackwell at his home in Santa Cruz, California. I had met him on a cruise in the spring. While it was a long trip, he kept his word and had me seen by several specialists regarding a maimed right foot as a result of surgery. A dividend was that I became familiar with an area of California hitherto unknown to me. Bob's house was on the edge of a golf course and he pampered me for the week I was there.

En route back to the cottage, I met my mother in Chicago so that we could take the flight to Toronto together. I was able, therefore, to help her get her dog through customs and disassemble his cage. Mary met us with my car and we drove north.

I had many guests visit that summer and all were a welcome diversion from my loneliness. The week of June 26th my family arrived—first Kent, Janice, and Tana, accompanied by their dog Zack as well as Tony Jr.'s dog Gus. Later in the week Elizabeth and Tony arrived. Having all my family with me had me in a state of euphoria.

That year, family members of the original RBYC members were inducted into membership and I was elected the new commodore. The meeting was held at the Davey's cottage.

My sons were incredibly helpful in taking care of chores I couldn't handle, including the digging of the grave for Tony's ashes at the Dwight cemetery behind Stewart Memorial Church. I have described the burial on July 6th in the section "Rocks and Shoals." Tony had requested a festive wake in his memory and that we did the following night at our cottage. It was a magnificent dinner party for 72 people on our lawn. The theme was "red, white and blue" and 150 helium balloons in those colors were sent aloft. A poem written by Margaret Ruscica (Appendix 7) was at each place setting and toasts were made in Tony's honor. My brother Murray rounded out the occasion with a magnificent display of fireworks. Tony would have loved his wake.

Two days later, the dedication of a stained glass window in Tony's memory was held during the Sunday service at the church. The window was magnificent and depicted many of Tony's favorite places, including his beloved spot on Pelican Point where he had smoked many a cigar. It had been arranged for by our Rat Bay Yacht Club friends and their one request was that it show a little sailboat on the water on the transom of which were the letters *RBYC*. I spoke—at length—about Tony, relating his life to the window. Janice had sketched the insert to the program for that day and Elizabeth sang the hymn *Morning Has Broken*. It was beautiful. Afterwards I had a luncheon for 20 people at our cottage. The following day Elizabeth and Tony Jr. left for Tucson.

A great joy for me that summer was the visit of Kent, Janice and Tana. I had them all to myself until July 21st. Kent did many projects to improve our property and cottage including the installation of a bannister on the stairway. It was intended for my mother's use but soon became a necessity rather than a luxury for a good many of us.

Kent & baby Tana on the beach - 1989

We spent a great deal of time on the lake—picnics at Breakfast Rock, boat rides up the Oxtongue River and trips to other towns on Lake of Bays such as Dorset and Baysville. Their main attraction was the ice cream shops which Dwight lacked.

The Sinclair family reunion was held at the cottages of my cousins Jack and Gordon on Lake Muskoka. Jack inherited his father's place there—Wit's End—and Gord and Linda had a lovely old home on an island on the lake—Dusquene Island.

Life would never be the same without Tony but when I left the cottage on August 18th to return to Tucson and my job I had a sense of gratitude that I had all those months with Tony at the end of his life as well as sufficient time to mourn and get ready to go on with life. I had been away from work for 1¼ years and how grateful I was to have my position at UA to engage me for many years to come.

1990 After a wonderful trip with my mother to France and Kenya, she and I arrived at the cottage June 10th. I had many guests over the summer including Wini Kirk and Joe Green. A particularly exciting event was a phone call on July 11th from Elizabeth and Tony telling me that she was pregnant. I was ecstatic.

Janice and Tana arrived on July 15th and Elizabeth and Tony six days later. Kent was unable to be there and we missed him. It was the typical active summer and, of course, Tana was the focus of a great deal of attention. I commented about her daily in my diary that year; she was my heart's delight.

The meeting of RBYC was at our cottage in 1990 and I assumed my role as commodore.

I was both apprehensive and delighted that Janice left Tana in my care when she returned to Tucson on July 19th. I have to admit that my adorable granddaughter exhausted me. What an active little girl she was!

Elizabeth was fighting morning sickness but bravely assumed the role of organist and soloist at our little church one Sunday, after which she retired to the bathroom and vomited. What a trouper! That night mother and I were invited to my sister's cottage that she was renting to a lovely couple, Lesley and John Brough. Their guest for the weekend was to be "The Phantom." Mother insisted I be there as she had accepted for me. I explained that it was impossible as I had Tana, and besides, we certainly weren't going to be meeting "The Phantom"—Colm Wilkinson—for whom Andrew Lloyd Webber had written *The Phantom of the Opera*. I was quite sure their guest was a member of the cast or some such thing.

Mother won and I arrived at her cottage with Tana on my hip and over we went next door for the little party. Imagine my amazement when I heard this deep, booming voice coming from the lake and I quickly realized we were indeed meeting the original and best known "Phantom." He was delightful and his voice enchanted Tana.

Summer ended when Elizabeth and Tony, with Tana, returned to Tucson. I followed the next day.

<u>1991</u> This was a particularly exciting summer for me as I now had two grandchildren visiting. William Maxwell von Isser arrived with his parents, Elizabeth and Tony, on his 5-month birthday—July 27th. Less than a week later Janice, Kent and Tana joined us.

I held the Sinclair family reunion at our place on August 3rd with 52 in attendance—the first time a Sinclair woman had hosted it— and a great success it was! As my diary noted, "It was a <u>perfect</u> day. I sailed through it—blissful. Exhausted. Elated."

Max's 1st jetski at 5 months of age with his dad - 1991

Family reunion at Pelican Point - 1991

Aldine in old tin boat Fair-Thee-Well - 1991

Kent, Janice and Tana had to leave early—on August 7th—as Kent was ill and needed to go into hospital in Tucson. Elizabeth, Tony and Max left the next day. I left one week later.

<u>1992</u> This was another happy summer with the traditional family activities, lively parties and the annual events that we had developed over the years. As was typical, my mother divided her time between staying at our cottage and her old white cottage—Birch Spring. I had many visitors, among them Howard Shenk and Merrill Dillon.

This year Kent and Tana—now 4 years old— came without Janice. Kent was at his best—full of fun and a very hard worker. Elizabeth, Tony and Max arrived on their 4th wedding anniversary, July 23rd, with the news that Elizabeth was once again pregnant. My diary recorded, "Thanks be to God." The following day it noted, "It is so incredibly good to have all my family here—safe and <u>sound</u> and <u>healthy</u>."

On July 25th we bought a new power boat which Kent "detailed" for hours. Kent taught me to drive it and Tony showed me how to "dock" it.

Kent getting ready for the sinking of the tub - 1998

That afternoon we engaged in another of our annual events—the sinking of the bathtub. Years before we hadn't known what to do with a leftover bathtub and decided to create a new tradition. Two people climbed with great caution into the tub, leaving it with only about an inch of draft, and paddled out into the bay. If they remained afloat any length of time, jet skis would be launched to make ever tighter circles around them, ultimately ending in "the sinking of the bathtub" in the middle of the bay. When the children grew old enough, they took over the duty with the same old tub. That night we had the annual RBYC meeting at the Davey cottage.

Annually, we were treated to hearing Elizabeth sing a hymn at the little church in Dwight. It always was a moving experience for the congregation and her family. Water skiing was a favorite activity for my sons and they both were incredibly good. We had a garage built that summer. The departure of Kent, Janice and Tana on July 29th came all too soon.

I took great pleasure in babysitting darling Max—a very precious child. Elizabeth was grateful for my help as once again she was miserable with morning sickness. For her it lasted all day. I was sad to see them leave on August 6th.

That day Howard Shenk arrived and we went for what was to be Ray Hickok's last social event. He was very sick with cancer. His lovely daughter Holly hosted the evening for just the four of us. Howard and I had gone by boat and returned to the cottage in the dark well after midnight. Later that night, Ray had a fall and broke his hip. He never fully recovered.

Babysitting Max - on Stanley the lion at the Hickok's - 1992

Another big event that summer was my sister's marriage to David Shand on August 8th at the little church in Dwight. Mary and Murray had a lovely dinner for them the preceding night and I hosted the wedding reception. It rained cats and dogs the day of the wedding so we had to move the whole party to Margaret Ruscica's cottage which was much larger than ours. The heavens opened and the rainfall was torrential. However, the weather did nothing to daunt the enthusiasm of the 60 guests who danced into the wee hours of the morning. That summer went on record as the coldest since 1887.

Mother, Howard and I left on August 13th. It had been another memorable summer.

<u>1993</u> The addition of Josef Alexander von Isser, who arrived in the world on March 23rd, was the big excitement at the cottage in 1993. How lucky I was to have all three of my grandchildren under my roof at one time. I was ecstatic. Janice didn't come that year and we missed her.

I had long wanted to stay at the cottage into the fall to see the glorious colors of the autumn leaves, to spend Canadian Thanksgiving with friends, and to see the first snow fall. To do this, I took a sabbatical leave from UA for the fall semester of 1993. All my wishes came true.

I had a great many houseguests over the months; Howard Shenk came twice. Other gentlemen visited as well—Al Marshick, John Maxfield, Merrill Dillon and Walter Hill. Sallie Lane, the most demanding and eccentric houseguest I have ever had, was there for a week also.

July 25th was a special day as my three grandchildren were christened in the little Dwight church. Elizabeth sang a solo and we followed this special occasion with a big luncheon at our cottage.

For many years I had heard of Ann Sinclair's cabin on an island on Cedar Lake in the northernmost part of Algonquin Park. I had been reluctant to accept her invitation to visit her there. It was truly remote and offered no amenities whatever. On August 19th I relented and Howard and I drove the long and difficult 5-hour trip to meet her in the little town of Brent, on the edge of the lake. Brent had a population of one!

We went by tin boat with her to the island; it lacked even a dock for landing. There were only three cabins on the entire lake! We spent several very quiet days there and returned to the luxury of our cottage—with electricity and running water! We were glad for the experience, but once was enough.

On August 22nd, Mother had my father's ashes moved from Mount Pleasant Cemetery in Toronto to the little

Aldine's mother at her father's grave in cemetery at Stewart Memorial Church 1993 cemetery in Dwight. She had noticed that many people went to Tony's grave to remember him, but nobody ever went to Dad's grave in Toronto.

The entire family gathered for the interment and returned to our cottage for a lovely dinner and evening. Now my mother is buried there as well. I have always kept flowers at our graves in the summer.

Another of my annual activities over many years was attending Al-Anon meetings in Huntsville once a week. I found it life sustaining to be with six nurturing women who had experiences similar to mine. One woman whom I particularly liked and at whose home we often met, sold her old farmhouse on Lake of Bays to Shania Twain who turned it into a magnificent cottage. Our meetings dissolved when death took the majority of our members leaving only two of us still alive. Those meetings had been a rich and comforting experience for me.

After my mother left at the end of the summer, Margaret Ruscica and I went to the charming village called Niagara-on-the-Lake, known for its local wines and for the many theaters that present plays by George Bernard Shaw and others. We stayed at the Prince of Wales Hotel and saw many wonderful plays.

When Margaret returned to Toronto, Merrill Dillon arrived in Niagara-on-the Lake for his annual reunion with old friends from Teheran with whom he had worked for many years. We stayed at the Oban Inn and had a fascinating few days.

Another short trip we took at the end of September was a visit to the home of my cousin Gord Sinclair and his wife Linda in Hudson, Quebec—just outside Montreal. Howard joined me. We spent time in Ottawa en route. After a lovely weekend at their home on a river, we went with them to their ski chalet in Jay Peak, Vermont. I remember getting very little sleep but having a great deal of fun!

After leaving them, we traveled through the Laurentians to the town of Arundel to visit friends—Johanna and Bob Earle. Never having been in this region, I was excited to see the sights and absorb the beauty.

On October 10th, having achieved all my goals for the summer, I returned to Tucson.

1994 After the coldest winter in Ontario in 43 years, I arrived at the cottage on May 12th. Over the years I always took a two-mile walk daily. This year I was rewarded with seeing trilliums growing—masses of them—a treat I usually missed as they are typically finished before my arrival. The trillium is the official flower of Ontario and it is forbidden to pick them. What a feast for the eyes they were.

The cold of winter continued and we had a heavy snowfall on May 26th, the day Merrill Dillon arrived for a visit. The day he left, Howard Shenk arrived so I never had a chance to get lonely. My mother arrived, with her big dog, Jock, in his kennel as usual, on June 15th. We couldn't know that it would be her last summer at the cottage as she died on October 22nd that year at age 86.

Max & Alex feeding the ducks

Tony holding Alex & Max - 1994

Kent, Tana & Janice - 1994

Alex on "solar powered" moon bike

While there were many exciting events at the cottage in 1994 with the visiting of friends and family from afar, the highlight for me was definitely my grandchildren. They were old enough to thoroughly enjoy their time on the dock, in the lake and on the beach. Tana was six, Max was three and Alex a baby of just one.

Tony's family arrived on July 16th and was able to stay for two weeks. I doted on those precious boys and was delighted when I was asked to take care of them while their parents did things independently.

All of Kent's family as well as Janice's friend, Georgette, came on July 21st. What fun it was to have all my family there at once with the laughter and joy that came from being at the cottage. Tana was old enough now to stay overnight at the Hickok camp with her dear friends Alexa and Kimi Hickok Smith. They have remained close friends all these years.

Tony rigging *Wet Dream*

My brother's sons brought their children over frequently, making a gang of happy cousins playing together. Janice and her friend had to leave early that summer—July 31st—but I had the joy of having Kent and Tana until August 7th. How hard my sons worked every summer to improve the cottage and keep it going.

Mom and I, with her beloved dog Jock, left for Tucson on August 17th and I was back at work at UA the following week.

<u>1995</u> I left for the cottage on June 1st knowing it would never be the same for me. For my whole lifetime I had spent summers there with my mother. For many years she had stayed primarily at our cottage with times alone at her own place. As my diary noted, "Mom's absence is pervasive and I miss her terribly." But as she would have wanted, the summer continued with its usual hectic pace.

I enjoyed both my gentlemen visitors—Howard Shenk who came for two weeks and Don Westby who stayed for over a month. On July 15th a huge tornado came through our area wreaking devastation throughout the region. It was quite terrifying and took down a big tree as well as our flagpole. We were without power for many days and had to learn innovative ways of cooking on a barbecue. Of course there was no water and we lived in quite a primitive manner for a time. Some people in our locale were without power for over a month! Margaret Ruscica lost many trees that were over 100 years old. What a mess it was!

Tana, Max & Alex on 1968 motorbike

On their ninth wedding anniversary—July 23rd—Elizabeth, Tony, Max and Alex arrived after having spent a week in Ohio with her family. Three days later Janice, Kent and Tana arrived. All my family together once again.

A big event on July 28th was the raising of our new flagpole which had been purloined from somewhere by our neighbor Paul Doughty. It took quite a gang to put it up and how happy I was to again see the U.S., Canadian, Ontario and Arizona flags flying.

Raising the new flagpole - 1995

The family gathering at the old white cottage before my mother's memorial service - 1995

Two days later came the events in my mother's honor. At 2:30 p.m. Murray, Carol and I interred our mother's ashes—along with those of her beloved dog Jock—next to my father in the little cemetery behind our church—Stewart Memorial Church. Later we had a beautiful service in the church at which my friend Don Westby played the organ and Elizabeth sang a magnificent hymn. The church was filled. Family and friends had come from far and wide. My mother had been much loved.

The final tribute was a huge dinner party at Pelican Point hosted by my brother, sister and me. My diary said, "It was the best party of the decade." Over 100 people attended. My brother completed the festivities with an outstanding fireworks display.

That summer, at age four, Max began his lifelong passion for fishing. On his first day he caught over 40 fish! All the children enjoyed the beach, the lake and many picnics at Breakfast Rock. I regained my interest in tennis and continued to play until my legs gave out years later.

I returned to Tucson on August 17th and was back to work at UA the following Monday.

Tana driving the boat - 1995

1996 Howard Shenk and I traveled to the cottage together on June 14th. He stayed 10 days. Murray and Mary completed the building of their gorgeous new cabin that summer and took us on a tour of it on June 20th. It retained the name Birch Spring as they had the old white cottage—the original Birch Spring—razed.

On June 27th Don Westby and his mother-in-law Mary Smith arrived. Don was a widower. His wife had been a friend of mine in high school. We showed Mary all the local sights and she left a week later.

Aldine sailing - 1996

The joy of my summer was having my family there for 11 days. All of Tony's family was there but Kent and Tana arrived on their own. Later Janice came with a dear friend of Tana's—Emily Kruger. What happy times all the children had together. They grew to love Pelican Point, and still do.

Don and I returned to Tucson on August 14th. Although he had become significant in my life, it was a short-lived relationship after we came home.

1997 My working days had come to an end. I spent my last day at UA on my 64th birthday—May 29th—after having been on permanent faculty there since 1975. This emancipation allowed me to be at the cottage from June 6th until October 6th. I took to retirement like a duck to water!

Howard Shenk, who had traveled to the cottage with me, helped in opening the cottage—a gigantic job. One annual task was the planting of many flowers around the cottage. Flowers are very important to Canadians and we certainly did our part spending hundreds of dollars a year to put color against our gray cottage. They have always been a gorgeous addition. Howard had to get back to work in Tucson on June 17th. I was alone, but my solitude was short lived as Sallie Lane came for a visit on June 30th. Although she stayed only a week, it was the week from hell. What a difficult woman she was!

My next guests were Polly and Jack Ledford who stayed only five days. They charmed everyone. Unfortunately their arrival on July 16th preceded by one day that of Kent, Tana and Tana's 11-year-old friend Jarreux De Muro. I was so excited to have them there. Five days later Janice and her good friend Tammy Wilder—Jarreux's mother—arrived. Tana water skied for the first time on July 29th, a red letter day! They engaged in lots of water skiing thereafter as well as canoeing and being pulled behind the boat on tubes.

The last day of July, Tony and his family arrived in the early afternoon so we spent hours on the dock catching up and watching Max and Alex who were excited about being there. I was adoring the role of grandmother and had all three of my darling

Tana at the beach - 1997

Tana with her beloved duck Warfield

grandchildren all to myself a great deal. One day I took them all to Huntsville to buy each a sweat shirt and, in turn, they could select a shirt for their parents.

Max caught a 17-inch rainbow trout in his Uncle Murray's trout pond—a favor my brother granted to few. Darling Elizabeth "taxidermied" it for Max. Another exciting adventure was Kent's catching three ducks for Tana. She adored all of them but when it came time to return to Tucson there was one she couldn't leave behind—Warfield. So back home he went with her on the plane.

I was sad on August 10th to receive a phone call from an old friend, Hal Grieve, telling me that his wife Bette had died. They had such a close and loving marriage. Months later Hal was in touch with me and our close relationship began, initiated by many weeks of daily e-mailing.

Howard drove to the cottage from Tucson that year arriving on August 14th and leaving on the 25th. More houseguests, Jeannette and Bob Renouf came on August 20th and there was not a day without heavy rain and mist during their entire visit. What a disappointment!

Merrill Dillon came for a visit in late August and, in spite of his advanced years, did many household projects. Also, he loved to hike and we trekked some magnificent trails in Algonquin Park. On September 3rd we left the cottage for a visit to the charming little town of Niagara-on-the–Lake where we stayed at the Queen's Landing Hotel. We saw several George Bernard Shaw plays as well as Chekhov's The Seagull.

My minister and dear friend, Susan Manning, shared the sad news with me that she had breast cancer from which she died in 2016. She asked me to take over the service and sermon for her at Stewart Memorial Church on September 28th while she took some time off. I would have done anything to help her and I quickly agreed to her request.

I took a scary trip to Montreal where my beloved cousin, Gord Sinclair, was being honored at a huge dinner to celebrate his 50 years in broadcasting. It was a frightening drive as there was a ferocious rain both going there and coming home and visibility was practically nil. Additionally, I got lost en route. Finally, I reached their home in

Hudson, Quebec and within an hour we went by stretch limo to the Queen Elizabeth Hotel where 500 guests assembled. It was a wonderful "roast" of Gord and a memorable evening for me surrounded by so many celebrities. I returned to the cottage the following day—exhausted.

I celebrated Canadian Thanksgiving with the Ruscica family at their cottage. The fall colors were magnificent.

1998 I spent a delightful week in Meshoppen, Pennsylvania visiting Hal Grieve on his scenic farm where we celebrated his 67th birthday on May 26th with almost 50 people in attendance. From there, we drove together to the cottage on May 27th and faced the big job of "opening." I was so glad to have Hal's help.

Having been very ill with atrial fibrillation all year, I felt lucky to have my 65th birthday on May 29th. I noted in my diary, "I am glad to be alive and reflect on what a truly privileged life I've had." Gord Sinclair arrived for a visit that day and, as the 30th was Murray's 67th birthday, we had a huge family party to celebrate both of us.

It was very cold on June 4th but Hal and I drove to the Visitor's Centre in Algonquin Park to introduce him to the history of the region. While there, a huge snow storm arrived and we returned to the cottage amidst beautiful scenery—the forest blanketed in white.

Hal left on June 10th, the day Howard arrived. He worked hard on the cottage and cabins and I was particularly grateful as my heart misbehaved all summer. Nonetheless, we did the delightful annual trips—up the Oxtongue River by boat, to Dorset by boat for ice cream, and picnics at Breakfast Rock. Annually Howard sang a solo hymn at the church service on Sundays and continued until age robbed him of his dulcet tones.

This was the year a qualifying Iron Man competition was being held locally. It drew people from near and far including my darling cousin Jennifer Sinclair and her husband Jay Cummings from Vermont. They had asked if a friend of theirs could stay with us as well—Jackie Simonson. They mentioned that she was ranked "the strongest woman in the world." I anticipated greeting a large woman with impressive muscles. Instead, Jackie was a very thin woman whom you would think a gust of wind could blow over. I guess her entire body was muscle and she continued for years holding her impressive title internationally.

Our whole household went into preparing for this event. It was Jennifer's first competition and, while getting ready for the day, Jay told her to stand still while he covered her entire body with Vaseline. We all wondered what the reason was for this. He explained that in the swimming portion of the event people would try to get ahead by pulling back the swimmer ahead of them. Vaseline prevented their managing to get a purchase. Both completed the competition, but their rankings held a little to be desired. It was the experience they were seeking, and they certainly did have an adventure that weekend.

Howard left on June 23rd and Hal arrived from Pennsylvania on June 25th and stayed until July 12th. I was glad to have his company and his great help with the cottage as my heart continued its erratic behavior. Nonetheless, I continued to take a two-mile walk daily as I had for many years.

I was thrilled when Kent and Tana arrived on July 15th and my diary noted that she was "enchanting." She had earned her yellow belt in karate on May 16th and was very much into sports. On her first day at the cottage she water skied, went out in the paddle boat, tackled the wind surfer and played on the beach. That night she and I took a ride in our power boat with Tana at the helm! It was her first time running the boat and she took to it like a duck to water. At age 10, she was a busy young lady that summer with sleepovers at the Hickok camp and visits to the magnificent Sharp cottage to play with their girls.

Max, Tony, Alex & Tana jumping - just before hitting the water - 1998

Janice and Tana's friend Caitlin Tavener arrived for two weeks on July 22nd and what a wonderful time they all had together. The annual family reunion was on August 2nd at the cottage of my cousin Jack Sinclair and his wife Pat at their Acton Island home on Lake Muskoka. It had belonged to my famous uncle, Gordon Sinclair. Elizabeth, Tony and the boys arrived at the reunion from their visit to Ohio where they had spent a week with her family. What fun to have all the family there.

Max, Tana & Alex on the beach - 1998

Alex, now five years old, learned to run the power boat and loved it. He is a natural at the helm. Max, now seven, spent time collecting turtles and frogs. Max continued his passion for fishing with

Alex driving the boat - 1998

224

great success. My grandsons were growing up! It was getting to the point where Alex could beat me at most board games that required anticipating his opponent's next move. Pelican Point was busy from morning until night. In the evening we often went out in the boat, sat on Pelican Point, watched movies or played games in the living room.

Movie night in workshop under Alex's artwork

Alex, Max & Kent in our workshop

Days were filled to the brim and I was sad to see all my family leave on August 14th but I had been lucky enough to have them there for a month.

Hal arrived for another visit on August 17th. A few days later we left the cottage to begin our wonderful journey through the Rocky Mountains and on to Vancouver where we embarked on our cruise to Alaska written about elsewhere in this memoir. We returned to Pelican Point on September 3rd. That summer Hal took his first and last sail in *Wet Dream*. He never liked sailing.

On September 8th, Hal left and Howard arrived. I was grateful to have his help in planning a big 60th birthday party for my sister Carol. As children we all had loved the square dances in the little town hall in Dwight. My aim was to replicate this experience for her. I rented the hall, found the musicians and caller, and made the dinner myself. We had rented tables and chairs and had decorated the hall to perfection. After dinner—for 50 guests—we collapsed the tables and the square dancing began. It was an unusual and very happy birthday party for my sister.

After I dropped Howard off in Toronto on September 18th for his return to Tucson, I went to Margaret Ruscica's home to stay with her for a few days. It was during the Toronto Film Festival and Margaret had "connections" allowing us to attend many of the movies and festivities.

Annually in mid-September my brother had friends visit him for a few

Aldine's annual visit with Murray's friends - 1998

225

days. They were men who had shared a house—The Gaylord Arms—in London, Ontario in the days when they were beginning their careers in finance. They had stayed in close touch over the years. I was always invited to join them for cocktails on one of their evenings together. They were all attractive, intelligent and successful and I enjoyed their company very much. I was sad to see these weekends end in 2014 when my brother died, the first of the group of about seven to do so.

On September 19th Merrill Dillon arrived for his annual visit and a few days later we took a trip to Niagara-on-the-Lake where we stayed at the Oban Inn. What a delightful few days we had, including visiting Niagara Falls with a wet ride in the boat *Maid of the Mist* that sails right up to the falls. We saw many plays at the charming theaters in the little town including, *She's Not for Burning, Lady Windermere's Fan*, and *You Can't Take it with You.* On my way back to the cottage I dropped Merrill at the Toronto airport for his return to Tucson.

Hal's next visit was on September 30th and he stayed with me until I left on October 10th for my flight to Tucson while he drove home to Pennsylvania. We had a lovely time giving and attending parties and readying the cottage for the winter.

<u>1999</u> This year I was able to be at the cottage from June 1st until October 1st. Howard Shenk was with me the first two weeks and was a great help in getting things up and running. My pleasure at being at the cottage was heavily dampened by the news that Carol's husband had pancreatic cancer. I talked to her daily and marveled at their courage.

Hal arrived just three days before we departed on June 23rd for a visit to Ireland. It was a marvelous trip and is recorded elsewhere in this memoir. On our return to the cottage, Hal built a wonderful raft to replace the old one that had disintegrated over time. The young people had such fun on the raft. Hal departed on July 18th.

Alex getting ready to go tubing

Max with huge frog - 1999

Janice, Tana & Kent - 1999

Two days later the family began to arrive—first Kent, Janice, Tana and their young friend Jarreux De Muro. Kent built a fire pit down near the beach that has provided many years of good times in the evenings roasting marshmallows and telling stories. Then Tony, Elizabeth, Max and Alex arrived after their visit with her family in Ohio. What a wonderful time they all had together playing on the dock and beach all day, enjoying big family meals, and playing games such as Balderdash in the evenings.

Hal and his grandson Greg arrived unexpectedly on their return from a trip to the aircraft show in Oshkosh, Wisconsin. What a houseful—11 of us now. It was a 24-hour circus at the cottage and, although I was exhausted by it, I loved seeing all my young people having such a good time.

Max, Alex & Tana in the paddleboat

The von Isser family at RBYC gathering - 1999

Tana remained after the family left for Tucson and I had her all to myself. We took a trip to Toronto for me to show her that fascinating city—the largest in Canada—including a visit to my childhood home and an elevator ride to the top of the CN Tower which was, at that time, the tallest building in the world. After several days she left on her own—with American Airlines escort service—for Tucson.

I returned to the cottage on August 19th, the day Howard arrived for another visit. On his departure, I was visited by a good friend, Jack Miller. He and I had a delightful few days before he continued his trip across Canada. Hal was the next visitor arriving on September 14th. He and I worked hard to finish cottage projects and close for the winter.

Hal and I spent a few days in Toronto before I departed for Tucson. Margaret Ruscica made sure we had a good time. We dined at elegant restaurants such as Avalon and went to the Princes of Wales Theatre to see a performance of *Cabaret*. We visited the Science Centre and walked through the huge underground shopping area below the Royal York Hotel. We were entertained by Mary and Murray at their magnificent home in Rosedale called *Drumsnab*.

I returned to Tucson on October 1st to find that Kent and Tony had opened my house, filled it with food, and had my car ready to go. I felt I was indeed the luckiest woman in the world.

2000 A new century! My summer at Pelican Point that year began on May 25th and ended on October 3rd. I did a major renovation at the cottage including repainting all the buildings, new tile and carpet throughout the cottage, new appliances and the addition of skylights in the kitchen. I was grateful to have two visits from Howard Shenk and two from Hal Grieve. They helped me enormously and saw me through a summer of

tenuous health. Atrial fibrillation plagued me all summer and required a visit to intensive care at the Huntsville Hospital and the necessity for an electro-cardioversion.

Hal with his big fish

That was the year Hal introduced us to the joy of kayaking. We all were so enthusiastic that we had bought four of them by the end of the summer and they have provided many moments of solitude as well as competitive challenges year after year. Another of Hal's good ideas was our buying a pontoon boat—often called a party boat—that would hold 10 people with ease. The young people have loved all the options it affords, and I have loved the ease of getting on and off the boat! While Hal made some wonderful additions to our cottage, the one he was most proud of was

228

the outdoor shower which is used almost exclusively by all the family. We do have two indoor bathrooms, but standing in Hal's shower looking out at the lake is a treat for everyone. He also added an outdoor "biffy" with a flush toilet!

I had the pleasure of seeing Marg and Don Donahue twice during the summer. They are dear friends with whom we have spent time every summer for many years. It is an enduring and treasured tradition.

It was the year of the death of Carol's beloved husband David Shand and his subsequent burial in our little church graveyard.

Tana arrived early that year and attended summer camp for two weeks—a well-known girls' camp, Tanamakoon. I think she weathered the experience with grace but never wanted a repeat performance. The rest of my family arrived bringing with them Tana's friend Ariel Porter.

Elizabeth & Tony with Alex & Max
in front of their tree - 2000

We were the hosts for the annual RBYC meeting and Kent happily relinquished his role as commodore. One of the children there had pink eye which poor Alex caught. He was furious, especially when it meant that he was unable to attend the Sinclair family reunion held at Mary and Murray's magnificent cabin. It was a great disappointment to him and to his mother who had to stay home with him. The reunion was well attended and was, of course, as spectacular as Mary and Murray would have it.

My beloved grandchildren were growing up, and all of them attempted water skiing that summer. They continued to put on plays for us and to videotape their adventures and our family activities. We still watch a few of these each summer to bring back the nostalgia of years gone by.

As the years passed, the young people followed in their parents' footsteps and began bringing their boyfriends and girlfriends to the cottage.

Tony on slalom ski

This will be my last entry for life at Pelican Point over the past 20 years. They were halcyon days that my family and I had been so fortunate to experience. They had enriched our lives and kept my family a close unit. There was, of course, sadness but balanced with so much joy. This memoir was written for my grandchildren; Tana was now 12 years old, Max was 9 and Alex was 7. They have their own memories of the years that followed and all the happiness that ensued. I'll leave them with those magical days to carry in their hearts forever.

Treasured years with my beloved family—I remember them all with great gratitude and a sense of having been blessed beyond measure.

Aldine on one of our three jet skis

18

‿‿

MY ADVENTURES IN REAL ESTATE

Putting the words "adventure" and "real estate" together seems like an oxymoron. Few would consider this profession very exciting. I did.

I'll begin at the beginning. As you can imagine, my mother Aldine Sinclair was terribly lonely when she moved to Tucson from Toronto having left her family, her friends, and even her country behind. Tucson was becoming an attractive place for Canadians to spend winters and soon my mother found that she was besieged by friends of friends who had heard that she lived here and might be able to help them find a home.

Mother took them all for scenic trips of the area and showed them various neighborhoods where they might be interested in living. Of course, she always had them for drinks or dinner as well. The people whom she had assisted would then find a real estate agent, again recommended by my mother, and buy a house.

My mother might have thought of entering the field of real estate on her own, but she was committed to and enjoyed helping me raise my sons while I was getting degrees and certificates. My parents always lived next door to us so my boys had two homes with a well-worn path between. Mother would fill in her spare time with lunching, playing bridge and entertaining friends.

My sons adored their grandparents. They were the first of ten grandchildren. Kent was the oldest and when he was learning to talk the closest approximation he could make to the name "Grandma" was "Mia." "Grandpa" became "Bumpa." The names caught and for the rest of their lives that is what they were called by our family and friends. It was so much easier to say Mia than Mrs. Sinclair and in that generation calling her Aldine would have been unacceptable.

When Tony and I moved our family to California from 1961 to 1964, my mother found herself rudderless. She had too much time on her hands and was bored. Then into her life came a woman named Marian Smith. Marian owned a real estate company and encouraged Mother to get her license. Soon the many friends who had previously sought her advice concerning homes to buy became her clients. She did very well in real estate.

Eventually Marian Smith decided to sell her company. My mother bought it and renamed it Sinclair Associates. It continues to be a very active company with my sister Carol at the helm and her daughters, Stephanie and Aldine, as associates. Carol is now 78 and goes to work daily.

Mother was incredibly successful and sold primarily high priced homes in the Catalina Foothills. She gained the reputation of being the most honorable woman in real estate in Tucson. If a couple had their hearts set on buying a certain home and she thought it wasn't right for them, she would tell them.

When we returned to Tucson from California, my mother encouraged me to hang a license with her. I really was not interested and couldn't envision it fitting into my schedule. However, I could see it as a source of extra income. Everyone pursuing a real estate license takes a course to prepare for the difficult Arizona real estate exam. I didn't have time, so I read the very lengthy textbook, took the test, and passed. My mother said she had never heard of anyone taking the test and passing without having first taken the course. Now it is required to take the course.

To encourage me, Mother turned over a lot of her clients to me and I generated quite a few on my own. I have mentioned Bette Layton elsewhere. She and her husband Jack bought their first house from me. Our dear friends, Johanna and Jim Stephens, bought their foothills home from me in 1968 and are still living in it and loving it more each day.

One of my clients was a quiet young woman named Linda See who had a daughter. I never sold her a house as she went on to marry Sir Paul McCartney and was the love of his life. I also showed houses to Barbara Kingsolver, as well as other celebrities.

Now let me step back and tell you about the houses Tony and I had lived in over our years together. Our first had been the house in which his parents had lived and that his father turned over to us when we married. (He moved into a little pink house next door that he had previously rented to Hal Grieve and his mother.) Our new home had been built by Indians in the old Ft. Lowell historical district in Tucson in the 1800s. Initially it had dirt floors and was of rude construction by any criteria. Over the years rooms were added, the floor covered, and eventually it had a bathroom. Let me hasten to say that Tony could not stand up straight in that bathroom; the ceiling was far too low, or he was far too tall.

Tony's father had turned it into a charming little villa with a great deal of Austrian charm. During one year when Hal was homeless, he lived in an old dilapidated trailer in the back. It had no electricity and no water. It did have a great many centipedes and scorpions. When I asked Hal how he did his laundry he professed that he didn't have any! He would shoot rabbits and cook them over a bonfire. Other food essentials he often had to steal as he had no source of income other than what he made at Gilpin Airport. He did have a motorcycle, a gift from his father, and rode it to Tucson High School every day—a good 15 miles away—for which I give him great credit.

Tony and I brought our first born son, Kent, home to this rustic dwelling. His crib was enclosed on all sides, including the top, so that scorpions could not fall from the ceiling into his bed. I once found a six-inch scorpion in Kent's room and screamed so loud that Tony came running. It was dead on the floor (having been very much alive) and Tony claimed that my screaming scared it to death.

Kent in his Thunderbird with Millie - 1960

When our son Tony Jr. was to be born, we knew it was time to find a larger, more suitable home. We bought a huge lot on the next street over, Glenn Street, and hired Tom Gist to build our house. It was perfect for our needs and was Tony Jr's first home. There was no Glenn Street actually. We had to have it bladed. There were no utilities available so we had to pay to have them all brought in and we were repaid as others built nearby.

Soon after completing our new home, we built a charming little house on our back acreage for Tony's father, Josef von Isser. It was designed by a creative architect, Veronica Hughart, who understood Josef and satisfied him both with respect to taste and comfort. He loved his little villa and died quietly in his sleep there at

Kent carrying newborn Tony home from the hospital - 1957

age 87 on January 17, 1972. On January 30th he was interred beside his wife –Dorothea Buhl King–in Evergreen Cemetery on Oracle Road in Tucson. Kent and Tony Jr. were pallbearers.

Our very good friends Barbara and Ed Hyde built next door to us as did our friends Persis and Stephen Congdon.

The most distinctive aspect of our new home was the pond we built. It is still well- known throughout the city. We waited until the boys could swim and then had it dug—wide and deep. Our boys had motorcycles at an early age—Kent was probably nine and Tony Jr. seven. In order to pack the sides of the pond—we had used bentonite to hold the earth—our lads would ride their motorcycles in circles around the inside of the pond. What a good time they had—around and around, up and down, scaring their parents but doing just the job that was needed. We had a solid, leak-proof pond.

Kent & Tony with grandfather
Josef von Isser - 1962

We stocked it with fish—tilapia, catfish, bluegill and the like—and encircled it with weeping willow trees. It had a dock and rowboat. Of course our boys and their friends loved it. The problem was that the water was opaque and it wasn't possible to keep track of what was going on underwater. I can't tell you the number of hours I spent counting heads to be sure all the lads were accounted for.

Tony holding Kent, Tony Jr. and
dog Millie - 1958

Tony also stocked the pond with gray geese. This was not to my liking. Geese make a mess and it took a good deal of my time keeping the place sanitary. Another problem for me was a severe case of jealousy. One of the geese, Ashley, had fallen head over tail feathers in love with Tony. Oh the carryings on and excitement when Tony came home from work every day. Into the pond Tony dove and immediately Ashley started having his way with him. Tony's back was a patchwork of scratches, and he

Kent & Tony Jr. in our pond - 1966

considered each a badge of honor. You see, he adored Ashley, too. It was all too much for me, but Tony thought it was enormously funny.

We also kept white geese in a closed-in yard. One year Tony decided they would be our Thanksgiving meal. I was horrified, but Tony was boss. He wanted to have our boys kill them by wringing their necks. It was Tony's wish that our lads would be prepared to survive in whatever circumstance they found themselves. That these geese were pets seemed to elude him. And so, one November day, the boys swiveled those geese and wrung their necks. Thanksgiving dinner gave them little pleasure that year.

The pond was, and is, truly beautiful—an oasis in the desert. We might well have lived there a lot longer had I not been selling real estate at that time.

My mother mentioned that a house had come on the market that might appeal to one of my clients, Al Marshick. Now, in my heart I knew that Al didn't really want to buy a house but, rather, he wanted my time and attention. One noon I raced from the university to meet Al to show him the house. It was love at first sight. Oh, not Al; I fell in love with that beautiful house.

This is its story. In the 1920s a man named John Murphey and his wife Helen bought an entire section of the foothills, 600 acres. (It is now the most valuable property in Tucson.) Mr. Murphey planned to subdivide it, but before he did he picked the most beautiful knoll on all that acreage to build his homestead house. It was on 10 acres. While building it, he and Helen lived in a tent nearby. A good friend of theirs, Josias Joesler, was an architect new to Tucson. He planned the house and Indians built it. Joesler is now a name in Tucson that commands attention. If a house is referred to as "a Joesler" the value of the property goes up many-fold.

This charming house was on Camino Real in the Catalina Foothills, a street many consider the most beautiful in Tucson. No descriptors I could provide would do it justice. Joesler had a specific style which always included a huge front screened-in-porch, odd angles, and miniscule bathrooms. This house had a tile roof and was built of mud adobe covered with white stucco. A large stucco wall enclosed a front patio. (Later we kept three noisy peacocks in this area.) Of course, the views of the Catalina Mountains were the best in Tucson and the windows and swimming pool took advantage of them.

Tony Jr. in our pool on his aircraft inner tube

John Murphey used an accent color of blue for trim and shutters, etc. It came to be known as Murphey blue, although its real name was Flemish blue. Our house painter, Joe Preter, teased me by referring to it as "bluish phlegm" thus reducing its charm considerably. Murphy beds were popular on Joesler porches, an attribute that Tony and I frequently took advantage of in the hot months.

Now I really hoped Al wasn't interested in a house, because I had lost my heart to this one. I phoned Tony who met me there after work. It has to be understood that we both loved our Glenn Street house and its unique pond so even thinking of moving was anathema. But we did.

Mr. Murphey had sold this house to build a more conventional home on Juan Paisano, a street he had named after himself—Juan in English is John. The Camino Real house was purchased by Pussy Voevodsky. We were only the third owners. Pussy eventually died and her two sons, whom we knew as friends, were the sellers. We bought it knowing we were getting in over our heads but determined to make this our new home. That was in 1969. To help out, my parents bought two acres of our land and built a magnificent house next door to us. Also, Katharine Merritt wanted a permanent place to come during the winter months and our large, complete guesthouse filled the bill.

Katharine spent three months there every year and, as Tony, our boys and I were gone all day, she needed a housekeeper/companion. We interviewed and hired a woman who became a part of our family and our lives—Marie Kelley. More about Marie later.

The bunkhouse

Our home included a stable and tack room. We had these rebuilt in 1970 to become The Bunkhouse, which became our boys' home. It was charming with two bedrooms, a living room, kitchen, and bathroom and the most wonderful fireplace we have ever had. It had wooden floors and ranch-like furniture and was perfect for our young lads, then ages 15 and 13. Unfortunately, it was a good 1/8 mile from our main house. They had freedom but there were boundaries that were closely monitored.

We were rigid about curfew when the boys had their own cars. To reassure us they were home, Tony put a big pipe across the road to the bunkhouse so that as they entered their front tires made a big "chunk-chunk" sound. When we heard the second "chunk-

chunk" of their rear tires we knew they were safely home and we could sleep peacefully. Years later we learned that the first of the "chunk-chunks" was the front tires, and the second was those same tires in reverse. Stories are still emerging of some of the hanky-panky that went on up there.

We always had dogs. At this house they typically were given free run of the property. But we did have a large dog run at the bunkhouse that our boys had built in 1973. Tony and I saw this as a good opportunity to give our boys a sex education lesson. Our female, Joey, was going into heat so we planned the event with great care and reverence. We explained to Kent and Tony Jr. that this was a natural part of life and gave great joy to its participants. We congregated at the dog run with our fold-up chairs.

Tony Jr. with Fido, Kent with Joey
on a 1951 Army Jeep

Both dogs, Joey and our male dog, were let into the dog run and spent no time at all in getting at it. Tony and I were calm and reassuring. I think the boys were beyond humiliated, but hey, we do the best we can as parents.

Tragedy struck. The mating was over, but the dogs were stuck. Yes, stuck. Mayhem broke loose as the dogs tried desperately to separate and the boys tried to help. It was beyond awful. Well, we all know the solution—a hose with cold water. I think this was the worst sex education lesson ever devised. I am surprised our boys ever became fathers. Their first visual exposure to the sex act was a disaster and I am sure scarred their minds permanently.

Of course the bunkhouse was an enormous attraction to our boys' friends. I never checked at noon to see if these friends had actually taken their girlfriends there for lunch or something else. I just didn't want to know.

And now the story of Marie Kelley, our full-time housekeeper for the ten years we lived on Camino Real. Marie was a force to be reckoned with. She was a tall, imposing and very handsome woman of black and Cherokee heritage. That combination should have come with a warning saying "combustible." However, although her loyalty was absolute, one was well advised

Tony Jr. driving 1951 Army Jeep

to stay out of her way when she was in one of her moods.

237

Marie Kelley

She lived in her own wing of our house that had a living room, bedroom, kitchen, sun porch and so forth. I became very spoiled. She did all the housework, cooking and laundry and even took our boys to dental appointments and so forth if neither Tony nor I was available.

I think the family would agree that nobody, but nobody, would have the courage to challenge my husband Tony. Marie had no compunctions whatever. For example, at dinner one night we all could tell Marie was in one of her snits. Watch out! Tony had two favorite vases that had been in his family for years. They were delicate. Marie was not. We heard a crash of glass and Tony was sure it was one of his vases. We heard her say, "I never did like those damn things anyway." Tony stood up prepared to reprimand her in the kitchen when we heard the next sentence. "Well, no use in having only one of those ugly things," followed by a second crash. Tony knew enough to sit down and be quiet.

On the hearth of the fireplace in the boys' bunkhouse was a beautiful ceramic rattlesnake in a coiled position. One day the boys heard Marie cleaning and dropping a few expletives. She hated that "damn" rattlesnake so one day she divined the ultimate solution to the problem. She took the handle of her broom and lit into that poor critter so that when she finished it was pulverized–just a haze of fine dust. And that was the end of that!

As you will have gathered earlier in these writings, Katharine Merritt was a very formal (and formidable) woman. During her annual visit, Marie had to wear a uniform—white in the daytime, black at night. She hated it but capitulated. However, she drew the line when Katharine rang a little bell to summon her to the table. No way any "damn" bell was going to tell her what to do! She had her limits, and we learned to respect them.

She absolutely adored Kent and Tony Jr. and was fiercely protective of them. If they skipped school, I never heard about it. And she picked their friends carefully. Two of the boys' friends at Green Fields School were scholarship students, Nicky and Curtis Simmons. They were delightful lads and we often took them camping with us. But they were black which did

Katharine Merritt with
Josef von Isser

not sit well with Marie. One day when she had them alone in the kitchen we overheard her tell them they didn't belong there and that they were not to come over any more and bother these folks. We did have a few words with her that time.

Marie had three children and I doubt she knew in any case what color they would be when they entered the world. The first one really had her nervous. She was only eighteen and was employed by a Chinese man—Mr. Yee–in his grocery store. They lived together. She was pregnant and terrified that she might be out on the street when the baby came. You see, she was quite sure the child would not look Chinese. Nor did it. A perfect little black baby appeared to the great delight of the "father." They named the child Forrest Wayman Yee, but I doubt there was much Yee in him. We all remember Forrest for his startling gold-colored eyes.

The next two were girls, one of whom, Linda, went into the Tucson Police Department. The other, Debra, married a red-headed fireman. Debra died in a traffic accident soon after her son, Yonseo Chaos, was born. Marie raised that precious child and he adored her until the day she died. We became very close to Yonseo.

Our household had four kitchens, seven air-conditioning systems—umpteen water heaters, and so forth. The time came when inevitably our lads would leave us. Kent had already gone to the mine in Quebec and returned to Tucson at the time that Tony Jr. was enrolling in a military academy prep school in Bandon, Oregon known as Millard. They both spent an academic year there — 1976-77 — Kent in catching up on academics while Tony Jr. was preparing to take his entrance exams for Annapolis Naval Academy. He had been nominated as a candidate there by Morris (Mo) Udall, a highly esteemed Arizona Congressman from 1961 until 1991.

Millard was a challenge for both boys. It was highly regulated with rigid standards imposed by the austere director and owner, Mrs. Millard. However, they excelled. A test was administered to all 80 students in attendance that year to determine in which of their colleagues they felt they could put the most trust. For example, if you had to be in a life threatening situation in combat, with whom would you choose to be. Believe it or not, my sons tied for second place. The school rarely had a tie. Kent insisted that Tony Jr. had about two one hundredths of an edge on his score. Since these scores were posted, I've always felt badly for whomever was at the end of the list. Our sons came home from that experience as much more confident young men.

Kent went on to attend Brooks Institute in Santa Barbara, California, unquestionably the finest school of photography in the nation, and graduated at the top of his class with a B.A. Tony Jr. decided his career choice was going to be in engineering and selected a program at the University of Utah in Logan. Later he transferred to Arizona State

University and completed his B.S. in Aeronautical Engineering Technology. He went on to build a stellar career in that field. With our boys having flown the nest our house became much too big for us. So we put it on the market and, thinking that so large and unusual a house would not sell quickly, I went off to Germany.

It was time, too, to say goodbye to Marie. That was hard on us all, but she was ready to lead a simpler life and perhaps settle down with Dave, a man who had been wooing her for years.

To our great surprise, our Camino Real house sold quickly. Suddenly, we were in need of a new home. As I have mentioned elsewhere, Tony was quite happy commuting

Our dining room - Camino Escuela

from Arivaca to Tucson Newspapers Incorporated where he was working at that time, but I knew we needed a Tucson home. We wanted to stay close to my parents so I found the perfect house on five acres one street over—Camino Escuela. It was a dirt road. The views were gorgeous. It was ideal for us and we bought it. It had the most magnificent dining room I have ever seen with adobe brick walls that rose to a height of 18 feet.

Although it was in an elegant neighborhood, the man who lived alone next door to us, Berkeley Charvoz, had a very simple house that might even have been referred to as a hovel. He made it clear from the outset that the less he had to do with us the better. I have never known a more unfriendly person.

Apparently his story was thus. Charvoz, the name by which he was always referred, had been a hit man for the CIA. He slept during the day and did target practice at night. He had an underground firing range. We were fascinated by the activity that went on over there but we kept a low profile. On his property were life sized boards jig-sawed to appear as replicas of men. We could see through our binoculars that he was a good shot indeed.

When Charvoz eventually died (we knew not how or why) I immediately made inquiries into the new ownership of his property as I desperately wanted to buy those five acres to add to our land.

His two sons were eager to work with me and consummate the deal as quickly as possible. However, there was a glitch. Charvoz did not have full ownership. Years before his wife at that time worked as a secretary for a lawyer friend of ours, Dick Duffield.

The wife, Diane, (now a friend of ours) had confided to Dick while working for him she was terrified of her husband as she was being used for target practice by him. He would make her lean against the headboard of their bed and then shoot bullets, encircling her head. He obviously was a good shot as she lived through this frightening experience.

Dick arranged to initiate divorce proceedings for her and he recommended that she get out of town—as far away as possible. She took his good advice.

When Dick learned of Charvoz' death, he contacted Diane and they reviewed her rights as a divorced widow. It seems that back when Charvoz was buying that house, he was a little short of cash and Diane put $2000 of her own money into it. This gave her complete ownership of the house upon his death.

Diane chose not to sell but went on to restore the house and live in it herself. Truly, it is now a showplace and very in keeping with the rest of the neighborhood. As you can imagine, Charvoz' sons were furious, and I was very disappointed.

We had memorable parties in our lovely home on Camino Escuela. People had their weddings there. Every year I entertained my full-time masters and doctoral students with a swim and dinner party. They were always a success, with one exception. My beloved graduate assistant, Bill Young, inadvertently walked through a floor length window on May 1st, 1981. He required hospitalization and a great many stitches. We are still close friends and write one another every Christmas. He, by the way, spent a semester living on the beach in Baja California with his wife doing the data collection for his dissertation. He used the Spanish test that I had written administering it to all the children of appropriate age in the nearby village. What a deal! Dr. Young has gone on to be a highly respected professional in Washington State.

One year the swimming party got a little out of hand. My students, who always felt very comfortable with me, decided to make it a nude swimming party. I didn't know how this would sit with other faculty members should they hear of it, but off came the swimsuits anyway and everyone had a grand time. I might mention that one young man was a redhead. He added a good deal of color to the party. My suit stayed on. Marijuana was a staple of this group. Some blew in my direction but with negligible results.

Our 1977 party was particularly filled with fun as Mike Manos, a very attractive Greek student in my doctoral program, taught everyone how to Greek dance. All my students and their dates or mates were there as well as Tony Jr. and his charming friend

Sarah. There were about 30 of us and the party continued into the wee hours of the morning.

Another party in April 20th, 1979 was to honor not only all my students but also their internship supervisors. There were 50 or more in attendance and it was a roaring success.

At our party in April, 1983, one of the students there presented a moral conundrum that will always haunt me. Her name was Cathy Campbell, a pretty young blonde woman who tended to stay very much to herself. We were surprised when she came to this big party, especially so as she brought her son River with her. He was about five years old and adorable. A few days later, quite by chance, several people in the program and I happened to be watching TV when a segment came on with pictures of missing children. River was one of them. The students came to me and we talked about what we should do. We simply couldn't decide how to proceed. We assessed the situation and decided that River was well cared for, loved his mother and that it was probably in the child's best interests to leave the situation alone. We didn't see that an alternative arrangement for River could be better than what he had. So we did nothing. Cathy graduated and left Tucson and I have not heard from her since.

That year, 1983, one of my students was married in our home in May. Dawn Ruitenberg and fiancé Bill Foster were thrilled to be able to wed at our swimming pool with an unobstructed view of the Catalina Mountains as a backdrop.

Another of my interesting students was Sherry Forgey. She had applied to my master's degree program in the education of children and youth with behavior disorders. When she came for her interview I was stunned. Sherry was a paraplegic in a wheelchair—and pregnant. I tried to convey to her that this was not an appropriate profession for her as the children who would be in her classroom were often violent and out-of-control. She was a very strong woman in every respect. She fervently believed she could move as fast, even in a wheelchair, as anyone else. I was convinced and she was both an excellent student and later a very fine teacher of autistic children.

von Isser family with Janice Angevine on Camino Escuela - 1982

We continued to have these parties until my retirement. The biggest was actually held in our Camino Escuela house with 80 people in attendance. We didn't get to bed until 3:30 a.m. that night! At another party in 1983 we hosted 50 students and in 1984 there were 70 there for a sit-down dinner on our patio. Clearly they were a success.

Tony always enjoyed these parties but wondered why on earth such fine young people would go into the profession of working with emotionally handicapped students.

Kent, Tony, Aldine & Tony Jr. on Camino Escuela

It was in this house that we learned of Tony's terminal cancer. For many years Tony had told me that if he knew he was going to die or if he ever intended to take his own life Tucson would never forget him. He was going to change the profile of the Santa Catalina Mountains. How? His plan was to fly a plane into Finger Rock altering its appearance forever. His back-up plan was to go to Mexico, sail off in his beloved sailboat and simply step off the stern. I was fully expecting some such termination to his life. But he didn't do it. A short while before his death I asked him why he hadn't ended his life sooner on his own terms. He vehemently replied that he "didn't want the bastards to think he couldn't take it."

Tony was ready to leave our big house and knew exactly where he wanted to live during his final days. We were lucky to find one place for sale in the townhouse complex he loved. We bought it on December 24th and moved in on December 27, 1986! In his final Christmas letter Tony wrote that his last three years were the happiest of his life.

By this time, my father had died (1984) and my mother bought a townhouse only three houses away from us in the same complex. Tony died in 1989 and mother in 1994. There were just too many memories for me there. I needed to move.

My niece Stephanie and her husband Tyler Meigs were planning to sell their townhouse very close by in another little community, Catalina Pueblo, where my sister lived. The house had and has never been on the market having had only one owner before Tyler bought it from her directly. And I bought it from Tyler directly in 1994 and moved in on April 29, 1995. Kent had done a magnificent renovation for me and it was fresh and modern and full of character. A bonus was that I now lived only two houses away from my sister Carol. I lived there alone until Hal and I tied the knot in 2008. I love it. It is beside one of the three pools in our little complex and I have a gate from my patio leading right on to it.

I want to add that we have wonderful, caring neighbors. It is almost like a community family here. One neighbor, Nancy Meister, has been a dear friend for years. She has a fascinating story to tell and I have recorded it in Appendix 6.

It is significant to tell the rest of the story regarding the sale of our beloved house with the pond. As I was a real estate agent, I planned to sell it myself. One Sunday afternoon in 1969 I went out to the road and was in the process of planting a "for sale by owner" sign when a car stopped. The driver, a woman, asked about it and I invited her to come inside and look. She phoned her husband who came immediately to see it, and they bought it. These people were Janet and Frank Marcus who remain close friends to this day and still live in the house!

Janet was a Tucson City Council Member held in high regard, with one exception—the pond. Tucson has a dearth of water and critics have complained that this is a blatant misuse of our resources. The pond remains and is a source of delight to all who see it. Frank was, at the time they bought our house, the Department Head of Cardiology at the University of Arizona Medical Center. As my heart problems increased he became my doctor and has seen me through many crises. Frank is still involved in research at UA and is at work every day.

As I have mentioned, that house was out in the country and crossing it is a deep arroyo called the Alamo Wash. Flash floods are a problem in this region and our wash was one of the worst. (It now has a bridge.) One afternoon Tony and I were sitting outside following a heavy rain when we heard a man's voice calling for help. We raced to find him and learned that he and his wife had crossed the arroyo in their car not knowing its depth when a flash flood hit them. Their names were John and Mary Sullivan and the water swept Mary from the car and rushed her downstream. We eventually found her body drowned on the desert. They had been returning from a church service and had seven children at home.

The Marcus family very much wanted to buy the little house that Tony's father had lived in, but Tony felt it would be a good rental. That meant, of course, that I would take care of it! So I cleaned and decorated and finally put it on the market as a rental. We had put a double bed in it. My first renters were two older women whom I knew at first glance would be trouble. They decided to rent it but, of course, it had to have twin beds to accommodate them.

Out went the double bed; in came the twin beds. At any hour of the day or night that they had a problem or needed a new light bulb, they would phone. I can't believe that a landlord is required to change a lightbulb! So, whether I was ready for bed or not, I would dutifully dress and drive over to take care of their issue.

They eventually moved on and left our little house. The next renter was an attractive young man about whom I had a very good feeling! I asked if he had a wife who would be living with him and he said he was soon to be married. "Oh," said I, "then twin beds won't do at all." Out went the twin beds; back came the double bed. He paid the first and last month's rent and told me he would move in two days hence. I left champagne and a fruit basket for the young couple.

When I phoned a few days later to inquire if everything was all right, there was no answer. Nor was there ever an answer which suggested to me that I had better check on the place. When I arrived I knew we were in trouble. The front door was wide open. I found the bed unslept in, and the fruit attracting flies. I also found a large suitcase in which were the remnants of what must have been a great deal of marijuana. Our lovely little villa had been used as a drop off point! I was very upset.

All was not lost, however. I phoned a young friend, David Sholin—the son of our minister–who was only too happy to collect the remaining marijuana. As I have never smoked, I haven't felt the full effect of "weed" but I did have him blow a little in my direction.

We did, by the way, sell the little house to the Marcus family who has enjoyed having their own family live there over all these years.

Having mentioned our other homes, I need to give credit to the three beautiful homes in which we lived in Palos Verdes Estates outside Los Angeles during our tenure there. We rented the first two and then bought a lovely place across the street from the school our boys attended. When we returned to Tucson, Tony wanted to keep it as a rental. I would have no part of that so we sold. Now each of those houses would sell for many millions of dollars. Ah, well.

My reason for leaving real estate was simple; I was shafted. As I mention elsewhere, Dr. Samuel Kirk had been seeking a real estate agent and had chosen me. This was to my great advantage and my great disadvantage. The Kirks were very specific about what they wanted in a house. I searched every listing, as did my mother, and immediately took them to see any house that came on the market that might suit their needs. I am not overestimating when I say I showed them dozens of houses. And if they heard or read of one of interest to them, over I went to take them to see it. It took countless hours so I suggested that they build just the house they wanted. No, they wanted to buy.

Over the next year I spent a great deal of time house hunting with Winifred Kirk and we came to love each other very much. In our research, we often traveled together. We were the best of friends. This was the advantage to which I alluded that came with this real estate experience. Now the bad news.

One Monday morning Wini phoned me excitedly to say that over the weekend they had found just the house they wanted and they had bought it—from another agent. I decided real estate was not for me. I am sure they didn't realize that morally they should have bought the house through me. But, I decided, if one's closest friends could do this, then I was a sitting duck for it to happen again. It certainly dampened my enthusiasm for staying in real estate sales.

The Kirks continued to be close friends. Sam had a devastating stroke on December 2, 1986 and was left without the ability to speak. His mind worked well but he couldn't express his thoughts. It must have been very frustrating for this august gentleman of letters to be rendered helpless in his last years.

I enjoyed my years in real estate and the opportunity it gave me to meet new and interesting people. However, when Tony became ill in 1986 I realized that this chapter of my life was over, but would never be forgotten.

19

୧୫୨୦

ADVENTURES WITH FRIENDS

ADVENTURES WITH KARL PATTISON

Karl Modjeska Pattison was a colleague at UA–a professor in the College of Engineering for 20 years. He was also a longtime friend of my husband Tony as they had worked together at Hughes Aircraft Company for many years. Frequently they took sailing trips together off the coast of Mexico and were, along with my father, members of the Tucson Literary Club. I include his middle name as it was a source of great pride to him. His paternal grandmother was the renowned Polish Shakespearian actress Modjeska. Yes, a single name—like Cher.

Karl Pattison - 1982

Karl came to our place in Canada for the first time in the early 1980s. In our cottage hang close to 200 photographs taken over the past hundred or more years— a chronicle of my family history. During an examination of each one, he suddenly stopped dead in his tracks. "But why is there a photograph here of my grandmother?" he asked. "No, no," said I. "These are only photos of my family." However, we removed it from the wall for closer inspection. On the back, where my father had carefully identified each one, was written, "We found this among Vada's photos. We don't know who she is but she is so impressive that we decided to include her." It was, indeed, Karl's grandmother verified later in Tucson in a book about her which contained the same photo. Now, how likely is that to happen!

Karl was born in 1921 and served in WWII as a B-29 commander. He is acknowledged as the only pilot ever to have landed a B-29 with three dead engines—a feat that would greatly impress any pilot. This occurred on an island in the South Pacific. Karl was flying missions over Japan. He was a tall man—6' 4"—and often referred to as "the gentle giant."

Another unusual story about Karl is that he ascended Mt. McKinley by himself—an act of atonement for an egregious sin he was convinced he had committed. It did indeed turn out to be a punishing experience. He barely missed falling into unimaginably deep crevasses on several occasions, and ran very low on food before he reached the summit. But of the greatest distress to him was that he had neglected taking toilet paper with him in order to reduce his load. Bad call! Snow and ice as a substitute only served to intensify the problem. He returned safely, expiated from sin, and lived until 2002.

My last anecdote about Karl is of a visit he made to Lake of Bays. Rat Bay, our bay on Lake of Bays in Ontario, Canada, is small and has been developed only in recent years. It must be noted that at the time this incident took place, there was not even a roadway on the other side of the bay. Well, one lovely summer day I was outside near our beach when I heard the strains of beautiful flute music wafting through the still morning air. Someone was in the wilderness on the other side of the bay playing Mozart's Piano Concerto No. 21, the theme from *Elvira Madigan* and Karl's favorite music. It was played, magnificently, once only. Then silence. I learned later that Karl had driven all the way from Tucson for that brief serenade, turned around and returned to Tucson—a drive of over 5000 miles!

PINACATES ADVENTURE

Although Karl was twelve years my senior, he was in far better shape than I. Hence, it was with great trepidation that I accepted his invitation to go with him to a region known as The Pinacates on February 25, 1983.

The Pinacates Volcano area is in the Sonoran Desert in northwest Mexico, a nearly unpopulated region between Arizona and the Gulf of California. It is a fascinating landscape of sand desert, lava fields, craters, fumaroles, and vents, all topped by a giant sprawling volcano. It covers an area of about 600 square miles and is under the aegis of the Mexican government. Karl had been there previously with adventurous friends willing to take a risk. His favorite formation was one he called "the fractured egg" and he was determined that I would see it. He had forewarned me that there was danger involved. It was at that time very infrequently visited and if we got into trouble there would be no one to help us. The road that existed was difficult to identify because of the shifting sand. There was no doubt that we would get bogged down in sand and that it would require great ingenuity to get us out. I would have to shovel while he gunned the engine—or I would have to act as weight on the vehicle—or whatever would get us rolling again. He took the only vehicle he thought would work for us, an old Volkswagen van (circa 1965) that he had outfitted for living with a little kitchen area, etc. (No indoor plumbing, however!)

We drove to Mexico, entered the Pinacate region, and many hours and miles later set up camp.

The "fractured egg" - Pinacates, Mexico - 1983

Day one saw us geared up and ready for the long trek to the fractured egg. Although the sun was bright, it was cold and I found myself shivering. The fractured egg is a geological structure growing out of the earth and abounding with fissures through which one could walk or crawl. These fissures wended their way throughout the egg, which in retrospect seemed enormous to me. I had no idea where I was or in what direction I should go when I noticed that Karl was missing, ostensibly playing a joke on me. Now, this wasn't fun. No time for playing hide and seek at this point, as far as I was concerned. When he didn't return immediately, I really started to shiver. The terror I felt was exacerbated by my tendency toward claustrophobia. If anything happened to him I was history. When he did return he had to endure my significant wrath.

We found our way out and started our return to the campsite. I had taken comb and lipstick in my pack, ever the female. Karl laughed when he saw me using them saying, "Aldine, you aren't going to see anyone but me for days." How wrong he was!

We had noticed a small aircraft circling high above us, a curiosity but not a concern. We should have realized that the government would patrol this area due to the possibility of drug exchanges, and what more suspicious vehicle could there be than an old VW bus! My terror was reignited when we found four Mexican federales with guns pointed at us when we arrived back at our camp. They had totally ransacked the inside of the van but, even though they found nothing suspicious, they were still convinced we were up to no good. My Spanish saved the day and eventually they relaxed and had a cup of coffee with us. Ultimately, they left. We breathed a sigh of relief and thought we were "out of the woods." They had told us they were a group of four government compadres who met once a year for a little R & R. No problem.

Aldine with federales - 1983

Until... Several hours later we were driving along, having experienced the requisite number of derailments due to getting stuck in sand, when we saw the same four oficiales blocking the road–with their guns aimed at us. Not good. We stopped. They seemed amiable and invited Karl and me to drive up a roadway at the end of which they told us was a well-preserved crashed airplane. Well, as pilots we were interested, but we really didn't see a way of refusing their invitation anyway. They had the guns. And climb we did, ultimately finding the promised aircraft.

Now the trouble began and that is the reason for my telling this story. They invited us—indeed they insisted upon us going down into a deep cave where they wanted "to show us something interesting." I knew in my gut that we were in great trouble, and so did Karl. It was with great reluctance that we acquiesced. Again, they had the guns, you see. There was quite a drop to enter the cave necessitating assistance even for the gentle giant. I had an agent on each side of me, as did Karl, descending further and further into the dark. That is when I knew for sure that we were going to be led to our death, our bodies so deeply buried in the mountain that we'd never be found. I was quite sure they wanted that VW bus, a real treasure for a Mexican even to this day.

Finally, I decided that I would not take another step toward my doom. If I were going to be raped and/or murdered it would be here and now. Enough was enough. I stopped and told them I would go no further. I stood resolutely while they made eye contact with each other for what seemed like a lifetime to me and appeared to come to a tacit agreement that maybe this wasn't a good idea. I guess they got cold feet and very courteously assisted us out of the cave and back to our van. Karl and I were aware that we had just lived through a close call. It may be the time I feel I came closest to death— although you'll read about other incidents elsewhere in my writing.

We were shaking like leaves as we drove on toward the McDougal Crater, a location of great interest to scientists. I had long been aware of it as there was a photo of it in the upstairs hallway of the old white cottage in Dwight. My father had been hired years before to take this picture while hanging out of an old plane that had no door on the passenger side. And my father had a significant fear of heights! I had seen it daily during my adolescent and adult years, and it carried a mystery about it that I longed to feel in person.

We reached the crater late in the day and climbed down as far as we safely could after which there was a significant drop off to the bottom. Karl felt he could easily get down into the crater and help me in and out. Now I am a risk taker but this seemed like potential suicide to me. What if Karl could get me out but then find that he himself was unable to do so? After considerable discourse, he realized I would not relent. I wasn't taking the chance. As I say, if anything happened to Karl I was finished.

We spent two more days exploring this primitive wilderness area and returned to Tucson. That was an adventure I was not going to repeat—ever!

MT. WRIGHTSON ADVENTURE

While it is not an exciting story, I do want to record that I did two significant climbs with Karl. One occurred in March, 1982 when we hiked to the top of Mt. Wrightson in southern Arizona. It has an elevation of 9, 453 ft. There is a good trail, but it is a long way from the base of the Santa Rita Mountains to the top, and I should have been in much better shape for it. We camped overnight at Josephine Saddle. I had left a cup of water outside the tent and found it

Aldine on top of Mt. Wrightson - 1982

frozen solid in the morning. Our second day would get us to the peak. I honestly thought I couldn't do it but with Karl's encouragement—no, insistence—and with crawling and clawing my way to the top like an Iron Man contestant, I did it. At the peak, which is a flat area about 30 square yards in size, is a registration book. I printed my name in bold letters.

I am sad to mention that the same year that we made our climb, a troop of Boy Scouts had gone on the same trip. A snowstorm overwhelmed them in the night and five lads died.

GRAND CANYON ADVENTURE

In April, 1982, I took another of my little "pat myself on the back" hikes that took Karl and me down an unmaintained trail in the Grand Canyon, the Hermit Trail. It was meant for only the intrepid hiker. It was a very steep, narrow path with a drop-off of thousands of feet. Additionally, there were large rocks that blocked the path in many places over which we had to climb. Add crumbly gravel to the mix and I had my work cut out for me.

On the rugged, dangerous Hermit Trail, Grand Canyon - 1982

Although the descent took seven hours, it seemed worth it when we reached the bottom and set up camp in that place that is one of the Wonders of the World. We swam in the Colorado River and watched the light change on the walls and columns as the evening progressed.

But the inevitable was ahead—the ascent. Karl, realizing that this would be difficult for me, took most of the contents of my backpack as well as his own. About a third of the way from the top I was finished—done. I couldn't go another step. Neither assistance nor encouragement was of any help. I hoped they had rescue teams for middle aged ladies who had overstepped their bounds. What would save me! Well, I'll tell you what happened.

Three energetic, but not overly polite, young women were coming up fast behind us. One saw me flagging and Karl carrying most of the load and said, "What, old lady, you're not up to it?" By damn, that rankled me! My adrenaline was surging, just what I needed. Suddenly I was practically flying up that trail with no difficulty whatever. That rude young woman saved the day. (I'm glad she never knew.) And the uphill hike took less than eight hours.

As a footnote to this story I want to tell you how it feels to get to the top of a long trail. One takes off one's backpack and feels a euphoria that almost defies description. It is akin to levitating.

COPPER CANYON ADVENTURE

One last story about Karl. This one requires a preface. In the early fifties when I started my course work at UA, it didn't take long for me to learn of the curse of the middle door of the university library. As a Presbyterian, I was conditioned to respect superstitions. I still do, to my embarrassment and chagrin. It was broadly known that if a student EVER passed through the middle door of the University of Arizona library he or she would not have even a chance of graduating. I joined the cadre of believers and never, but never used that door. I was determined to graduate.

Eventually the time came when I was to receive my Ph.D. I would indeed graduate. My father, Murray Sinclair, a feature writer for the Arizona Daily Star, wrote an article about my long-standing avoidance of using the middle door at the library. But, he added in his column, that on the day I received my degree I would, for the first time, enter the library through that very door. He specified the date—Friday, December 13, 1974. Could there have been a more ominous date?

In short order my father received a letter from W. David Laird, Dean of the University of Arizona library from 1972 to 1990. In it he wrote that he and his staff had read the article and harbored serious concerns that the venerable old library might not be able to withstand the trauma to which it would be submitted on that day. To protect it, the middle door of the library was to be locked at that time. And so it was that for the first and only time in UA history no one **could** use the middle door. A few years later the library was moved to a more modern facility. I was on the library Board for a while. (As an addendum, the first house Tony and I lived in was on San Francisco Boulevard. It was later bought by David Laird and his wife Dr. Helen Ingram who still reside there.)

Because there were so many obstacles to my ever graduating, I decided that if that middle door was an omen of doom, I might perhaps be wise to avoid all middle doors at the university. And I did.

This soon morphed into a fear of middle doors throughout Tucson, even the world. If one could be contaminated, then perhaps they all were. Who could be sure! Yes, it was inconvenient for others, but they respected my determination. Regrettably, these many years later I still will not pass through a middle door and the weird thing is that I don't think it is weird!

Now to my story. Karl and I had long wanted to backpack down into Cañon del Cobre—Copper Canyon–in the northwestern part of Mexico. This is the home of the Native American Tarahumara tribe. The Spanish discovered them throughout the State of Chihuahua in the 1500s. They are a nomadic tribe moving seasonally to accommodate their crops of corn, beans, squash and tobacco that are their staples.

These reticent people live a quiet life throughout Copper Canyon isolated from the Mexican culture. They number between 50,000 and 70,000 and are famous for being fleet of foot. Wearing only leather thongs, they can run for hundreds of miles, seemingly without tiring. They catch deer barehanded. Their homes are in caves, under cliff overhangs, or in small cabins of wood or stone. They are incredibly private and see few outsiders.

Karl and I were going to descend the canyon on our own and hoped to meet some of these people. Many tourists think they have visited the Tarahumara when they take the train—the Chihuahua Pacífica–from the coast of Sonora to Chihuahua. In fact, they see the fall-out from the tribe—the Indians who want to make money and sell their wares along the train track garbed in their unique regalia. We were seeking the real experience.

Because we would be carrying everything we needed for a week in our backpacks, we were incredibly careful about weight. We took tea, but we removed the staples from the teabags to make them weigh less! Our towels were about 12" by 18". It would be cold down in the canyon so some items were, of necessity, heavy. We took whistles and mirrors for contacting each other in case we became separated.

We had thought carefully about gifts for the Tarahumara whom we hoped to see. We had small tools for the adults and balloons for the children.

We were incredibly excited about this experience which we were doing over spring break from the university. We had timed our departure from Tucson late on a Friday— March 12, 1982—after my last class. I was in such a hurry that I literally ran from the elevator in the Education Building to meet Karl at his car outside. Someone noticed my haste and opened the door for me—yes, the middle door. Without thinking I raced through and then almost gagged when I realized what I had done. I knew without doubt that our trip was <u>doomed</u>, irrevocably <u>doomed</u>. Karl tried to make light of my gaffe, but he had seen it and he too knew that we were in trouble.

We flew on a plane filled with flying feathers from hens and small animals of many species to the town of Ciudad Obregon. After what my diary noted was "the noisiest night of my life" we endured a three-hour bus trip to the seaport of Los Mochis (the flies) where we spent the night. A seafood restaurant had been recommended to us so it was with watering mouths we went there and took a table at the sea's edge. Karl ordered the local clams. I dislike clams so chose to have their delicious Mexican food. Karl, however, was insistent upon my having at least one of his clams. I capitulated. Bad move.

The next morning we boarded a train for the nine-hour trip through the Sierra Madre Mountains to reach our destination–Creel, Chihuahua. This railway was considered an engineering miracle and passed through magnificent country. However, according to my diary, we found Creel to be "the most barren, depressing, windy, cold place I could imagine." It was from Creel that we planned to "thumb" a ride with any passing truck driver who would be able to drop us near a canyon trail—the beginning point for our adventure.

Although we had felt queasy on the train, it wasn't until the moment that we checked into our humble motel for one night, than the inevitable doom hit us. The clams were Satan's tool. For days our illness showed no mercy. We were so sick that I thought my insides would come out—one direction or another. We were living in our own filth barely able to take care of ourselves. We were running fevers. I honestly wondered if I'd ever see home again—and we were on a time line. I had to be back in Tucson after spring break to teach my classes. I didn't see how that would ever happen. The minute that we both felt strong enough to travel, we decided to return to Tucson. Certainly the backpacking trip was out.

We limped to the train, pounds lighter than when we arrived, and made the long train trip back to Los Mochis. There we were unable to find room in a hotel and had to take a taxi out of the city to finally find a place to lay our heads. The next day we made our way back to Los Mochis, took the bus to Ciudad Obregon, and flew to Tucson. There Karl collected his truck and we headed into Tucson. Alas, the truck was breaking down and drove slower and slower until it finally stopped. We were stuck on the highway— and we were exhausted.

My darling son Kent, who was on spring break from Brooks, came to our rescue. He brought his own truck, towed Karl and his truck to Karl's house and then he and I went home—at last.

I believe it was the most horrible trip I have ever taken and I never took even one step into Cañon del Cobre. Now do you believe the curse of the middle door?

Karl Pattison married the widow of one of his old students, retired from UA in 1990 and died on February 12, 2002 at the age of 80.

ADVENTURES WITH MARGARET RUSCICA

OUR EVENING WITH PRINCE PHILIP

Everyone should have a friend like Margaret Ruscica—ebullient, unique, and loyal. She abjures sleep but maintains an energy level that would compete easily with that of marathon runners. And she wrings every moment out of life that her 4 to 5 hours of sleep a day afford her.

Margaret Ruscica

She loves fine dining, her family, and her friends. I am lucky enough to be in the latter category. Also, she loves theater, but prefers sitting only in the front row, center. For this she is willing to line up in the wee hours of the morning, months ahead.

One summer in 1993 when I was alone at the cottage, Margaret phoned from her home in Toronto and asked if I would like to join her in attending the opening of a new IMAX film on Harbour Front in Toronto on October 13th. It was sponsored by the World Wildlife Fund and its president, Prince Philip, would be there along with a host of Ontario dignitaries. The event included a reception, the film and dinner. We would be in the lesser priced area, which was quite all right with me.

My concern was clothing as I was in the north woods, it was cold, and I had nothing appropriate to wear. When I joined her in Toronto she bedecked me in her best finery and jewelry and the result was that I looked quite elegant.

Off we went for a gala evening. We had to cross a long bridge to the Pavilion which had been decorated to coordinate with the film we were to see—tropical plants and lots and lots of smoke and steam. We were quite giddy with the moment when we encountered the hosts who asked whether we were Jaguars or Cougars—the two levels of admission. Margaret said that while we felt like Jaguars, we were, in fact, Cougars. Bad call. We were ushered with pomp to the appropriate reception area. And there was Prince Philip, Duke of Edinburgh. "Oh, oh," said Margaret, "we're in the wrong place!" I thought it was rather wonderful and encouraged her to stay. I then asked if she'd like to join me as I was going over to chat with Prince Philip, with champagne in hand. She blanched and couldn't believe I had such gall.

He was reticent but charming. I sent my warm regards to his wife.

Eventually, they called us for the film. We were in the first queue—as Cougars—and I heard people ahead of us giving their row letters to the ushers. "Say Row M, Margaret. Say Row M." She did and we settled ourselves in the center of Row M and awaited the festivities. Security came along to check Row L which I had suspected was where the dignitaries would be seated. I asked the nice man if he'd mind checking to see if he could find the lipstick I had dropped, a black cylinder. He found it and gave it to me without comment!

In time the theater filled and Prince Philip took the seat directly in front of me. Margaret was ready to pass out. She was as upset as I've ever seen her and she longed to retreat and join the Jaguars. Well, the place had filled and there was no possibility of that so she stuck it out. Half of who's who in Ontario was in attendance—quite a thrill for me. I was annoyed when Prince Philip chatted with the men on either side of him disturbing my concentration and came very close to tapping him on the shoulder to ask him to please hold it down.

Now the fun began. Spotlights were focused on the Prince and we who were sitting immediately behind were also the center of the spotlight activity for all of Toronto to see. Margaret truly was ready to pass out. Far below in the audience she saw her friends and family—Jaguars—whose mouths dropped open to see us amidst all the fanfare.

It was an excellent film—*Seven Years in Tibet*–made in Korea, but as soon as Margaret could escape, she did. I am not sure she has ever forgiven me, and she continues to blanch when the subject arises.

MY EXPERIENCE WITH SHIRLEY MacLAINE

Again Margaret called me from Toronto while I was alone at the cottage up north and invited me to join her and two other women for a single performance by Shirley MacLaine. I had always been enchanted by her and grabbed the opportunity.

Margaret and we three ladies went to a lovely restaurant prior to the show. I sat on the inside of a banquette and loved the opportunity to be in a gracious setting after several months of roughing it. I had lamb. Suddenly I couldn't breathe. I couldn't swallow. I couldn't cough. My esophagus was totally blocked and I knew I was in big trouble. I was also in shock. One of the ladies, seeing that I was in serious distress, asked if I were all right. I shook my head, no. She saw that I had little time before I would pass out and screamed for a waiter to come to perform the Heimlich maneuver. I was almost unconscious but took the last of my energy to put my hands on the table to push myself up to get out of the confined space. With that exertion, up came the lamb and a good deal else all over the table. It seemed to be coming out of my nose and eyes but rather than feeling embarrassed I felt a surge of enormous gratitude to be alive. I was in a state of grace and elation.

Margaret asked whether I wanted to continue with the evening. On an all new high, I most certainly did. We were, as expected, in the front row, center. That amazing woman, Shirley MacLaine, came on stage and never left it even once during the two hour performance. And she is only a year younger than I am! Her costume changes were subtle and happened in the background—unnoticed by the audience. But what made this event unique was that from the moment she started her performance until her last bow she rarely took her eyes off me, yes, me. We had an instantaneous psychic connection. She has always been known to have a unique communication with the "other world" and must have realized that I had just suffered a near death experience. All around us in the audience people were looking at me—wondering what my relationship was with Ms. MacLaine. This connection between us was palpable— uncanny. Never have I had such an experience of feeling one with another person— whom I had never met.

When we left the theater, several people approached us to ask about the phenomenon they had just witnessed. It was inexplicable—and unforgettable.

20

ೞ

MY UNUSUAL BEAUX

Since I became a widow at age 55, my husband having died in early 1989, I had almost twenty years of being single before I married Hal Grieve in 2008. I had many gentlemen friends during that period, most of whom were relatively normal but some of whom were—well, unusual.

One of these friends, Joe Green, whom I will mention frequently in this memoir, was traveling in Australia. He visited a former colleague, Paul Moffitt, whom I had known years earlier. Paul asked for news of Tucson, and Joe mentioned that Tony von Isser had died. Paul and Joe had been driving at the time. Paul suddenly stopped his truck and looked at Joe disbelievingly. Apparently he had eyes for me years previously when he and I were psychologists on a federally funded model preschool Indian project for handicapped children in Arizona. There was a team of us who visited all 22 Indian (Native American) reservations in Arizona. More is written about this project in a separate chapter.

Paul had been married during the time of the project; his wife Sue was a darling. They subsequently divorced. When Joe returned from Australia he warned me that I might be hearing from Paul. Indeed I did. I was in Canada at the time Paul phoned. He wanted to visit me in Tucson when I returned but insisted the date be set for the time of the first new moon thereafter. He was convinced that relationships had a better chance if initiated with a waxing moon! That should have been my first clue.

In truth, it was a terrible time for him to come to Tucson as the semester was just beginning and I was overwhelmed with work. But he did indeed arrive on September 9, 1991. He unpacked in my guest room. We went swimming, to my mother's house for a drink and out for dinner. About midnight I heard moans coming from Paul's room. He was in agony. He had to get to the hospital. All I could think was that I was exhausted and what had I gotten myself into this time!

Paul insisted I go into the examining room with him. Ugh. My relationship with Paul had always been professional and this was very uncomfortable for me. The medical team suggested I step out while they catheterized him but Paul beseeched me not to leave him. I closed my eyes, willing time to pass quickly. After many hours, he was discharged with the diagnosis of a kidney stone which they assured him would pass in time. Off we went at 3:00 a.m. to find an all-night pharmacy to fill his prescription for pain.

Bed, when it finally came, never felt so good. My guest room was at one end of the house and mine at the other end, door closed.

Paul settled in. His diet consisted of vegetables—period. He drank only tea, but never Earl Grey tea which was all I had. All the clocks and fountains had to be turned off as the noise disturbed him. There were jeans hanging over doors and my perfect little house was soon disassembled. I felt as though I was living with Crocodile Dundee. It just wasn't working—waxing moon notwithstanding.

Every morning I received a report as to whether the kidney stone had passed. No joy. I had provided Paul with a little sieve so that he could find it should the blessed event occur. One night I heard cries of elation emanating from the other end of the house, but coming closer. He threw open my door with the hallowed sieve in hand containing—yes—the kidney stone.

When the time came for Paul to return to Adelaide in New South Wales, Australia, I took him to the airport counting the minutes until the plane departed. As he left he handed me a beautifully gift-wrapped little box that I was sure contained an engagement ring. He asked me not to open it until the plane had taken flight. He had assumed that we would marry and had already asked his two daughters if they would prefer to live in Australia or the United States.

Well, it wasn't an engagement ring; it was his kidney stone, the most treasured gift he could think of leaving for me. OMG.

He spent the winter (summer for him) carving from eucalyptus trees he had hewn himself. He carved a remarkable portrait of me as well as a beautiful box that he inscribed with a tender message. He said he planned to deliver them to me in Tucson. I strongly urged him to mail them but he needed to be sure, absolutely sure, that I received them. I did not encourage another visit so was quite surprised when I had a knock on my office door at UA one morning and there was Paul, gifts in hand.

I did not invite him to stay with me so, mission accomplished, he turned around and flew back to Australia. The carving is hanging in our cottage in Canada and the charming box decorates a table in Tucson. While we are in touch by e-mail and at Christmas, I have not seen him since. Nor did he marry again.

My sons Kent and Tony Jr. were not keen on Paul and decided they needed to find a replacement for him in my life as quickly as possible. (They didn't need to worry; I had never succumbed to Paul's charms, although I did love his Australian accent.) They spoke to a good friend, Rick Small, who had a broad range of friends. Enter Howard Shenk. On October 5, 1991 the young people had a cocktail party to introduce Howard and me, assuring me that this was a fine and philanthropic man I was about to meet. They were right.

Howard qualifies as unusual in that, of all my beaux, he is the only one who became a life-long friend and an important part of my life. Our friendship has weathered a quarter of a century and is stronger than ever. My grandchildren have adopted him as a surrogate grandfather and there is never a family gathering, large or small, in which Howard is not included. He is indeed a part of our family. And a truer friend there could never be.

Knowing I had some excellent recipes, Howard suggested I write a cookbook for my family. Neither he nor I could imagine the magnitude of the project or its popularity upon completion. Howard printed close to 150 copies for distribution and they were gone as quickly as warm, chocolate chip cookies! It is long and colorful and in many of the copies the recipes are on the right page while on the left page there are family photographs taken over the years at our cottage. These copies have 205 pages! The title of the book is *Pelican Point Favourites*. It should be mentioned that it was also Howard's idea that I write this memoir.

I have made many wonderful trips with Howard over the years. One of our many memorable trips was traveling in Guatemala and climbing the Maya ruins that I write about in another chapter. Another was a month on the South Island of New Zealand where we left not a stone unturned. High on my agenda of "must do's" there was bungee jumping off the Queenstown Bridge, where the whole movement began. As I had passed my 60th birthday, the jump for me was free. However, Howard, six years my junior, was years away from reaching 60 but he could have taken advantage of the "jump naked, jump free" offer. He decided he'd rather pay. Well, I got out on the bridge, all weighed and chalked with statistics, walked out on that plank and looked down. Suddenly all the reasons for not doing this surfaced in my mind. Of primary importance was the upcoming commitment I had to work at the University of Canterbury for two months. A close second was my love of life. Once I backed off (literally) Howard–with great relief–was exonerated from having to jump. He told me later that he had felt honor bound to make the jump if I did, and he still breathes a sigh of relief that it never came to pass.

Howard and I love singing hymns. On his annual visits to the cottage in Canada we would walk two miles daily singing from the depth of our souls. We both know from memory verse after verse of dozens of hymns. Many people carry bells and noise makers while walking on our road as a warning to any nearby bears. Our singing took care of that problem.

An admirer early on had been a Submarine Commander in WWII. He was sufficiently affluent to afford gifting me with magnificent jewelry. One piece deserves special comment. He designed and had made for me a bracelet of large gold rose buds into each of which was set a diamond or a ruby. He had created a message in Morse code wherein the diamonds are "dots" and the rubies are "dashes." When read from left to right it says A-V-S (Aldine Virginia Sinclair, my maiden name). When turned around the Morse code reads, from left to right, I-L-U. It is a stunning piece and always draws attention. It was accompanied by earrings and a brooch.

One potential romance had to be aborted before it ever took off! My beloved friend Kate Altaffer had taken it upon herself to play match maker. She phoned one day to ask if I remembered George Hilliard. Indeed I did! As a young woman I had been captivated by his intellect and stature; he was 6' 5" tall! Although George was 11 years my senior, Kate and her husband Dabney thought that a dinner party the following Saturday would be nice for reacquainting us. I concurred. She then phoned George to invite him and he responded, "I would have enjoyed that very much, Kate, but I'm getting married on Saturday." And a lucky man he was to have won the heart of Emily Adams, a truly lovely and gracious lady. They were wed in late October, 1989 and had many happy years together before George died in 2011.

Dr. Peter Riplog was dashing, highly intelligent and handsome. I was introduced to him on the tarmac at the airport in Sedona, Arizona where our regional 99s group (an international affiliation of women pilots) was having a fly-in to have lunch. It was December of 1992. We were immediately attracted to each other and the great romance began. Pete was unique in that he had graduated summa cum laude from Stanford

University with a Ph.D. in aerospace engineering. He was immediately snapped up by Hughes Aircraft Company to be their chief rocket scientist and ultimately plant manager. His job was basically to sit in his nicely appointed office and think. Yes, just think. He was supposed to generate brilliant new ideas having to do with missiles and the like.

I want to point out that I never dated a man whom I did not know personally or to whom I had not been introduced. And, with rare exceptions, I dated only men who had either not been married or who were widowers. Pete was in the latter category.

Years ago I had formulated a series of requirements for a man who might garner my attention. At the top of the list was intelligence, and Pete fit the bill. Second came honor, then loyalty, sense of humor and so forth. In time, Pete went to my mother to ask if he might marry me. My mother had her own criteria for an appropriate spouse for me and she quickly responded with "You're too old and too short." I guess that about said it. Our romance ended sadly when Pete developed pancreatic cancer and died on June 5, 1993.

Walter Hill was another charmer. I had been introduced to him by one of my graduate students, Jennifer Hill, who thought that her grandfather and I would really hit it off. Jennifer had a story of her own. She was a stunningly beautiful young woman. One night while getting in her car in a parking lot on the university campus she was approached by a young man asking to borrow a pencil. While turning to find one for him, she was shoved violently into her car and the young man drove off, holding her at bay with a knife.

She was terror stricken as they drove north out of Tucson and hours later, on the Black Canyon Highway north of Phoenix, they had to stop for gas. The driver headed for a strange little gas station off the highway. Jennifer went to the ladies room and stayed there as long as possible while peeking out the door. Fortunately, two men came in to gas up their car. She went screaming out yelling that she was being kidnapped. The young man sped off in her car and soon, the Highway Patrol having been summoned, squad cars abounded. They had the highway closed to the north and south and the kidnapper was soon apprehended. He later admitted that she was being taken to a remote location in northern Arizona to be used as a "sacrifice" in a bloody cult ceremony. To my knowledge, he is still in prison.

Walter and I developed a nice friendship and he was one of many who came to the cottage for a visit. Although he was well into his 70s, he spent only a long weekend. That was a long trip from Tucson for anyone at any age for so short a time.

I noted in my diary that I always had fun with Walter. He was attentive–and loved the ladies. In December of 1993 he took me to Chicago and what a whirlwind weekend it was with shopping at the most elegant stores and dining in very sumptuous restaurants.

In Tucson, Walter took me to dinner frequently, but always to the same place, Le Rendezvous, an elegant French restaurant. There they knew me by name and we had our special table. I felt pampered. Walter was a restauranteur owning the well-known Charles Restaurant in Tucson. (He also held all the Kentucky Fried Chicken franchises in Southern Arizona.) Of course he knew all the other major restaurant owners in town.

Some months after Walter died, I was taken to the magnificent Anthony's Restaurant and had an opportunity to talk with Tony, the owner. I mentioned having been a friend of Walter Hill but that for some reason Walter had taken me only to Le Rendezvous. "Oh," said he, "that was yours, was it?" It seems that Walter had a number of ladies on the string and, in order to save embarrassment and confusion, each one had her own restaurant. I had a good laugh over that. I felt lucky to have been assigned to my favorite!

Dr. Joseph Green, whom I mentioned earlier, and his wife Ruth had been long time friends of ours. Ruth died, as did Tony, so Joe and I struck up a friendship as a couple. It was never romantic but we traveled a great deal together. Joe was the first child psychiatrist in Tucson. Hence, we were also colleagues and attended conferences together. It was at one of these conferences in Chicago that Joe introduced me to the eminent psychiatrist Dr. John Werry from Auckland, New Zealand. That meeting had a big impact on my life. He is the professor who arranged for a position for me at the University of Canterbury in Christchurch, New Zealand for my last sabbatical leave, about which there will be more in another chapter.

Long before I departed for New Zealand, Joe had casually mentioned that he might visit me while I was there. Nothing more was said until I received a phone call months later when I had been in New Zealand for several weeks. Joe announced that he'd be arriving in Christchurch two days hence and was planning to stay with me. (I was living in faculty housing.) I was furious. I had no forewarning and I wasn't at all sure that I wanted him there at all. Joe was a high maintenance friend. I explained that I could not meet him at the airport as I had a dinner engagement. When he suggested he join me, I assured him he would be much too tired after the long journey. "Not at all," said he.

Now, there are very strict rules for social comportment in New Zealand and I was fairly sure they wouldn't include inviting an additional guest to a small dinner party at the last minute. The hostess, however, took the request with good grace.

Some of the rules of etiquette included never, ever using the word "fanny" which is the word used in New Zealand for the unsavory four letter word c–t. While it isn't a word that comes up in everyday conversation, Joe did wear a fanny pack when hiking and often alluded to it. So I told Joe that it was completely off-limits to mention it in conversation. I added that under no circumstance during his visit should he ask the host for ice in his drink. They neither had nor used ice.

Well briefed in appropriate behavior, Joe and I went to the home of Dr. Warwick Elley and his wife Val for an intimate dinner. I was honored to be included as Dr. Elley was a world renowned specialist in issues related to literacy, as well as being a dean at the University of Canterbury. I had heard that he invited to his home visiting professors from abroad as there weren't very many of us at that time (1994). I introduced Joe and even before we sat down he advised everyone that he had been briefed on what he could and could not say and knew that he should not use the word "fanny." Mouths dropped open. I was humiliated and furious—really, really furious. And then, when asked what he would like to drink he added, "with ice, please." My evening was shattered. And it went from bad to worse. We did nothing that evening to dispel the image of the "ugly American." I must add that I never heard from the Elleys again.

As I say, although I loved Joe as a friend, he was difficult. I had to do all the driving as Joe was nervous about driving "on the wrong side." And he claimed he got sick if he was not seated looking forward in trains, which we used frequently for travel. Hence, I saw everything we had just passed.

Joe is gone now and is one of my old friends whom I truly miss.

Let's go on to the motorcycle rider. Now, I've always loved motorcycles as my husband and two sons had them for as long as I can remember. A friend, Ben Storek, never got over passing a woman on a motorcycle on Glenn Street and then realizing it was his friend Aldine. He mentioned that incident for the rest of his life.

My motorcycle beau was a university colleague with whom I enjoyed going to theater and movies. Since he is still alive, he shall remain nameless. I knew I was held in high esteem by him when he invited me to join him and a cadre of his friends on their annual motorcycle trip—1000 miles down the Baja Peninsula in Mexico, the second longest peninsula in the world. The longest is the Malay Peninsula in Southeast Asia. I was quite excited when we met as a group to finalize our plans until I learned that they made the journey in the **nude**. Can you imagine! I love an adventure but that was too over the rainbow even for me.

Over many years, one exciting suitor was a man named Merrill Dillon. Now, while he never really specified his profession, he alluded to having an affiliation with "the company"—the CIA. Many friends of his had this impression as well. It was borne out by the frequent number of sudden trips he made in spite of his advancing years. He did not look threatening in the least, but I suspect there was a violent streak not far below the surface. He was the perfect operative, old and appearing to be innocuous.

One time Merrill returned from Alaska with a broken arm—allegedly due to an exchange of gunfire wherein he had to jump off a bridge.

I once mentioned to him my intense hatred for the doctor (Dr. Trudeau) who was responsible for the catastrophic care my son Kent received following his devastating accident in a gold mine in Chibougamou in Northern Quebec (and ultimately for his death). Merrill said he would take care of it. The wheels in my head turned, and I practically freaked out when I realized his intent. I told him that just the amputation of one finger on his right hand would be sufficient, and then I retracted even that. I hope it never happened.

Merrill loved coming to our cottage in Canada annually. Everyone doted on him and he had my undivided attention. Hence, I was very surprised when he phoned one August that he would not be visiting us. That was 2001. Of course he couldn't tell me what was preventing his coming, but I sensed it was important.

When I returned to Tucson, I had dinner with Merrill and heard the story. Merrill had been selected as one of a team of six going on an important mission. Several suspected terrorists had fallen through the cracks and needed to be found ASAP. The team met in Atlanta and split up into two groups. Merrill's team followed the trail of the terrorist to whom he had been assigned as far as Miami. Then—nothing. The mission had failed, ultimately causing the deaths of thousands of people.

I asked Merrill if they ever discovered the whereabouts of the missing terrorists. "Oh, yes," said he. They had been two of the terrorists who took down the Twin Towers in New York City on September 11, 2001. I still get tears in my eyes when I think of how close it was to not having happened and how inexcusable it was that the terrorists fell off our intelligence radar.

Soon after Tony died, I met in South America Dr. Robert Blackwell, a physician from Santa Rosa, California. As I was traveling throughout the spring of 1989, I didn't make contact with Bob again until I was at our cottage in Canada, alone, in May. Initially I rejected his invitation to visit him but soon found that Lake of Bays can be very lonely at that time of year and decided I would go. It was a long trip but I had a wonderful time meeting his friends and family and seeing beautiful places in that part of California.

In the fall of 1989, my mother, sister and I went to San Francisco for a lark and invited Bob to join us. The poor man! We led him a merry chase wanting to see and do as much as we could fit into a day. Although he knew San Francisco well, he found himself going the wrong way on one way streets, up the down hills and down the up hills and putting his perfectly maintained Mercedes Benz in jeopardy around every turn. I think he was thrilled when our departure day arrived and he could kiss all those ladies goodbye. That was, as I recall, the end of that relationship.

There were other beaux such as the Chair of the Department of Education at a Tucson psychiatric facility whom I had known professionally, Bill Gordon. He was also the leader of my grief group when my husband Tony died. Ours was a tempestuous relationship that ended in his betraying me. I was relieved when he ultimately moved to Alaska.

Dr. Ralph Shelton's introduction into my life caused me considerable trauma. I was taking a walk alone on a remote road near Arivaca when I heard someone approach from the rear on a bicycle. He intercepted me and said, "Oh, I thought you were my wife. She is lost and I am looking for her." There are some weird people in the Arivaca area and I was quite sure he qualified. Satisfied that I was not his wife, he introduced himself. He was a retired professor from the University of Arizona having had a distinguished career. He and his wife had chosen Arivaca for their retirement home.

In fact, his wife was indeed missing and there was an intensive search to find her. She had wandered away from a psychiatric institution in Tucson and was later found dead on the desert. This was not a good beginning to a relationship so Ralph and I fizzled rather quickly. I am happy to say he is now happily remarried.

And there was the head of the Reading Department in the College of Education at UA, Dr. Kenneth Smith, whose principal attraction was that he, too, was a pilot. His flying left a great deal to be desired, especially his taxiing skills on the ground. He kept forgetting he had wings and narrowly missed defacing both the hangars and his aircraft. He went on to marry a lovely woman.

Handsome Don Westby swept me off my feet with his quick wit and sense of humor. We were briefly engaged but over time the laughter was not enough to hold the relationship together—and Bob's your uncle.

And there was the fetish collector, Louis Drypolcher, to whom I was introduced in Mexico but with whom I was geographically incompatible as he lived in New Mexico. (Let me hasten to explain that in the Southwest a fetish is an object believed to have magical powers.) En route from Mexico to New Mexico he stopped for a visit with me in Tucson. During dinner he made a rude suggestion as to how we might spend the rest of the evening. I told him he might have waited at least until after dessert before making such a proposal, and I immediately sent him on his way, without dessert. He drove a Volvo that he prized. In his escape he bumped into a post in my carport and smashed his rear window. It was raining heavily and he begged to stay. I taped garbage bags in his rear window to protect his luggage from getting wet, and off he went never to be seen again.

John Maxfield won a place in my heart with his dancing skills. I had met John on a cruise in 1991 and we became good friends. On October 18th, I visited him at his lovely home on a golf course near Williamsburg, Virginia, and on December 17th he came to Tucson. The next summer he drove to the cottage. John had expectations for the visit that I chose not to fulfill, so his stay was brief and the relationship was over. I am quite sure our elderly neighbor at the cottage, Dorothy Thompson, was curious about all the gentlemen who came to visit me. I hope her imagination didn't run rampant as the reality would have sadly disappointed her.

I had dated a man in Toronto, John Thomas Sereny, who telephoned me in Tucson in 1994 to advise me that he was seeking a wife. Lucky me; I was a candidate! He came courting and stayed at Canyon Ranch in Tucson. I passed on his invitation to spend the weekend there with him. The relationship was doomed from the beginning. This was a man whose car—a Ferrari Testarossa costing just under a quarter of a million dollars— hinted at the size of his ego and his need to be noticed. It was obvious to me that the future Mrs. Sereny would always be his second love. Even his license plate was testimony to his first love—JTS 001. He was number one. Sayonara, Sereny.

Jack Miller does not quite qualify as a suitor, although the thought of a relationship crossed both our minds. He is an old friend of Elizabeth from Creston, Iowa who has visited me at the cottage and who spends time in Tucson every winter. He is a hero to our family as he constructed at our cabin in Arivaca a set of stairs from the living room to the loft that are unique and impossible to describe. Suffice that one would not be able to climb that stairway if inebriated as it requires concentration and coordination even when fully sober. Jack's photo is always on display near the stairs to remind us of his great kindness and of his amazing carpentry ability. Jack has written his own memoir and it is captivating.

Fred Daily was one of the nicest men a woman could ever meet and an important part of my life in 1995. He was a widower, and a gentleman in every sense of the word. His mother was Mexican and his father a gringo. Actually Fred was ¼ English, ¼ Irish, ¼ French and ¼ Mexican. He was very proud of his heritage; his forbears had been part of the famed group called the Buffalo Soldiers where they served as officers. They began defending the Southern Arizona border in 1913. They were stationed in Ft. Huachuca for 18 years and during that time protected our nation from Mexican revolutionaries as well as bandits such as Pancho Villa.

Fred was heavy. He never drank alcohol but was addicted to Coca Cola. He owned a roofing company but even the frequent climbing of ladders was not enough exercise to keep his weight down. He needed to lose one hundred pounds. I recommended that he give up coke and walk two miles a day and that within a year he would have lost those hundred pounds. He did just as I had suggested and became a lean and very handsome man. He reduced from 280 pounds to 180. Fred came to the cottage and was well liked by all. Complications in my personal life required that I stop seeing Fred. He is a splendid man whom I miss. He was a widower who never remarried.

Dr. Carl Oppenheimer was a scientist in Texas who came to Tucson to court me in 1996. When I went to Costa Rica he asked me to collect some earth from the edge of the Poás Volcano—earth with very special properties. He was involved in a project to develop a product that would soak up instantly and completely the oil from oil spills the world over. This earth was part of the necessary formula. I don't know whether the project came to fruition, but I did end up with a lifetime supply of septic tank treatment that we use in Canada.

Suitors came and went but either they were not sufficiently interesting to mention, or they left me with memories I would rather not recall. Never in all those years did I live with anyone. That would not have met with the approval of my children.

And then there was dear Hal. He and Tony had been good friends and flying buddies back in the 1940s in spite of Tony having been five years his senior. Tony introduced me to Hal on October 6, 1952 on the UA campus. He had heard that his good pal Tony was getting married and thought he had better check this out. Although he lived in Pennsylvania, he hitchhiked to Tucson which provided the opportunity for us to meet.

When Hal's wife Bette died in 1997, Hal came courting from Pennsylvania where they had lived on a farm in the hills above the Susquehanna River for many years. He decided to move back to Tucson where he had been raised and where his mother, Marion DeGrazia, lived. He stayed at the DeGrazia Gallery in the Sun. Hal frequently proposed marriage and indeed he met every single criterion on my "have to have" list mentioned previously. I just wasn't ready for marriage.

In 2007, life-changing events occurred in my health that boded well for me to live longer than I had anticipated. Having done all he could to control my escalating atrial fibrillation, my beloved cardiologist, Dr. Peter Ott, performed the ultimate surgery from which there was no turning back. It is called an AV node ablation which severed the connection of my heart so that I now have no natural heartbeat whatever. I became, and continue to be, totally dependent on a Pacemaker, a wee battery that keeps me alive. (Dr. Joseph Alpert at university hospital refers to me as "our robot lady.")

Although I had received at least a dozen proposals of marriage over the years, I had never wanted to give up the life of a single woman. Kent had quietly told the family that if, in fact, I ever did marry he hoped I would pick Hal.

After careful thought, I realized that it was time to settle down and Hal was indeed the man with whom I wanted to share the rest of my life. His requests for my hand in marriage had run out years previously—he had given up—so it was up to me to conjure a way for him to propose once again. I planned the perfect setting—the front porch at our cabin in Arivaca with champagne and romantic music. It was October 31, 2007. The scene was set. I had told Hal that something very special was going to happen that afternoon. He didn't have any idea as to what was ahead.

And so I suggested we drink to my healthy future and a new and exciting chapter in my life that was now wide open—the sky was the limit. I had new hopes and dreams. No clue! So I asked what his hopes and dreams for the rest of his life were. He said his life was just as he wanted it. So I asked if he was happy with our relationship as it was. Totally delighted, said he. So I suggested he think "outside the box" at some wonderful but crazy possibilities. Still no clue! "Well then, let's look at this from a different paradigm." (He didn't know the meaning of paradigm.) I was just giving up when he said, "Are you talking about *marriage!!*" "Oh," said I coyly, "that's a wonderful idea." He was awed—dumbstruck. So down on one knee he went and said those four precious words—will–you-marry-me? Hence, we wed at the little Mission in the Sun (the chapel) at the DeGrazia Gallery on January 5, 2008. I was blessed with his love and devotion for almost nine years before he died on December 2, 2016.

My journey with many beaux was great fun and never boring! Again I am a widow, blessed with many happy memories. And I am deeply grateful for having had loving relationships throughout my life.

21

⊂≋⊃

MY SPIRITUAL JOURNEY

As I have sought within myself to make an honest appraisal of my spiritual journey, I have realized that my early history had a profound effect on what was to come.

Born in Toronto, Canada of a rigid Scots family, boundaries and protocol were established early in my life. Oh yes, the men did, and do, wear kilts to major events—family reunions, marriages, funerals—and bagpipes are a doleful constant in my memory. We attended Timothy Eaton Memorial Church. Toronto had strict rules for Sunday behavior. There were no stores or movie theaters open, only one drug store per area was available, and people knew enough to gas up their cars before the Sabbath. Add to these restrictions those of my family—no card playing, no work, and precious little laughter.

I knew right from wrong—there was no gray—and I determined early to be a "good girl." I have spent my life being a "good girl." It is difficult for me to determine to what extent this pursuit influenced my faith. Somehow morality, good works and success were integral to my relationship with the church. Even as a young girl, I attended church faithfully whether or not my parents went with me. Was I being a good girl or was I pursuing God? I'm not sure. Certainly as I grew older I followed the rules imposed by the church and a strict father. No drinking, no smoking, no sex. With respect to the latter, I hope he meant that restriction to last only until marriage. My two sons are evidence that I interpreted it that way. I broke none of these rules. I was a good girl.

Sunday was God's day to me and over time I came to see that, in fact, it was my day with God. For many years I attended church in Tucson faithfully. I spend four months a year in Canada and I attend the little church in the hamlet near our summer cottage regularly. I used to sing in the choir. Actually, on many Sundays I was their choir.

I love going to church, although I do not think it is essential for me to be there to please God. It pleases me. A few

Aldine in Stewart Memorial Church choir - 1991

experiences send the proverbial shivers up my spine. One is at take-off when flying a plane alone and another is the sound of voices raised in singing beautiful old hymns.

When I was twelve, my family moved to Tucson to accommodate my father's ill health. One of our first tasks was to find a church home. The options were legion as we were of the United Church of Canada which includes several denominations in the U.S. With our Scottish heritage, we chose the Presbyterian church where I remained until I moved my church home to St. Philip's in the Hills Episcopal Church in 1989. This change occurred at the time of my husband's death. The outpouring of love from St. Philip's was in sharp contrast to the total lack of contact or concern I received from St. Mark's Presbyterian Church.

Throughout my life, I have needed to prove myself to those I love. This is a requirement I place on myself. No one has ever demanded my perfection. I married the man of my dreams when I was 19 years old. Having spent my life trying to be perfect for my father—a powerful figure in my life—I now turned that attitude on my husband. I had to prove I was worthy of him and being godly meant being good. I was. It must have been tiring for him. In my quest for proof of my worth, I succeeded in amassing many university degrees, licenses and skills. Each one was a patent of nobility that testified to my goodness. Oh, if only my eyes had been opened earlier. If I had known then that perfection does not equate with goodness and godliness, I wonder what my life would have been. How dreadful for my sons to have had a mother so hell-bent on succeeding. I thank God that they became the two finest people I have ever known. God's grace in action again.

It is interesting that gender plays such a strong part in my journey. First I needed to please my father, then my husband, and God was certainly a father figure. It took a long time for me to realize that I do not need to impress God; he truly accepts me as I am, a repentant sinner.

Several events in my life fortified my faith in God, the hereafter and the integration of soul and spirit. Such experiences cannot be expressed in words—they were far beyond that limitation. One was the loss of a child I was carrying. I began to miscarry a child I desperately wanted. I felt, experienced, witnessed the soul of the baby leaving her mortal body. Waves of spiritual communication surrounded me as the little one departed this life for another. I knew to the millisecond when the fetus died. This was the most profound spiritual experience of my life. I buried our baby on the desert near our home in Tucson.

A second experience occurred immediately after I had a medical test which required the injection of dye into my veins. I returned to the cubicle to dress and then it happened. I was dying. I did not feel as if I were passing out; I knew that I was dying. And I did. When the doctor had returned from the x-ray clinic to his office, he was told that his patient had died. I believe that God intervened and decided it was not my time. I returned to life. Stunned faces stared down at me as I awakened. A year later I saw one of the nurses who had been in attendance during this incident and she said, "It was impossible; you were dead." Again, words do not exist to express what I felt as I "came back." A calm and beauty and clarity greeted me unlike any I have known before or since.

In the spring of 1989 I was very sick with atrial fibrillation and in hospital five times for almost three weeks. In the emergency room a medical procedure was tried in an attempt to get my heartbeat under control. Without my permission, and I would not have given it, I was injected with a medication that stops the heart for about twenty seconds—like rebooting a computer. I am told by a loved one who was sitting there with me that twenty seconds seems like an eternity when the heart monitor is flat. I felt the identical sensation of leaving life that I had felt the other time. Believe me, you know when you are dying. The procedure, by the way, was not successful.

Death and dying have become of increasing interest to me as I age. In the hospital I was close to death at one point; they could get no blood pressure reading, but I was conscious. I closed my eyes and saw a tunnel; I opened them and saw the white light. I was amazed that I was not afraid of death. I am afraid of the process of dying and the possible pain and indignity associated with it.

I have identified events that have influenced my spiritual journey. They have molded me to believe more strongly in the ultimate will of God and in His love for me.

I cannot pinpoint where I am on this spiritual journey. It is a work in progress. I love God unfailingly and totally. He is a pervading part of every minute of every day and prayer is a part of my thought process. Every daily occurrence warrants a little chat with God. For example, when I arrive home safely from driving in Tucson, I thank God. I beg for understanding when I do something stupid. In all, I have had a remarkable life full of loving family, rewarding pursuits and incredible opportunities. I have seen the world and smelled the flowers. For the most part I have enjoyed good health, and I thank God as I think He personally provided the grace for all of this to occur. Thus, God touches my life in every event I experience, big or small.

I want to add that I was on the Vestry of St. Philip's In the Hills Episcopal Church where I was a member. It was a great honor.

I no longer attend church in Tucson. I am, at the moment, without a church home and I am at peace with this. God and I remain as closely bonded as ever, perhaps more so since the death of my older son Kent.

Two churches have had an enormous impact on my life. One of these–Stewart Memorial Church–is in Dwight, Ontario, Canada about three miles from our cottage. Elsewhere in my writings I have mentioned a stained glass window inside that church in memory of my husband Tony. There are also stained glass windows for my mother, father, grandmother (Ella Gertrude Eagen) and my aunt (Ella Mae Walker.) The lovely Bible on the altar is in memory of my uncle, Alan Walker. We all started attending that church in 1933 and continued to worship there annually until those mentioned were taken in death.

Stewart Memorial Church - Dwight, Ontario

In the small graveyard behind the church lie my parents, my husband and my son. It is where I hope to be someday.

Another church played a major role in the lives of all my Tucson family. While seeking a new church home when we moved to Tucson, my brother Murray came home one day and said he had found it! Now, when a teenage boy gets excited about a church you have to know that there is a girl involved or else it really is a unique church. Both were true in this case. The girl was Suzanne Bradley and the church was the fledgling St. Mark's Presbyterian Church.

The great attraction at the church was its charismatic, handsome and engaging minister, Dr. Paul David Sholin. Dave was 28 and three years out of Princeton Seminary when Mountain View Presbyterian Church (its initial name) came into being. The son of missionaries, he had been born in Olavarria, Argentina. Dave was raised primarily in Spain and so his fluency with Spanish attracted him to this area. He was enormously appealing to young people who called him Dave (or Rev) and who loved the many gatherings around bonfires with Dave playing the guitar. His charm extended to older people as well and his congregation increased rapidly.

The church was Mountain View from its start in 1948 until 1964 when it was decided that something biblical would be more appropriate. It was then named St. Mark's Presbyterian Church.

Dave officiated when my husband Tony and I were married and he christened our children. He married Kent and Janice and was our pastor at the services for both my mother and my father when they died. He even came to the cottage several times. My father was a member of the church Session and I was a deaconess. I was director of Vacation Bible School for several years.

Dave and I became very close over the years. I found his profound faith contagious and have recordings of dozens of his powerful sermons. Dave was grateful to find in me someone who had a passion for the Spanish language and who could listen to him read poetry in Spanish for hours on end. We'd both end up in tears; it was very moving poetry.

Dave was a great help to me in planning my extensive trip to work in South America. I will always hold a special place in my heart for him.

By the way, I gave Sunday morning sermons at both of the churches I have just mentioned. I preached at Stewart Memorial Church in July of 1970 and in September of 1997. I delivered the sermon to the congregation at St. Mark's Presbyterian Church on August 29, 1971. (Appendix 7) I was deeply touched to have been considered worthy of this honor.

Dave preached his last sermon at St. Mark's Presbyterian Church on December 30, 1984. He died many years later at age 92.

Christians are always works in progress. My journey of exploring my faith is far from over. I echo Martin Luther King's observation that "Faith is taking the first step even when you don't see the whole staircase." Every morning upon awakening I thank God for being alive yet one more day and for the opportunities that day holds.

22

C3&O

ROCKS AND SHOALS

Before arising every morning I say a prayer to God thanking Him for the amazing life I have led—so full of love, friendship, beauty and adventure. And always I express my gratitude for the day ahead and all the promise it holds.

All of us have disappointments, big and small. That is part of life. In this memoir I have addressed the experiences I have had that enhanced and fulfilled my life. I have skipped over most of the rocks and shoals, but they were there.

However, some events affect us so deeply that we never really recover from their impact. These are the life-changers after which we are never the same person.

ANTHONY KENT von ISSER
August 26, 1926 – January 8, 1989

The first I will recount is the death of my husband whom I have adored from the second I met him until this very moment. In 1986 he was diagnosed with mesothelioma, a death sentence. No one recovers from this devastating kind of lung cancer typically caused by exposure to asbestos.

Its existence was discovered quite by accident in March, 1986 through a routine physical exam which included a lung x-ray. Several doctors reviewed the x-

Tony

ray and couldn't identify the spot they saw. It was sent to the CDC in Atlanta. It was unfamiliar to them as well. Interestingly, diagnoses of difficult diseases are often accomplished through a process of elimination. They systematically reject the problem it clearly is not and eventually end up with a short list of what it could be. Further testing isolates it to its final diagnosis—in Tony's case, mesothelioma. While Tony's was not typical, there was nothing else they could call it.

The year 1986 was fraught with angst. Tony had to face a great deal of pain and uncertainty. On March 10th I wrote in my diary, "It is all a blur of Tony's incredible valor, strength, dignity and of my unbelievable pain and heartbreak. I am so deeply in love with him and honor him more each day."

Tony with Kent and Tony Jr. - 1986

After our visit to an oncologist, Dr. Michael Boxer, I realized that we knew nothing about what was ahead for us. I phoned Dr. Boxer and asked him to be realistic and specific with me. It was then March. He said he doubted that Tony would see Christmas. We phoned Kent and Janice in Billings, Montana where they were living. Janice, a nurse, heard the death knell after hearing only "meso." They quickly sold their house, left their jobs, packed and moved to Tucson to be near Kent's father.

As Tony evaluated his life, he felt he had missed out on only one thing—a grandchild. Well, Kent and Janice went into action once again and soon were assuring him that he would indeed see a grandchild. That is real love. (Tony Jr. was not yet married and could make no such offer.)

Dr. Boxer's pessimism was unacceptable to us. We immediately switched to University Medical Center where a team went into action and ultimately extended Tony's life to three years. In the last Christmas letter he wrote that these were the happiest years of his life. Tony's doctors were exceptional. Dr. Sydney Salmon, head of the cancer center, was with us and supported us every step of the way. Tony had a shunt installed which continuously fed cisplatin, his chemotherapy, into his tumor. It was not effective.

Dr. Jack Copeland, UA Medical Center's miracle man at that time, performed two thoracotomies in order to scrape out the cancer from the tumor on the exterior of his lung. In both cases, we were told that this was a stopgap measure and that the cancer would come back. Tony was ultimately offered a third such surgery, but they were so ghastly that he didn't want to go through it again.

At that time we were living in the lovely house on Camino Escuela. Tony very much wanted to move to a smaller home with fewer demands and he knew exactly where he wanted to go—Catalina Townhouses on Campbell Avenue. It didn't matter to him which of the townhouses we moved to; he loved them all. I was lucky to find that one was for sale. We bought it on December 24th and moved in on December 27, 1986.

We continued to live our lives, Tony showing amazing courage through it all. When asked by people, "Do you ever wonder, why me?" His response was always, "Why not me." During this time I was asked to be Acting Department Head of the Department of Special Education. My first response was, "Absolutely not." As I have said, it is difficult for me to say no, so when they pled their case I finally relented with the caveat that at any time Tony needed me I would leave wherever I was to be with him. This actually happened at a Deans' meeting. A message was brought to me and, without a word, I got up and walked out. Tony had just found out his cancer had returned and he needed me to be with him.

When it became clear that Tony had only months to live I immediately arranged for a year's leave of absence from UA. My dean urged me to just show up occasionally so that they could keep my job for me with full pay. This time I said a resounding no and made clear that the next year, 1988, belonged entirely to Tony. I would not leave his side for any reason during that time.

Tony took a leave from his job at UA, too, and we headed for Canada in May, at the end of the spring semester.

Our 35th (and last) wedding anniversary with family in Arivaca - 1988

During this time our beloved Elizabeth entered Tony Jr.'s life and they fell very much in love. They were planning their wedding for the summer of 1988 and knowing that Tony would be unable to make the trip to Tucson for the occasion, they decided to take the wedding to him. And so on July 23, 1988 Elizabeth and Tony Jr. were wed in the little church in Dwight, Ontario that has been so much a part of our lives. Afterwards there was a joyful reception at my mother's old white cottage on Lake of Bays. Both Tonys were jubilant that day. Tony managed to walk all the way down the hill to the church and back again.

Elizabeth's wonderful family understood the problem and came en masse to Dwight for the wedding. Her mother, father, three sisters, aunt and many nieces were there. We billeted them in every room we could find in our cottage and that of my mother. What was leftover was the old bunkie with bunk beds and no facilities whatever—except electricity—and that is where Elizabeth and Tony Jr. spent their honeymoon! The wedding was magical and the marriage is one of the happiest I have ever known.

Our granddaughter Tana had been born on May 2nd so we even had a grandchild present. Sadly, Tony did not live to see his magnificent grandsons, Max and Alex.

Knowing that Tony had very little time left, I made arrangements in Huntsville, Ontario for handling the inevitable. I thought Tony would choose to die at the cottage. But the first snowfall came and he said it was time for us to go home. We returned to Tucson on October 12th.

Tony made one final attempt to save his life. He spent October 24th at University Medical Center (UMC) with many hours of appointments. He had a "simulation" for radiation. They recommended two treatments a day for five days a week for seven weeks. He was warned the side effects could be devastating. I wrote in my diary, "He is so sick now—I am heartbroken. Then he had a simulation in hypothermia. It was miserable for him. What a nightmare. He will die if he doesn't do it and it will kill him if he does. And he is <u>so courageous</u>."

Tony with his grandchild, Tana
Christmas - 1988

Tony looked at his options and told the doctors at UMC that if they could give him even a 5% chance that it would cure him he would do it. They could not. Tony continued going to work as long as he could drive. We had his last Christmas in 1988 with Tana on his lap.

During the many months of Tony's deterioration, Kent and Tony Jr. were at our house almost daily. They quietly helped and supported us in every way they could.

The day after New Year's, Tony told me he was going into our bedroom and would not be coming out. He climbed into bed, took off his watch (which he never did), and shared his last wish. He wanted no one, absolutely no one, to come into the bedroom thereafter. We never had hospice. I took care of him entirely. It was frightening for me as I have no nurse's training whatever. When oxygen tanks were delivered, it was up to me to transport them into the bedroom and connect the tubing. I was nervous that I would do it wrong.

Tony refused food and water. He soon began to hallucinate and went into a coma. He was gasping for breath and clearly in pain. I phoned his doctor who wanted to put him in hospital. I would not do it. Tony had been clear about his wishes. Therefore, liquid morphine was prescribed so that I was able to give it to him by mouth.

Tony was suffering so much that I prayed every night that this would be his last. Occasionally he stopped breathing, but our dog, Stacy, sensing that something was not right, would nudge and rouse him, and he would take another breath.

I never left his side and slept with him until his last breath—on Sunday, January 8, 1989 at 4:40 a.m. As he had made me promise, there was to be no service for him in Tucson. (The university had a service but I did not attend.) I received over 300 letters, cards and donations in memory of Tony.

In his obituary I requested that in lieu of flowers donations be made to the Cancer Center at the University of Arizona Medical Center. So much money was sent that the director—Dr. Sydney Salmon—had a room at the Cancer Center named in Tony's honor. There was a dedication ceremony at UMC to which all the donors and my family had been invited. The crowd was enormous and Dr. Salmon spoke and presented a plaque to go on the door of the room for Tony. In the

Dedication of room (1937A) in UMC Cancer Center

speech he gave, I was very touched when he said that of all the patients he had ever treated "there was never as devoted a wife as Tony's."

I took his ashes to the cottage to be buried in the little cemetery there as he had wanted. Since this could not happen until the summer, I had all spring to plan for his interment. It had to be special as he was a unique and special man. And it was.

My first thought was that it was too bad that Tony could not be buried in all the places in the world that he had loved, but then I realized that all the world could be buried with him. It became a cause for me to do this just right.

I started collecting earth and water from all the places he had lived, loved and worked during his lifetime. When assembled, seventeen areas were represented:

- Earth dug up from his family graveyard at his castle (the Gaudententhurm) in the town of Partschins in the Tyrolean Alps by a cousin, who also sent a photo of them digging it

- Earth from Carmel, California that I dug up there near where he lived as a child
- Earth from the Black Oak Cemetery near the ranch in Canelo in Southern Arizona where he had lived as a boy
- Water from the Pacific Ocean where he had served in the Navy
- Earth from our homes in Tucson:
    o 4749 San Francisco Boulevard
    o 4949 E. Glenn Street
    o 4615 Camino Real
    o 5300 Camino Escuela
    o 6294 N. Campbell
- Earth from Pelican Point—our cottage in Canada
- Earth collected by a friend in Alaska with whom Tony had worked in construction
- Water from Lake of Bays
- Earth from his parents' graves in Tucson
- Earth from our beloved Cañon del Oro
- Earth from Arivaca
- Water from the Sea of Cortez where he loved to sail
- Sand from the Grand Canyon sent by a friend with whom he flew there

Drs. Edith & Peter von Solder digging up soil from the von Isser graveyard, the Gaudententhurm, Tyrol - 1989

His colleagues at work had sent a tee-shirt with 38 signatures to be buried with him. Our

Tony's burial - July 6, 1989
Elizabeth & Tony, Mother, Aldine, Kent, Tana & Janice

book group in Tucson* had sent one of Tony's favorite books, *Dr. Zhivago*, signed by all the members. We also added a cigar and a bottle of rum.

The day of the burial, July 6, 1989, was lovely. My mother joined us—Kent, Janice, Tana, Tony Jr., Elizabeth and I. At the cemetery we formed a circle around a hole the boys had dug. Each of us in turn told the part of Tony's life represented by the earth and water as we placed it in the grave and stirred it into the ground with his ashes. Then the tee-shirt and book were laid on top and finally a good cigar and a healthy sprinkling of his favorite rum.

After we covered the hole, his gravestone was placed on top. Kent had gone into Cañon del Oro in the Catalina Mountains near Tucson to find the rock that Tony always moved from one campsite to another to be the cornerstone for the new fire pit. (It took all my wiles and a few tears for me to be able to take it on the airplane from Tucson to Toronto as it weighed so much.)

As Tony had wanted, there was not a religious word spoken but, at his request, most of us had a tot of his favorite cheap Mexican rum as we said our final goodbye. He had added that it would be quite all right with him if we chose to relieve ourselves of said rum on his grave. Even as he neared death, he kept his sense of humor.

The stained glass window in Stewart Memorial Church - Dwight, Ontario

Tony and I were members of a very small yacht club—The Rat Bay Yacht Club (RBYC) that had only six members. The other four members had a magnificent stained glass window made in Tony's memory which pictured the clouds (in which he flew), the point of land on which he sat at our cottage, the pine trees that surrounded the point, and our beloved Rat Bay with a little red sailboat on the transom on which was etched "RBYC." Also, on the window, in addition to Tony's birth and death dates, is the final part of the poem "High Flight," "… put out my hand and touched the face of God." (Appendix 8) It was a favorite of Tony's written by a 19-year-old U.S. pilot who had gone to Canada to train in order to be able to fly in WWII. He died in a crash in England two weeks after writing this now famous poem.

At Tony's request we had a whoop-it-up wake for him at our cottage that included dozens of friends, red, white and blue balloons being sent off into the sky, and amazing fireworks detonated by my brother skilled in such matters. Margaret Ruscica read one of her tender poems that still brings tears to my eyes when I read it each summer. (Appendix 9)

Tony was bid adios in just the way he would have wanted. It was unique and special, as was he.

* The book group held an important place in our lives and its members constituted many of our closest friends. We joined this august group of intellectuals in 1966 and, although over time it could not sustain the emotional entanglements that inevitably

emerge in a closely knit group, the individual friendships survived. Tony and I alone remained unscathed but the distress we felt for our beloved friends was heartbreaking.

The Book Group
Top: Ruth & Joe Green, Aldine & Tony, Mary Rose & Dick Duffield
Bottom: Marjorie & Michael Martin, Cathy & Ben Storek

JOSEF KENT von ISSER
March 28, 1955 –October 5, 2014

I can think of no greater loss than that of one's own child—at whatever age. My beloved son Kent died when he was 59, by his own hand. Yet my heart is full of gratitude that we had him as long as we did. In those 59 years he gave more love, kindness, and caring than would be typical in several lifetimes. He lived a full life—just in fewer years.

My husband Tony had made clear to me that he wanted two sons and would like to have the first by the time we had been married two years. Ever the dutiful and loving wife, our first son—Kent—was born on our second wedding anniversary!

Even as a small child, Kent was a risk taker. He thrived on excitement, speed and living on the edge. While we loved him with all our hearts, he kept his parents on edge, too. As his parents, Tony and I strove to build Kent's confidence in himself, always severely lacking. I wrote a letter to my parents in Tucson while we were living in California which tells of our joy in his successes. Part of the letter follows:

Kent with his parents Tony & Aldine
Christmas - 1957

"Kent's initial dread of his first swim meet unexpectedly turned into genuine enthusiasm. The meet was with a Santa Monica team. Kent participated in the 9-10 year old category which put him with older, more experienced kids. To our complete joy he did beautifully. He was in three events and came home with three ribbons. Granted they were third place ribbons, but it was physical proof to Kent that he did mighty well. He was bursting with pride! He admitted he loved every minute of it and can hardly wait till the next meet. Tony and I were much more nervous than he as we wanted so desperately for Kent to see himself in the limelight. And he did.

This success came the day after he got his report card. It was a thing of beauty. Academically it left something to be desired, but every 'effort' grade was high—for the first time in his life. With the report card came a note which I shall quote. '...I feel that if a medal were to be given to a child for displaying the greatest improvement in behavior and effort during a given time, Kent would receive it.'"

I wish this brief exposure to self-appreciation had lasted. It did not.

As a young person, Kent lived a balance between being a good boy and a bad boy. It kept us on our toes. His wife Janice reported to me that on the very day he died he had said to her, "Kent von Isser you are a good man—but a bad boy!"

The event that was the source of his ultimate demise occurred many years ago when he was 19 years old—in 1975. Both my husband and my brother, Murray Sinclair, thought that Kent needed to get away from home and his protective mother. (Tony said I made a Jewish mother look like a heartless shrew!) Hence, against all my protestations, Kent was sent to work underground in a contract gold mine—Chibex—in Chibougamou, Quebec, Canada—way, way up north. My brother owned the mine.

The day before Kent left on January 7th, I noted in my diary, "I am really upset over Kent's leaving. It will be like losing a limb." Little did I know what lay ahead.

Kent never should have been there. The miners were all professionals, French Canadian, and tough. They did not speak English; Kent did not speak French. They had no patience with an American kid who was the nephew of the mine's owner. He was terribly lonely there, and scared. During Kent's tenure at Chibex, he witnessed one decapitation and heard of another. It was a very dangerous place for him to be. And it was January and very cold.

I had made clear to my brother that it was essential that Kent have Workmen's Compensation papers before he went down in the mine. Our health insurance did not extend to Canada. The mine superintendent, Mr. Babcock, was of the same opinion. Until Kent had these documents, he would not allow him to work. Murray phoned the mine daily to check as to whether or not Kent had been sent down into the mine. He had not. Finally Murray spoke directly with Mr. Babcock who reiterated that he did not allow anyone to work in his mine without the proper papers. My brother responded, "Mr. Babcock, that is not your mine—it is mine—and Kent will go down tomorrow." He did.

It was only two weeks later, January 29th, that the ladder on which Kent was working 2000 feet below ground gave way due to an unexpected explosion. He took a fall that rolled him to within a foot of a hole that went down hundreds of feet. He was lucky there. He was unlucky in that his leg was severely broken in three places—the beginning of the events that spiraled down to pain and suffering for the rest of his life.

I have all the letters Kent sent me from the mine and it was almost as if he were prescient. He wrote that he was terrified underground, and didn't understand why he was there at all.

He was put in hospital in Chibougamou. The doctor, Dr. Trudeau, applied a cast— much, much too tight a cast. Kent phoned us that he was in terrible pain. We tried to find Murray; he was in New York City. When we located him, we asked him to have Kent moved to a Toronto or Montreal hospital. He told us he'd be back in touch, but he never was.

As the days went by, the incredible pain Kent was experiencing turned to numbness and his toes turned black. The nurses begged the doctor to remove the cast. He refused. One night, contradictory to the doctor's orders, the nurses decided to remove it. As they cut into it, the cast began to open of its own accord. This was a more serious problem than they could deal with and so they left the cast on.

With only one flight into Chibougamou each week, I had to deal with everything by phone. I needed to talk with Dr. Trudeau but he claimed to speak only French. With great difficulty, I arranged a conference call from Tucson that included a French interpreter I had located. I pleaded with Dr. Trudeau to please, please remove the cast. I said that as Kent's mother I was begging him. He responded, in perfect English, "If you do not like the way I am treating your son, you can come and get him."

Mr. Babcock took the situation into his own hands. He had Kent flown to St. Michael's Hospital in Toronto by an ambulance plane on Saturday, four days after the accident that had occurred on January 29, 1975. Kent had not urinated since the accident and the flight was excruciating for him. He arrived at the hospital with uremic poisoning and a fever of 104 degrees. The surgeon, Dr. John McCullough, went to the hospital to see him immediately after hearing of Kent's condition, even though it was a Saturday and the day of his daughter's birthday party. He assessed the situation, saw how damaged the leg was and opted to do an amputation the following morning.

Tony and I flew to Toronto immediately and found that they had not removed Kent's leg after all. The doctor thought he could save it—and he did, making it the most damaged leg that had even been saved in Canada. My sister Carol, a nurse who lived in Toronto at that time, told me that when the cast was removed Kent's leg exploded like a watermelon. It was gaping open from knee to ankle. We estimate that it was three feet in circumference. Gangrene was running rampant.

Carol took her children to visit their cousin. Although his leg was under a sheet, they could see its size. One by one, they each passed out on the floor.

Kent had one surgery after another. A plate and screws were installed. Through some miracle, the leg remained, although the doctors made no guarantees. They thought that eventually they might have to remove it. Considerable skin grafting was required.

Fortunately, Kent had a wonderful sense of humor which had to be put into play one day when he had been prepped for surgery, was lying ready and waiting when he suddenly found himself alone in the operating room. Linda Lovelace, of *Deep Throat* fame, was in emergency at his hospital and garnering a great deal of attention, including that of his surgical team!

Kent "on furlough" with girlfriend Helga at Lake of Bays April, 1975

Kent was in St. Michael's for many months. My loving sister Carol took him home for furloughs occasionally and she and her family visited him regularly. I went to Toronto to be with him every other week throughout the spring, leaving behind in Tucson Tony, Tony Jr., Katharine Merritt who was in residence, and my job. It was a long and awful spring.

Kent was, of necessity, on heavy pain medication. He was hallucinating. I asked the doctors to please reduce the high level of narcotics he was taking. They asked me if I wanted him in unbearable pain or seeing things that weren't there. The answer was obvious.

I couldn't possibly take the reader through this interlude in Kent's life and describe adequately the horrors he endured. For this injury he had eleven surgeries. There were still more that needed to be done even at the time of his death. When he finally was released from the hospital, almost a year later, he was addicted to prescription drugs.

I will mention two related issues here. First, Kent had no insurance in Canada. How was I to pay the bills that had accrued over this time? My brother suggested I get a good lawyer. However, he offered no suggestions as to how I might accomplish this and left for Cameroon for six weeks. I was distraught.

Finding a lawyer was no easy quest as my criteria were stringent. He had to be familiar with Workman's Compensation law as well as immigration issues. As well, he needed to be French-speaking and able to travel with me to Montreal. My cousin in Montreal, Gordon Sinclair, had found a law firm there who would accept this case and the many years of negotiating it would require before Kent would receive Workman's Compensation retroactively.

Feeling alone and abandoned in Toronto, I had no idea how to locate a lawyer there. The story of how I found one is a remarkable tale. It occurred quite by accident one night after I had spent the day with Kent in hospital during one of my bi-monthly visits in Toronto to be with him. I was housesitting for my sister in a small community north of the city while she and her family were vacationing in Florida. My aunt had suggested I visit a friend of hers—Peter White, an elderly retired lawyer—who might be able to give me some leads. I wended my way to their home where I had drinks with him and his wife. Although they were gracious hosts, they were of no assistance whatever.

Upon leaving their home, I found that it was snowing heavily and it was very, very cold. Laden with bags of Kent's laundry and inadequately dressed for this weather, I took up my post at a nearby bus stop in the dark of night. Fifty minutes later I was becoming panicky as there had been no sign of a bus. Life looked very bleak. I was lonely, cold and discouraged. However, fate stepped in when suddenly a car stopped in front of me with a lone, male driver–an attractive one at that. Lowering his window, he asked me if I was waiting for a bus and advised me there would be no more busses that night. What was I to do! Breaking every rule of safety I had ever been taught, I jumped at his invitation to drive me to the nearest subway station.

Well, the drive ended up at the beautiful Prince Hotel where we had a "nightcap" and got to know each other. The gods were taking care of me that night as this man who appeared from nowhere turned out to be…a lawyer! And…he spoke French. Further, he had all the necessary qualifications to deal with this complicated case. Was this possible? What a relief it was when he agreed to become my attorney. By the time he dropped me off at my sister's home, we were old friends with big plans. His name was Robert Kay. He and I went to Montreal several times that spring. In addition to taking care of my legal needs, Robert became a good friend and spent many weekends that summer at the old white cottage.

Kent and I flew together to Montreal twice in 1976 to deal with associated problems. The matter was finally resolved on August 22, 1979 after years of angst and doubt, but in the meantime every bill had been paid.

The second issue had to do with a lawsuit I initiated. You would think that this accident would be justification for such an action. However, lawsuits were almost non-existent in Canada at that time, and they still are few and far between. This was the cause for our having difficulty in finding lawyers to take the case. Doctors censured their own. I was seen as an uncouth American by suing Dr. Trudeau. I was not seeking a monetary award; I just wanted this cruel doctor to have a day in court. He was, of course, convicted of malpractice which was confirmed by a hearing of his peers. (I lost, rather than gained, monetarily with an award of $5000–less than the attorneys' fees. I gave the money to Kent. I have never regretted the lawsuit. Dr. Trudeau was seen for what he was—an incompetent and insensitive physician.)

Years later, April of 2013, Kent wrote me a letter that included this reflection on his accident and his life:

"Honestly, you couldn't make this up! The only way this could unfold the way it did is if it really happened. ... every step of that journey was a story unto itself. It's a miracle I survived. But that seems to be what I do. Anyway, from the split second of that explosion, my life was changed forever. ... It was one hell of an experience and I can't imagine what it was like as a parent. I pray that never happens to me."

I do not want this to be a recitation of Kent's medical woes. I merely want to establish that his life-changing experience at the mine created the perfect storm that framed the events of all that was to come for him.

On December 11, 1975, when the doctors in Toronto could do no more for him, Kent returned to Tucson to live. He meant his arrival to be a surprise for the family, but I got wind of it and we were all there to greet him. His good friend Randy Sharp met him at the airport and when he arrived at the house he just casually walked in the back door. Oh the whoops of joy! We were so glad he was finally back with us. He looked wonderful and seemed happy, and he walked pretty well without his cast.

As he was planning to go to university, Kent decided to join Tony Jr. who was registered to attend Millard—a military academy prep school in Bandon, Oregon. Kent thought this experience would hone his academic skills that had rusted during his convalescence. They were there for the fall of 1976 and graduated on January 27, 1977. The physical demands placed on the students were grueling but Tony reported that Kent ran every lap that he was capable of with the other students.

Every year Millard required that a form be completed by all their students, the purpose of which was to have them rate their colleagues according to their courage, honor—in short, to whom would they most readily trust their lives in a combat situation. Of the 80 students in the school, my two sons tied for second place! I did indeed raise some splendid men. How awful it would have been to be the student who placed 80th on the list when the results were posted on a bulletin board.

On August 21st, 1977, Kent moved to Flagstaff, Arizona to attend Northern Arizona University (NAU). He could not find an appropriate area of study and returned to Tucson to find a job. On September 17, 1979 he went to work for Pima Mines south of Tucson and by October 8th had received two promotions. Sometimes his shifts were not to his liking—from 11:00 p.m. to 8:00 a.m. He knew that hard physical labor and driving enormous trucks were not compatible with either his physical limitations or his intellectual capabilities.

Photography had always been a passion for him and we were thrilled when he was accepted to Brooks Institute of Photography in Santa Barbara,

California–unquestionably the best school in the country for this area of study. He began his studies there on August 25, 1980 and from the beginning was a stellar student. Shortly before he graduated, Tony and I received a letter from the President of Brooks advising us that Kent was the top student in his class with a grade point average of 4.0. That was April 16, 1983.

Can you imagine the pride and ineffable joy we felt when Kent graduated with a B.S. degree on June 10, 1983. A phalanx of family and friends arrived to share in the ceremony and the experience—my mother and father, Tony Jr., Janice Angevine (Kent's wife-to-be), Midge and Jay Angevine (Janice's parents), Johanna Plaut, and Tony and I. Our hearts soared with his great success. That night my parents hosted a party for him at the Santa Barbara Biltmore adding more people to the entourage of celebrants, one of whom was Ann D'Agostino who had been his "landlady" during his tenure in Santa Barbara. In fact, it was from the kindness of her heart that she took in a few Brooks students as roomers as she enjoyed their company and having young people around. She lived on Alston Road, in a very upscale neighborhood. She even allowed Janice to visit him there; they were engaged to be married.

Kent's graduation day from Brooks Institute of Photography - June 10, 1983

Kent looked happy and proud that day having had moments in his childhood when he wondered if his life would ever gel. It was amusing that both of my very handsome sons looked so much alike at that time that Tony Jr. was repeatedly congratulated on his great achievement. They did, indeed, look almost like twins.

Kent in Montana

On August 5, 1983 Kent accepted a job with a company called Design Works in Billings, Montana. That seemed so far away to me, but it was time for Janice and Kent to build a life of their own. They moved together to Billings on August 12, 1983.

Having been in love with Janice since the day they met in the fall of 1977, Kent announced that they would be married in Tucson on May 19, 1984. They returned to Tucson on May 14th and the festivities began. Tony and I hosted the rehearsal dinner at our home on May 18th. On the 19th, our minister, Dr. Paul David Sholin, performed the wedding ceremony at St. Mark's Presbyterian Church. The bride and her bridesmaids were radiant and Kent, and his best man Tony Jr., made my heart soar with pride.

As my father had been in hospital at Tucson Medical Center for quite some time, he

The wedding - St. Mark's Presbyterian Church
May 19, 1984

Janice & Kent flanked by her parents, Midge & Jay Angevine and Aldine & Tony. A handsome wedding party.

was unable to attend the ceremony. But, as sick and weak as he was, he insisted upon a family photograph being taken in which he, in a wheelchair, was surrounded by loving family who had come from far and wide. These included my brother Murray and his son Murray, both in kilts. What courage and determination it took on the part of my father to dress for the occasion and to

Aldine & Murray Sinclair surrounded by their family

pick the spot on the lovely grounds at the hospital for the photograph. It was the last time he was outside, as he died shortly thereafter on June 1st.

Kent and Janice loved Arivaca and picked our fifth-wheel there as their honeymoon destination! I don't think they ever regretted it. They returned to Billings on May 27th

Newlyweds Janice & Kent - 1984

but Kent returned on June 3rd for the memorial service for my father which took place on June 4th, again at St. Mark's Presbyterian Church with Reverend Paul David Sholin conducting the service. What a sad time for Kent as he had always adored his grandfather, Bumpa.

Kent, always accident prone, broke his foot while moving an air conditioning unit on June 10th. There were so many highs and lows for him that year–1984.

Kent and Janice loved their life in Billings, each being away from family for the first time—a very positive step for them both. They loved the winter months there and the little home they had bought. Disaster struck for all of us when Kent's father Tony was diagnosed with a terminal form of cancer—mesothelioma—in March, 1986. Tony phoned to let Janice, a nurse, and Kent know of his illness. Janice heard only the first syllable—meso—and instantly knew Tony was very ill. They soon sold their house and moved to Tucson to be near Kent's father. What a loving act that was!

In fact, Tony was given less than a year to live but

Kent in Saguaro National
Monument, Tucson - 1985

with incredible courage and determination stretched it to three years. He claimed they were the happiest years of his life.

As he reviewed his life, Tony expressed few regrets. His greatest disappointment was that he would never see a grandchild. Kent and Janice wasted no time in making that wish come true and on May 2, 1988 presented him with his beloved granddaughter, Tana Jay von Isser, who has lit up all our lives since that day. Tony held her on his lap on Christmas morning, 1988, only 13 days before his death.

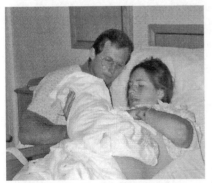

Janice & Kent with their newborn
baby, Tana Jay von Isser - May 2, 1988

Janice, Grandmother Aldine, Tana & Kent on Tana's first birthday

Kent loved Tana with all his heart and soul and was an outstanding father. When I wrote Kent once that I would, if I could, trade places and assume for myself his suffering to save him from it, he responded:

"Thank goodness parents can't do that because we would be depriving our kids of a horrible but incredibly valuable experience. Anyway, here I am, broken but not finished. Apparently, the powers that be have more lessons for me to learn. Bastards!!! Love you mom, Kent."

On November 6, 1990, Kent had the grand opening of his own photography studio. It attracted a large gathering of significant people in Tucson, and everyone was in awe of his magnificent gallery and his spectacular photographs. Without question it would have been a great success had he not discovered that running a business was not his forte. In time, he moved on to other pursuits. His favorite job was his last—at the DeGrazia Gallery where he was a jack of all trades. He thrived on the work and he loved the people.

Kent the photographer

Over a period of time, Dr. Paul Dempsey, a Tucson plastic surgeon, performed magnificent restorative work on Kent's leg. Kent's sense of fun extended to his leg as well. Truly, it was deformed (and ugly) beyond belief. When wearing shorts in public, people would, of course, stare at his leg. If anyone had the courage to ask what had happened he would simply respond that it was a shark attack. And it looked like just that.

Later the thin layer of skin covering his leg muscles, tendons, etc., wore away and more surgery was necessary to protect the infrastructure. Dr. Dempsey took a huge slab of hip from below Kent's waist to graft to his leg. The new and even weirder appearing leg bothered him less than the cavity in his abdominal area that had been the donor site. He was incredibly self-conscious about it and spent the rest of his life assuming positions that would make it less obvious. His was such a monstrous looking leg now that his boss at the DeGrazia Gallery, Lance Laber, suggested he get a booth and charge admission to see it. Kent thought this riotously funny. He never lost his appreciation for the ridiculous.

Not only was Lance his boss, but also his good friend. They often took trips to Kino Bay together or to the White Mountains in Arizona to fish. Kent didn't like fishing, but he thoroughly enjoyed his time with Lance.

Still, Kent was always in pain and succumbed to pain killers when it became untenable. He was admitted to drug rehabilitation centers several times and for many months at a time.

Herein, I will add an aside. Dr. Dempsey was a paragon in our community and loved flying. One blustery March day he went flying late in the afternoon to do "air work" in his new twin engine airplane. I had picked the same day to go flying as I needed to improve my skill in landing in heavy crosswind conditions. Later that day, an announcement came over the radio and TV reporting that a prominent Tucsonan had just crashed near Tucson International Airport. My family knew I was flying that day and jumped to the conclusion that it must be I. In fact, it was Paul Dempsey, whose skills have never been replaced in this community, who died. Sadly, Tucson lost a fine plastic surgeon and a good man.

Kent was now without a surgeon in Tucson who was capable of doing the very fine restoration required on his leg and hip. The remaining surgeries were delayed, and some of them never transpired at all. While the situation was not perfect, he felt he was better off leaving well enough alone.

On November 2, 2001, Kent had been alcohol and drug free for 15 years before his health began to deteriorate further. He was plagued with Epstein-Barr and his liver started to fail. In his last years he was in debilitating pain all the time. I could recite a litany of the procedures he endured but in recent years alone he had a knee replacement, an ankle replacement, and a pacemaker installed. While in hospital he caught the dreaded C-diff infection which incapacitated him. He had a stroke. His kidneys were failing and he was told that it was necessary for him to start dialysis treatments. Then back pain started with a vengeance. Kent could see he was on a downward spiral with respect to his health–unrelenting pain and his inevitable reliance on painkillers.

On December 1, 2013 after he had had his ankle replacement surgery, Kent wrote me an email. It said:

> "I just re-viewed the photo of my tortured lower limbs. Wow! And the funny part is that was a good day. I'm beat to pieces, yet so grateful for the love of my family and the incredible life I've had. If I were to write a book its title would be *Broken, but not Finished.* I don't seem to know how to throw in the towel! But, 'mother of glory,' I can't even reach my 'boot straps,' much less pull them up yet another time. I am not being a cry baby, but I'm quite content to live every minute of this arduous descent. God is good."

Part of an email he sent me only months before he died said:

> "You're an incredible woman, an amazing mother and an impossible act to follow. And I am grateful for your high expectations. I have to admit that I am glad we cannot go back in time to possibly make different choices. I am comfortable being the flawed individual that I am. Sitting here, now, it is crystal clear that I made countless poor choices. But I doubt that I would recognize the mistakes had I not made them. So, going back without the benefit of hindsight would likely be an endless continuous loop. Best to just move on."

A letter I received closer to his death said:

> "I really want you to know how grateful I am that you are my mother. Although you set the 'bar' impossibly high, all of your efforts to raise two good sons were not wasted. Although incredibly different, Tony and I are truly good honorable men. I love my brother and have watched him keep his sights on 'the prize' until he has, over the course of a career, achieved his goal. Wow! My little brother, my role model! I can only hope that watching me make poor choices helped keep him on his path."

Kent had a strong faith in God. After his death, Tana found this tender insight into his faith on his computer:

> "Just a thought to contemplate, paraphrased from Romans 5-6-7
> Imagine that each person you come in contact with is a puzzle for you to put together. Usually when assembling a Jigsaw puzzle you have all the pieces as well as a picture of what you are constructing. But what if you had the picture, but not all the pieces? What if you didn't even know what pieces were missing or what to look for?

We start by realizing there is One who already knows everything about each and every one of us. God sees the complete picture. He has all the pieces, and He truly understands us. His love and compassion for us are not defined by how easy we are to get along with. He loves us despite our difficult parts, and He sets us a beautiful example of how to do the same with others."

Having provided so much history, I now want to say more about my remarkable son. There is no question that he was unique among men and, as his daughter Tana told me recently, there are no words that can do him justice.

One of his innumerable admirable qualities was that he treated everyone equally. He truly lived his life by the golden rule and his license plate read "Live the golden rule."

Kent's motto was "nothing is impossible" and he proved it by building his own beautiful house from scratch. His brother-in-law and good friend, Sam Angevine, would pitch in when Kent needed an extra hand. He and Janice designed their own unique home built on three acres of desert land in the Catalina Foothills in Tucson with magnificent views in every direction. They broke ground in 2003 and began living in it in March, 2005. That is the same year Kent contracted polymyalgia rheumatica, a debilitating painful disease which was probably caused by the stress associated with the overwhelming task of building their house on his own. But all their sacrifices were worth it to them. It is about 4000 square feet in size, charming throughout, and was their pride and joy. What beautiful parties they had on their patio! Janice continues to live there.

Kent's sense of humor was often ribald and his love of life was contagious. He had an infectious laugh. He was always very close to his cousins and an example of the kind of humor he would share with men was characterized in a letter he wrote to his cousin Scott after he had been in Tucson visiting in March, 2014.

-----Original Message-----
From: Kent [mailto:jkentvonisser@comcast.net]
Sent: Saturday, March 22, 2014 11:12 PM
To: Sinclair, Scott
Subject: By the way.....

Your family is out of this world great! Your sons absolutely blew me away. Now, I have to say this cautiously, but your wife is SCARY smart. Or quick witted, or just a serious force to be reckoned with. Whatever it is, she's awesome and you are the bravest man I have ever known! You must wear Kevlar boxers! Seriously, she is awesome. But (and please don't misconstrue this) my balls retract when I am in a conversation with her!
Her horse is a gelding right? It was his idea, in my opinion! Okay, once again I've gone too far. She is fantastic!
Better go. Kent

People loved being with Kent as they would be exposed either to his incredible sensitivity and kindness or to his quick wit. Kent thought on his feet and never missed a chance to throw in a quip or a pun. He often signed his name *José*–Spanish for Josef, his first name.

One could only marvel at Kent's mechanical skills. He could fix anything, but his particular interests were in motorcycles and cars. When he was a teenager he once told me he was sure he could disassemble and reassemble a car engine even if he were blindfolded. And hubris was not in Kent's lexicon. He took great joy in shocking little kids with one of his tricks. Once, when cleaning a motorcycle as a teenager, he caught his finger in a rotating wheel and severed about a third of it. While Tony and I took him to the hospital, Tony Jr. was assigned the job of locating the remainder of the finger. He did, but not in time. Thereafter, Kent would gross people out by sticking his finger up his nose. It looked as if it went right up into his head due to its short length.

His prowess as a motorcycle rider and a jeep driver was legendary. In Arivaca one time, he borrowed Tyler Meigs' new and very powerful BMW motorcycle to take "a little ride." He rode to Amado—a distance of a little over 40 miles total—along a twisty, hilly road. He was back in 15 to 20 minutes! As I say he was a risk taker, but riding that fast on that road was absolute craziness.

On a jeep ride with Kent - April, 1991

One Sunday he invited me to go on a jeep ride with him to the back side of the Catalina Mountains. We left the roads completely and drove up canyons with boulders the size of small cars, and he never got stuck once! One would have to have seen his driving skill that day to have believed it.

Another of Kent's pleasures over the years was mountain biking. One of the incredible places he rode was to the top of Charleau Gap in the Catalina Mountains, a challenge for any biker.

Kent had a keen interest in aviation for a while. One of his many amazing feats was soloing in a Cessna 150 at Tucson International Airport on his 16th birthday, March 28, 1971—the earliest age allowed for solo! He was a natural pilot and flew magnificently. As he did not yet have a driver's license – he was only 15 – I took him to the airport for his flying lessons. The air traffic controllers

Kent's solo flight on his 16th birthday - March 28, 1971

300

knew me well and allowed me access to the tower whenever I wanted. I enjoyed listening to Kent's radio communications and watching him fly from a good vantage point. One day, the tower advised Kent to make a right downwind for landing. He was making a left downwind approach. The tower corrected him and he complied. I unadvisedly went on the radio to assure him that all pilots had made this error in their careers and said reassuring words. Kent was deeply humiliated and never really forgave me for that intrusion in his life. He was quite right and I spent many years apologizing. Sadly, I believe it was this incident that resulted in his loss of interest in flying.

He was a craftsman who could take a raw piece of wood and turn it into a thing of beauty. Our home is replete with inlaid bowls he made of mesquite which he had harvested from a fallen tree on our property. The headboard in our guest room is magnificent—a mosaic of mesquite that is a piece of art in itself. He had made it for me as a birthday gift and installed it on October 31, 2001. He also built our mesquite dining room table to the measurements I gave him and it is a daily reminder to me of his incredible skill and imagination.

He saw beauty and captured it skillfully on his camera. His photography was phenomenal and its nuances and composition spoke to his great talent. We have the gift of many of his photographs throughout our house. He loved music—all kinds. He wrote poetry and expressed himself magnificently through the written word. He was a very private man. He loved life, in spite of all the arrows it flung at him. One of his favorite places on earth was our cottage in Canada close to which he is now interred. You will read more about this in the chapter concerning our life in Canada. He was a fantastic water skier and loved dousing people with the huge spray he created.

And Kent loved his pets—dogs and cats—with a passion. He was almost inconsolable when one of them died.

Kent and I shared a close relationship; we trusted and loved each other deeply. I had written Kent a letter in which I stated, "…being the mother who saw and continues to see her beloved son in distress has been a life-altering event for me. Not a day goes by that I don't fervently pray to God for surcease for you from the day to day challenges that never seem to go away. I pray for you to have happiness, a healthy body, freedom from pain, and from addiction, and a higher awareness of your own magnificence. I ask God nightly to please let me see your life this way while I am still alive." It was not to be. I finished the letter with, "I love you with all my heart, Kent, and admire you beyond what words can say."

While I was in a state of shock to receive from his daughter Tana the phone call on a Sunday night that Kent was gone, I don't think it was really a surprise to anyone else in the family. They had seen the signs and heard his hints of what he ultimately planned. I, optimistically, always thought he would get well.

Kent was loved by all. I don't think there was anyone he ever met who did not enjoy his company, admire his courage, and have a good laugh hearing his outrageous and engaging stories. He was certainly adored by his family.

Late in his life Kent wrote me a note that broke my heart but expressed his feeling of worthlessness which ultimately was too much for him to bear:

"Mom, this trip down memory lane is possibly my attempt to explain to myself why I am so fucked up right now. I hate being the center of attention and especially dislike having physical ails define who I am. It really pisses me off. I've tried to never be a complainer. But my health issues make me feel like just that. … Look at my role models. Dad, Hal, you, Al Marshick, Uncle Murray. I was surrounded by overachievers and thrill seekers! And I would have fit right in if it weren't for the distinction of being insecure and very self-conscious. Not traits of any of my role models."

Following Kent's death, the outpouring of love was monumental. I received almost 200 remembrances. They came in the form of flowers, food, contributions made in his name, cards, e-mails, letters, visits and phone calls. I was deeply touched and responded to every tribute personally. I wish Kent could have read them to see how much he was loved and appreciated.

Warren Susman, an influential cultural historian, wrote that America had shifted from a "Culture of Character to a Culture of Personality." My son never had to make this shift. He was strongly endowed with both.

Throughout writing these memories of Kent, I have chosen to let him speak for himself where it was possible. As my beloved Tana has reminded me, "There are limits of language to describe experience and that some feelings are not of the verbal world." Kent was lovingly buried at Lake of Bays, a place he enjoyed all his life, and a Muskoka rock bearing a plaque in his memory rests beside the graves of his father and his grandparents. On the plaque is written the first line of a poem Kent loved, *Requiem—* "Under the wide and starry sky," by Robert Louis Stevenson. (Appendix 10)

I have the honor every day of remembering that Kent was my son and of acknowledging his strength of character, his tenacity, his warmth and tenderness, and his love for his family and friends. His heart will beat with mine forever.

Kent's gravestone - Stewart Memorial Church, Dwight, Ontario

MURRAY MALCOLM SINCLAIR
May 30, 1931—February 14, 2014

Carol, Murray & Aldine - 1991

My brother Murray and I were born two years and one day apart. Hence, we always celebrated birthdays together. However, as people we could not have been more different. His flamboyant and reckless style was 180 degrees from my reticent and rule-following behavior. We both, however, were abundantly endowed with the Sinclair determination and tenacity.

Murray died at age 82 having used up every available resource his body could provide. He outlived cancer beyond a span anyone could have anticipated. He smoked, drank, caroused and should have burned his body out many years earlier. He suffered in his last years, but he never complained nor did he slow his pace significantly.

Murray, our sister Carol, and I lived in Toronto until we moved to Tucson, Arizona in 1945. Murray returned to live in Toronto permanently in 1953. He married Ann McHardy-Smith, a beautiful and cultured girl with an infectious laugh and with whom he had three wonderful sons. I adore my nephews Murray, Scott and Craig, all of whom live in Vancouver. Sadly this marriage ended in divorce. Ann died in 2012 at the age of 73.

Murray's second marriage was to a woman who filled all his needs and who was the love of his life, Mary Johnston. They produced a son, Christopher, and a daughter, Candice, each of whom inherited the charm of their mother and the wit of their father.

Uncle Murray was greatly admired by my two sons, although riding with him in either a car or a boat was off limits for them. He was a maniac behind the wheel! His last car was a Tesla.

Mary, Candice, Christopher & Murray - 2013

Murray was an inimitable character and a true Scotsman. A licensed pyro-technician who often tried to blow up his closest friends, and inadvertently himself, he lived much like the fireworks he loved–fully and with color. He laughed loud, spoke his mind and took particular pleasure in a good story, a magic trick, and especially a great joke. Boundless energy, a twinkle in the eye, and an indomitable optimism marked both his work and private life.

As a prominent Bay Street financier, Murray was known for his entrepreneurial zeal and business acumen, relying on his keen intellect and honed market instincts for the enormous success he achieved. He loved going to work every day and was passionate about "the deal." Murray was once referred to in Barron's Magazine as "a Canadian gentleman of venturesome cast." Believing that the best business was not conducted from behind a desk, Murray traveled widely and cultivated lasting relationships throughout his long career.

Murray was an aspiring lumberjack who spent countless hours manicuring his forest for the birds and wildlife he loved at his Lake of Bays home, Birch Spring. He could often be seen tearing across the lake at any given hour in one of his many speed boats with a rooster tail behind him and a bottle between his legs.

He was as colorful and dynamic as the art he collected. Few were immune to his infectious sense of humor and unique personal style. The outfits he wore were colorful to the extreme, and rarely did anything match.

Mary and her daughter Candice arranged a memorial service for Murray that would have totally delighted him. It was held at the Ontario Museum of Art in Toronto on May 14, 2014. It could be compared to the Big Top—over the top. More than five hundred were in attendance and there was action in every part of that huge room. There were jugglers on eight foot stilts, and members of the Circque de Soleil in every corner doing their acts with silks. Musicians were omnipresent and going from table to table were magicians who boggled us all. And Mary had arranged for his favorite color, orange, to be used throughout.

There were only five speakers; I was one of them—the only woman I might add. His son Murray was the master of ceremonies and captured the character of his father brilliantly. The evening ended with dancing and appropriate ribaldry.

Murray was buried in the cemetery behind our little church in Dwight, Ontario near his parents. A brilliant and charismatic giant of a personality, Murray's credo was, *"We're not here for a long time, we're here for a good time."* He lived to that end each and every day. Murray will be missed but never forgotten.

Murray with his family - 1983
Murray, Christopher, Mary, Candice, Craig, Scott & Murray Jr.

Murray & his family at their home in Cabo - Christmas, 2013

HAROLD JOHN GRIEVE, JR.
May 26, 1931 — December 2, 2016

When I started this memoir, I could never have imagined that the last change I would make would be to acknowledge the death of my husband, Hal Grieve. He died from pancreatic cancer on December 2, 2016 leaving a big hole in my heart and in my life. I know how blessed I am to have known him for so long and to have been married to him the last nine years of his life.

Fifty-six years after meeting Hal, we were wed on January 5, 2008 in the Mission in the Sun at the DeGrazia Gallery. I was 74 and he was 76 years of age. We both found new love in old age and shared many happy years together. He and my husband Tony had been close friends when they were in their teens, although Tony was five years older than Hal. You will have read about this friendship in an earlier chapter. They were indeed kindred spirits.

In 1952, Hal had heard that his friend Tony was to be married. He decided he had better get to Tucson to check out this unlikely rumor. Hence, he thumbed his way from Pennsylvania to Tucson and found that indeed it was so. I met Hal on October 6th of that year.

Hal was born in Pittsburgh, Pennsylvania on May 26, 1931, the son of Marion Sheret and Harold John Grieve, Sr. The marriage did not last long and Hal's mother became a veritable gypsy–always on the move from place to place as the whim or the job dictated. As a result, Hal remembered having attended about 24 schools at the elementary and middle school levels, followed by ten high schools, before he finally graduated in 1950. His last year of high school was in Meshoppen, Pennsylvania where he met the love of his life, Bette Prevost.

Wanting to start a family right away, they could hardly wait to get married. However, there was a problem. Neither could qualify for a marriage license because they were too young. While Bette's parents gave permission, Hal was unable to find his mother. She was now married to the famous Tucson artist Ted DeGrazia and they were spending most of their time hanging out with Diego Rivera and Frida Kahlo in Mexico. Hal couldn't locate them so his mother's permission could not be obtained.

They did research and learned that the legal marriageable age in North Carolina was 13. So off they went by bus to Elizabeth City, North Carolina, to tie the knot. It was a happy marriage that produced three children but was cut short by Bette's death in 1997. Sadly, their son Scott died at age fifty-six. Hal's daughter Linda and her husband Randy Childers live in Park City, Utah. His son Greg lives with his wife Jo Ann on the farm that Hal and Bette had built in Pennsylvania. Hal visited them there every year.

Hal and Bette moved from job to job in Pennsylvania, none lucrative or satisfying. He decided to be in touch with his old buddy Tony in Tucson to ask if there might be a job for him at Hughes Aircraft Company. Tony assured him that if he came to Tucson there would be a job waiting. So, on Tony's word, they packed up their old car with all their possessions and their two children and headed west. Both were happy with their new jobs in Tucson and life was good. Another baby came.

Over the years, the von Isser and Grieve families would join together for picnics, camping trips and the like. Bette, however, had placed a caveat on their moving to Tucson. She insisted that after twenty years in Tucson they would return to Meshoppen and her roots. Hal kept his word. They went back to Pennsylvania, built a house and lived there until Bette's death in 1997. Hal had always had a soft spot in his heart for me, so after an appropriate length of time, he came courting—via e-mail. We corresponded daily for months until Hal moved out to Tucson permanently on New Year's Day, 1998. We were married ten years later.

Hal was blessed with four grandchildren and nine great-grandchildren, all of them very precious people. He counted himself richly blessed and left this life with peace in his heart.

Hal & Aldine - 2010

Hal & Aldine - Our wedding day, January 5, 2008

Hal & Aldine - Our engagement

Aldine & Hal - 2016

Hal's last summer - 2016
Tana, Max, Tony, Elizabeth, Shireen Singh, Alex,
Aldine & Hal

23

❧

SUGAR AND SPICE

...and everything nice. Into one's life come people and events one never could have planned for that are the sugar and spice of life. My son Tony heads the list.

ANTHONY K. von ISSER

Tony holding Tony Jr.

Tony Jr. with his grandfather
Josef von Isser

We all thrive on sunshine, and Tony is my sunshine. He has brightened and warmed my life since he was born on October 8, 1957. What a happy lad he has always been and kindles the spirits of all who know him. It would be difficult to find anything about Tony that isn't pretty perfect.

Tony was born in Tucson and had another name entirely. I won't mention it as he has always

disliked it. I was confused when people started referring to him as Tony and I always corrected them. Oh," they would say, "well, he told us his name was Tony."

When we moved to California in 1961, I enrolled him in school as Tony von Isser, his choice, and he has been Tony ever since. So, you can see that he has a mind of his own and considerable determination.

Tony was taken home from hospital as a baby to our Glenn Street house. He loved it there. He remembers the joy of living in wide open spaces with freedom and lots of dogs who were able to run free. As you will read elsewhere, we had a big pond in which he and his friends could swim, boat and fish. An idyllic life for an active lad. He developed a garden at that house, syphoning off water from the pond for irrigation.

Tony Jr. - 1961

I asked Tony to tell me the worst moment of his childhood. He did not hesitate. He recalls vividly how frightened he was to have come home from school one day to find no one there to greet him. This never had happened before. Then he saw telltale signs that something bad had happened, and he was all alone. After what must have seemed like a long time to him, he saw his father and me on either side of Kent, holding him up, walking toward the front door. He was both relieved and horrified as Kent was swathed in bandages from head to foot looking something like a mummy.

Kent, 2 ½ years older than Tony, had come home from school and decided to experiment with gunpowder he had seen stored in the carport. He made a trail with it along the ground with a big pile of it at the end. He lit it, watched it creep along the ground, and was there at the pile for the finale. That finale came as a blast that burned him badly and set him on fire. He raced for the pond and jumped in to extinguish the flames.

It was at this point that his father came home and took him immediately to hospital. I followed soon thereafter. We knew Tony could take care of himself for a while, but didn't take into account how scared he might be at our absence.

Tony loved summers at Lake of Bays in Canada, and winters spent camping in Cañon del Oro in the Catalina Mountains. You will read much more about these adventures in other chapters of this memoir.

When Tony was four we moved to California. We lived directly across the street from the school in which he was enrolled in kindergarten—Malaga Cove School in Palos Verdes Estates. We left California to return to Tucson to live when he was seven years old. For the remainder of his elementary school years he attended Whitmore School on Glenn Street near our house.

Tony Jr. with Fang

Middle school is difficult for all youngsters, and Tony did not like the school he attended during those years. It was a private boys' school—Green Fields Day School. In fact, Tony didn't like school at all until he attended Catalina High School. There he met the teacher who would change his life, Richard Huerta who taught welding. Tony loved that class and really liked Mr. Huerta. He was in that class for four years and became so adept at welding that he was made Assistant Teacher for a while. You will know how important welding class was for him when I tell you that even on Senior Ditch Day he went to school so that he would not miss it!

Tony is a skilled welder and has been doing metal work for over forty years. His metal sculptures are magnificent and sought after by all who see them. He rarely takes an

order on consignment but could be kept busy full time if he wanted to make it a business. He prefers to do it for his own pleasure. Both his home in Tucson and our place in Arivaca display a great many of his unique and very beautiful sculptures that he has welded over the years.

A memory that Tony treasures is always that of having lived next door to his grandparents—Aldine and Murray Sinclair. As I have said elsewhere, there was always a path from our house to theirs. When we lived on Glenn Street, they built a house next to ours. When we moved to Camino Real, they again built a magnificent house beside us. Both my boys

Aldine's parents in their beautiful home next door to us on Camino Real adored their grandparents who were like second parents to them.

I thought Tony might find it difficult to leave our Glenn Street house with its wide open spaces and a pond. Such was not the case when we moved to the Camino Real house in the foothills about which you will read in the "real estate" section of this memoir. It had ten acres and gave him ample space to drive his all-time favorite vehicle—a 1951 army jeep for which he paid $500. He bought it when he was 12 years old. And the dogs could continue to run free!

At age 16 he needed a proper vehicle to drive to school, so on October 5, 1973 he sold his beloved jeep in favor of a 1973 Datsun pickup. He had already sold his motorcycle on September 26th for $390. Young people want to get their driver's license on their 16th birthday. Tony was no exception so I took him to the Motor Vehicle Division on his birthday, October 8, 1973. It was closed! What a disappointment. We returned the next day and he became legal to drive. He was ecstatic.

Tony could handle discomfort, hard work and tedious studies but he could not stand blood. One day at Catalina High School, where both boys were in attendance, there was a safety film being shown in the auditorium. Attendance was mandatory for all students. There was a good deal of blood and gore as car accidents were being shown on the screen. Kent heard a <u>thud</u> in the auditorium and said, "Yup, my brother's here." Tony had passed out cold!

As I have said, we gave our lads a good deal of freedom. In late August when Tony was still 16 he took his truck with his small camper on the back and off he went with his close friend, Corky Chandler, to San Diego. When they returned to Tucson, we didn't hear a lot about their adventures but we did discover that they had slept in the camper in parking lots!

Both Kent and Tony were members of the Jack Kramer Swim Club in Palos Verdes Estates, California when we lived there in their grade school years. This club recruited swimmers when they were young to develop a team that would eventually train seriously for the Olympics. The grueling schedule and the intense competition did not suit our boys, or us, so we withdrew them from the club. They were, after all, only 8 and 6 years old. However, swimming has always been one of Tony's fortes and swim team was one of his passions during high school. He regularly placed in swim meets and on April 30, 1975 broke all his previous times—58.3 seconds on the 100 yards and

25.1 seconds on the 50 yards. We were so proud! Swim practices started early—6:30 a.m.—so we had a lot of early starts to our days.

All our family was enormously pleased when Tony Sr. rejected a job in California to become the head of labor relations for the entire Hughes Aircraft Company. He was convinced he would be dead of a heart attack or alcoholism within ten years if he accepted that position. The boys were delighted when we returned to Tucson at the end of the school year in 1965. We moved back into our old home on Glenn Street that my parents had been watching over for us while we were in California. During our absence they built a house next door.

Tony enjoyed entering science fairs and won first place in a competition in Tucson in 1974. He had built a small wooden bridge that could hold 79 pounds! He tried his hand at golf and with his buddy—Corky Chandler—entered a golf tournament at Tucson National on January 9, 1976. That interest didn't last long.

Tony Jr. in hang glider

Another pursuit was hang gliding to which he devoted every spare moment on weekends for several years. During this time he worked as a janitor for El Corral Restaurant six days a week. He didn't have a lot of spare time. But he could always fit in time for tennis and continued to be an outstanding tennis player until his knees gave out. He and I loved playing tennis together and did so both in Tucson and in Canada. I remember one wonderful game we had on New Year's Day of 1979 when we played three sets together at the Tucson Raquet Club. He won two of them and I won one. I don't know if we were well matched or if he "gave" me one set!

Tony Jr. assessing the TP job!

Bowling held a prominent place in his life during his teenage years, too.

When Tony turned 17 in 1974 he was already over 6' 2" and my diary tells me he had decided he didn't want to get any older. It was in honor of his birthday that a group of girls got together and TPed the bunkhouse on our Camino Real property in

315

which our boys lived. They hit it with over 60 rolls of toilet paper. They even put rolls of toilet paper on poor Fido who looked like a mummy when Tony found him. The area looked very festive but took a while to clean up.

In 1975 he sold his drums—to the relief of the whole family—and turned his interest to building a go-cart.

At one time, all four men in my family worked at Tucson Newspapers Incorporated. Tony Jr. stuffed newspapers, Kent delivered them, Tony was the Personnel Director and my father was a columnist.

Tony Jr. - 1975

On New Year's Day in 1975 while Tony was 17, he worked all day at El Corral Restaurant as a janitor and that night as assistant to the bartender. And he was underage even to drink, for goodness sake!

During his teens, Tony frequently went with us to our fifth-wheel trailer in San Carlos, Mexico. Sometimes we flew there ourselves in a small plane. Other times we flew to Guaymas commercially and thumbed a ride to our trailer. Occasionally we drove from Tucson. Often Tony would take friends there with him—Corky Chandler and Kurt Richardson among them—and they would have wonderful adventures. Often they would go off in our Montgomery-six, a very small sailboat, for activities on other beaches and to sail the ocean.

Tony loved living at our house on Camino Real which I describe in detail elsewhere. I failed to mention, however, that it had a huge workshop—a necessity for the guys in my life—and a rooftop deck where Tony remembers sleeping many a night. Of course, there was the bunkhouse there that gave my sons a great deal of freedom—possibly too much— but Tony would never disobey the rules. He is and always has been a rule follower. By sticking to the safe track, he thinks his life was made much easier.

Tony on his Yamaha 80 on Camino Real.

After high school, Tony had thoughts of going to the U. S. Naval Academy at Annapolis, Maryland having been nominated for this opportunity by Morris Udall, our U.S Representative from Arizona from 1961 to 1991. In order to prepare for the entrance exam he attended Millard, a military academy prep school in Bandon, Oregon for the academic year 1976-77. He worked hard there: it was a grueling schedule both academically and physically. Kent attended with him and they shared conflicted feelings about the experience. It was demanding and worked them to their limits, but they both came away feeling that every painful hour had been worth it.

After he completed Millard on January 27, 1977, Tony took up flying with a vengeance. He went to Tucson International Airport for instruction almost daily and made his first solo flight on April 22nd with three perfect take-offs and landings. He was on such a high that he fairly glowed. There was a party in his honor that night and we awarded him a little trophy.

I have to admit I worried somewhat as while flying over Green Valley one day he had two near mid-air collisions. On August 29th, 30th and 31st he took solo cross countries to Phoenix, Wilcox, Bisbee/Douglas, Yuma, Gila Bend and Casa Grande. He started night flying in September of that year, and loved it.

The day Tony soloed – December 31, 1977

On December 31, 1977 Tony became a licensed pilot. There was much excitement in the family and lots of celebrating with champagne and balloons. (Tony, however, did not drink the champagne as he has never had an alcoholic drink in his life!)

On September 19, 1977, Tony began his college education at Utah State University in Logan, Utah to study Agricultural Engineering. Thinking ahead, he disassembled his Yamaha 80 motorcycle, shipped it to Utah, and put it back together again when he arrived. Now he had transportation! He made good friends at university, learned to ski and enjoyed many skiing weekends. He continued his love of skiing even after leaving Utah. On January 3, 1981 he went with friends for a long skiing trip–nine days—that took them all the way to Montana. He has always been an outstanding water skier and, in addition to water skiing in Canada every summer, he often went to the Arizona lakes, such as Roosevelt Lake in 1984.

Finally he had started to enjoy school. However, he discovered his passion was in aeronautics and the program that suited his plans for the future was at Arizona State University (ASU), in Tempe, Arizona. He left Utah State at the end of the spring semester—May 30, 1979—and began the fall semester at ASU on August 26, 1979. While home that summer, he bought a used Volkswagen Sirocco that he loved. Sadly it was run into on January 4, 1980. No harm came to Tony, but he was very upset by the condition of his car.

Tony had his own apartment in Tempe, while attending ASU that I often used when I had to stay in the Phoenix area. Often he wasn't even there, as he came to Tucson almost every weekend. We loved having him live so much closer than he had in Utah. Tony had planned to buy and assemble an experimental aircraft kit and it was with great relief that his father and I learned that on September 11th of that year he decided against it.

I am the luckiest mother in the world to have as conscientious a son as Tony. No matter where he   lived, if he was not with us on a Sunday he always phoned his father and me—always. That has never changed and I can be assured without doubt that every Sunday I will receive a call from him. There could be no more faithful and thoughtful son than my beloved Tony.

Tony had a black Labrador dog named Fido. They mutually adored each other. Theirs was a heart- warming relationship of unconditional love. As an example, Fido once made the mistake of almost catching a skunk that sprayed him liberally before making a getaway. Nothing eliminated the overwhelming skunk smell on poor Fido. Even a bath in tomato juice was to no avail. No one would go near him for days—not even Kent's dog Rover. But Tony—he let Fido sleep in bed with him as always, an expression of his total devotion.

While Tony was away at ASU, Fido registered his displeasure by refusing to stay home. Daily we had to drag him home from my parents' place—his preferred choice of residence during his "abandonment." So beloved was Fido to Tony that my mother took Fido to an artist to have his portrait painted. Tony received it for Christmas in 1974, and it still holds a prominent place on the wall of his den. I still get teary remembering the day we had to say goodbye to Fido—May 12, 1981.

Tony is the only member of the family who has been to our cottage in Canada in the winter. On December 26, 1981 he flew to Toronto and went north with his Uncle

Murray, Mary, and his cousins—Murray, Scott and Craig—to stay with them at their cabin. He didn't return to Tucson until January 5, 1982 having had the time of his life enjoying the snow and all the sports available in wintertime only.

Tony Jr.'s graduation from Arizona State University – May 14, 1982

His program at ASU was called Aeronautical Engineering Technology and he thrived on the coursework. He graduated with a B.S. on May 14, 1982. All the family was there to celebrate and I noted in my diary that, "It was one of the most exciting days of my life." Tony, of course, was on a cloud. In the spring of his last semester, a recruiter— Dick Switz from Hughes Aircraft Company–came to interview students. He had his eye on Tony and the interview took place over dinner. That evening—April 23rd–he made Tony an offer on the spot—to be a Manufacturing Engineering Rotator in the El Segundo, California plant. Tony was one of the few graduates who already had a job lined up before he even finished university.

Tony was encouraged to take time off before he moved to California as he had just graduated from university and needed a breather. He did, and went to our Canadian cottage for a month before he made his move to the coast on June 29, 1982. He was earning $25,000 per year, a kingly sum at that time.

Once Tony was settled in his new home in Playa del Rey, I could hardly wait to visit him. On October 18, 1982 I flew to Los Angeles, took a taxi to his apartment and made myself at home. I found it quite luxurious for a young man just starting out, although I knew he felt he was only camping. He arrived home early from work at 4:30 p.m.—with a bottle of wine. Tony didn't then and never has had alcohol so I knew this was a special treat just for me. We went to the Magic Castle in Los Angeles for dinner— always an exciting adventure—and had a delightful evening together. I slept on a spare bed in his bedroom.

On May 10, 1983 I visited Tony again and was surprised when he invited me to meet his boss at Coco's Restaurant in Manhattan Beach Mall. My diary noted that "I couldn't believe Tony would invite his boss to lunch to meet me. I am so flattered—and it was great fun. Clearly Tony's boss thinks he is wonderful. Boss is 42, attractive and witty."

In his new job, Tony rotated from one position to another to determine what phase of production he wanted to pursue in depth. This was a one-year assignment, but before the year was over, he was sought by Hughes in Tucson to accept a position with them. He came to Tucson for an interview on May 26, 1983 and jumped at their offer as his family lived in Tucson and he loved the open spaces.

He started at Hughes Tucson on August 8, 1983 and bought a new car on September 5th—a copper-colored Nissan sport truck. His first job at Hughes Tucson was as an assembly engineer and he quickly moved into supervision. Tony did not aspire to climb the corporate ladder. That came with a price he was not willing to pay and a balance of life that he did not want for his future. He was repeatedly offered impressive positions, but he maintained a level that gave him time for a personal life.

However, on October 14, 1986 he was named Engineering Supervisor for all production engineering for the Phoenix missile. I remember how excited he was and what a challenge he faced. In March of 1995 he was given another promotion and raise. Hughes had been taken over by Raytheon but his position was not altered.

On October 5, 2001, Tony received what I believe is the highest award given at Raytheon. He was selected to receive the title of Senior Principal Engineer with Honors. The Honors selection process was initiated by peer nominations to acknowledge people who have demonstrated exceptional leadership and technical skills. A recognition dinner followed but, due to the events of September 11th, it had to be delayed until March 1, 2002.

Tony Jr. on Camino Escuela

He received a plaque and a cash award as well. The Director of RMS Engineering, Stu Roth, wrote, "Congratulations on being recognized for your technical excellence!" Even Tony was a little overwhelmed by this rarely awarded tribute.

Another interesting professional experience was his invitation in September of 2004 to the Pentagon. His exceptionally high clearance rating allowed him to wander throughout the facility. He was attending the production rollout of the new Tomahawk cruise missile which was being introduced to the military in the inner courtyard of the Pentagon. His responsibilities included setting up the display of the missiles. It was an exciting experience for him and another honor bestowed upon him.

Tony's last job was demanding to the maximum. He was the building manager for a plant that was at a very high level of spacecraft integration. He had total responsibility for the building and had to be the first one there to open it in the morning, and the last to leave at night in order to be sure it was buttoned down securely. This meant that for years he had to arise at 4:15 a.m., leave the house by 4:45 a.m. and have the building open and ready to go at six in the morning. Often he had to drive out there on weekends to accept delivery of a shipment. Some of these deliveries were of a single item that arrived in a huge, air conditioned truck and that item could well have been worth over several million dollars.

His job was to supervise the third stage element integration and test which included the kinetic warhead assembly. Tony, who is by nature precise, has said that this was <u>very</u> precise and detailed work with precision that was of the highest possible caliber. Nothing could be overlooked as the fate of a large city population might depend on that warhead. As Tony says, they took attention to detail to an extreme level.

Special shoes had to be worn in the building. No one could wear a wedding ring and risk it falling into the assembly. Even Tony had to wear a hairnet, and Tony is bald.

He loved his work there, and the people he worked with, but after a 32 year career with Hughes and Raytheon, it was time to retire and take advantage of the pension he had accrued. He was 56 years old.

Tony Jr.'s house – 1641 E. Waverly

I'll return now to the story of Tony's new job at Hughes in Tucson in 1983 when he began his permanent life here. He immediately went house hunting, found what he wanted, and made an offer. It was accepted on September 18th and, as my diary reported, "...he was so excited he practically can't function." The house at 1641 E. Waverly in central Tucson closed on September 28th and the very next day Tony hosted his first party in it. It was glowing with warmth and love and he even had a fire going in his fireplace. Those in attendance were my parents, Carol, Terry, their children Aldine and Ted, their daughter Stephanie and her new husband Corky Chandler, Karl Pattison, my husband Tony and I. He was suitably praised for his home and for his gracious party and was given useful housewarming gifts.

Then the work began. I was delighted to be able to help Tony get settled in his new house. We had such fun buying supplies and curtains and turning it into a real home. Beginning on October 16, 1983 we started painting the entire house. It had to be done at night and on weekends as both he and I worked. I noted in my diary, "What a job!! Only for Tony!" One night four of us got together and painted the entire living room. Once the entire place was painted, I waxed the floors. It looked beautiful and Tony was thrilled. Tony's first houseguest was his old boss from California, Don Bilderback. Tony became quite adept at entertaining and I remember his sit-down dinner party for 12 family members on August 25th of 1985.

Shortly after my father's death, my mother decided she needed a companion—a dog. She could never have a pet due to my father's allergies, and now she was going to fulfill a dream—a dog to love. My sister and I quickly found an irresistible litter of pups. Mother was drawn immediately to a black lab that she bought and named Jock. They were inseparable for the remainder of her life. I took one look at Jock's brother and lost my heart to him. I named him Angus. That summer, 1984, when Tony was at the cottage he and Angus bonded; they became close friends. I quickly saw the writing on the wall—this was Tony's dog in every respect. I gave him to Tony who abbreviated his name to Gus, and they were good buddies for many years.

Everything in Tony's life was falling into place, but there was one critical element missing—a wife. Now it has to be said that Tony was a very handsome and appealing young man, and many special young ladies came into his life. It seemed that every year a different one was visiting us in Canada. He always checked them out at the cottage, as he had to be sure they would share his passion for Lake of Bays.

They all were lovely—Molly Thomas, Sarah Finley, and Sarah Winkler, whose father was a general. Tony Sr. kept saying, "Marry her. She's perfect. You'll never find a better wife." And he was right. Each was a gem and they all loved Tony and Lake of Bays. But Tony was not yet smitten.

And then, into his life came Elizabeth Anne Sikula. He had found her–the woman of his dreams—and we quite agreed that she was a very special young lady. I wondered if he would check her out at Lake of Bays. Well, this is how it went. He drove from the cottage to the airport in Toronto to pick her up for her first visit to the cottage on August 1, 1987. He quickly learned that Elizabeth couldn't even swim! She was afraid of the water so that pretty much limited their water sports. Did it matter to Tony? Not even a smidgeon. She was

Elizabeth Sikula - 1988

his girl. They had started dating in 1986 and were married at Lake of Bays in 1988. You'll read all about the wedding elsewhere in this memoir. Well, Tony knew what he was doing. He did indeed marry the perfect girl who is the joy and the collagen of our whole family. If I had a daughter, I could not ask for one whom I could love and admire more. She is creative, loving, and thoughtful and delights one and all with her charming laugh and wonderful sense of humor. I could go on with superlatives for another paragraph, but suffice that she learned to swim and can jet-ski with the best of them. We all adore her.

Tony Jr. & Elizabeth – the day they told us of their engagement – April, 1988

Elizabeth & Tony with Aldine's family & Gus

Tony and Elizabeth built a lovely natural adobe house on Camino Real that they moved into on December 21, 1989. It was stunning with a magnificent view of the Catalina Mountains. When they designed it, they had not taken into consideration that children might come along. And indeed

Tony Jr. with his parents on his wedding day

Tony & Elizabeth in front of the tree they planted after their wedding

they did—William Maxwell on February 27, 1991 and Josef Alexander on March 23rd, 1993, my beloved grandsons. This house was not appropriate for child rearing so in the fall of 1993 they found a house higher in the foothills which worked well for them for many years.

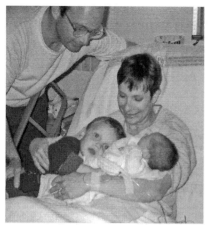

Elizabeth holding Max & newborn
Josef Alexander, with Tony looking on

Hamlet with Tana in "swimming
pool" in Arivaca

Tony & Elizabeth with Alex sitting on Max

Elizabeth and Tony have had many pets over the years but perhaps the most unusual, and most troublesome, was their miniature pot-bellied pig named Hamlet! A constant companion, Hamlet even went to Arivaca for celebrations. However, a problem arose. When Max was just a little guy learning to walk, his progress was considerably hampered by Hamlet who took great pleasure in bumping into Max and knocking him down. Another annoyance was his proclivity for finding and swallowing odds and ends including pieces of Elizabeth's jewelry. When her loveliest pearl earring went missing, she knew where it had to be and declared this to be her final "search." It was recovered but Hamlet was given to a couple who thought having a pot-bellied pig would be great fun! Even having had full disclosure of Hamlet's habits, they willingly accepted him.

After their boys left home, they decided it was time to move. Somehow we assumed that they would downsize. Not at all. They found their dream house in a beautiful neighborhood in the Catalina Foothills with incredible uninterrupted views. It has almost two acres of property and they have done a great deal to enhance their home, patio and pool areas.

They have 4000 square feet of living space with a huge garage and a 1000 square-foot workshop that Tony had built and in which he now spends much of his life. With its six bathrooms, three fireplaces, an office and den for Tony and two studios for Elizabeth, their house has lots of space for all their activities. There is also a guest house. They love it and use every inch of it. Elizabeth spends countless hours in her studios designing and creating jewelry. As well, she is a recognized artist and her magnificent paintings have traveled the nation to be displayed in art shows. She has ample space for working on all her many projects.

Elizabeth and Tony have always been very active in their church life with Elizabeth having been involved in drama teams as well as solo and group singing. They have put their hearts and their souls into their spiritual life. An impressive and emotional event took place on November 9, 2003 when Tony, Max and Alex were baptized. The baptisms were consecrated with full immersion and there was not a dry eye among us.

Every Friday night Elizabeth and Tony have a cocktail party from 5:30 p.m. to 7:30 p.m. inviting their family, friends, and neighbors. It always seems to be made up of a different group of people every time and it is always interesting and great fun. It is the highlight of my week.

Now that Tony has retired, he has time to be with Elizabeth and work in his fantastic workshop. He creates magnificent metal sculptures that surround their home. He often goes off-road riding with friends and covers much of Southern Arizona in this pursuit. He works hard at our place in Arivaca keeping acres of grass mowed, by hand, to stave off the ravages of potential fires. The dry desert can go up in flames quickly. Watching over and maintaining it is a big responsibility for him.

Thanksgiving in Arivaca is one of his favorite times of the year and he makes it special for everyone who joins us for that celebration there. In 2015 we had 40 people come, and eight dogs. What fun we had! Tony provides all manner of exciting activities including potato guns, a pneumatic golf ball canon, and a pumpkin catapult that Kent made years ago. There is something new and challenging for every age at every gathering and everyone tries his hand. And as everybody brings food for the table, we don't go hungry!

Tony's passion for many years was, and continues to be, the restoration of antiques. He loves to rehabilitate old farm equipment—tractors especially—as well as old furniture and safes. He has a vast collection of safes, some weighing as much as 1500 pounds and one that is 130 years old.

Tony has traveled a great deal but the family trip he loved most was to Tahiti followed closely by our trips to Costa Rica and Jamaica. I have written about these in other chapters.

Tony is an avid reader of anything to do with World War II. He and Elizabeth visited Normandy Beach in October, 2015, an emotional experience for them both. He is a pilot and has for many years studied aircraft and aircraft types. I am confident that were you to put a photograph of any plane in front of him he could not only identify it but provide its history as well.

I asked him what would be on his wish list for the future. He responded without hesitation that someday he would like a barn or hangar, and a runway. He used to have a tennis court on the list but gave that up when his knees and ankles balked.

People have always been attracted to Tony. His gracious charm, enthusiasm for life and sparkling wit appeal to all—old and young alike. Still, if I could ascribe only one attribute to Tony it would be that he is honorable. That is the highest characteristic I could bestow on anyone. He is a man of integrity and humility. Upon the death of his older brother Kent in 2014, Tony became the oldest son of the oldest son in the von Isser family and became the new Count Anthony von Isser. His dignity and courtly manner make him a fine head of this ancient family.

The day after his brother died, I wrote a letter to Tony. The letter included, "While I know you never want center stage, you need to know that you have been my strength and my hero throughout the years. You have gone about your life with dignity, enthusiasm, and dedication. You truly are a paragon." I added, "You are my rock and my center, and I thank God every night that my life has been graced and blessed by you. Your love for your wife, your children, and for me is steadfast, unflagging, unconditional, and nonjudgmental. Thank you for all you are and for being my beloved son." I signed it with "I love you more than words can say."

He is my son. He is my sunshine.

CAROL ELLA SINCLAIR

My precious sister Carol. Although she is five and a half years younger than I, my first memories are of her. She has always been my best friend—someone I love and trust unconditionally. The fact that she is my sister is icing on the cake.

Carol - 1941

When we were small and living in Toronto, we shared a bedroom. Although Carol was in a crib, she would crawl into bed with me and we would spend many happy hours in each other's company. Scratching each other's backs was one of our favorite pastimes. We carefully counted and tallied so that each got her fair share. I know I frightened her with some of our "games" such as my shouting that a train was coming and we had to get under the covers quickly. I rather think she enjoyed being scared but still I have regrets as I wonder what irreversible damage I did to her psyche.

Murray, Carol & Aldine - 1940

She has always enjoyed telling people that she is my <u>much</u> younger sister but I have never taken umbrage. She was an adorable child with curly blonde hair and could wind all of us around her little finger.

Carol was my maid of honor when I married Tony in 1953. She was all of fourteen years old with braces on her teeth. I was a mother at age 21 when she was only 15. We were living very different lives at that time— each going her own way. Still, when she moved to Toronto in 1959 to go to nursing school, there was a big gap in my life. In Canada at that time, nursing was a highly respected profession. She earned her Registered Nurse's degree at Wellesley Hospital in 1961. Nursing was a different field then with enormous responsibility and very strict rules. She wore a uniform with the

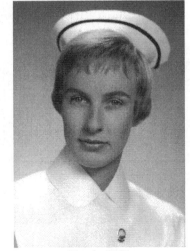

Carol - 1961

327

typical "British" nurse's hat. Carol made very close friends during those years, women with whom she is in touch regularly to this day. Annually her nursing class has a reunion in or near Toronto and Carol never fails to attend.

Carol in her kilt at the old white cottage - 1958

However, her nursing career was short-lived as she met and married Terence Edward Belsham with whom she raised three beautiful children, Stephanie, Ted and Aldine. I adore them all, and Stephanie is my goddaughter as well. I feel honored.

It wasn't until we were adults that Carol and I became close and have shared thick and thin with each other.

Carol has had more than her share of "thins." She was stricken with lung cancer when she was only 37 years old with three small children. Her doctors gave her a one in fifty chance of surviving. Her lung was removed but there was no accompanying chemotherapy or radiation. She, too, has the incredible Sinclair survival gene and, having beaten the odds, is now a healthy and very beautiful woman at age 78.

Carol & Aldine - 2007

Aldine, Stephanie, Carol & Ted - 2013

Finding that she was unhappy in Toronto, Carol bought a beautiful house in the Catalina Foothills in Tucson on February 3, 1981. She and her children moved there permanently on April 11, 1983. In September of 1989, she and Terry were divorced. Carol never returned to her nursing career but chose instead to join our mother in real estate. Her first job, as a secretary to our mother, began on October 18, 1983 but she quickly earned her real estate license and soon thereafter her broker's license. She continues to go to her office every day at her real estate company, Sinclair Associates, which she has owned since 1984. Prior to that it was owned by our mother who had purchased the company in 1963.

Carol & David at their wedding reception - 1992

Eventually Carol met the love of her life, David Shand. David was Canadian. They were married at the little church in Dwight, Ontario in 1992 after which there was a beautiful reception. As well as being a joyful party, it was also memorable because of the weather. Ontario can have huge rain storms and on this day the skies opened and it rained like billy-be-damned. This added a dimension of hilarity to the occasion. How could that happen on one's wedding day! One aspect of that wonderful marriage was that Carol and David had such good times together and laughter was de rigueur. She was totally happy, and smitten. She met David on a blind date. He went home with her that night and never left. He had moved to Tucson to become involved in southwestern art.

Sadly, David died of pancreatic cancer on July 3, 2000. Since then, she has chosen to remain single.

Carol was my matron of honor when Hal and I were married in 2008. We have each stood beside the other for our four weddings—hers both performed in Canada and mine in Tucson.

Carol had a bad fall in April of 2015 that left her with bleeding clots in her head and a degree of paralysis on her right side. She is still recovering from that incident. How brave she was to have a cochlear implant in 2016 to restore her hearing of which she had been deprived for many years. One would never notice that she had these setbacks as she continues to be vibrant, optimistic, and productive.

I am extremely proud of my little sister and her incredible tenacity. She, like so many Sinclairs, is a wonderful story teller and when in her presence there is never a dull moment.

Carol has her own story to tell and all her family has encouraged her to write her memoir. Hence, I shall leave it to her to put her mark on history with her own words.

24

⊗⊗

MY PEN PAL

As one looks back on life, there is a deep appreciation for very special relationships that have been long-standing and deeply rooted. One of these for me is with a woman whose friendship I treasure, and yet I have met her only twice in the almost 75 years I have known and loved her. Her name is Margaret Collin.

This is the story. During WWII I attended Oriole Park School in Toronto, Ontario. Canada had entered the war in 1939. In the third grade (1941) I was blessed with a teacher who had imagination and compassion. She was aware of how difficult life in England was at that time and recommended that each of us have a "pen pal." What a life-altering event it was for me to draw the name of Margaret Cock. Our lifelong correspondence began.

Margaret's family had come from Wales but later settled in Essex in 1907. They were farmers and took their cows and horses with them—the cows traveling by train. At the beginning of WWI in 1914, they felt vulnerable living so close to London so returned to Wales. In 1919 they moved back to Essex and bought the same farm they had sold when they left there in 1914! That farm was Haye Farm which I later visited. Margaret lived there with her parents until 1975 when she married Jim Collin. She and Jim moved to Feering and I find their address so charming that I just have to acknowledge it:

> Little Patches
> World's End Lane
> Feering
> Colchester, Essex

How many times have I sent a letter to that address! Margaret does not have a computer so, even at 84, writes each letter in longhand. We cannot correspond by e-mail. Our letters go back and forth several times a year. I have quite a collection! Knowing of my interest in the royal family, she frequently sends me news articles and brochures about them.

Aldine standing beside pen pal, Margaret Cock, on our visit to meet her family

When Tony and I visited England in 1954, a priority was a visit to Margaret and her parents. We traveled by train through beautiful countryside. They could not have been more cordial or more welcoming, and to this day I remember the sumptuous feast they presented us.

The second time I met Margaret was for tea at the Berkeley Hotel in London. She had come to see Katharine Merritt and me while we were on a brief visit to England.

Sadly, Jim died several years ago while they were on a Mediterranean Cruise. They did not have children.

I believe Margaret is the longest-time friend I have. I will love her always and cherish the friendship we have developed over so many years.

25

ೞ౫ಬ

MY DIARIES

I am thought by many to be obsessive-compulsive. They are absolutely correct. Some habits in my life permeate so deeply that I think I would go into withdrawal if their availability to me were denied.

One such habit is writing in my diary. I started this addictive behavior when I was 11 years old and have indulged in it every day since. Yes, I have written in my diary daily for 72 years. That constitutes a considerable number of volumes recording a great many memories. Many are sad; most are moments of sublime happiness. It is about the latter that I am writing in this memoir. I believe I have been the luckiest woman ever born in spite of the rocks and shoals life puts in front of all of us.

My diaries are stored in two fireproof boxes. The first holds the books that record my life until I married. That box will go to my grandchildren. The second is from 1953 until the present and the contents will be sunk in the deepest part of Lake of Bays upon my demise. They are not to be read. I hope it will be done with a little pomp and ceremony given the thousands of hours of my time that have gone into their creation!

As a footnote to a comment above, I want to share one of life's lessons that I was blessed to learn. I mentioned that my diaries were not to be read. Why? Well, early in my marriage, Tony and I were invited to a picnic on the desert in Tucson by two impressive couples—Ann and Bill Woodin and Joseph Wood Krutch and his wife Marcelle. Bill Woodin was a founder and director of the Arizona Sonora Desert Museum and a herpetologist by profession. He was an usher in our wedding. Ann was an author. Dr.

Krutch, who died in Tucson in 1970, was a renowned writer, critic and naturalist. He was tall, taciturn and very distinguished. His wife Marcelle was a charming French woman and a dear. She was not prepossessing in terms of appearance, but her inner beauty shone through. Her husband adored her.

At the picnic, Marcelle drew me aside saying she wanted to share some thoughts with me. Clearly I was a woman totally smitten by my charismatic husband, and she felt I needed some womanly advice. It was brief, but it hit home with me. She said, "Aldine, you love your husband very much, but every woman must have her secrets." I have never forgotten her words and they have been a creed that has served me well.

PART TWO

MY TRAVELS

26

❧

GREECE

<u>1967</u>

I had a love affair with Greece. It lasted many years and was enabled by my husband's godmother, Katharine Merritt. When I last saw Greece in 2008, it was but a parody of its former glory. But I knew it when it was vigorous and exciting.

As has been written in the chapter *My Unusual Marriage*, my husband Tony was eager for me to embark on new adventures. In 1967 Katharine Merritt had mentioned to him that she was going with three others on a road trip through the Peloponnese Peninsula in Greece that summer. Aha! Tony saw an opening for me to begin my life of exploring new horizons. He was going to make sure that this trip would be my initiation. He was a pretty smooth talker and, with some effort, inveigled Katharine to include me in the party. This wasn't easy for many reasons. One was that the car that had been rented for the trip was small and fitting five people into it was going to be a squeeze.

Prudie and Peter Mennell and their daughter Lindsay were Katharine's guests. As Peter was a British Ambassador, Katharine had visited them in many countries over the years. She was to be their hostess on this trip as a way of reciprocation. Lindsay was Katharine's goddaughter. Another glitch in my going was that Katharine had planned to share a room with Lindsay. Now I would be with Lindsay while Katharine would be on her own. To say that I felt like an interloper would be an understatement, but Tony was determined. Peter, being a diplomat, acquiesced to my joining them—probably reluctantly. He would be doing all the driving.

And so it was decided. I would be passenger number five!

I would not have chosen so early a "start" date for our newly envisioned life-plan of independence for both Tony and me.   Kent was only 13 and Tony Jr. 10 years of age. I had never been away alone—ever—and had no desire to leave my lads when they were so young. My parents offered to take care of the boys. They lived next door to us on Glenn Street at the time. Plans progressed. Tony prevailed.

As I departed Tucson for my first solo adventure I was reluctant and scared. With a sinking heart, I waved a tentative goodbye through the plane's window. As soon as we were airborne I burst into tears.

I met Katharine in New York City and spent a few wonderful days as her guest visiting the Metropolitan Museum and attending theater. All of this was new to me, and soon I had left guilt and concern behind and embraced with enthusiasm this unfamiliar hedonistic lifestyle. Katharine and I flew to Athens together where we rendezvoused with the Mennells. I couldn't believe my good fortune in flying first class, which was Katharine's only mode of travel. Soon, however, she put a damper on it for me. Her habit was to set her watch to the time of the place we were going. Hence, even if we were to be served a sumptuous meal on the plane, Katharine forbade it as it did not coincide with the appropriate time to eat at our destination. She never suffered from jet lag!

This was a good year to travel in Greece as there were exceedingly few tourists. On April 21st of   that year the Greek coup d'ètat had been initiated by a group of colonels. The degree of dissention and violence was unpredictable so most people chose not to include Greece in their travel plans that year.

We were going to be exploring the Peloponnese Peninsula in the southern region of Greece. A   land that is mountainous in the interior with deeply indented coasts, it is separated from the central part of the country by the Gulf of Corinth. At that time there was no bridge to connect these bodies of land. In 2004 the Rio-Antirio Bridge was constructed to link the western Peloponnese with mainland Greece.

The Mennells were British and very curious about every aspect of history, anthropology, biology, geology, mythology, etc. They had established an ambitious itinerary for us. I was in constant amazement at the beauty and history that unraveled before us day after day. My education was considerably expanded!

We visited places hitherto unimagined by me. They included Patras, Kalamata, Corinth, Sparta, Nafplion and the ancient city of Messene. We explored the theater of Epidaurus. A highlight for me was our time in Olympia—the site of the Olympic games in classical times. There we saw the Temple of Hera and the ruins of the Philippeion as well as the Palaestra.

We were indeed crowded in our little car but Peter was gracious about the extra weight in the car (me) as we bounced along the winding dusty roads. I have never known a more vocal back-seat driver than Prudie. She was forever yelling at him to "HOOT," which meant to blow the horn at a driver who offended her. I would have hauled off and bopped her had I been Peter, but he was ever the gentleman. I just cringed in the back seat.

We stayed in Xenias which are government managed hotels that represent the historic Greek concept of hospitality. This attitude of taking care of travelers came from ancient Greek times and is mentioned in Greek mythology. Each Xenia was unique and charming.   We learned enough Greek phrases to be able to comport ourselves appropriately. I adored Greek food that was for me unique and irresistible. I was not ready for ouzo as I had never had an alcoholic drink at that point in my life.

I was well aware that I had caught the travel bug and I knew I wouldn't be seeking a cure. I was enchanted by this experience. So taken was Katharine with Greece that even before we left the country she had arranged to charter a yacht for the following year and planned to invite selected friends to join her on a cruise of the Aegean. And so it began. The first of these cruises was to be in 1968 and thereafter they occurred every even numbered year for many a year to come.

Imagine my surprise to return to Tucson at the end of the trip to find that everyone had thrived in my absence!

1968

Tony was covetous of his limited vacation time from work. He didn't waste it on any pursuit that did not hold great appeal to him. However, anything to do with the sea— and the grandiose life-style we anticipated—was enough to convince him that a cruise on the Aegean would be time well spent. Indeed it was.

And so, at the end of June, I went to New York City to spend a few days with Katharine before flying with her to Athens once again. Tony was to meet us in Athens later. Katharine's guest list varied slightly from cruise to cruise but there were a few who, like Tony and me, were on all of them. We became close friends. These included Prudie and Peter Mennell as well as Katharine's friends in Stamford, Connecticut—Jan and Ames Richards. Usually there were only eight of us on board—occasionally ten. Therefore, the Mennells, the Richards, Katharine, Tony and I formed almost the full contingent.

Often one of the other passengers was a stuffy British man named Guy Meek. His biases were from a different era and he did not disguise his contempt for some of my American ways. He was of the school of thought that one would never write a letter to two people. It was either to the wife or to the husband, but never both. Simply not done! Also he tatted! One would typically find him on deck totally immersed in his needlepoint. Katharine, however, doted on him and, his ostensible good breeding notwithstanding, he could not disguise his disdain for her and all the rest of us. Guy visited often in Tucson, too, until his death in April, 1976.

The *Christabel*

Of our many cruises on the Aegean Sea this was the least memorable and the only one we took on the ship *Christabel*. It was a beautiful yacht—120 feet in length. It was owned by a doctor who named the ship after his wife. He was reluctant to let it out for charter, but Katharine came very highly recommended. The crew was substantial in number and the chef was inspired with each of the meals he prepared.

Katharine always queried her guests prior to departure as to their food and drink preferences. My mind boggles as I recall the cases and cases of liquor that were on board to accommodate each person's taste, and most of them were still on board when we left. Katharine was of the "old school." Hence, we dressed formally for every evening meal in spite of the heat and humidity of the Greek summers. This was not to Tony's liking. It gave him pause for thought; was the discomfort worth it? Fortunately, the "wine-dark sea " won. I thought there might be a mutiny of the gentlemen aboard, all of whom abhorred this tradition. Here they were on vacation on a yacht and they had to wear a suit and tie each evening. It wasn't as difficult

Dining on the yacht – Katharine with Tony on left

340

for the women aboard as long dresses were in style during that time.

Often we would go ashore after dinner, which was served late, and we were an obvious source of amusement to the Greeks in the tavernas we visited. Being young and ebullient, we joined in the Greek dancing. American men in suits did not fit the image!

Aldine at the Acropolis - 1968

There are more than 150 inhabited Greek islands. I have been to about 70 of them. Each morning on board we would sit down with the captain of the ship to discuss the day's plan. We could go wherever we wanted whenever we wanted. Typically we consulted a map, identified our current location, and decided our route for the day. We could stop and swim at whatever beach caught our fancy. We would usually tie up at night near a town so that we could go ashore and enjoy the local flavor.

Each of these cruises lasted two weeks. What an indulged and satisfied group disembarked at the end of each of these voyages.

1970

This year I struck out a little deeper into my adventurous life. My sons were now 15 and 12 years of age and each had plans for the summer months. Kent was going to work as a ranch hand at Katharine's ranch–the Three Rivers Ranch–which was located inside Yellowstone Park near Jackson Hole, Wyoming. When Yellowstone was founded, Katharine's father, Schuyler Merritt, was given a 50-year lease before he and his family would have to vacate the land. (Yellowstone Park was founded in 1872, first run by the Department of Interior and then for 30 years–until 1917–by the US Army. Thereafter, the Park Service took over.) Although their lease was probably up in about 1922, Schuyler Merritt was able to have it extended so that Katharine continued to visit the ranch until well into her 70s.

When the lease ran out, the ranch buildings were completely disassembled. Kent visited the site some years later and commented that one would never have known there had been a ranch house there.

Kent, and later Tony Jr., had the wonderful experience of working there for a month every summer during their teenage years. My husband Tony and I were frequent visitors at the ranch as well.

Meanwhile, Tony Jr. would be visiting our Tucson neighbors—Barbara and Ed Hyde and their family–on Nantucket Island, their summer home. He would be taking tennis and sailing lessons with their son Ted. With Marie Kelley, our housekeeper, at the helm on the home front now, I knew that my sons would be sent off with clean clothes and lots of cookies. Later in the summer we would, as always, be at the cottage in Canada together.

Our 1970 Greek cruise embarked from the beautiful harbor at Vouliagmeni where we boarded our yacht, *Dorita*. The ship was magnificent—120' of luxury. The owner rarely allowed it to be used as a charter and always sent his nephew as an escort. He joined us on all the cruises in the years ahead. Fortunately we liked him very much and he was a tremendous help as we planned our journey day by day. His name

The *Dorita*

was Michael Kanalidis and he apparently had a background in medicine. Certainly he was connected to a great many powerful Greeks as you will see later.

The guests this year remained the same as on the previous cruise which was very much to our liking. This summer Katharine chose to explore the Adriatic Sea and Yugoslavia.

We headed west passing close to Albania where no visitors were welcome at that time. We spent a good deal of time in the Bay of Kotor with its fascinating villages and views of ancient times.

This was quite different from last year as the opportunities for swimming on warm beaches were few and far between. Still, we docked at interesting ports every night and continued to sightsee on shore after dinner. The mood in this area was far less frivolous than that of the ports on the Aegean.

An interesting port of call was Kõrtula—the second largest island in the Adriatic. What a fascinating place to visit with its ancient structures and rich history. We spent several days there.

Dubrovnik was a significant destination—a new experience for us all. It was, in those days a city of charm and character. It still is considered one of the ten best preserved medieval walled cities in the world. It was that very year—1970— that Dubrovnik had been demilitarized to protect it from war. That was not to be. As we know, it was later besieged by the Serb and Montenegran soldiers and suffered significant damage from shelling.

At the time we were there, it was delightful to walk along the wall surrounding the city. We enjoyed the shops and the interesting articles that were for sale. We spent several days there exploring the city and the surrounding area.

Piling into two taxis one day, we drove 50 miles to the ancient town of Mostar. It is, without question, one of the most fascinating cities I have ever seen. The Nereiva River passes through it with a bridge above that is probably Mostar's most recognized landmark. It was built in the 16th century and is awe inspiring.

Aldine & Tony overlooking Mostar - 1970

However, we had a heart stopping and terrifying return trip to Dubrovnik—an experience none of us would ever choose to duplicate. While it is only a two hour drive, it was the longest ride I have ever taken. The road was exceedingly winding and narrow with frequent precipices that dropped off hundreds of feet.

While waiting for us to do our sightseeing on foot, our taxi driver must have imbibed a great deal of alcohol. He was close to being incapable of driving. We wove all over the road as he repeatedly fell asleep at the wheel. We prodded him. We yelled at him. It was hopeless. We all were terrified and honestly doubted we would survive this horror. It would have been unwise to stop as we didn't speak the language and thought that eight people standing by the side of the road would be an oddity but not reason for a rescue. And we could well have put ourselves in further danger. We held on tight, prayed, and survived. Never have I been so relieved to reach a destination–Dubrovnik. Now we needed a good stiff drink. Yes, I was drinking by now, Tony having introduced me to the demon brew with Ripple wine!

We went as far north as Split, a large city that is considered just over 1700 years old. In fact, it was founded as a Greek colony in the 4th century BCE. It held little attraction for us.

We returned to Vouliagmeni to disembark the *Dorita*, all of us feeling that for future cruises we would remain on the Aegean Sea.

1972

As mentioned, Katharine Merritt chartered her cruises on the even numbered years. Tony and I were very excited about this one as we knew what luxury and beauty awaited us in Greece.

On May 31st, two days after my 39th birthday which was well celebrated, I departed Tucson bound for NYC. Although I was staying at Katharine's apartment on East 51st Street, she herself was in London at the time. Katharine insisted that her guests have breakfast in bed which was always a source of discomfort for me. It was up to her old housekeeper Delia Cahill to bring me breakfast and never, no never, would Delia sit down while I ate. She loved to talk with me as she was lonely but her attitude of servitude would require her to remain standing through the duration of our conversation. She was in service with the Merritt family from the time she had come to the U.S. from Ireland at age 16 until she died.

Katharine was a member of the very exclusive women's club, the Cosmopolitan Club, and arranged for me to have the use of it while she was absent. I met friends there for lunch.

On June 1st, I flew from Kennedy Airport to Frankfurt, Germany where I had a layover of many hours before continuing on via Lufthansa to Genoa. On June 3rd I embarked on the cruise ship *Enrico C* for an interesting voyage.

Our first port of call was Casablanca. I had met a lovely man, Ensio, and his son Marco. I want to point out that in all my travels alone Tony had encouraged me toward *carpe diem* in spite of whether or not the event appeared appropriate or conventional. Another of Tony's requests regarding my independent travel was that I meet some nice man as soon as possible—someone who could keep an eye on me. I was following orders. Ensio, his son and I took a three hour train trip to Marrakesh passing through barren and poverty stricken areas. Camels abounded. We visited the mosque and palace and had lunch at what was to become one of my favorite hotels over time—La Mamounia. We spent hours at the marketplace Jemma el Fna with its legendary snake charmers and fascinating wares. We were back at the ship that evening.

The next day we arrived in Tangier where I spent the morning sightseeing with a trip along the coastline, a visit to fascinating caves and then to the Kasbah. The ship sailed that afternoon taking us very close to Gibraltar. That evening we were in Spain, and I went ashore with friends in Torremolinos to visit a discotheque and then to El Madrigal to see the dramatic flamenco dancing. That night I had three hours of sleep but what a colorful and memorable experience! The next port of call was Malaga followed by a day at sea.

On June 10th I disembarked the ship and flew to London where I stayed at the elegant Berkeley Hotel with Katharine.

The following day I took a train into the countryside to visit a lovely family whom I had known for some years—Major and Mrs. Hamish Robertson–near Meopham. They toured me through their lovely gardens and along country lanes to their very old church. I returned to London by train and met my beloved pen pal, Margaret Cock Collin for drinks and dinner at the Berkeley with a walk later to Trafalgar Square. Oh how good it was to spend those hours with her.

The changing of the guard at Buckingham Palace captivated me, and I could never watch it often enough. So, the following day I left Katharine to do some sightseeing on my own. That night we went to Drury Lane to see the musical *Gone with the Wind*, a great treat. It was time to leave for Greece.

We had an early departure flying from London to Athens the following day. I was thrilled to be invited by the British Airline captain to sit in the cockpit for the landing— after which he invited me out for the evening. That was not to be. I already had a dinner engagement with an old friend, Stratis Mytinileous, and so I left Katharine with other of her guests who were going on the cruise, including Guy Meek once again. We were staying at the Grande Bretagne—a stately hotel in the center of Athens.

Stratis treated me to an unforgettable Greek evening starting with a tour of his yacht followed by dinner at Kuyus at Tourklimano. The following day he drove me in his open car to the cliffs on the other side of Varkisa. We picnicked and swam in the gorgeous ocean water. Stratis was clearly developing fantasies that were not going to materialize so I knew it was time to end the friendship. My fidelity to my husband was sacrosanct.

Whenever I visited Athens, I always spent time with John Paraskevopolis, a professor at the University of Athens, whom I had known while he was working at the University of Illinois. He was consistently a charming host and took me to an enchanting rooftop restaurant in the Plaka for dinner. Afterwards, as we were driving through Athens for him to take me to my hotel—The Astir Palace—he told me he had to run to his apartment for a moment. We parked on the street in front of his building and he suggested I go up with him. I refused. He told me that my being in a car alone at that time of night would be very unsafe. I weighed the options and the decision wasn't long in coming. I knew I'd be safer alone on the street than in his apartment with him. He made many more such attempts to capture my fancy—unsuccessfully.

Katharine never understood, but typically accepted with grace most of my independent adventures in Athens. We had met a group of people in the hotel, one of whom was a doctor. He invited me to join a swimming party down the coastline. We drove to the top of a hill, having parked his car off the highway, and started our way down a winding dirt path to the beach. I could see a group in the distance. As we drew closer, I saw that they all were naked. Humiliated and outraged to have been drawn into this debauchery I, in a huff of indignation, admonished him firmly to tell his friends to put their clothes on immediately. As if! This, I learned in time, was the way Greeks preferred to swim. I was such an innocent and while "the doctor" continued on toward the beach I made a reverse turn and headed back up to the highway. And there I was—alone. Adrenalin still surging through me, I walked until a bus came by that I could flag down for the remainder of the trip into Athens. I was in time to join Katharine and the others for drinks and dinner. I had learned a lesson.

I longed to see the Parthenon by moonlight. Once a month—at full moon—all artificial lighting was extinguished at the Acropolis so that it was lit entirely by moonlight. As my visit to Athens happened to coincide with this event, I was determined not to miss it. So, on the appointed night after everyone had gone to their rooms for the night, I slipped out quietly and headed for the Acropolis. It was a sight I shall never forget— spectacular in its full glory.

I returned to the hotel about 2:00 a.m. intending to return quietly to my room with no one the wiser. It didn't go that way! When I entered the hotel lobby I found there were police everywhere and Katharine, fully dressed, looked frantic. She had gone to my room to ask for help with something and found me gone and the bed untouched. She had gone berserk and had called in a missing persons report. She was about to phone the American Embassy. They were initiating an all-out search for me as Katharine was sure I had been abducted. I was in hot water and severely scolded. I probably deserved it.

Tony was due to arrive at 2:35 p.m. the next day—June 16th— and my excitement knew no bounds. As it happened, an engine on his aircraft caught fire and fell off when only an hour outside of NYC. His flight did not arrive until 10:45 that night. He, however, was filled with enthusiasm and energy so off we went at midnight to Kuyus in Tourklimano for hors d'oeuvres and wine. Bedtime was very late that night!

We set sail on our cruise on June 17th from Vouliagmeni traveling around Cape Sunion and between the mainland and Makronissos with a stop to swim somewhere near Megalo. We hugged Avia on the right and arrived at Chalkris at 7:30 p.m. Running with the current we went through the bridge at 1:00 a.m. It was a long and fascinating day.

Every day included a good deal of swimming—sometimes off the fantail of the ship but more often at beaches on islands along the way. The second day we moored off the island of Aidipsos before lunch, which was a very big affair daily. We wended our way to a favorite Greek island of mine, Skopelos. Before dinner—on board—we went for a walk in the village and returned for coffee in the square after dinner. I felt as if I were living a in a dream.

Ginny Richards, the daughter of Jan and Ames Richards of whom I have spoken, often joined me in snorkeling at delightful beaches on unpopulated islands. I found wonderful treasures at the bottom of the sea—urns and vessels of various shapes and ages—which I treasure in my home to this day. Tony, in the meantime, was sailing in one of the dinghies; he capsized once but managed to right himself. We docked for the night at Alonissas. It wasn't very attractive looking so we did not go ashore.

The next day was our typical schedule of swimming, eating and sunning. We

Tony with the *Dorita* in the background

anchored near a beach on Skiathos where Tony and I swam ashore, sunned and swam back to the ship. That night we tied up at the town of Skiathos—thoroughly Greek and absolutely delightful. We went ashore for coffee after dinner.

The last of the guests—Peter Leslie, a British gentleman—arrived from Athens to join the group. We sailed again to Skopelos where Peter and I swam to shore from the ship. While others sunned, he and I walked to a lovely inland lake. After a delightful afternoon we all swam back to the ship and sailed to Skyros arriving at the tiny village

about 7:30 p.m. After dinner we went ashore and later Tony and I joined five Greek men for drinks, dancing and music. Oh what a happy-go-lucky lot the Greek men seem to be while their wives often appear dour.

I mentioned that our escort, Michael, knew a great many influential Greeks. One day we sailed past Skorpios, the magnificent island owned by Aristotle Onasis and where he married Jackie Kennedy. Suddenly a helicopter swooped above us with a woman hanging out the window enthusiastically waving to us indicating that she wanted us to pull in at Skorpios. She recognized the *Dorita* and Michael. Michael made the appropriate gestures to indicate that it wasn't possible. Jackie could not have known that the boat was chartered. Still, it was fun to have that transitory vignette. Eventually, by the way, the island was sold to a Russian billionaire for one hundred million dollars.

An eight-hour trip on the following day took us from Skyros to Lesvos where we tied up at Port Sigri. Since it was a barren and poor area, Michael had dropped us off at an island to swim. I took a very long walk along the beach—alone—and came upon a huge lighthouse. An old Greek gentleman who made it his home took me inside and gave me a tour. It was fascinating. The ship was tied up at Lesvos that night.

Having presented a glimpse of the way we spent our days, I will consolidate the remainder of the trip by noting a few highlights. This was the summer Ginny Richards, the youngest member of our contingent, met one of our ship's sailors—Tassos. More to come later.

We visited many islands including Chios, Samos, Pythagoria and arrived in Kusadasi, Turkey from where we traveled on to Ephesus. We resumed our island hopping to Samos, Patmos, Mykonos, and Delphi, Kea, Hydra, Spetsai and Poros. Some islands we visited multiple times and many I have not mentioned at all as they were just for swimming or picnicking.

Aldine on Santorini - 1972

We disembarked from this magical trip at Vouliagmeni on July 9th. Tony and I immediately met up with friends from Tucson and began our odyssey with them that I write about in another chapter. Each of these cruises had its own personality and this one ranked as very special.

1974

Tony and I flew together to London where we met Katharine at the airport and flew on to Athens. Our gorgeous hotel, the Astir Palace, was at Vouliagmeni. Our room was on the top floor with its own terrace and gardens. Katharine did spoil us, and we loved it. One evening we took Michael and the owners of the *Dorita* out for dinner. They were absolutely charming Greeks and obviously wealthy.

An interesting event occurred. While I was ascending to our room by myself one afternoon, I found I was accompanied in the elevator by one other person—a very beautiful and exotic looking Greek woman using a cane. It slipped quite naturally from my lips to politely lament that no such beautiful woman should be incapacitated. "Oh, my dear, it is nothing. But thank you for your thoughtfulness." Upon reaching her floor the elevator door opened and who was standing there but Aristotle Onassis. She told him she had just met this lovely young woman. He bowed and they proceeded on their way. How could I not have recognized Maria Callas right away!

The following night my friend John Paraskevopolis took Tony and me to Geros tou Moria for a memorable Greek dinner at the Plaka. Later, while driving us back to our hotel, John turned to Tony in the passenger seat beside him and said, "Many women come to Greece in the summer looking for an amorous encounter. You are fortunate to have a wife who is faithful to you." I was surprised at his candor.

We began this cruise on June 17th sailing from Vouliagmeni. We were caught in some heavy winds which the captain identified as a full-fledged *melteme* (Greek hurricane). Thus, some of us spent time in our cabins suffering from *mal de mer.*

To the chagrin of her parents, a spin-off from the melteme was the solidifying of a budding romance between Ginny Richards and one of our sailors, Tassos. While sailing in heavy winds, some chair cushions on deck blew into the ocean. In dove Ginny to save them. Then in dove Tassos to save Ginny. Panic on board ensued and what seemed to me to be a major rescue at sea was initiated. All were safe in the end.

Ginny's parents, Jan and Ames Richards, were pillars of their community in Stamford, Connecticut and had long planned the perfect marriage for their one and only daughter Ginny. She was the apple of their eye. It was very difficult for them to accept the love affair going on between this unlikely couple.

One night we were entertained with brilliant Greek dancing by Ginny and Tassos. The magic between them was palpable. Now mind you, Ginny spoke not a word of Greek, nor did Tassos know English. I guess love has its own communication.

Instead of the proper and more typical marriage that they had planned for their daughter, Ginny and Tassos were married at the beginning of our 1976 cruise in a big,

Aldine in Greece - 1974

fat Greek wedding on the island of Aegina where the young couple took up residence.

Life was idyllic on the cruise with many unique moments but I will simply mention some of the islands we visited along the way–Poros, Hydra, Serifos, Spetsai, Sifnos, Ios, Milos, Santorini, Astipoalaia, Kos, Pserimos, Kalamos, Leros, Patmos, Noxos, Mykonos, Delos and Tinos.

The cruise terminated on July 1st. Tony and I took Katharine to London and flew together to Miami. Tony went to Tucson and I to Cuernavaca, Mexico to enroll in a two week course of intensive Spanish. I have written about this elsewhere.

1976

Prior to embarking on our biennial cruise, my parents, sons and I had a wonderful Mediterranean cruise that is written about in another chapter. We ended our trip in Athens on June 19th. I met Tony at the airport as he had arrived from Tucson that day. We returned to the ship to join my parents and our boys for lunch. That night we went to Geros tou Moria for dinner in the Plaka and went to the Sound and Light performance at the Acropolis. It was our last night all together.

On June 20th we disembarked our cruise ship and took a ferry to Aegina to join this year's contingent of guests on the *Dorita* which was docked there. Mother, Dad and our sons had lunch aboard and returned to Athens for their flight to Tucson. It was a 24-hour trip for them!

In the evening the Dorita guests attended Ginny and Tassos' wedding. We truly had a taste of Greece. The wedding was lovely and was followed by a Greek party to end all Greek parties with music and dancing into the wee hours of the morning.

On this trip we were without many of the previous *Dorita* guests and added quite a few new ones. Ginny's brothers, Chris and Van, were with us as well as Johanna Plaut who was a frequent visitor to our home in Tucson. We were delighted that a British couple with superb senses of humor–Marcia and Tony Melville-Ross–joined us this time.

On our second day out, a terrific wind came up causing enormous waves. On our five-hour trip from Hydra to Seriphos everyone was seasick—except Tony. It was more comfortable to be outside in the fresh air than below in our cabins. Hence, people were retching over the rail and it was generally unpleasant. The wind persisted for another day so we were unable to leave Seriphos. Ultimately, we braved the seas, still high, and sailed to the island of Ios.

A few days passed in relative calm with opportunities to swim off many beaches—seeing many more nude bathers. I was becoming inured to the sight. At Ios the ship dropped several of us off to swim to the beach and then take a strenuous walk to the village at the top of the mountain. We descended the other side and walked to the harbor where the *Dorita* had sailed to await us.

We enjoyed relatively calm sailing for a few days and then yet another *melteme* struck. The captain estimated the wind at about 50 knots. We pitched and rolled and were generally miserable. This was the most uncomfortable of all our cruises. It had not been easy on Katharine–now 90 years old—who had often chosen to stay on board while we went ashore. We all suspected this would be the last of our cruises;   Katharine simply was no longer up to it.

In spite of the weather we stopped at a great many islands including Aegina, Poros, Hydra, Seriphos, Ios, Santorini, Naxos, Paros, Mykonos, Delos, Tinos, Andros, Petali and Kea. We picnicked and swam at many more, the names of which I often didn't know.

The wind gave us no surcease. It continued to blow all the way to Vouliagmeni— our last port of call and the end of an era.

It was our last cruise with Katharine and time to say goodbye to friends whom we had come to treasure and whom we knew we would never see again. There were many hugs, a few tears and promises to stay in touch. While I subsequently took many more trips to Greece and cruises on the Aegean and Ionian Seas, none was ever as opulent.

Katharine continued to visit us in Tucson during the winter for several more years. She died at her home in Connecticut at the astonishing age of one hundred and a half years.

On July 4th, Tony returned to Tucson and I flew to Toronto to spend the remainder of the summer with my family at our old cottage. It was necessary for us to make one side trip on August 10th—to Montreal.

Kent and I drove through Algonquin Park, saw the Parliament Buildings in Ottawa, and arrived in Montreal in the late afternoon. Kent was there to see doctors for his "examination of discovery." This was relative to the ghastly injury he had at a mine in Chibougamou in northern Quebec the year before.

We visited the stadium where the Olympics had recently been held. Montreal is a very beautiful city situated on an island.

Kent then drove back to the cottage while I flew out of Montreal bound for Tucson on August 13th. Having been gone since May 27th, it was time to get back to work at UA. The new semester started for me only three days later.

27

⚙

NORWAY

ALONE ABOARD *THE METEOR* –TO THE NORTH CAPE–1969

I had been a sheltered young woman never having lived in a dorm, or sorority house, or even attended a summer camp. When Tony arranged with his godmother, Katharine Merritt, for me to join her on a trip through the Peloponnese in Greece in 1967, it was the first time I had ever been away from home alone. I thought that as long as I was going to be in Europe, I would take advantage of a situation that might not come again and expand my wings even further. A part of the world I had always dreamed of seeing was Norway–and it was calling.

Striking out on my own truly was a terrifying experience but I had planned to soften it by meeting a good friend, Ann Woodin, in Holland for a few days. I flew from Athens to Amsterdam and checked into the Amstel Hotel which was our meeting place. The reception desk handed me a note Ann had left for me: she had taken a trip on the canals and was sorry she would miss seeing me. My heart sank.

Because this was a big, clean and friendly city, I felt comfortable in sight-seeing on my own. Many people spoke English which was a great boon. Still, I had to become accustomed to their use of the vernacular. I remember standing at an intersection not knowing which way to go to find a certain museum. I stopped three young women to ask for directions. They said, "Obviously it is right there," pointing across the street. I took that as a rebuke for my stupidity. Then I realized that the word "obvious" to them meant that it was visible. I was far too sensitive and they, in fact, had used the word correctly.

I have enjoyed returning to Amsterdam many times and always appreciate having the beautiful Amstel Hotel as my home base.

My big test now faced me. There was no one meeting me in Bergen, Norway, and to me it seemed a very distant and formidable place. I arrived in the evening. It was cold, wet and dark. I was scared. I took a taxi to the lovely Norge Hotel and checked in. Loneliness overtook me. I was miserable and very frightened. I did not leave the hotel that night or the following day. What a scaredy-cat I was!

When the day came for my departure on a cruise ship I checked out of the hotel, took a taxi to the pier, and went on board. This "obviously" turned out to be a magnificent experience as I have been traveling ever since—a great deal of it alone.

Let me describe the ship. It was a very old, small wooden Norse cruise ship named the *Meteor.* I did not realize at the time that this was a ship unlike any I would ever see again. It had no horizontal stabilizers or other modern effort toward making a passenger's voyage more comfortable. My "cabin" was no bigger than a clothes closet and the door into it would open just enough for me to squeeze in before it was blocked by the "bed"—a glorified cot. It did have one luxury—its own basin and water.

One of the great assets of this ship that I would come to appreciate more and more was its size. Because it was so small, it could enter fjords that were inaccessible by larger vessels. I saw Norway then as I have never seen it since. And I was utterly convinced that there was no more beautiful country anywhere on Earth. I haven't changed my mind.

The first evening I ventured toward the dining room barely able to walk as the ship was lurching for a fare-thee-well. We were out at sea and the waves were enormous. Upon entering the dining room I was quickly noticed by two couples. The gentlemen leaped to their feet and ushered me to their table. I will never forget their kindness throughout the entire cruise. We became close friends and I wrote them annually until their deaths.

As a single woman, I was an anomaly on board and people made sure I was never on my own for long. The hostess for this cruise was Mary Borchsenius, a kindly, middle-aged lady. If I had a problem, she solved it. I mention her again in a cruise I took of Norway years later. One issue I had to deal with was clothing. I had come from Greece where lightweight clothing was appropriate. Here I needed warm clothes and a jacket that could stave off the very cold weather ahead. Mary collected bits and pieces from here and there and I soon had a wardrobe that took care of all my needs.

Our first port of call was Geirangerfjord and a visit to the town of Geiranger. I had never seen such beauty. It overcomes one's senses. We had tea at the Stalheim Hotel as I took in the sight of waterfalls glistening on the steep slopes of the fjord.

I will mention the fjords and towns into which we traveled—Alesund, Molde, Trondheim, and the spectacular Stavangerfjord and Levangerfjord. Then Bode, the Lofoten Islands, Hammerfest and Harstad. The town I remember most enthusiastically was Tromsø. It was considered the northernmost city in the world and there was a pervading sense of friendliness and intimacy. We were taken by small boat up a long river to see vistas that never would have been available to cruise passengers on larger ships. During the afternoon and evening of the day we were there, we—as couples or individuals—were guests in private homes. I enjoyed a delicious Norse meal with a lovely family—an unforgettable memory.

Tromsø contains the highest number of old wooden houses in Northern Norway, the oldest house dating from 1789. This town, north of the Arctic Circle, is a cultural center for its region. The Arctic Circle is the most northerly of the five major circles of latitude that mark maps of the Earth. The region north of this circle is known as the Arctic, and the zone just to the south is called the Northern Temperate Zone. North of the Arctic Circle, the sun is above the horizon for 24 continuous hours at least once per year.

I was very excited about crossing the Arctic Circle and was awarded a certificate to recognize this occasion which is framed and on the wall of our cottage in Canada. I was a novice traveler and still very much in awe of these new experiences.

On our route going north, our last port of call was Honningsvag. It is the northernmost village in Norway and "gateway" to the North Cape—our ultimate destination. It was a bumpy and uncomfortable 22-mile trip by bus from there to reach the North Cape (NordKapp)—ostensibly the northernmost part of Europe. There one encounters a 1,007 foot high cliff with a large flat plateau on top where one can stand and watch the midnight sun or the views of the Barents Sea to the north. It was difficult walking and there were no amenities of any kind at that time. It was a rugged, never-to-be-forgotten experience.

The very handsome first officer of the *Meteor*, Evand Legland, had taken a fancy to me and made this cruise all the more exciting as I had opportunities to visit the bridge and see sights on shore that were not privy to other passengers. And I was naïve. One night he invited me to his cabin. Well, Evand invented the concept of "man cave"—music, lighting, and yes, a bed. Really, what was I thinking being in an officer's quarters at night. I eventually extricated myself unscathed but only after shedding some very convincing tears.

Later he told me that many nights he had entered my cabin while I was asleep and just looked at me. I was never aware of this, thank goodness.

Ships company – Mary Borchsenius second from right, Evand Legland fourth from right

One man on board who did not take a fancy to me was Charles Weigland, a delightful man from Australia who was in the cabin next to mine. Finally, when he could stand it no longer, he asked me to please not wash my "smalls" in the wee hours of the morning. I had no idea I was keeping him awake night after night.

We were soon to be back in Bergen and ready for disembarkation when Evand furtively advised me that there would be an extra suitcase joining mine outside my cabin at the time of departure. Indeed there was and I was mighty curious as to what it could contain that he himself could not take off the ship. This was to be his last cruise with passengers. He went on to become the captain of Norse cargo ships and developed a reputation for being one of the most respected maritime officers in Norway.

He met me as we left the ship, arranged a taxi to take us to the airport and kindly saw me off—his suitcase carefully stowed in the trunk of the taxi. I will always wonder with what contraband I left the *Meteor!* Sadly I must report that a short time thereafter the *Meteor* caught fire and was left merely a cinder.

I was excited all the way back from Bergen to Tucson. I had missed my family terribly, but I had caught the traveling bug for which I never found a cure.

DENMARK AND NORWAY WITH MY FAMILY—1979

S pring semester of 1979 was over leaving me in a state of exhaustion. Tony took the situation in hand and spirited me off for a week of sailing on the Sea of Cortez. It was heavenly to be together before my exit for the summer.

Soon after our return to Tucson it was time to leave for Europe. Kent and Tony Jr. took my parents and me to the airport for our departure to Toronto. I should have seen the omens of impending trouble. Even before we boarded the plane, both my handbag and suitcase handles broke. In for a penny, in for a pound, I shipped my ailing suitcase directly to Copenhagen–my ultimate destination–while I flew to Toronto with my parents.

After saying goodbye to Mom and Dad at the Toronto airport, I flew to Copenhagen, Denmark–a long flight that was filled to the gills. It was Friday, June 1st when I arrived—the beginning of a four-day holiday in Denmark. My suitcase was nowhere to be found. Alas. In the nature of full disclosure, the baggage people conveyed to me that it wouldn't be available until the following Tuesday after the long weekend. Here I was en route to a lovely resort in Denmark on Jutland for a week of rest and pampering. And all I had to wear was the dress on my back!

Finally, resigned to my loss, I climbed on an SAS bus that was headed to the downtown train station where I would board my train to go north, only to find that the bridge over to Copenhagen was closed due to a workers strike. We sat on the bus for two hours in the heat, which did nothing to improve the condition of the only clothes I had—those I was wearing! Finally I reached the train station where a strange old lady took me under her wing and helped me find the train to Helsingor. Upon arrival I boarded a bus for the Marienlyst Hotel where I was to stay for a week. I had read about Marienlyst and knew that it was considered one of the best hotels in all Denmark. It was situated on the Jutland peninsula, a part of Northern Europe that forms the continental portion of Denmark and the northern portion of Germany.

I arrived mid-afternoon—24 hours after leaving Tucson! As my diary noted, I was "hot, tired, discouraged, dirty and no suitcase." Later in the day my period started. Could it get worse? It did.

Peter Marquardt, an old friend from Germany, joined me on June 2nd. I was glad for his company but I'm not sure he was glad for mine. I remember being rather unpleasant that week—and I didn't smell very nice. We did have some lovely moments—sitting by the ocean and walking for miles. It is a beautiful region and the resort was lovely with a swimming pool that had undulating waves. But I didn't have a swim suit and couldn't use it!

We took a ferry over to Helsingborg, Sweden where we walked through the ancient Mary Church and Castle Karnan—a medieval tower in southern Sweden. It is the only part remaining of a larger Danish fortress which controlled the entranceway to the Baltic Sea. That evening we danced the night away with me still in the clothes I had initially donned in Tucson days before.

On June 4th we took an hour's bus trip north through beautiful countryside to Dronningmolle where we found a glorious beach. Nude bathers abounded. Well, admittedly, perhaps one half of the people there were wearing the bottom parts of their bathing suits. It was great fun to sit and people-watch! Neither Peter nor I deigned to join the tumbling mirth of naked swimmers.

Back to the hotel and voilá, my suitcase had been delivered. Oh the pleasure of bathing and putting on clean clothes. My vacation had begun! Until the next day when I awoke bathed in sweat and running a high fever. Poor Peter. I think he had a different concept of how our week would go. Now he became difficult. What a pair we made!

After my night of shaking and sweating, Peter brought me breakfast in bed. Although I was on the mend I had one more anomaly to deal with. At that time a fever would cause my left eye to swell terribly and I would look truly grotesque. Peter took one look at me that day and went for a long walk—alone.

It was that day—June 6th–that my parents, my brother Murray and his wife Mary, and my sister Carol and her husband Terry Belsham arrived in Copenhagen. I was surprised that Mary had come as she had told us in February that she was pregnant! Peter and I made good use of this our last full day together—June 7th. We walked to the Kronborg Castle—a stronghold in the town of Helsingor, Denmark immortalized as Elsinore in William Shakespeare's play *Hamlet.* It was one of the most fascinating castles I had ever seen, but it was terribly cold inside.

Back to the hotel we went and to my astonishment my phone rang. Carol was calling to tell me that they were all downstairs in the hotel having coffee as part of a tour they were taking. My family had known Peter for years so we all had a lovely hour together.

The following day, June 8th, Peter and I packed up and took the train to Copenhagen. He checked into the Admiral Hotel which was a charming old warehouse. After lunch he took me to the pier where we said our goodbyes and where I joined my family. I would not see Peter again until he visited me in Tucson for a week in December, 1980.

My family and I embarked on our gorgeous ship, the *Royal Viking Sky,* for our North Cape cruise along the coast of Norway to celebrate my parent's 50th wedding anniversary.

Our first day aboard was "at sea" and, as none of us felt well, it was a good time to kick back and do nothing. We did attend the Captain's welcome aboard party and enjoyed the floor show that followed.

On June 10th we arrived at Geirangerfjord in the morning. Carol, Terry and I went ashore to take a long and lovely walk. On our departure later in the day we sat on deck to watch the beautiful scenery. How lovely the coast of Norway is!

Trondheim was our next port of call and we all took a 9:00 a.m. bus tour visiting a large and very old cathedral as well as seeing the city. We had tea on deck later in the day to listen to the band as we sailed out of Trondheim at 6:00 p.m. Our evenings at dinner together were always very lively and we soon were identified as the "noisy" table. Murray was always up to one antic or another which kept things lively for everyone.

I made a point the following day of being up early to see the Svartisen Glacier—the second largest glacier in Norway. It was magnificent. That night we stayed up until midnight because it was daylight outside, but we didn't see the midnight sun.

On June 13th we docked in Honningsvag. It was raining and foggy and very cold. Of course, we were at the northernmost part of Europe so what could we expect? I remember Mary, a careful but inveterate shopper in those days, going on a major shopping trip in this very dreary little town. She found a store that sold handmade woolen goods and thought they would be nice for the baby when he arrived later in the year. It was a marathon shopping trip unlike any these staid salesladies were likely to have seen previously. Mary loaded up on one of everything they had and now had her baby's layette. The shop was virtually emptied!

Often at dinner Mary did not join us. She was engrossed in reading a book called *Princess Daisy* —all the rage at that time—by Sidney Sheldon. She often missed our day trips as well saying, "If you've seen one fjord, you've seen them all." That was our Mary and we loved her.

At 5:30 p.m. that day we all climbed aboard a bus for the hour-long trip to the North Cape. I was terribly excited once again to have this amazing experience. The road had opened only two days before as it had been impassible due to many days of heavy rain. Even though we couldn't see through the windows due to so much flying mud, my enthusiasm was not remotely dampened. It was literally freezing at the North Cape and all my family thought they would perish. I, however, had a long-standing plan—to take home with me the northernmost rock in all of Europe. So out I went by foot to the edge of the North Cape. I reached out for the furthest rock that I could carry and now was the proud possessor of a souvenir I still can look at daily. That night we did indeed see the midnight sun. What a thrill for me.

Hammerfest was our next port of call. Although all the rest of the family went ashore soon after we docked at 8:00 a.m., I wanted to spend this day alone. I climbed to the highest point within walking distance for the gorgeous views. I walked through the town and bought a "Viking" for Janice—a little figure that poured forth power and history.

This was one of many Royal Viking cruises that included a very special member of the crew—Stefano Fattori—who always managed to be our waiter and who became almost a part of the family on these trips. He often took Carol and me (and included Mary and Murray on this voyage) to parties in the crew's quarters which were much more lively than those taking place on the decks above. Stefano and I sent letters and audiotapes to each other each winter. This particular night Carol and I went to bed at 3:00 a.m. in full daylight!

I had fallen in love with the town of Tromsø on my visit there a few years earlier and I thoroughly enjoyed renewing my acquaintance with it on June 15th. That night's entertainment was a costume parade and everyone went all out in being creative. It was great fun. One woman was wearing only her slip on which she had put a sign saying "Freudian Slip." I have used that idea myself since then. My family had a wonderful champagne party that night—with Stefano, of course—that went on until 5:00 a.m. I often wondered how Stefano managed his heavy duties during the day while getting no sleep at night!

My father and I often had little contests that we took quite seriously. This year's had to do with amassing little mint candies. Outside the dining room at night was a bowl of mints. Guests typically took one or two when leaving. Our challenge to each other this time was to see which of us could accrue the greatest number of mints during the cruise. We established rules and set the starting and the completion times. I was absolutely convinced I would win as I had so many places I could stash the mints—in my purse, pockets, etc. I was sure I was a shoo-in. Was I ever wrong! Now I won't say my dad gloated, but he certainly took a good deal of pleasure in having whupped me. I couldn't believe he had collected twice the number of mints as I had.

A day at sea was very welcome and all of us spent it in doing healthy activities on the ship to compensate for our debaucheries at night. That evening the captain had a Skoal party followed by an amazing Norwegian buffet. We then were treated to Norwegian dancing and somehow the party went on again until 5:30 a.m. However, with only two hours of sleep I was up and ready for our day in Gudvangen. Part of my diary entry today was "It can't go on this way!!" But it did. Mary, Murray and I spent the day together exploring and walking. No one could verbally do justice to the Norwegian coastline. It has a grandeur all its own.

Having missed exploring Bergen during my visit here nine years ago, I took advantage of my new courage and independence and saw every inch of the city visiting the Norse museums and wandering through residential neighborhoods. It is a wonderful old city. It was less than 50 degrees F. and raining but one expects that kind of weather in Norway. I noted in my diary that although I was sleep deprived I was happy and laughing a good deal of the time. It is wonderful to be with my beloved family. (Tony again had chosen not to join us on this trip but I don't think he would have enjoyed the intensity of so many hours of family time on board. He needed his privacy.)

The next day we arrived in Stavanger where the whole family took a launch up the Lisefjorden. It was absolutely magnificent with sheer cliffs on each side; the views were literally breathtaking. We sat on the bow until the very cold weather forced us inside. It was a clear day which was a great boon.

That night was the official celebration of my parent's anniversary. The captain was having his farewell party followed by a memorable dinner. Cruises were very different in those days. Each night we were presented with a very elaborate menu for that evening. Every one of them was worthy of being a keepsake and I still

Aldine in Norway

have quite a few stored at the cottage in Canada. Tonight's was very special indeed. There was quite a fuss made over my parents and the captain came to shake their hands. Imagine 50 years of marriage. They had been wed in Toronto on July 27th, 1929. Murray was now 48, I was 46 and Carol was only 40. Stefano joined us later for our last evening together.

Years later, in 1989, my mother and I took a Royal Viking cruise in Australia. Upon boarding, one of the first things I asked was whether or not Stefano Fattori was on that cruise. Imagine my disappointment when I learned that he had left the ship only that morning for a three-month holiday. I have never seen him since.

We arrived in Oslo on a beautiful day and took a four-hour city tour. Later I phoned an old friend, Mary Borchsenius, who joined us for dinner on the ship that evening and stayed until after midnight. What a lovely surprise that was.

We had another day in Oslo. My mother, Carol, Terry and I walked to the ferry and took it across the bay to stroll through the lovely residential areas. We then returned for the last afternoon on our beautiful ship. It always had non-stop activities–many of which we had taken advantage of—and this would be our last chance. We kept very busy that afternoon.

June 23rd arrived, heralding our departure from the ship and our long flight back to Toronto. I remember this cruise as one of great beauty and continuous happiness and laughter. It was but one of many of my trips to Norway but stands out as the most luxurious and the most fun. And now began our summer at the cottage in Canada with all its own adventures!

28

SPAIN, MOROCCO & PORTUGAL – 1973

I have visited Spain many times but none was quite as much fun as being there with my parents, Kent and Tony Jr. in 1973.

We had flown to Madrid on June 8th and stayed at my favorite hotel there—the Palace. As tired as we were upon arrival, we walked that night to a superb Spanish restaurant–La Barraca—dining on paella and sangria. We all loved it.

We wasted no time the following day in beginning our exploration of the city–first to the Prado and then to the Royal Palace. Both were awe inspiring. That night we went to a memorable restaurant—Casa Botín—and on to Zambas for a colorful flamenco show.

On Sunday we enjoyed more sightseeing and attended a bull fight. My father had gone frequently to Nogales, Arizona from Tucson to see these events and interview the toreros. He deemed the Madrid fight excellent. We had dinner at El Bodegón.

Our tour of Spain began the next day. I rented a car—a Fiat 1430—and drove to El Escorial where we took a tour. Then on to Valle de los Caídos and then to Segovia. Each location is steeped in history. Our destination was Avila, one of my favorite places to visit. We even named one of our Tucson homes "Avila."

We took a beautiful, mountainous road to our next stop—Toledo. It is fascinating. For the most part we were staying in Spain's paradors. Some years before, the Spanish government had converted old monasteries, convents, palaces, fortresses, castles and other historic buildings into luxury hotels. These buildings were maintained by the state. Each was distinctive and charming. Reservations for them had to be made as much as a year in advance. I had done so. The word parador is actually a contraction of the Spanish words para and dormir, which translate to "for to sleep."

Tony & Kent in Toledo, Spain - 1973

When we were settled into our parador in Toledo—Conde de Orgaz–we drove into the old city and visited Santa Tome with El Greco's painting of the Burial of Count Orgaz. We saw El Greco's home and the cathedral and wandered the streets.

The next day we drove over 250 miles along a winding road with fumes from trucks making the hot day even more uncomfortable. It was not pretty countryside but we ultimately arrived in Córdoba. Having seen Toledo, the family could only be disappointed by this big modern city. We did, however, enjoy the lovely parador—La Arruzafa.

Our next destination was Granada. I had tried desperately during the previous year to obtain rooms at the parador there but it was fully occupied. That parador, located within the grounds of the Alhambra Palace, is magnificent, elaborate and elegant. It is one of the landmarks of Spain. We had lunch there after which I approached the desk. I simply asked if they had any rooms available. They responded with, "Are you Mrs. von Isser? We have been trying to reach you to advise you that we do have space for you." I was stunned that, without having said my name, they knew who we were!

If I could go back in time and change a decision I had made, this certainly would have been one of them. Because I had booked another parador on the top of a nearby mountain and had already paid a $25 deposit, I opted that we go on. What a mistake. It was a long, tortuous and dangerous drive up into the Sierra Nevada Mountains. The parador was a ski lodge at over 8000 feet for goodness sake! My father got asthma, the boys lost the car keys, and I was frustrated. I was, after all, doing all the driving!

Leaving as early as possible the next day, we drove straight to Málaga, a long, winding, but very pretty drive. We had lunch on the patio of our parador— Gibrafarro—with a beautiful view of the city and the ocean. We decided, however, to cancel our reservation in order to go on to Algeciras as we were nervous about missing the hydrofoil the next day.

And what an exciting day we had on the following day. First there was a hydrofoil boat ride to Tangier where we met our guide—Sharif Mohamed Bacalli. We drove in two taxis into the hills where we rode camels. The trip continued on through the city, through the Kasbah and to a wonderful Moroccan restaurant—Hamad—for lunch. Later in the day we flew Air France to Marrakesh and took a taxi to the exotic La Mamounia Hotel where we had dinner in the beautiful garden.

My father had been looking forward to visiting the souk (marketplace) Jemaa el-Fna as, although he disliked snakes, he wanted to write a feature about snake charmers. To enhance the story, he had his picture taken charming a snake. He was indeed proud of that. After we dropped my family back at the hotel, our guide Abdul Harim took me on a private tour of places he thought I might enjoy seeing. I discovered that his itinerary was not to my liking. Opium dens were not on my "must see" list.

Aldine's father, Murray Sinclair with snake in Marrakesh

The next day was a Monday, the only day of the week that a Berber souk is open. With Abdul as our guide again, Kent, Tony Jr. and I headed into the High Atlas Mountains. We visited a Berber village and were invited into one of their homes. It was fascinating. Later we went to an ancient Berber Jewish synagogue. We saw a very old mill on a river. After lunch in the mountains, we returned to the hotel to collect my parents who had chosen to spend the day resting. We returned to Jemaa el-Fna. My father wanted a repeat performance with the cobras!

Aldine on a camel – Tangier, 1973

It was insanity on my part but I discovered in a rug store in the souk two beautiful hand-made Moroccan rugs that I felt I couldn't live without. They were thick and big—10 X 12 feet—and weighed a great deal. The merchant offered to send them to Tucson but I wasn't going to let those rugs out of my sight. Even though they rolled them up tight for us, they still were two huge and heavy bundles. My family thought I was out of my mind. Later I agreed. We still had a long way to go on this trip. As an aside, the rugs were in our homes in Tucson for many years and are now in my bedroom at the cottage in Canada looking much the worse for wear.

We tried something new the next day—a buggy ride. It lasted three hours and we covered over seven miles. We visited the Saadian tombs, went through the Kasbah, and past the El Badi Palace. We went to the Jewish quarter to shop where my father was pick-pocketed! We had yet another visit to the Jemaa el-Fna; it was full of mystery and intrigue and we found it irresistible.

The meals at the hotel were wonderful and we chose to eat in the garden in spite of rodents and cats running around. Mother had a habit of carrying a roll of toilet paper in her purse. At the end of a meal, she would wrap up rolls or whatever remained to take back to our rooms for the boys to have when they got hungry, which happened frequently. One night she left her purse partially open only to discover that a varmint had stolen the toilet paper and was making off with it at full speed. Alas, we watched in dismay as the toilet paper unrolled as the rodent ran away with it. Yards of it were trailing along behind it and the other guests didn't know whether to laugh or be offended. We were just plain embarrassed.

We spent a day enjoying the beautiful hotel. La Mamounia is a jewel. Its grounds are magnificent and the swimming pool is surrounded by tropical foliage. Kent and Tony spent a good deal of time in it.

Our last day there was June 20th, and we used it well. We took a long buggy ride that was delightful and ended up, as seemed to be the case daily, at the Jemaa El-Fna where I engaged in a frenzy of shopping. Having restrained myself on previous visits, I bought all the things I had had my eye on for days. Unfortunately, like the rugs, they were big. What was I thinking! I bought a hassock and camel bag for Tony that I still keep in my little office. Now we had all of this to carry as well as the rugs for the remainder of the trip!

The next day we flew to Tangier once again where we boarded a ferry for Cadiz, Spain. I rented another Fiat 1430 and took the family on a lovely drive to the beach where we all swam in the ocean. Heavenly!

On to Seville via a toll road. On this highway we had a totally gross experience that had other drivers shaking their fists at us. It was a three-lane road; we were in the middle lane. Now picture this little Fiat with five passengers and heavy baggage—very heavy. We were sitting mighty close to the road as we drove along. Suddenly I saw in front of us a big dead dog. I looked left and right—traffic on both sides. We all saw that dog loom up in front of us and there was no way to miss it. Even though I straddled it, we hit it with our undercarriage! What a mess. Blood, gore, hair and body parts were flying in every direction. My boys were mortified. My parents were horrified. And other drivers were ready to kill me. We really had chosen too small a car for this trip!

I became totally disoriented in Seville and could not find our hotel. It took me over an hour of driving in circles to eventually locate it. By the time we did find it—the Hotel Colón—I was in tears of frustration. I had a lot of responsibility as all the plans and their implementation were mine to execute. We turned ourselves over to our guide, Pilar, for the remainder of our visit.

We were ready the following day to leave for Ayamonte, Spain where we stayed at a wonderful parador, De la Luz. We spent the afternoon at the beach and even my father swam that day.

On Sunday we took the ferry across the river that separates Spain and Portugal. The roads we encountered were bumpy and we realized anew that five people in one tiny Fiat was incredibly uncomfortable. Add to that the weight of the rugs tied on top, all manner of packages and luggage and we knew there were difficult times ahead. Of course, every night all of this had to be moved into the hotel. My lads were kept busy hauling cargo but uttered few complaints.

Finally we arrived in Praia da Rocha, Portugal and checked into the beautiful hotel Algarve. Later we crossed the very hot beach on wicker paths to swim in huge waves in the ocean.

We drove to Lisbon the next day through beautiful countryside where the people we encountered were both handsome and simple. The Spanish and Portuguese languages are not as similar as one might think but most of the Portuguese people were able to understand my Spanish and made every effort to communicate with me. The roads to Lisbon were mountainous, winding and bumpy and we all were tired and ready for our hotel. But I couldn't find it. I drove around and around the city following maps and my family's instructions. It was hopeless. I eventually stopped and flagged down a passing car asking—in Spanish, of course—how to find the Hotel Flórida. He indicated I should follow him. I couldn't understand why we kept seeing the same landmarks over and over as we dutifully stayed behind him. We seemed again to be going in circles. And we were. He, too, was totally lost. He apologized profusely. He was unable to help us and wished us well as he went on his way. Eventually, we did find it. I think that is the night I had a little too much to drink!

We loved our swims at the Algarve and our visit to Lisbon. My father, a reporter, had made plans ahead to visit and interview the exiled king of Italy, King Umberto, at his home in Cascais. He was gracious and charming. I was glad to see that being exiled hadn't diminished his elaborate style of life!

We drove to Sintra and Estoril where we had lunch by the sea. We took city tours and explored on our own. We dined in fine restaurants. One was Gambrinas —and another was in the hotel purported to be the best in Europe—Avis.

On June 28th we left Lisbon and flew to London where we stayed at Brown's Hotel. All we managed to fit into our schedule that day was a walk to Piccadilly Circus.

We wasted no time the following day in seeing as much as possible of London. Hiring a private guide for the morning, we were able to make stops at Westminster Abbey, the Tower of London—where we saw the royal jewels—and watched the changing of the guard at Buckingham Palace. We spent much of the afternoon at Madame Tussaud's Museum which the boys found awesome. That night we were invited as guests to witness the locking of the Tower of London. It was an ancient and impressive ritual.

For our last day in London we visited the British Museum and took a boat trip down the Thames River to Greenwich and back.

Sunday, July 1st, our day to return to Tucson, was fraught with problems. My father was terribly ill and didn't think he could make the trip. We agonized over what to do and decided we needed to get him back home and with his own doctors. For a man of ill health he had been very courageous during this extensive and exhausting trip.

Our flight overseas had been cancelled requiring considerable juggling of airlines and schedules. At Kennedy airport Tony Jr. left us to take a flight to Toronto where he was met by his Aunt Ann. She saw him safely off to the cottage on the bus the following day.

We didn't reach Tucson until 12:30 a.m. and Dad was in bad shape. It took him several days to recover. I was thrilled to see Tony who met us at the airport. I think we all breathed a sigh of relief to be home after such a long and demanding trip. Nonetheless, as I reflect on that arduous journey, I realize how significant a time it had been for me as I can recall to the smallest detail each of the days I spent with my fantastic family.

29

♋

HAWAII

KAUAI WITH MY PARENTS AND SISTER—1974

In my diary I described this as "the most wonderful holiday of my life." I enjoyed many wonderful trips as the years went by but this one was indeed special.

My sister Carol, who was living in Toronto at the time, had been ill with pancreatitis and my parents thought the best place for her to recuperate would be Hawaii. And indeed she did rally! Once she recovered from jet lag, she was out dancing every night!

I had been visiting a friend in Los Angeles so met my parents and Carol at the airport there on January 7, 1974. I was 40 and my sister was 35 years old. We flew to Hilo on the island of Hawaii. The following day we took a tour from 8:30 a.m. until 5:30 p.m. which took us to Rainbow Falls, an orchid garden, the Halemaumau Crater, Kilauea Volcano and on to the black sand beach at Punaluu. Then we went to South Point, the southern-most tip of the U.S., followed by a lovely drive to Kona.

We checked into the beautiful Keauhou Beach Hotel. The next day I rented a car so that we could sight-see independently. That night we drove 60 miles to the Mauna Kea Hotel for dinner. It was an impressive evening.

On by plane for the short hop to Maui where we stayed at the Royal Lahaina Hotel. I rented a Mazda station wagon and we drove about 30 miles along the magnificent shoreline. I spent a great deal of time playing tennis in Maui. And we spent altogether too much time lining up to buy gas as it was during the time of the gasoline shortage. While it cost only 58 cents a gallon, it was difficult to find.

We had a magnificent drive from Lahaina to Hana which is one of the most isolated communities in the State of Hawaii. One reaches it by driving the Hana Highway, a long winding 52 mile long road along Maui's north shore. It is a difficult drive as there are so many twists and turns. Hana is also known as the place Charles Lindbergh chose to retire in the 1970s. He died there in 1974 and is buried near Hana.

After dinner one night Carol and I went out to dance and had a very embarrassing experience. We had met two nice gentlemen—cattle ranchers from the Midwest—with whom we were dancing and having cocktails. They insisted upon paying for the drinks and the evening was going well. I think they had expectations. What followed was truly unexpected but I am sure our "dates" didn't think so. They had left to go to the men's room when Carol suddenly felt as if she were going to pass out. I needed to get her back to our room quickly. When our friends returned to our table, we were gone. I can't imagine what epithets went through their minds as I am sure they thought they had been duped. I promise that was not the case—but it was convenient!

Our favorite place to visit on the islands was Coco Palms Hotel on Kauai–to which we had flown from Maui. Coco Palms was set in a coconut grove, possibly the oldest in Hawaii. We arrived in time for lunch and I had scheduled a tennis lesson for that afternoon with their pro—John McDonald. At lunch I shared with my family a little scuttlebutt I had already heard. In what I thought was a lowered voice, I told them that my tennis pro had previously been the Roman Catholic priest for the island. However, he had fallen hopelessly in love with a beautiful young parishioner named Kathleen. He left the church and they were married. John McDonald was a haole, a term used in Hawaii to refer to individuals of European ancestry in contrast to those of native Hawaiian heritage.

Alas, the islanders were now in a state of anger and confusion. Were the marriages he had performed over the years still sanctified? Were their children baptized? And what about all those funerals! I told my family in sotto voce that there had been a raging scandal. Well, at the next table I noticed three people attempting to overhear our conversation. It didn't occur to me that this would cause a problem. Until—I went for my tennis lesson and there was my new instructor–John McDonald–who had been one of the three at the next table. Now, what are the odds! He seemed to take the incident in stride and the lessons continued throughout the week. He was a good instructor, by the way, and my serve improved significantly.

Another John, Big John, was a force and presence who was known by anyone who ever stayed at Coco Palms. He was an icon. And indeed he was a big Hawaiian and very charming. He certainly charmed me and escorted me to delightful places on the island and lovely evenings of music and dance. And always he had a magnificent and fresh lei delivered to my room daily.

I had rented a station wagon and took the family on daily drives. One gorgeous drive was along the shoreline to Hanalei. It was a perfect day and so clear that we could see the top of the mountain. The surf at Haena was very high, at least 10 feet.

That night my little sister didn't get back to the hotel until 3:00 a.m. I think she was making great strides in recovering from her illness.

I played tennis every day—some days with Big John and other days with the pro who asked me to join in playing doubles. I noted in my diary that I played very well that week. Such was not always the case.

One of the traditions at Coco Palms was a nightly torch-lighting ceremony. As darkness fell, a conch shell blew that echoed from deep in the coconut grove. A big drum beat and was answered far down the lagoon. Hawaiian youths ran through the grove igniting dried coconut husks buried in containers. Loud speakers carried the voice of Grace Guslander telling the meaning of the ancient tradition. It was indeed an impressive experience. That was followed by a private cocktail party hosted by the Guslanders under a ramada surrounded by waving palm trees. The guests were always charming, the conversation interesting, and the Hawaiian music enchanting. We were invited to these soirees every evening during our visit. On one occasion a song was dedicated to my family and we were all presented with beautiful leis. My parents and the Guslanders became great friends and my parents made Coco Palms a default vacation spot for many years to come.

All good things must come to an end and soon we were on our way back to Tucson where Tony Sr. and Kent met us. How wonderful to receive big aloha hugs from both of them.

AT THE MAUNA KEA WITH TONY – 1974

The women pilots association—the 99s—was having its international conference in Hawaii. Even though I had been there only months earlier, one can never get too much of this beautiful state. Tony and I decided we'd attend the conference and then explore the islands further independently.

On April 26th we flew to Honolulu where I spent the next few days with the 99s while Tony explored the many marinas. Boats were always his passion. There were many cocktail parties in the evenings and Tony enjoyed sharing stories about flying—his other passionate interest.

Convention over, we flew to Kaanapali airport on Maui. At our request the pilot—Art—flew the Cessna C402 low and slow over Maui following the coastline and the road to Hana. It was breathtaking. He then flew us across the ocean at 900 feet and then into canyons at the north end of the island of Hawaii. In due time we landed at Kamuela (Waimea) and took a limousine to the incredible Mauna Kea Beach Hotel where we spent five blissful days.

We passed much of our time on the beach and swimming in the waves. One evening we took a cocktail cruise on a catamaran with Tony doing most of the sailing. We snorkeled, played tennis until we developed blisters, ate and drank. We were in heaven.

Our next stop was Hilo where we stayed at Waiakea Village. We returned to Tucson on Sunday, May 5th— a fat, happy and thoroughly rested couple.

WORKING AND PLAYING WITH MY PARENTS AND SONS – 1975

Having been invited to conduct three workshops in Hawaii, I extended my sights and saw a golden opportunity for my son Kent. Having completed all the surgeries the doctors could perform to that point, Kent was given a furlough from St. Michael's Hospital in Toronto. He returned to Tucson on April 30th and he, Tony Jr. and I left for Hawaii on May 3rd. My parents were going to follow two days later.

We flew to Honolulu and on to Kahului on Maui where we were staying at the Royal Lahaina Hotel. The following day I rented a car and we took the long, beautiful drive to Hana where we had lunch. The boys were quite taken with the magnificent scenery, and I was glad to see more of the area than on my previous trip.

That night I drove into the town of Kahului to meet with the workshop directors to plan the program. Each workshop lasted for three days. I arrived at work the following morning at 7:30 a.m. and worked all day teaching the administration of a learning disabilities test—the ITPA. The participants included ten people from the district covering Maui, Molokai and Lanai. They were bright, eager and easily absorbed the information. Elver Higashi, the director, stayed all day and was a charming host.

I left in time to meet my parents at the airport and take them to the hotel. Mother didn't feel well and Dad had asthma. Not a good beginning. Tony Jr., now age 17, had spent the day joyfully swimming in the ocean and diving in the waves. My heart broke for Kent, now age 20, who was so pale, weak and thin and burdened with a cast. Still the freedom of being out of the hospital setting was enough to keep his spirits up. This interim was to give his leg bone time to heal. If it did not, a bone graft would be necessary.

While I had been working, the boys had taken their grandmother on a train ride to Lahaina. Elver wanted to take me out for the evening but I chose to go with the family to the Maui Surf for dinner and a floor show.

The last day of the workshop Tony Jr. drove me to Kahului—1 ½ hours of driving for him. I couldn't have asked for more wonderful people with whom to work. Elver took me to lunch. Somehow, I knew I would be seeing him again.

The family picked me up at the end of the day and we left for Kauai where I was met by Toshiyuki Hirabayashi—the curriculum specialist for Kauai—who greeted me with a lovely lei. He drove me to the Coco Palms Resort. The boys rented a car and, with my parents, went independently. We attended the Guslanders' cocktail party and had dinner, after which I was really ready for bed. Big John—whom I mentioned in the first Hawaii story—had called me on Maui and had asked me for a date that night. I was so tired from working on Maui that only sleep appealed at this point. No date.

The second workshop began the following day. Toshiyuki picked me up at 7:30 a.m. I was taken to Lihue where I met the staff. The workshop was not nearly as successful this time. The participants were speech and hearing specialists, psychologists and special education teachers. The group didn't gel and they showed little enthusiasm for the subject—again the ITPA.

I was totally worn out at the end of the day but joined my parents and the boys for the nightly cocktail party with a lovely torch lighting ceremony. Later I joined Big John for a delightful evening. For a big man, he danced divinely.

Toshi picked me up again the next day to continue the workshop in the State Building in Lihue. There was a controversy among my students as to who should be responsible for administering the ITPA. Professional toes were being stepped on and this wasn't a problem I could solve for them. As well, I was losing my voice; I noted in my diary that I was nauseated from exhaustion. Thank goodness it was Friday and I had the weekend to rest and recuperate.

That night we were guests of the Guslanders in their home—a great honor. One of the dishes they served was chili and I commented on how delicious it was. Apparently Elizabeth Taylor and Richard Burton had been guests there and this was leftover chili from their visit. Liz would eat chili from only one restaurant in southern California and therefore had the chili flown to Hawaii. Being very interested in this story I asked, "When were the Burtons here?" Their response was—three years ago. Oh, oh.

All seemed well as the next day began, and then it hit. We had serious food poisoning. That is, everyone had it except my father who did not eat chili. It was just as well, as Dad had a colostomy from having had colon cancer years before. Wasn't he the lucky one. Kent was in dire straits. He had a fever and chills. With a cast on his leg and severe diarrhea he had a very tough day. Tony Jr. and I rallied and managed to get in some tennis.

We still were not up to par the next day but Tony Jr. and I were able to play tennis (he was a fine tennis player) and later I met Big John for more tennis. I took all the family for a drive to Spouting Horn in the afternoon.

That night at the cocktail party my mother was honored as the "mother of the year" with the appropriate pomp and ceremony. Kent had heard that this was to occur and had bought her an orchid.

On Monday a man whom I had met the year before, Bob Cole, picked me up and drove me to Lihue for the last day of the workshop. It went quite well. Toshi

Hirabayashi and three of his colleagues took me to lunch at the Plantation Garden at Poipu. It was lovely.

After work Tony Jr. picked me up and we two flew to Honolulu leaving Kent with my parents on Kauai. Ethel Muratsuko, the director of the workshop I would be conducting there, met us at the airport and took us to the Waikiki Outrigger. Tony went off on his own while Ethel and I had dinner on the rotating "Top of Waikiki."

And so began the third workshop on May 13th. Working in Hawaii and being a tourist were two very different experiences and trying to blend them had been difficult. When working, one saw the seamy side of a community with its picayune conflicts and the sad lives many of them led. Alcoholism was rampant in Hawaii at that time as were both child and wife abuse. What a contrast to life at Coco Palms!

Ethel picked me up each day at 7:00 a.m. to take me to the workshop site in the leeward district—a good 45 minute drive. The group I would be teaching was the largest yet and kept me incredibly busy and working late to accommodate their individual needs. I realized that three-day workshops conducted by only one person were incredibly demanding. However, I know I did a good job and was invited back to work with them again in the fall. I, however, had no intention of going through this torture again.

Tony Jr. had a wonderful time on his own in Honolulu during the day. Each night we had dinner together and shopped for items to take back with us, and for Kent to take back to his girlfriend in Canada, Helga. At the end of the third day Tony Jr. and I met at the airport and took a return flight to Kauai where we were met by my parents and Kent—happy to see us back.

We attended the nightly cocktail party; oh, how ready I was for this beauty and elegance. Later Big John and I went dancing and I didn't get to bed until 2:15 a.m.—not very smart on my part.

My vacation had officially begun and I was eager to take on the role of tourist. The days flew by with lots of swimming, tennis and ice cream. This trip had been very beneficial for Kent who looked like a different person.

We returned to Tucson on May 19th where we were met by Marie, our housekeeper, as Tony was at a meeting of the Tucson Literary Club. On this night my father was unanimously invited to become a member of the Literary Club, a very great honor from a group of men whom he enjoyed for the rest of his life.

Kent left Tucson to return to hospital in Toronto on May 28th. His leg bone showed no sign of healing so a bone graft had been scheduled. It took place on August 7th. It wasn't until December 11th that Kent was finally released from St. Michael's Hospital, almost a year after the mining accident. The doctors had done all they could for him.

He returned to Tucson in time for Christmas. What a joy it was to all the family to have him home at last!

KAUAI WITH MY PARENTS – 1976

Coco Palms on Kauai, Hawaii had become an annual destination for my parents. In 1976 they arranged their visit to coincide with my spring break from UA and invited me to join them. As I loved it there too, I was quick to accept.

Leaving Tucson on March 12th, we flew to Honolulu and then on to Lihue, Kauai. We were assigned gorgeous connecting rooms and attended the nightly cocktail party Grace and Gus Guslander, the owners of Coco Palms, hosted every evening. After dinner we listened to the marvelous singing of Larry Rivera.

I awakened the next day to a phone call from Elver Higashi with whom I had worked the previous year. We had become good friends. I passed the day playing tennis, lying in the sun and shedding all the stress from life in Tucson. Later my parents and I drove to the spectacular Nawiliwili. I

Aldine's parents, Murray & Aldine Sinclair, at Coco Palms - 1975

ended the day at the tennis court for the final games in the tournament and joined my parents at the cocktail party.

After church with my parents the next day, I received a phone call from Elver telling me he was arriving for a visit that afternoon. After picking him up at the airport, we went for a picnic at Haena Beach. Elver joined us for dinner before returning to his hotel. He was a charming Japanese man whom my parents enjoyed very much.

After playing tennis the following day, Elver and I picked up my parents to have lunch at the Plantation Garden Restaurant in Poipu Beach and later we dropped him at the airport for his return flight.

And so the wonderful relaxed week continued with lots of tennis and swimming and lovely drives every day. One we particularly enjoyed was to Waimea Canyon with its many lookouts. We had lunch at the lodge there. Other activities included ukulele lessons for my mother and me and lots of bridge playing for my parents. Typically, I went for nightcaps after dinner with friends I had met there.

We watched canoe races from the beach in front of the hotel. Once again we were invited to the Guslander's home for dinner—this time with no unpleasant gastric consequences!

Taking an afternoon on my own one day, I had an exciting adventure at the Waipahee Slide. It is located near Kealia and required almost a half hour walk to reach this natural slide in the Waipahee Stream with a pool at the base. The stream and pool were nestled within a reserve above Anahoa. I was alone and unaware of the dangers associated with the slide. The water into which one slides has been known as the "bottomless pool" and has claimed many lives over the years. After heavy rains a strong whirlpool may develop that can suck swimmers into its vortex. I had two thrilling slides into the pool totally unaware of the potential hazard. I was indeed fortunate to have that unique experience as, only three years later, it was closed to the public, never to reopen.

Casual sightseers are now discouraged from trying to access it by five miles of rough road, blocked first by a locked gate and later by a wire cable. Then there is a 20 minute walk through ferns, scrubby trees and brush. While it was once something of a tourist attraction, it is now unavailable to the public.

I wasn't surprised to hear from Toshiyuki Hirabayashi, another gentleman with whom I worked the previous year. He took me to the Plantation Garden Restaurant to "pick my brain" for a couple of hours. He was grateful for the workshop I had given the year before.

The heavenly life as a tourist at Coco Palms continued until March 21st. I had to be back in Tucson Sunday night in order to go to Mexico City the next day. While I proceeded home to Tucson, my parents went on to Kona on the big island of Hawaii.

Tony and my sons met me at the airport. Replete in my diary were comments about how very handsome my sons were—actually I often used the word "gorgeous." And they were.

And so, tucking away my memories of a deliriously relaxed and happy week with my parents, I proceeded the following day to Mexico City with Winifred Kirk to work with professionals there on the final problems associated with the development of the Spanish adaptation of the ITPA—a test for learning disabilities about which you will read elsewhere in these chapters.

KAUAI WITH TONY – 1983

Our 30th wedding anniversary was approaching on March 28, 1983. Tony and I thought Hawaii would be the perfect place to celebrate. We were right.

We flew to Los Angeles on March 11th where we checked into the Hyatt for the night. Within minutes Kent arrived from Santa Barbara where he was attending school at Brooks Institute of Photography. We had a wonderful time with him catching up on his life and absorbing all his enthusiasm for his education at Brooks. He was radiant and doing very well there.

We drove to Tony Jr.'s place in Playa del Rey where, to our delight and surprise, our sons toasted us with champagne and presented us with gifts. One was a beautiful silver champagne bucket engraved with our names and the date of our marriage. I treasure it to this day. As my diary said, "We were <u>touched</u>!!" Additionally, Kent gave us a beautifully framed photograph he had taken and Tony Jr. gave us a remote control radio for Tony's model sailboat. Off we went to the Magic Castle in Hollywood for a happy family dinner.

Tony and I flew to Kauai the following day, rented a Mazda and drove to Waiohai Hotel on Poipu Beach. It was gorgeous. We had been upgraded to a deluxe room and indeed it was. We found flowers from friends and bottles of champagne in recognition of our impending anniversary.

Among our activities that week were drives to Hanalei, Haena and other places at the north end of the island including the lookout there at 4000 feet. We went to Waimea Canyon where it was cold and windy. Tony had fun going to the harbor at Nawiliwili to look at boats. We swam a great deal on the beaches of Kauai which are spectacular and we did a lot of snorkeling.

The management of our hotel kept us supplied daily with fresh fruit and cheese trays and, with such a lovely room, we were quite happy spending a good deal of time at the hotel. We did just as we had planned—spent precious time together, relaxed, swam, took sightseeing expeditions and ate. We were sated with all the goodness of life when we returned to Los Angeles on March 19th and again checked into the Hyatt Hotel.

The following day Tony Jr. picked us up to drive us to Palos Verdes Estates where we had lived for three years in the early 1960s. It was fun to see our old home and the school where I had taught. After lunch at the hotel and our goodbyes to Tony Jr., we flew to Tucson. I had a hunch that all was not well with my father and discovered that he had been in El Dorado hospital for several days having experienced the worst asthma attack of his life. We went right over to see him. I commented in my diary that, "He and Mom are incredible!!"

The next evening, Monday, was the meeting of the Tucson Literary Club. Dad had been preparing his essay for that occasion for over a year; Tony had to present it for him. That must have been a great disappointment to my father. On March 24th, over a week after entering the hospital, my dad went home. He was very frail and it was heartbreaking to me.

HONOLULU WITH MY MOTHER – 1984

One day Mother announced that her daughters were fat. She was quite right. She told us each to lose 20 pounds—she would finance it. Carol chose Nutrisystem as her program. I would have no part of spending that amount of money just to go on a diet, so I joined Weight Watchers at $5 weekly.

By November of 1984 Carol and I had reached our goal—or, should I say, Mother's goal. We were svelte and 20 pounds lighter. Mother felt I had been short-changed on the deal and thought it would balance the situation if she took me to Hawaii—to a real estate convention.

Mother had us booked on a DC-10 to Honolulu and in the elegant hotel where the convention was to take place. I was excited about this. However, fate stepped in. She and I had a friend, Jane Ward, who heard of our plan and begged to be included. She needed to get away. Her husband had died and she was lonely. It isn't that she missed her husband so much, she would tell us, but she did miss sex. Jane was an old, withered, highly unattractive and unappealing woman whom nobody could believe had been married to a handsome New Zealander. She insulted people and when the barbs stung my family members I rebelled. I told her husband Bob that he had to get her under control. "Oh," said he, "she's just a straight shooter."

After Bob died, Jane continued to live alone but she decided that she would commit suicide. It became almost a game as Jane would threaten, take action, and call my mother. Mother would phone 9-1-1, meet the paramedics at Jane's house, and save her—time after time after time. It was consuming a lot of my mother's time and energy. Mom drove by her house every morning to be sure the newspaper had been picked up. If it hadn't, Mother took action. We knew that one day Jane would be successful, but my mother felt honor bound to prevent it as long as she could.

Back to the trip. I did not want Jane to go. I didn't like Jane. Mother, in her infinite kindness, said we must include Jane. Among other inconveniences, we could no longer stay at the conference hotel—it was filled. Mother found an acceptable, if not exceptional, hotel nearby. Jane asked for the specifics of our plans and when she discovered that we were going on a DC-10 she threw a fit. "Why, that is the most dangerous plane in the air today," she complained and added that in no way would she risk her life in it. This from a woman who was attempting suicide weekly!

Mother changed the reservation for the plane which meant that we would no longer be a part of the cadre of realtors flying to Hawaii together. I was disappointed.

In the end, Jane decided not to go at all.

Mother and I flew to Honolulu on November 7th. At 7:30 a.m. the following morning we registered for the conference at the Hilton Hawaii Village ready to begin classes the next day. We had a lovely time taking a tour of Oahu, meeting friends for lunch, and being taken for a Thai dinner that night by my charming doctoral student of years ago, Mike Manos.

Mother awakened the following morning with atrial fibrillation—a family curse. She couldn't attend classes. What was I to do? Well, I felt I would forego responsibility and spend the day sunbathing and swimming on Waikiki Beach while Mother rested and recuperated. I was delighted when she was well enough in the evening to have a fantastic dinner with me on the third floor of the Hyatt Regency Hotel. This conference wasn't so bad after all! We spent our free time during the week doing the usual tourist things—sails at sunset on a catamaran and shopping at wonderful Hawaiian malls.

We dutifully earned our real estate points in classes the following day and were guests of our beloved friend, John Riley, for dinner at Ilikai that night. The agony of having to spend all day in classrooms again the following day was relieved in the evening when I took a favorite friend of mine—Michael Hewett, son of Frank Hewett— and his girlfriend Jan to John Domino's for dinner. Here I had just come off a Spartan regime of eating and I was faced with delicious meals noon and night. It just wasn't fair. I want it duly noted that I actually lost weight on this trip. How was that for self-control!

On our return to Tucson, Mother decided that, having lost so much weight, I now needed a face lift. I really didn't want one but she was unrelenting in her insistence. So, on December 27, 1984 I signed in with Dr. Paul Dempsey and did the deed. The speed with which I recovered was truly amazing. On New Year's Day, Tony and I attended the annual party of Lois and Eric Ramsay—a well-attended event. I hoped I would receive some comments—even compliments. Nary a word. Finally, in frustration I asked my beloved friend Cathy Storek if she noticed anything different about me. She hemmed and hawed and finally suggested that maybe I was wearing a new dress? It is unbelievable that less than five days after surgery I had no bruising whatever—and apparently I looked pretty much the same. And it had cost $1000! Over the years gravity took over and Dr. Dempsey's excellent work was for naught.

As for Jane Ward—she finally outfoxed my mother. On her way to church one Sunday morning, my mother dutifully checked that Jane had picked up her newspaper. She then went on to church. Jane knew when mother returned home after church so called mother at the appropriate time to be saved—except that on that particular Sunday

Mother did not go directly home. Later than usual she found Jane's phone call on her answering machine, went directly to Jane's house, and found her and her dog in their Cadillac dead. Jane had put a hose in the exhaust and killed herself and the dog with carbon monoxide. So endeth Jane on August 9, 1987.

THE BIG ISLAND WITH TONY, ELIZABETH, MAX AND ALEX—1998

Elizabeth and Tony were very excited about a trip they had long planned through the Panama Canal, a first for them. I was to have taken care of Max (7) and Alex (5) in their absence. Sadly, atrial fibrillation (AF), which had haunted me for many years, picked that spring to hit me with a vengeance. In fact, I was in hospital with AF attacks five times that year—1998–for a period spanning three weeks.

Quite wisely Elizabeth and Tony cancelled their trip as their babysitter could not be depended upon to be able to perform. They both have always been amazing in their flexibility and in their love for me. They decided that if I couldn't be left home with their children, they would change the plan and take me with them as their guest to a different destination—Hawaii. How very kind of them! Of course the boys were excited to be included.

I exacted promises from them about how we would handle any medical emergencies I might have and we made decisions as to methods for dealing with each. I was not at all well at that time.

We flew on April 3rd to Kona on the big island of Hawaii where Elizabeth and Tony had rented a beautiful villa with a lanai that overlooked the ocean and the beach directly in front of it. It was part of the Outrigger Kanaloa at Kona, in Keahou.

Our days were magical. We found beautiful beaches where the boys could snorkel in the tide pools and explore the shore for shells and other treasures. While I watched over the boys, Elizabeth and Tony would shop and explore on their own. As the days went by, the boys became more adventurous and wore face masks and fins into deeper water. They were thriving.

Lunch at the Mauna Kea

On Palm Sunday we went to the magnificent Mauna Kea hotel for Sunday brunch and spent the afternoon on the beach there.

On some days I would walk with the boys for as many as two miles to find their favorite places to swim and play. Typically, the shoreline in that area is lava-covered, the reason for our having to search out sandy beaches with mysterious tide pools to explore. Often Elizabeth and Tony would bring a picnic and join us for fun in the sun at lunch time. I was delighted that they had plenty of time to themselves and I lapped up every minute with my precious grandsons.

Now, I have always perceived myself as the perfect grandmother but that perception was severely jeopardized during one of my visits to the beach with the boys. I had my eye on them constantly in the distance, assuring myself they were safe at all times. One day, however, I was approached by the police and told that I was to leave the beach with my grandsons immediately. Unbeknown to me, my angelic Max and Alex had been tossing sand, first toward one another and then, apparently, in a more generalized manner. Complaints were made to the authorities, I was fingered as the "responsible" party, and we were unceremoniously ushered off the beach. I was sure I'd be in deep trouble with their parents!

Kona was nearby and the boys loved the submarine ride there. They went several times. One day we visited the incredible Hilton Hotel at Waikoloa with its monorails and boats. It had 62 oceanfront acres and was situated just north of Kona. We walked through its tropical gardens with waterways and enjoyed seeing the exotic wildlife. We took the museum walkway with its Asian and Polynesian artwork and watched a show with children playing with dolphins. It was a magical experience for us all.

Elizabeth & Tony with their boys

One of my favorite sightseeing trips was to Waipio on the north coast with its magnificent views. This area is considered one of the scenic wonders of Hawaii. We traveled down into the Waipio Valley by van where we were met by our informative guide—Hanalei—and taken on a two-hour tour on a wagon drawn by mules. Max and Alex were able to take the reins—a big thrill for them. We passed 1200 foot waterfalls and saw wild horses, taro patches, and fresh water rivers. It was a spectacular, albeit a somewhat uncomfortable, journey.

Max & Alex at Waikoloa Hotel

Another day Elizabeth and Tony took off for a helicopter flight. No sooner were they airborne than the pilot found that the wind was much too strong for a safe sightseeing tour and had to land. What a disappointment.

We often found excellent restaurants for dinner such as the King Kamehameha Hotel where there was a colorful luau with Hawaiian dancers. Another was the Kona Surf where manta rays came to frolic. Often I chose to let the four of them go off for dinner together and I enjoyed time alone on our lanai.

When the time came to return to Tucson, I wrote in my diary, "Our last wonderful day in Hawaii after one of the most special weeks in my life. Elizabeth, Tony and the boys were so good to me and I thrived."

Upon our return home on April 10th, I found I couldn't sleep well without "my boys" nearby. The following day was Easter when twenty members of my family gathered for dinner giving us ample time to tell of our wonderful experiences in Kona.

My reprieve from bad health was short-lived. Three days later I was back in hospital with AF. How lucky I was not to have had a problem in Hawaii!

KAUAI WITH MY SONS AND THEIR FAMILIES—1999

Would I plan a family trip this way again? Never! Having taken my beloved family on many previous trips as one unit, I had decided in 1999 to spend time with them separately—a week with each son and his family. I missed the synergy and energy generated by my young people when they were together. While it was wonderful, it just wasn't the same.

On March 26th I flew from Tucson to Kauai with Elizabeth, Tony, Max (8) and Alex (6). We drove to Lihue where we were met by our friends Bette and Jack Layton who presented us with leis and helped us get organized. We drove on to Poipu where I had rented a gorgeous condominium/bungalow on the Kiahuna Plantation – 35 acres of tropical paradise. Our place, right on the beach, had two bedrooms downstairs and a huge living room, dining room and kitchen upstairs. We were in the lap of luxury.

We spent our first full day there with a visit

Alex, Max & Tony enjoying the surf

to Waialua Falls and later swimming in the ocean. Even I braved the waves but my diary noted that I got tossed around a lot and occasionally Tony had to pull me out. Later we took a trip up the Waialua River to the Fern Grotto. It was Hawaii at its loveliest.

A trip to Waimea Canyon was on the docket for the next day. As we drove along the shoreline road, we saw many humpback whales leaping in the ocean. We had a picnic and enjoyed breathtaking scenery.

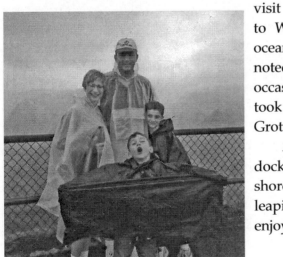

Elizabeth, Tony & their boys

Aldine with Bette Layton at Princeville Hotel

My friend Bette Layton had recently moved with her husband Jack to Kauai as permanent residents. The next day Bette took me under her wing to show me all the interesting places she had discovered in her new life there. We had lunch at di Amici on Poipu Beach in Kilauea. We drove through Princeville, her new place of residence, and she showed me the bed and breakfast that she and Jack were arranging for me that night— Hale Ho'o Maha at Hanalei. Later we had drinks at their new home followed by dinner at the Princeville Hotel. The meal was outstanding and the hotel magnificent.

Hale Ho'o Maha was the strangest B and B you could ever imagine. It had no curtains on the window and no lock on the door. My room was Spartan and without its own bathroom. The management was a couple straight out of the sixties with braided hair and colorful tattoos. I felt neither comfortable nor safe. I was angry with myself for allowing this intrusion on my time with my family and was quite ready to leave when Bette picked me up the following day to return me to Kiahuna Resort. When I arrived, I found I was alone for a while as the rest of the family was off on a snorkeling expedition. That night we dined at the lovely hotel restaurant–Piatti's–which had been voted the most beautiful restaurant on Kauai.

Leaving Alex and me behind the next day, Elizabeth and Tony took Max on what was to have been a fun-filled day of fishing. Max loved fishing. There were six people on the boat—all adults with the exception of Max, who received lots of attention. He was allowed to sit on the fly deck. Elizabeth and Tony, however, noticed that the sea was becoming exceedingly rough and the boat was starting to roll significantly. Although Max was oblivious to the severe swaying of the boat and happily eating a bag of Doritos, Elizabeth sand Tony were close to throwing–up on a much more stable deck below. They were miserable, but there was no turning back. Max was in his element.

Once out in deep water, Max joined the rest on deck and the crew got to work. Everyone had a line in the water—and everyone knew how much Max wanted to catch a marlin. Suddenly one man's pole bent almost to breaking—"Fish ON!" The man was quickly ushered to a deck chair and strapped in. The fight lasted quite some time, but once the big fish had tired, the man was kind enough to ask Max if he wanted to reel it in. Can you imagine Max's excitement! Out of the chair came the man and into it went Max. Elizabeth and Tony were frantic as they watched their son fighting to bring in such a catch, especially after it breached the water and they saw how big it was. They insisted Max relinquish his seat to the adult! The fish was huge—eight feet in length!

Max with the swordfish

After hauling it aboard, the crew tied it to the back of the boat and, as they returned triumphantly to shore, Max was able to touch and examine the day's bounty. His excitement, however, turned to sadness. This magnificent creature of the sea was dead—and they had killed it. A few tears flowed on their return to our condo. Still, Max continues to enjoy looking at his photograph standing beside that behemoth of the sea. What a catch!

Alex enjoying the beach

In the meantime, Alex and I were thoroughly enjoying ourselves and not subjected to mal-de-mer in the least. We ate ice cream, walked on the beach and watched movies. All of us topped the day off with dinner at Brennecke's, a beachfront restaurant which is considered to have one of the best views of any place on the south shore.

Friday, April 2nd was our last day together before the "changing of the guard." That night this part of my family was to return to Tucson while Kent and his family arrived. Elizabeth and Tony spent their remaining time on Kauai by going on an all-day tour in a van that visited all the sets at which movies had been filmed on Kauai. They found it fascinating.

I, in the meantime, had my two darling grandsons all to myself for the day. They went to a craft camp in the morning followed by lunch and snorkeling at Poipu Beach. They loved it and so did I.

In the evening we headed to the airport to say aloha to Tony and his family as they departed and aloha to Kent, Janice and Tana (10) as they arrived for their week on Kauai. There were hugs all around and I felt sadness at an ending but excitement for a beginning.

Kent, Janice and Tana loved their new "digs" and barely settled in before they headed for the beach where they spent considerable time throughout their week on Kauai. On Easter Sunday, April 4th, we drove to a gorgeous beach—Polihale Beach—that is by far the longest stretch of beach in the state of Hawaii. It is necessary to drive on a dirt sugarcane road to reach this remote beach on the western side of the island—the most westerly publicly accessible area in Hawaii. That day the sea was violent and the waves were high so, wisdom being the better part of valor—we returned to the hotel to swim. We had a magnificent dinner at the Piatti Restaurant that night.

Tana with a flower in her hair

Leaving Tana with me, Janice and Kent were off before daybreak the next morning for a day of adventure. They drove to the north end of the island to hike the Kalalau Trail. This trail runs along the Na Pali Coast and is approximately 11 miles long. They had been told that experienced hikers could complete the round trip 22-mile trek as a day hike, but the average hiker needs two days minimum. Janice and Kent accomplished it in one day and even these inveterate and intrepid hikers found it a formidable undertaking.

The trail is notable for its remoteness, beauty, difficult terrain and dangers. *Backpacker Magazine* listed it as one of the "10 most dangerous hikes in the US." *Outsider Magazine* rated it as one of "the 20 most dangerous hikes in the world." As I say, Janice and Kent loved a challenge. They had almost found their match that day and came home exhausted. We had

Janice on a difficult & dangerous trail

dinner in the condo that night! Tana and I were spared that agony and spent our day swimming at Poipu Beach and browsing in the nearby shopping center.

The following day we rented a 4-wheel drive jeep and took a magnificent trip into inner Kauai starting with Opaeka'a Falls–a spectacular 151-foot waterfall–and then followed rugged hunting access roads into the bush. You will read in another chapter of Kent's remarkable prowess with driving in difficult situations. His skills were put into action that day. I think we would have gone on for hours longer had the gas gauge not indicated to us that it was time to start home and to have a swim on our beach.

Kent, Tana & Janice

The surf was heavy that day so I chose to walk on the shore while the others braved the water. It was an exhilarating experience for them but not as exciting as the activity they chose for the following day.

Janice, Tana & Kent readying for their
helicopter ride

Janice, Kent and Tana were up early to take an extended helicopter trip over Kauai. They were in a Hughes 500 with no doors. Although I am an experienced pilot, I had always abhorred flying in a helicopter so chose to sit this one out. We spent most of the following day on the beach. It was heavenly.

On April 9th it was time for our return to Tucson. We had lunch at the Princeville Hotel where we had the Laytons join us for lunch–elegant but expensive. We then drove to Anini Beach and spent time sitting in Lydgate Park.

The inevitable departure time had arrived so that evening we drove to the airport. I had been in Hawaii for over two weeks and needed to get back to reality. The life in Hawaii is all too soporific and could easily become habit forming. I was quickly brought back to earth in Tucson with mountains of mail and laundry that had accumulated. But I have to admit to having a bit of a spring in my step as I drifted through the next few days filled with memories of family and the beauty of the islands.

MAUI WITH MY SONS AND THEIR FAMILIES–2001

Every adventure in Hawaii was a special occasion and our family trip to Maui in April, 2001 was no exception. Our entourage included–Kent, Janice and Tana— Tony, Elizabeth, Max and Alex— Howard Shenk and me.

At the Maui airport, we rented two cars and drove to Makena where I had rented two spectacular condominiums at the Makena Surf. We were on a beautiful beach and spent much of our time in the ocean. The size of the waves and the temperature of the water were perfect. Our first night there, Kent cooked hamburgers on our terrace while we watched whales frolicking in the distance. We had found nirvana!

Succeeding days were spent in group activities of various sorts as well as trips to explore the region. One of these was a four-hour zodiac (an inflatable boat) trip with Blue Water Rafting to a good snorkeling area, but the sea was high and the long stretch of water we had to cross to explore caves by boat made us truly miserable. It was very bouncy and very uncomfortable. We were reminded of this the next day by our aching muscles. However, the snorkeling was magnificent and well worth the discomfort we had endured. Upon returning to the landing, Tony, Elizabeth and Janice decided to go out for two hours more while Kent, Howard and I returned to play on the beach with the children.

Another group trip was to Molokini Island by zodiac for more incredible snorkeling. Molokini Island is a crescent-shaped crater which forms a small, uninhabited island. It is considered one of the outstanding snorkeling and diving areas in Hawaii. Maui truly is a swimmer's paradise.

On another occasion, we took a trip to the other side of Maui—West Maui—to visit the Iao Valley which was very lush and crisscrossed with streams. There we climbed the Iao Needle—a vegetation-covered lava remnant rising 1200 feet from the valley floor. We found a trail to a windy overlook which was one of the steepest I have ever encountered. It was very beautiful, but cold. We enjoyed a picnic lunch there.

We explored tide pools and Tony and I encountered some huge turtles while snorkeling together. Countless hours were spent in the ocean. One neighbor who was staying there with his family was the actor Adam Arkin. I had always been attracted to his acting style, and he was handsome as well. One day while snorkeling, I lost one of my fins. He noticed and came to me asking if he could help. Off he went into the surf spending about half an hour in the retrieval of my fin which now had special importance to me! Kent, Tony and the children would often meet up with him and his children on the beach after dinner for a last swim and some good conversation. They were close in age, Kent having been born in 1955, Adam in 1956 and Tony in 1957.

Each family opted to do side trips individually, as well. Janice and Kent took a grueling 12-mile hike along the ocean's edge on abandoned lava fields. That day Elizabeth and Tony took their boys and Tana to Lahaina to spend the day snorkeling—their favorite activity.

Lots of time was spent in playing games and reading and in being together as a family. It was a memorable holiday well suited to all the age levels and we came home to Tucson happy and mellow.

The day after our return to Tucson was Easter—April 15th—and my sister Carol celebrated the occasion by having us all for a special Easter dinner with all her family. We entertained them with our adventures in Hawaii.

A happy family

Janice with Tana

Tana & Kent

Elizabeth & Tony

Elizabeth, Tana, Janice & Aldine

Tana, Alex, Max & Kent

Tony, Alex, Max & Elizabeth

CRUISE TO HAWAII WITH HAL– 2010

N ot all memorable trips elicit good memories. Hal and I had thought that a cruise to Hawaii would be a romantic way to celebrate our second wedding anniversary. We did spend a great deal of time in bed, but not in a romantic way as we both were sick during most of the trip!

This was to be a totally relaxed two-week cruise visiting several Hawaiian islands. We boarded the *Golden Princess* in Los Angeles on January 3, 2010 and spent four days at sea as we crossed the Pacific Ocean. And what delightful days they were, filled with time to relax, nap and read. The second night out the captain had a formal party for which Hal wore a tuxedo. I noted in my diary that he looked "devastatingly handsome." The sea was often rough and I had several episodes of feeling decidedly queasy.

Our first port of call was Hilo. I was relieved when I was able to use my cell phone to call Tucson. I had been worried about Max who was on a skiing trip to Utah. In fact he <u>had</u> been injured, dislocating his shoulder, breaking his arm and sustaining nerve damage to his right hand which he was unable to use. I was distraught—and felt helpless.

Honolulu was our next stop where we took a ferry over to the *U.S.S. Arizona* Memorial which had been constructed above the sunken ship. It was a very moving and sobering experience. We continued exploring Honolulu but returned to the ship early as Hal had been felled with a nasty cold. He felt miserable.

On Kauai the next day we purchased all manner of medications to deal with Hal's cold. I was perfectly happy not to travel far on that island as it held golden memories for me that I did not want to dilute.

On Maui Hal felt well enough to take a tender to shore and go on the long excursion to the Iao Valley about which I had told him such glowing tales from my previous experience there. We took a tram ride through the plantation and returned to the ship

Aldine & Hal

where he was glad to get back in bed. I had never seen him with a worse cold.

The next day, at sea, I came down with Hal's cold and was content to spend the day in our cabin which had a lovely verandah. We both rallied in the evening, Hal again in tuxedo, and attended another of the captain's formal dinner parties. It was followed by a Mariners' Club party for passengers who had traveled on this line previously. Out of more than 2000 passengers on board, I was one of only 106 who were Elite members which implied having taken a great many cruises and provided a number of special services. Later we went to the theater to hear an incredible guitarist.

After a night of chills and fever, I spent the following day in bed feeling very sick indeed. Hal brought soup to me but nothing, not even reading, could catch my attention that day. I just lay there, which is most unusual for me. I was beginning to wonder about the wisdom of our taking such a long cruise.

The next day was a repeat, but I did rally sufficiently to join Hal in the dining room for dinner. The following day looked a little brighter for both of us; we were on the mend. Hal donned his tuxedo once again and we attended another party hosted by the captain. Hal had his photograph taken with the captain but I looked so awful that I refused to join them.

We docked in Ensenada, Mexico the next day, a new experience for both of us. It was our last day on the ship and we were ready to go home. This had been a long and tedious trip—not what we had anticipated at all. The next day we disembarked in Los Angeles with very long security check lines and hours of waiting for our flight. I started coughing and couldn't stop—I could barely breathe. It was the worst coughing fit I had ever experienced and I found it quite frightening.

How good it was to see Howard awaiting us at the airport in Tucson on January 17th. He whisked us home and I must say bed that night was a welcome sight. I gave serious thought to never going on another cruise, but fortunately time dimmed the memory and we had many more wonderful trips.

Both of us visited our doctors the day after our return. Hal was prescribed an antibiotic and cough medicine but chose not to have them filled. My diary indicated that, "He later admitted that he loves his coughing and accompanying sound effects. I couldn't believe it!" I, on the other hand, obeyed instructions from my doctor and started taking a Z-pack antibiotic. We made a full recovery. And so did Max after his disastrous injuries. All was well with the world once again.

30

CUERNAVACA, MEXICO CITY & MÉRIDA – 1974

After leaving Tony in Miami following our Greek cruise in 1974, I flew to Mexico City, took a taxi to the bus station and then a bus to Cuernavaca. I had set aside two weeks that summer to take a total immersion course in Spanish at Centro de Artes y Lenguas. The purpose was to improve my fluency in both spoken and written Spanish. I was involved in writing a test, in Spanish, for monolingual Spanish speaking children for diagnosing learning disabilities.

I stayed at a lovely old inn, Posada Arcadia, where the personnel knew that they were to speak only Spanish to the students at El Centro. Classes were held daily for six hours with a recess during which we sang Mexican songs. I was exhausted every night but my Spanish improved by leaps and bounds. However, serious homesickness was setting in.

Time was given us for travel so one day I took a bus to Tepoztlán where I took in all the sights. On another day I joined three ladies–from U.S., England and Australia. We hired a taxi to go to Taxco as all the buses were full! The countryside was beautiful and the town was enchanting.

In an attempt to lose the weight I had gained on the cruise, I had subsisted on bananas and nuts eaten in my room. One night I couldn't resist a real meal in the dining room and joined a baroness from Austria and a purser from a ship. They were interesting company indeed. Another dinner companion–Robert Jones Schaeffer, a professor of Latin American history at Syracuse University– took me to a delightful restaurant called Las Mañanitas.

On another occasion he suggested we skip school to have a day of rest and see more of the area. We packed a satchel and off we went in his car to see a remarkable pre-Columbian ruin—Xochicalco—that had incredible views from the top. On to a bathing resort—Las Estacas—with its river of running water that was exceedingly clear. We swam and lazed for hours. Dinner was at a beautiful inn—Cocoyoc—much of which was built in the 16th century.

School continued to be challenging. We were reading books by B. Traven—*Macario*– and by Octavio Paz—in Spanish, of course. Eventually, it was time to say goodbye to my fellow students and professors. I knew that my experience here had been time well spent.

I traveled by bus to Mexico City where I stayed at the Hotel Camino Real and had dinner at the famous Foquet's. I squeezed in as much sightseeing as possible, enjoying particularly a return visit to the Archeological Museum at Chapultepec Park. I left Mexico City to fly to Mérida on the Yucatán Peninsula. Eighty miles from there is Chichen-Itza, an amazing Maya ruin where I spent four hours tramping through the ruins and climbing the temples. Then, time to leave.

I was ready for my favorite part of the summer—at the cottage with my family. I flew to Toronto and took a bus north to the nearest town, Huntsville, where I was met with great enthusiasm by 11 members of my family before they took me to the cottage. I was home!

31

∽৪৯

TAHITI

TAHITI WITH MY ENTIRE FAMILY – 1975

Tahiti. Even the name conjures visions of deep blue water, dramatic mountains and beautiful girls. All were accurate. My father made good on his intention to celebrate my having earned a Ph.D. by taking the whole family to Tahiti. We had many family holidays together over the years and across the world, but this truly was the most spectacular.

The adventure started on October 17, 1975. My parents and I flew to Los Angeles where we met my brother Murray and his wife Mary, and my sister Carol and her husband Terry Belsham, all of whom had flown there from Toronto. Tony Jr. was to join us the following day as he had to remain in Tucson to take the ACT exam. Kent was in hospital in Canada. I felt very guilty that we all could go off to enjoy such splendor when he was confined within four walls day after day. My husband Tony had elected not to use his vacation time on this trip. (And my father was paying for everything— except my brother's bar bill!) Tony and I did go to Tahiti together in 1977.

My brother had access to an amazing place in Los Angeles—the Castle of the Brotherhood of Magicians. Membership was limited to only the most outstanding magicians throughout the world. It was the ultimate goal of magicians to be invited into membership. We had dinner there and saw magic tricks that defied even the most vivid imagination. To say that the sleight of hand was unbelievable would be an understatement. We went from one room in the castle to another and from one incredible experience to another.

The seven of us departed for Papeete, Tahiti at midnight. I am sure no one on board that long trip had much sleep as Mary was on a high and kept everyone amused or engaged in conversation. Nobody seemed to mind as she made for fascinating entertainment. From Papeete we flew in a small plane to Huahine, an island with only one hotel at that time. We drove around the island for a couple of hours, swam, snorkeled and soaked in the beauty of this exotic paradise.

Tony Jr. arrived at 12:30 p.m. the following day having traveled for 21 hours. He was immediately in love with Tahiti, and this primitive island with dirt roads only was a good introduction. We loved exploring on bicycles every day. Our "rooms" were darling thatched-roof cottages. We took many drives around the island and did a great deal of snorkeling and swimming. Some of us walked to the end of the reef to watch the waves break. It was spectacular. We took a little boat to an island for a picnic.

It was cold on Huahine and a hot shower would have been welcome. However, there was no hot water in our cottage! As I say, it was quite primitive but I think I liked this island best of all.

After three days on Huahine, we took a 15-minute flight to Raiatea, the next island we visited. Tony Jr. and I were given the best "room" at the hotel. Actually it was a thatched roof hut. We took turns on each island with a different family having the special room which then became the party room. Many of our rooms were at the end of long boardwalks so that our dwellings were perched on stilts above the ocean. Each room had a glass window in the floor or a door that could be raised to that we could lie on our stomachs and watch the sea life cavorting below.

We hadn't enjoyed good weather on this trip and on Raiatea it continued to rain and the wind blew so hard that it made huge waves. It was noisy in our room with the wind roiling up the surf below. We all took a van ride around this beautiful island—so tropical and scenic. We never failed to have excellent meals with a great deal of very fresh seafood available.

My staid father thought it was time for me to buy a bikini. I stood out in my old-fashioned, one piece, body-covering swimsuit. This is the father who scolded me if I walked out of my bedroom in Tucson wearing only a slip! So into town we went to buy the bikini riding in bicycle carts that two people could pedal. I wasn't then and I have never become comfortable in a bikini—and I had the body for it in those days!

The room that Tony Jr. and I shared seemed to be the one in which we all congregated. What good times we had swimming off our little porch and generally enjoying one another's company.

One day all seven of us went in an outrigger canoe out on the ocean. We went up a river and then to an island to snorkel. The marine life was unbelievably colorful and beautiful. Home for a hot shower; this island was far more civilized that Huahine had been.

On our last day in Raiatea, with the rain still pouring and the wind still blowing, we went for a trip in a big cruiser. It took us across the ocean to the town of Tiva on the island of Tahaa. From there we went to yet another island where we enjoyed the snorkeling immensely. Unfortunately, my father took a fall. Traveling was difficult for my parents, but they loved being with their family and thus were willing to endure the inevitable discomforts. The trip back to Raiatea was wet and rough but we had great fun and laughed our heads off.

Outrigger canoe ride

In the evening we all played "the bottle" with the little band. It amazed us to learn that beautiful music can emanate from a bottle merely by stroking it gently with a spoon!

Breakfast was a source of great amusement to us as the "lovely" Tahitian beauties would serve us each morning with disdain and lethargy. How could they be such wrecks morning after morning. They didn't bother combing their hair or wearing shoes and they fairly threw our plates of food at us. However, by evening they had sobered up and defaulted to their affable demeanors.

Tony Jr. and I had little sleep that night as the winds were strong and there was a very heavy surf beneath our room. Hence, we were up earlier than usual and ready for an exciting new day which would take us to the island of Bora Bora. It was pouring rain, as it had every day, and we waited all morning for the weather to be suitable for a take-off in the small aircraft.

We finally reached Bora Bora and what a lovely island it was—worthy indeed of all the photos used in advertising Tahiti. It was necessary for us to go by boat from the airfield on a reef to the mainland and then we were taken by their van to the hotel. The hotel was gorgeous with beautiful grounds and charming thatched bungalows once again.

Tahiti

Carol and Terry drew the best room this time. Since it was raining so hard, Tony Jr. and I slept the afternoon away and later joined the others for cocktails in the Belshams' room. It was elegant! That night at dinner we were entertained by fantastic Tahitian dancers.

Again the next day the weather was foul with heavy wind and rain. Tony Jr. and I were in an open-air room exposed to the elements. There was no glass in the windows. Everything in our room was blowing; even a lamp blew off a table! Our enthusiasm, however, could not be quelled so off we all went for an exciting trip in a glass-bottomed boat. We saw beautiful fish, a five-foot shark and enormous manta rays only 30 feet from the hotel. Later we would swim with those very manta rays!

In the afternoon we went on a lagoon cruise that provided plenty of time for snorkeling, one of our favorite pastimes in these beautiful waters. Tony Jr. and I followed up with a little ping-pong and later we went exploring in a little outrigger canoe. What fun he and I had together day after day. Mary and Murray returned to Toronto. We would miss their high spirits and outrageous behavior.

Bora Bora is often used as a setting for fashion magazines to show off their merchandise and their models. And the models were exquisite. Somehow, however, they equated beauty with privilege and often were unreasonable in their demands. We didn't like them; they were haughty. Nonetheless, all people enjoy looking at a pretty girl. These girls, however, showed off a little too much of their prettiness and frequently sunned on their balconies in the nude. Well, who could help but take a peek. Their responses to our glances were not very ladylike and we were pleased when they finally packed up and hit the road.

And now it was time for me to hit the road. My last day on Bora Bora was October 26th. I used it well. After breakfast we all gathered to go by motor boats to the barrier reef. My diary noted that it was "frightening, rough, and very uncomfortable." Later my mother, Tony Jr. and I went for a bike ride. We swam, had lunch and took a spectacular circle island tour.

After a Tahitian dance show on the beach that was sensuous and graceful, we enjoyed yet another magnificent Tahitian dinner. Afterwards I had drinks with José Remus, a psychologist from Mexico City.

Our plan to go sailing the next day was thwarted yet again by the heavy wind. After swimming and lunch, I took Le Truck (the name given to their van) to the boat that would take me to the airport. Having said goodbye to all the family, I flew to Papeete. I shopped in town and was driven back to the airport by a delightful Tahitian gentleman who presented me with a shell lei. The supervisor of Pan Am very kindly hung a lovely mother-of-pearl necklace around my neck and made sure I was given three seats across on the aircraft so that I could get some sleep. Everyone was very kind to a woman traveling alone. After a stop in Los Angeles I arrived in Tucson at 7:00 a.m. where I was met by a friend who took me directly to the university.

I noted in my diary that "This was one of the most beautiful trips of my life—full of love and laughter and the joy of being together." But it was over and I had to get back to work. I spent the morning at my office sorting mail and solving problems. I taught my special education seminar at 12:45 p.m. and an Educational Psychology course at 2:00 p.m. I took notes at an Educational Psychology faculty meeting at 3:00 p.m. and taught an important Behavior Disorders course from 4:00 to 6:30 p.m. Along the way I bumped into my department head who asked how my week away had been. I reported that it had been a trip to Tahiti in my honor and that my family was still there. He seemed truly upset that I hadn't requested the full time off so that I did not have to leave Tahiti early. I'm afraid my work ethic got in the way and I regret to this day that I hadn't had the courage to ask for a longer time off when I had put in my request. Alas.

My husband Tony picked me up at UA at the end of the day and I must admit I was very tired. What an incredibly long day it had been for me. The first thing I did was call Kent at the hospital in Toronto and learned that he had his plaster cast removed the previous day and that his doctor said he was over the hill—on his way to recovery. We were ecstatic. He would have more surgery next year. On December 11th he was released from their care and returned to Tucson to live—at long last!

The perfect ending to a perfect trip. In retrospect I do not remember the dreadful weather we had day after day in Tahiti. It is all a meld of happiness and good times. Isn't it wonderful when we remember all the highlights of a trip and not its inconveniences!

TAHITI WITH TONY – 1977

Having heard how very beautiful Tahiti was from Tony Jr. and me, Tony thought it was time he and I should spend time there together. I was thrilled. We rarely had trips all by ourselves.

We left Tucson on March 7, 1977 flying via Los Angeles to Papeete, Tahiti. We arrived at 5:00 a.m. and waited for the first flight to Huahine. We were staying in the best room at the Bali Hai Hotel there—bungalow number one, right on the beach.

Tony's first order of business was to go swimming, and he instantly fell in love with the magical Tahitian waters. We spent most of that day resting and swimming. The next day we rode bicycles around the island, walked to the reef, and did lots of swimming. This has to be the most romantic place in the world for a holiday.

An all-day picnic was on our agenda for the next day. We took a boat to a small island where the snorkeling was magnificent. It rained bucketsful on our return, making the trip even more fun. We finished the day with another bicycle ride.

We loved Huahine and time passed so pleasantly that I was surprised when a baggage cart arrived to pick up our luggage. I said to Tony, "Are we leaving here today?" Indeed we were and we had all of 20 minutes to pack before we were on our way to the airport for our flight to Bora Bora. We took the boat from the airport on a reef to the mainland. Then there was the long bus ride to the hotel. We went swimming as soon as we unpacked but found strong undercurrents.

Tahiti

While on Bora Bora we took a ride on a glass-bottomed boat, sailed, canoed, rode bicycles and swam. It was wonderful. Friends of ours, Lilianne and Bob Selby, were moored nearby in their sailboat. We swam out to their boat to have drinks with them and to hear about their long voyage from the United States.

Our next island was Moorea. Again, we had the long boat ride to the airport on the reef and flew to Papeete where we transferred to a small plane that would take us to Moorea. We stayed at the Bali Hai in one of their wonderful bungalows on stilts over the water. We could watch the marine life through an aperture in the floor.

We had glorious weather day after day so the following day we went on the *Liki Tiki* to a beach where we snorkeled and had a delicious hamburger and beer lunch. That evening we enjoyed banjo music and Tahitian singing after dinner.

On our last day on Moorea we went on a fascinating interior island tour. Our guide, Albert, did a wonderful job in telling us all the local lore and in showing us through plantations and around the beautiful bays.

Raiatea—the next island on our itinerary—is always a beautiful place to visit. While we were there, we went on a speed canoe trip to Tahaa and from there to a motu (a very small island) to snorkel. We rode bicycles. We watched a fire walking ceremony. We took a small outrigger canoe to a few nearby islands and swam and laughed and thoroughly enjoyed ourselves. We hired a guide, Philip, to take us in a speed canoe up the Faaroa River and on to a magnificent little motu to snorkel.

Tony in Tahiti

On March 23rd we flew to Papeete where we spent an interesting day. We went on a private all-day sightseeing trip around the island with an excellent driver—Roland Hunter—stopping to have lunch at the Gauguin Museum. At night we dined at the Maeva Beach Hotel and saw Tahitian dancing at its best.

The following day we took the long flight back to Tucson arriving at 12:10 a.m. We were met by Kent and Tony Jr. who were full of stories for us. We drove to their bunkhouse with them and chatted by a fire until 3:30 a.m. It was good to be a family again.

During our absence both boys had been taking flying lessons. Tony Jr. had driven to Northern Arizona University and Utah State University to check them over as potential schools to attend. Kent had flown to the University of Miami and did not find it to his liking. Katharine Merritt and Johanna Plaut were in residence at our place. My parents had just returned from a trip to the Caribbean.

Kent had bought a new Sirocco car as well as a new off-road Volkswagen. Tony Jr. had started a little business making and selling metal sculptures. How could all that have happened when we were away only two weeks!

32

༺ஐ༻

VISITING THE FAMILY CASTLE IN THE TYROL – 1976

The year 1976 was indeed a year of travel for me with time in the spring to teach in Hawaii and many weeks in the fall working in South America. Of course, there was always our time in Canada in the summer, and, as it was an even numbered year, the biennial trip with Tony and others on a private yacht in Greece in June and July.

However, having finally convinced my parents to start a life of travel, I was not going to let the momentum pass. Dad had been reluctant to leave home given his serious health constraints but once he got a taste of the excitement of seeing new parts of the world there was no stopping him. My parents had caught the travel bug!

We had decided that this year we would take Kent and Tony Jr. to see their castle in the Tyrol in the north of Italy and follow up with a cruise on the Mediterranean. It had been a demanding year for me so, prior to meeting them in Venice, I treated myself to a repositioning cruise aboard the *Royal Viking Sky* which left from Miami en route to Funchal on May 30th. Funchal is the largest city in Portugal and the capital of Madeira.

I really needed rest and spent almost every day sleeping and reading. That was, of course, the purpose of the trip. We arrived in Funchal on June 7th and took an all day trip around the island of Madeira visiting Canico, Santa Cruz, Machico, Porta da Cruz, with lunch at an inn in Faial. Madeira was incredibly beautiful with high hills, deep valleys and many streams.

On to Monte via Ribeiro where I took a sled-ride down to Funchal which was great fun. Later I took a flight to Lisbon where I spent the night. The following day I flew to Venice, with long stopovers in Madrid and Rome.

Seasoned traveler that I considered myself to be, I confidently rented a car at the airport believing I could easily find the ship where my parents and sons awaited me. After driving for over an hour, I realized I was hopelessly lost and close to tears. Some kindly man finally led me to the port at Arriba Sete Martyr, put me on a private water taxi and sent me off to the ship. With much relief I boarded the *Golden Odyssey* and fell into the arms of my loving family. Our journey had begun.

As I say, the main purpose of the trip was for Kent and Tony Jr. to see the ancient castle of their heritage—the Gaudententhurm. It is in a small Tyrolian village in the Alps—Partschins–near the town of Merano in northern Italy. We got an early start in our rental car and hours later reached our destination. My father, a newspaperman and feature writer, wrote an article about this experience. He will tell the story far better than I. Hence, I turn the dialog over to my dad.

A FAMILY WHOSE CASTLE ISN'T THEIR HOME
By Murray Sinclair
Tucson Daily Citizen—Saturday, October 16, 1976

Visiting an ancient European castle can be fascinating, but would you want to live in one? A very real question for Kent and Tony von Isser both of 4615 Camino Real. Because, apparently, an Italian castle started in 1348 (that's about 100 years before Christopher Columbus was born) and still kept up by their relatives is theirs for the asking.

The boys are back from a visit to their potential inheritance on the slopes of the Alps near the entrance to the Brenner Pass and they've made their decision: they prefer Tucson, or at least the U.S. The life of noblemen isn't for them.

But why don't they claim it anyway, live the good life for a few months, and then sell for a nice bundle of cash? Even if they didn't believe it should stay in the family (which they do), they couldn't. More than 35 years ago the Italian government named it a National Historic Site and cut taxes to a minimum.

At the same time the government decided that no structural change, inside or out, could be made without official approval. Months of delicate negotiations were needed before permission was given to install modern indoor bathrooms.

The family can live on in undisturbed peace indefinitely, but if the time comes when they no longer want it, and the attending expenses, the government will probably take over the upkeep and admit the public. After all, there aren't many buildings around that were started in the 1340s.

What's it worth? There is no way of telling. But the furniture alone would bring hundreds of thousands of dollars at any of the major New York auction houses. Specifically, the boys' father, Anthony K. von Isser, is the No. 1 heir followed by Kent, 21, and then Tony, 19.

Actually, the Gaudententhurm—the name of the compound—isn't a castle at all, but that's what it's called by the people of Partschins (where it's located) and nearby Merano. More accurately, it is a manor of the style once favored by wealthy land owners—a type of building characteristic of south Tyrol.

The foundations of the original part of the building are supposed to be 12 feet thick. Perhaps this is an exaggeration, but they're thick, really thick. They were laid by Gaudens von Partschins, a peaceful fellow who had no intention of leaving himself at the mercy of bands of rascals wandering through the mountain pass below. So he built himself a fortified tower which also served as his residence.

And he built well. The tower, to which the remainder of the manor has been added, is in as good condition today as when it was built 628 years ago—if you ignore the worn steps of the spiraling stone stairway. The boys were properly impressed.

They'd flown from Tucson to Venice the day before. The city was covered with smog. So was the Mediterranean from Greece to Malta to North Africa. Now, as they drove northward with their mother and us, their maternal grandparents, only a hazy outline of the tops of the Alps could be seen because of the polluted air.

Car rentals are dreadfully expensive in Italy. We had a small Fiat for one day— 12 hours to be exact. When the Mastercharge bill arrived they'd charged us $142.67. The toll road into the Brenner Pass is as good as the freeways in Arizona.

Some of the lower walls of the Alps are pockmarked by shells from U.S. howitzers fired as American troops inched their way northward in World War II. Partschins and Merano are about 180 miles from Venice. For centuries the area was part of Austria—until Austria went down to defeat with Germany in World War I. Then this section of the Tyrol was sliced off and made part of Italy, one of the victorious allies. That was well over 50 years ago, but large numbers of the residents still regard themselves as Austrians rather than Italians. Road signs are given in Italian and German, which doesn't help much when the driver understands English only.

Merano was easy to find. Getting to Partschins, a picture-postcard village on the side of the mountains, was a different matter. Once there, the rest was easy. We just called to anyone convenient "Gaudententhurm?" and followed the direction they pointed. An ancient, wrought iron gate was open, because we were expected. A narrow dirt driveway bordered by grass and stone walls led to the manor, a three-floor, 50 foot high, ivy-covered mansion, shaded by a towering chestnut tree.

The number 1620 over the main entrance wasn't a street address but the date the doorway and that part of the building were added. An artist and servant live on the ground floor, paying minimum rent and acting as genteel house-sitters. Dr. Peter von Sölder, an anesthetist and descendent of the maternal side of the family, his wife (a dentist) and their two teen-age sons hurried up from Merano.

For years the von Sölders lived on the second floor of the Gaudententhurm. Their sons were born there. Berta von Sölder, an aunt, had the top floor until she became elderly and, with a companion, moved into Merano. The doctor and his family soon followed her. Now they use the manor for an occasional weekend but only the second floor. The top floor is still Aunt Berta's.

All three floors are filled with beautifully preserved, centuries-old furniture and crystal chandeliers worth a fortune. Polished inlaid tables; sideboards and china cabinets; chairs that were old when Napoleon was defeated at Waterloo; chests, bookcases and side tables—most inlaid and all freshly polished—fill the rooms. The walls are covered with portraits of early day von Issers: Johann Simon who bought the property: Anton Simon and his grandson and wife, the former Josephine von Preuzu Lusenegg und Korburg.

There's an army chest from the time of Prince Eugene, filled with antique toys. A small leather trunk from 1780 still contains six bottles of wine. Religious objects fill several cabinets. One room the size of a small ballroom (perhaps that was its original use) is crammed with excess centuries-old furniture for which a dealer would give his eye teeth. Some of the windows are bottle bottoms set in lead, a method used before flat glass panes were known.

Doors hidden behind curtains open into small, secret rooms, all furnished. Once the compound included a chapel where the family and the workers worshipped. Now it is a large Roman Catholic church used by all the people of Partschins. The sound of the original bells is still heard in the valley far below. The church cemetery remains undisturbed, the burial place for a dozen generations of von Issers and the Hendls, Stachelburgs, Ealthenhofens, Rolandins, Drouzers and Bauers who owned the property before them. Some of the grave markers have toppled over and now lean against the church.

The stable and carriage house are no longer used but the barns, almost as stout as the main building, are in good repair. The boys wandered along the stone paths in what was once a large, formal garden. The paths need repairing. The round goldfish and lily pond in the center is still filled with water, but the fish and plants are gone. The lawns are cut but not manicured as they once were.

A little background now, about the von Issers, the information coming from the general historic collection of heraldry and titled families in the Royal Bavarian State Library. The records before 1530 are lost. By then the Isers were apparently well known in the Alpine region of upper Bavaria and the record is complete. Possibly they took their name from the Isar Valley in which they seem to have lived.

When they moved into the Tyrol, the name moved with them. As was the custom, different branches of the family distinguished themselves by adding the names of places. The record shows a Mountain Iser, Hillside Iser, and Iser in the Forest and a half dozen others. They were plain, hard-working valley farmers trying hard to make ends meet.

There wasn't a general or a person with a distinguished place in society among them.

So why were they elevated into the aristocratic realm of the Austrian Empire? Long before the family prospered members shared what they had—food, clothing and shelter—with the poor. The record in the library says: "They gave incessantly, assiduously and indefatigably—often beyond their means." They helped the aged, homeless, widows, orphans, waifs and those rejected by their communities.

When they didn't have enough grain of their own, they bought and made it into bread for the needy. Even so, they became large land owners. The record says: "Word of their good deeds and charitable work finally reached Vienna...ultimately coming to the ear of the sovereign...who in recognition of their long standing noble acts honored Blasius Iser, his two sons and two brothers by bestowing upon them a patent of nobility." This was in 1682. It would seem that old Blasius was particularly proud of the honor. Wanting to distinguish his branch of the family from the others, he added an extra "s" to his name. So did the rest of the family, and it's been Isser ever since.

Some years after Blasius died, Bavarian and French troops fought their way through the Brenner Pass and into the Tyrol, doing the customary pillaging and burning. Unfortunately for the von Issers (the Emperor's patent authorized the "von"), one of the documents missing when the invaders were chased back home was the parchment elevating them to knighthood. Empress Maria Theresa corrected this in 1774 by granting Johann Simon von Isser, a merchant, another patent of nobility. This hand-painted and lettered scroll with a seal the size of a tea plate hangs on the Tucson von Issers' living room wall.

Forty–four years later, just to make sure that the job was well done and would last forever, Emperor Franz II invested Anton Simon von Isser with the title of nobility all over again. The king was obviously impressed with Anton's actions when another wave of invaders had come through the pass. Although a civilian, he raised two companies of riflemen. When Austrian troops retreated, he emptied his granaries and then used his own money to buy wheat. He also bought badly needed ammunition and lead.

Emperor Franz also changed the family name to Isser von Gaudententhurm. His document was just as impressive and more detailed (the translation takes four typewritten pages) than the scroll signed by Maria Theresa and says in part:

"...from now on Anton Simon Isser von Gaudententhurm, his legitimate heirs and heirs of their heirs, male and female sex, shall be honored and addressed as noble persons by everybody...and are entitled to all privileges customarily given to noblemen, and like other nobles...of the Holy Roman Empire take part in tournaments, receive fiefs and dispense justice."

The boys from Tucson liked the idea of receiving fiefs and dispensing justice (traffic fines alone could be considerable) but decided that the Italian government would probably dispute their rights. The family tree starting with Christian Iser in 1530 fills three typewritten pages and includes a flock of gentleman farmers, several nuns, innkeepers, a salt miner, clergyman, university professors, merchants, a mayor, collector of customs, judge, governor, physician, major on the general staff of the Austrian Army and a mining engineer. The last two listed on the tree are Kent and Tony.

Josef Max Kaspar von Isser, the boys' grandfather who died in Tucson in 1972, continued the good works for which the family had been noted for centuries. During World War I, when he was a German officer, he was twice decorated, including the military cross, for his work in breaking enemy codes. When peace came, he returned to Innsbruck. That's where he met Miss Marian Lindsay, a wealthy American who was running a relief project for the poorest of the poor with her own money.

Von Isser volunteered to help. For three years he was her unpaid assistant. In this capacity he found and saved a convent of shut-in nuns dying of malnutrition. For this he was honored by the Pope with the Papal Cross.

In 1922 he met Miss Dorothea King, another American. They were married in 1925. Because of her health, they came to the U.S. and settled in Tucson. That's when he shortened his name to von Isser. Kent and Tony have been glad he did. Fellow students and teachers at Catalina High had enough trouble with von Isser without making them struggle with Isser von Gaudententhurm.

Tony & Kent at entry to the
Gaudententhurm

The boys had taken a casual interest in their family history but they learned a lot more from Dr. von Sölder as they toured the grounds and buildings. As he walked them to the car when they were ready to return to Venice, he told them: "We have been keeping this up only until the von Issers return. When are you coming back to claim your heritage?" "It's beautiful, really beautiful," one replied, which was being as noncommittal as you could get.

In the car, Kent said, "It should be used." "You're right," agreed Tony, "but not by us."

Sated with information and history as we returned to Venice, we were nonetheless excited about the next part of our adventure. It was Kent and Tony Jr.'s first cruise so they were quite overcome by all the amenities available. Kent was 21 and Tony Jr. 19 at that time.

We spent the following day seeing Venice, first by a private taxi boat for two hours followed by a walk to St. Mark's Square. While the boys climbed up the bell tower with its magnificent view, my mother and I celebrated with a glass of Campari—her first.

We, like most people, were sad to leave Venice when we set sail for our first port of call—Dubrovnik. I was fortunate to have visited there in 1970 on one of Katharine Merritt's cruises when it had far fewer tourists and when the lifestyle seemed simpler. On this trip I found the city considerably changed and not as appealing.

We hired a taxi and embarked on a two-hour tour that took us up winding roads for dramatic views and down into the old town, the Plaka. Tony Jr. and I walked the high and narrow wall at the sea's edge and thoroughly explored this fascinating city. (Kent was still healing from his accident and could not accompany us.) I have been there several times now and never fail to fall under its enchanting spell. Later we sailed through the Bay of Kotor.

Kent and Tony Jr. took advantage of every activity the ship had to offer from skeet shooting and swimming to magic shows and Pirates Night. Tony Jr. even danced with his grandmother and me—an all-time first that perhaps he'd prefer to forget. I had noted in my diary on September 9, 1971 that I had taken Tony Jr. to his dance class that day and "he hates it."

Corfu was our next destination and, having been to Paleokastritsa, previously I was confident the family would overlook the difficult drive to get there in order to take advantage of its magnificent views. The monastery there has a museum dating from AD 1225. It was a day we all enjoyed.

We visited Sicily. Next was Malta, which I have always loved. It has a special golden glow that I've never seen elsewhere. We took a guided tour that left no corner unexplored including a visit to Mdina–a walled town situated on a hill in the middle of the island. The town is still confined within it walls and has a population of just under 300. The boys were greatly impressed with the church there.

On to Tunisia arriving in La Gaulette, the port city for Tunis which is the country's capital. We took a four-hour bus trip which included a walk through Sidi Bu Said. Then to Tunis where we visited the Bardo Museum and shopped in the souk (marketplace), which left much to be desired.

We were delighted that our next day was at sea, a time to rest and catch up with ourselves. The highlight of the evening was the Greek dancing performed by the crew. I have always loved Greek music and their unique dance style. I noted in my diary that Kent went to the pool today and did not seem inhibited by his ugly leg. That was a big relief for me.

Mykonos was our next port of call and we wasted no time in getting on the first tender to the town. We enjoyed the beach, shopping and basking by the wine dark sea.

Rhodes was next and again we made an early start to go to the town of Lindos. Even my 72 year old asthmatic father climbed all the steps to the Acropolis on top. The view made it well worthwhile. That evening Tony Jr. and I went into the town of Rhodes to walk through the castle and The Street of the Knights.

Eventually, we arrived at our last port of call–Athens. My parents, Kent and Tony Jr. immediately headed for visits to the Acropolis and several museums. I had other plans. My husband Tony was arriving from Tucson and I

Tony, Mother & Kent

414

was thrilled to be going to the airport to meet him. That evening my parents, Tony, the boys and I went to my favorite Greek tavern, Geros Tou Moria, in the Plaka, certainly one of the most picturesque places in Athens. We went on to see the Sound and Light performance at the Acropolis. A wonderful, happy day.

Sunday, July 19—the last day of our family trip. We all took a ferry to the island of Aegina where we had lunch on the yacht *Dorita* before Mom, Dad and the boys returned to Athens and their departure for Tucson. For Tony and me this was the beginning of yet another of the amazing trips we took with Katharine Merritt as her guests on a yacht. Much more about that in another chapter.

This was the day of Ginny Richards' marriage to her beloved Tassos, a crew member on the *Dorita* whom she had met two years previously. Ginny is the daughter of friends, Jan and Ames Richards of Connecticut, who went on every one of the Dorita cruises with us. It was the Greek wedding to end all Greek weddings with an unforgettable reception. Everyone participated in the Greek dancing. It was an enchanting evening. The following day we embarked on our cruise aboard the *Dorita*.

33

CRINO

EUROPE, SCANDINAVIA AND THE BRITISH ISLES—1977

What an exciting trip I had with my sister Carol and my parents in May of 1977! Carol, an anglophile, had never been to London and was excited beyond words to be seeing all the places about which she had read for so many years.

I flew to Toronto on May 14th where I was met at the airport by a throng of family—my parents, Carol, her husband Terry and their three children, and my brother Murray, his wife Mary and Murray's sons Scott and Craig. It was like a family reunion. I would love to say that this gathering was just to meet me, but in fact it was to bid farewell to my parents, Carol and me as we left for a long trip to Europe. We soon boarded a British Airlines Boeing 747 where our seats were on the uppermost floor.

I knew we would have a busy few days in London as Carol was determined to visit every nook and cranny in that city. Unfortunately Dad was ill for a good part of this trip, but the first day my mother, Carol and I took a bus tour which drove first to the changing of the horse guard at Buckingham Palace. One poor guard fainted twice while we were there! On to Westminster Abbey and the Parliament buildings. Although I had been to all of these places, I was seeing them anew through the eyes of my sister who was totally ecstatic to actually be there and not just reading about them.

Later in the day Carol and I took a bus to Piccadilly, walked through Soho and Carnaby Street and took a taxi to the Parliament buildings where we lined up for ages so Carol could go inside to see the ancient Westminster Hall.

It was cold and rainy the next day, but Carol and I headed out early to visit the Old Curiosity Shop and see once again the Tower of London followed by a visit to St Paul's

Cathedral. Later we walked the Strand and Fleet Street and visited book shops, one of Carol's favorite activities in life. Later we picked up my parents so that my father and Carol could have their first visit to Madame Tussaud's wax museum. For dinner that evening we went to a restaurant built in 1667—Ye Olde Cheshire Cheese. We had great fun.

Mother with Carol & Aldine

On May 18th we traveled to Southampton where we embarked on our cruise ship—*The Royal Viking Sky*—my second voyage on it. It was Carol's first cruise and on a truly gorgeous ship.

Our first port of call was Amsterdam where Dad missed out on almost everything because he was ill. What a good sport he was! My mother, Carol and I walked into Amsterdam to Dam Square where we took a taxi to the Amstel Hotel, always one of my favorites. After lunch, we visited the Rijksmuseum and saw many Rembrandts—my favorite of which was Night Watch. Later we drove through residential districts, along canals, past parks and windmills and into the Jewish district. We visited Anne Frank's house. I was very touched by that experience and the following day I read the book *The Diary of Anne Frank.*

Carol and I stayed up much too late every night and certainly did not get enough sleep. It was on this cruise that I met a lovely German gentleman, Peter Marquardt. We developed a close friendship and later I had the privilege of visiting him and his family in Germany and he visited me both at the cottage in Canada as well as in Tucson. Carol became friends with his traveling companion, Herr Schuler. We spent the following day traveling on the North Sea and passed oil derricks, one of which had blown up only two weeks before, an event that drew international attention.

On this day Dad had to see the doctor on the ship. His health had always been tenuous. He managed to join Mother, Carol and me to hear a lecture given by the author Irving Stone, a fellow passenger. We also attended a lecture that introduced us to the Shetland Islands, Skye and Ireland. That evening Peter, Herr Schuler, Carol and I walked on deck as we passed through Sognafjord to Aulandsfjord. It was magnificent.

We arrived in Norway on a gorgeous day. Mother, Carol and I went to Flam where we took a train up into the mountains to Voss having a delicious smorgasbord lunch there. We took a bus trip past beautiful waterfalls to the Stalheim Hotel where we had tea while looking at what might be the most gorgeous scenery in the world. Mother was now sick too so Carol and I spent the evening in the ship's Buccaneer Club watching a floor show and dancing with some of the ship's officers until the wee hours.

The following day we arrived in Bergen, Norway where I had visited in 1968 on another cruise to the North Cape. Mother was now in bed sick, but Dad was able to join Carol and me for a tour through Bergen. In the afternoon Carol and I returned to town to take a funicular up the highest hill. It was magnificent. At last the four of us were able to have dinner together. It was a happy celebration.

The next two days were highlights for us. Our ship moored off the stark, intriguing island of Mainland—the largest of the Shetland Islands. We took a tender into the town of Lerwick where we took buses to travel all around the island. We never saw a single tree. It was stark beyond belief, but not depressing. I think tourists rarely visited there. We went to Jarlshof and the Pictish Ruins. This area provides an insight into the way of life of its inhabitants during the late Bronze Age, Iron Age, Pictish era, Norse era and the Middle Ages. It was a fascinating and eye-opening experience. The sun set that night at midnight!

The following day a small group of us—my parents, Carol, Peter, Herr Schuler and I—took a tender to the magnificent Hebrides Island of Skye. We walked to the wonderful MacLeod Dunvegan Castle. We continued to walk for miles while I absorbed the very essence of this island—its sounds, its scent and its very air. I heard a cuckoo bird. It was on this island that Carol had a deep and spiritual experience in which she somehow connected with her ancient past. She walked by herself for hours and has never had so profound an experience since. She will never forget the Isle of Skye.

Later in the afternoon Peter and I played ping-pong. We were very well matched. Carol went off on her own that evening returning to the cabin very late. She had been partying in the crew's quarters and rued the experience the next day. Unfortunately, the sea was very rough that day and our tender ride to Dun Loaghaire on the Irish coast was wild. Even Dad made this trip as he very much wanted to visit Dublin. We found it drab but interesting. Dad and I visited the wonderful Trinity College Library.

Although Carol had no sleep the previous night, that afternoon she and I played ping-pong with three delightful Irish customs officers who remained aboard our ship until we sailed that night.

The next morning found us moored off the coast of Ireland. We had a tender ride to the town of Cobh where we took buses for a wonderful drive through County Cork, through the city of Cork and on to the famous Blarney Castle and its world renowned Blarney Stone. Mother, Carol and I climbed the narrow 90 steps to the top and tentatively approached the Blarney Stone. My remarkable mother lay down under the stone and did indeed kiss it. She was unbelievable! It was quite terrifying to be hanging over space while one did the kissing but hundreds of thousands have done it and presumably no one has yet died in the act. Being obsessive-compulsive about germs, I also hated thinking how many people had kissed that stone before me!

After returning to the ship, Carol and I played ping-pong with Peter and Herr Schuler. (Can you believe we never called him by his first name? I don't think we even knew it. I do remember him saying to us each night "shlaf gut"—sleep well. Carol and I continue to say it to each other frequently.) The captain had his farewell party that evening. I was of mixed emotions. I was very excited that on the following day my sons would be joining us as the cruise continued. However, I would also be saying goodbye to my beloved sister and to Peter to whom I had become very attached.

After a morning of playing shuffleboard with Peter and watching the gorgeous scenery pass by, we arrived in Southampton. There, with many parting tears, we said our farewells to Peter who was returning to Germany and to Carol who was going home to Toronto. During the cruise, she had suspected that all was not well with her and this was confirmed in Toronto when she saw her doctor. Sadly she received the diagnosis of lung cancer. I did not learn this until later in the summer and all our lives changed as we faced this tragedy as a family. Carol was only 37 at the time, with three small children.

I was to have met my boys Kent (now 22) and Tony Jr. (now 19) at Southampton. Our wires got crossed and when I returned to the ship I found that they were already settled in their cabin and looking for me!

And so began the next phase of this trip which I shall write about in the next chapter. What an amazing and long trip this was!

34

CRESSO

EUROPE, SCANDINAVIA AND RUSSIA—1977

Early in my children's lives, I had determined that they would see as much of the world as possible before settling down to their adult responsibilities. And they did indeed see the world—far and wide. Kent (22) and Tony (19) joined my parents and me on a cruise in May, 1977 that would take us to many countries on two continents.

We were aboard the *Royal Viking Sky*, a beautiful ship with only 210 passengers on this cruise. My parents and I had met my sons in Southampton and sailed to our first port of call, Amsterdam. Our first evening there we took a fabulous canal ride and then walked along Canal Street where the prostitutes sat in windows tantalizing the passersby with their sensuous bodies and come-hither looks. It was quite an eye-opener for my lads!

The next day, May 29th, was my 44th birthday. (I was only 21 when Kent was born.) To celebrate, we took an all-day tour through the countryside, along the beaches and ultimately to the enchanting town of Madurodam. We spent a considerable amount of time there as we were fascinated by the concept of this village. It is a miniature park in the Scheveningen district of The Hague. It is home to a range of 1:25 scale model replicas of famous Dutch landmarks, historical cities and large developments. Everything, including flora and street decorations, is modeled to scale. The little people—its residents—have their clothing changed according to the season! It was named after George Maduro, a very handsome Jewish law student from Curacao who fought the Nazi occupation forces as a member of the Dutch resistance. He died at Dachau concentration camp in 1945.

We had lunch at The Hague and traveled on to Delft and Rotterdam. That night we had a wonderful dinner on board the ship with birthday cake followed by a floor show and I felt thoroughly feted.

Kent greeting the captain, followed by Tony and my father in his Sinclair tartan trousers

The following day we visited Marken and Volendam. Marken forms a peninsula in the Markermeer and was formerly an island in the Zuiderzee. I had been to both places in 1968. That evening the captain had a cocktail party. We sailed at 1:00 a.m. en route to our next port of call–Hamburg. The harbor there was huge! We all took a city tour and were impressed by how modern and clean the city was. We stopped at Alster Lake and the botanical gardens and drove through the infamous red light district of St. Pauli and the Reeperbahn, also known as the world's most sinful mile.

We had our first damp, cold day on June 1st but spent time on deck watching the beautiful Kiel Canal pass by. Kent, Tony Jr. and I played lots of ping-pong and then watched in fascination as we went through the locks of Kiel. That night the crew put on an impressive Parisian review floor show, and when my parents departed for the night the boys and I went to the Buccaneer Club to dance. Kent left early but Tony Jr. stayed right there with me as I danced away the evening with one of the ship's officers. Tony Jr. then saw me to my room at 1:00 a.m.!

We arrived in Visby, Gotland after a gorgeous day on the Baltic Sea. Gotland is a Swedish island. Our ship had moored at some distance from land and so we took a tender to shore and joined a small group for a wonderful tour of the island. The scenery was beautiful. Although it was very cold that day, the boys and I walked the last three miles back to the harbor. That night we were entertained aboard the ship by Swedish dancers.

We arrived in Stockholm the next day. It was astonishing to my family as we approached the city to see how much the scenery reminded us of our beloved Lake of Bays in Canada. Sailboats zipped around us and with the sun glimmering on the ocean it was a scene of great beauty. My parents, sons and I took a morning tour including a visit to the spectacular city hall, and a walk through the old city where we saw the warship Vasa. It had sunk on its maiden voyage in 1628 and was raised in 1961! It was still being restored at the time of our visit.

At night, Tony Jr. and I walked into the old part of the city and saw some truly strange sights—weird looking people carrying strange objects such as snakes, and overdosed drunks lying hither and yon. We were glad to get back to the sanity and the safety of the ship.

My mother, my sons and I took a two-hour "under the bridges" canal trip. Stockholm is on 14 islands connected by 52 bridges. We went to the huge NK department store to shop and then returned to the ship. The boys and I were on deck for our departure at 4:00 p.m. marveling at the beauty of the scenery. I was enjoying so much the company of my sons and spending time with them together and individually. Both were in university so these moments together were precious.

During the night we arrived at Helsinki, Finland. This visit was a first for me and I was excited to be seeing at last this country about which I had only read. We were lucky to have a lovely day, and Helsinki was a fascinating city. The city tour took us to Senate Square, an ancient cemetery, a unique "rock church" and the Olympic stadium. We returned to the ship where Kent and I lay in the sun and took a sauna. At night my parents and I went to a concert followed by a floor show. We were enjoying every minute of this amazing trip to distant lands.

At eight o'clock the next morning we arrived in Leningrad, Russia where we went through a difficult process of customs and immigration. Dad had chosen to stay in Leningrad so my mother, sons and I went immediately to the airport for a flight to Moscow. When we saw our aircraft we almost went into shock. It was ancient and not well maintained. The tires were so thin that the boys—both pilots–doubted they would last through taxi and take-off. After a very rough take-off roll through many potholes, we were at last airborne. The interior of the aircraft was truly disgusting; my "sick bag" had already been used! (I took it back to Tucson with me as a souvenir and had it in my office at UA as a "conversation piece.")

We were met at the airport in Moscow and taken to the Metropol, a grand old hotel about which books have been written. There was an interesting custom in the hotels in Russia. On each floor there was a lady at a desk; she was the key lady to whom you must give your key when leaving the hotel. On your return, it was available once again. We had lunch and set out on a tour of Moscow—a very clean and impressive city. While we saw many areas of the city, we concentrated primarily on the Kremlin and Red Square. We visited several churches there.

We felt very out of place in Moscow and were objects of considerable scrutiny. The Russian people whom we saw were dour and poorly dressed. It seemed as if all the women had hennaed red hair. We realized how very foreign we must appear to them and indeed we did feel like fish out of water.

The mood that night, however, was very different indeed. We attended the world renowned Moscow circus–an incredible experience. The people were immensely proud of their circus and we noticed throughout the evening that we were being checked for our reactions. They lit up when they saw us having a good time. Their entire demeanor was more relaxed and affable in that venue. We made sure they saw how impressed we were, and it gave us enormous pleasure to see them so happy.

At midnight we took the Red Arrow Express back to Leningrad arriving at 8:30 a.m. My father was glad he had made the choice to remain in Leningrad as he had not felt up to taking the demanding side trip to Moscow. He had enjoyed himself thoroughly in our absence as he had visited places that had long been of interest to him. We went to the Europa Hotel where we had breakfast and set out on a day of exploration. While spending several hours at the Hermitage Museum, we learned that it had 12 miles of corridors, a thousand rooms and three million exhibits. As my diary noted, "We had to gulp it, not sip it."

We did more sightseeing and returned to the ship to clean up. We hadn't even brushed our teeth ashore as we were afraid of the water! That evening we were treated to a special floor show on board—Russian musicians and dancers.

Leaving Leningrad at midnight, we had the next day at sea. We were in need of time to take care of laundry and letter writing. (There was no texting in those days!) At night the captain had a cocktail party after which there was dancing. To my delight, the captain approached our table and invited me to dance. After several dances, he walked me back to my family. Later I learned from the crew that in all their years with him they had never seen him dance with a passenger. I was very flattered.

We had another day at sea before arriving in our final port—Copenhagen, Denmark. I was truly sad to be leaving this lovely ship that had been my home since May 18th and it was now June 10th—23 days later. Upon disembarking, my parents, sons and I took a taxi to the Hotel Arthur Frommer. After checking in we took a tour of the city stopping to see the famous "little mermaid" that was, to my disappointment, small and unimpressive. As my husband Tony loved pipes, I searched for and found the perfect Danish pipe for him.

Later we took a canal trip through the entire city of Copenhagen and its harbor. We had dinner and spent the evening at the incredibly lovely Tivoli Gardens. The boys went on some terrifying rides there!

On June 11th we left Copenhagen and took a flight to Glasgow with an intermediate stop in Stavanger, Norway. It was very cold in Glasgow and we weren't impressed with our hotel. As it was the Queen's Jubilee year, all hotels were fully booked and we accepted what was available. We did, however, go to a magnificent restaurant for dinner—Malmaison. As our plans for a rental car went awry the next day, we spent longer in Glasgow than we had intended. This gave us time to attend church in the impressive Glasgow Cathedral followed by wonderful coach tour of the city.

It rained heavily the following day, the day of our departure from Glasgow. The boys got soaked loading our little rental car and finally we all piled in "like sardines, and wet" as my diary noted! Dad was all for calling the whole thing off. I know he didn't feel well most of the time, and this was a very long trip for my parents—a month so far. Nonetheless, off we went driving through beautiful countryside passing Loch Lomond. Of course, we had expected to see Nessie but she didn't make an appearance that day. What a disappointment!

As Tony Jr. was too young to qualify as a rental car driver, Kent had offered to do all the driving—his first experience in driving on the left side of the road. Throughout the entire trip he made the error of driving on the right side only once. That was an impressive record and I was very proud of him. We ended this day, June 13th, at a beautiful little village—Strathpeffer—where we stayed at a magnificent, expensive 100-year-old manor named Ben Wyvis Hotel.

In better frames of mind the next day, we set off to drive through the highlands of Scotland that took us through beautiful, rugged country with moors and lochs. We all were delighted with the experience and my father, with his strong Scottish roots, was thrilled to be seeing the land of his ancestors. We drove through Dingwall and Ullapool and had to take a ferry boat once to continue on our drive. We were lucky there was very little rain that day so that our views of the scenery were excellent.

My father had the added problem of dealing with a colostomy so we stopped early that day in Thurso. I was glad for the shorter driving day as I sensed that my mother wasn't feeling well, but she would never have complained. I knew they both wanted to see Scotland, but I was sure they would be ready to leave for Tucson the following week.

It never became dark that night and it was cold, very cold. The next day we headed for the most northerly point in Britain—near the town of John O'Groats. The day was lovely and the scenery along the ocean was spectacular. We stopped in the town of Wick to mail invitations to the Sinclair family reunion we were hosting at the cottage in Canada later in the summer. We thought it would be fun to send them from the place that was the seat of the Sinclair clan. It seemed that practically every person we talked with there had the name Sinclair—which was pronounced Sink-ler. Later we stopped for woolen goods in Beauly.

We stayed that night in the beautiful Culloden House on the magnificent Culloden Moor. It was just outside Inverness—an expensive 22-room mansion. My father had looked forward for many years to seeing and exploring the historical area of Culloden but was unable to join us the following day. It broke my heart that he had to spend it in bed as he was ill. I was sorry he was missing so much but very proud of him for making the effort. The rest of us visited many parts of the region including the impressive Dun Robin Castle.

While Dad felt better the following day, he stayed in bed while my mother, my sons and I drove into Inverness where we took a 2 ½ hour boat trip that traveled all the way to Loch Ness. Still the monster did not make an appearance! In getting there, we went through the Caledonian Canal, passed through Dochgarroch Loch and right into Loch Ness. It was a cloudy but pleasant day (for Scotland). It was thrilling to pass by Aldourie Castle. Dad joined us for dinner that night and we decided to go straight through to Edinburgh the next day.

My diary identifies Culloden House as "the most beautiful inn I have ever visited." It will remain in my memory forever. Rather than put my father through another day of driving through the Highlands of Scotland with another short stop at a hotel at night, we drove to Edinburgh. Along the way we stopped at the awesome Blair Castle, the town of Perth, and to the Firth of Forth Bridge—an impressive sight indeed. Kent did a marvelous job of driving on this day but I know it was stressful for him.

Tony, mother, Kent & Aldine - Edinburgh

It was a relief to return the rental car the following day with the help of our bellman, Jack Anderson. In the afternoon we visited Holyrood Palace after which we took a fascinating taxi ride around Edinburgh—a good way to do it as Dad was with us and still not feeling his best. At least he had a chance to see the city about which he had read so much.

On Sunday, June 19th, Father's Day, the five of us went to services at St. Giles' Cathedral. It was magnificent. Later we visited Edinburgh Castle which was indeed interesting. It had been a nice day again; we were lucky with the weather. At night we went to the Two Inn Restaurant for dinner and later went to

Lawnmarket where we attended a program of readings of Sir Walter Scott. It was excellent.

We spent our last day in Edinburgh shopping for a kilt for my brother Murray and then walking the Royal Mile to visit the John Knox house. At night we dined at the oldest restaurant in Edinburgh—The Beehive Inn. At this point we all were saturated with food and none of my clothes fit me! Definitely it was time to go home, which we did the following day—June 21st. We had been "on the road" since May 14th!

We flew to Toronto where my sister met us at the airport. We all were going to stay with her—except Kent. He flew directly back to Tucson as his plan was to drive back to Canada towing a jet ski he had ordered some weeks previously.

Among the many people I phoned that night were Winifred and Sam Kirk. They gave me the news that I was now officially an Assistant Professor at UA and on tenure track. I was ecstatic, as universities typically do not hire their own graduates. They had made a rare exception in my case. I did, by the way, receive tenure the first time I applied.

And so our summer in Canada had begun!

35

ॐ

GERMANY—1978

For many years it was my habit to travel to Europe every summer. I had always wanted to see the Rhine and Mosel River regions in Germany so I was quick to accept an invitation from a good German friend and his mother to visit them.

Peter Marquardt and his family were from Mainz. It was the summer of 1978. I flew to Cologne to meet him as he was working there at the time. I was delighted to start the trip in this city as I had long wanted to visit the Cologne Cathedral.

Work on this cathedral started in AD 1248. It now is the largest Gothic cathedral in Northern Europe and boasts the second tallest spires. These towers are 515′ tall and are of openwork—a significant factor in my story. Its two huge spires give it the largest façade of any church in the world.

On the first day, while Peter went to work, I couldn't wait to get to the cathedral. It was early morning in late May and there were no tourists visible, none whatever. There was no ticket booth and no one to ask if I might take the stairs to the top of the steeple. I saw no one, but someone saw me. What a foolish woman I was to go inside alone, and it came close to costing me my life.

I knew it would be a long climb but I was sure I could do it if I took my time. At a point, I stopped to catch my breath. Suddenly an attractive young German man raced by me heading up the stairs. In a few minutes I continued the ascent and eventually found him stopped, ostensibly to catch his breath. I smiled and went on. Again as I climbed he raced past me as I rested. I had no inkling danger was ahead. When I caught up with him again, about 2/3 of the way up the spire, he was waiting for me. His intention was clear when he grabbed me and started ripping at my clothes. I screamed and I screamed, but there was no one to hear me. My screaming was out of control and I could see panic in his eyes. He started moving me over to the large opening on the spire where I have no doubt he intended to push me out.

I made a quick decision. Whatever he had in mind for me couldn't be worse than plummeting to my death. I stopped screaming and cooperated. Fortunately, God was looking after me for in the distance above we could hear the voices of women descending. There wasn't time for him to accomplish his wicked deed so he fled down the steps and disappeared.

When the women reached me I had reassembled my clothing but looked terror stricken, I am sure. I was gasping for breath. They smiled and fanned themselves as if to communicate to me that it was a long and arduous climb indeed. They had no idea.

As my diary reminds me, "He really roughed me up."

I eventually exited the spire and again there was no one in sight. My first impression of Germany left a great deal to be desired.

After Peter and I started our journey along the Rhine, it didn't take long for me to see that Germany is beautiful, perhaps one of the most beautiful countries I have ever seen. We stopped at all the cities and towns along the way and I found people gracious and welcoming. We often had dinner at the homes of friends of his, and while none could speak English, I soon found that I could follow the basic conversation and Peter translated my thoughts to them. One such evening, we went for drinks to the home of Seka and Berndt Haufmann and on to dinner at the beautiful home of his friends Bert and Margit Steinoff. We spent another evening with them having dinner on the top of Hotel Steigenberger in Frankfurt.

Peter was a recovering alcoholic. While he never drank anything with alcohol, he insisted I have a taste of all the regional wines as well as their local beer. I am not a beer drinker but–when in Germany do as the Germans. I noticed over time that my abdomen was swelling—larger and larger each day. It was dreadfully uncomfortable and I feared that if I had been pricked with a pin I would have exploded. Eventually I learned that the local beers are not pasteurized. An unpasteurized beer is "live" beer containing living micro-organisms such as yeast. To my chagrin they were using my stomach for fermentation and I wasn't happy. My beer drinking days were over and my body subsequently returned to normal.

It is impressive that Germany subsidizes alcoholic rehabilitation centers, and Peter showed me where he had lived for a period of time during his recovery. I do believe everyone should have the availability of professional help when they give up drinking, and I was impressed that Germany makes this possible for all its people.

I remember a lovely drive along the Rhine one Sunday morning. Peter mentioned that we were close to a very beautiful vineyard—Schloss Vollrads. It was a private residence, and I was concerned that we were intruding as we drove along the entrance road flanked on each side by huge trees. When we neared their home, we pulled over and stopped. To our amazement the most beautiful music was being played on a piano within—Eine Kleine Nachtmusik by Mozart. I was entranced and could visualize in my mind a beautiful young German girl at the piano on this magical morning. I have never forgotten that moment as I was deeply touched by the experience. Later that day we also visited Schloss Johannisberg and Monastery Eberbach.

I later learned that Schloss Vollrads has centuries of wine making history and traditions. Upon returning to Tucson, I ordered a case of this marvelous wine and, while it is not inexpensive, it is indeed a splendid wine.

I had many such lovely experiences with Peter. It is so much better to see a country with someone who has an involvement with it.

And now I want to tell you about Peter's family. They lived in Mainz. I was honored to visit them there and to hear their story. They suffered terribly during World War II. They were <u>not</u> Nazi sympathizers and lived every day in fear. They would not put the Swastika in their window. Peter had an older sister who was drawn into the Nazi youth movement and excoriated her parents for their refusal to cooperate with the regime. Peter's father (also Peter) was taken in for fingerprinting and, of course, the inevitable tattoo of an identification number on his arm. Not long after that Peter's father disappeared—he was just gone. Peter's mother was terrified of her own daughter and convinced she had turned them in. She knew that she had to take Peter somewhere safe.

A brave lady indeed, she packed a suitcase, left their apartment, and headed for the railroad station. There was chaos everywhere as other Germans were attempting to flee as well. Mainz was an industrial city and very much a target. Peter described the anguish of his mother pushing and shoving in an attempt to get on a train. Finally they succeeded and left Mainz.

Frau Marquardt had no idea where the train was going or where she would find safe haven for herself and Peter. Perhaps a day later when they were in the countryside, she and Peter departed the train. They walked and walked until they came to a farmhouse. They asked if they could be taken in, and were refused. Eventually they found a family that reluctantly accepted them. They were never kind to Peter or his mother, but they were safe.

When the war was over they returned to Mainz. Their apartment had been shot up and was in ruins. I saw the bullet holes still there on the walls of the stairwell to their apartment. Their daughter had disappeared and Peter never saw her again. And, of course, the father was gone.

They resumed life and perhaps a year later Frau Marquardt heard a knock at her door. When she opened it she was horrified by what she saw—an emaciated old man, dirty and unkempt, who could barely communicate. It was Peter's father. He had been interned in a prison camp in France and released when the war ended. How he ever found his way home is a mystery.

When I visited the family, Frau Marquardt went to enormous trouble to make my stay pleasant. She was so impressed to have an American woman visiting. Unfortunately, Peter was often at work and I was left with his parents. His mother would spend ages in the kitchen preparing delicious meals, but that left me alone with Herr Marquardt. He, of course, did not speak English and I did not speak German. But it really didn't matter as he had lost his mind and had only jumbled thoughts. So, I would carry on a meaningless conversation in English while he would respond with meaningless German. It was an uncomfortable situation.

Years before, Peter's father had been an excellent carver of wood. When I departed Germany I was given a charming box he had carved which I still see daily in my office and which I treasure. I also received a magnificent coffee table book of photographs of Germany entitled "Schönes Deutschland"—Beautiful Germany.

A side trip Peter insisted we make was to Munich to visit the Dachau concentration camp. Dachau was the first of its kind opened by the Nazi government in 1933. The camp is now a memorial to the more than 40,000 people who died there and over 200,000 who were imprisoned there during the Nazi regime.

One would wonder why the Germans would want to expose the world to this dreadful episode in their history, but that question was answered at the entrance to the camp with a sign saying "We must never forget what we did. We could do it again." Peter and I visited the museum and watched a film in English (they are shown all day and in many languages) which told the whole ghastly story. We followed this by a visit to the crematoria in front of which are huge photographs of the bodies stacked outside them waiting for removal. It was a grizzly and unforgettable scene. We visited the barracks and saw names scratched and written on the sides of bunks. It was heartbreaking and all too real. Although this was a sobering excursion for me, I found it extremely moving and very informative about the Holocaust and the devastation it wrought.

Meanwhile, back in Tucson, Tony and I had put our beautiful hacienda on Camino Real on the market to sell. It was time. Because it was large and rambling, I did not think that it would attract attention quickly so I felt free to go to Europe. Well, my mother was an incredible salesperson and received two offers on the first day it was shown.

Although I phoned home frequently from Germany, we had arranged that if something important arose, such as the selling of our house or some other emergency, that I could be reached through a "code." From wherever we were in our travels, Peter would call his mother every night to check on any incoming calls from the United States. If the person calling said, "Canada, Canada, Canada" it meant that I should phone home right away.

One night when we called her we heard a frantic "CANADA, CANADA, CANADA" and I knew my trip was over. It was an abrupt end to a fascinating experience but I returned to Tucson the next day.

I have lost touch with Peter, but I remember well the visits he made to my family both in Canada and Tucson. He was a good man. To my knowledge, he never married.

Travelogues can be boring but I would like to mention some of the interesting places I visited while with Peter. We walked a great deal—often dozens of miles a day and much of it on forest trails and in small villages. I truly preferred walking as when Peter was on the autobahn he rarely drove less than 180 km per hour. My heart was often in my mouth.

Peter had a special birthday dinner for me at Weinhaus Sankt Peter in the Ahr Valley. I drank their incredible Sekt and had venison and kiwi.

Peter took a good deal of time off from work while I was there, so one Saturday we left his home in Brühl and traveled to Oestrich-Winkel where we stayed at the lovely Hotel Schwan. We visited wonderful castles and walked through Ruine Rheinfels. We wandered through interesting Boppard and also Bacharach. Later we drove by the Lorelei.

One day when I was on my own, I took the Köln-Düsseldorfer ship for a trip along the Rhine. Much of this I had seen with Peter by car. I walked to Sessellift and ascended to the top on the chair lift. There were few people up there and I remember being nervous.

We visited Ulm and its cathedral and climbed the highest steeple in the world there. As I have mentioned, the second highest is in Cologne. We went to Augsburg—a fascinating town from the Middle Ages. There we climbed to the top of the City Hall for the magnificent view. While in Ulm, we also toured the Dom Cathedral followed by St. Ulrich Cathedral.

On we went to Königsbrunn and visited friends of Peter's there. We drove on through beautiful countryside approaching the Alps and Austria on our way to Füssen.

From Füssen we drove to the base of Neuschwanstein. A half hour walk—in the rain—took us to this magnificent castle which is, of course, world-renowned. We continued on to Steingaden where we visited the impressive baroque church—Wieskirche, located in the foothills of the Alps. Our next stop was Franziskaner where we walked through many churches. Next on our agenda was a visit to the Olympic grounds where we climbed to the top of Olympic Tower. That night we went for drinks at the home of Peter's friends Alexander and Marita for aperitifs and later to a wonderful restaurant—Schwarzwaelder.

In Munich, where we had visited Dachau, we had a stark awareness of the other side of life when we visited the magnificent Schloss Schleissheim. Other towns we enjoyed were Nürnberg, Wuerzburg and Marktheidenfeld. Peter also took me to the area where he had lived during the war years with his mother.

Certainly Peter did everything possible to make this the most comprehensive tour of his country that he could. I have been to other parts of Germany on other trips, but the area that I visited with Peter was truly Schönes Deutschland.

36

⊗⃝

CANEEL BAY AND THE VIRGIN ISLANDS—1980

On my 47th birthday, May 29, 1980 my darling parents took their family on a very special vacation to Caneel Bay in the Virgin Islands. I was particularly excited about this trip as it was one of the few family holidays when my husband Tony accompanied us.

Caneel Bay is set on a 170-acre peninsula in the Virgin Islands near seven picturesque beaches. It is located on the northwest side of St. John, one of the U.S. Virgin Islands. The hotel in which we were to stay was known as a Rockresort and was one of the early members of Laurance Rockefeller's hotel chain. Rockefeller had the resort buildings designed to blend in with the landscape, and the lighting of it is such that guests were easily able to see the stars at night. The resort was a member of Leading Hotels of the World. We knew we were going to a little bit of heaven.

We rendezvoused in Miami–my parents, my brother and his wife, and my sister and her husband– flew to St. Thomas and took a bus to the boat that carried us all to Caneel Bay. To our astonishment, my parents went "skinny dipping" in the ocean that night—privately, of course. Clearly they were indeed in the spirit of things.

Each of us had a private cottage and the hotel lived up to its worldwide reputation of being gorgeous. What a life of luxury we led there with lots of time for snorkeling, reading, sun bathing, hiking and swimming. May 30th, the following day, was my brother Murray's 49th birthday and Tony took us all to dinner at Turtle Bay to celebrate. That night the partying went on very late and I noted in my diary that my parents got no sleep whatever.

Our adventures the next day included sailing for Tony and me and a tour around the island of St. John for all of us. It was absolutely breathtaking. We were served rum punch making all of us a bit tipsy—with the exception of my father who didn't drink. He had taken a vow of abstinence at age 12 during a church service. He had kept to his promise. Dinner that night was at Turtle Beach.

In memory of my beloved Auntie Irene who had recently died, my father chartered a power boat from 9:00 a.m. until 6:00 p.m. We traveled all over the British and U.S. Virgin Islands stopping for lunch at Little Dix Bay. We swam, snorkeled and enjoyed every minute of this special time together. I should note that, for the first time in my memory, my father broke his pledge of abstinence and had a rum punch. Now, my father did not know how to drink liquor. So, with rum punch in hand, he simply slammed back that drink in two gulps. He hadn't learned about sipping. I think that was his first and last drink and it packed a powerful "punch." My father was

A mellow group – Tony, Murray, Dad, Carol, Aldine & Terry. Mother and Mary in front

feeling no pain and took on a much more relaxed persona for the remainder of the day. What a joyful time that was.

During a succeeding day, we took time out from swimming to take a boat and a taxi to the town of Charlotte Amalie on St. Thomas for shopping and sightseeing. We often had dinner at the Sugar Mill.

Another day we took a boat taxi to Trunk Bay where we found the most beautiful beach I had ever seen. We snorkeled around the island and saw magnificent and colorful fish. During our time at Caneel Bay we took time to visit Cruz Bay. These forays provided an opportunity to spend time with my sister and brother, both of whom lived in Toronto, reliving nostalgic moments in our lives and appreciating each other's company.

Each evening we'd go for drinks before dinner to a different cottage and rum continued to be a favorite staple late into the night.

On June 5th it was time to leave, knowing we had shared a moment in time we would neither repeat nor forget. One photograph that was taken on the infamous day of my father's debauchery was enlarged to 22 by 24 inches and I have looked at it every day of my life in Tucson since then—a constant reminder of my parents' love for us and ours for each other.

We flew via St. Croix to Toronto where Tony and I picked up our car and drove to the cottage arriving at 10:00 p.m. We were dumbfounded to see how much work Kent and Tony Jr. had accomplished there in our absence—both inside and outside. This was our first summer in our new place on Rat Bay; it had been basically a shell when we bought it. Tony and I found that we now had a lovely paneled bedroom with gorgeous views. Our boys had even put up curtains and made our bed for us. It was the beginning of yet another memorable summer on Lake of Bays.

37

CRED

BERMUDA—1981

My brother Murray and I had birthdays separated by only one day—plus two years. To celebrate these occasions in 1981, my parents took Murray and his wife Mary, Carol and her husband Terry, and me to Bermuda for nine days. Mom and Dad always hosted these family trips with great panache and this was no exception.

We arrived at the gorgeous Coral Beach Club having left Toronto together earlier that day, June 1st. Our accommodations bordered on perfection. We had a big cottage with four bedrooms –each with a bathroom—and two living rooms and kitchens, one on each of the two levels. One living room was 32 feet long! We were in heaven.

I remember that we were provided with fresh flowers daily and fluffy towels that seemed to be replaced hourly. They were used appreciatively as the beach was right outside our front door and we swam frequently.

It seems that my father fell ill on all our trips. Having been unwell his entire adult life, I thought him very valiant to go on these family excursions. This time his heart was misbehaving and my mother told us that asthma was wearing

At dinner in Bermuda – Mother, Carol, Aldine, Dad, Murray, Mary & Terry

it out. Dad never complained but we all worried. He did indeed die almost exactly three years from that date on June 1st, 1984.

It was a week of luxurious dining, scenic sightseeing, and late-night drinking—sometimes until 3:00 a.m.!

The last day was dampened by my brother's admission that he was in trouble with the Ontario Securities Commission, having been charged with defrauding investors of vast amounts of money. He was truly upset and sorry and we all were greatly saddened by this news. Eventually his problems were resolved—he had to pay a $1,500,000 fine over three years. As I say elsewhere in these chapters, *Barrons* magazine referred to him as "a Canadian gentleman of venturesome cast."

On June 9th we all returned to Toronto. The following day Mother, Dad and I flew to Tucson where we were met by Tony Sr. and Kent. Everyone fared well in my absence, but I had missed them!

38

⊙ॐ⊙

ALASKA

ABOARD THE *SUN PRINCESS* WITH MY PARENTS – 1981

Mixing business with pleasure, my parents and I attended a real estate course on a cruise ship in Alaska. I left our cottage in Canada on June 20th and flew to Vancouver, British Columbia where I met Mom and Dad who had flown there from Tucson. We immediately boarded our ship, the *Sun Princess*, for our cruise to Alaska.

I did manage to fit in a real estate class on our first day at sea amid trips to the gym, the bridge, and to see a film about Alaska. The captain had a cocktail party followed by dinner, a floor show and dancing–a nightly routine.

Juneau, the capital of Alaska, was our first port of call and there was time in the morning before we docked for Mother and me to attend

Aldine with her parents

a class. Later she and I left the ship to go to the Mendenhall Glacier and with a group of ten "shot the Mendenhall." There were occasional moments of excitement on the river but the scenery alone made the trip worthwhile. Dad, in the meantime, went on a flying tour to see glaciers.

Aldine with her mother at the Mendenhall Glacier

Glacier Bay, which we visited the following day, was spectacular in spite of mist and rain. Mom and I had to leave the deck, however, to attend real estate classes. What an inconvenience, but it was necessary for my mother and me to accrue 24 hours of real estate class credit every two years in order to maintain our licenses. Aboard a ship was a much nicer way to do it than attending Hogan's School of Real Estate in Tucson!

On June 25th we reached Ketchikan and that morning I took a three-hour walk with a very nice man I had met. Mom and Dad weren't up to that and I was delighted to have company. But it was back to reality in the afternoon when Mother and I attended more classes.

As the next day was at sea, the full day was taken up with real estate school. At least we were getting lots of hours toward our goal. Fortunately we didn't miss seeing the magnificent Misty Fjords as we entered it.

We couldn't believe that we were already back in Vancouver on June 27th where we took a bus tour of that very beautiful city. The following day we visited Vancouver Island and the city of Victoria which were accessible by ferry. We stayed in the famous old Empress Hotel where we had tea in the afternoon– one of the gracious daily events for which it is famous. Mother and I took a city tour.

I had long heard about the magnificent Butchart Gardens and was thrilled with our visit there the following day. I took many photographs of the flowers and made them into colorful note cards to give friends. Mom and I also visited the anthropological museum but didn't have sufficient time to do it justice. My diary used the word "fantastic" to describe it.

On June 29th our four-hour ferry trip back to Vancouver seemed like no time at all as the

Aldine's parents – Aldine & Murray Sinclair

weather was beautiful, as was the scenery. That night we boarded a train to begin our journey across Canada. The roll of the train made sleeping a delight but my mother wakened me early so that I would miss none of the gorgeous scenery through which we were passing. British Columbia was beautiful beyond description. We passed lovely forests and rivers, saw many deer, and were thrilled to at last see the Rocky Mountains which terminated near Banff.

Soon we were on the plains and eventually reached Calgary. We checked into the Sheraton Hotel and didn't have dinner until almost 11:00 p.m.—much too late for my parents. We had a short night as early the next morning we were picked up by friends of my parents and taken for breakfast to the rotating tower of the hotel, followed by a thorough tour of the city. We were impressed at how progressive and modern it was.

Again this trip had been more than my parents could handle and Dad was having bad asthma while Mother was miserable with sciatica. Still, we boarded a DC-10 later in the day to fly to Toronto where we met Tony who had just arrived at the airport having flown from Tucson. Murray also met us and, while he took our parents home to his place, Tony and I boarded a train that took us to Huntsville, the nearest town to our cottage on Lake of Bays.

There we were met by Kent who had done a wonderful job of preparing for our arrival. He informed us that Tony Jr. had finished summer school and made Bs in both physics and finance. He had worked hard to achieve this and was ready to come to the cottage later that week. We had a delightful few days alone with Kent whose company we enjoyed so much and who had worked hard at the cottage in our absence making significant improvements both inside and outside. A new summer in Ontario had begun!

THE ROCKY MOUNTAINS AND ABOARD THE *MAASDAM* WITH HAL–1998

Until I entered his life, Hal had not traveled a great deal. We always laughed over one experience he had the first time he came to visit me at the cottage in 1998. He had not been to Canada before and while driving he was listening to the radio. An announcer came on saying, "And now a bulletin from south of the border." Hal's first thought was, "Now what are those crazy Mexicans up to?" He quickly realized that it was the United States that was south of the border! Hal became a seasoned traveler.

In August of 1998 we had a fascinating trip that took us through western Canada and Alaska. We departed the cottage on August 20th and flew from Toronto to Calgary, Alberta arriving mid-morning–in time for a full day of sightseeing. It was a vibrant, modern city and left us both with a favorable impression.

Banff Springs in Alberta was our destination the next day. Surely it is one of the most beautiful places on earth—nestled in the Rocky Mountains. We took a tour of the area and stayed in the stately Banff Springs Hotel.

Hal & Aldine with Banff Springs Hotel in background

En route to Kamloops, British Columbia the following day, we made a stop at Lake Louise, known as one of the most beautiful sights in Canada. Then we took a magnificent drive through the Rocky Mountains stopping for lunch at Rogers Pass—again spectacular. We visited several national parks, one of which was Yoho National Park along the western slope of the continental divide. Another was Glacier National Park that has one of Canada's largest cave systems. We ended the day at Lac le Jeune near Kamloops, staying at an inn beside the lake–much of which is in the Lac le Jeune Provincial Park. We fell in love with this area and the wonderful people we met.

After a long walk beside the lake the next day, Hal and I left for Vancouver. We made many stops along the way and passed through several very long tunnels. We had lunch at Minter Garden reaching Vancouver late in the day.

444

Before departing on our cruise at 5:00 p.m. the following day, Hal and I spent many hours exploring Vancouver, a stately and elegant city. We walked for miles along the streets and surprised my nephew–Scott Sinclair–by dropping in to see him at his downtown office. Now we were ready and eager for our trip to Alaska, Hal's first time there, and headed for Canada Pier to embark on our ship, Holland America's *Maasdam*. It was beautiful.

Aldine & Hal – after shooting the Mendenhall

After a day at sea, we arrived in Juneau in teeming rain. Nonetheless, we took the Mendenhall white water trip and got thoroughly soaked. Even my rubber boots were full of water and my feet were in pain they were so cold! I noted in my diary that I was thoroughly miserable. Well, from my experience, occasional discomfort is just part of traveling.

Skagway was our port of call the next day and Hal and I exited the ship to take a long walk—the length of the town. Later we took a bus to the virtually abandoned gold rush town of Dyea. From there we hiked the first two miles of the historic and scenic Chilkoot Trail–a 33-mile trail that ends in Bennett, British Columbia. It had been a major access route from the coast to the Yukon goldfields in the late 1890s. The trail was very steep and a challenge for me, but I did it! Atrial fibrillation continued to be my nemesis. We went on from there to the Taiya River where we boarded an 18-foot raft to float down to Dyea. It was mighty cold!

We were at sea the next day and spent considerable time in Glacier Bay which was fascinating. It was a cold, rainy and windy day so we did most of our sightseeing from inside the ship.

Aldine & Hal at the Chilkoot Trail

We were lucky the following day to find the sun shining as we entered Ketchikan. After walking through the town, we went on a memorable five-hour adventure. We flew in a de Havilland Otter over mountains, valleys and fjords with amazing vistas of

445

Alaska. The pilot stayed as low as possible to afford us views of wildlife below. What excitement when we spotted mountain goats, bears and such!

Landing on Misty Fjords, which is about 40 miles east of Ketchikan, we transferred to a catamaran power boat to explore the fjords by water. The beauty left us breathless. We loved every minute of this excursion.

In the evenings on board ship we dined well and enjoyed floor shows. We danced every night—a favorite activity for Hal. We were impressed with every aspect of our shipboard experience. On the last evening aboard, the Captain had an "alumni" party for those of us who had sailed on this line previously. Years later, when I was traveling with Tana, I received a medallion for having taken 30 cruises. It was an easy way for me to travel and see the world.

On August 31st, Hal and I disembarked in Vancouver, checked into a beautiful hotel—the Waterfront Center Hotel—and took a long walk through Stanley Park along the waterfront. We followed that with an almost four-hour tour of the city. The next day we took the ferry to Victoria, had lunch at the Empress Hotel, and spent hours at Butchart Gardens where once again I took dozens of photographs. It was always such a magnificent place to visit. It was almost midnight before we arrived back in Vancouver and both of us felt ready for a good night's sleep.

The next day we had the long journey back to Toronto not arriving at the airport there until almost midnight. The following day we returned to our beloved cottage having been away for over two weeks. The first thing I did was call Kent and Tony Jr. All was well with them and their families in Tucson.

Hal was now hooked on travel—especially by cruise ship. We did it many more times.

ABOARD THE *SUN PRINCESS* WITH ALL MY GRANDCHILDREN – 2006

Every grandmother's dream is to have all of her grandchildren alone with her on a trip. My dream came true. Having taken Tana to Europe when she was 14 years old, I planned the same type of experience for my grandsons when they were old enough. The time had come—2006. Max was now 15 and Alex was 13. I should mention that I was then 73! The boys very kindly invited Tana—their cousin who was 18—to join us and they selected the destination—Alaska.

If I had been nervous about being responsible for Tana in Europe three years earlier, my worries were now trebled! I thought of all the things that could go wrong, but the moment I met them at the airport in Dallas I was off and running.

I had been at the cottage in Canada while the young people were still in Tucson. On July 1st I flew to Dallas and my first worry was over when we found each other after their flight arrived from Tucson. We flew on together to Seattle where we stayed in a strange hotel—Hawthorne Suites—with all of us in one room! It was cozy but fun and a good beginning to a magnificent trip together. Having traveled a circuitous route from Ontario to Seattle, I was mighty tired when I hit the bed that night.

On July 2nd we took a limousine to the pier and boarded our ship—the *Sun Princess*. The boys had a cabin next to the one Tana and I shared. Our first day on the cruise was spent at sea giving the young people a chance to explore the ship, work out in the gym, and enjoy their new independence. There was a formal dinner in the dining room that evening, followed by a party hosted by the ship's captain. Afterwards, the four of us enjoyed a riotously funny floor show. So far, so good.

At our first port of call—Ketchikan— we got up at 4:45 a.m. to be at the gangway at 6:10 a. m. to embark on a wonderful, fun excursion. The first part of it was a jeep safari through the mountains followed by a canoe trip on a lake. We stopped on the shore at the edge of the lake where we sat by a big bonfire, had soup, and drank hot chocolate. There was time for an interesting nature walk before we returned to the ship.

Alex, Max, Tana and Aldine – on our canoe trip

It was a gorgeous day in Ketchikan—unusual for that time of year. As it was the 4th of July, there was a parade that we were able to watch from the deck of our ship. It was a charming spectacle. Then Tana suggested that they "catch a tan in Ketchikan" and off they went to the swimming pool. We went to both a movie and a floor show that evening and I could tell that my young people were enjoying this whole experience immensely. That was a second concern assuaged.

How fortunate we were to have glorious, sunny weather again the next day. I arose very early to go on deck to see the magnificent Tracy Arm fjord. It was absolutely breathtaking with icebergs, glaciers and waterfalls dropping from majestic snow-covered mountains. I suspected the young people hadn't had much sleep the night before, but nonetheless I wakened them to witness this awesome spectacle—one they might never again have the opportunity to see. They were grateful—I think.

We sailed on to Juneau where we disembarked to join a group that was going to "shoot" the Mendenhall River–the run-off from glaciers. Hence, it was cold water. We climbed on a raft for the trip down the rapids, some mild and some quite substantial. Since my young people and I were at the front of the raft, we were quickly soaked from the spray and waves. I thought my feet would literally freeze as, in spite of wearing boots provided by the rafting company, my socks were soaked. My plight was recognized by a fellow passenger in the rear who took off his own socks to lend me so that my feet could heat up. How kind of him. I returned them to him, clean, later in our cruise.

We were wet, tired and cold when we returned to the ship at 7:00 p.m. that evening but we were ready for a gracious dinner at 7:30 p.m. It lasted until 9:15 p.m., a long time for young people to sit and be served course after course of food. I went to bed while they went to the "gym." They seemed to spend a lot of time at this gym and I wondered what other activities went along with their gym time! Fortunately, I trusted them completely and they all checked in when they went to bed. At least, I assumed they went to bed. Oh, the innocence of a trusting grandmother!

Skagway was our next port of call and our streak of good weather was over. It rained. However, a little shower wasn't going to alter our plans and we took a delightful narrow-gauge railway trip from Skagway to Fraser, British Columbia—a distance of 27.7 miles. The scenery was spectacular and the experience memorable.

When we returned to the ship Tana and I were ready for a nap while Max and Alex played ping-pong. Max skipped dinner that night as he wasn't feeling well but the rest of us dined together and went to a comedy show. We had a quiet evening with Max and Alex in their cabin, Tana doing a work-out in the gym and I, with a glass of wine, reading in the atrium. This down time was a welcome respite for us all. We had undertaken a busy trip indeed.

I noted in my diary the next day—which was spent at sea—that "The children won't remember this day fondly. They were all seasick." The ocean was very, very rough with our cabin window being underwater a good deal of the time. The boys spent the day in their cabin while Tana and I proceeded to have lunch and take a nap. All of us went to dinner followed by the captain's party. I noticed that the boys had eaten very little, but it turned out to be too much! We made a hasty retreat to our cabins but, with three children throwing-up and only two bathrooms, it was a disaster. Poor Alex had no choice but to vomit on the floor of their cabin and the stench was pretty awful.

Somehow we all ended up in my cabin with Alex, sure he was dying, lying on my lap. I knew well the misery of *mal de mer* having experienced it frequently on the Sea of Cortez, and my heart went out to them. A "hazmat" team in full regalia arrived for the clean-up of the boys' cabin, but nothing, absolutely nothing, would remove the smell of vomit. I pitied the passengers assigned to that cabin on the next cruise who would have to endure the odor.

The next morning we were told by our room steward, Bastin, that seas as high as we had endured the previous night were rare anywhere the ship traveled in the world. Well, one more of life's experiences for my young people.

That day we were at sea until we arrived in Victoria, British Columbia at 5:00 p.m. It was there that Tana experienced a life altering event. Excited that she could use her cell phone once again, she immediately phoned Tucson. I watched the color drain from her face when she received the tragic news that her dear friend Lacey had been killed in a car accident. Tana has never fully recovered from that shock and loss.

Tana needed time to herself while the boys and I had dinner. They ate heartily after their seasick event the previous night.

We arrived in Seattle the next morning and arose to find that our bathroom was flooded. We were relieved to leave the ship and take a tour of Seattle with a visit to the Space Needle. We checked into the Sixth Avenue Inn, again sharing one room. I was exhausted, but we walked a long distance to see a movie—*Superman Returns*—before closing up shop for the night.

The next day was long, difficult and emotional. Tana wanted desperately to be in Tucson for her friend's memorial service that day. She was inconsolable and I was terribly concerned about her. I was up at 2:30 a.m. to get ready to depart and then wakened the children. We were in the lobby before 4:30 a.m. awaiting the shuttle that would take us to the airport. It did not arrive until 5:10 a.m. and I remember being a nervous wreck. I doubted we would have time to make our flights. We were indeed the last people to board the aircraft. The plan was for all of us to go to the cottage in Canada, but Tana was able to get on standby to return to Tucson. She needed to be there for Lacey and her mother.

Because we were using American Airlines advantage mile tickets, we had to fly to their hub airport, Dallas. Tana went on to Tucson while the boys and I flew to Toronto. Darling Hal met us and drove us to the cottage; we arrived at 11:00 p.m. There was much excitement about being there and none of us got to bed until 2:00 a.m.—Hal and I separately, of course. We maintained proper protocol to model moral behavior for my grandsons. I had been up for almost 24 hours!

It had been a trip with many high points, and one very low point for Tana. I was grateful that everyone had enjoyed the adventure and come out of it unscathed. There are photographs of our various experiences on walls throughout the cottage which are reminders to me of a very special time in my life with my beloved grandchildren.

39

CR&O

CENTRAL MEXICO — THE GOLDEN CIRCLE OF CITIES — 1985

Mexico has magic, but no area more so than the golden circle of Mexico, mystical places with names like Guanajuato and Pátzcuaro. My classes at the university had terminated for the spring semester making it the perfect time to explore that region that had held my imagination captive for many years.

I embarked on this trip on May 17, 1985 with my friend Karl Pattison. We flew to Guadalajara, Jalisco for an overnight stop. After renting a Volkswagen Beetle the next day, we took a long and interesting drive to Guanajuato, in the state of Guanajuato. This city is located in the center of Mexico—northwest of Mexico City. The average altitude in this state is 6611 feet, so it was quite cool.

The next day, my diary records that "I had one of the most fascinating days of sightseeing of my life." We saw Indian dances in the city center (el centro), and visited a market place and several local mines. We attended a colorful fiesta at Mina Cata village. We returned to Guanajuato and discovered festivities going on in all parts of the city as we drove through the winding streets.

We spent three more full days in Guanajuato and every moment there was a treasure. We had breakfast at the famous Castillo de Santa Cecilia which we found magnificent but not gracious. We took a long drive on the high roads around the city and stopped at El Cubilete—a small mining village—and returned to Guanajuato visiting en route a huge, garish statue of Jesus on top of a mountain, Cristo del Rey. We put in a lot of miles that day.

As Karl wanted to make Guanajuato our headquarters, we took long day trips to other areas.

We left early the next day headed for San Miguel de Allende. Driving at high elevations, over 8000 feet in many places, we arrived in San Miguel in time for lunch at the famous Jacaranda Restaurant. We found the city to be charming, colorful and fascinating. It was a long and fulfilling day.

I was very distracted the following day, May 22nd, as Kent was having surgery on his leg in Billings, Montana where he and Janice were living. I was distraught that he was having yet another general anesthetic and would have to endure more pain. What a relief when I talked to him on the phone and heard that all had gone well.

One of the places we visited that day was the birthplace of Diego Rivera. This famous artist played a small part in Hal's life. His mother, Marion DeGrazia, and her well-known artist husband, Ted DeGrazia, frequently visited Diego Rivera and his wife Frida Kahlo at their home in Mexico City during the late 1940s. Marion, Ted, Frida and Diego were often a foursome over the years with some stormy and steamy time spent together. Years later we wanted to take Marion to see the movie *Frida* and she would have no part of it. She said she detested the woman!

Perhaps the most unusual and mystical place we visited in Guanajuato was the Museo de las Momias. During a cholera outbreak in this vicinity around 1833, a considerable number of bodies had been buried in a local cemetery. Between 1865 and 1958 a local tax was imposed requiring relatives to pay a fee to keep their family member interred. If they were unable or unwilling to pay the tax, the bodies were disinterred which is what occurred with nearly ninety percent of the remains.

It was discovered that about two percent of the bodies had become naturally mummified over time. These remains were stored in a nearby building and, in the 1900s, began attracting tourists. Cemetery workers charged visitors a few pesos to enter the building which was ultimately called El Museo de las Momias.

Due to the high frequency of deaths during the epidemic of cholera, many of the bodies were buried immediately to control the spread of the disease. It is thought that in some cases, the dying may have been buried alive by accident resulting in horrific facial expressions. One of these was Ignacia Aguilar. She suffered from a strange sickness that made her heart appear to stop. During one of these episodes, her family was convinced that she was dead and had her buried. When her body was disinterred, it was noticed that she was facing down, biting her arm, and there was a lot of blood in her mouth.

You may be sure that a lot of the mummies were in grotesque positions which made our visit there all the more eerie. Although a law was passed in 1958 that prohibited disinterring, this museum still exhibits the original mummies. You would have to see them to believe their excellent preservation. They seemed almost to be living, so real did they appear. There were hundreds of them, old and young, and it almost embarrassed me to look into their faces as they seemed to be looking back at me. Nonetheless, gross or not, this place had become one of the biggest tourist attractions in Mexico. It certainly was an experience I'll never forget.

Museo de las Momias - Guanajuato

Enduring heavy truck and bus traffic, we traveled to Morelia the next day. We had arranged to stay in a very beautiful hotel—Posada de la Soledad. Karl took one look and decided it was too fancy for his comfort. It became clear to me that Karl did not like big cities, so after touring Morelia we drove on to Querétaro in north-central Mexico—the capital of the free and sovereign state of Querétaro. It is one of Mexico's smallest states. As it was just another big city we continued on to Pátzcuaro, Michoacán. We both fell in love with it immediately and checked into the Hotel Los Escudos on the main square. We found it to be an unspoiled old colonial town with marvelous architecture.

Pátzcuaro sits on the southern edge of Lake Pátzcuaro, famous for its whitefish, and was founded in AD 1324. Since the Mexican Revolution, it has worked to maintain its colonial and indigenous look. Houses are made of adobe and/or wood and generally have tiled roofs.

Throughout this trip we had seen few tourists, and this was true in this city as well. Having done little shopping on this trip, we made up for it in this region. I bought fabrics, a painting I still love and local crafts. We drove to a high outlook—El Escribito—and on to the town of Santa Clara known for its fine copper ware. As I have been known to do on trips, I went on a shopping binge buying 12 large copper plates, vases, candlesticks, bowls, etc. I forgot that copper needs frequent attention to keep it shiny and rue to this day some of my purchases.

After breakfast on May 25th, we went down to the wharf to take a boat to the island of Janitzio on Lake Pátzcuaro, accessible only by water. On the highest point of the island stood a statue of José Marie Morelos, a hero during the time of the Mexican

Independence. It was accessible by climbing a long stairway. We were disappointed with the island so didn't stay long.

Later we visited the village of Tzintzuntzan on the north shore of Lake Pátzcuao known for its pyramids and unique festivals, the most significant of which was their annual celebration of the Day of the Dead. They also had well-made straw products.

I have a passion for primitive art, particularly indigenous ceramic statues and sculptures. Those of Michoacán were the most creative and colorful I had ever seen. Buying four of them was a whim I could not subdue, knowing full well that they would be very difficult to carry. I simply couldn't resist! Indeed, they were charming but when packed became large and heavy packages. As my diary said, "Now how to get them home?" I am so glad I managed it as having them to see and enjoy daily for lo! these many years has given me great pleasure. (In fact, I gave one to my sister who loves this sort of art almost as much as I. Hers was of *The Last Supper*.)

One that I kept was a delightful representation of eight Mexican cowboys, four on each side of the sculpture facing each other, engaged in a folk dance. Their elbows were out, heads lowered, and hands in front of them. My son Kent, who always had a vivid imagination and a quick wit, was quite right when, upon seeing it for the first time, commented that, "It looks like a bunch of guys having a pissing contest." I giggle every time I look at it.

We finished the day having a delicious dinner of the local whitefish for which Lake Pátzcuaro was so well known.

The following day Karl fell ill with *tourista* (surely not the result of the fish!) but soldiered on to fulfill the busy day we had planned. We drove to Uruapan for breakfast at the delightful El Paraiso. On to the famous Parícutin Volcano near the Tarascan town of Angahuan that is the closest village to the volcano. We walked for hours to reach the area covered by lava from the 1943 eruption of Parícutin. The lava covered every village in the area leaving only one building standing—a church which rose out of the bleak and barren sea of lava. It was an amazing sight. We found this whole area fascinating. It had been a hot and difficult walk and I was exhausted. The panacea for this fatigue was to drive on to Uruapan for ice cream and a lovely walk through the Parque Nacional.

We had loved our visit to these golden cities of Mexico but it was time to go home. Our last day, May 27th, required a tedious six-hour drive to Guadalajara with only one five-minute stop. We took time to drive around Lake Chapala to explore the American colonies such as Ajijic. We were not impressed.

After a night in Guadalajara, we flew to Tucson to be greeted at home by Tony and Tony Jr. who were eager to see all the items I had purchased and to hear about our adventures. I was eager for a report on Kent only to learn that he was still in considerable pain. Also, the previous week my mother had been in great discomfort from a bladder infection and had passed a kidney stone. As well, my niece Stephanie had had a miscarriage the previous day, and our housekeeper Marie had to have her gall bladder removed and would probably never work again. After 16 years working for us both full and part-time, we were saddened by this news. It was the end of an era. And nobody had taken care of the house the entire time I was away! Fortunately, my mother eased my path back into reality by taking Tony, Tony Jr., Carol, Terry and me to dinner at the Plankhouse that night.

The next day I celebrated my 52nd birthday.

40

THE ORIENT AND BEYOND — 1986

The orient was calling. I had long been captivated by the sibilant names of exotic places—names that roll off your tongue such as Cebu, Sabah and Sarawak. I was ready to yield to the seduction of the South China Sea.

While I rarely succumbed to the luxury of a semester of sabbatical leave, this seemed the time. It was the spring semester of 1986 and, having mentioned to my family my plan to take a trip, I suddenly found that I was to be joined by my mother, my sister-in-law Mary and my brother Murray. Mom was now 78 and I was 52 years old.

My mother and I left Tucson on January 11th to spend a few days in Vancouver en route. We visited there with her friend Margaret Ashley who made sure we saw everything of significance and beauty in that magnificent city. Not a stone was left unturned. We also had opportunities to see my nephew, Murray Jr., who had moved to Vancouver from Toronto. He and his lovely friend, Leann Wolfin, entertained us as did friends of theirs.

On January 14th we met Mary and Murray at the airport and flew on Cathay Pacific Airlines from Vancouver to Hong Kong. We spent our first day there visiting the Stanley Market, and Repulse Bay and taking a sampan ride to the floating village of Aberdeen. We drove up to Victoria Peak where the views were wonderful and took the tram line down. In the evening we met dear friends from Toronto for dinner—Marg and Don Donahue. Mary and I shopped late into the night!

On January 17th we embarked on our cruise ship—the *Pearl of Scandinavia*. Our first port of call was Canton, China—now known as Guangzhou. We took a bus trip from eight in the morning until six at night passing through incredibly depressed and depressing areas. It seemed obscene to have a 12-course meal for lunch while the local people were going hungry. It was a memorable day complete with time for shopping.

Mary, Aldine & Murray at dinner on the ship

We spent two days at sea before reaching Manila arriving at 6:00 p.m. which gave us time to go ashore for sightseeing and drinks at the gorgeous Manila Hotel. The following day we took a long trip to Pagsanhan Falls—one of the most famous falls in the Philippines. We were taken in canoes up the Pagsanhan River through many rapids to the falls—a two hour trip. The return was much faster as we were going with the rapids rather than against them. The scenery was tropical and mystical.

We had another day at sea before arriving in Cebu on January 23rd at 7:00 a.m. Cebu is an island in the Philippines. Mother and I walked into Cebu City and realized that this was not a safe place for two women alone. We

Mother & Aldine – canoe trip on Pagsanhan River

hired a guide and taxi for the rest of the day and visited many fascinating places. We saw a cross left there by Magellan, the Santa Niño Church, a century-old home that had been converted to a museum, the university museum, the market place, and a Taoist temple where Mother and I "spoke with God." I note in my diary that Mary and I stayed up until 1:00 a.m. that night dancing with the ship's officers.

Yet another day at sea before arriving in Kota Kinabalu, Malaysia where we visited the city with its enormous contrast of wealth and poverty. We joined Mary and Murray for lunch at a gorgeous hotel. Mother and I continued our sightseeing and returned to the ship ready to sail for Borneo.

Aldine in Kampong Ayer, Brunei

On January 26th we reached Brunei, a beautiful and very wealthy country. The four of us took a four-hour bus tour visiting an excellent museum in Bandar Seri Begawan, the main city. We walked through an incredible village on stilts—Kampong Ayre. It is a water village over Brunei Bay. We then viewed the awe-inspiring billion dollar residence of the Sultan of Brunei. We were fascinated with Borneo and visited both Sabah and Sarawak, two Malaysian states on the island of Borneo.

We had two days at sea before reaching Bangkok where we disembarked. Our four days in Thailand were fascinating and very varied in scenery and activity. The first day we acquainted ourselves with this city through a bus tour that stopped for a long visit at the Royal Palace and the Chapel of the Emerald Buddha. Mother and I checked into the lovely Hilton Hotel while Mary and Murray stayed at the Oriental—the loveliest hotel in Bangkok. We were on different budgets. We joined them for a wonderful Thai dinner and a performance of Thai dancers.

Mother & Aldine in Bangkok

The following day Mother and I were up and ready to go. It was a wonderful day. We took a bus through the countryside and a boat ride that took us through canals to the floating market at Damnoen Saduak. On for a visit to the world's tallest stupa (pagoda) at Nakhon Pathom and later lunch at the Rose Garden—a floating restaurant. After lunch we attended a very colorful Thai show.

After taking Mary and Murray out for dinner that night, we returned to our hotels in Bangkok. Rather late, I had a telephone call from Mary. Frantic, she told me she thought she had just been raped and begged me to come to her hotel. I grabbed my passport, said a fleeting goodbye to my mother and ran to the street. There I hailed a tuk-tuk and after a wild ride to the Oriental met a very upset Mary. (A tuk-tuk is a motorized version of the traditional pulled rickshaw.)

She explained that she had gone to the spa for a massage. The masseuse did a wonderful job until the finale when she climbed on Mary's back. Mary soon realized the woman was not wearing underwear. The massage continued but rather than using her supple hands she used her genitals. Up and down. Up and down. Mary was horrified and managed to extricate herself, pay the woman and flee—to call me! I sensed that this was not the emergency I had anticipated and tried to get Mary to calm down. Mary absolutely insisted that I have a massage to verify that she was not just imagining the whole episode. I have had a good many friends who have had massages in Bangkok and I didn't doubt for a moment any part of her story. Still, to placate her, I had a massage—and I don't even like massages! Suffice that Mary's considerable beauty had put her at risk while my massage was *de rigueur*. Her angst assuaged, Mary went off for a good night's sleep. I still had to hazard yet another harrowing tuk-tuk ride through downtown Bangkok at night to get back to my hotel!

On our last day in Bangkok, Mother and I hired a "fast boat" and had a fantastic ride through the khlongs (canals). Bangkok was crisscrossed by khlongs and so had gained the nickname, *Venice of the East*.

We had loved this colorful visit to an incredible country, but it was time to go home. We flew to Hong Kong for the night. The following day, February 2nd, we had time to pick up the ultra-suede suits and coats we had ordered on our previous visit before going to the airport for our flight back to Vancouver.

Mary ran into trouble at customs in Vancouver. She had taken with her to Asia her lovely jade jewelry that she had purchased on a previous trip to Hong Kong. Mary has very beautiful and expensive jewelry. In checking her baggage, the customs officer found the jade jewelry and asked for the sales receipt. Of course she didn't have one and explained that this was old jewelry that she had taken with her on the trip. During this interrogation, Mother and I had to leave to catch our plane to Los Angeles and then to Tucson. We later learned that Mary was unconvincing and was charged duty on her own expensive jade!

Tony met us at the airport; I was thrilled to be home and with him again. Little did we know then that on March 4th—only one month hence–Tony would receive the diagnosis of mesothelioma, a lethal cancer. Our days of *joie de vivre* were coming to an end.

Later I wrote in my diary "Spring has been a blur of Tony's incredible valor, strength, dignity and of my unbelievable pain, heartbreak and love for him."

41

CRID

SOUTH AMERICA WITH MY MOTHER—1989

Everyone handles grief differently. My approach was unconventional but effective. I fled. My home was unbearably lonely without Tony who died on January 8, 1989 at age 62. I was 55 and a widow. I was bereft. The thought of the months ahead in adjusting to a life without my love was unimaginable.

Having taken a year's leave of absence from UA, I did not need to return to work until August. I wanted to get away, as far as I could. Somehow, I thought this would assuage my unfathomable grief. I decided to go south. Argentina looked like a good destination. My mother, then 80 years old, asked if she might go with me. I welcomed her company.

Although I had known for three years that Tony's illness was terminal—mesothelioma—I never accepted the reality of his dying. It came as a shock to me and I was in no way prepared for it. Having made no plans for what was ahead for me, it took some pretty fancy footwork to pull this trip together as quickly as we did. With passports in order and dogs arranged for, we departed Tucson on January 25th, a mere two and a half weeks after Tony's passing.

Our flight to Buenos Aires seemed interminable. We flew first to Phoenix where we had a long wait. Our next flight was to Atlanta with another long wait. Finally in Miami we were told that our flight was oversold and we had to go on standby. It was now late and we were exhausted. There was a solution however—first class. We bit the bullet and enjoyed a delightful flight to Buenos Aires arriving at our hotel, the Sheraton—at 1:30 p.m.! We had been traveling for 23 hours.

I note in my diary that I was excited to be in Buenos Aires but that so much sadness had come with me. I was missing Tony terribly and noted that my grief was less easily managed when I was tired. In other words, I was a blubbery mess.

The following day we took a four-hour city tour. I remember being surprised at the simple grave of Eva Perón. I had anticipated something grander for the woman who was the first lady of Argentina from 1946 until she died in 1952.

Later in the day I bought two items—a red cashmere sweater and a red poncho. Even 27 years later they are in perfect condition and I wear them frequently. Mother and I were joining a group to take a cruise and met with our fellow travelers that evening. We even attended a tango show at Casa Blanca; my mother was game for anything!

On January 28th we boarded the *Ocean Princess*, a small ship of only 12,000 tons. January 29th, the three-week anniversary of Tony's death, caught me off guard and I was inconsolable. I realized how grateful I was to have my mother by my side. The following day we docked in Montevideo, Uruguay. There we took the city tour and enjoyed the lovely people and the many activities available to us.

We were quite surprised with our port of call the next day—Mar del Plata, Argentina. We had never heard of it, yet it is a major fishing port and is the biggest seaside beach resort in Argentina. The beaches were gorgeous and its people delightful. While my mother had a nap in the afternoon, I went swimming at one of the beaches. The swimmers were scantily clad and the sun was strong. We had a busy evening that kept us up until 2:00 a.m. I am sure no one would have known I was a grieving widow but if they had caught me in my moments of solitude they would have had no doubt. I noted in my diary on February 1st that "I was awake almost

Mother & Aldine

all night reliving Tony's death, grieving, silent weeping." I wondered if it was any better being away than it would have been had I remained home.

We spent the next two days at sea. Mother kept me busy—classical guitar concerts, fashion shows, floor shows, movies and midnight buffets.

Mother & Aldine

On February 2nd we moored off Florianopolis, Brazil, a city with 42 beaches. It also is the surfing mecca for that region. It was necessary to take a 30-minute ride in a tender to reach shore, and another 30 minutes on a bus to arrive in the town. The weather was lovely and the views magnificent. Still, we were glad to return to our cabin on the ship.

The following day we reached Santos—the largest seaport in South America. There we took a funicular to the top of a hill for incredible views. Any other time I would be enjoying every moment of this cruise. However, as noted in my diary "I am ready to go home. Miss my boys and Tana. Need roots. Somewhat depressed. My life has been only Tony for over three years, and I don't know what I am going to do without him." (Tana was almost eight months old at that time.)

Rio de Janeiro was our final destination. We were there for several days and they were memorable as this was the time of *Carnival*. Although the prospect of trusting my life to the cable cars dismayed me, we nonetheless took a trip up to Sugar Loaf Mountain. It was magnificent and the views truly breathtaking. That night we enjoyed an evening out—from 8:00 p.m. until 1:00 in the morning! We had dinner at a sumptuous restaurant and watched a samba show.

We had been fortunate to meet two lovely gentlemen on board the ship, Richard Corcoran and Robert Blackwell, who were delighted to escort us on all these outings. I stayed in touch with both of them until their deaths.

The next day was the 4th week since Tony had died. Although I wasn't in tears quite as much, I noted that I was desperately sad. Mother's birthday was approaching and I knew exactly what she would like for a gift. She had long mentioned how very much she would enjoy having an aquamarine ring. So we headed for H. Stern and she found her heart's delight—the perfect ring. She wore it daily the rest of her life and now I wear it with happy memories of my lovely mother.

Attending *Carnival* was a daunting experience. Rio is an incredibly dangerous city at all times   but during *Carnival* it goes crazy. No one goes to work that week and all conventionality is abandoned. People become crazed animals. We were warned again and again about the danger on the streets at this time. Rio has charm but it lacks dignity. Men thought nothing of urinating against a wall on the street. Graffiti was rampant and disgusting.

Rio's *Carnival* is considered the biggest in the world with two million people in the streets every day. This festival that precedes Lent began in Rio in 1723.

Prior to going to the big event—the parade– at 7:00 p.m., we were issued tee-shirts; everyone had to wear them before they were allowed to leave the ship. They were for identification and security. We were taken from the ship to waiting buses by armed guards who accompanied us to the Sambadrome where the Carnival parade took place.

When we arrived at the stadium, locked gates were opened to allow the bus to enter. We were in a cage. When the gates behind us were locked, a new set of gates was opened. The security was amazing. Were one to have to go to the bathroom one was escorted by an armed guard.

The parade is made up of samba schools—groups of people who represent a neighborhood or other social group. There is a theme each year that influences the way floats are decorated. A full year is spent on preparing the floats.

The performance goes on for 24 hours and is a spectacle that defies description. The people of Rio, no matter what their economic level, spend a year preparing their costumes and floats which are opulent and original beyond imagining. We were told that people allowed their children to go hungry in order to save money for *Carnival*—the most important time of their year. They live for it.

And they die for it. While my mother and I were there we saw at least one death occur before us, possibly two. The floats are built to be very high with curvaceous beautiful women in magnificent costumes adorning every inch of them. Typically there was one stunning young lady at the top of each float and we could see that all of them appeared to be on very precarious perches. While sumptuous and glittery,

The parade – Carnival in Rio

the floats were not well built and often could not sustain the weight on the top level. We witnessed one young woman fall many feet to her death. A cart came along, picked up her body, and left the arena. The parade continued as if nothing had happened! We saw a second such incident, but we thought, and hoped, that the girl might still have

464

been alive. I understand there are as many as two dozen deaths associated with the parade annually.

As I say, the city goes insane at this time. No one works, not even taxi drivers. Everyone is participating in *Carnival*.

Usually the stands are packed for every minute of the 24 hours of parade. We, however, returned to the ship at a reasonable hour as my mother's back was hurting from sitting on the concrete seats. It was to be our last night on the ship. We were packed and had placed our suitcases outside the cabin at the appointed time as we were disembarking early the following morning. In the middle of the night my mother, in a cold sweat, awakened and gasped, "I packed my passport in my suitcase!" We knew we were in serious trouble as the American Embassy would be closed for the week and there wasn't a hotel room available in all of Rio. We absolutely had to leave as scheduled. Mother was so upset that she ran in the bathroom and threw up.

Suddenly I had a thought. With so little attention to responsibility at this time, maybe the suitcases had not yet been collected. And there they were, outside our cabin door. We retrieved them having had the scare of our lives.

The next day we left the ship and were taken on a very beautiful drive through the Brazilian countryside. We spent a lovely day visiting charming towns—Petropolis and Teresopolis. We returned to Rio at 6:00 p.m. and were dropped off at the Copacabana Club for drinks and dinner. Our flight was not due to depart until 1:00 a.m. so we had ample time to relax and enjoy the company of two Brazilians whom we had met. We managed to communicate through their Portuguese and my Spanish.

We were taken to the airport at 9:30 p.m., the beginning of a nightmare that still leaves me trembling. The ensuing events were terrifying in the extreme. The roads to the airport were empty of traffic. We entered the terminal to find there were no agents—none whatever. The place was deserted. There appeared to be no other flights departing this late. We were taken by our tour guide through long, dark empty corridors to our waiting area. Hours went by. The passengers for this flight were sitting ducks—absolutely, unequivocally vulnerable. One o'clock came, then two o'clock. It was dark and scary. No flight crew was in evidence.

There was no option to return to the city. We would have no protection whatever getting to the highway and then there would be no taxis. We were stuck and frightened. Finally at 3:00 a.m. the flight crew from hell arrived. They were red-eyed and drunk. At no time in my life would I have boarded a flight with that motley group. I weighed whether I would rather die in Rio—the victim of violence—or in the air in that aircraft. It was a tough decision.

Going forward seemed the best option. We boarded a plane that should have been in a museum—a very old and tired DC-8 with linoleum floors and seats turned this way and that. My seat belt refused to buckle and the interior was filthy. There was no service whatever. No water. No food. The crew was surly as well as inebriated. I got my mother settled across three seats so that she could elevate her very swollen ankles. This was her 81st birthday—February 7th—and she was exhausted. Bear in mind that we had left the ship early in the morning and had no opportunity to rest all day.

The plane finally took off at 3:30 a.m. en route to Miami where we arrived three hours late—but miracle of miracles, we did arrive. We had missed our connecting flight so did some rapid rescheduling to St. Louis, Phoenix and ultimately Tucson where Tony and Elizabeth met us at 8:00 p.m.—midnight our time. I don't know how long we were traveling but I think it was about 40 hours. It seemed interminable.

I anticipated going home to bed but found that I had a visitor—Wini Kirk—who stayed for two hours to chat. By the time I could finally lay my head on a pillow, I couldn't sleep. My body and brain knew not what day it was much less what time!

I was home. The emptiness of the house overwhelmed me with sadness. My indomitable mother, however, carried on with her unfailing enthusiasm for life and invited Carol and me for drinks on our first night home. She certainly did set the bar high!

I have visited most South American countries now except Paraguay. Each is distinctive. I have also been to all the countries of Central America with the exception of El Salvador.

42

CR&O

AUSTRALIA AND ASIA—1989

Having been in Tucson for a month since returning from South America and a respite from my loneliness, I felt ready to escape once again. I had already gone as far south as was reasonable so I decided that this time I would head west. Australia sounded just right. In the year following my husband Tony's death, I traveled to six of the seven continents.

I departed Tucson on Thursday, March 9, 1989 to fly to Los Angeles and from there on a Qantas 747 to Cairns, Australia. As I was in business class, I had to climb stairs to get to the top level where my seat was located. To my embarrassment, I tripped on the top step—quite by accident, I swear. Who was there to catch me but the plane's captain. He asked me where I was going. I thought this was quite amusing as he, of everyone aboard, should certainly know where we were going—and I told him Cairns. I pronounced it as I read it. He found that delightful and said, "Oh, that's how you say it." I learned quickly that it is pronounced "cans" as in tin cans. We chatted and I mentioned I was a pilot. He saw me to my seat.

Before take-off I was approached by an attractive young blonde woman who told me that the captain requested my presence in the cockpit. So forward I went, astounded by how high off the ground we were, and was strapped in securely for take-off. Now, ordinarily I would have loved this opportunity, but either they forgot I was there or they thought I was having too good a time to want to leave. In fact, I had paid a princely sum for business class and was eager to return to my seat and the comforts it had to offer. Finally I thanked them profusely and got myself untethered.

Sometime later, the young blonde woman came through the cabin to check with the passengers to assure that they were comfortable. Most gave her cursory attention at best. They thought she was a flight attendant while I knew differently. She was the first-officer! I have to admit she looked very tiny in right seat in the cockpit.

We arrived in Cairns early in the morning on Saturday; I had lost Friday completely. I was joining a group of 21 people for an exciting itinerary—a trip I had dreamed of for years. We congregated that evening for dinner. I was so pleased to meet my new mates. Early Sunday morning we met to embark on a spectacular journey. In Cairns we boarded a train; the railway line was a hundred years old. We traveled into the mountains to Kuranda seeing waterfalls and magnificent scenery along the way. Our destination was the Great Dividing Range that separates the tropics and the outback. It is the third longest mountain range in the world. The views were breathtaking.

Visiting the Great Barrier Reef was another highlight. We were taken by boat for a several-hour trip to the outer reef which included time for the group to snorkel. What an amazing experience! Later I went snorkeling by myself. I note in my diary that "it would be so wonderful if Tony were with me as he'd love this." I continued to miss him terribly.

Nevil Shute (a pen name) was for many years my favorite author. He was an English novelist and an aeronautical engineer who spent his later years in Australia. I have collected every book he wrote. While I loved them all, *A Town Like Alice* was at the top of the list. I had longed someday to visit Alice Springs, then a town of 25,000 inhabitants with four traffic signals. My group and I flew to Alice Springs, which is in the center of Australia, where we went to Anzac Hill with its magnificent views. We visited many places that had previously been just images in my mind. They included the old overland telegraph station, the Alice Springs well and the flying doctor's museum. I was entranced with it all.

It was very cold the next day. We were taken by bus into the outback where groups of Aboriginals live. They weren't cold. They condescended to putting clothes on, as they were prepared for our visit, but typically they lived naked year round. We were taught how to throw a boomerang; I never did get the hang of it.

Visiting an Aboriginal camp

468

They showed us how to cook lizards and witchetty bugs—grubs from rotten trees that are a great delicacy to them and a source of oil which they need in their diet. Some are as long as six inches; I ate one. Not bad at all! We were there for almost three hours and no one wanted to leave. But the cold and rain were penetrating and it was time to go. I have since done considerable reading about this culture and am mesmerized by their nomadic way of life.

Off to the airport where we were flown to Yulara and driven on to Ayers Rock (pronounced "ez"). There we were given the opportunity to climb this phenomenal sandstone rock formation that is one of the most recognized landmarks in Australia. I found it tough going. We viewed it at sunset, champagne in hand, struck by its magnificence as the light on it changed as the sun went down turning it various shades of red. We were there several days before flying to Sydney.

My mother had wanted to come with me on this trip but had not been feeling well after our recent return from South America. I discouraged her as she was now 81 years old and it is a long flight to Australia. She was not to be put off. Finally she was cleared by her doctors to travel and immediately made plans to fly to Sydney to join me.

When I arrived in Sydney my mother was already in our hotel room having arrived early that morning. She was unfazed by the trip and asked where we were going for dinner! We had ample time in Sydney to take city and harbor cruises and enjoy the beauty.

Our special table on the ship

On March 18th we boarded our cruise ship for the next almost three weeks—the *Royal Viking Sea*, a favorite ship of ours from the past. We were seated for dinner at a table for seven and I don't ever remember being with a group for that length of time that I enjoyed as much. We laughed and chatted and became very close. I think we were the envy of the dining room as we were having such a good time together.

One couple, Josie and Jack Zamel, were Australian. Jack had been raised by an immigrant widowed mother from Lithuania. They were very poor and Jack had no prospects for an education. His mother knew no English. But she had dreams for her son whom she knew to be brilliant and who had always said he would love to be a doctor. Unknown to him, this determined woman obtained the application forms for the University of Sydney and, with help, completed and submitted them. One day a letter came for Jack which bewildered him. He was a laborer and not used to receiving mail. Imagine his surprise to find in the envelope a letter admitting him to medical school with full tuition!

Jack went on to become a very successful doctor. He was the head of the team that developed the first sleep apnea machine to assist with breathing at night. He ultimately worked for the Nera Corporation and was highly regarded in the medical research field.

It was Jack who taught me a bit of Australian. I often had difficulty understanding what he said because of his heavy Australian accent. While on deck one day, he said to me, "It looks as if we're in for a "rine share." I finally "got" it—a rain shower!

Another couple at our table, Lisa and Steve Schmidt were unmarried at the time and enjoying life. They had no money worries and were seeing the world. They became quite chummy with many of the more affluent guests on board such as the Pulitzer and the Bacardi families. I am still in touch with the Schmidt family every Christmas. Ted Bell was our seventh table companion.

In Canada that summer I had visits from both the Zamels and Lisa and Steve. The latter couple had a kayak tied on the roof of their car and had just come from a visit with the Bacardis on their island in the Caribbean.

Our first port of call was Hobart, Tasmania where we took tours and saw Tasmanian devils, koalas and kangaroos. Afternoon tea was served to the wailings of a bagpipe band. Mother was definitely not feeling well, and a visit to the ship's doctor and a prescription for antibiotics were necessary. I was awake the entire night assuring myself she was breathing.

After a day at sea we reached Melbourne, took the appropriate tours, and set sail for Perth, Australia—a four day trip at sea. Perth is the furthest western major city in the country. The driving distance between Melbourne and Perth is 2126 miles and I am told that in taking the train one traverses one stretch–300 miles in length– that is without a bend or a curve.

It was now March 28th, Kent's 34th birthday and my first wedding anniversary without Tony. I was very weepy. Upon returning to my cabin after lunch I found the most enormous bouquet of flowers arranged for by Kent and Janice, Tony and Elizabeth. I was deeply touched and went to the bow of the ship and cried my eyes out with gratitude and with sadness.

Aldine with the Balinese dancers

After spending many days at sea, Bali was our next port of call. This lovely island easily convinced us that the glowing reports one hears of Bali are justified. It is very beautiful as are its women. I was photographed with a group of gorgeous and graceful Balinese dancers and I must say I felt like a duck among swans!

Singapore, which I had looked forward to visiting very much, was our next port of call. Its rigid code of conduct was infused in us before we left the ship. If one so much as spat on the street one would go to jail. Drugs were anathema. We all behaved ourselves and admitted that their strict rules worked. It was as clean and orderly a place as I have ever seen.

Mother had made steady improvement as the days went by but I think this trip was hard on her.

On to Hong Kong where we spent several days shopping, sightseeing and having dinner with the Zamels and the Schmidts. We knew then that the friendships would continue.

On April 11th I had been away from Tucson for five weeks (and had gained ten pounds.) It was time to go home. We flew from Hong Kong to Tucson via San Francisco. Tony Jr. met us at the airport and that evening Mother had the whole family for drinks!! Now 11 months old, Tana was walking! I had been gone too long, and I knew I had to settle down and adapt to my new life alone. It wasn't easy.

43

❦

SAFARI IN KENYA AND ADVENTURES IN PARIS—1990

In 1990, my intrepid mother announced to me that she was not going to die before she had seen Paris and gone on safari. Mother didn't mince words; she meant it. Hence, I thought I'd better get a move on as she was then 82 years old. I can't believe the enthusiasm and energy she exuded throughout this unforgettable trip.

I must preface this story with my own disability at that time. On May 1st I had delicate reconstructive foot surgery at the Mayo Clinic in Scottsdale. The surgeon was Dr. Kenneth Johnson, renowned throughout the world as the ultimate foot surgeon. He had written the seminal book on foot surgery. Well, every doctor has a right to blow it occasionally. He did with me. I am still dealing with the fallout from the errors he made. Doctors in Tucson who see me can't believe that this icon created the disaster my foot has become. There is a chapter in his book entitled *Surgical Cripples;* I should have been cited!

I attempted to return to see Dr. Johnson only to learn that he had died in a plane crash. He was another of my surgeons who bought a light twin engine aircraft and pranged while learning to fly it.

I had finished the semester at the university and flown to Toronto on May 15th in a foot cast. I noted in my diary that I was so exhausted I fell asleep in the bathtub at Mary and Murray's house where I was staying.

The next day I drove to the cottage. It was cold and windy that year and I was very much looking forward to joining my mother in Paris on May 21st. She flew from Tucson and our plan was to meet at our hotel in Paris—Hotel Castiglione. She was to have taken a taxi from the Paris airport, and I became quite frantic when she didn't arrive when I expected her. Alas, her plane was two hours late in arriving, but I had no way of knowing this. Think of it, the woman was 82 and had flown from the southwest in the U.S. to Paris in one hop!

Mother arrived and as I noted in my diary, "looking elegant and full of vigor. Amazing!" After dressing for dinner, we walked to Place Concorde and on to Hotel Crillon for a drink. We returned to the hotel for dinner and our welcome beds. Mother was less tired than I!

Not wanting to miss a beat, we were up early the next day for our bus trip to Versailles, my mother's first visit there. It was all she had dreamed it would be, and more. I was thrilled to see her so happy. Unfortunately, Mother twisted her hip getting out of the bus and developed sciatica. We returned to Paris and went to the Eiffel Tower for dinner and on to the Folies Bergère which lasted from nine o'clock to midnight. It seemed to take forever to get back to the hotel and then neither of us could sleep!

After perhaps two hours of sleep, we were up at 6:00 a.m. for a fourteen hour trip to chateau country. We visited Chateau de Blois and had lunch at a lovely restaurant on the outskirts of Tours. We continued to the magnificent Chateau de Chenonceau. There was a lot of walking and stair climbing at Chambord, so Mother remained on the bus to rest her hip. I couldn't believe the pace this woman was keeping. We also saw, but did not stop in, Chaumont, Amboise and Cheverny. It was nine o'clock before we got back to Paris and Mother was ready for dinner!

We were up again early on May 25th to take a wonderful tour of the sights of Paris. The Louvre and seeing the Mona Lisa was a thrill for Mother as she had dreamed of having this experience all her life. We also spent time in Notre Dame, but it was difficult for both of us to walk long distances. Mother never complained about the pain she was enduring with sciatica, but then, I don't ever remember her complaining about anything ever!

At 8:30 that night we took a taxi to De Gaulle Airport and flew Air France to Nairobi, departing at midnight. We had dreadful seats in the windowless front of a jumbo jet. On my right was a large bearded man in extremely dirty casual clothing. An enormous dog lay on his lap but seemed to prefer mine.

We endured this trying flight arriving in Nairobi at 8:30 in the morning. I had decided that if we were going on safari it was going to be the best—Abercrombie and Kent. Also, it was a flying safari so we wouldn't spend a lot of time on bumpy dirt roads. We were met by their agent and taken to the Safari Club Hotel. By this time, my foot, still swathed in bandages, was swollen and Mother admitted to being a "wee bit tired." Hence, we took the remainder of the day off.

By morning we were eager to meet with our guide, Humphrey Meme, and the other seven guests in our group. Our first destination was a visit to the home of Karen Blixen which is exactly as it is described in so many books about her. Absolutely charming! One couple was so unpleasant (always keeping us waiting while they "made out" in covert locations) that they were soon dismissed from the group and now we were a party of seven for the remainder of the safari.

Mother in front of Karen Blixen's house

Mr. Kent, of Abercrombie and Kent, invited us to his home for drinks and later took three of us on to Tamarind for dinner. (My understanding was that there never had been an Abercrombie involved in the tour outfit. Mr. Kent simply thought it added a certain panache to the name of his company and tacked it on.) It was an exciting day for me—full of firsts.

Elephants at Ambroseli

We were up early the next day to depart from the airport at 6:30 a.m. to fly to Ambroseli Reserve. Without delay, we were picked up to go in jeeps looking for animals. We were very lucky as we saw lots of elephants very close to us, watering their babies. There were a great many zebras and wildebeests, some not ten feet away. I was quite overwhelmed.

We returned to our hotel, Ambroseli Serena Lodge, for lunch, a rest, and a swim. At 4:00 p.m. we reassembled and did another run–this time seeing a cheetah, baboons and impalas. We were back in time to see Mt. Kilimanjaro at sunset. It was magnificent. We spent the evening dining and watching others dance. I was shackled in my cast.

On May 29th I turned 57 years of age. I had been a widow for two years and during that period of time had visited six of the seven continents. I never made it to Antarctica. We were up at 5:15 a.m. that morning to go on an early game run. A rhinoceros crossed right in front of our van. Exciting! Back to the hotel for postcard writing and lunch. There was time to sit by the pool before our next sojourn into the bush at four o'clock.

Before dinner I was able to climb a little hill for another look at Mt. Kilimanjaro. It was known that it was my birthday so there was added gaiety that evening and Mother and I drank much too much. Not a good idea. We did not sleep well.

Ready or not, Wednesday found us up early needing to pack and leave for the airport at 7:30 a.m. to fly to Nyeri. There, we took a van to the magnificent Aberdare Country Club. Mother had a headache and didn't feel well. She skipped lunch. Nonetheless, off we went again at 2:15 p.m. to drive to The Ark, our next stop. It was a fascinating, lush, very basic inn located at an elevation of 7500 feet.

Mother became very ill, as did half of our group. I was terribly worried as we were in the wilderness with no medical help and she was in bad shape with serious stomach flu. I did the best I could for her, and never left her side. We had open areas that served as windows in our room and elephants wandered by. Mother missed all of this.

In the morning, more members of our group were ill. However, we had to move on to the Nyeri Airport to take our plane to Samburu. Mother and I liked it there immediately as it is so much like Southern Arizona at 3200 feet. While Mother was better, she spent most of the day in bed and had only soup for dinner. I went on the game drive and saw beautiful desert terrain as well as baboons, elephants, giraffes, zebras and several kinds of impalas.

Both Mother and I felt much better the following day—I having fallen victim to the bug as well. Everyone in our group had been ill. We took a long, dusty and very bumpy drive through beautiful countryside arriving at The Mount Kenya Safari Club at 12:30 p.m. My diary reminds me that it was "magnificent beyond description." We had our own lovely cottage with a fire going in the fireplace at all times. Although we were on the equator, we were at 7000 feet and it was cold. The grounds were gorgeous. A magnificent dinner with many courses was served at eight o'clock.

Another thrilling experience for me the next day was joining a young woman I had met for a horseback ride up Mount Kenya. It was incredibly beautiful as we rode higher and higher. There were just the two of us and I admit to having felt a degree of discomfort at being in a wilderness area with which I was totally unfamiliar. My friend, Pat Rechnich, seemed at ease and knew the terrain so I settled down and put my life in her hands. We didn't get back to the lodge until after dark. My mother was pacing the floor and definitely not happy with me. In my haste to join her for dinner, I bumped my injured foot which commenced to bleed copiously. I was quite scared that I had done it serious injury. (Oh dear, might this have accounted for Dr. Johnson's regrettable failure with my surgery?)

Aldine with her mother at the equator

Following an early breakfast the next day, we went by van to the equator. There was, of course, the demonstration of water circulating different directions on either side of the equator. I had been on the equator in Ecuador in 1976 as well. Still, it continued to fascinate me.

We flew from the Nanyuki airport in a twin Otter to Maasai Mara over beautiful countryside—the Aberdare Mountains and Rift Valley. We were delighted with our accommodations, a large tent at Kichwa Tembo (Elephant Head) Camp. We were intrigued with their hot water system. They placed big drums outside our tents under which a fire was kept lit until the water became hot. Then the fires were allowed to die out and we enjoyed the hot water only if we were there for it or if there was enough left. But we were on safari and didn't expect all the comforts of home.

Mother was certainly back to her spunky self. We were assured that on the afternoon game run we would see lions. Strict rules were given—stay absolutely quiet and do not put any part of your body outside the jeep. Our private group was small so this shouldn't have been a problem.

Indeed we did come upon three huge male lions and because the guide deemed that they had recently eaten and appeared lethargic it was safe to drive right up beside them. As I say in my diary, "we were cheek to cheek."

Now, mind you, we were in an open jeep. There were no windows and only a tarp for a roof. What a wonderful opportunity for photos. We all were in thrall and remained very, very quiet.

My mother wears a large gold family ring occasionally. On this day she had it on her finger. Who could have known what my darling and

"Cheek to cheek" with a lion

energetic mother would think of next. None of us was ready for what followed. Without warning, my mother put her hand outside the jeep and, with her substantial gold ring, banged loudly on the side of the jeep. Additionally, in a loud voice she bellowed, "Let's get some action here!" This roused the attention of the lions. They began to rise to their feet. The terror in the jeep was palpable. The guide turned pale. Mother was silenced.

The jeep crawled away with everyone saying a silent prayer that the lions wouldn't come after us. Mother was quite unfazed by the incident. The rest of us were not. We felt lucky to see another day.

Mother had been keeping an incredible schedule so chose to take the next morning to rest. She needed it, and the day ahead promised to be strenuous. At 6:15 a.m., I met with three others of our group at the "airport" where we boarded a Cessna 206 (5YAHZ), an aircraft category in which I had considerable flying time. We flew to Rusinga Island Fishing Camp on Lake Victoria—the second largest lake in the world, boasting 26,600 square miles. Only Lake Superior is larger. It is, however, the biggest tropical lake in the world. Lake Victoria is divided among three countries—Kenya (6%), Uganda (45%) and Tanzania (49%).

Aldine with her catch at Lake Victoria

The flight was about one hour in duration. The camp was absolutely beautiful and managed by four young people who served us breakfast.

The four in our group, along with a guide, took a boat out onto the lake where we fished for many hours. This was all a dream come true and I could scarcely believe it was really happening to me! We were lucky to have a gorgeous day—not always a guarantee. We all caught a great many fish–big ones–the largest of which was 25 pounds.

In the afternoon we made the return trip. I did all the flying on both legs. What a thrill! I definitely logged the time in my logbook when I got back to Tucson,

We returned to camp to pick up my mother who was very excited about our upcoming visit to a Maasai Mara village. We all were fascinated with the Maasai way of life. They are a semi-nomadic people. Their wealth lies in the number of cattle and the number of children they have. A respectable number of cattle would be a herd of about fifty. I do not know how many children would be considered "respectable," but it is known that any man with a dearth in either category is thought to be a poor man indeed. Because of the high mortality rate, they do not name their children until they are three months old.

Aldine with Maasai children

The Maasai had always lived on a diet of milk exclusively. With droughts and a drop in the size of their herds, they have had to turn to legumes as well. They augment this Spartan fare for special occasions, such as a wedding, when they kill a cow for the celebratory feast. This luxury occurs infrequently. Their cattle are their wealth and their lives depend on them as they rely on their milk to live. They also drain blood from cattle on rare occasions to provide additional nourishment to someone who is very ill or for pregnant women.

All the Maasai are circumcised in their youth. The story is that young men must kill a lion prior to circumcision. This is now a tradition being frowned upon as the lion population is in jeopardy. The surgery is accomplished without the use of anesthesia and to exhibit pain would cost a young man his opportunity to become a junior warrior. Girls must endure this mutilation as well or they would be considered unmarriageable. Marriages continue to be arranged.

The people took a great liking to my mother. We were invited into their "homes"–crude mud dwellings in which they share their space with the livestock. Mother had her photograph taken with the chief of the tribe of the village we visited. They both wore broad smiles. It was so colorful and charming a photograph that my mother used it for her Christmas card that year. This was a fascinating experience and has left indelible pictures in my mind.

Mother with the chief of the Maasai Mara village

Later we went on a game run to see hippos. When we finally got to bed that night we both were exhausted. This was difficult for my mother to admit but I had no such compunctions.

The following day we went game viewing on exceedingly bumpy roads from 8:30 a.m. to 12:30 p.m. I note in my diary that my mother "was incredible." The second game viewing was at four o'clock that afternoon. We actually saw another cheetah, the fastest animal in the world. Later there was a storm that left us without electricity, and it was cold.

That evening we had a very special treat. We had been advised ahead of time that there might well be one formal evening and that we should take appropriate garb. Humphrey Meme, our guide, had indeed planned such an event. We were driven in jeeps to a place beside a river in which there were a large number of hippos. Hippos are unpredictable and dangerous so the location selected was given careful consideration. On the bank of the river a tent had been erected and tables set with linen cloths and fine silver and china. There were lit candelabras as well. It was elegance in the jungle. The meal was delivered by jeep and served by waiters in uniform. This entire trip was a study in contrasts!

We flew from the Kichwa Tembo camp at Maasai Mara the following day, June 7th, to Nairobi where we settled into a room at the Nairobi Safari Club that had been provided for our use prior to our departure later that night. Now I went shopping in earnest. I rarely buy jewelry for myself but I had my heart set on a gold bracelet that is known as an elephant hair bracelet. The natives of Africa typically make them from the tail hair of the elephant and believe they bring good luck to the wearer of the bracelet. They are delicate and very intricate in the manner in which they slide open and closed. These had been replicated by jewelers in gold and, although very expensive, I was thrilled to have one that I wear with delight to this day.

Mother and I had dinner with my friend Pat that night at a famous restaurant—Alan Bobbes. The food was delicious after the basic fare provided us throughout our tour. At midnight we flew Air France to Paris arriving at 8:45 a.m. Somehow we were able to sleep on the trip and arrived relatively rested and raring to go.

Having checked into the Hotel Duminy Vendome, which I described in my diary as "small and tacky but clean and quiet," Mother and I started out on our exciting day. However, it turned into a nightmare which I remember with trepidation to this moment. My amazing mother and I <u>walked</u> from the hotel to the Musée d'Orsay where we spent many hours enjoying the art in this magnificently converted old railway station. We had lunch there and continued in amazement seeing the work of the impressionists—Monet, Manet, Pissarro, Cézanne, Gauguin, Van Gogh and so forth. We were in awe of the works of Rodin and my mother finally saw the original of Whistler's Mother. This trip was all she had hoped it would be—until…

We exited the museum in the late afternoon to find that it was raining heavily. Knowing we could not retrace our steps on foot to the hotel in this deluge, we jumped into a taxi. Then panic set in. Neither of us remembered the name of the hotel. I couldn't tell the driver where to go (although later I wanted to!) but kept yelling *droit* and *gauche* when I thought I saw something familiar. The fact is that we were hopelessly lost and I was faced with a problem I didn't know how to solve. We hadn't brought our passports, or a room key, or anything that would help the police relocate us. Hence, there was no point in getting the police involved.

The taxi driver became exasperated and finally told us to get out—in the rain! How rude of him. So there we were, two ladies alone and lost in Paris. While it doesn't sound serious, it was, and we were both terrified—and wet.

My ingenious mother suddenly had an inspiration. Across the street from where we stood was a store whose legendary name was familiar to us both—H. Stern. Mother was confident that someone there would speak English and be able to suggest a way for us to extricate ourselves from our dilemma. She was right. A group of the salesladies congregated and interrogated us about every detail of the hotel that we could recall. I remembered that there was a restaurant on the corner near the hotel. I described it. With their help, we were able to recall other details as well. Finally one woman jubilantly proclaimed that she knew where it was. Not only had she saved us, but she kindly took us to the hotel. There it was—no longer seeming small and tacky but built of gold—the most beautiful hotel we had ever seen! Since this episode in our lives, I have encouraged travelers going abroad to be sure to take some identifying item from the hotel with them. A traveler's credo should be *never leave your hotel unless you know how to get back to it*.

We felt a sense of obligation to go to the restaurant on the corner for dinner and it was delightful. An omelet and wine—what could be smoother on the tummies of two traumatized ladies.

On June 9th, after a memorable trip together, Mother and I took a taxi to De Gaulle airport where we had to say our goodbyes. My mother returned to Tucson and I flew to Toronto. I learned later that Mother's flight from Chicago to Tucson was cancelled and she didn't get home until midnight Tucson time! I have always adored and respected my mother, but she set the bar impossibly high for 82 year old women on this trip. Mother and I went on to make many more trips together until she died at age 86. There will never be another like her!

In Toronto I stayed with my brother Murray and his wife Mary and spent hours in making myself presentable to go to the gorgeous wedding of Lisa and Jim Ruscica accompanied by Ray Hickok. The reception that followed was held at the Four Seasons and the whole event was quite spectacular. I was tired but ebullient.

The following day my nephew Craig drove me to our cottage on Lake of Bays. I was so tired I began to hallucinate. I actually believed I was looking at a herd of elephants. I am sure they were trees but you couldn't have convinced me.

And so began another summer at our cottage in Muskoka in Ontario.

44

cx/cx

ABOARD THE *ROYAL VIKING SUN* CRUISING U.S. PORTS–1991

The Gulf War was looming in the summer of 1991. My mother and I were quite sure that a trip to the Mediterranean that we had anticipated with much enthusiasm would be cancelled. We were right.

However, the Royal Viking line did not give up easily. They changed their itinerary to one of visiting cities on the east coast of the U.S. and renamed the cruise "Springtime Americana." As Mother and I had never visited some of these ports of call, we eagerly accepted this new plan.

On May 11th we set sail from Montreal, Quebec on the *Royal Viking Sun*, a gorgeous ship, and began what was to be one of our favorite cruises. We spent a day traveling up the St. Lawrence River. The scenery was magnificent. Our first port of call the next day was Cape Breton Island in Nova Scotia, one of the Maritime Provinces in eastern Canada. My early education had been in Canada, and the intrigue of this region had captured my interest many years earlier. It lived up to my expectations. I saw for myself where so much Canadian history had occurred and it was fascinating for me.

Although it was a very cold and dark day, we took a four-hour tour from Sydney to Bedeck to visit the Alexander Graham Bell Museum which was, as we expected it to be, impressive. We could see the Bell home in the distance. It is

Alexander Graham Bell Museum – Cape Breton Island

interesting to note that Alexander Graham Bell Jr. and his wife Jackie were neighbors and friends of ours in Tucson. Later we had a lovely drive across the island. That evening Mother and I were ready for some night life on the ship so we attended the singles party. My mother won a prize!

Two days later we were in Boston and my nephew Ted was there to meet the ship. He was in law school in Boston. The three of us took a tour of Marblehead and Salem and had a good time wandering the streets. We returned to the ship for lunch and had fun showing Ted all the lovely nooks and crannies of the elegant *Sun*.

New York City was the next port of call, and it was a thrill to pass by the Statue of Liberty and Ellis Island on our way into New York Harbor. It was a beautiful day and we took a wonderful tour all over Manhattan. On board ship I had met a lovely gentleman, John Maxfield, a resident of Virginia who knew New York City well. That afternoon, while Mother rested, he introduced me to parts of the city I had missed on all my previous visits. What a wonderful afternoon it was and we capped it off with a beer at Rockefeller Center.

The next two days we were in Baltimore, a new city for Mother and me. We took the mandatory tour of the city and, while our initial impression left something to be desired, we grew to like it more and more as the day progressed. Later in the day, the Royal Viking Line—intent upon pleasing us—took everyone on board the ship to the National Aquarium. Their treat included drinks, dinner and dancing. It was a spectacular, fun-filled evening although we had altogether too little time at the aquarium. I tucked into the back of my mind that another trip there should be added to my bucket list.

Another wonderful new experience was provided by the ship's company again the next day. Bedecked in our finery, Mother and I ventured forth to see the famous Preakness races. What a gala event! We were quite surprised to learn that very few people watch from the stands. Most join parties in the village in the center and watch the races on TV. It is just as well as it was a cold day. We were amazed with the elegance of the spectators and the grandeur of the venue.

The following two days we were at sea and the ocean was very rough with waves as high as 12 feet. I spent the days fighting seasickness but somehow managed drinks with my mother and John both nights followed by dinner and a floor show.

John, a widower, became a good friend. He visited me both in Tucson and at the cottage in Canada. I visited him at his lovely home on the edge of a golf course in Virginia.

Hamilton, Bermuda was our next port of call where Mother and I boarded a tender to ride to shore. There we met the bus that would take us on a four-hour tour of the island. It included visits to the aquarium, the zoo, and Crystal Cave. It all was very beautiful. While Mother returned to the ship in the afternoon, John took me by taxi to Elbow Beach. There we lay in the sand and swam in the cold ocean. We just made it to the dock in time for the last tender back to the ship.

Mother & Aldine with clowns on the ship

After dinner that night we all enjoyed the funniest Liar's Club I had ever seen. The following day was another spent at sea and full of happy activities on the ship.

The following two days we were in Charleston, South Carolina which we found charming but hot and humid. We spent a great deal of time walking and shopping in the market.

In Savannah, Georgia the next day, Mother and I took a three-hour tour and were disappointed to find that it was a rather run-down city. We were happy to return to the ship and its endless interesting activities. In the evening the captain hosted a Skald party and a Norwegian dinner followed by Norwegian dancing. It was delightful.

We reached Ft. Lauderdale, Florida on May 27th and flew to Tucson. There we were met by a lovely man who had been courting me, Fred Daily. After we dropped my mother at her home, Fred asked me to marry him. I was not expecting this at all and was quite clumsy in my refusal. I cared deeply for him but marriage was not in my plans. I couldn't get Tony out of my heart.

My 58th birthday was two days later and I was thrilled to see all the family at a party in my honor, especially my grandchildren—Max, who was now three months old, having been born at 12:27 p.m. on February 27th. And, of course, my precious Tana was there.

Mother surveying a
sumptuous feast

Mother and I often reminisced about our delightful trip—"Springtime Americana."

45

CRITICAL ornament

EXPLORING IRELAND — 1999

Ireland with its fascinating lore, history and landscapes had been beckoning Hal and me for months. When the University of Arizona announced its trip to the Emerald Isle we leapt at the opportunity. Every moment we spent there was pure magic and will remain in my heart and mind forever.

We flew from Toronto to Dublin and then Shannon, Ireland on June 23, 1999 and traveled to Ennis where we stayed at a lovely place—The Old Ground Hotel. It was a beautifully restored 18th century manor house situated in the middle of the town. The group of which we were a part consisted of 28 members of the Alumni Campus Abroad Association. This was to be an educational tour and indeed it was.

Our first day was filled to the brim with learning and sightseeing. At 9:00 a.m. there was an excellent lecture on the history of Ireland. This was followed by an orientation tour of the city with stops at the Old Friary and a local church. We went on to Knappogue Castle for lunch and a tour of the castle. It was a tower house built in 1467 in the parish of Quin in County Clare. What an austere place to dine. We felt surrounded by spirits of yore.

Our next stop was Quin Abbey–the main attraction in the town of Quin–followed by a visit to Craggaunowen Project—a recreation of Ireland's history. It was an open air museum set in 50 acres of woodland with a picturesque lake and provided several examples of early historic dwelling places. It was indeed sylvan and had a feeling of mystery about it.

We were quite ready to return to the hotel to change and then attend a panel lecture at 6:00 p.m. followed by an evening to "meet the people." The Irish folks whom we met lived up to all the preconceived ideas we had about these hearty people—witty, charming and vivacious.

The following day began with two fascinating lectures, one about the Irish famine and the other about Irish authors. Our bus then took us to Durty Nelly's in Bunratty for lunch. If one wanted to find the quintessential Irish pub, this place would fit the bill. It was charming. Later we visited Bunratty Castle, a large 15th century tower house in the center of Bunratty Village in County Clare. We went on to Folk Park which is a living recreation of the homes and environment in Ireland of over a century ago. It features over 30 buildings in a "living village."

In spite of the cold and rain the next day, we wasted no time as our tour had a full itinerary planned. We started in The Burren described as a karst landscape—an irregular limestone region with sinkholes, underground streams and caverns. It covered 250 square kilometers of land. We saw the Paolnabrone Dolmen—a portal tomb in the Burren dating back to between 4200 BC and 2900 BC. Imagine, over 7500 years old!

On we went to a small harbor village in County Clare called Ballybaughn. The name alone would attract you to it. We had lunch there at the quaint Whitehorn Restaurant.

Our next stop was Newtown Castle, a 16th century tower house within the Burren area. My diary noted that the walk we took there was very difficult. We finished our day with a trip to the Cliffs of Moher, one of Ireland's most breathtaking natural wonders. It ranked as one of the most popular tourist attractions in all of Ireland.

Hal in Ireland

Our daily lecture started us off the next day, followed by a bus trip that took us north through Gort—a town in the south of County Galway in the west part of Ireland– and on to downtown Galway City. We were given a tour as a group and then had independent time to wander through the arts district.

Lunch that day was at Thoor Ballylee—another 15th (or 16th) century tower. It was also known as Yeats' Tower as it was once owned and inhabited by the Irish poet William Butler Yeats. During lunch, we enjoyed an audio-visual presentation on the life of Yeats. We had a delightful walk to the old mill there.

Our next stop was to the former home of Lady Gregory on her estate, Coole Park. Lady Gregory—

Isabella—was a close friend and literary colleague of Yeats and was a dramatist and folklorist. Together they had weekly salons with well-known authors of the day. Lady Gregory married Sir William Gregory and, although he was 35 years her senior, they produced one son. Sadly he was killed in WWI while serving as a pilot. We took a long walk through the woods of Coole Park and returned to Ennis.

I remember well that evening back at the hotel. One of the most exciting experiences one can have in Ireland is sitting at the feet of a really good Irish storyteller. After dinner we met Eddie Lennihan who had to be the finest storyteller in all of Eire. A traditional Irish storyteller is known as an Irish shanachie. Eddie had us on the edges of our seats totally mesmerized by the drama with which he presented his stories. I had been plagued with atrial fibrillation throughout this trip, and Eddie almost did me in! I was totally in thrall and in such a state of agitation—even terror–that I knew an all-out attack of AF was pending if I didn't get out of there fast. Can you believe I had to leave in the middle of one of his stories? It was that exciting! Hal very sweetly bought a cassette of his stories which still continues to give me the "willies."

We had been looking forward to our visit to the Aran Islands the next day. They are a group of three separate islands located at the mouth of Galway Bay that are accessible by water only. While driving to the ferry port, Rossaveal, we went through Connemara, a district in the west of Ireland. We reached the port and boarded the ferry.

We docked at Inishmore Island, the largest of the three islands, with a population of 840. Being in the Aran Islands made me feel as if I had stepped into a bygone era. The people maintain their own language and customs from centuries past. It was an enchanting place, and it felt enchanted. After a fascinating drive around the island, we had lunch at the foot of Dún Aengus—the most famous of several prehistoric forts on the island.

It was a cold and rainy day, and the terrain was limestone rock and very barren. Imagine living your whole life there, and many did! I remember almost freezing to death on the ferry trip back to the mainland.

It continued to be rainy and cold the next day–our last with the group. I noted in my diary that "It has been an incredible trip—just marvelous." We took a bus trip down to the Ring of Kerry and around the lakes, stopping at Ladies View–a well-known viewpoint. It was magnificent—even in the rain.

That evening we had our "graduation ceremony." I won first prize in the limerick contest! After our final dinner together, we enjoyed wonderful Irish musicians and dancers.

Having said our goodbyes, the group left to return to the United States while Hal and I set out on our own. After renting a car, Hal took a good part of the day "practicing" the art of driving on the left side of the road. We knew our itinerary going forward included some very narrow roads.

On the following day, we left the Old Ground Hotel that had become like a second home and drove to Dingle—a charming village and the only town on the Dingle Peninsula. En route, we spent an hour in Tralee—the largest town in County Kerry. We drove through the Conner Pass which is considered to be one of the most beautiful drives in all Ireland—as well as being one of the highest points in the country. That night we had dinner at the well-known Doyle's Seafood Restaurant which we found rather pricey.

Again the next day it rained. This hampered our ability to fully appreciate the absolutely magnificent countryside through which we were driving. In my diary I noted, "…the visibility was <u>awful</u>. Darn. I've always wanted to drive the Ring of Kerry and I could see very little. Hal did a wonderful job on <u>very</u> narrow, winding roads." We spent the night in Kenmare, a small town located at the head of Kenmare Bay.

We couldn't believe it when we awakened to another day of rain. Nonetheless, we drove all around the Beara Penninsula along the southwestern coast through spectacular scenery—albeit viewed through the mist—and stopped in Adrigole, a fishing village of only 450 people. We had friends living there—Geraldine and John MacConnell.

Geraldine and John had an interesting history. They had owned a gift shop outside our hamlet of Dwight in Ontario that drew people from far and wide and earned them many awards. They decided to return to their roots in Ireland and moved—lock, stock and barrel—to this tiny village with few inhabitants. They established their new gift shop and, after only a year in business, were voted the finest gift shop in Ireland. They excelled in what they did. Certainly they liked living in remote places! We returned to Kenmare where again we spent the night.

We left Kenmare—in the rain—the next day and drove through gorgeous scenery to Killarney, a town in County Kerry. After a lovely, long walk there, we continued on to the charming village of Adare where we checked into the Carrabaun House, a bed and breakfast with a magnificent garden. Adare is in County Limerick.

The following day we drove to Foynes Flying Boat Museum and later to the Curraghchase Forest Park—a 774 acre forest in County Limerick. Hal's driving was superb as he navigated the very narrow lanes to the Celtic Theme Park and then the Heritage Museum. We visited the elegant Adare Manor Hotel. Although we couldn't afford to stay there, we had heard about it and wanted to see for ourselves what all the hullabaloo was about. It lived up to all its rave reviews. This magnificent hotel was first mentioned in history books as a manor in 1226!

July 7th, our departure day, was long and grueling. We left Adare, drove to Shannon and from there flew to Chicago and then Toronto arriving at 2:00 a.m. (5:00 a.m. in Ireland). We hunkered down in Toronto for the night—absolutely exhausted. The next day we were revved up and ready to head back to the cottage. It was good to return to our beautiful lakeside home.

While I have had many wonderful visits in Ireland—about eight—I remember this as the one in which I felt most connected to these unique people and their beautiful country.

46

CRBO

THE PANAMA CANAL—2001

As many cruises as I had taken, the Panama Canal had eluded me. I had no idea what I had been missing until Hal and I embarked for San José, Costa Rica–the first leg of our adventure—on January 24, 2001. I was delighted when we landed in San José, the country's capital and one of my favorite destinations, and checked into the Hotel Palacio. A note in my diary at the end of our first full day said, "A wonderful day. Having fun. Excited."

The following day we took a tour that took us through the Cloud Forest—in clouds, of course, and in a torrent of rain. There were mud slides on the highway; it was wet! We slogged through the rain on slippery paths to get to the rain forest where we took an aerial gondola ride for an hour or more—in the rain. We were 150 feet above ground level which did not sit well with my acrophobia. The forest canopy was magnificent and the ride ended at a lodge where we had lunch. We were given time for a long walk through the rain forest, in the rain, before we returned to the bus for the trip back to San José.

The Poás Crater was our destination the next day, a place I had visited many times before. It was socked in, wet and windy! Lunch was at the Britt Coffee Plantation where we had an interesting tour as well. Back at the hotel I sat by the swimming pool to read and later we enjoyed a delicious Costa Rican dinner.

January 28th was our last day in Costa Rica. We spent it walking through San José and later boarding a bus to take us to Punta Caldera to board our ship. En route we stopped at Grecia and Sarchí—mandatory stops for every Costa Rican bus ride, it would seem! We were pleased to find that we had a lovely cabin on the new cruise ship—*Amsterdam*.

By visiting Nicaragua the next day, I had been to all the countries of Central American except El Salvador. We had taken a tender and then a bus for the 1½ hour trip to the town of Granada. As we drove through the countryside, I found the views of true poverty both upsetting and sobering. I noted in my diary that, "The contrast to our ship was mind boggling." We stopped for coffee in Granada and, while sitting with a group of fellow passengers, a woman noticed she had been robbed. None of us had seen the culprit sneak up, abscond with her purse, and disappear. The thief was clearly an expert. I was not disappointed when we returned to the ship and left the sad plight of the Nicaraguans behind.

The luxury of the ship was welcome as we spent the following day at sea cruising through the beautiful Golfo Dulce where I had been before. And then we entered the Panama Canal. We had been prepared for the experience through lectures and films but the reality was awe- inspiring.

The Panama Canal

Both Hal and I remembered well the following day at sea. The ocean was incredibly rough with waves 18 to 24 feet high and Force 10 winds. Eventually we reached Curacao, a colorful Dutch colony, and took an island bus tour through Willemstad to Chobolobo, famous for its liqueur. We continued to an old country estate—Brievengat—and later walked through the town stopping to have a beer beside the canal.

Hal parasailing

Another port of call was St. Thomas, again a repeat for me, where we docked in Charlotte Amalie. Hal and I passed on shopping in this shopper's mecca, preferring to take a taxi to Megan Bay to lie in the sun and swim. It was heavenly!

On February 6th we arrived in Half Moon Bay in the Bahamas and took a tender to shore. What a gorgeous island! Hal and I chose to be independent once again and headed for the beach. Hal went parasailing—his first experience with it—and soared to 500 feet! We took a nature walk and Hal went kayaking while I lay on the beach and swam. A glorious day!

All too soon, the adventure was over leaving us with indelible memories. We disembarked at Ft. Lauderdale where we took a paddle boat ride on the inner waterways passing incredibly expensive homes with yachts parked at their docks. What a life!

Hal's son-in-law Randy Childers met us at the airport in Tucson and, in contrast to our trip in the tropics, it snowed in Tucson the following day!

47

⊂ℑ⊅

WITH TANA IN EUROPE ABOARD THE *PRISENDAM* —2002

I had always dreamed of someday having a granddaughter whom I could take to Europe. My dream came true. Having already traveled on a great many family expeditions, and having visited the cottage in Canada annually, Tana was already an experienced traveler. But a cruise through the British Isles, France, Spain, Norway and Denmark was of a different dimension. She was 14 years old and well able to take care of herself if my health failed. This cruise ranks at the top of the list as one of my most memorable trips abroad.

When the trip began on June 12, 2002, I was at our cottage in Ontario and Tana was in Tucson. By the time we met at the Toronto airport, Tana was tired—very tired—having had only three hours sleep the previous night. We had a long delay in Toronto but finally boarded a Boeing 747 and, crammed into our seats, took off across the ocean. It was a horrible trip with several people having medical emergencies en route. It seemed that bodies were lying on every available spot on the floor. Tana was seated beside a large and gregarious woman who was a talker! That was not a night Tana would get any sleep whatever.

We arrived at Heathrow, took a bus to Southampton, and boarded our ship—a Holland America vessel called *Prisendam.* I had been aboard this ship before when it had belonged to the Royal Viking Line and it was considered quite luxurious at that time. Well, things had slipped. Tana and I shared a cabin adjacent to the cables that were hydraulically raised and lowered for dock mooring. The noise they made was unimaginable!

Tana was so exhausted from two days without sleep and all the difficult traveling she had endured that she quite literally passed out on her bed. Later, she didn't even remember having boarded the ship! And one may be sure that she did not hear the racket of the cables being raised when the ship sailed!

All the angst and fatigue were soon forgotten after we settled into our cabin the following morning—a day at sea. Our cabin number, by chance, was 333—Tana's favorite number! We met our table-mates; they were old and staid but my gracious granddaughter entered into our evening dinners with them with enthusiasm and interest. My first task was to find a woman I trusted to whom Tana could turn if my atrial fibrillation got the better of me. I met Jean Wegener–a lovely, gentle lady who willingly accepted the responsibility and recorded all the necessary information. Jean and I are still in touch every Christmas; she was a friend to remember.

With that off my mind, I could sit back and relax. The captain had a "welcome aboard" champagne party followed by a floor show that evening. We were off and running.

I will never forget the delightful port at which we arrived the following morning— La Rochelle, France. It is a city in southwestern France and a seaport on the Bay of Biscay. It was founded in 1152 and Tana and I immediately fell under its enchantment during a tour through the city and the surrounding area. We walked a great deal to fully absorb the beauty and charm all around us. That evening Tana attended a teen gathering and connected with some young people her age.

In the morning we awakened to find that the ship was cruising up the Garonne River to reach Bordeaux, France, one of the most delightful cities I can remember having visited in all of France. The old town had been well preserved and Bordeaux has the highest number of preserved historical buildings in France, except for Paris. We took the city tour which included a visit to a vineyard offering wine tasting. Bordeaux wines had always been favorites of mine. We were delighted to have a good deal of time to explore the area as the ship docked there for the night.

Tana at Saint-Emilion, France

We had a very full day ahead of us when we arose on June 17th. Tana and I walked into the city center, took many photographs, and visited the local museum. In the afternoon we took a tour to Chateaux La Croix de Gay in Pomerol and on to Saint-Emilion—a fascinating 13th century town dating back to Roman times. It was surrounded by walls that offered magnificent views. We also visited the

498

catacombs and a number of tombs from the 11th and 12th centuries. My diary noted that "It was <u>very, very</u> hot that day." The evenings on board ship were always delightful with excellent dinners and superb entertainment.

Tana and I were on deck as we docked at Bilbao, Spain the following day. The sky was overcast which seemed perfect for this region. Leaving the ship, we took a shore excursion through the old city. We walked for what seemed like miles, and were fascinated at every turn. The Guggenheim Museum was a source of amazement to us. Some of the art exhibits boggled one's imagination. I remember one that was a pile of debris encircled by yellow crime-scene tape. At first I assumed it was construction underway. Then I realized that this was "art." As they say, beauty is in the eye of the beholder! Both classical and modern art were on display.

After dinner that evening Tana attended a teen party which seemed to go on rather longer than I had expected. When she returned, I pretended nonchalance when, in fact, I had been on pins and needles. It was a big responsibility for me to have this beautiful young lady under my wing. I have long had a "cookies in bed" addiction; they seem to soothe me into sleep. I often waited until I thought Tana was asleep before I indulged but she always seemed to catch me, commenting "Having your cookie fix, Nana?" I finally gave up trying to disguise it. She even helped spirit them into the cabin so I wouldn't run out!

Neither of us will ever forget the magic of the next day spent in La Coruña, Spain. We took a six-hour shore excursion to the awesome and unforgettable Santiago de Compostela with its marvelous buildings and squares. Of course we visited the ancient cathedral where the remains of St. James the Apostle lay and placed our fingers in grooves where his had been—along with those of millions of people whose visits had preceded ours. The cathedral had initially been built as a shrine to St. James and became the most famous pilgrimage site in the Christian world. The deep feeling of spirituality the cathedral exuded and its beauty and mystique have never left our minds. Tana and I often reminisce about that experience.

We were treated to wine, hors d'oeuvres and local dancers in the afternoon. The event was held in the majestic courtyard of what had been the former home of King Ferdinand and Queen Isabella of Spain. It was steeped in history as their wedding had taken place in the year 1469. And, of course, the royal couple had authorized the expedition of Christopher Columbus to the New World. We were quite overwhelmed with all we had experienced that day. However, we returned to reality on our trip back to the ship where we had a delicious dinner and outstanding evening entertainment.

We were glad the next day was at sea–time for me to nap and exercise and for Tana to work on her computer. We were crossing the Bay of Biscay—a first for me. That evening the ship's company hosted a formal event. Tana looked adorable in her pink evening gown. After dinner and the floor show, we attended the officers' black and white ball. It was elegant and memorable. We went to bed late that night!

Tana in Waterford, Ireland

We docked in Ireland the next day; it was rainy and overcast as one might expect it to be in that country. We spent the day on our own taking a one-hour bus ride into the town of Waterford where we had lunch at a pub and shopped. That night there was another teen party. I noted in my diary that, "I worried but all was OK." My imagination often took over and I could envision her falling off the stern of the ship and other such horrors.

Belfast was our port of call on June 22nd on another rainy, cold day. I had been there years before and found it considerably changed. Clearly Bill Clinton was their hero as there were many statues of him throughout the city. As well, there was a street named in his honor. The people thought he had made a big impact on their lives and felt deeply indebted to him. Tana and I took a fascinating four-hour tour. We were grateful that most of it was inside a bus as it was raining very hard that day. We followed the road along the Ard Penninsula and stopped at a pub in Donaghadee for lunch. It was a charming experience with lovely young Irish girls dancing and lots of Irish music. What a cozy spot that was!

That night the ship passed close to Scotland and in the morning on the starboard side we could see the mainland clearly and on the port side a wonderful view of the Orkney Islands. It was such a lovely day we were able to have lunch on deck. In the evening, the captain held a Mariners' party for people who had traveled on their line before. I received a medallion as I had taken a considerable number of cruises. I was photographed alone with the captain and his first officer. Tana was impressed. Later, the crew put on their floor show. It was, again, a late night for Tana and me.

At 11:00 a.m. we arrived in Kristiansand, Norway. We had glorious weather there. Tana and I took a 45-minute coach trip to Grovane driving alongside the Otra River. Grovane was a railway village. There we boarded a narrow-gauge railway and traveled to a spot called Beiholen where we

Tana & Aldine in Norway

stopped to have coffee and lefse by the river. Lefse is a traditional soft Norwegian flatbread. We returned to the ship satisfied that we had caught the flavor of this region.

Oslo, Norway was our next port of call; we arrived to another beautiful day. Tana and I walked along the pier to embark on *The Helena*—an old Norwegian sailing vessel that had been well restored. We enjoyed a three-hour water tour along Oslofjord. As my diary noted, "It was very beautiful—but not Lake of Bays."

We returned to the ship for a Norwegian lunch and then retired to our cabin to start packing for our departure. I noted in my diary that "Tana is such a darling and such fun to travel with. We've both seen and done enough, however, and although we <u>loved</u> the cruise, we're ready to go home." That evening Tana went to another teen party and didn't return until late. Enough of these teen parties, thought I! Still, as anxious as they made me (she was out of my sight, for goodness sake) I am glad she made these age-appropriate contacts. That night it was very windy and the boat rocked us to sleep.

On our last day—June 26th—we disembarked in Copenhagen, Denmark with a long trip ahead of us. However, we took time to take a tour of the city before heading for the airport. While awaiting our flight, I noticed a friend walking past. "Betty," I called out to her, and she looked over quite surprised to see someone she knew in the airport in Copenhagen. It was Betty Dovenbarger, a good friend of Joe Green who is mentioned throughout this memoir. Tana was quite amazed at the coincidence.

We flew British Airways to Heathrow where we changed terminals and took British Airways to Toronto. Howard Shenk met us there and drove us to the cottage. We were exhausted and took a day or two to adjust to our radically different environment. My dream had come true. I had taken my precious granddaughter for her introductory tour of Europe. And it had been perfect!

48

❧

COSTA RICA —2003, 1997

I was fortunate to have many trips to Costa Rica, a delightful country to visit. Two of these visits stand out as unique and memorable. I will tell these stories in order of my preference rather than chronologically.

WITH MY FAMILY—2003

I took my children and their families on many trips through the years, but our visit to Costa Rica was particularly special and very luxurious. My family included Kent, Janice and Tana, Elizabeth, Tony, Max and Alex. Our friend Howard Shenk also joined us. It truly was the trip of a lifetime and was particularly unusual as we were a private party, not part of a group. I had arranged for private vans, buses, and airplanes throughout which made our travel comfortable and easy.

We rendezvoused at the Tucson Airport from which we flew to San José, the capital of Costa Rica. There we stayed at an old mansion downtown—Granja de Oro–which boasted 32 rooms. An interesting fact about San José at that time was that there were no street addresses. How people found one another or mail was delivered remains a mystery to me.

It is also significant to mention that Costa Rica has no military and its population is more than 96% literate. Also, they were the first country in the Americas to ban recreational hunting. And the people are lovely—helpful and kind. You realize quickly that you are visiting a country that is every tourist's dream.

While staying in San José, we took a trip to the Poás Volcano, my third visit there.

The family on the beach at Manuel Antonio

After two days in San José, we flew in two Cessna 206s (single engine aircrafts) to a primitive airport in Quepos and from there to our destination—Manuel Antonio. We checked into our individual family huts at Tulemar Bungalows, each perched high above the tropical rainforest with a breathtaking view. They appeared rustic and charming, but had every convenience one would need, especially air conditioning. It was hot! Our days there were spent in exploring Manuel Antonio State Park with its incredibly diverse population of animals, and in taking a small open boat to Damas Island where we wended our way through the mangroves and were treated rather rudely by monkeys.

Swimming was, of course, a priority, but the waves were big and more than once my brawny lads had to pull their mother out of the ocean. The long, winding road down to the beach was physically demanding whether going up or down. Fortunately, transportation was only a phone call away from either our bungalows or

A rude monkey

Tony & Elizabeth in the pool at Tulemar

the beachside bar making the trip much less exhausting. Drinks at sunset in the negative edge pool were special, as were the iguanas who sauntered among our feet looking for scraps of food during dinner at the open air restaurant.

We left Manuel Antonio regretfully, promising we would return one day, and were flown in Cessna 206s once again to San José. From there we boarded a private twin engine Otter for the 40 minute flight to Tamarindo on the Pacific Coast in Guanacoste.

We loved our accommodations there–a resort named Cala Luna. Again each family had its own villa, each of which was 1350 square feet in size, and each with its own swimming pool! While there we spent considerable time at the beach, went on a long snorkeling expedition, and took a rough kayak ride in the Tamarindo Estuary. This estuary was home to much wildlife—beautiful birds and, more importantly, crocodiles! Despite its small size and population, Costa Rica ties with Brazil for the most reported crocodile attacks in the Americas.

Kent was especially fond of using his paddle to poke any crocodile that ventured too close—much to the chagrin of the rest of the party. We thought the crocs might have their revenge when Kent upended his kayak in the water but, fortunately, there weren't any near enough to reach him before he managed to right himself!

The most exciting event of the day was yet to come, however. While waiting for our van ride back to the resort, we encountered a VERY drunk caballero who wanted us to pay for rides on his horse. Although we politely declined, he became very belligerent, drew a knife and slurred "I will keeeeel you!" Our guide assured us that if we just ignored him, he would eventually go away–which he did—but it made for a great story!

Tony with Alex, Max & Tana in waterfalls near Xandari Plantation

Every night was a special treat as we dined outside on beautiful patios and the sunsets always seemed to be spectacular.

Eventually we headed out to the airport to a hovel masquerading as a terminal and left Tamarindo for a flight aboard our private twin Otter to San José. There we were met by our private bus which drove us to our most beautiful hotel of all—The Xandari Plantation. Again we each settled into individual villas and, while the young people took a strenuous hike to the many natural waterfalls and pools, I took advantage of the peace to simply enjoy the magnificent views.

There was big excitement the next day as the young people (everyone but Howard and me) took a dramatic white water expedition that lasted almost four hours. It was classified as a Class III-IV, which means there were many scary moments, lots of hard work, and a few close calls. Near the end of the ride, the guides encouraged everyone to jump off the rafts and ride the white water with nothing but their life jackets! While not a strong

Reventazón rafting trip

swimmer, Elizabeth didn't want to be the only spoil sport, so decided to join the rest. She immediately regretted it, but managed to make it to the calm waters along with the others—albeit choking and gasping for breath. Everyone was proud of her for "jumping" outside her comfort zone.

Meanwhile, Howard and I hiked to a waterfall where we swam and lazed away the afternoon. Dinner was, as always, a spectacular event with views we will never forget.

The next day was April 9th, memorable as the day that the statue of Saddam Hussein was toppled in Baghdad. I watched it happen on the TV in the lobby while we waited for the van that would take us to the airport in Arajuela.

As I wrote in my diary, it was the "best trip of my life" but I think I often wrote that at the end of trips. The best part was being with my family and seeing them so engaged in every aspect of that amazing country and its wonderful people.

WITH THE UNIVERSITY OF ARIZONA – 1997

This incredible trip was under the aegis of the University of Arizona and provided excellence every step of the way. There were 24 of us in the group and my traveling companion was a good friend, Larry Littlefield. Ours was a strictly platonic relationship. I was blessed that among the passengers were people who became and continue to be very dear friends, Bette and Leonard Cooper. Leonard recently passed away.

We flew from Tucson to San José during my spring break from UA and checked into the Hotel Herradura. The first day we visited the Britt Coffee Plantation, coffee having been a major industry in Costa Rica since the late 19th century.

Aldine with Larry Littlefield in San José

Day three provided me with the first of four visits I have made to the Poás Volcano, an impressive sight. It is one mile wide. Then on to La Paz Waterfall, reputed to have therapeutic effects. We stayed that night in a gorgeous resort, El Tucano. The following morning we departed for a full-day excursion to Cano Negro Wildlife Refuge where we boarded a boat for a 2 ½ hour trip on Rio Frío. My diary notes that we passed many fields—coconut, nutmeg, pineapple, orange, and sugar cane–as well as seeing a great variety of wildlife.

Larry and I took time off the next morning to enjoy lying in the hot springs, swimming and writing postcards. What a beautiful setting it was! Arenal Volcano was another famous destination in Costa Rica and that afternoon we could see why this would be so. It is the most active volcano in the country as proven to us when we took a long hike up the volcano and heard the spewing of lava and the sliding of rocks. That evening we were treated to the inspiring sight of glowing red lava as well.

We reluctantly departed the gorgeous spa, El Tucano, the following day and went by bus with our group to Sarchi, a typical destination for tourists as it boasts a great many shops and markets. I was not impressed with the quality of the work.

And then began the most exciting part of our trip—our cruise from Puntarenas on the Pacific coast. We boarded the M/V Temptress Explorer, a very small ship indeed, that evening. The captain welcomed us with a cocktail party and an introduction to the crew.

Early the next morning we packed our cameras, dry socks, etc. and traveled by zodiac crafts to shore where we donned hiking boots for the jungle trek in the Curu Biological Reserve. I found it a bit disappointing. Back to the ship for lunch, after which we set sail for Tortuga Island with time there for a lovely swim. That night we were treated to a wonderful picnic on the beach.

February 10th presented us with another zodiac ride to shore, this time for an almost three-hour hike into the forests and along the beaches in Corcovado National Park. It was gorgeous. We saw macaws and other tropical wildlife. Back to the ship to travel to San Josecito Beach where we disembarked once again, this time for lunch on shore. We swam and snorkeled; it was lovely. That night we enjoyed the captain's farewell dinner. It had been a wonderful day—difficult hiking at times, but well worth the effort.

The next morning we anchored off the coast of Golfito on Golfito Dulce. We took, as my diary says, "a very difficult, steep and arduous hike through forests and jungles to a camp where an American man lives." What a surprise that was. That an inaccessible, isolated location such as that would appeal to somebody to make his home seems unfathomable to me!

Later that day we left Golfito in a twin Otter to fly to San José. It rained all day and the return trip was an incredibly rough ride. As there wasn't enough room in the Otter for all of us, some women were left to take smaller planes back to San José. They arrived terrified and in tears from the wild ride they had experienced. Not a good way to end a wonderful trip!

Our final event was a poolside cocktail party at the hotel that night with some of the best paella I've ever eaten. Paella is an ancient dish from the area of Valencia in Spain. It is a combination of a great many different kinds of food—meats, seafood, poultry, vegetables—that, with spices, creates an aromatic and flavorful stew. The origin of its name is interesting. In olden times in Spain, neighbors would congregate from time to time for a fiesta at a nearby home or farm, bringing with them whatever they had that could go into the paella. The word paella was initially "para ella"—for her. The woman of the house was given all the staples and from these she would create the paella. As people arrived at the gathering they would present their foods and say, "para ella" later to be shortened to paella.

This trip with the University of Arizona was well-organized with a great deal of variety and a good blend of leisure time interspersed with hiking and exploring. I loved every moment of it.

49

∽

PUERTO PEÑASCO, MEXICO —2004, 2005, 2006

Our trips to San Carlos, Mexico had been curtailed by the danger associated with driving there due to aggressive drug cartels. We accepted the next best alternative for our jaunts to the ocean—Puerto Peñasco, known by Americans as Rocky Point. Located only 214 miles from Tucson—a convenient getaway for us–it lacked the beauty and charm of the more southern destinations.

Although I had been there many times previously, Hal and I started our annual trips in 2004. We had decided to spend New Year's Eve there, arriving on December 30th. I will quote my diary to sum up my evaluation of life for the year we were leaving behind. "Last day of the year—and it was a good one. Hal and I have lots of aches and pains— but I am <u>happy</u> with my life—which has been an amazing life. I am a very lucky lady. Slept late. Laughed and ate and read on our 'front porch.' Not much of a hotel but the best around. We drove all around Cholla Bay and downtown and walked the busy streets and El Malecón. Had beer overlooking rocks. Dinner at Happy Dolphin and early to bed." And so farewell to 2004!

The succeeding days in Rocky Point were spent in kayaking on the days that weren't too windy, and in absorbing the unique ambience of Mexico. On January 3rd it was raining so hard that we decided to cut our vacation short and left the hotel at noon. It was a long trip back to Tucson as we ran into a horrendous rainstorm that Hal said was the worst he had ever driven in. I was terrified as the road went through a dangerous Indian reservation. Hal insisted, however, that we were at the front of the storm, and we needed to get back to Tucson before the arroyos ran and the road closed.

We reached Tucson, a bit the worse for wear, at 5:30 p.m. and spent a delightful evening with Kent and Tony.

Later in 2005, Hal and I visited Rocky Point once again. It was a pleasant getaway destination. Much of our time there was spent in trying to locate a good place to bring the entire family the following year. We spent hours kayaking, although we found that the swells of the ocean were fairly substantial. Some days we were confined to kayaking only in the marina to stay well away from a fairly vigorous ocean. It was a lovely few days and we returned to Tucson rested and content.

In 2006, we decided to recognize Kent's 51st birthday—March 28th–with a family trip to Rocky Point. We had rented a magnificent house on the beach that belonged to friends of Elizabeth and Tony—Susan and Rick Wedel. They are remarkable people and Rick is their family physician and mine, as well.

There was ample room for us all—Kent, Janice and Tana—Tony, Elizabeth, Max and Alex—Hal and me. Hal had to sleep with the boys as he and I were not married at that time. The place came with a staff—Anita and Jesus—who took care of the cleaning and provided our dinner every night.

Max, Tony & Alex in the surf

What wonderful times we had over the next week. During the day we kayaked, walked the beach and played in the surf. Sometimes the tide was so high that it came right up to the steps of the house. Kent and Tony played football, hit golf balls, and flew kites with the children. At night we played games such as Balderdash and watched movies. One day when Kent took the young people beach exploring, he was stung by a sting ray. It caused him considerable pain but there was nothing we could do to help. One simply lived through it.

It was a delightful week in a lovely environment—one more of our happy family trips.

High surf

50

ೲ

MAYA RUINS AND CENTRAL AMERICA—2004

Although I had previously explored some of the Maya Ruins having visited Mérida and thus Chichén Itzá and Uxmal, I had long wanted to see and learn about them in depth. Out of the blue, a friend – Howard Shenk – received a brochure intended only for British clients advertising just such a trip. He had no idea why he was on the mailing list but we both were delighted when our applications were accepted.

The date of departure, March 13, 2004 was only six weeks after I had major surgery– a hysterectomy at age 70! Thus, I was on pins and needles awaiting the approval of my physician for me to take this taxing trip, granted only the day before we left. And taxing it was!

It was the wee hours of the morning when Howard and I reached Panama. We felt fortunate to find a driver loitering around the airport who was willing to take us to the ship. It was scheduled to depart later that morning. Alas, the driver was an unpleasant, uncommunicative man but we counted our blessings for finding a ride at all at that time of night. It wasn't long before we changed our minds about this and suspected our lives were in serious jeopardy.

Off this driver took with a screech of tires and a curse. After a few miles, we found we were not on a highway at all. He had turned off on a dirt road that grew narrower and narrower as we proceeded. Howard and I looked at each other in terror silently acknowledging that we were quite certain we were being hijacked. We felt helpless but in my best Spanish I asked the driver where he was taking us. More cursing. Eventually we entered a village and the car slammed to a stop in a cloud of dust.

Without a word, he opened the door and off he went, leaving us alone in the dark. We had no idea where in the Southern Hemisphere we were and had forebodings of disaster—robbery, dismemberment, the whole thing! It turned out that he had friends in this village who would lend him money to buy gas to get us to the ship. We were indeed wrecks when we finally left him and his "taxi" on reaching our destination.

As I say, it was very, very late now and not a soul was in sight. We managed to find our cabins on our own but had read that there was a mandatory boat drill that night and we fully intended complying with that mandate. We waited an hour. The sun was starting to come over the horizon. We decided that perhaps we had missed the boat drill. Duh! Our trip had begun.

Now, this was no ordinary cruise. The *Minerva II* was the only vessel in the P & O Line run by the British for the British. There were about 500 passengers, only eight of whom were American or Canadian. I couldn't begin to tell you how impressed I was with the British curiosity and stamina. We traveled under some very difficult circumstances and there was nary a complaint.

Howard in front of the *Minerva* II

The trip began in Panama and ended in the Bahamas. We anchored at little known ports of call. Ours was the first cruise ship ever to visit La Ceiba, Honduras. The reason for each of these ports was their accessibility to Maya ruins. Many of the excursions on land were very long with Copán, Tikal, Quiriguá, Lamanai, Cobá, Chichén Itzá and Uxmal being up to twelve hours in length.

Aldine in Antigua, Guatemala

I must admit that one of the trips I took that required 12 hours had nothing to do with the Maya. Seven of us flew in a Cessna Caravan from Santo Tomás to Guatemala City and then on to Antigua. I had the good fortune to sit right seat on both legs and for those of you who fly I want to mention that take-offs were done with full-flaps. I was uncomfortable with this and pointed out "the oversight" to the pilot who advised me that full-flaps were *obligatorio*. Ah, well. Antigua was the Colonial capital of Guatemala until its destruction by earthquake in the 18th century. It was breathtaking in its beauty and charm.

Aldine translating for the guide on Maya ruin tour

The countries we visited in addition to Panama were Costa Rica, Honduras, Guatemala, Belize and Mexico. While in Honduras, we toured the ruins at Copán, an impressive experience. Our guide was a cheerful man who quickly admitted he did not speak English very well. He was right! Our frustrated group, knowing I spoke Spanish, asked if I would be kind enough to translate for him. He was delighted and gratefully relinquished his pointer to me. I did a credible job and everyone was happy!

What a wonderful way to be indoctrinated into the "Mysteries of the Maya"–the name of the cruise–on a British ship on her maiden voyage with intellectually zealous and physically intrepid passengers. Among the passengers were Peter O'Toole and Countess Mountbatten, daughter of Lord Mountbatten of Burma. They were treated like everyone else, queuing up with the rest of us. As well, there were no fewer than sixty medical doctors on board. Peter O'Toole was rather shy but never failed to greet me warmly with his familiar sweep of his arm. There was a magnificent library aboard—with not one piece of fiction. You were going to be educated whether you liked it or not!

There were seven guest speakers aboard, each acclaimed in his field. Topics addressed many areas of the regional culture and terrain:

–Maya art and architecture and the enduring culture of the modern Maya
–European colonization and conflict between old and new worlds
–The Central American ecosystem
–Maya beliefs and confrontation with Christianity
–The Meso-American barrier reef system (2nd largest in the world)
–Comparison of pyramids in the old and new worlds
–Cracking the Maya code
–The anatomy of a rainforest
–Wildlife of the neotropics
–The impact of the United States on Central America
–The real pirates of the Caribbean
–Pre-conquest religions (Maya, Aztec) and blood sacrifice

Two weeks sped by and all too soon we reached Freeport in the Bahamas. We flew from there back to Tucson. I certainly got my wish—an in-depth exploration of one of the world's fascinating destinations.

51

☙

JAMAICA WITH MY SONS AND THEIR FAMILIES—2005

While far from the most luxurious of our family trips, Jamaica was considered by all to be one of the best. What made it so special for them I am not quite certain. Perhaps it was because every aspect of it was out of the ordinary.

We departed Tucson on March 26, 2005. Our group included Kent, Janice, Tana (16), Tony, Elizabeth, Max (14) and Alex (12). Our friend, Howard Shenk, came with us as he often did. As Howard had arranged for the two of us to fly first class on a Boeing 777, we arrived in Jamaica rested and enthusiastic. However, the rest of my family had taken other flights that ended as a trip that could only be described as a nightmare. We were all to have arrived in Montego Bay about the same time and take the long drive to our destination together—we in a rental car and they by a limousine provided by our villa. As they had been rerouted due to flight problems, we had no idea what their new schedule was.

Howard was chagrined that he was denied a rental car as his driver's license had expired. How lucky were we that we saw a man brandishing a sign saying "von Isser." The intention was that this man was to provide the transportation for the rest of the family. We were saved. We explained to him that we didn't know when the others would arrive, but we were ready to go.

We knew soon enough that we had averted disaster by having an experienced Jamaican driver—Garfield—at the wheel. The two hour trip to the villa was over treacherous winding roads—sometimes only one lane wide—and, as it was nighttime, it was very dark. Howard counted his lucky stars that he was not the driver and when we finally reached the villa it was with a sigh of gratitude for having survived the trip.

And then the waiting game began. We had no way to be in touch with my young people. We could only wait anxiously for their arrival which didn't occur until 1:30 p.m. the following day. They were met by Garfield and, although it was in daylight, the driving experience was no less scary for them. Add to that that Alex, who was prone to carsickness, retched during the entire trip. They all were exhausted when they arrived. What a beginning!

The villa that I had rented for this holiday—the *Buccaneer*—was isolated and remote. It was situated on the top of a hill overlooking the ocean and had a winding path down to the "beach." Sadly, Hurricane Ivan had gone through that area the previous fall and the beach was strewn with logs and debris of every sort. We could have been dismayed. But there was something magical about this bougainvillea-covered place and its attached cemetery.

Looking down on Treasure Beach

The villa, which was basically open-air, had four bedrooms in strange locations. Tana and I had to go through her parents' room to reach ours—not always convenient. And it had four bathrooms, always a plus. The house reminded us of a hacienda with tropical plantings and exotic plants and flowers escaping from every crevice. It had no wall separating the living room from the patio—just an iron gate that could be closed and locked but was left wide open during our entire visit.

Interior of the Buccaneer

The place harked back to generations past and had the advantage of coming with two ladies—Susie and Rima–who were to serve our every need—barefoot. They stocked the refrigerator, made the meals–which were very basic–and laughed a lot. Garfield—Susie's husband–was our man "Friday" and another man, Seifert, spent a great deal of time there as well. We came to love these dear people. All our meals were eaten outside and were delicious.

Our happy group – Alex, Tony, Elizabeth, Max,
Aldine, Howard, Susie, Rima, Janice, Kent & Tana

Seifert on the porch

Beside our swimming pool was the graveyard. We never understood its proximity to the pool and the house but it was a wonderful spot to sun and hang our towels.

March 28th was Kent's 52nd birthday, reason for fun and celebration. There was an upper deck where we spent the evening telling stories. There was never a dearth of family memories for reminiscing.

One day was especially memorable. Garfield took us in a Jamaican "canoe/motor boat" up the Black River to a wonderful place to swim. Everyone took turns jumping into the river from a rope attached to a tree. Tana was in the process of swinging over the river when we spotted a huge crocodile nearby. That activity was quickly scotched.

Alex, Tana & Max in the pool

Later we were taken to a most unusual place for lunch—the Pelican Bar—which was three miles out into the ocean and built on stilts on a reef. It was a

Swinging from the tree

Embarking on a boat trip

517

thatched roof structure—open on all sides—with a menu of fish and lobster. A man named Floyd was the owner, host, chef and waiter. While our meal was being prepared, we swam in the ocean surrounding the "restaurant." When we were summoned for lunch, we found that there were only two chairs so we sat on the floor to dine. The fish was served whole—head and all. For those who were squeamish about the head being attached, Janice came to their aid and ate heads and all. We returned home through a very rough sea which made for a wild ride but lots of fun.

Pelican Bar

Having nowhere accessible to go if we left the villa, we had dinner at home every night. Afterwards, we would sit on our porch and watch the activity on the beach. There was a thatched hut there that was referred to as a bar. It was a gathering spot for local people who congregated nightly, built a bonfire and smoked "weed." From the happy sounds emanating from below, we knew what a good

Alex with his fish lunch – head and all

time they were having. Every evening, the prevailing wind from the ocean carried a heavy residue of their marijuana smoke up the hill for us to enjoy. I'm not so sure I didn't get a buzz on one night—it was that thick!

This area was a hub as the local people were fishermen and brought their catches there daily. The beach, known as Treasure Beach, had previously been the place where pirates gathered. As most were of European background they were fair skinned. In intermingling with the local Jamaican girls, a generation with lighter skin emerged. Jamaicans are typically very dark skinned, but on this part of the island they look more European. We found them to be very handsome people.

Walking through the debris on the beach each day, we were able to find some good areas to swim in the ocean. We had to be exceedingly careful and children were supervised at all times. A reef protected us from the ocean but there was a very strong riptide. The best spots to swim were close to the reef where the water was deep. There were, however, spaces in the reef where the riptide could suck you through and out into the sea.

One day Howard and I were swimming alone out there. I thought I was being careful but suddenly I found myself being pulled inexorably toward the reef. I screamed for Howard to help me. He, I have to add, is not entirely comfortable as a swimmer or in the water. No one else was nearby to see my dangerous situation. I will always remember Howard coming to my rescue, grabbing my leg and, with all his strength, pulling me back to safety. Had he not caught me, I would have been dragged through the jagged reef and would have had no way back to shore. Unquestionably, he saved my life.

Nine of us in Susie's van!

Susie had the availability of a rickety old van that would barely hold all of us. It was uncomfortable in the extreme and I often ended up sitting on the floor of the backseat under the feet of the people seated. Nonetheless, this was our transportation and Susie was a pretty good driver. One day she took us for a ride to "see" Jamaica. We found it to be an arid, hot, third world country.

We drove to Lover's Leap with its 1750 foot drop to the ocean where indeed there had been a lot of jumpers. She took us to a secluded but very dirty beach. Additionally, the undertow there was far too strong for any of us to swim. That was followed by lunch at an outdoor restaurant on the beach that tourists rarely visit—Ochies. We definitely had Jamaican fare there.

On our next stop, she hit the jackpot—a hardware store. My family loves odd bits and pieces of things and they found invaluable treasures here including brass and copper nails of which they bought many pounds.

On other days, a highlight was the visit of the local vendors who arrived with their many arts and crafts. There was a good deal of haggling before firm prices were established. Basically, this was the main contact we had with local people.

One night we were the guests of Elizabeth and Tony at Jack Spratt's for pizza and wandered through the famous Jake's Resort.

During the days we spent time together and time on our own projects. We collected shells and artifacts, swam in the pool or ocean, painted, played

Max & Alex feeding local pigs

games and listened to Max play his guitar. We took naps, read, chatted and ate. As I say, this was a favorite trip of us all. It was a time for family to be together in an intimate and carefree setting. We returned to Tucson on April 5th loaded with all manner of treasures such as chains and nails. Everyone was happy which made me happiest of all.

52

 consider

THE CARIBBEAN ABOARD THE *QUEEN MARY 2* –2006

Perhaps our most disappointing cruise was aboard the biggest ship in the world at that time—2006. We had flown to New York City prior to embarkation on the *Queen Mary 2* and stayed at a Holiday Inn at the south edge of Central Park. The weather was dreadful on our day of embarkation, January 3rd. It was very cold with strong wind and sleet. I elected to stay in the hotel in the morning but Hal braved the elements to fulfill a dream. He wanted to be on NBC's Today Show—as part of the audience panned by the cameras standing outside the studio. And there he was! I was so pleased his hope had been realized. He was a celebrity!

We boarded the *Queen Mary* 2 late in the day amidst great confusion. The crew was simply not ready for their next load of passengers. We settled into our delightful cabin, excited at all that lay ahead. The next two days were spent at sea giving us an opportunity to explore this behemoth. To our surprise and chagrin we discovered that it was not nearly as luxurious as other ships we had taken. The company appeared to be pinching pennies. We did not have robes for our cabin nor were there sufficient towels.

However, the captain's party was lovely, the meals excellent, and the floor shows varied. And I spent every evening dancing with my favorite beau, Hal. He was a superb dancer. Our first port of call was Charlotte Amalie on St. Thomas. We had visited there before and spent our time buying gifts to take home to our families. One new item was a tee-shirt that changed color in the sun!

After another day at sea we reached Curacao, again a repeat for us. We made a trip to shore but chose to enjoy the remainder of the day in activities on the ship. On all the cruises I have ever taken, I walk the promenade deck daily for two miles both for exercise and to stave off the effects of rich meals. On this ship three laps was equal to 1 1/3 mile. It was enormous and simply walking from one event to another onboard ship would probably have sufficed for my daily regimen.

On January 9th, the captain had a party to honor passengers who had previously sailed on the Cunard Line. I think I set the record for having sailed over the greatest number of years. Tony and I had traveled on the *Parthia* from New York City to Liverpool in September, 1954—52 years earlier!

After another day at sea, we arrived in Cristóbal Colón, Panama. Howard and I had been there 20 months previous when we took a cruise aboard the *Minerva* 2 but we had seen little of the area as we had arrived at night. Hal and I took an excursion that left at 8:45 a.m. and returned at 3:30 p.m. We toured the modern city as well as the old city and found it fascinating and full of history. It was a much a more interesting visit than we had anticipated.

I had been excited about our arrival in Costa Rica, one of my favorite countries to visit, on January 11th. Hal was up at 3:00 a.m. and ready to go. However, the voice of the captain came over the loudspeaker announcing

Hal on St. Thomas

that it was too wavy for the tenders to safely carry passengers to shore. Everyone agreed that it didn't look too rough at all and that the captain was merely saving time, fuel and money. What a disappointment for us all.

Both Hal and I had developed bad colds on this trip so accepted gratefully the reality that we would be at sea now until we reached New York City. The captain made up for having missed a significant port of call by hosting a magnificent dinner with escargot, lobster and baked Alaska. It was marred, however, by a wine steward who had become increasingly rude as the days went by. I had to take him to task. As my diary said, "It upset me to do it but I would have been more upset if I hadn't."

On the last day of our cruise, January 13th, the wind howled and there was lightning, thunder and rain. We did quiet things as we both continued to feel miserable with colds.

Disembarking the ship was a nightmare and we were glad to see the last of *Queen Mary* 2. We were never tempted again by the cruise offers that came by mail. When we arrived in Tucson on January 15th, we had traveled for 23 hours straight. Hal dropped me off at home and bed never felt so good.

I would happily have spent the following days in bed as I continued to have a chest cold and fever but I had committed to taking care of Max and Alex which was always a joy for me. Elizabeth was at art school in Scottsdale and Tony, of course, at work. The boys had the day off from school. Alex showed me his Honor Roll certificate and his new ipod. I took the lads to a movie and then to a guitar store. Guitars had become a serious passion for Max and he played well. The next day I picked Max and three of his friends up after high school and was there when Alex came home from school. I loved my time with my boys but was glad to turn them over to their parents when the time came.

Wednesday I was so sick I never even dressed. By Thursday I was too sick to drive so Hal took me to the doctor who diagnosed a bacterial lung infection and prescribed a powerful antibiotic and heavy-duty cough syrup. It took weeks for me to fully recover. The *Queen Mary* 2 was not an experience I ever wanted to repeat.

53

☙❧

THE GAUDENTENTHURM AND THE MEDITERRANEAN — 2008

It was serendipity. Unexpected moments of magic and experiences that transform us forever occur so rarely. My family was particularly fortunate as this happened when they were all together and could share equally the gratitude and euphoria that events had converged as they did.

In 2008 I decided the time had come to take my whole family for a visit to the ancient home of the von Isser family—the Gaudententhurm–in a small town called Partschins in the Alps in northern Italy known as the Tyrol. I had taken my sons to visit the old castle when they were teenagers and now it was time for their children to have the same opportunity.

After considerable coordination with the von Isser cousins in the town of Meran in the Tyrol, a time for the visit was established. Tony Sr. and I had been in touch with this family—the von Sölders—since the early 1950s when we had visited there for the first time. The patriarch, Dr. Peter von Sölder, was deceased but his widow, Dr. Edith von Sölder was alive and very well in spite of her advanced years. Her children and grandchildren were excited to be meeting their cousins from the United States. All were of similar ages but of disparate cultures and language. One would think this might have created a problem. Not at all.

Our rendezvous in Europe was the first hurdle. Kent, Janice, Tana (20), Tony, Elizabeth, Max (17) and Alex (15) had flown together from Tucson to Venice where they immediately boarded a train to take them north to Meran. They were met there and welcomed with open arms by the von Sölder family.

Hal and I had flown from our cottage in Canada on June 4th arriving in Venice the following day. There we boarded the ship on which later we all would take a cruise—the *Emerald Princess*. We knew we couldn't handle the strenuous days with the young people in Partschins and Meran so we awaited them on the ship.

Tony and Max exploring
Partschins on
Max-von-Isser-Straße

And a strenuous, fun-filled time they had. The emotional connection with their cousins was immediate and the days that followed exceeded any experience they had ever known. They were welcomed into their homes and hearts and the magic of that time has never faded. It will remain for each of them a joyful interlude in their lives.

One incredible experience they recall was the opportunity they had to visit one floor of the old castle that had been locked since Edith's husband had died many years before. It housed ancient von Isser treasures—family heirlooms, furniture and paintings. They were in awe. Tony and I had seen these treasures 54 years previously, and I was thrilled that they too were able to witness so much of their family history.

With their cousins they went hiking and sightseeing. They spent hours visiting and getting to know one another—language differences not being an impediment. New friendships were forged that will exist forever. We are all on Facebook now so continue to send messages and photographs. I would so like to write about each of those beautiful Austrian cousins but suffice that they are handsome, intelligent and worldly.

My young people were on a very high "high" when they joined us on the ship after their trip to Northern Italy, and they didn't come down for days. It was wonderful to behold and exceeded all my hopes and expectations. The purpose of the trip had been fulfilled.

The von Isser men in Partschins –
Tony, Max, Kent & Alex

However, this was just the beginning of a longer adventure. We sailed from Venice on June 6th and spent the following day at sea. Regrettably, I experienced every cruiser's nightmare–none of my luggage had made it to the ship and I was without even a toothbrush. Frantic calls were made to Heathrow in London where we had changed planes begging them to locate my bags. Leaning on the mercy of the man with whom I spoke I said, "But sir, I am on my honeymoon and I have to wear my husband's underwear to bed!" His response was that as I was on my honeymoon I shouldn't be wearing anything at all to bed. What a cheeky thing to say! In fact, Hal and I had been married only a few months and this was indeed our delayed honeymoon.

For several days I wore the clothes in which I had traveled—jeans and a sweater–even to the formal dinner night on board. I had not even taken a carry-on bag with me as I didn't want Hal to have to deal with it during our travels. Big mistake. I could have purchased clothes on board the ship but I was sure as we approached each port that my luggage would be waiting for me. It never turned up—until months later when it was delivered to our cottage in Dwight. I tried to be a good sport about this debacle, but it did put a damper on my enjoyment of the trip.

Dubrovnik, a Croatian city on the Adriatic Sea, was our first port of call. I had been there several times before, once with Kent and Tony Jr. We landed in the city by tender, after which the families went their own ways and enjoyed this ancient, fascinating city. Many photographs were taken to record their long walk on the wall that surrounds the city. It is 1.2 miles long. Hal and I entertained ourselves by having a beer in an outdoor café. We always met as a big, and noisy, family in the evening for dinner on the ship. Tana and I often went off on our own for long talks after dinner. I treasure those moments with her.

Corfu, our next stop, enchanted everyone. It is a Greek island on the Ionian Sea. The young people walked to the old town while Hal and I took a taxi to tour the island with many stops to enjoy the magnificent vistas. Calamari, one of Hal's favorite foods, was on our menu for lunch, and it was delicious. His day had been made. Finding good calamari had been one of Hal's quests in life; he rarely had been satisfied but kept on searching for it as if it were the Holy Grail.

Kent, Tana & Janice lunching in Corfu

On June 9th we reached Katakolon, a small, sleepy port town on the western coast of the Peloponnese Peninsula of Greece. The weather was magnificent and the young people went ashore to take an excursion to ancient Olympia. On their return, they had time to shop in town. I was very touched by what they had bought—rather gaudy

Our group at dinner with ladies in their matching dresses

Greek dresses for each of the women in our group that we all wore to dinner that night (and never again). Their colors were intoxicating—turquoise, red, pink, and yellow—and they were replete with shiny ribbon! This was their loving attempt to level the playing field as they had their lovely frocks while I continued to wear jeans and sneakers. I am sure that all the other diners were aghast at our ensembles and probably were wondering, "What are they thinking?"

Janice and Elizabeth lent me whatever clothes they could that would fit me. Janice had provided me with a bathing suit that day so that Hal and I could visit the Lotus Spa pool with its "eternal wave" machine. That night Alex won a sports competition on board while Max, who had taken his guitar, serenaded everyone.

Those dear boys had found a stick on the beach at Katakolon to assist me in walking. I was a little wobbly, I admit. The stick developed quite a history. When we returned to the U.S., the stick was discovered by a security dog in the airport in Philadelphia. Its hormone-driven master, a strident woman who would brook no infraction of the law, was confiscating the stick. Well, I was emotionally involved with that stick as was known by my family. We were told that it could not go on board as it was natural wood that could harbor some horrible fungus, or whatever. Kent asked if it could go in a suitcase and be sent as baggage. I am sure that when she agreed to that option, she was confident it would not be an issue as the stick was about six feet long and could not, of course, fit in a suitcase. She didn't know Kent! He broke the stick in half, put it in Hal's suitcase (I didn't have one) and we were free to go. When Kent came to the cottage later in the summer, he worked miracles reviving the stick with glue and dowels, and I continue to use it to this day. What memories it evokes!

Athens, with all its memories for me, was our next port of call. We landed in Piraeus where I hired a van and the nine of us had a private tour that covered much of the city and surrounding area. We stopped for a walk up to the Acropolis and later had lunch on the terrace of a picturesque restaurant in the Plaka. Back at the ship, each was on his own in the late afternoon and Hal and I chose to nap. After dinner that night there was a hilarious comedy show.

Family at Olympic Stadium

Who knows where the young people went for the remainder of the evening and night!

Young people love Mykonos, our port the next day, and mine were no exception. We all went ashore to explore the town and enjoy the beaches. Hal and I, content with our advancing years, chose to sit in the shade at a quaint café for lunch and a respite. I bought a few more sundresses to see me through the cruise. Hal and I returned to the ship to swim in the lovely pool and get some exercise. That night I felt quite elegant at dinner in one of my new gowns. Things were looking up.

Kuşadasi, Turkey was a total surprise for us all. I had been there years before when it was a simple port whose main purpose was to provide a dock for ships to stop for disembarkation of passengers taking the excursion to Ephesus—the main attraction. How changed it was! There were stores abounding providing the best shopping I had ever seen anywhere. I bought a stylish red leather jacket that continues to be a staple in my wardrobe. I also added a blouse to my limited wardrobe.

Ephesus created quite an impression on my family. It is a famous ancient city that was founded in the 10th century BCE. It was a long day for them and all were glad to return to the ship for some "time out." We met in the Crooners Lounge, as was our habit, before having dinner in the fabulous Da Vinci Dining Room. The evening's entertainment followed and everyone enjoyed the floor shows immensely.

Santorini—unforgettable and magnificent. I had been there many times but never failed to fall under its spell. While all the young people rode donkeys to the village on the top of the island, Hal and I, with our brittle bones, were perfectly happy to go by incline tram. As we roamed the charming, cobbled streets, I made use of my stick to assist me in climbing the hills. Suddenly I was bumped into and almost knocked over by an aged, black clad crone who was racing up the hill hell-bent for election! Ahead we watched her stop, sit down on the road, arrange herself, place her alms basket in front of her and assume a convincingly pathetic position complete with tears—a crippled old widow with no means of support. We roared with laughter, and I secretly wished I had her vigor and chutzpah.

Alex ascending trail on Santorini

Tana on her donkey - Santorini

We all joined for lunch at a terraced restaurant overlooking the Aegean. There is no denying it—the views of Santorini hanging over the Aegean defy the imagination. It is spectacular in the real sense of the word. Back at the ship that night, we enjoyed a floor show featuring a hypnotist and I continued to wonder why people would put themselves in such an embarrassing position on stage as volunteers in front of all those strangers. Hypnotism had always fascinated me, and I am one of those who can be "put under" with the least provocation.

The next day at sea gave everyone a chance to unwind and enjoy the beautiful ship. I spent time at the pool reading and swimming. Before dinner we all congregated to have our family photograph taken. Later we enjoyed the floor show and Hal and I took a romantic walk on deck followed by a nightcap—for him. We wanted this cruise never to end. Having all of my family together filled my heart with pleasure.

Elizabeth hiking up Vesuvius

We docked the following day at Naples, Italy— one of my least favorite cities. Neither Hal nor I felt up to the exertion of the demanding visit to Mt. Vesuvius preferring instead to spend the day on the ship. Mt. Vesuvius is best known for its eruption in AD 79 that led to the destruction and burial of Pompeii and other settlements.

The report we received from the climbers on their return was that it had indeed been a tough trek to the top of the mountain and they were physically exhausted. And after their visit to Pompeii they were emotionally drained as well. This experience had a profound impact on all of them. Everyone took a much needed rest before dinner.

Max had made many friends on the ship and arranged for our last dinner on board to include the families of all his new buddies. It was a big and happy group and everyone had a stupendous time.

We arrived in Rome on June 17th where we disembarked for our return home. We were up before 4:00 a.m. and all nine of us headed for the Da Vinci airport arriving there at 5:45 a.m. We flew US Air to the airport in Philadelphia in rather cramped quarters. It was a sad moment for me when we left there to go our separate ways—Hal and I to our cottage in Ontario and the rest of the family back to Tucson. Unquestionably, it had been a memorable trip that none of us will ever forget—filled with synergy, harmony and love.

After a night in Toronto, Hal and I returned to the cottage. How good it felt to have my own things around me—especially clothes and cosmetics, both of which I had been denied for so long. It was mid-September when I received a phone call from Pierson Airport in Toronto. They wanted directions to our cottage so that they could deliver my luggage! I couldn't believe it and I wasn't really sure I wanted it anymore; there were such unpleasant memories associated with it. When I opened the first suitcase, I realized what I had been denied during the trip. It was devastating. All those nights without my crossword puzzles, to which I was addicted, and all the cosmetics that would have staved off the punishment of life at sea. But what I also found was my address book which had probably been the greatest loss of all. The circle was complete and I was at peace.

The von Isser & von Sölder families

Sylvia von Sölder, Christine Schönweger, Janice von Isser, Christof, Edith, Felix, Elisabeth, Maximillian, Anna, Otto & Phillip von Sölder, Elizabeth, Tony, Tana, Max, Alex & Kent von Isser

54

∞

THE AZORES AND BEYOND—2011

Hal had turned 80! We decided that such a significant event called for a celebratory cruise. On May 4, 2011 we flew to Ft. Lauderdale, Florida, spending a night there before our departure the next day.

Our ship was the *Grand Princess* and the cabin to which we were assigned was dreadful—a great disappointment. The ship was full so we had no alternative other than to embrace it with dignity. The trip, however, turned out to be very much to our liking with interesting ports of call and superb excursions.

We spent six days at sea crossing the Atlantic—a time when a lovely cabin would have made the days more comfortable. As it was, our bed was pushed against a wall leaving no walking space beside it. Thus, I had to crawl across the entire bed to reach my niche in it. Of course, I had neither a bedside table nor a lamp to read by at night. Our furniture was one desk chair. It was in the very bow of the ship so we knew this would be a rock and roll trip. We had not meant to economize, but someone had to draw the short straw in each category on every cruise, and it was our turn. Two nights into the cruise, the ship had to make an unscheduled stop in Bermuda to disembark a very sick passenger. Hal, always Johnny on the spot, had barely let the poor man's bed cool before he was at the purser's office begging him to allow us to move to it. No luck.

But, one adapts and we turned our cabin into a cozy nook that fitted our needs and where we spent many happy hours.

We passed our days attending classes, hearing lectures, and learning to line dance! The meals were superb and the floor shows outstanding.

Our first port of call on May 12th was Punta Delgada, the largest city in the Azores. We were on Säo Miguel, the largest of the nine islands that make up this archipelago belonging to Portugal. We took an excellent tour by bus through the countryside, stopping at a pineapple greenhouse after which we took a walk through a botanical garden. We stopped frequently along the way for passengers to disembark and view the magnificent valleys and hills. Säo Miguel was very beautiful and this excursion explained the reason for it being known as The Green Island.

Hal & Aldine on Säo Miguel Island

The next two days were again at sea. I had counted on spending a good deal of this free time at their internet café but sending an email proved to be impossible. I very much wanted to be in touch with home as my brother was having serious cancer surgery in Toronto. Later we learned that all had gone well.

Cobh, Ireland was our next stop—a place that Hal and I had visited previously. We knew just where we wanted to go this time—the fascinating Immigration Museum. This port has a remarkable maritime history. It was the departure point for 2.5 million Irish people who immigrated to North America between 1848 and 1950. Cobh—then known as Queenstown—was well known as it was the final port of call for the RMS *Titanic* when she set out across the Atlantic on her ill-fated maiden voyage.

Another notable tragedy associated with the town was the sinking of the RMS *Lusitania* by a German U-boat in 1915. While 700 passengers were rescued, 1,198 died. The survivors and the dead alike were brought to Cobh, and the bodies of over 100 who perished in the disaster lie buried in the Old Church Cemetery just north of the town. Ireland has always been a destination that fascinated us.

We arrived in Dublin the following day to very windy and cold weather. We were able to spend considerable time in St. Patrick's Cathedral but, due to very tight security in the city at that time, we couldn't visit Trinity University. The security was in place in preparation for the arrival the following day of Queen Elizabeth, marking the first time a monarch had visited there in almost a century.

Glasgow, Scotland conjures a dark city with cold and dreary weather. That is how I remembered it from a visit almost sixty years earlier and that is as it was when we arrived there the following day. We took a long city bus tour ending at the Kelvingrove

Gallery and Museum. Hal and I went off on our own and, sated with Scottish history and lore, made our way back to Greenock where our ship was moored. Later in the day we were treated to bagpipe music and a Scottish dancing program. As I am of primarily Scottish blood, the pipes never fail to elicit a powerful response in me—both physically and emotionally. They are played at all our Sinclair family events—weddings, funerals, baptisms and family reunions among them.

Never having been to Wales, I was excited the following day when we docked at Holyhead and took a bus tour through the countryside stopping briefly in a town that the Welsh claim has the longest name in the world. It was Llanfairpwllgwyngyllgogerychwyrndrobwyllllantysiliogogogoch which translates to The church of St. Mary in the hollow of white hazel trees near the rapid whirlpool by St. Tysilio's of the red cave. For the local people, of course, the name just rolled off their tongues but we tourists were tongue-tied. We continued on to Beaumaris Castle—an austere edifice to be sure. It was very cold there. However, I found the scenery lovely, green and gentle, and could understand why Wales held such a great attraction to the three million people who lived there. They were very proud of their homeland, their culture and their language.

We did considerable walking on our own that day and enjoyed mingling with the local people before returning to the ship. A formal evening was planned with the captain hosting an elaborate party.

Our next stop was Falmouth, Cornwall in southwest England. It was the first lovely day that we had and we took full advantage of the sunshine and warmth. We had a delightful bus tour throughout Cornwall stopping in the town of Marazion on the shore of Mount's Bay. We had been looking forward to experiencing Cornish clotted tea–plain tea with scones, jam and incredibly rich clotted cream. It was all I had hoped for–delicious—the most scrumptious tea I have ever had. From the charming teahouse, we had a spectacular view of the iconic St. Michael's Mount—an impressive castle offshore accessible by land only during low tide. Happily weary, we returned to our ship at 5:00 p.m. in time for a late dinner.

Hal in Cornwall

The following day was the last of our cruise with a visit to the city Hal had been dreaming about—Paris. This was his first time there although I had been there several times—the first with Tony in 1954—57 years earlier!

It was a three-hour drive from the ship in Le Havre to Paris where we had many hours to explore the city. We loved the cruise on the Seine and wandering the streets.

Hal was thrilled to have his dream come true but he considered our one day there quite enough. He found it crowded and altogether overwhelming.

By the time we returned to the ship, we had been exploring France and Paris for over 12 hours. While I was frantic with fatigue, I noted in my diary that, "Hal is always so even and keeps me sane." Our tiny cabin was a welcome sight and we quickly showered and prepared for our last night on board the *Grand Princess*. Indeed it had been a grand trip.

We disembarked in Southampton on May 21st having been away from Tucson for 18 days. Flying back required 24 hours of travel to reach the Tucson airport where we were met by Howard. When we arrived home, we found that he had provided our house with lots of food—so very kind of him. One of my first tasks was to phone Toronto to learn of Murray's condition. Mary reassured us he was making a good recovery.

Hal in front of the Eiffel Tower

We were home in time for Alex's graduation from Catalina Foothills High School on May 25th. After the impressive evening ceremony, the graduates were invited into the gym which had been decorated magnificently and provided with ample food and activities to keep the young people occupied for the entire night. Alex left at 5:00 a.m.— a happy camper!

A couple of weeks later we noted that National Geographic Magazine had named the ten best places in the world to visit that summer–2011. The Azores and Wales were among them, but the number one spot went to <u>Muskoka</u>, the location of our summer cottage in Ontario. Just think, we were spending the summer at the place considered the best in the world that year, and we had already visited two of the others during our trip. All very exciting!

55

C3&O

THE MARITIME PROVINCES IN CANADA—2011

Alex had completed high school in May of 2011 and asked a special favor of me. Could he have four of his friends come to the cottage in Canada for a week of play before they settled down to university? Now, I have never, ever lent the cottage to anybody and here was Alex asking to have a group of energetic teenage boys there to celebrate their freedom. Did I think twice about it? Not at all. I was delighted they were planning this spree, although it meant that Hal and I had to get out of Dodge.

We started our departure day—August 6th— by taking Kent, Janice and Tana to the bus terminal in Huntsville for their trip to the Toronto airport and then their flight to Tucson. Alex and I had already made a grocery run–$450—in preparation for his visitors. Alex is a phenomenal cook/chef and had planned some rather exotic meals. Drinking alcohol is not legal in Canada until age 19 so we had no booze on board. I might add, however, that a "secret Santa" –Mary Sinclair—had left a case of beer for them at the front door after Hal and I had left.

I spent the morning making sure all sheets were changed and the cottage spotlessly clean. Alex wisely stayed out of Nana's way as I was a whirling dervish when I got going. His friends were to arrive on the 9:00 p.m. bus. One lad, who had flown from Germany, had spent the night on the floor at the airport awaiting the arrival of his friends the next day so that they could all come north together.

There was only one fly in the ointment. Hydro (the electric company) had reminded us for weeks that in order to make an equipment transition it was necessary for them to turn off the hydro for 12 hours—from 8:00 p.m. until 8: a.m. on August 13th and 14th, Alex's last night there and the day of their departure. How were they ever going to awaken, have breakfast, pack and leave early in the morning when it was still dark outside? I had outlawed the use of candles but they did have ample flashlights. Their bus was to leave Huntsville at 8:00 a.m. I had arranged for them to leave my car at a designated spot in Huntsville for us to pick up later. I had to put this conundrum in Alex's hands.

During the week Alex was using the cottage, Hal and I had decided to make a trip to the Maritime Provinces in eastern Canada as he had never been there. At two in the afternoon, we said goodbye to Alex, leaving him on his own, and headed east through the magnificent Algonquin Park. Later we lingered in Ottawa, Ontario, the nation's capital, and enjoyed the beauty of this gracious city and the stately Parliament Buildings. Our goal for that evening was a town I have always referred to as the "armpit of the world"—Hawkesbury, Ontario. We stayed there in what must have been the seediest motel we had ever encountered. It was a lark just because it was so awful. We found a swinging café for dinner and considered the whole experience a "hoot."

The following day took us through Montreal and Quebec City. This was not easy driving for Hal as the French Canadians refused to speak, write or recognize English as a language in any way. This included all the highway signs. Hal depended on my two years of university French to help him translate what he was supposed to do next on the highway or in the cities. He was not at all happy! In the rest of Canada, all signs and labels had to be in both English and French. This applied to every can of soup or box of cereal. In Quebec they went so far as to require that grocery stores have only the labels in French visible on the shelves. Now really!

We were exhausted by the time we checked into a Best Western Motel in Edmundson, New Brunswick. And we were bleary-eyed when we started out after breakfast the next day and drove without stopping (except for gas or a bathroom break—or a quick trip into the woods). My diary noted that, "We were on serious back roads–no civilization for many miles—and I loved the beauty of the countryside." We drove across the entire province of New Brunswick and took a bridge more than nine miles long onto Prince Edward Island. On my previous trip there with Tony, there had been no bridge whatever and it was necessary to cross by ferry.

We continued to the charming town of Charlottetown where we found a quaint motel in which to stay—the Banbridge Inn. We sat on rockers on our little front porch with a glass of wine before going downtown for a delicious seafood dinner. Hal had been craving lobster fresh out of the sea. If he couldn't find it there he believed he wouldn't find it anywhere.

We spent another day in Charlottetown driving throughout the island and finding it delightful in every respect. We felt so ready to go home, but Alex had another five days there. Hence, we continued on the next day for what evolved into a long and exhausting trip. We traveled via Woods End Ferry to Nova Scotia in rain. I have failed to mention that it had rained every day of the entire trip so far! We drove all day on a lovely scenic route on the East Shore.

Hal found the highways there very confusing and frustrating. I remember Halifax as only a blur of lights through the windshield wipers. We were looking for a nice motel but seemed blocked at every turn and drove on into the night—in the rain—to a town called Truro. There we found a room in a Super 8 motel. We had a very late dinner and finally got to bed at 11:00 p.m. This had not been a relaxing trip thus far.

The following day I was the one who was truly frustrated. Even Hal was exhausted by the trip now and it continued to rain cats and dogs. As we were traveling primarily in Canada, I had taken only my Canadian passport with me. We intended going from New Brunswick into Maine for the route home that we had planned. At a little place called St. Stephen, we attempted to cross the border into the States. The U.S. customs official took our passports—U.S. for Hal and Canadian for me. He then asked me to provide proper identification. I told him that my passport was current and should be sufficient. It wasn't. Not enough documentation, he said. He gave us an out suggesting we tell him we were only going into Maine for the day to shop. I would have no part of that—a lie and, I thought, unnecessary. I became a bit chuffed which did my cause no good.

Clearly they were not going to let me into the U.S. with only a Canadian passport which I felt quite sure must be illegal. All the Canadians I know travel with only their Canadian passports. However, knowing Hal was tired and worn, I admitted to the official that I also had a U.S. passport—but not with me. Suddenly, his attitude changed and he pointed me toward the customs building. It was huge and gray and looked very much like the waiting room in a prison. Not a soul was in evidence except for one woman behind a wicket who looked most unwelcoming. I told her that my Canadian passport was proving to be insufficient to allow me to cross the border but that I did have a U.S. passport at home. She pecked away at her computer and said, "Oh, you're a pilot." The FAA must pop up first. In any case, I was now legal to cross and we entered Maine officially. I was seething.

In Maine we could see Mt. Katahdin that Kent, Janice and Tana had climbed so many times. It is a tall and very steep mountain in the Appalachian chain that rises 5,267 feet and is the highest mountain in Maine.

We took the scenic coastal road to Bangor and on to Newport where we stopped for the night—at another seedy motel! Dinner was at McDonald's. Would Alex ever know the torture I was being put through on his behalf?

Another nightmare—truly scary—occurred the following day, an experience that still sends shivers up my spine. While we drove only 463 miles that day, my diary noted that it seemed like hundreds. We had crossed from Maine into Quebec—still south of the St. Lawrence River. Having carefully checked our map, we had identified the back roads we intended to take that would join the highway leading into Montreal. As a backup, we turned on our GPS and decided to follow it to the letter. It guided us through little back villages and narrower and narrower roads. Finally the roads were dirt roads and this didn't seem right to us. Now, however, we had no alternative but to adhere to the guidance of the GPS.

We drove for miles with no civilization in sight—not even a mailbox along the way. It was then that the GPS told us to take the next right–a muddy country lane where we had to dodge water-filled ruts in the road. This was all wrong and I was scared. With fences on both sides of us, we could not turn around. We had to follow it to the end, and end it did—at a padlocked gate. I was now terrified. I was sure that our GPS had been hacked and that we had been led astray for nefarious purposes. I was nearly hysterical by the time Hal was able to turn us around and get us out of there. We drove back toward where we had started and were able to find a route that ultimately took us in the direction of Montreal. I was beyond exhausted when we finally reached Montreal where we drove for hours—literally hours—covering the same terrain over and over in our attempt to find our way to the highway going west toward Ontario—and home. We were feeling vulnerable and helpless—trapped in Canada's second largest city.

We stopped for help but nobody would speak to us in English. In frustration in one gas station   store I said loudly, "I know you understand me and I think you are all very rude not to help me." One brave woman followed me out of the store and gave me some guidance. Hal said he would never drive in Quebec again, and he meant it.

It was eleven at night when we finally reached Cornwall, Ontario and, desperate to find a motel we took the first exit into the city. We soon came upon a gaudy, neon-lit truck-stop motel but—any port in a storm! While Hal kept the truck running, I ran in to see if they had a room available. The bar I had to pass through was filled with rowdy, noisy and heavily tattooed revelers. Not good! I approached "reception"– the check-out counter in the truck stop–and asked if they had accommodations available. When she responded with "By the hour or day?" I made a hasty retreat, jumped in the truck, and told Hal to "gun it."

Nothing was available along the second exit, but on the third we struck gold. We found a lovely motel—a Best Western–the nicest we had on the entire trip. Our room was gorgeous–elegantly decorated and with a fireplace. But we were so tired we were beyond caring. The dining room was closed so we went to bed hungry. What a trip!

We drove practically without stopping the following day—ignoring the beautiful sights and oblivious to Ottawa and Algonquin Park. When we stopped at a motel outside of Dwight we had driven over 2700 grueling miles. We could hardly wait for morning and our return to the cottage. We planned to be there at 8:00 a.m., after Alex and his buddies had left. Then it hit us. Hydro was off in Dwight. The nice waiter at the cafe there told us to be sure to take buckets of water back to our room as there would be no other way to flush the toilet. Oh, and they wouldn't be serving breakfast the following day due to the outage!

There we were—so close to home—with no light to read by and no way to flush the toilet. When we reached the cottage the following morning, we found that Alex and his friends had indeed left and everything looked perfect. Bless their hearts. There was a note of gratitude signed by all of them. Would I go through it all again for Alex? Of course–without batting an eye. The boys had taken copious photographs and later presented me with a collage of all their activities—or at least most of them, shall we say! It hangs on a wall at the cottage and tells the story of all the happy moments they shared at our cottage, Pelican Point.

56

CRES

ABOARD THE *RIVIERA* IN THE CARIBBEAN—2013

Although we had sailed on the Caribbean Sea several times, Hal and I were delighted to find a luxurious cruise that landed at ports of call we had not previously visited. We were excited about this trip and anticipated it with great enthusiasm.

On February 11, 2013 we flew from Tucson to Miami, Florida where we checked into an elegant hotel downtown—the Hyatt Regency. A drink at the bar renewed our energy and we dined that night in the River Front Restaurant. This was an excellent beginning.

We embarked on our lovely ship—the Oceana Line's *Riviera*–the following day and were thrilled with our beautiful cabin which had a verandah and a large bathroom complete with bathtub. The next two days were spent at sea, which was much to our liking as my diary claimed "it is probably the best cruise ship I've ever known."

Our first port of call was Road Town, the capital of Tortola in the British Virgin Islands. We took a group excursion in an old-fashioned open-air wagon and toured the entire island. The roads were very steep and narrow and, as we were in a British country, we drove on the left side of the road. I did some great shopping at an inland market and made many cell phone calls back to the States. We returned to the ship for a delightful evening of dinner and dancing.

St. John's, Antigua was our enchanting destination the next day. Antigua is an island in the West Indies that I had visited several times before. We took a four-hour guided tour that included four stops. I found there to be a great deal of walking in our explorations. When we returned to port, Hal and I shopped and enjoyed the local color.

I had been invited to this island a few years earlier by my beloved cousin Gordon Sinclair whose daughter was being married there. I had been unable to attend, but when Hal and I visited the very location where the wedding took place it had special meaning for me.

Everyone I knew who had visited Barbados had raved about it so Hal and I had been eagerly awaiting our visit to this island. Barbados is a sovereign island country in the Lesser Antilles. We were disappointed in it for many reasons.

First, we arrived on a Sunday and took a taxi to downtown Bridgetown. The cab driver dropped us and left. To our dismay, not only were there no stores open—none—but neither was there a restaurant where we could have lunch. We decided to return to the ship but the streets were deserted with not a taxi in sight. After walking a long way in our attempt to find help, we finally were able to hail a passing car that stopped to see what we needed. Imagine our relief when the driver was not only willing to return us to the ship but offered to give us a comprehensive tour of the island en route.

Secondly, while we were grateful for the opportunity to see the island, it fell far short of our expectations.

Castries, the largest city on Saint Lucia as well as its capital, was our next destination. Saint Lucia is a sovereign country in the eastern Caribbean on the boundary with the Atlantic Ocean. We took a guided tour that had four stops, and we found it the cleanest and prettiest island of our trip thus far. I found that all the walking on these excursions taxed the limit of my energy. I noted in my diary that, "My heart just won't do it." It was disappointing for me to realize that our wonderful trips might be coming to an end.

There were amazing specialty restaurants on the ship. The previous night we had been delighted with the food in Red Ginger—an exotic Asian restaurant—and on this night we ate in Jacques, an elegant French restaurant.

Gustavia on St. Barts was our next stop. The name St. Barts is actually an abbreviation in English for its actual name—Saint Barthélemy. It is an overseas collectivity of France and is an island fully encircled by shallow reefs. Unfortunately, when we arrived there Hal was feeling very sick with a cold but didn't want to miss that day's tour. We took a tender to shore followed by a long bus ride around the island. By the time we returned to the ship Hal was shaking with fever and headed directly for our cabin and bed. We watched movies to distract him from his misery and had a quick dinner at the buffet that night.

Fortunately the following two days were spent at sea as Hal was very ill. He went to the ship's doctor both in the morning and the afternoon of each day to be administered shots of antibiotics. He was being carefully monitored as neither of us was young—Hal was 81 and I was 79. We pulled ourselves together in the evening for our last meal aboard a cruise ship. Hal loved Italian food so we went to the restaurant Toscana—a delicious ending to our hundreds of lavish meals on ships.

Why had we not seen the pattern ages ago? On every cruise we would start out with good health. As the days progressed, Hal would inevitably get a terrible bacterial infection and soon thereafter I would have it as well. We had to face the music—this was going to be our last cruise. It had been such a convenient way for us to travel but the repercussions to Hal's health, and to mine, were devastating—and expensive. He had mounted up hefty bills visiting ships' hospitals. This one came to over $2500 and Hal spent the next year attempting to get his insurance company to reimburse him. He finally won, but the unpleasant experience finished any interest he had in cruising ever again.

We disembarked in Miami and waited many hours at the airport for our departure to Tucson on February 22nd. Elizabeth and Tony met us at the Tucson airport in spite of entreaties that they not come near us and risk getting our germs. They came anyway, the dears, and had filled our refrigerator with all manner of healthy and appealing food. I was deeply grateful as by then I, too, was very sick and glad not to have to go to the grocery store for many days. And my darling sister Carol provided us with nature's cure–chicken soup. Again, it took us ages to regain our health.

A few days later Max had his 22nd birthday. He had flown to Tucson from New York City for the occasion. He was living there permanently and working as a fashion model—very successfully I might add. I commented in my diary that, "He is so handsome and so <u>happy</u>." As time went along he had become a highly popular and very sought after model internationally. For many weeks, photos of him appeared on all the city buses in New York City. As well, there were mammoth-sized images of him on buildings throughout the city during men's fashion week in 2014. People frequently mentioned to Elizabeth and Tony photographs they had encountered of him in the stylish men's magazines. The important thing is that he was loving life. His favorite city was Tokyo where he spent two months in 2015 and three months in 2016.

We were glad to be home and with our family. My life's goal had been to see the world. Mission accomplished. I could now sit back and relive all the memories I had accrued through so many years of travel. What a lucky woman I have been!

57

☙❧

SHORT BUT MEMORABLE TRIPS

O ver the years, I took myriad short trips—some professional and some just for fun. Most were routine, but others stand out as special. I will mention some of them.

1952-2016 — Guaymas and San Carlos, Mexico

Alpha and omega. The beginning and the end. The first and the last. Tony and I had been courting for only five months in 1952 when he invited me to go to Guaymas, Mexico with him. In those days, a young lady would never have been permitted by her parents to go off with a young man—unless they were properly chaperoned. Thus it was that on our first trip together we had the company of two friends of Tony's father— Mary Lewis and Pauline Granicher. Fortunately, we adored them both, and in spite of their advancing years they were full of spunk. We departed Tucson for the 365 mile trip south in time to reach Guaymas by 4:00 p.m. We stayed in the magnificent hotel—Playa de Cortez—I, of course, sharing a room with the ladies. There was time to swim before dinner after which Tony and I had private time to lie on the beach.

Oh, how in love I was and our first day there was magical. Tony and I rented a small row boat and went out on the ocean to explore. Anchoring at a small island quite a distance from shore, we tried our hand at fishing. I had great luck landing both a trigger fish and a very beautiful mackerel. Later we all went into the town of Guaymas, which was little more than a fishing village then. After a lovely dinner at the hotel, Tony and I again had time to snuggle on the beach.

The next morning was very stormy, giving Tony and me a reason to go shopping—for special cigars that he loved. After lunch the weather had cleared so we chartered a yacht and went deep-sea fishing for six hours. The sea was very rough with big waves. Tony and I were in heaven as we stood on the bowsprit while the sea spray flooded over us. What magical moments! I even caught a shark that day! Although it turned cool that night, Tony and I had time alone together before going our separate ways.

We had heard of the lovely views at a place called San Carlos and, on our last day, we took the opportunity to drive there and see for ourselves. There was nothing but a dirt road and a few scattered buildings but, having seen the pristine white beaches that stretched for miles, we knew we would return.

And we did return– dozens of times over the next many years. Each visit had its unique purpose and many of them are recorded throughout this memoir. Some of the richest moments of our lives were spent there together.

But all good things must come to an end–omega. For me it was with Hal and my family in May of 2016. We were the guests of my beloved son and daughter-in-law—Tony and Elizabeth—as well as their son Alex and his girlfriend Shireen Singh. Elizabeth had arranged for two gorgeous adjacent condominiums right on the beach near San Carlos at Bahia Delfin. How to describe such beauty! We looked out on the Sea of Cortez and the startlingly beautiful peaks of Tetas de Cabra.

Maintaining her high standards, Elizabeth had arranged for a condo with three bedrooms—one for her and Tony, another for Shireen and a third for Alex. But times had clearly changed over the intervening 64 years. Young people did not require the degree of supervision imposed on Tony and me so many years previous. They could well have put Hal and me in their third bedroom instead of renting a separate condo for us!

Dinner at Blackie's – Shireen, Alex, Aldine, Hal, Elizabeth & Tony

San Carlos had bloomed over time and had a wide variety of excellent restaurants. Some were formal, such as Blackie's with its walls covered with photos and murals of Frida Kahlo with whom Hal's parents had a <u>very</u> close relationship along with Frida's husband Diego Rivera. Many good stories were told the night we went there for dinner.

On the other end of the spectrum was The Soggy Peso, a casual restaurant on the beach where there seemed to be as many dogs as patrons. How often does one have the opportunity to run one's toes through the sand while eating dinner!

Hal was now 85 and I was almost 83 but we didn't allow age to interfere with our enjoyment of every moment there. A highlight was a "sunset cruise" which we thought would be tame but beautiful. On

On the beach at the Soggy Peso

the contrary, it was an exciting time for us all. Our excellent crew was determined that their six clients on-board were going to have an experience they would never forget. And they came through! Quite suddenly we were surrounded by a school of dolphins—many, many of them—leaping and cavorting around our boat. They were magnificent and we all were shouting with the sheer joy of being entertained and sought out by them.

We were on a high that got even higher as we moved into a pod of whales and their calves. There must have been 20 of them surfacing and diving, spraying and plunging. We couldn't believe our good luck. I had been whale-watching the world over and had never encountered so many at once, or as close as these were. I felt I could have reached out and touched them, although I know they were at least 10 feet away from our boat.

Hours having passed, it was time for us to return to port, stopping to see the sun setting on the horizon as promised. Not a moment of those happy times together could I ever forget. It was my last visit to San Carlos and my last trip with Hal, and it ranked among the best.

1962 — Cuban Missile Crisis—California

Tony, our sons and I were living in Palos Verdes Estates, a community close to Los Angeles, California, in the early 1960s. The Cuban Missile Crisis occurred in 1962. It was a 13-day (October 16-28) confrontation between the United States and the Soviet Union concerning Soviet ballistic missile deployment in Cuba. It was the closest the Cold War came to escalating into a full-scale nuclear war. The world was probably saved from disaster as a result of tense but successful negotiations between John F. Kennedy and Nikita Khrushchev.

Tony was well aware of the threat to our family during this time as Los Angeles most certainly would have been a target. We could only imagine the panic and devastation that would occur were this to happen. We knew that Tucson would also be a target due to military installations there, but Tony decided he would rather die in familiar and peaceful surroundings rather than in pandemonium. We chose to evacuate to Cañon del Oro north of Tucson.

So seriously did we take this crisis that Tony took time off from his job at Hughes, I arranged for a substitute teacher for my students, and we removed our boys from school. We packed our camper with the food and supplies we anticipated needing and headed for Arizona. To our surprise, the highway was not jammed with people trying to escape the impending holocaust. Everyone seemed oblivious to the danger.

We set up camp in the mountains north of Tucson, radio at our side, and waited to see what was going to happen. Will the world ever know how close we came at that time to WWIII? When we felt safe, we returned to our home and our lives in California. We never told anyone of what we had done, nor did we ever regret our decision to take charge of our own lives during that time.

1967 — Grand Canyon

Katharine Merritt visited us for three months every winter for many years. One year she

On the trail at the Grand Canyon –
Aldine in light colored coat

decided to treat my family to a trip into the Grand Canyon. She had chosen New Year's Day. The Grand Canyon is very cold at that time and 1967 was no exception. It was snowing that day and temperatures hovered around 10 degrees. While Tony and our two sons, Kent (11) and Tony Jr. (9) were appropriately clothed, I was not. I had worn old levis and fabric sneakers. What a mistake!

As I mounted my mule for the trek down the Bright Angel Trail, I heard a resounding ripping of cloth. The crotch of my jeans had picked that moment to fail me. Astride a saddle, I was exposed to the elements and risked severe frostbite. Someone found a safety pin that helped my modesty but not my comfort.

I have a tendency toward acrophobia and as we started down the trail I soon learned that it was often narrow and at the edge of a precipice overhanging a drop of thousands of feet. And the trail was icy and slippery! I cannot begin to relate how totally miserable that experience was. I was frozen in places I'd rather not mention and my feet were in untenable pain. I could do nothing but go forward. We made it down to the Phantom Ranch where some first aid was given to me and my clothing.

To say this was one of the most unpleasant adventures of my life would be an understatement!

Early 1970s — Miami and Malibu

Throughout the early 1970s I made frequent trips to visit Dr. Herbert C. Quay, head of the Department of Psychology at the University of Miami, and Dr. Frank Hewett, Head of the Department of Special Education at UCLA. Herb lived in Miami, Florida while Frank lived in Malibu, California, both delightful destinations although the purpose of these trips was work. Herb was assisting me in writing my doctoral thesis. His input was invaluable. Frank was assisting me in my work with emotionally handicapped children and ultimately in helping me develop my program at UA. They both were highly regarded in their fields and each was an author of many books. How fortunate I was to have their insight, friendship and help. And I was lucky, too, to be able to enjoy swimming in the Atlantic with Herb and in the Pacific with Frank. Both had homes on the ocean.

1975 — Acapulco, Mexico

Mother and I needed to accrue credits toward our real estate credentials. What nicer place could we choose to do this but Acapulco, Mexico? There was a real estate convention there from September 10th until the 14th. We thought it would be nice to have our husbands accompany us.

I also intended to work with a colleague developing the Spanish edition of the ITPA test—a long-term project for me as it was not published until 1980. My associate was Jan Duran who flew in from Mexico City.

We stayed at the beautiful Acapulco Princess where it was reported that the very eccentric Howard Hughes was in residence. It was a gorgeous setting with five swimming pools each with an exotic feature—slides, waterfalls, suspension bridges, etc.—and beautiful outdoor restaurants. Tony and I swam under a waterfall to a bar with stools that kept you mostly submerged.

It rained a great deal during our visit but one doesn't seem to mind tropical rain. I managed to fit in the real estate classes, consulting with Jan, and having fun with Tony and my parents. A successful trip for us all.

1975 — Kino Bay, Mexico

An unusual trip for Tony and me occurred in late November, 1975. While we had spent considerable time on the beach at Kino Bay in Mexico, we had never stayed in the town. Wini and Sam Kirk owned a beautiful condominium on the beach at Condominios Jaqueline. They wanted us to visit for a few days and picked me up early on November 26th. We drove to Hermosillo where we made a stop to consult with Enrique Vásquez — the director of the language institute there—concerning the ITPA test we were developing together.

The following day, Tony flew to Hermosillo where we met him at the airport. It was a pleasant few days with lots of margaritas, beach walking, and card games. Ordinarily it is an eight-hour drive from Tucson to Kino Bay but returning to Tucson with Sam driving his Mercedes hell-bent-for-election we did it in six. That was the last time I was willing to put our lives in Sam's hands on the highway!

1976 — Mexico City

A typical trip to Mexico City, of which there were many in the final preparation of the ITPA—a learning disabilities test in Spanish—occurred on March 22nd. Winifred Kirk, the co-author of the test, and I flew to Mexico City and checked into my favorite hotel— The Genova. We arrived at 7:00 p.m. and went to work. We met with Paz Beruecos and other professionals until 2:00 a.m.

Wini and I had time the next day to visit enchanting little Mexican hotels such as Bamer, El Cortés and Montego. Later we met with a few colleagues and had dinner with two charming gentlemen–one a matador and the other Luis Echeverria's personal pilot—Edmundo Salinas. Echeverria was the president of Mexico from 1970 to 1976. We went to La Gondola Restaurant and listened to their fascinating stories.

After two more days of intense work, we returned to Tucson. What a surprise my sons received. They were at the airport to meet their grandparents who were just returning from Hawaii and there I was—home a day earlier than expected. We also learned that Sam Kirk was in hospital with an intestinal infection.

1976 — Chicago

A typical professional conference was that of the Council for Exceptional Children (CEC) held in Chicago from April 5th to 9th. While some of the speakers were excellent such as Dr. William Rhodes and Dr. Edwin Martin, I usually found conferences rather uninteresting. This one, however, left me with an indelible scar. One of the workshops that was high on the list of choices for many participants concerned sexual adaptations for the physically handicapped. This was not my field so I had not enrolled in it. It wouldn't have mattered. The workshop had been full for months.

One had to have a special pass to be permitted into this course. Strictly by chance, I was walking past the room where this group was meeting when a young woman came out the door and told me she was going on to a workshop more relevant to her needs. She offered me her pass. While I wasn't eager to attend, I was curious. So I slipped in while everyone was preparing to lie on the floor. I joined them wondering what was to come. After we were guided into a relaxed state, the speaker started. "Recall a time in your life when you urinated after having held it in for a long, long time." "Recall your first orgasm—really experience it." Well, on he went with the most personal suggestions you could imagine. I was lying on the floor with everyone around me in deep meditation so escape didn't seem possible.

I thought the next segment must surely get down to specific interventions for working with special needs individuals, but no. Three movie screens appeared on the stage. The films we were to see were introduced and the cameras rolled. I did not consider myself a prude, but these shocked me to the core. I will merely hint at the content but suffice that, having never seen pornography, these were inconceivably upsetting to me. One was a handicapped woman in a shower "pleasuring" herself. The second was of a young handicapped couple "working around" their handicaps–very successfully I might add. The third would not be appropriate for young people even to hear about.

I was sickened by the exposure to a situation I had not anticipated. I literally fell into it with no preamble or preparation for what the content was intended to accomplish. At the first possible opportunity I left, returned to my room and threw up. Somehow I felt sullied. I didn't leave my room the rest of the day.

So much for professional conferences.

1976 — Ann Arbor and Toronto

A short but significant trip was to Ann Arbor, Michigan to consult with one of the major figures in my field–Dr. William Morse. We met on May 14th in the education building at the University of Michigan. At that time, special education was in the forefront and there were ample federal funds to accommodate special meetings such as this. He received $300 for this consultation which was a considerable amount of money at that time.

I left him to go to the airport to fly to Toronto where I was met by Kent, my sister and all her family. Kent had preceded me by a few days in order to see his doctor, John McCullough. We all stayed at Carol's home and were up until 3:00 a.m. chatting and catching up. The next day Kent and I traveled to Montreal to meet with his lawyer.

The following day was very important. I was truly stressed about it. Dr. McCullough was meeting with us to discuss Kent's future with respect to his leg. He decided he was finished with Kent—that he had done all he could. There would be no more surgery. (Of course, as time went by Kent had much more surgery on his leg in Tucson.) The plates and screws would remain. No cosmetic surgery was planned. And his floppy toe would simply remain floppy. The family was overjoyed and Kent breathed a big sigh of relief. Now he could get on with his life.

1976 — Wyoming

One of our favorite places to visit was Katharine Merritt's ranch, Three Rivers Ranch, near Jackson, Wyoming. It had been in her family a great many years and was then on a fifty-year lease as her father, Schuyler Merritt, had agreed to ultimately cede it to Yellowstone Park in which it was located. The lease expired late in Katharine's life so our sons were able to work on the ranch in the summer during their teens for many years. It was beautiful there beyond description.

It was September 3rd and already very cold at the ranch. We depended on open fires to keep us warm. Their year round caretakers were Inez and Jerry Jacobson. Inez did all the cooking and Jerry was the ranch foreman. They became close friends over the years and sadly Jerry died in 2006 and Inez in 2014.

Our activities that week included lots of hiking; one walk was to the Snake River. We swam in Jackson Lake. We rode horseback. And we ate and drank a great deal. Katharine had asked us to drive a car back to Tucson for her use in the winters. We were happy to extend our little vacation and spent nights en route home in Logan, Utah and Flagstaff, Arizona. It is interesting that Tony Jr. started his university education in Logan, and Kent started his in Flagstaff!

That was but one of our many trips to Wyoming which has to be one of the most beautiful states in the nation.

1979 — San Francisco

While I typically resisted attending conferences, there were compelling reasons in this case to make an exception. First, it was being held in San Francisco. Second, it was the ACLD conference (Association for Children with Learning Disabilities) and would be attended by everyone of importance in this field. And lastly my expenses were being paid by the University of Illinois. How could I not go!

In addition to attending fascinating meetings and going to memorable parties, I managed to fit in several trips to Fisherman's Wharf, Ghirardelli Square and Chinatown. Some of us went to Finocchio's for their female impersonator floor show which was quite a risqué thing to do in those days. And I promise I did do a good job of promoting the Spanish adaptation of the Illinois Test of Psycholinguistic Abilities (SITPA) of which I was co-author and was the purpose of my going to the conference. This one was worth the exception I made!

1979 — est in Phoenix

I was fortunate to have the opportunity to participate in one of Werner Erhard's Seminar Trainings—better known as *est*—that were offered throughout the world from 1971 until 1984. Anyone who has had this experience could never forget its powerful effect. Sam Kirk and I had decided to attend it together. It was to be held in Phoenix for two consecutive weekends. We knew it would be demanding, grueling and uncomfortable both emotionally and physically. It was.

The purpose of this 60-hour course was to "free oneself from the past" which was accomplished by "experiencing" one's recurrent patterns and problems rather than repeating them.

There were 200 participants at these seminars, all of whom agreed to follow the ground rules which included not wearing watches, not talking unless called upon, not eating at or leaving our   seats to go to the bathroom except during scheduled breaks separated by many hours.

The first day, Saturday October 13th, sessions started at 8:30 a.m. and terminated at 2:30 a.m.—18 intense hours. The only meal break was at 10:30 p.m. The intention was to subdue us—to break us down—to make us vulnerable to suggestion. Werner Earhard was the leader and he brooked no sissies.

The second day started at 9:30 a.m. and featured the "danger process." It was upsetting in the extreme with screaming sessions interspersed throughout the day. At one of these seminars, this experience caused one man to suffer a heart attack and die. Earhard was not held responsible. Sam and I returned to Tucson that night arriving home in the wee hours of Monday morning.

Sam elected to do the driving the second weekend, too—October 20th and 21st. He dropped me off on Friday night at Tony Jr.'s apartment in Tempe where I was staying and picked me up on time for our 9:00 a.m. beginning on Saturday. Midway through the morning Sam stood up and walked out. Enough was enough. He never consulted me about it so there I sat wondering how on earth I was going to get back to Tucson.

A kind man drove me to Tony Jr.'s apartment at 3:00 a.m. and somehow I got back to the final training session on time the next morning. This is the day we were supposed to "get it" and indeed I did. When enlightenment came to me I was euphoric and grateful for every awful moment of that difficult training that had been so full of misery and discomfort. Some nice man drove me to Tucson arriving at 4:30 a.m. Sam had made a mistake in leaving. He missed the ultimate moment of ecstasy when the puzzle that is one's life suddenly fit together with a new clarity.

Although I had only a little over two hours of sleep, I awakened on Monday refreshed, relaxed and ready for the day. So impressed with my new attitude were Tony and Tony Jr. that they themselves, individually, went to *est* when it was again presented in Phoenix.

Tony Jr. went in April, 1980 and as my diary reports, "He was blown away by the experience." Tony and I went to his "graduation" on April 12th. Loved ones are encouraged to be there when a person completes the *est* experience. We didn't want to miss that magical moment. We drove to Phoenix and waited until 3:00 a.m. before we could join Tony. It was worth it to see his euphoria; he was on a cloud.

1979 — Toronto

Vada Irene McKinnon. I loved many of my beloved aunts and uncles but none more than Irene. She neither wanted to, nor anticipated, living as long as she did—to age 102. She died on October 29, 1979. We all were devastated. I adored Auntie Irene to the extent that as a child I "changed" my name to Aldine Virginia Irene Sinclair. On October 31st, I flew to Toronto for her funeral that was to be on November 1st. Visitation was at Bedford Funeral Home and, given her advanced age, we had not expected many to be in attendance. How wrong we were! The room was filled to overflowing! The flowers were lovely. We went in limousines to Mount Pleasant Cemetery for the graveside service. It was a rainy, dull day, which was to be expected. My brother Murray and his wife Mary had a magnificent reception at their lovely Toronto home. My parents and I then returned to Tucson.

This is a good place to note that Mary and Murray lived in one of Toronto's unique homes— Number 5 Drumsnab, a street on which there were only eight houses. Theirs was Toronto's oldest house having been built in the late 1700s on 150 acres. It had a buttery and a bakery and, having been modernized, an indoor swimming pool. The grounds were lovely, although the acreage had been reduced to only a little over an acre as Toronto grew—a huge lot in their part of Toronto–Rosedale. We all were sad when they sold it.

1981 — Kino Bay, Mexico

Tony and I had several trips to Kino Bay for visits with Wini and Sam Kirk at their condominium on the beach—Condominios Jaqueline. On January 8th, however, Wini, Sam and I went there for a working weekend. I always promised myself that I would not submit my life to Sam's driving ever again, but I did and we were lucky to survive the trip unscathed. Tony decided he would not join us as he was to be interviewed for a job at Gates Learjet that he wanted very much.

Tony had retired from Tucson Newspapers, Inc. in August of 1980 and found that life in retirement did not suit him. He was eager for this new job which he was offered and accepted on February 11, 1981. In the interim he had spent several months at our cottage in Canada and at his retreat in Arivaca. His work with Gates Learjet did not have the appeal he had anticipated so he retired yet again, this time on April 30, 1982. As Tony had very much enjoyed his colleagues there, we had a dinner party for them— 40 guests–on the following Sunday so that he could share a proper goodbye with each one.

Wini and I spent an entire day preparing for a full-day workshop I was to give in Hermosillo, Sonora on January 10th. None of the participants spoke English so I presented the entire workshop from 9:30 a.m. until 6:30 p.m. in Spanish. When we finished I was exhausted and glad to return to Kino Bay for a margarita, or two.

Sam capitulated and allowed me to be the driver on our return to Tucson—an almost eight hour trip. It was a successful, although very tiring, weekend!

1981 — New Orleans

New Orleans was once a great drawing card to those who wanted late nights, good music and oodles of atmosphere. And so it was that a few friends and I took the plunge into debauchery on Friday, February 13ᵗʰ, a daunting date! We checked into the Maison Dupuy—a charming old hotel in the French Quarter. We had dinner at Brennan's and went on to the Hilton to hear a Pete Fountain concert. It was fantastic! Drinks at the Rain Forest on the top floor there followed before we called it a night.

Although the weather was not good, we spent a good deal of time walking in the French Quarter and drinking altogether too many of the famous New Orleans "hurricanes." We listened to incredible music and knew it was time to move on.

We headed for Cancún on February 16ᵗʰ and stayed in a balcony suite at El Presidente. There was time for walking on the beach and eating in good restaurants— Carlos and Charlie's, Chokos and Tere, and Hugo's.

We returned to Tucson on February 20ᵗʰ. I wanted to be home to celebrate with some of my favorite people the following day—Misty and Gary Grynkewich. Their daughter, Julia, was baptized at St. Philip's Episcopal Church and I was her godmother. What an honor! Afterwards, Misty and Gary's families came for a champagne party at our house and stayed for hours. What fun and how special! Their second child, Jeffrey, is also my godchild. I am proud of them both, and love them very much.

My niece Stephanie Meigs is a goddaughter with whom I am very close. Another godchild who will always be special to me is Jenny Duffield, the beautiful daughter of my dear friends Mary Rose and Dick Duffield. I am sad that I am no longer in touch with another goddaughter—Celia Ann Aldine Martin Romaine. I love them all.

1981 — Camp Lake, Ontario

Ordinarily I would put this in my chapter about summers in Canada, but one location needs special attention. It was called Camp Lake. We referred to the very basic cabin there that belonged to my sister-in-law, Ann Sinclair, simply as Camp Lake. It required a strenuous trip to reach it as it was accessible only by water. We had to take canoes on the roofs of cars to launch at a landing after which followed a long paddle to reach the cabin. It was easy to plan when to go into Camp Lake but the departure was always subject to the weather. Karl Pattison went there alone in his wherry one summer and had to remain days longer than he intended because of heavy wind. It was blowing so hard and the waves were so big that even that intrepid adventurer was trapped. Once Ann barely made it out in the late fall when the ice started forming and the snow was ferocious. And, I believe it was there that Kent proposed to Janice.

On August 7th a gang of us from the cottage went in to Camp Lake—my parents, Carol and her husband and their children Stephanie, Ted, and Aldine, my nephews Murray and Craig, Karl Pattison and my son Tony Jr. and I. We were bursting at the seams. There was a small main room with a fireplace, two tiny bedrooms and an outhouse. We used the lake for keeping clean. We talked, played games and told ghost stories late into the night. What a happy time it was for us all.

The cabin at Camp Lake

There were only three other cabins on this big lake, but we never saw anyone in them. Many happy times and youthful adventures occurred there that the young people still talk about. We all were sad when Ann had to sell the place but none of us will ever forget it.

1981 — Alpine, Arizona

Tony and I took another short trip with Wini and Sam Kirk to their cabin in Alpine, Arizona in the White Mountains of northern Arizona on October 30th. We arrived at 11:30 p.m. and it was exceedingly cold! Sam had a pond there which he stocked with fish. We had a relaxed time playing cards and taking walks. I noted in my diary that "I am so relaxed I can hardly move." Just what the doctor ordered!

1981 — Hawley Lake, Arizona

A favorite place to visit was Karl Pattison's cabin at Hawley Lake that he himself had built in about 1960. As it was on the White Mountain Apache Indian reservation, he had only a lease on the property. It was situated on a beautiful lakeside site in the White Mountains of northern Arizona at an altitude of 8200 feet. This meant the summers there were cool while there was plenty of snow to play in during the winter. I visited him there for the first time on November 9th, 1981 and continued until 1985. Each time I was there was a unique experience largely due to weather conditions. We always had peaceful times with lots of exercise including canoeing on Hawley Lake. One of our many hikes was to Cyclone Lake—a four-hour trek. We often walked around the perimeter of the lake—a distance of two miles. The lake was 300 acres in size.

I remember one incident on March 12, 1984. I was not feeling well so rather than walking around the lake we chose to drive. On the other side of the lake, Karl's truck got stuck in the snow. He tried everything he could think of to extricate the vehicle but it wouldn't budge. By then it was dusk and the dark of night was approaching—and it was very cold. Nonetheless, we started our long walk back to the cabin. Were we ever lucky when two Apache women saw our distress and gave us a lift home in the back of their pickup truck. Karl was very embarrassed, but I was immensely grateful!

Aldine at Hawley Lake

One visit was in the dead of winter with many feet of snow and very cold temperatures. Karl's only shower was outside with a cloth curtain surrounding it—a curtain that concealed only one's body as Karl liked to look out on the scenery while he showered. One day a neighbor passed by who noticed me in the shower and came over to say hello. Unfortunately she was a talker and couldn't have realized that Karl's little water tank produced a limited amount of hot water. Why I didn't simply tell her I that I *had* to exit the shower I'll never know, but there I stood with ice water beating down on me for an interminable length of time freezing my rear end off. When she finally left I was frozen to the bone. It took hours for my body heat to return to normal!

My last visit to Karl's cabin was on April 26, 1985. We arrived at Hawley Lake very late at night in a heavy snowfall. It was quite spectacular as the snow was deep on the ground and all the trees were white. It was 24 degrees outside and only 35 degrees in the cabin. The water line was broken and needed immediate attention. Our purpose in being there was to spend the weekend searching for a piece of property onto which Karl could move the cabin. We found land he liked in Nutrioso, Arizona. Unfortunately, it was not on a lake.

The Apaches terminated the leases on Hawley Lake in 1985 so Karl was forced to disassemble the cabin log by log and move it to the land he had purchased in Nutioso near Alpine, Arizona. His enthusiasm for visits there was never the same.

1982 — New Orleans

One CEC (Council for Exceptional Children) conference I attended sent chills down my spine– quite literally. It was held in New Orleans in the late winter. In an effort to save money, I elected to stay at a motel on the outskirts, rather than in the big convention hotel downtown. The consequences of this decision were close to disastrous.

I entered a rather run-down office to check in, but hey, I wasn't expecting luxury. I was told how to locate my room and set off to find it. It was a long walk through increasingly dilapidated hallways under construction where sheets of plastic were hanging to take the place of walls. I passed many workmen who ogled me; they surely knew which room I had been assigned. I was nervous. I had seen no other hotel "guests" and deduced I might well be the one and only. It was now nighttime and, although the room was definitely on the "seedy" side, I thought I could tough it out. I should have run when I could.

As the door didn't lock securely, I propped a chair against it. Then I discovered that there was no hot water and, worse, no heat in the room. The office was now closed but I couldn't have handled returning down those long halls alone in the dark anyway. So, putting on all the warm clothes I could find, I eventually went to bed. I am not exaggerating when I say that I almost froze during the night. Desperate and frightened as the cold was so intense, I even got under the mattress to try to find warmth! That didn't help a bit. I thanked God when morning came and I was still alive, but I was no longer thinking straight. I believe I was close to hypothermia. Almost frozen and sleep deprived, I made my way to the office. My lips were blue and numb, but I was able to let them know in no uncertain terms that it had been unconscionable for them to have sent a woman to that room. They sheepishly agreed and did not charge me.

I made a beeline for the downtown Hyatt and was lucky there was a room available. When I opened my suitcase, a wave of arctic air wafted from it. Everything inside was close to frozen!
Never did feeling safe and taking a hot bath feel so good!

1982 — La Paz, Mexico

Mexico was always a favorite destination for Tony and me. One special place was La Paz on the eastern coast of the Baja peninsula. On November 10th we flew with my parents and our mutual friends Jane and Bob Ward to Guaymas where we were to catch a flight across the Sea of Cortez to La Paz. However, as the plane of the president of Mexico was due to arrive, we were held up for several hours. Finally our flight left and we headed for La Paz. We checked into a hotel right on the beach—the Gran Baja—and were ready for a week of wining and dining. Sadly, our first night there my father had a bad asthma attack and my parents knew they had to return to Tucson as soon as possible. The first flight out was not until the next day! Taking masses of cortisone and staying in his room, my father was able to endure the wait.

The Wards joined my parents in leaving the following day, so Tony and I were on our own. We drove to the harbor at Pichilingue and located some lovely isolated beaches in the area.

The following day we drove to Cabo San Lucas. We were anticipating dreary scenery but instead found it to be spectacular with magnificent desert growth all along the way. The problem we encountered, however, was the condition of the road which was badly in need of serious repair. There weren't just potholes but whole sections of the road that just dropped away without any warning signs. We were on our mettle to navigate a safe arrival at Cabo where we had lunch at the beautiful Finisterre, clearly the best hotel in the area at that time. It had views to both the Pacific and to the Sea of Cortez. You may be sure our return trip to La Paz in the dark was done at a slow speed and with great concentration. Once we were safely back at the hotel, we deemed it a lovely trip and a delightful experience.

Our last full day there was spent in enjoying various beaches, our favorite being Balandra Beach, and taking a two-hour trimaran cruise at sunset. We were the only passengers. This trip to La Paz was one of many and that enchanting old town never failed to please us.

Tony and I had our last trip to La Paz together in late October of 1985. He was dealing with health issues and this destination was always a source of serenity for us both. We had a lovely room at Los Arcos Hotel and a steak dinner on its patio under a full moon. Heavenly! We spent our days swimming and snorkeling at Balandra and Tecolote beaches. They were so very beautiful and there was never anyone else in sight to intrude on our intimate and memorable time together. Such moments of tranquility were few and far between thereafter.

1983 — Dwight, Ontario

It was spring break and Tony and I felt adventurous. As he was retired his schedule was open, and he spent many months of the year at the cottage. This was to be our destination for a week. We were met in Toronto on April 1st by a friend who drove us north in our Ford Galaxy. Our lake, Lake of Bays, was still frozen solid.

Our second night there we went for dinner to Carol and Terry's cottage nearby. It was snowing and so very beautiful. Friends—Margaret Ruscica was one of them–were there, as well as my former sister-in-law Ann, a lovely lady. Mom and Dad phoned that my father was back in the hospital with a fever of undetermined origin. We worried so much about him that I hesitated going away because he always seemed to become ill in our absence.

We tried using our car one day but it became entrenched in mud and we were stuck at the cottage. There was lots to do—hanging pictures, cleaning the cottage, cooking, taking long walks and getting our place ready for the summer. As the weather was so bad we spent a good deal of time drinking rum toddies in front of the fire. Life was good.

One activity that we enjoyed "off season" was wandering along the shoreline and peeking in cottage windows. It was fun to walk around places that we looked at from the lake all summer but rarely had a chance to see up close.

Eventually we rescued our car from the mud and headed to the nearest town to buy groceries so that we could have a dinner party. We created a delicious dinner and delightful evening. Our guests stayed until 2:00 a.m. On Sunday, April 10th, it was time for me to get back to Tucson as I had to be at work the next day. Tony did not return to Tucson until May 19th. From the Tucson airport I went directly to see my parents. Dad had lost 16 pounds after so many hospitalizations. I think he counted every day of life as a dividend by then.

1983 — San Francisco

Much of what I taught my students in my "methods for changing behavior" class was about ways of bringing joy into our students' lives. All had emotional or behavioral problems and their lives were typically bleak. Thus, I was intrigued by a conference being held in San Francisco the topic of which was *The Healing Power of Laughter and Play.* I flew there on April 28th and checked into a wonderful 100-year old hotel—the Sheraton Palace. The conference began that night.

It continued for the full day on April 29th but I slipped out to have lunch in the revolving restaurant at the top of the Hyatt Hotel. Again the next day there were few breaks, but I found the content of the lectures fascinating. On the final day the course terminated at 1:00 p.m., and I immediately took a bus to the Golden Gate Bridge. I walked all the way across and back and thoroughly enjoyed the exercise, the scenery and my solitude. Another bus took me to Fisherman's Wharf where I loved strolling and gawking. I had dinner at Alioto's and walked all the way back from the wharf to the hotel arriving exhausted but content. The following day I returned to Tucson.

1983 — The Gila River, Arizona

I had heard mixed reviews about tubing down the Gila River in Arizona. Some found it beyond exciting while others found it terrifying. I concur with both. I came close to losing my life on the Gila. The Gila is a 64-mile-long tributary of the Colorado River. Karl Pattison and two of his colleagues had scheduled a "float" on the Gila for August 28th and invited me to join them. Always up for an adventure, I accepted.

I was given ample warning by them of what situations to avoid such as getting sucked into a vortex of the river when approaching a tree. It could mean smashing into a tree that has fallen across the river with such force that it could cause death or else suck you under the tree. The river runs at about 5 to 8 mph in some places. It flows erratically and has stretches of river with class I to II whitewater—even up to class IV in some places. My companions were, of course, experienced in this endeavor and wanted to encounter the greatest number of challenges and thrills possible. I had neither the training nor the strength.

I avoided some dangerous situations. What I wasn't prepared for was getting sucked underwater, which would require considerable strength to overcome. Worse, if

Karl & Aldine at Gila River

one was being swept along underwater and became entangled in roots it could be very serious. Everything moved so fast that I could not predict what lay ahead. I was very unhappy about this whole experience, in a state of terror, and wanted nothing more than for this horror to end. It did. I was underwater, became entangled, and was helpless—at the edge of the river. I could see above the water but I couldn't get to the surface. By chance–God's grace once again–one of the participants, Seth, saw my dilemma, reached down and was able to pull me to safety. I was in a bad way—half drowned. This experience resulted in considerable shaking, substantial bruising, and a deeply-felt gratitude for surviving. Karl was very upset by my close call and very apologetic. I am sure he felt there was no challenge I couldn't meet. He found out differently.

A few weeks later I had a totally different experience on the Gila. Karl, two of his friends, his pregnant daughter Marylka, Carol, Terry and I piled into Karl's Volkswagen van and headed for Winkleman, Arizona to "shoot" the Gila. This time we avoided the dangerous section and tubed down the tranquil lower half–twice. We had a picnic on the shore and found it to be a beautiful and peaceful day. In May of 1984 a group of eight of us spent a day on the Gila and a week later 14 of us enjoyed that tranquil experience—so unlike my introduction with Karl in 1983!

1983 — Guaymas, Mexico

At 4:00 a.m. on October 5th Tony left with his sailboat to drive to Guaymas for the annual Columbus Day race. Two days later my brother-in-law Terry Belsham, Tony Jr. and I flew to Guaymas where we were met by Tony and taken to that enchanting hotel—Playa de Cortés. We had a swim in the pool, some margaritas and left for a skipper's meeting in San Carlos. Tony was ready for the big race.

Later we had dinner at Las Playitas in Guaymas where the waiters sang the beautiful song *Las Mañanitas*—the equivalent to *Happy Birthday to You*—to Tony Jr. whose birthday was the next day. He turned 26 years old. It was a happy time.

On October 8th Tony, Tony Jr., Terry and I went to San Carlos where we joined 50 other sailboats participating in this sailing competition. It was a beautiful sight with the white sails wafting in the wind as they awaited the starting horn. It was a hot day but our discomfort went unnoticed as it was all so exciting and we did some good sailing. Later, a friend drove us back to the Playa de Cortés where we cleaned up and went for dinner to the home of very good friends who were full time residents of Guaymas, Joy and Jean Vidal.

The following day we had to say goodbye to Tony Jr. who was due back at work the next day. Tony, Terry and I took a taxi to Las Playitas to board our sailboat *Aldine* for the return race to San Carlos. As my diary noted, "It was very windy with high seas and I was terrified." We had drinks on the boat on our return. After changing in the hotel, we returned to San Carlos for the victory banquet. We had come in 14th out of 23 boats in our class. The following day Terry and I returned to Tucson. Tony went on for some solo sailing and returned to Tucson later. After cleaning up his sailboat he headed for Arivaca, and more solo time!

1983 — Mexico

By the end of 1983 I was tired from a year fraught with problems and disappointments. A little holiday was in order. Karl Pattison kindly offered to drive me to interesting destinations in Mexico. Our first stop was Hermosillo, Sonora, parts of which are very beautiful as its name implies—Hermosillo translates to "beautiful."

After a few days there, we drove for five hours to reach Los Mochis, Sinaloa. I could never relax in the car as Karl had chosen to take his aged Volkswagen "bug" on this journey—a very small and uncomfortable vehicle. Mexican roads are dangerous and Karl was known for falling asleep at the wheel. I was constantly on guard. At the hotel in Los Mochis we discovered there was no hot water, not unusual in small motels at that time. This was not quite the luxurious interlude I had envisioned for my rest cure. It got worse.

Our next destination was Mazatlán, Sinaloa—a considerable distance with few intermediary gas stations. I happened to glance at Karl's face during our drive and for the first and only time ever I saw that he was incredibly nervous. The gas indicator was on "empty" and we were in the middle of nowhere–a bad combination in Mexico. Then came a miracle! We did indeed run out of gas. It occurred quite literally at the same time that a gas station materialized unexpectedly—and we glided on empty to a pump. We were so lucky.

Mazatlán was a great disappointment—I compared it to Coney Island–so we decided to leave and take the ferry across the Sea of Cortez to La Paz on the Baja peninsula—a place we knew and liked. After a two-hour wait for the ferry, we were told there was no room for the car. Back to Mazatlán we went to spend New Year's Eve at Señor Frog's—which lived up to its reputation of being very noisy and great fun.

We eventually wended our way back to Tucson via Culiacán where again our motel had no hot water. But the worst was yet to come. Our next stop was Guaymas, Sonora. There was no water whatever in our hotel there due to recent storms. Water, however, was readily available if one collected it in buckets as it streamed through the ceiling in my room! There were at least a dozen leaks pouring water. I had to move my bed to find a place to sleep without being dripped upon! I remember that it was so awful that there was nothing to do but laugh. We simply doubled over with laughter. Perhaps it was part hysteria! It rained all night and I had little sleep. My room was awash. You may be sure our departure the next day was very early in the morning. I noted in my diary that "I had had it" and wanted to go home. And when we reached it, home never looked so good. I had left on this trip with visions of quiet beaches and time to rest. I returned frustrated and exhausted. So much for "dream" trips.

Sadly I learned that my father had a stroke the day before my return and was in hospital, his fifth visit in a year. He also had sustained three broken vertebrae in my absence. As always, my parents were optimistic and uncomplaining. How I admired them.

1984 — Sedona, Arizona

Tony and I were ready for time alone. We sought a destination that could afford us intimacy, beauty and mystery. People come from the world over to experience the magic of Sedona and it is practically on our doorstep. We shared very happy days there in January taking jaunts into the red rock area and exploring Oak Creek Canyon–as well as nearby ghost towns. The evening of January 22nd was devoted to watching the Super Bowl, a diversion indeed from the unique aura and history that had surrounded us for several days. It was a memorable time for us and preceded a spring fraught with concern as Tony dealt with serious neck cancer that required a complete neck dissection and reconstruction.

1985 — San Francisco

ACLD (Association for Children with Learning Disabilities) was having its conference in San Francisco that year—far too tempting a location for Tony and me to ignore. On February 20th we departed for SFO. I have to admit to attending very few conference meetings but Tony and I had a wonderful five days together.

We wasted no time in taking a cable car to Fisherman's Wharf where we had dinner at Scoma's. The next day, after attending the keynote speech at the conference, I joined Tony for dim sum in Chinatown after which we walked to Fisherman's Wharf. We took a ferry around the bay and under Golden Gate Bridge. Later, while Tony went to the marine museum, I went to Ghirardelli Square for shopping and a butterscotch sundae! Tony and I met and took a ferry to Sausalito where we walked the waterfront and had dinner overlooking the bay and watched the sun set on San Francisco.

After making an appearance at the conference the next day, Tony and I took a four-hour drive to Yosemite National Park to view the famed El Capitan, Half Dome and the falls. What a glorious experience for us both.

Sated with the good life, we made our way back to Tucson. Kent and Janice had stayed at our place during our absence but had left to return to their home in Billings, Montana the previous day. They left our house spotless!

1985 — A Cruise on the Caribbean with my Mother

It was my spring break from the university and Mother was ready for a trip. Dad had died less than a year earlier and Mother was still very fragile emotionally. The trip would have been perfect had it not been for *Danny Boy*. It must be admitted that my father had a dreadful voice—truly awful. But I remember as a child what pleasure he took in singing that song at the top of his lungs. It is a vivid auditory childhood memory.

Mother and I sailed out of Tampa on March 16th on the Holland America flagship *Nieuw Amsterdam* with about 1400 other passengers. On the first evening the band struck up with *Danny Boy*. It was too much for Mother. That was the 59th anniversary of her first date with my father. There were many tears.

We visited wonderful ports of call—Cozumel in Mexico, Montego Bay in Jamaica and Georgetown on the Grand Cayman Islands. We were fascinated that this last place had an elevation of only 81 feet at its highest point. And it was that night that an Irish tenor sang *Danny Boy* on the ship. Mother was ready to go home.

It was also that day that Tony started his new job as Employee Relations Director at the University of Arizona—his last job and the one he loved above all others he had over his professional career. He continued working there through his terminal illness and finally had to give it up when he could no longer drive.

Mother and I returned to Tucson on March 23rd. The following day she hosted lunch at the Arizona Inn for my sister-in-law Ann Sinclair, her sons Scott and Craig—who were visiting Tucson from Toronto—as well as Tony, Tony Jr. and me. I am quite sure she was glad to be home.

1985 — Carefree, Arizona and Anaheim, California

The CEC (Council for Exceptional Children) conference was in Anaheim in 1985 but I preceded it with a wonderful, carefree few days visiting Johanna Plaut in her luxurious home in Carefree, Arizona. On April 15th I met my mother at the airport in nearby Phoenix and off we went to Anaheim to attend the conference. Too often these events are a boondoggle for professors wanting an excuse for a little holiday. That could even be said of me! This was, however, an opportunity for me to reconnect with old colleagues. A great deal of our time was spent going for drinks to people's rooms and reminiscing.

Our second day there, Mom and I went to Disneyland from 10:00 a.m. until 5:30 p.m. Mother was 77 at the time. We took a four-hour tour and then went off on our own. There was a great deal of walking involved but my mother was always a good trouper.

The following day I dutifully went to an enormous arena for the opening of the conference and the keynote speech. I abandoned my mother for the afternoon—a great relief for her as she needed some rest—and was taken by Frank Hewett to his home in Malibu where I met his newly adopted son Ted, a troubled teenager. After dinner, Frank drove me all the way back to Anaheim where Mother announced that she was ready to go home. She was bored and she missed her dog Jock. We were back in Tucson the following day.

1985 — Navajo and Hopi

As my diary said on April 29th, "It is snowing and I am leaving Hawley Lake for the last time and I'll never see it again as Karl has to move his cabin in July." Having spent so many happy times in that beautiful place I remember the sadness I felt. However, it was time for me to get to work so Karl drove me to Show Low, Arizona where I met my colleagues Dr. James Chalfant and Dr. John Bradley. We three were going to be teaching on the Navajo Reservation for three days.

We left Show Low early the following day so that we would have time for sightseeing. We visited the Petrified Forest and the Painted Desert and drove through magnificent country. Eventually we arrived in Chambers, Arizona which, as my diary noted, "is nothing but the Chieftain Motel which is 90 miles from where we are working but there is no motel closer to Chinle and Chinle Motel was full." We raced off to reach the BIA (Bureau of Indian Affairs) at 3:00 p.m. From there, Jim and I drove to Many Farms, Arizona where we each taught a class until 6:30 p.m. When we returned to Chambers, we talked and drank until the wee hours of the morning. I noted that I got only three hours of sleep.

We left at 6:00 a.m. the following morning and drove to Chinle. After a quick breakfast we hopped in a truck to do a tour of Canyon de Chelly that lasted until 2:15 p.m. My diary tells me, "It was magnificent. I loved it. We had best driver—Joe Thompson—and got stuck many times in a rapidly flowing river that covered the floor of the canyon and through which we had to drive all day. Incredible scenery and ruins."

We all changed quickly at the lodge where we were staying and raced to the education center. I

John Bradley & Jim Chalfant

was driven to Cottonwood, Arizona for the day's presentation. We drove on to Ganado, Arizona where we stayed in two cabins at the Indian Junior College. I remember going to bed exhausted. No partying that night!

Jim, John and I left at 7:00 a.m. the next day to drive to the Hopi mesas. We walked through Old Oraibi, visited the Cultural Center, and left to wend our way through small villages stopping at pawn shops with heartbreakingly low prices on their rugs and jewelry. We dropped Jim in Cottonwood and John and I continued to Many Farms to teach our last classes. Many hours later we were back in Show Low where we stayed the night before returning to Tucson the following day.

1986 — New Canaan, Connecticut

Katharine Merritt died at a very old age, almost 101, at her home in Stamford, Connecticut. Although Tony was ill he was determined to go to her funeral. On September 20th Tony and I flew to New Canaan, Connecticut where we were met by our friend Johanna Plaut who took us to her home to stay. We attended the service and managed to spend time with our old friends Prudie and Peter Mennell and with Jan and Ames Richards whom we knew well from our Greek Island cruising days. We found New Canaan charming. We returned to Tucson on September 23rd.

Johanna Plaut was the fifth wife of a very wealthy man who was much older than she. When he died she never had to worry about money again. She was generous in the extreme and financed a good many of my flights to Toronto when Kent was in hospital in 1975. We had become close friends. When she was in Arizona during the winter we visited back and forth between our place in Tucson and her Arizona homes in Carefree and in Patagonia where she had a ranch. After Tony died, I visited her often as we both were widows and enjoyed each other's company. Johanna died on September 21, 1993 of brain cancer.

1989 — Guaymas, Sonora

For many years Tony and I had dear friends, Joy and Jean Vidal, who lived in Guaymas, Sonora, Mexico. We saw them annually when we participated in the Columbus Day sailing races. Jean's early years were spent in France where he was born. His father, an engineer, was part of a group of people who decided to move from France to Santa Rosalia on the Baja Peninsula of Mexico. With them they took everything that would make their lives comfortable and familiar, including school teachers and doctors. Theirs was a French community and only French was spoken. Many years later the community returned to France while Jean and his family moved to Guaymas. Jean was at a great disadvantage. He spoke no Spanish whatever. Ultimately he learned but continued to have a very heavy, and charming, French accent.

His life was further complicated when it was necessary for him to go to university and he had elected to go to Occidental College in California. But he didn't speak English. He learned. He and their four children are all tri-lingual.

The spring that Tony died, 1989, the Vidals took me under their wing, and I spent many long weekends with them. Flying commercially from Tucson to Guaymas was easy and inexpensive. What good times they planned for me—swimming excursions, shopping and even a side trip to Alamos. One fascinating experience was a visit to the Yaqui Indian community, Vicam, near Ciudad Obregón some distance from Guaymas. The Sonora Yaquis inhabit the valley of Rio Yaqui. It was Easter time and their religious ceremonies were in full sway. I was fascinated with the rituals, the haunting music and the deer dancers. I visited the Vidals six times during that year and will always appreciate their kindness in making available to me these escapes from my loneliness in Tucson.

1989 — Santa Cruz, California

I left Tucson as early as possible to go to our cottage in Canada thinking that I could reach once again to the unfamiliar to sustain me through my grief. Tony had died in January. I should have known better. Tony's presence was pervasive at the cottage. I arrived there on May 11th and didn't leave until August 16th, just two days before I returned to work at UA for the fall semester.

I spent hours a day writing letters to every person who had been in touch with me following Tony's death. There were at least 300. It took weeks. Finding that living alone with little human contact at the cottage was becoming oppressive, I took advantage of an invitation from Dr. Robert Blackwell whom I had met on the cruise in South America earlier in the spring. He lived in Santa Cruz, California on the edge of a golf course. It was a very beautiful area. Bob was a widower. I had been having a very difficult time with one foot following unsuccessful foot surgery in 1988. Every step I took was painful.

Bob had phoned frequently over the months and knew of my deep concern for my foot. He invited me to visit him, tempting me with the offer of seeing many specialists who were friends of his and could advise me about my foot. I accepted. On June 8th, long before my family arrived, I drove to Toronto, stayed with my brother and his wife, and flew the next day to San José where Bob met me.

He made good on his promise. I saw a multitude of physicians and endured endless tests. I saw orthopedic surgeons, neurologists, podiatrists, psychologists and nutritionists.

I was wined and dined in elegant style. It was a week of pampering, sightseeing, and visiting with his family. Still, it was time to go back to the cottage in Canada so I left on June 16th. I flew to Chicago where I met my mother at her plane as she was en route to Toronto. I wanted to help her get through customs in Toronto and take care of locating her big dog Jock in baggage. Also, it was necessary for somebody to disassemble Jock's cage and tie it on the roof of my car. It was an annual fiasco but we muddled through. My sister-in-law, Mary, met us with my car, and I drove Mom north to the cottage where she stayed with me.

1989 — San Francisco

Although she was now 81, my mother was determined to miss nothing while she could still travel. On September 15th my sister Carol and I took her to San Francisco for a long weekend. We were met at the airport by my Santa Cruz friend Bob Blackwell who drove us to our hotel—Hotel Rafael. After taking us to dinner, he escorted us on an evening of debauchery, which was what my mother had requested. First we went to Finocchio's—a club that features female impersonators—a place that Mother had long read about in her tabloids. She wasn't disappointed. That was followed by a visit to a "strip joint." She loved it.

September 16th was my sister's 51st birthday. I was then 56 years old. Bob left that day but we were joined by my ebullient friend Al Marshick. We all were such close friends that we provided him with a mattress and allowed him to sleep on the floor–four of us in one room! We did the tourist type activities all day ending it with a special dinner for Carol at the Marrakesh Restaurant. Al insisted on taking us to his favorite bar—The Edinburgh Castle. We sat on stools at the bar and Carol and I soon declared we thought we were falling in love with the handsome bartender. Al laughed and said it would be a waste of our emotions as this was a gay bar. I had noticed there was a plethora of men there! Mother had another new experience and was giddy with pleasure. After satisfying our mother's rather innocent proclivity toward prurient pleasures, we returned to Tucson on September 18th.

The following weekend I visited Al at his home in Oxnard. Time spent with Al was always memorable and our exciting activities left me exhausted and ready to return to Tucson.

1989 — Tacoma

My mother, Carol and I took another delightful trip together on November 10th as I had a long weekend. We flew to Tacoma and checked into a Holiday Inn in SeaTac which is located between Seattle and Tacoma. The purpose of our trip was to visit Carol's son Ted who was in law school at Puget Sound. We had a wonderful few days, albeit all of them rainy, and left having had a delightful time with my nephew.

1990 — Fun at Lake of Bays and CEC Conference in Toronto

The boondoggle was a weekend in winter time at our cottage in Ontario. The excuse was a CEC (Council for Exceptional Children) conference in Toronto. The date was April 21st.

I flew to Toronto where I was met by my sister-in-law, Ann Sinclair, who drove me to the cottage. The weather was gloomy–cold, rainy and foggy. Arriving about 10:00 p.m., we immediately phoned friends inviting them over for a drink and a good chat. We sat by a roaring fire until they left at 3:00 a.m. I noted in my diary that it is always exciting to come to the cottage, but much less so without Tony.

The lake was still frozen solid; it had been a long, hard winter. Wasn't I lucky that the next day was gorgeous with the first sunny day since February!

The weekend was spent in visiting art galleries and craft stores, hiking to our local falls as wide as I had ever seen them, visiting with friends, and dining out. On Sunday night Tony Jr. phoned as he does every Sunday and has for many years. I count on those calls. What an attentive and loving son.

Monday came and reality arrived with it. Ann and I drove to Toronto where I stayed with my brother Murray and his wife, Mary. The next day I took the subway to the Royal York Hotel, the CEC convention center, to register and attend sessions and business meetings. The following day I heard the keynote speaker, Dr. William Morse, who is well known in my discipline.

I attended a performance of *Les Miserables* with Mary and Margaret Ruscica. We barely made it home before a major blackout hit Toronto.

On April 26th I returned to Tucson having enjoyed every minute of my visit to the cottage and an excellent conference. I loved the flexibility of being a university professor!

1990 — Visit to Sonoran Missions

Although it was only a three-day trip, my visit to nine historic missions in Sonora, Mexico with the Southwestern Mission Research Center made a lasting impression. There were 32 of us in the group; I was traveling with Winifred Kirk. The first day, October 19th, we explored the missions in Cocóspera, Imuris and Magdalena where we saw the bones of Father Eusebio Kino.

This Jesuit missionary, who had a profound impact on the development of northern Sonora and southern Arizona, was also a geographer, explorer, cartographer and astronomer. For the last 24 years of his life he worked with the indigenous Native American population in the region then known as the Pimeria Alta. He was born in Italy in 1645 and died in 1711. By the time of his death he had established 24 missions. The most famous one near Tucson, a beloved local treasure, is San Xavier del Bac.

That night we stayed in Santa Ana where we had a happy margarita party. The second day we visited five missions—Atil, Oquitoa, Tubutama, Pitiquito, and Caborca, where we spent the night. On our last day we stopped for lunch in San Ignacio and arrived in Tucson at 6:00 p.m. I decided immediately that I wanted to make the trip again—but I never did.

1990 — Chicago

Having been invited to attend the 37th annual meeting of the American Academy of Child and Adolescent Psychiatry, I flew to Chicago on October 23rd. The following day I spent from 8:30 a.m. until 5:00 p.m. at a symposium concerning psychoses. It was fascinating. That night I had dinner with Dr. Herbert C. Quay, an author of many erudite books and the head of the Department of Psychology at the University of Miami. We had dinner at an Armenian restaurant—Sayat Nova. Later in the evening I met Dr. Joseph Green, a child psychiatrist whom I knew in Tucson. We attended a presentation of the movie *Cinema Paradiso* which was followed by a

Aldine with Joe Green in Chicago

discussion of the content by professionals in the field of

mental health. I felt quite humble in this assemblage of intellect. After a nightcap with Joe, I welcomed the oblivion of slumber.

The following day I attended a lecture given by Herb Quay on "aggression." I noted in my diary that, "I understood practically nothing." The afternoon was spent in lectures addressing the subject of "suicide." Later Joe Green took me to the Field Museum where there was a huge reception given by the Brown School.

After a full schedule the next day, which focused primarily on issues associated with ADHD (Attention Deficit Hyperactive Disorder), Joe Green and I attended a Menninger reception at the elegant Tremont Hotel. This was followed by a Wisconsin reception. These psychiatrists like to party!

On the final day of the conference, my wish came true. I was introduced to Dr. John Werry, a professor in the Department of Psychiatry at the University of Auckland in New Zealand. I was hoping to spend my final sabbatical year in New Zealand and needed a contact. Dr. Werry could not have been more encouraging and urged me to be in touch with him when I was ready to make plans. Our meeting resulted in my teaching at the University of Canterbury in Christchurch on the South Island of New Zealand in 1994. I have dedicated a full chapter to this amazing experience.

I returned to Tucson on October 28th sated with a new awareness of the intricacies of our brains   and of the difficulty in finding treatments that will successfully direct our deviant thought processes back to mental health.

1992 — A Strange Experience

Because it was a favorite story of my grandchildren, I must include this anecdote in my memoir. On November 14th, my mother and I had driven to Scottsdale, Arizona in her Lincoln Town Car for a weekend of fun.   We checked into our hotel and went off for dinner and a movie.

My mother was very particular about keeping her car locked. As I pulled into the movie theater parking lot, I rolled down the window to ask directions. I forgot to close it. We parked, I clicked the lock button, and we went to see "A River Runs through It." On returning to the car I noticed that I had forgotten to close the window and, rather than upset my mother, I quickly raised it before she could notice. What I should have done was to have checked the floor of the back seat for an intruder. We exited the parking lot and stopped at a stop sign in a dark area.

Suddenly, while driving across a long bridge, there was a very, very loud and sharp rapping on the roof of the car. It frightened us both. A few moments later it happened again—bang, bang, bang on the roof, as if it were somebody signaling with a ring or other metal object to someone inside the car. We were sure that the message was "now is the time." With great apprehension, I asked my mother to see if there was anybody on the floor of the backseat. There was not.

My mother was truly freaked out. I could think of nothing but speeding up the car so that whoever was on the roof of the car would fall off. I thought he must have jumped on at the stop sign. I raced along the highway knowing I would not stop until there was help. Eventually we came to a Jack-in-the-Box and I pulled in and went to the order window. I asked if there was anybody on the roof of the car. I am sure they thought we had had one too many earlier in the evening because they could see no one.

Mother and I returned to Tucson the next day and I mentioned the incident to Kent. He climbed on the roof of the car and saw clearly the scrapings where fingernails had dug in as well as an indentation that he was sure had come from a belt buckle. He had us check it out as well to verify his findings. Clearly, someone had been on the car. Well, Tana and Max were quite captivated by this story and asked to have it repeated time and again. I embellished it only with sound effects; the story was true. The roof of the car was repaired but my mother never quite got over that scary incident. I had always thought she was unflappable, but this experience rattled her thoroughly and forever more.

One more little car story about my mother took place the same year in April. It was a Friday and Mother was driving across a busy divided Tucson road—Campbell Avenue—and did not see a car approaching rapidly from her right. A young woman in a BMW was coming much too quickly down the hill and rammed into Mother's car. The police came and asked her questions to verify that she was mentally alert. She was quite indignant because of course she knew who the president was! She was 84 at the time. I went with her in an ambulance to the hospital. She was released and I took her home with the admonition that she rest.

Mother always had a cocktail party on Friday night. And the beat went on. Twelve people attended the party that night and Mother seemed none the worse for wear. She was truly remarkable.

1992 — Albuquerque

My good friend Merrill Dillon was part of a unique cadre of about 80 people who met annually at locations all over the U.S. and Canada. He invited me to join him for several of these occasions. My first was in Albuquerque, New Mexico on August 29th. This group was made up of Americans who had lived in Teheran, Iran between 1962 and 1979.

The Shah of Iran, seeing his people struggle financially and unable to find jobs, had brought into his country many businesses that were willing to locate there. The caveat was that they would provide the management of their companies but their employees had to be Iranian. It was a very successful program until the Shah left Iran for exile in 1979 as the last Persian monarch and Ayatollah Khomeini took over. He became the supreme leader of Iran and soon sent the Americans packing. Merrill had been the manager of one of the companies—Rayovac–and had loved the life in Teheran.

With so few Americans living there, they quickly bonded and developed lifelong friendships. These annual meetings were a reunion of these old friends. They had known Merrill's deceased wife, Ruth, and I wondered if they would accept his new and much younger friend. They did, and I enjoyed several reunions with them before Merrill died. Others were at Niagara-on-the Lake in Ontario in 1993 and in Las Vegas in1994.

Shortly after our plane landed, we took a bus trip with them to Isleta—an Indian pueblo. In the evening we went by bus to the base of Sandia Peak where we went 2.7 miles by tramcar to a restaurant –High Finance Restaurant—for dinner. It was at an elevation of 10,378 feet. The views from there take in 11,000 square miles of New Mexico.

We spent the following day in Santa Fe, always a mystical location for me. On our last day in Albuquerque, we shopped in Old Town and visited the Natural History Museum. On Monday we returned to Tucson arriving in time for me to teach my 1:30 to 4:30 p.m. colloquium and still have time for office hours. I did call some of these short trips too close!

1992 — Long Lake, Wisconsin

Joe Green, a dear friend in Tucson, talked often of his family cabin on a lake in Wisconsin. On September 25th I finally had the opportunity to visit it and see the glorious area about which he had spoken with such fondness. I flew to Minneapolis where Joe picked me up for the very long drive to his place on Long Lake.

The color of the fall leaves was spectacular, and I was delighted with the serenity of the area. My first two nights there I slept for more than 11 hours. What a boring guest I must have been! Joe had a 140 horsepower motor on his boat so we took several trips down the lake stopping for picnics along the way. Sitting by candlelight in the evenings and hearing the sounds of the forest was sublime.

It was a lovely weekend in a region I had not seen previously, and Joe and I reminisced about that lovely visit for years to come.

1992-93 — A Cruise to the Mexican Riviera with my Mother

Mother with Aldine –
Mexican Riviera cruise

Mother and I took another of our delightful cruises together over New Year's at the end of 1992. We embarked from Los Angeles on December 29th after a nerve-jangling trip that resulted in our being the last to board our ship, the *Fair Princess*, for a 10-day trip along the coast of Mexico. We visited lovely ports of call—Puerto Vallarta, Zihuatanejo, and then Acapulco. This town elicited many memories for me as it had been my honeymoon destination with Tony exactly forty years previously. It is incumbent upon tourists in Acapulco to watch the divers of Quebrada, always a heart-stopping experience even though I had seen the spectacle several times before. These intrepid Mexican men dive from a height of 115 feet into the ocean below which varies in depth from 6 to 16 feet, depending on the waves.

Our next stop was Mazatlán which had been my favorite town on a similar trip my mother and I had taken only two years before. It continued to hold great appeal for me. Our last port of call was Cabo San Lucas, always spectacular. We returned to Tucson on January 8th having enjoyed a pleasant interlude in my otherwise frantic life.

Aldine with Quebrada divers
in Acapulco

1993 — Montreal, Vermont and the Laurentians in Quebec

In the fall of 1993 I was on sabbatical leave from UA. Thus, I was able to extend my time at our cottage in Canada—hopefully until the first snowfall. Howard Shenk was visiting and accompanied me on a fascinating trip to Quebec and Vermont. We drove through Algonquin Park–always a magnificent experience–stopping briefly at the visitor's center that is steeped in local history. We drove through many snow flurries adding to our excitement.

The entrance to Algonquin Park is only 12 miles from our cottage. The park is absolutely pristine and strictly regulated. It is about one quarter the size of Belgium in area, and has over 2400 lakes. Ontario claims to have 750,000 lakes! Canada has more lakes than all other countries in the world put together.

We stayed that night in Ottawa, the nation's capital, at the elegant Chateau Laurier. The following day we drove to Hudson, Quebec—just outside Montreal—where we were visiting my beloved cousin, Gordon Sinclair, and his wife Linda—a beautiful woman and special friend. The following day we drove into Montreal—actually an island—and took a three-hour tour of the city. It was very beautiful and is the second largest city in Canada. Toronto takes first place, while Vancouver is third.

Afterwards, we drove to Jay Peak in Vermont where Linda and Gord had a gorgeous ski chalet. There were eight of us, and we spent a delightful few days together walking, shopping for wonderfully made local crafts, eating and sleeping.

Our next destination was in the Laurentian Mountains in Quebec–the town of Arundel–to visit Johanna and Bob Earle. They were excited about the place they planned to take us for dinner. We were very alarmed by it. We drove for at least an hour into the mountains with roads becoming narrower and bumpier. We truly worried about where we were being taken, but eventually we came to a small mountain inn with excellent food. They were gracious hosts but we were ready to return to the serenity and comfort of our cottage. We departed the next day and took another scenic trip through Algonquin Park. We were home!

1998 — Hal's Farm, Meshoppen, Pennsylvania

Imagine approaching your 67th birthday without ever having had a party in your honor! Such was the case for Hal in 1998. Things had to change and I meant to change them. Hal was going to have a birthday party in 1998! I suggested that we have a full-fledged event at his home in Pennsylvania. He was instantly excited at the prospect of showing his farm to me and introducing me to all his family and friends.

I flew to Newburgh, New York on May 18th where Hal met me and we set out on the three-hour drive to Meshoppen, his "home town." Meshoppen is a very old community with about 500 residents. It had its own post office and Hal had attended Meshoppen High School. It was dark during our drive so I saw little of the surrounding countryside. Once we arrived at his home, family started arriving to see Hal and to meet me. His son Greg, daughter-in-law Jo Ann, and their children Courtney and J.R. (Gregory junior) dropped in, as did his mother-in-law, Jessie Oliver. My worry that Jessie might have difficulty in accepting another woman in Hal's life was quickly eradicated when she drew me into her ample bosom. I was charmed by them all.

When I awoke in the morning I was in awe of the beauty that surrounded me. Hal's place was set on 20 acres high on a hill overlooking the Susquehanna Valley and the river below. It was magnificent—really breathtaking. Hal kept 13 of his acres mowed and it looked like a lovely country estate.

Hal and Bette, who had known each other since before their high school days, had built this home themselves and moved in upon its completion in 1980. They lived a blissful life there until Bette's death from ovarian cancer in 1997.

Aldine dozing in her chariot

Hal's magnificent pond

Our days passed, each with its own special surprise. One of my favorite activities was being towed in a cushion-lined trailer behind Hal's tractor high into the wilderness of the hills where we often spotted deer and other wildlife. What joy that brought me. Another was swimming daily in an acre-sized pond Hal had built that had a gazebo and many weeping willow trees beside it. Getting in the water every day was sheer bliss for me with two minor drawbacks. The first was that while in the pond I was constantly being nipped at by bluegill fish. Secondly, I was unable to fully relax knowing there were "man-eating" size catfish at the bottom of the pond—20 feet down. Well, they were big—at least three feet in length. Now who could relax wondering when one of these "predators" might surface?

We walked daily—the two miles I always walked when traveling—often to the quarry that had been Hal's destination for his two-mile runs–a part of his life for 30 years until his knees balked. It is also where he went to cry his heart out when Bette died. She had always been his sweetheart—the one and only—and her death left him bereft.

I often walked alone and foolishly took a route that required climbing a very, very steep hill which I named "Hell Hill." It really was hell to get up that hill which had to be at a 25 degree angle of bank at least.

One night we went to the nearby town of Tunkhannock where Courtney and J.R. were playing in a concert at the high school. We visited many of Hal's family including Ellie Grieve, his stepmother, as well as his aunt Virginia Sheret—age 90—who had us over for dinner at the old Sheret farmhouse where Hal had spent many of his summers growing up. Jeanne Jayne, Hal's sister-in-law, along with her boyfriend Russ Testos, were among our many visitors.

We attended church at Russell Hill drawing many stares from curious friends who wondered about the fancy lady Hal had on his arm, and we visited Bette's grave.

The 26th of May arrived—Hal's birthday– and we were ready for the big event. Hal had never known of a party such as this to have been given in this area. I had sent out printed invitations well in advance. We were delighted that almost 50 people came and stayed late into the night. Some were people Hal had not seen since his high school days—greatly changed, he noted. I was exhausted at the end and grateful that I was told to sit down while friends and family undertook the cleanup. What good and kind people they were.

Hal blowing out the candles at his big birthday bash

Still, I could never quite get used to some of their country ways. It was a very casual culture and people never knocked at doors when they arrived for a visit—expected or not. They simply walked in. I always made sure I was appropriately clad when I was outside my bedroom.

I think I passed muster with the local people, but definitely I was an anomaly in this Appalachian community. Many of these people had never traveled outside their own county–Wyoming County. Truck drivers from that area were seen as world travelers.

These annual trips to Hal's farm continued for many years. During the winter Jo Ann and Greg lived in Hal's house and moved to their smaller home next door for the summer. Greg had a car repair garage right beside their home—Greg's Garage—and the pattern of their lives worked perfectly. Eventually, at Hal's insistence, they moved into Hal's house permanently. During my visits thereafter, we stayed in a motel in Tunkhannock and visited the family. All good things must end, as did my visits. Hal continued to fly there for a week at the beginning of our summer. After a family visit, he drove his pickup truck to our cottage in Canada for the summer and returned to the farm in the fall to leave the truck and fly back to Tucson. He had the joy annually of watching his grandchildren and great grandchildren grow older.

1999, 2002 and 2003 — Santa Fe

My good friend, Howard Shenk, was the director of AHOF, the Arabian Horse Owners Foundation. Frequently horse shows were held in Albuquerque after which he would go to Santa Fe for rest and relaxation. I was often invited to accompany him. After meeting him at the airport in Albuquerque, on October 30, 1999, we drove to Santa Fe staying in a lovely hotel north of the town—the Bishop's Lodge. Our large room had two Murphy beds and a fireplace that provided us with warmth and atmosphere.

We visited the Georgia O'Keeffe museum—a woman whose art had always fascinated and repelled me at the same time. In Tucson I had attended a Chautauqua—performances popular in rural America until the 1920s to provide entertainment and culture. This one featured the life of O'Keeffe and I found her to be enigmatic and narcissistic. Add to that that she painted while nude and I inexplicably found that her lifestyle and subject matter—female genitalia in disguise—were offensive to my sensitivities.

My sensitivities were further assaulted when Howard took me to a world famous spa called Ten Thousand Waves. I was aware ahead of time that there were hot tub arrangements for many proclivities. There were those for men and women together—either in the nude or with a bathing suit. Others were for nude men only. Others for nude women only. I made amply clear to Howard that I wanted my dignity and privacy preserved and under no circumstance was he to subject me to nude males. I was clear on that!

Our first indulgence at this spa was to have a massage—my treat. Actually I don't like massages but—when in Rome! That was to be followed with a soak in a hot tub. And where did Howard take me—to the nude men's spa! I will never be able to eradicate from my scarred mind the number of—well, you know—that I took in at one glance when we entered. I was furious—albeit mildly fascinated. Most of the men were Asian. I found my way to the fully-covered women's Jacuzzi leaving Howard to lounge with his gender. Nudity had never been a problem for Howard. My Scottish upbringing, however, took rather a dim view of it.

We spent countless hours on Canyon Road visiting the shops and finding all manner of arts and crafts that would beggar the pocketbook but inflamed our senses. It was a delightful few days with a very dear friend.

Howard and I took another such trip to Santa Fe on March 18, 2002. This time we stayed in a suite on the 5th floor of La Fonda Hotel with a fireplace and a corner porch; it was quite luxurious. Our days were spent in visiting nearby pueblos such as San Ildefonso, Santa Clara and the charming town of Taos, New Mexico. We walked the length of Canyon Road awed by the beautiful art galleries and tempting shops.

Several days later we returned to Albuquerque, where I had met Howard when I flew from Tucson. We visited the excellent Natural History Museum and attended an

IMAX performance   about bears. It was very impressive. A highlight of that day was my introduction to Krispy Kreme donuts. It was memorable!

From the pine trees and cool air of Santa Fe to the heat I encountered when I returned to Tucson on March 21st was notable. The temperature in Tucson was in the 80s—hot for March.

My final trip to Santa Fe with Howard was in October of 2003. While I had loved my delightful autumn interludes in Santa Fe with him, I soon realized that this would be my last. The weekend was marred by my shortness of breath and atrial fibrillation–the catalysts for my pacemaker installation shortly thereafter. Clearly I could no longer tolerate high elevations.

By chance, Howard had arranged for a second-floor room with no elevator in the Plaza Real. I looked up that long flight of stairs and doubted that I'd make it through the next few days. We spent our time there exploring the stores and galleries on Canyon Road and eating in excellent restaurants. I was constantly lightheaded and unable to breathe easily. It was a relief to drive   downhill to Albuquerque where we roamed through "Old Town" and saw an IMAX production called *Ocean Oasis* about the Baja Peninsula.

I was glad to return to Tucson and had a pacemaker installed the following month. I had the best of Santa Fe, and it almost had the best of me!

2000 — Cabo San Lucas, Mexico

Both because of its proximity to Tucson and its enormous charm, Hal and I took many short trips to Mexico, this one to Cabo San Lucas at the tip of the Baja peninsula. February 1st, we spent four delightful days at the Hacienda Beach Resort in a room with

a lovely veranda and a view looking right out onto the ocean. We were serenaded by merry mariachis that evening at dinner.

During our days there, we spent time walking in town and on the beach and drinking tequila—at least Hal did. He loved the margaritas there and, to his delight, found a restaurant—Margaritaville– that not only made excellent margaritas but also the tastiest calamari Hal had ever experienced.

Hal & Aldine in Cabo San Lucas

One day we walked to Plaza Gloria to board a 110 foot "tall ship" for a whale watching cruise. It did not disappoint. Whales were frolicking all about us—as exciting an experience as can be imagined. We were literally jumping with joy in witnessing this magnificent spectacle and brought home many photographs to memorialize it. The halcyon days slipped by too quickly and we were back in Tucson on February 4th.

2000 — Bisbee, Arizona

Bisbee! Who has ever heard of Bisbee? Well, let me tell you that it has been named by AARP as one of the most "alive" places to retire in the U.S. And it was runner-up as one of the "quirkiest" towns in America. What more does one want for a weekend retreat?

Bisbee is built on steep hills with small and oddly shaped homes. One of its drawing cards is the Copper Queen Mine which features in its lobby a Fairbanks Morris engine. Tony Jr. has had– in his vast inventory of machinery over the years–an identical engine with a serial number only ten digits different from that of the one at the Copper Queen. Both were made in 1918 and are now collector's items. There were probably only 500 such engines that have ever been in existence. What a coincidence!

I have taken advantage of this unique destination throughout my life and have always chosen to stay at the Copper Queen Hotel as it has one room that is haunted. It truly is. I have never planned far enough ahead to get that room as people make their reservations for it far in advance. However, incidents of spooky things happening in that room during the night are well documented by the hotel. John Wayne stayed there several times. Our favorite restaurant was a charming little place called Le Chene Bistro.

One of the trips Hal and I made there was on February 25, 2000. We took a long route driving past beautiful Parker Lake in southern Arizona and stopping in Tombstone, Arizona. We were real tourists that weekend and even made a trip into the Copper Queen Mine.

One day we drove to Douglas to have lunch at the historic Gadsden Hotel. Hal and I used to play a game—identifying people (mostly men) whom we thought were pilots. Pilots just have a look about them. I spotted one, but didn't have the nerve to approach and verify. Later, we saw him on the street and I simply stopped and asked him if he was a pilot. It turned out he was—and with a great many hours under his belt! One more tick on my scorecard.

While in Douglas, we took a detour to cross the border into the small town of Agua Prieta, Mexico seeking medication for my brother-in-law who was dying of pancreatic cancer. We made a hasty purchase as we saw danger lurking in the streets and headed back to Bisbee.

We left on the 27th in order to be in Tucson that night to celebrate Max's 9th birthday. He has always been a lover of weird food, but the best we could do for him that night was sushi at Sakura. I adore that lad!

2000-2001-2002-2003 — San Carlos, Mexico

Perhaps it was one's first view of the rugged mountains—Tetas de Cabra—reaching toward the azure sky or maybe it was the first glimpse of the Sea of Cortez glistening in the sunlight. But, when one turned onto the road leading to San Carlos, the world fell behind and one grasped the magic of this unique and charming area.

San Carlos is mentioned in one context or another throughout this memoir. Hal had been there with Tony decades before but renewed his enthusiasm for visiting there with me in 2000. We made trips annually for years to come.

Rather than individualize each visit, I will write a composite of our time spent there. We stayed at Condominios Pilar, a delightful resort at the edge of one of the pristine white beaches for which this area is known. Swimming in the ocean was always a great treat, in spite of having to fend off sting rays and watch for jellyfish, the poison of each being incredibly painful. We spent hours in kayaks exploring nearby islands as well as mysterious little coves.

On our first visit, Hal went off on his own in a kayak to seek peace and do a little fishing. He succeeded in the former, and failed at the latter. He recalls vividly his first independent venture. While paddling along, he suddenly was surrounded by "sharks." At least, that is what he thought accounted for the many dorsal fins encircling him. To his enormous relief, he discovered that rather than hostile sharks they were inquisitive dolphins. His initial terror became delight with his new aquatic friends who stayed with him for quite a while.

Another boating adventure that we loved was taking our kayaks to a nearby estuary. When the tide receded, it drew our little vessels along with it. How beautiful and exciting that was! We also went out on professional fishing boat trips; Hal loved them while I would rather have been reading on the beach.

We often spent time with beloved friends who had time-shares there—Gail Harris and her husband Roger Fox, and Roz Leydet and her friend Ed Johnson. The restaurants in San Carlos were outstanding and very varied in their locations and cuisine. Some were right on the beach and without floors so that we could run our toes through the sand as we ate. Others were quite formal—even exotic.

For all of us, napping and sipping margaritas were other favorite pastimes.

When the U.S. government discouraged traveling in Mexico due to the dangers associated with drug cartels there, we respected their advice. What a disappointment! There simply wasn't another destination that quite compared. But we embraced all those happy memories!

2000 — Vancouver and California

We had been invited to the wedding of my beloved nephew Scott Sinclair and his beautiful and vivacious bride-to-be, Danelle. It was to be in Vancouver, British, Columbia on May 5th. As it was a long way to go for a wedding, Hal and I decided to extend our time away and make it into an adventure.

Hal drove to Vancouver so that we would have his pickup truck, and I flew there on May 4th. It was a long trip for me, too–eight hours of travel. Having been invited to the rehearsal dinner that night, Hal picked me up wearing his new suit while I had dressed to the nines for the occasion before leaving Tucson. The problem was that no one had told us where the party was to be held. So there we were in our finery in Vancouver with no place to go! We had a quiet dinner alone.

Before the wedding the following day, Hal and I walked for hours in Stanley Park although it was very cold. It even snowed! We attended the beautiful wedding at 6:00 p.m. and, having come from so far, and as we were family, we expected to be joyfully received. We weren't; we never even met the bride. I was noticed at the reception by my darling nephew Murray who asked me to tell a story about Scott at the podium from which people were making speeches. I do not do well at impromptu speaking, botched it, and was embarrassed.

As no post-wedding festivities were mentioned to us for the following day, Hal and I departed Vancouver planning to take a ferry to Victoria. Alas, we missed a turn and ended up in the state of Washington. Soldiering on, we took a ferry to Point Townsend and on to Port Angeles where we stopped for the night. We had seen beautiful scenery all day long, but it continued to be cold.

The following day we drove through the magnificent Olympic Peninsula passing gorgeous lakes, streams and climbing through mountains passes. We took a long walk on the unique black sand of Pacific Beach. Such beauty everywhere we looked! That night we reached Cannon Beach, Oregon–a charming little village. We spent the night at The Wave Hotel having a

Hal on the beach on Pacific Coast Highway

room with a fireplace and that looked right onto the beach. All our previous disappointments were erased.

Although we arose to a drizzling rain the next day, we took a leisurely walk on the beach. We had loved this little town but left for a long day of driving through gorgeous countryside and having magnificent views of the coastline. Oregon is a beautiful state indeed! We stopped for the night in Gold Beach, a mere 35 miles north of California.

The following day it rained hard and we found the 310 miles of driving difficult indeed. We drove along the spectacular coastline and climbed through mountain passes. We couldn't resist driving 25 miles along the Avenue of the Giants to view the magnificent redwood trees in spite of the driving rain. How delighted we were to reach our destination—Mendocino, California. Our hotel room in the Mendocino Hotel again had a fireplace, which was a welcome treat after a cold and wet day. The hotel had been built in 1878 and oozed charm, although we found it a bit pricey. We enjoyed the luxury of our room that night.

Our destination the next day was San Francisco which took us along beautiful, winding roads. Hal's lovely cousin, Sherie Goddard, lived in Mill Valley so we made a stop there to visit her and her husband George en route. Later, after checking into the Grosvenor Suites on Powell Street in San Francisco, we took the cable car to Fisherman's Wharf for a long walk and dinner at Scoma's. Delightful!

Our days in San Francisco were filled with moments of awe and joy. We took a tour of the bay, shopped on Pier 39, walked through Chinatown taking time to eat their outstanding dim sum, visited the maritime museum and lusted in the stores in Union Square. We dined in fine restaurants and reminisced about all the variety that this wonderful trip had offered.

On May 13th I flew back to Tucson while Hal drove in order to get his truck home. What a wonderful time we had, and to this day Scott and Danelle remain some of my favorite people on earth.

2000 — Kentucky

Admittedly, driving the back roads of Kentucky had not been on my bucket list, but when Howard Shenk invited me to attend the wedding of his niece in Lexington I accepted—with reservations, however. Somehow I have never felt at home in the South.

We flew to Lexington on October 4th. Before the wedding the next day, we saw the sights of the city and visited the children's museum—one of Howard's great interests. The wedding of his niece Lauren to David Fouts was lovely and followed by a delightful reception.

The following day Howard and I started out to explore the back roads of Kentucky. I was totally charmed as we wended our way through territory utterly unfamiliar to me. Our destination was a Shaker village that I had been forewarned was alcohol free. While I was not a big drinker, I did enjoy a glass of red wine in the evening. Giving Howard plenty of notice, I pointed out one liquor store after another as we drove along where we could have picked up a bottle before entering the abstemious town of Pleasant Hill. Men! Suddenly we were there–too late. Howard remembers my ire.

Pleasant Hill is the site of a Shaker religious community that was active from 1805 to 1910. It became a National Historical Landmark and was the largest registered Shaker community in existence. It was situated on 3000 acres of farmland and featured 34 restored 19th century buildings. We stayed at The Inn at Shaker Village which was charming and very reminiscent of days gone by. As my bed was very high off the floor, it required a little stairway for me to reach it! I wondered about people who had a tendency to fall out of bed. I hoped I would not be one of them as one could sustain serious injury! However, having gone to bed stone-cold sober, I was not in danger of losing my bearings.

The next day we visited the enchantingly restored shops and walked the colorful streets. We took a paddleboat—The Dixie Belle—on the Kentucky River and while it was great fun it was very cold. We continued driving the beautiful back roads to Louisville. En route we stopped at Berea College, distinctive for having been the first college in the Southern United States to be coeducational and racially integrated. Additionally, it charges no tuition. Every student admitted is provided a four-year scholarship.

We also passed by Churchill Downs, the racetrack famous for holding the annual Kentucky Derby. I was particularly interested in it as a good friend of ours—an older woman—Freda Chambers—had a strong family connection. Freda's maiden name was Churchill. The racetrack was named for her forbears John and Henry Churchill who had made the land available to their nephew—Colonel Meriwether Lewis Clark, Jr., grandson of the explorer William Clark. His efforts resulted in the development of the course.

Freda married Arthur Chambers. They were neighbors of ours in Tucson. Tony Jr. found a treasure trove in the outbuildings at the Chamber residence which held all manner of machinery and equipment. One item, a Honda 1968 motorcycle, had been used by the austere gentleman, Art Chambers, for surveying property in the late 1960s. Tony fell in love with it, bought it, and transported it to our cottage in Canada where it has been for 36 years and is still used annually.

Of greater interest was the use to which it was put in 1989 when Elizabeth and Tony were married. It was the vehicle on which they left their wedding reception in Dwight, Ontario to go on their honeymoon. Mind you, their honeymoon was spent in an old bunkie on our cottage property only two miles away. Hence, it was a very appropriate vehicle for the occasion.

Louisville was my point of departure for Tucson while Howard remained in Kentucky to visit family. The trip I had approached with a jaundiced eye turned out to be absolutely delightful, and Howard was a charming host.

2001 — Las Vegas, Nevada

An easy weekend destination for Tucsonans is Las Vegas, accessible easily by either flying or driving. Over the years I made many visits there both with Tony and other friends. Once was with Howard Shenk. We flew there on January 14th and checked into a suite in the Treasure Island hotel. We spent a good deal of time walking from one hotel to the next taking in the spectacular ambience of each. The mind boggled at their extravagant decorating and unique themes as each attempted to outdo the other with respect to grandeur and unexpected surprises. In the evening we attended an incredible show—"O"– at the Bellagio Hotel. It was a performance by Cirque de Soleil and was both elegant and awe-inspiring.

We continued our exploration of the magnificent hotels again the following day and dabbled in a little gambling. Back to Tucson we went on January 16th having ogled our way through that mecca of fantasy—Las Vegas.

Yet another visit to Las Vegas was with Bob Munns, perhaps the oldest friend I have. We were playmates as children in Toronto, boyfriend and girlfriend in our teen years, and friends forever. After his wife Diane died, he came to visit me in Tucson. One of the many side trips we made was to Las Vegas, his first visit to Fantasyland. We stayed at the lovely Mirage Hotel. He couldn't wait to see all the sights and we walked for hours from hotel to hotel stopping for an expensive lunch at Caesar's Palace.

Bob went exploring on his own the following day; I slept late recovering from the aches and pains incurred during our lengthy sight-seeing expedition the previous day. Then, once again, we hit the strip walking to Bellagio and on to Monte Carlo and New York-New York where we had lunch. Bob went on without me. I took a taxi back to our hotel and dived into a hot bath to assuage my aching bones. That night we went to the Rio and saw the dinner show *Tony and Tina's Wedding*. It was a riot!

Bob was a glutton for punishment and off he went the next day to absorb more of this fairytale city. We had dinner that night at New York-New York after which we saw a terrific stand-up comic show with Rita Rudner.

We returned to Tucson on December 8th and went that evening with Howard Shenk and his friend Joanne Triplett to the lovely Christmas performance annually presented at the renowned Mission San Xavier del Bac. What a contrast—from the tinsel of Las Vegas to the serenity of San Xavier and the beautiful Christmas carols sung by the Tucson Boys' Chorus.

2001-02 — A Cruise down the Mexican Coast with Hal Grieve

Although I had taken the "Mexican Riviera" cruise many times before, it was new territory for Hal and I was caught up in his excitement to have a romantic trip together  over New Year's. He had selected a Royal Caribbean ship—*Vision of the Seas*—that departed from San Diego on December 30th. After a day at sea to rest, we were ready to celebrate New Year's Eve and what a celebration it was! My diary notes that there was much "gaiety, noise and fun." Our first port of call was Cabo San Lucas where Hal had time to go to his favorite restaurant there—Margaritaville—which served us

Hal & Aldine on Mexican Riviera Cruise

memorable calamari washed down nicely with– a margarita, of all things!

On to Mazatlán where we took a 3½ hour walking tour of the old city. It was fascinating! Puerto Vallarta was our next port of call followed by two days at sea. Suddenly we were back in San Diego and couldn't believe a week had passed. The cruise was all we had hoped it would be and set the tone for a wonderful year to come.

2002-2003 — Road Trip to Sandy, Utah

Hal's daughter Linda and her husband, Randy Childers, had been encouraging us to visit them at their home in Sandy, Utah. We knew they were planning to leave there soon, so we got a move on and left Tucson by car on December 29th. Our first stop was Sedona, Arizona, a popular destination for people the world over. Its aura of mystery with an overlay of the spiritual was captivating. The air there was seductive and after a good night's sleep we left to drive through Oak Creek Canyon.

The views as we rode along were breathtaking. There was snow on the mountains and tree branches providing a unique dimension to all we saw. We ended the day in Page, Arizona where we visited Glen Canyon Dam and the associated museum. It was fascinating.

The following day we drove to Kanab, Utah where we stopped for coffee and then took back roads north toward Salt Lake City. The freeway was impassable due to snow. The scenery was gorgeous with the pristine snow and colorful hills. We had hoped to find a nice motel to spend our New Year's Eve but finally counted ourselves fortunate to find anything at all in that remote area. We celebrated in a 1960s type motel—Roberta's Cove—in Nephi. Just being together and feeling snowed-in in that rural location made the ushering in of 2003 a memorable occasion.

We reached Salt Lake City the next day and found the hotel in Sandy where a room had been reserved for us. It would be difficult to describe the Castle Creek Inn as it was indeed a castle with only 10 rooms, each with a unique motif. Ours was called the Canterbury room and had a fireplace and huge Jacuzzi. Linda and Randy were superb cooks and had us to their home for dinner where they served exotic Japanese food.

The next day was cold which set the mood for the day Linda and Randy had planned for us—a trip in the mountains and a visit to the location where the winter Olympics had been held the previous year. They showed us through the town of Park City, to which they ultimately moved.

On January 3rd we left Sandy and traveled to Cedar City enjoying the scenery all along the way. We stayed at a delightful inn—the Town and Country. The following day we drove to Las Vegas stopping in Kolob Canyon—a part of Zion National Park. We checked into the Aladdin Hotel—always comfortable if not elegant—and started our jaunt along the strip to visit hotels and shops. That night we saw the Cirque de Soleil production of "O" at the Bellagio Hotel and I was just as impressed as I had been the first time I saw it. Hal was quite overcome by the spectacle and took every opportunity thereafter to watch these performances either on stage or on video.

We reached Wickenburg, Arizona the following day having visited the impressive Hoover Dam. It was a dreadful day of driving as the roads were narrow and there were high winds that blew sand and dust. We were ready to go home and the next day, January 7th, we barreled back to Tucson. Being back in my own bed again felt so comforting after many days away.

2005 — Clear Lake, California

The relationship between Al Marshick and me had been adversarial at best, contentious at worst—albeit we had a crush on each other for 63 years. Al had lived the world over, part of it in Saudi Arabia where he could quickly amass a considerable amount of money as an engineer in order to pay off his five ex-wives. Ultimately, he settled with his brother Ken in Clear Lake, California, although I am sure their arrival was unsettling for many of the residents there. Al and Ken took vigor and chaos wherever they went!

I had been a widow for 16 years when Al invited me to visit them on February 18th. He had suggested marriage several times over the years but I knew it hadn't worked with the previous five wives, and it was not likely to work with me. It just wasn't on my bucket list. I did, however, end up marrying the third of the "three musketeers" mentioned earlier in my memoir. Good decision!

Girding up my loins for whatever lay ahead, I arrived at the Sacramento airport on schedule where Al met me. There was a good deal of air turbulence en route making it an uncomfortable trip. I saw this as an omen. The drive to Clear Lake took us through Kelseyville, and Soda Bay with beautiful scenery all the way. Ken's house was on a hill overlooking the lake. I was quite overwhelmed with the beauty of the area, and their views were spectacular. Deer roamed the hills. It was indeed bucolic.

It rained continuously my first day there, a good time for the brothers to spend teaching me the nuances of a computer—each trying to outdo the other with his wisdom. It was dizzying! At night we met scads of their friends for dinner at a Mexican restaurant.

During my visit Ken and Al went to great trouble to assure my comfort and to provide many   comprehensive tours of that beautiful area. When my departure day arrived, they drove me to Sacramento through spectacular countryside.   It had been a more serene visit than I had anticipated. Perhaps I was disappointed.

Hal met me at the Tucson airport–flowers in hand. We had dinner on our way home and when he left me at my front door I was unprepared for what I found inside. He had strewn flowers throughout the house. What a darling! Why did I continue to reject his proposals—until 2007!

A footnote to this story concerns Al's last visit to see me in Tucson at the end of 2007. As he, his brother and I sat on my patio drinking wine, I told him I was going to marry his old flying buddy Hal Grieve, and he became ashen. He said he had always thought I would eventually relent and tie the knot with him. Given his state of mind, and that I was now engaged, I asked my sister Carol if she would have them at her house for the night. She, too, adored them both so quickly acquiesced. She lived three houses from me.

What a fiasco she endured that night! They stayed up late drinking. When she thought they had finally settled down, she undressed in her bedroom and was down to her skivvies when Ken thrust open her door in a panic announcing that the toilet was overflowing. Out she ran to grab the plunger—her house being more important to her than her modesty—and took care of the load Ken had left in the toilet. What a mess she had to deal with!

Not quite ready for bed, Al—a cigar lover—stoked up an old stogie right outside her bedroom window so that smoke was wafting in threatening to choke her. She was not pleased. In the morning, Al ran his hat through her dishwasher creating more plumbing problems. She happily bid them adieu!

After they left, she found one more catastrophe to deal with. Carol had urged Ken, who slept on her navy blue sofa, to use the sheets that she had offered him. He said a blanket and pillow would be fine. Carol, a meticulous housekeeper, was chagrined to find during her tidy-up that Ken was a skin-shedder. Her sofa was covered with a fine layer of the molt he had distributed–particularly from his feet–and it simply refused to succumb to any measure she used to remove it—a vacuum, damp cloths and a whisk broom. She had that reminder of Ken for several weeks before the skin peelings wore off!

I never saw Al again. He developed esophageal cancer which rendered him without speech. He refused to learn how to use the gadget that would enable him to create vocal sounds and chose to become a recluse until he died on December 15, 2012. He was 82 years old. All three of the original trio of pilots are gone now, each having succumbed to cancer.

2005 — Pasadena, California

Hal was a skeptic. I am not. Being a good sport, I accepted his invitation to join him in attending   the annual conference of The Skeptic Society to be held at Cal Tech in Pasadena, California on May 12th. My thoughts were—nothing ventured, nothing gained. We spent the first night in Blythe, California in a Motel 8. Being together made it an adventure instead of a challenge. However, life looked much brighter the next day when we arrived in Pasadena and stayed at a Westin Hotel.

We attended a session of the conference that night and waited almost two hours for the program to begin. Not a good start! I noted that it was fun, but not educational—

music, magic and mind reading. The next day was the presentation of a series of lectures—reports of research. Truly, we both fell asleep. Hal called it quits. Enough was enough. Later we drove through Old Pasadena and had dinner at Club 21. I noted that Hal was in a weird mood. I should think so! Identification through association, I suspect.

The status quo was regained the following day by a visit to Hal's cousin, Rene Sheret and his wife Bobbie—a darling couple. After two hours with them we started our trip back to Tucson arriving home on May 16th. Hal never suggested another skeptics meeting, and I noticed that we no longer received their mailings. I may have damaged his enthusiasm, or maybe he saw the light!

2013 — Cabo San Lucas with my Siblings

It is fitting that I end this long list of short stories with a trip I took with my sister Carol Sinclair to the home of my brother, Murray Sinclair, and his wife Mary. My brother was dying of cancer and his son Murray wanted very much for there to be a reunion of the siblings before his father died. He orchestrated it well. It was March 21st when we gathered at their place in Cabo San Lucas.

Mary and Murray had lovely homes—one in Rosedale in Toronto, a magnificent cabin in Dwight, Ontario and a third near Cabo San Lucas on the Baja Peninsula of Mexico. The latter is where they spent their winters. It is a luxurious place with a spectacular view of the ocean.

Over the years a wall had grown between Murray and me. We were polite, but not close. This had happened to Carol, too, to a lesser degree. Hence, it was with some trepidation that I embarked on the trip to Cabo.

In arranging this meeting, young Murray had sent all of us photographs he had amassed that covered the years of our lives together since childhood. He extracted a promise that we would gather together over a glass of wine some evening during the visit to look at them and reminisce. We complied. It was a very moving experience for me, requiring a considerable amount of Kleenex. It was a time of catharsis and bonding, just as young Murray had planned.

In spite of my alienation from my brother, I had repeatedly acknowledged my respect for the dignified and courageous manner in which he had accepted his illness over the years. He had endured unbelievable pain, and I don't think I heard him complain even once. Mary was incredible in her unflagging devotion and in the unwavering care she gave him over the last years of his life.

As hosts they were without equal. We were wined and dined and shown every nook and cranny of the magnificent gated community in which they lived, as well as the area thereabouts. Carol and I were thoroughly spoiled and sad to leave when our departure day arrived.

It was indeed our last time together as brother and sisters. Murray died less than a year later—on Valentine's Day of 2014. Mary continues to live in the lovely homes they created together.

And so my stories end. I have enjoyed recalling, reminiscing and sharing these moments in time that made up the tapestry of my life—some tender, some sad and some comical. I have lived by my father's credo—that every day is a gift and that not a moment should be squandered. What a lucky woman I have been!

CONCLUSION

And so my story is told.

I thank God daily for blessing me with a life filled with love, beauty, adventure and opportunity. Most of all I am grateful for the amazing people who have made my life so rich an experience, especially my beloved family.

I hope that, even in a small way, I have lived by the credo so simply expressed by MotherTeresa:

> Let no one ever come to you without leaving better and happier.
> Be the living expression of God's kindness.
> Kindness in your face
> Kindness in your eyes
> Kindness in your smile

Aldine von Isser
Tucson, Arizona
2017

APPENDIX 1

THE AMERICANS

Gordon Sinclair

Gordon Sinclair
Radio Station CFBR 1010
2 St. Clair Avenue West
Toronto, Ontario, Canada

"LET'S BE PERSONAL"
Broadcast June 5, 1973
CFRB, Toronto, Ontario
Topic: "The Americans"

The United States dollar took another pounding on German, French and British exchanges this morning, hitting the lowest point ever known in West Germany. It has declined there by 41% since 1971 and this Canadian thinks it is time to speak up for the Americans as the most generous and possibly the least-appreciated people in all the earth.

As long as sixty years ago, when I first started to read newspapers, I read of floods on the Yellow River and the Yangtse. Who rushed in with men and money to help? The Americans did.

They have helped control floods on the Nile, the Amazon, the Ganges and the Niger. Today, the rich bottom land of the Misssissippi is under water and no foreign land has sent a dollar to help. Germany, Japan and, to a lesser extent, Britain and Italy, were lifted out of the debris of war by the Americans who poured in billions of dollars and forgave other billions in debts. None of those countries is today paying even the interest on its remaining debts to the United States.

When the franc was in danger of collapsing in 1956, it was the Americans who propped it up and their reward was to be insulted and swindled on the streets of Paris. I was there. I saw it.

When distant cities are hit by earthquakes, it is the United States that hurries into help... Managua Nicaragua is one of the most recent examples. So far this spring, 59 American communities have been flattened by tornadoes. Nobody has helped.

The Marshall Plan .. the Truman Policy .. all pumped billions upon billions of dollars into discouraged countries. Now, newspapers in those countries are writing about the decadent war-mongering Americans.

I'd like to see one of those countries that is gloating over the erosion of the United States dollar build its own airplanes.

Come on... let's hear it! Does any other country in the world have a plane to equal the Boeing Jumbo Jet, the Lockheed Tristar or the Douglas 107? If so, why don't they fly them? Why do all international lines except Russia fly American planes? Why does no other land on earth even consider putting a man or women on the moon?

You talk about Japanese technocracy and you get radios. You talk about German technocracy and you get automobiles. You talk about American technocracy and you find men on the moon, not once, but several times ... and safely home again. You talk about scandals and the Americans put theirs right in the store window for everyone to look at. Even the draft dodgers are not pursued and hounded. They are here on our streets, most of them ... unless they are breaking Canadian laws .. are getting American dollars from Ma and Pa at home to spend here.

When the Americans get out of this bind ... as they will... who could blame them if they said 'the hell with the rest of the world'. Let someone else buy the Israel bonds. Let someone else build or repair foreign dams or design foreign buildings that won't shake apart in earthquakes.

When the railways of France, Germany and India were breaking down through age, it was the Americans who rebuilt them. When the Pennsylvania Railroad and the New York Central went broke, nobody loaned them an old caboose. Both are still broke. I can name to you **5,000** times when the Americans raced to the help of other people in trouble.

Can you name me even one time when someone else raced to the Americans in trouble? I don't think there was outside help even during the San Francisco earthquake.

Our neighbours have faced it alone and I am one Canadian who is damned tired of hearing them kicked around. They will come out of this thing with their flag high. And when they do, they are entitled to thumb their nose at the lands that are gloating over their present troubles.

I hope Canada is not one of these. But there are many smug, self-righteous Canadians. And finally, the American Red Cross was told at its 48th Annual meeting in New Orleans this morning that it was broke.

This year's disasters .. with the year less than half-over… has taken it all and nobody…but nobody… has helped.

APPENDIX 2

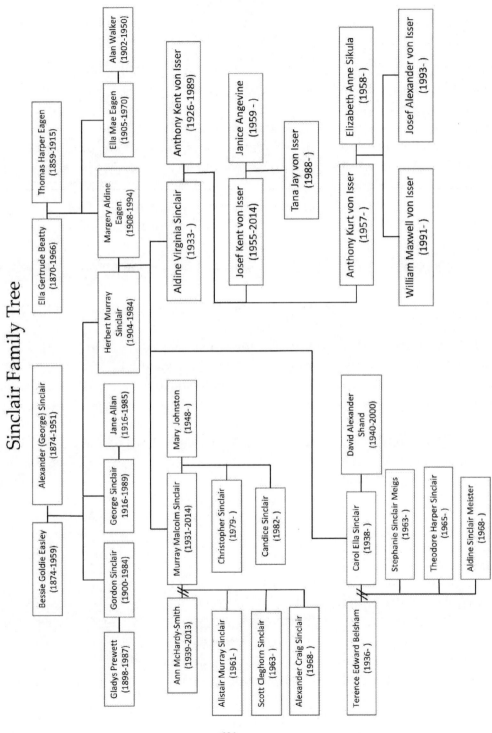

Sinclair Family Tree

APPENDIX 3

A WHALE TALE

Somewhere out there *Aldine Baby*, my Venture 24 trailerable sloop, has a friend. The friend is a whale. They became acquainted last May during two weeks of single-handing on the Sea of Cortez.

We were four hours out of Guardian Angel Island en route to Dog Bay on Tiberon Island. The knot meter read about two, in light air, but due to current several bearings had confirmed that speed over the bottom was in reverse. It was going to be a long passage.

The sound of whales spouting, common enough on the Gulf, was a welcome diversion. On this quiet day, by looking sharp, two or three long, black shapes could usually be seen.

Normally whales intercepted by sailboats simply continue on their way or shyly submerge until a prudent distance is re-established. In the habit of Mexican fishermen, who want no part of whales, we have frequently given way to these mighty leviathans even when the rules of the road didn't require it.

Later on the whale who was to become our companion slowly passed at right angles some hundred yards ahead. I watched him with casual interest. I believe I spoke some sort of greeting. After nearly two weeks alone, and this my third single-handed Gulf sojourn, I was no longer self-conscious about talking aloud to myself or to anything else.

The whale was soon clear and forgotten. I twiddled the autopilot course knob and went back to reading. A few minutes later I noticed the whale had changed course. He was now paralleling us going the opposite way. I began paying attention. He next surfaced, then sounded 50 yards astern, heading toward us beneath *Aldine Baby*'s gentle wake. I dove for the camera. After a suspenseful wait, he reappeared well ahead.

I told him out loud to mind that Venture 24s have a five-foot draft. I had no trouble remembering that many mysterious disappearances on long distance races and ocean passages were thought to be the result of collision with whales. While I didn't expect him to return, for good measure the Sea Gull

Tony's whale in close pursuit

outboard was fired up to make clear *Aldine Baby* was not one of his kind.

But the outboard seemed to act like a magnet. He made another wide, leisurely 360, spouted some 100 feet astern and homed in on the fantail once more. Though submerged, he left a path of swirls and eddys on the surface. Standing on the rail I looked deep into the water trying to spot him. He came in view perhaps six or eight feet down and along the port side, moving just faster than the boat. He was big. Very big. Very, very big! Or maybe my boat was just smaller than I thought. I had turned on a tape recorder trying to record the sound of his blow and thus recorded my own words and feelings of the moment:

"Whale, I don't blame you for being attracted to *Aldine Baby's* smooth, white bottom but hear me well—she's mine and she's a boat! You can look but you can't touch! (Pause) Please...Sir...Excellency...Your Highness..." He finally surfaced too far ahead for a picture or recording.

But the next pass was different. It was a plain, old-fashioned buzz job. I couldn't see where he came from but he surfaced and spouted while crossing the bow only six feet ahead! I captured both the photo and the sound, as well as spray from his blow hole complete in all its pungent glory. I told him he'd never make it with *Aldine Baby* without first inhaling a bucket or two of Listerine.

The friendly whale stayed with us about four hours. He seldom came as close as on those first few passes but there was no doubt we were being squired all the while.

I really wasn't overjoyed with this attention. Our fate seemed to hinge entirely upon his judgment and sense of decency. There was little to be done other than run the motor and raise the keel, neither of which seemed to make any difference to him.

When our whale finally went his own way, I was almost sorry. He had been a companion on a lonely sea. No harm had come. It had been a fascinating, unusual experience. Besides, it's nice, in a different sort of way, to feel wanted by a whale.

When night came we were sailing easily in light air under overcast skies. It was very dark. The sound of spouting whales was all around. By looking deep into the water, the phosphorescent outline of whales, porpoises and schools of fish could frequently be seen followed by luminous streaks of turbulence. The sea beneath was busy and aglow. It was like looking down from an airplane at night upon a network of highways. The sight was a wonder; the feeling kind of spooky.

I nervously assumed *Aldine Baby's* own luminous outline would clearly mark her presence but hoped it wouldn't also tweak the curiosity of nearby whales. I remember imagining, even wishing, that somewhere out in that blackness, escorting safe passage through his spouting brethren, was our friendly whale of the afternoon.

The night went without incident. Perhaps our whale had been out there after all. Who knows? I wonder where he's been since then and where he is right now.

By Tony von Isser
4615 Camino Real
Tucson, Ariz. 85718
1-15-73

NOTE TO READER: Tony's articles always alluded to him and his boat as "we."

APPENDIX 4

THE HISTORY OF CHARLIE THOMPSON ROAD

Having lived on Charlie Thompson Road for the past 84 summers, I have many memories of life as it was there long ago. This history will introduce the magic of the region of Muskoka where I spent the summers of my childhood and my adolescence, as well as the years there with my children and grandchildren. It will also introduce the people who made a profound impression on me and who molded my summer experiences.

Charlie Thompson Road begins at the top of a hill beyond the little church to which I have gone all my life and at which my parents, my husband Tony, and my son Kent are buried.

The first cottage on Charlie Thompson Road is where I spent so many summers of my life. The initial dwelling was built in 1888 and was used as a hunting cabin by the Charles Cunningham family from Rochester, New York. Later that building became the Dwight library and was called the Birch Spa Library. In the early 1900s, the Cunninghams added on to that rough log cabin and created a three-story white cottage which they called Birch Spring because of the pure spring water that runs through the property, surrounded by birch trees. The property still bears that name.

My uncle, Alan Walker and his wife Elma, purchased that property in 1945. Although they had no children, they wanted a permanent summer place where my parents could bring their children each summer following my father's enforced move to Arizona as a result of asthma.

Looking down Charlie Thompson Road from top of hill - 1943

My brother Murray Sinclair and his wife Mary took possession of the property in 1979 and built a magnificent cabin with well-groomed grounds on the Birch Spring property. Considering it a safety hazard, they burned down the old original white place that was there for so long and in which my family and I had spent so many summers. It had been a beacon at the top of Dwight Bay and I will miss it forever.

Charlie Thompson Road continues for five miles with a loop at the end. Therefore, it receives only local traffic. At the beginning of the road, Dwight Bay can be seen to the south but as it progresses, and climbs a hill, it approaches Rat Bay to the east. It isn't visible, however, until you reach Libby and Gord Duncan's beautiful home—Rats' Cabin. They are beloved friends who are always at the ready to help us in any way. Their cottage–their year-round residence—was featured in the winter 2014 edition of Our Home magazine. At the end of the road on the loop, one sees what is called North Bay on many charts—the water between Dwight Bay and the "big lake." Our very dear friends, Barbara and Wayne Twaits, have a charming home there that has, in addition to its strong flavor of Muskoka, a hint of Mexico as well. It also is their permanent residence.

That covers the geography of the area, but its magic is yet to be told. That lies in the stories of how the road developed and of the colorful people who lived beside it—many for a long, long time. I am one of those.

We will begin with Charlie Thompson for whom the road was named. Who was this Charlie Thompson? This is his story. The tale goes that when Charlie and his brother were very young, they walked a cow from Toronto to Dwight—a distance of about 170 miles. Apparently, once Charlie saw this area, he was determined to make it his home someday. There is an old barn on the original Charlie Thompson property which still bears a sign saying 1897. This belonged to his extended family as did the old log cabin there. Sadly, over time, these folks ran into financial trouble and told Charlie that the property was his for the taking. They simply deeded it over to him as they could no longer afford to stay there. This windfall had about 200 acres of land which included the entire peninsula along which Charlie Thompson Road runs. The property was called Tapawingo Farm and we now have the original sign hanging on our bunkie, a gift to us from a good friend of Charlie's, Don Rowntree. It is a treasure that evokes many memories.

Charlie was a Toronto boy and, as was the tradition in his youth, he joined with friends on Saturday nights at the Maple Leaf Ballroom. It was there that he met Dorothy who was from a prominent Woodstock family. They fell in love and married in 1929, just three weeks before the Great Depression hit. As was true with so many young couples at the time, they had no financial resources whatever. So Charlie borrowed his father's car to take his bride on their honeymoon to Walker Lake, not far from Dwight, thus introducing her to the beauty of Muskoka.

In time, he brought her to the log cabin on the farm to live. It wasn't an easy life for Dorothy. She had to get used to snow coming through the spaces between the logs and to living in a one room cabin with no amenities. They did, however, have a root cellar that depended heavily on the snow coming at the right time in the winter to insulate the cellar from bitter cold snaps.

Dorothy was a great baker of pies. One day she had just finished making two berry pies and was waiting for them to set when all hell broke loose in their cabin. Charlie had decided to dig a cellar but came upon a boulder down there that he just couldn't budge. Well, the answer of course was dynamite. He had, however, neglected to mention this plan to Dorothy who was in the kitchen above when the explosion occurred. Pie filling was scattered far and wide and Dorothy's temper was acutely tested. This was, as I say, only a one-room cabin but Charlie bought three pigs that had to live indoors with them in the winter. Dorothy, as a properly raised young lady, had to adjust to a whole new way of life.

While the cabin had few comforts, they had wonderful times there with picnics and hayrides and such. On one of these hayrides, the wagon came loose and Charlie fell off, was dragged by the horses and was trampled very badly by them. He had been given up for dead but Dorothy somehow got him to Toronto General Hospital. They gave her little hope for his survival but eventually he made a miraculous recovery.

Dorothy and Charlie had very little money. Charlie took a job in Algonquin Park— 12 miles away–for a few years, and life was tough for them. Every Monday he would walk to his job in the Park and every Friday he would walk back to the farm and Dorothy. He had two horses that worked in the Park as well. He was paid $5 a week for his work and $5 for each of his horses which meant that his weekly income was $15. They made do by shooting moose and deer and by making and selling maple syrup. Dorothy baked all their bread and was skilled in the kitchen. I was often the recipient of her fantastic oatmeal cookies.

While Dorothy and Charlie never had children, they raised two nephews. One, Bill Wilson, was the son of Dorothy's brother while Don Oliver was the son of Charlie's brother. Dorothy and Charlie, it should be mentioned, were related. Amazingly, her nephew was the image of Charlie while Charlie's nephew looked just like Dorothy. It was Dorothy's job to see that these lads got to school at Portage every day. In winter there was a high, snow-covered hill that had to be climbed as well as ice that had to be crossed. When she was unsure as to how thick the ice was, Dorothy would crawl over the ice to test it. If it was safe, the boys would follow behind her. What determination!

Charlie eventually amassed enough money to be able to attend Shriner's Conventions all over the world. In 1962, Dorothy and Charlie built a more gracious home near the mouth of Rat Bay which they accomplished entirely on their own. Dorothy herself did the roofing job and painted the entire cabin.

Charles Washington Thompson was born in 1904 and died in 1984 at age 80 of prostate cancer. He had three brothers and three sisters. He was an active member of Stewart Memorial Church, and I remember well that he took collection every Sunday, always dressed in suit and tie. There is a lovely stained glass window there in his memory.

Dorothy was born in 1910 and died in 2003 at age 93. She lived on Charlie Thompson Road until shortly before her death.

But back to the beginnings of Charlie Thompson Road. Initially, it was not a road at all but a trail used by the Hutcheson Lumber Company to clear-cut the entire hill. It was also used for taking hydro lines up and over the hill to Portage. The road had no name until the time of Charlie's death. A neighbor, Bill McPherson, circulated a petition requesting that the hitherto unnamed road become Charlie Thompson Road. This went into effect the day before his death.

Over time, Charlie amassed a fortune. He was an astute business man and saw the potential for the peninsula he owned. His idea was to improve the road for the purpose of selling off lots to people to build cottages beside the lake.

Among the first places built was one my sister Carol eventually bought on the loop. She sold it in 2012. Most of the original cottages on Charlie Thompson Road beyond his old farmhouse have either been torn down and rebuilt into veritable mansions, or have been added on to. My sister's place was razed and in its place is a spectacular new home. While the new cottages are quite magnificent, our own place is an exception. Ours is definitely a cottage.

It is interesting to go way back in time to the early residents in the Dwight area. I remember well old Mr. Keown who owned the second home on Charlie Thompson Road. This is his story. He had come from Ireland and was drawn to this area because of the Land Grant Act. The government was not entirely kind in encouraging immigrants to come here as farmers. In the beginning, the land was not bad for farming but the topsoil was very shallow and soon wore out. Nothing was known of rotation of crops or fertilization so the settlers had to turn to other means of livelihood.

Initially, Mr. Keown built a place near Oxtongue Lake. It was but a shanty. Eventually he grew lonely and decided he needed a wife. So, he walked to Orillia—75 miles away–to put his name in for a "mail-order bride" from Ireland. Life was difficult in Ireland at that time and families often had to reduce their load by sending their eligible daughters away to marry abroad. Often these girls were very young. Having registered for a bride, Mr. Keown walked back to his place on Oxtongue Lake. To his surprise, during his absence it had been moved into by a black family who had come to Canada via the underground railroad to escape slavery in the United States. He thought the situation over and decided that they needed it more than he did. So he gave it to them and left to move to the west shore of Dwight Bay where he built a lean-to on the property that is now owned by our dear friend, Margaret Ruscica.

Word reached Mr. Keown in the spring that a group of brides was soon to be arriving in Orillia. This time he took a buckboard down to meet her. The pairing of couples was something of a lottery—each groom having been given a number as had each arriving bride-to-be. When their number was called they had to locate each other. I remember Mr. Keown as being no more than 5' 2" so he had a long stretch to look up and introduce himself to his bride as she was a girl 6 feet tall!

Back they went to the lean-to to start their lives. They arrived at night and when the bride looked outside she saw what she thought were people. She was crushed with disappointment the next morning when she realized that what she had seen were, in fact, tree stumps. They were quite alone in the wilderness. Old Mr. Keown was a diminutive, earnest man with only one tooth. My sister remembers that tooth as having a spectrum of colors—black, yellow, green and more. He died in his nineties. We estimate that he was born in about 1850.

Ultimately the Keowns built a proper house on Charlie Thompson Road. I remember it well as a child. They had a barn and a chicken coop. My sister's great delight was collecting eggs for the Keowns. Their only child, Bert, lived with them. I recall Bert as a wonderful man with a twinkle in his eye and a wicked sense of humor. One of the many stories about Bert was the time he went hunting and shot a deer—out of season. He wasn't sure how he'd get it home without being caught. He was deep in the woods. Intrepid Bert dragged that deer to the Oxtongue River, threw it in, climbed aboard, and paddled it home—down the river and across Dwight Bay.

Bert kept about a dozen cows which he led out every morning, walked them along the lane that would become Charlie Thompson Road, and let them loose in a huge field—adjacent to our cottage. And every night he would lead them home and milk them in the barn. Now, this exercise with the cows meant a great deal to me personally as I grew up awakening every day to the sound of the cow bells. They were a part of my summer life and to this day I can hear them clearly in my mind.

Farming was difficult but the Keowns managed to grow a vegetable garden and sold their produce. My friend, John Burgar, remembers one morning when he and his sisters went to the Keown's to buy produce. Mr. Keown was in his suspenders, shaving with a straight edge blade, and the air was blue. Apparently wolves had devoured his twelve lambs the previous night and he was irate and desperate.

Another source of income was for Bert to sell ice. He had two Fjord horses and in the winter he would cut up ice on the lake and keep it over the winter. In the summer, the horses would pull a wagon with the ice as Bert delivered it to cottages. He knew the dimensions of everyone's ice box and would cut accordingly. I remember well him placing the ice in a burlap sack, throwing it over his shoulder, and putting it in our icebox—sawdust and all. My parents would carve out a piece of the ice large enough to accommodate their putting the milk against it.

When old Mrs. Keown died, there was need for a housekeeper and the Keowns hired a woman named Sadie Woodcock. Sadie was at that time a married woman, although she hadn't seen or heard from her husband in many years. That was in the 1930s. As time went along, it was clear to everyone that Bert and Sadie were in love. But she couldn't marry him as she was still legally married. Every summer Bert would come to our old white cottage, Birch Spring, for a cup of tea and a chat and every time my outspoken elderly grandmother, Ella Eagen, would ask him when he was going to make an honest woman of Sadie. Those tea parties lasted well into the 1970s.

Word finally reached Sadie that her husband had died. Well, into Huntsville went Sadie and Bert and Bert told the municipal clerk that they were going to get married then and there. As everyone knew how long they had waited for this moment, bans and other requirements were overlooked and, at long last, Bert made an honest woman of Sadie. That happened in the 1960s.

One sidebar here is that Sadie had an infamous sister by the name of Viola McMillan. She was credited with the development of the Prospectors and Developers Association of Canada. Also, she issued stock on the Toronto Stock Exchange for a claim near Timmins. It turned out that it was effectively a scam and many people lost millions. She ultimately went to prison for eight months and was publicly disgraced. A long way from Sadie back on the farm!

Across the road from the old Keown place are two very old cottages. One is called Cobble Cottage. It is a lovely example of fieldstone construction. It was built as the club house for the Stewart family's Tennis Club and was home to two grass courts. Beside it is the cottage called Beacon Lodge. It was built in 1924 to house their staff with the materials left over from the clubhouse construction.

My family started renting these cottages in 1931 when my brother was two months old. My first summer was in 1933 at age two months hence making 2016 my 84th summer in Dwight. My sister Carol didn't come along until 1938. When my family started going to Dwight, the roads from Toronto were quite primitive and it took my father nine to eleven hours of driving to get there. Imagine my family starting out from Toronto. They had to take spare tires in case of flats, all their linens and equipment for babies such as cribs. It sounds like a monumental task.

We had few comforts but fell in love with Lake of Bays, a lifelong love affair. A friend of ours, Jane Tate, was to be married to a man—Charlie—whose work would take

him all over the world. She insisted, therefore, that her wedding vows include "love, honour, and Lake of Bays." This is the kind of attachment one develops to this region.

We did not have electricity (hydro) but used coal oil lamps. My mother cooked on a two-burner wood stove. We drew water from a pump outside the cottage. Daily we walked through the woods to fill pails with the legendary spring water that flows through the Birch Spring property. We were given permission to swim in the lake as the cottage did not come with lakefront privileges.

An annual event was Bert Keown taking us into the old boarded-up cottage — Birch Spring – later to become our summer home. What an exciting treat that was for us children! There were hundreds of bats that were inconvenienced by our visit—which was delightfully scary

Aldine in her kilt carrying firewood into Beacon Lodge - 1938

to us. My sister and I remember vividly one such occasion on a July 12th, the day of the annual Orangemen's Day Parade. It always passed by that property to taunt the Cunningham family who were Roman Catholic and from Rochester, New York. The marchers wore determined faces and passed in grim silence along the road until they

reached the hill overlooking the Cunningham home—Birch Spring. Then they'd let loose with fifes and drums and let out shrieks and blasts against their enemy. Clearly Catholics were not held in high regard in the early days of the area. Carol and I were quite impressed with seeing the colorful sight as they passed. Two years after we moved into that property, my father went up to see the group and told them that the Cunninghams were gone and we were Protestant. They never came again.

The Sinclair family at Beacon Lodge – Murray, Carol, Mom, Dad & Aldine

Below our places—we rented both Beacon Lodge and Cobble Cottage over the years— was the summer home of the Chisholm family. It was built in about 1920. The Chisholms had made their fortune by inventing the pea podding machine. I was a frequent visitor there as there were young people my age with whom I played. My friends were the grandchildren of old Mrs. Chisholm–Ruth Ann, Carolyn and Alastair Souter. What fun we had and what mischief we engaged in. When old Mrs. Chisholm died, the cottage was inherited by ten descendants. While they had every intention of keeping it and sharing the expenses to maintain it, it ultimately had to be sold. The new owners are our beloved friends Lesley and Simon Stubbs who make an annual pilgrimage each summer from their homes in England and France.

The Hickok camp is next to the Stubbs' place. The first actual cabins built on both the Chisholm and the Hickok properties were built in 1905 and my brother was shown a receipt by Alastair Souter indicating that each building had cost $25. Later, in the 1920s, Stephen Rae (referred to by his family as S. Rae) and Justine Hickok purchased their property, subsequently known as Totem Lodge as there were as many as 10 magnificent totem poles built there over the years.

In the early years there were no roads to this area. To reach their property, the Hickoks and their guests had to take a train to Huntsville and then a steamer across Fairy Lake and Penn Lake to North Portage. There they boarded the narrow gauge railroad to cross over to South Portage on Lake of Bays.

That railroad, the Portage Flyer, was in operation from 1904 until into the late 1940s. From there they boarded another steamer which would take them to

The Portage Flyer – Aldine inside with Carol looking on - 1942

their destination on the lake. This was the only way to reach the cottages in the early years. Of course, it required having a dock that could accommodate

Aldine watching the Lake of Bays steamer arrive - 1942

a steamer, or landing at a neighbor's dock. It was also the way that people bought their food. A big boat would go to the docks around the lake where people would gather for their purchases. Birch Spring had a very long dock.

The first of the Hickok camp's many buildings is known as the Bat House and was the source of many

The Kodiak bear at the
Hickok's Totem Lodge

hours of fun for me and my siblings when the Hickoks were not in residence during the WWII years. They then built the main lodge with its wonderful old front porch and magnificent view of Dwight Bay. Housed therein are many artifacts amassed over the years by S. Rae's two sons, Ray and Alan, who were great adventurers and sportsmen. One impressive relic is the stuffed remains of what is thought to be the largest Kodiak bear ever shot. It is a grizzly that was killed by Ray Hickok on Kodiak Island. It is immense and looms over the dark room in which it is located standing some 10 to12 feet tall and weighing close to 2000 pounds. It is an awesome sight for both adults and children alike. Another heirloom is a stuffed lion that they named Stanley. He, too, was a source of fear and fascination for generations of children.

Alan Hickok, on a fishing trip to South America, caught a 20-foot marlin off the coast of Peru, not far from Cabo Blanco, weighing 1540 pounds. It is the second largest fish—a black marlin—ever caught. This is how the story goes. The world record was a fish caught in the same area two years before Alan caught his, and Alan's weighed 20 pounds more. Alan caught his fish at 9:00 in the morning and he continued to fish all day. On their return to land, the captain said that Alan's big fish had probably lost about 100 pounds through dehydration during the day. He suggested that they dangle it in the water over the side of the boat to allow the fish to reabsorb the water it had lost. Alan flatly refused fearing that the sharks might attack it. Hence, he lost out on the world record but he had the fish, and it now is housed in the Smithsonian Institution in Washington, DC. Photos of it hang in the Hickok cottage.

But it wasn't always a privileged life for the family. As a young couple, S. Rae and Justine started a business selling belts made of seal skin that they contracted for with Eskimos. While S. Rae made the belts in his garage, his wife went from door to door selling them. Ultimately their little enterprise grew to become the Hickok Belt and Buckle Company and, I was told by my brother, had 7000 employees at one time.

In time, their retreat on Lake of Bays became quite a lavish site. The family would arrive by airplane, a PBY amphibian flying boat, which landed on the water and drove right up onto their beach. What a stir of excitement there was on our bay when the Hickoks arrived. Their lifestyle was unlike anything else in the area. Justine insisted on formal dinners every night that were served at 6:00 p.m. sharp by their butler Sam and his wife Eve, the cook. Sam and Eve were great fishermen and came every night to the cribs off the dock at our old white cottage. Rarely did they miss an evening of fishing. Then they would return to camp to prepare their own dinner. The cribs to which I refer were the foundation for the old steamer dock that had been in front of our cottage.

The Hickoks had tennis and badminton courts and John Burgar, who lived next door, remembers parties there with glaring headlights and blaring music that went on deep into the night. Many celebrities were among their frequent guests. One, Al Rockwell, was owner of Rockwell International that built the space shuttle. Ray knew that even as a lad my son Tony was fascinated by aviation. During one of Rockwell's visits, in 1978, Ray invited Tony over to meet the great Al Rockwell. What a thrill for Tony. Prominent on a wall in Tony and Elizabeth's house in Tucson is an enlarged photograph of Tony with Al Rockwell's arm draped over his shoulder. Tony became a space engineer with Raytheon and a pilot, as was my son Kent.

Another visitor, definitely an eccentric, was W. H. "Boss" Hoover who was the founder and owner of the Hoover Vacuum Company. As he was afraid of flying, he would arrive in an elaborate 40-foot two-decker bus equipped with its own movie theater. I am told by Alan Jr. that he had at least 1000 movies on board.

Tragedy struck the Ray Hickok family in 1970. Ray and his wife Sally had five children, three boys and two girls. Holly, their older girl, was to be married and she and her parents had gone to their home in Rochester, New York to make preparations for the wedding. The other four youngsters were left up north with Dorothy and Charlie Thompson to watch over them. Two of the lads, Ray Jr. and Chris–a good friend of my son Kent–borrowed the family car one evening to take home a friend who had spent the day with them. They had a head-on collision on the old bridge at Marsh's Falls and all three lads were killed. The pall of sadness over that accident has never been fully eradicated. For many years, huge photographs of his two lost sons hung in Ray Hickok's cabin. The remaining children—Holly and Kimberly, both of whom I adore–and their brother Tom continued to spend time at camp every summer.

There was further trouble. Twice the Hickok company business expenses exceeded their income and the company floundered. And twice it was brought back to being a profitable company. Ultimately, however, the company was sold to the Tandy Corporation. Totem Lodge now belongs to the Hickok heirs who maintain its mystery and subtle elegance. For many years, Charlie Thompson was caretaker of the Hickok property. S. Rae died in 1945 at the age of 62. Justine died some years later. Ray and Alan are now deceased.

The next drive on the left is that of the Burgar family. It has a wonderful history. John Burgar has spent summers there all his life, the last 54 with his wife Carolyn. John's father, John Sr., was a sniper in WWI stationed in a very dangerous area of Belgium. He was injured and taken to England for recovery. There he met a volunteer, Queenie, who helped in his nursing care. Eventually they came to Canada and were married. Sadly, she died of flu in the '20s.

A kind woman by the name of Adda Berger (no relation) had a deep concern for the returning wounded veterans and decided to build a cabin to which veterans could be invited for rehabilitation. Adda was from the Welland area, a spinster and a school principal in Toronto. The place she chose for her philanthropic retreat was Dwight Bay. This was in the 1920s. Getting to her place required the arduous trip by train and steamer that I have mentioned. My brother, Murray Sinclair, who was familiar with the history of this area as well as being very knowledgeable about the Group of Seven—famous Canadian artists–told me that over time Adda entertained every member of the Group of Seven at her Dwight Bay retreat. It is known that A. J. Casson—one of the seven–actually did a painting of Dwight Bay.

John Burgar Sr. was a frequent guest at Adda's place and continued to stay in touch with her even after he married his wife Ada in 1928. (It is interesting that, just as Queenie had nursed John in England, Ada—John's second wife–had nursed John Sr.s' parents when they caught flu and died in the 1920s, as did Queenie.)

So fond of John was Adda, that when she died in 1933 she left her cottage to him. Additionally, she left $500 to each of his children—Beth, Mary and John—none of whom she had ever met. Young John's first summer here was in 1933, as an infant. He and I were born and began spending our summers here the same year—1933. We have been lifelong friends.

By the time John Sr. and his family owned the place, a basic lane off Charlie Thompson Road had been built. Still, while their father John was working during the week they had no car. Hence, as I mentioned earlier, the children were dispatched to the Keown place to buy vegetables and they either rowed or walked to Woodcock's store in Dwight to buy other essentials. Their water came from a spring box with a spout.

Above the Burgar's cottage is a roadway that has grown and been added onto considerably since its early days. Initially the cottage, now owned by the Ruscica family, was naught but the lean-to built by Mr. Keown. Eventually, the property was owned by two sisters, spinsters, the Misses Fahey who spent summers there for many years. It was a very simple structure indeed.

When they became too old to enjoy the place, the Misses Fahey rented to a Dr. Campbell. My sister remembers it well as she babysat for the Campbell children and she found it to be a terrifying experience. She was only 13 years old and there she was with two small children, no telephone nor hydro and beset by ghosts. She swears she could hear and feel ghosts. (Margaret Ruscica tells story after story about the ghosts who still inhabit the cabin. Margaret, who has owned the place for well over forty years, would not, for all the tea in China, pass a night alone in that cottage. She isn't afraid of the ghosts. She just prefers not to spend the night with them. She would often bunk in with us for the night.)

In time, the Faheys sold to a Toronto man, Ted Carr. He made many additions and refinements, including a stable with horses, and made it the place it is today. His family was devastated when they found out he had sold the cottage right out from under their noses, while they were visiting in Florida. He had sold it to Tom and Frank Ruscica in the late 1960s. Because the Carr family had not anticipated the sale, they had left all their clothes and food thinking they'd be back there the next summer. Margaret and Tom moved into a fully furnished home called Bay Meadow.

Tom built a big guest cabin in 1967 and a tennis court which he was very generous in sharing with the neighbors. I remember large groups of us gathering there on summer afternoons to participate in "daiquiri doubles." We'd play a few games, rotate off the court for a quick daiquiri, and then back into the game we'd go. The tennis deteriorated rapidly but I am sure the gaiety could be heard across the bay.

A friend of Frank Ruscica was John Candy, the actor. John had a home in Mississauga and had visited Frank many times at his cottage, as both were avid fishermen. He had his heart set on buying Frank's place on Lake of Bays, brought his wife up to see it, and a deal was struck. Frank, however, tarried too long at the cottage finishing the roof he was building and by the time he got to Toronto to sign the papers, John had changed his mind. As his friends knew he was a passionate fisherman, they discouraged him from buying on Lake of Bays. The rumor John heard was that the water in the lake, on a scale of 1 to 10, was only a 7—hence, polluted. Sadly, the deal was lost. Tom and Frank Ruscica are now deceased, but Margaret and her family continued to spend summers there.

The next lane on Charlie Thompson Road is called Millman Road. The properties that this lane serviced were owned by a family with three branches—the Millmans, the Mabees, and the Floyds—all from the Ottawa area. They lived way out at the end of Dwight Bay. They were very private and reclusive people who built simple dwellings right on the shoreline as there were high cliffs close behind them. Private property signs were everywhere and you may be sure there were no "droppers in."

Their privacy was intruded upon when tragedy struck in the early 1970s. This is the story as I understand it. Joe Millman's wife, while preparing a meal at her kitchen window, looked out to see her husband returning from a little fishing trip. He was alone. He stood in the boat to show her the size of the fish he had caught. She went down to the lake to meet him, and there was no sign of him. Nor has there been to this day. He simply disappeared. The search began. The lake was dragged without success. Then the RCMP became involved as there was concern that he might have been kidnapped. His profession was working in intelligence with the Canadian government. Eager to find him, dead or alive, they brought in dynamite thinking that possibly his body was stuck somewhere under a rock. Lake of Bays is very deep in that area. All their efforts were for naught. (It is sad to note that Joe Millman's son, Tommy, also died from drowning.)

As a child, I had gone with my family on picnics to an island in Rat Bay. Some people like the name of our bay—others loathe it. Apparently it was originally named Muskrat Bay but shortened for convenience, certainly not for esthetics.

Charlie Thompson decided this island should be developed, too. As he was a law unto himself, he bypassed any thought of regulations and permits and put in a causeway from the "mainland" to the island. Unfortunately, without a culvert to allow fresh water to move from the lake into the bay, a swamp has developed on the inland side—but a pretty swamp. This causeway was built in 1972.

Three lots were established on the island. Our cottage was the first one built–in 1975–so when Tony and I purchased our place on November 13, 1979, we were the only ones on the island. What heaven it was! All that space with natural growth, absolute privacy, and a profound sense of silence and serenity. Dan and Joan Poyntz were the next to build—an enormous place—and finally Treacy and Bob Canavan. We call our location "The Island" and most local people know it as such.

His peninsula on Rat Bay has grown beyond Charlie's wildest dream. Rat Bay has become a sight-seeing destination with boats coming from around the lake to see the many big new places on both sides of the bay, all of which have been built in such good taste that they feel just right. I am in awe of the wonderful people who live on the bay and on Charlie Thompson Road. It is a dream come true to live among so many amazing, accomplished, and kind people. Many of them—I can count at least seven families on our end of the bay—are year-round residents.

One wonders what might have been had Charlie Thompson not had the imagination and motivation to develop this magnificent part of Muskoka. From a simple farmhouse, he created an unforgettable area. Our cottage represents continuity in the lives of my children and grandchildren. They travel far and wide during the year, but they can count on our little place, Pelican Point on Rat Bay, to be there—just as they remember it–year after year. In 2011, National Geographic named the top ten places in the world to vacation that summer. Muskoka was number one! It has become such a popular destination for Americans that there is discussion in the Government of Ontario to create an international airport in Muskoka. What a privilege it has been to live in this magnificent area.

APPENDIX 5
MAP OF OUR AREA OF ONTARIO

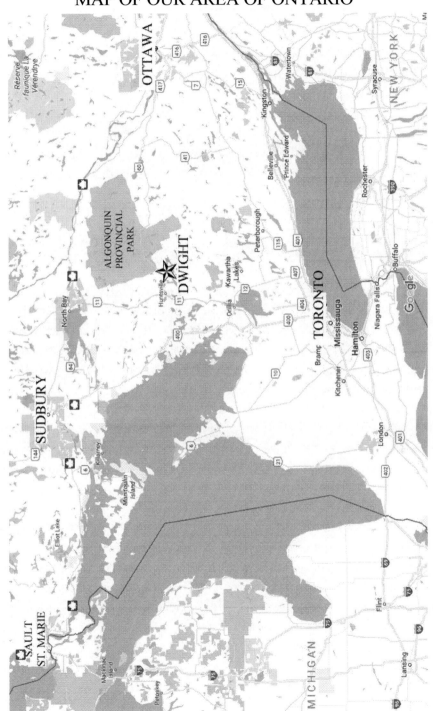

APPENDIX 6

NANCY MEISTER

I am honored to have a friend like Nancy Meister—a unique and generous lady, and a person who makes a difference in people's lives. She was our hospital counselor at University Medical Center when my husband Tony was going through cancer treatment. She was wonderful!

Possibly the most significant difference she made in someone's life was that of Alejandro Toledo. This lad was born into an impoverished family of indigenous peasants of Quechua heritage. He was the eighth oldest of sixteen brothers and sisters, seven of whom died in childhood. He was born and raised in the village of Ferrer in Perú in 1946.

Although his father wanted him to go to work at age 11, he was encouraged by teachers to continue his education by working nights and weekends. He was the first in his family to graduate from high school.

This is where Nancy Deeds enters the picture, along with her future husband Joel Meister. In 1965, they arrived as Peace Corps Volunteers in Chimbote, Perú—a city on the northern coast. Chimbote had grown from a population of 10,000 to 100,000 due to migration from the Andes to the coast. This influx of people was the result of the El Niño current having brought great numbers of fish to the region that could be used in the fertilizer industry, thus making jobs available to them. Alejandro had moved to Chimbote with his family when he was eight years old.

Nancy and Joel were looking for a place to live and work in Barrio San Isidro and encountered Alejandro standing in front of his house. It appeared somewhat better built than most as his father was a mason. It had, however, dirt floors and was without electricity or running water. They approached Alejandro telling him that they were looking for housing.

A small room in front had been used as a "tienda." Alejandro asked his parents to rent the room to Nancy. Joel built a straw mat "estera" nearby. The family welcomed the additional income. In the year that followed, Nancy and Joel recognized young Alejandro's enormous potential and considerable charm and taught him English at night using a kerosene lantern. They gave him his first book. Nancy and Joel became close to the Toledo family and even traveled with Alejandro to the Andes to meet his grandfather in Ferrer, Alejandro's home town.

Over time, they talked with Alejandro about a world outside Chimbote and encouraged him to apply for a local civic group's scholarship to study in the United States with the agreement that he would ultimately return to his own country. Indeed, he was chosen to receive a one-year grant. When he arrived in the United States, Nancy helped him get into the University of San Francisco's special program for non-English speakers. Nancy and Joel lived in San Francisco at that time.

Toledo went on to receive a B.A. degree in economics and business administration at the University of San Francisco by obtaining a partial soccer scholarship and working part-time pumping gas. Nancy had arranged for him to live in the home of two professors as a baby sitter for their two young sons. That job did not last long as the couple decided he was not sufficiently "polished" for their liking.

Toledo later attended Stanford University, earning both an M.A. degree and a Ph.D. there. After the completion of his education, he returned to Perú and, while pursuing a career in economics, entered the world of politics. The bottom line is that he earned the love and admiration of the Peruvian people and was elected President of Perú in 2001. He was the first indigenous president there ever!

Toledo has had a remarkable career, receiving honorary doctorates from 52 prestigious universities around the world. He has lectured in more than 30 countries. Talk about a "rags to riches" story! He continues to this day to speak out on the relationship between poverty and economic and social development.

Through all these years, Alejandro has never forgotten the significant difference Nancy's help and inspiration made in his life. He has stayed in touch with her and has visited her in her home in Tucson. She and her charming husband, Jay Book, live across the street from us. To my knowledge, Nancy never asked for any favors in return until 2006. She and a friend were hiking the Inca Trail in Perú. Her partner died on the trail in a remote part of northern Perú. Nancy needed support and guidance in arranging for his cremation. Who better to call upon than her friend, Alejandro Toledo.

A post script here is an incident that took place during one of Toledo's visits to Harvard University. He was at a restaurant in Harvard Square with Nancy and Joel's son Adam, who was a Harvard student at the time, when he recognized the couple that he had worked for when he was at the University of San Francisco in 1965. They were attending their son's graduation. The couple also recognized Alejandro and asked him how he liked his job. They assumed he was a waiter in the restaurant! Alejandro was proudly able to tell them that he was teaching at the Kennedy School of Government at Harvard!

P.S. My precious niece Aldine Meister is married to one of Nancy's two sons—Matt Meister.

APPENDIX 7

Sermon I delivered at St. Mark's Presbyterian Church
August 29, 1971

KNOWING THE UNKNOWABLE

You have just heard Dr. Sholin read from the 15th chapter of Matthew. Listen again to the 28th verse. *Then Jesus answered her, "O woman, great is your faith! Be it done for you as you desire." And her daughter was healed instantly.*

Faith, that so often defined and yet undefinable word. Knowing the unknowable.

Is faith necessarily a matter of belief in God, or in religious doctrines? Is faith of necessity in contrast to or divorced from reason and rational thinking?

Perhaps a Charlie Brown cartoon can help me illustrate some aspects of faith.

Picture Charlie Brown and Lucy and Linus lying on the grass staring at clouds. Lucy begins: "If you use your imagination you can see lots of things in the cloud formations. What do you think you see, Linus?"

"Well, those clouds up there look to me like the map of British Honduras in the Caribbean. That cloud up there looks a little like the profile of Thomas Eakins, the famous painter and sculptor. And that group of clouds over there gives me the impression of the stoning of Stephen. I can see the Apostle Paul standing there to one side..."

"Uh huh. That's very good. What do you see in the clouds, Charlie Brown?"

"Well, I was going to say I saw a ducky and a horsie but I changed my mind."

In this cartoon lies the paradox of the two possible approaches to God—that of doctrinal acceptance or of direct appreciation. Eric Fromm names these "rational and irrational faith".

The day before yesterday I returned from Canada where I had spent six weeks visiting with family in the cottage we have gone to since I was a child. And every summer we have gone to the little white church in the village. Each Sunday the minister tells a children's story after which we sing a hymn and they are dismissed for church school.

I listened particularly carefully last Sunday as the children sang a song we all have known since childhood—*Jesus loves me this I know / For the Bible tells me so.* This is an example of doctrinal acceptance. Children begin in their faith by believing what they are told to believe.

In the cartoon, Linus's visions have been preconditioned by a background of education and knowledge which he superimposed on an existent reality. In the same way, in the doctrinal approach to faith, a knowledge of the scriptures and dogma causes us to superimpose a mist of preconceived thought which may tend to conceal the true reality of God.

To Charlie Brown, the formation of clouds contains within itself the true reality— and his interpretation is secondary to that reality. This approach has variously been termed "the mystic or gnostic approach to God."

The poignant message in the cartoon lies in the fact that we are first tempted to admire the brilliant correlations made by Linus and to ignore the simple observations of Charlie Brown. How sad that Charlie Brown felt overwhelmed and humbled by Linus and quietly retreated. He felt terribly inadequate.

Doesn't this remind you of a Christian? Somehow we have been misguided into believing that humility and self-disapproval are synonymous. For Christians, the problem may be further compounded by the mistaken notion that God wants us to stop loving ourselves. Many of us feel so guilt-ridden that we see self-hatred as being the only way of dealing with our sins that will be pleasing to God. We tend to equate misery and sanctity.

God's love for us is neither partial nor tentative. It is not dependent on our good behavior, or even on our faith. He loves us, and each of us is of infinite worth in His sight.

Eric Fromm states that self-love is the ultimate basis for all love both of fellow man and of God. This was implied by Jesus when he issued the second great commandment: Thou shalt love thy neighbor as thyself.

Fromm tells us that the process of emerging into life, of waking up, requires one quality as a necessary condition—faith. And love requires the practice of faith.

To have faith requires courage, the ability to take a risk, the readiness even to accept pain and disappointment. Whoever insists on safety and security as primary conditions of life cannot have faith. Whoever shuts himself off in a system of defense, where distance and possession are his means of security, makes himself a prisoner. To be loved, and to love, require courage—the courage to judge certain values as of ultimate concern and to take the jump and stake everything on these values.

Love is an act of faith, and whoever is of little faith is also of little love.

In his book Love and Will, Rollo May tells us that in all stages of human development the experiences of love and death are interwoven. Love is a reminder of our own mortality. When a friend or member of our family dies, we are vividly impressed by the fact that life is evanescent and irretrievable. But there is also a deeper sense of its meaningful possibilities and an impetus to risk ourselves in taking the leap.

To Unamuno faith is the substance of hope, and hope in its turn is the form of faith. Until it gives us hope, our faith is a formless faith—vague, chaotic, potential. It is but the possibility of believing–the longing to believe. We must believe in something, and we believe in what we hope for—we believe in hope. We remember the past, we live the present, we only believe in the future.

To believe what we have not seen is to believe what we shall see. Faith, then, is faith in hope; we believe in what we hope for.

This was echoed by Paul in the eighth chapter of Romans which was read here the first Sunday in August. The 24th verse says, "For we are saved by hope: but hope that is seen is not hope: for what a man seeth, why doth he yet hope for."

Love makes us believe in God in whom we hope and from whom we hope to receive life to come. Love makes us believe in that which the dream of hope creates for us.

To Kierkegaard, either God exists or He does not exist. If God does not exist, it is idle to follow the arguments for the proof of his existence. If He does exist, then there is no need to illustrate the fact.

Possibly Christ himself wished to deny the rational or provable approach to faith when at the time of his trial he refused to perform a public miracle which he knew would forever remove man's need for purely subjective faith.

Knowledge without love, says Unamuno, leads us away from God, and love, even without knowledge, and perhaps better without it, leads us to God, and through God to wisdom.

To believe in God is to love Him, and in our love to fear Him; and we begin by loving Him even before knowing Him, and by loving Him we come at last to see and discover Him in all things.

APPENDIX 8

HIGH FLIGHT

Oh! I have slipped the surly bonds of earth
And danced the skies on laughter–silvered wings;
Sunward I've climbed, and joined the tumbling mirth
Of sun-split clouds – and done a hundred things
You have not dreamed of – wheeled and soared and swung
High in the sunlit silence. Hov'ring there
I've chased the shouting wind along, and flung
My eager craft through footless halls of air.
Up, up the long delirious, burning blue,
I've topped the windswept heights with easy grace
Where never lark, or even eagle flew;
And, while with silent lifting mind I've trod
The high untrespassed sanctity of space,
Put out my hand and touched the face of God.

by John Gillespie McGee

APPENDIX 9

GOODBYE TO TONY
Margaret Ruscica

You had to leave us Tony,
There was nothing you could do.
Your body was host to the dread disease,
That was slowly spreading through.
You fought it with such courage.
A lion till the end.
And everyone who knew you,
Was proud to call you friend.

This was your final summer,
And oh you used it well.
If despair was your companion,
You were not going to tell.
I'm sure that many, many times,
You wished there was more time,
But you didn't age and wither,
You left us in your prime.

There were so many pleasures,
Before the reaper won.
You held your grandchild in your arms,
Saw the wedding of your son.
I'm sure that as you sat there,
Alone beside the lake,
The thought of leaving everyone,
Was more than you could take.

I remember well the day you left,
It makes my eyelids sting,
You gave a jaunty little wave,
Saying, "See you in the spring."
We watched you driving up the lane,
I think we knew that night,
That for Tony there would never be,
Another spring in Dwight.

So you went back to Tucson,
To give it one more try,
Hoping for the miracle,
It was too soon to die.
The miracle did not happen,
It was not meant to be,
But you were blessed in one way,
You died with dignity.

One less burden for you,
As despair you tried to hide.
You died at home in your own bed,
With Aldine by your side.
She was beside you night and day,
As into sleep you'd drift.
And never did she weaken,
As she gave her final gift.

And so one day in January,
You gave up with a sigh.
For you the pain was over,
It was time to say goodbye.
But for all of us who mourn you.
Your friends and family,
We cannot help but wishing,
It did not have to be.

I'm sure we all fear dying,
Is there heaven, is there hell?
But Tony faced it bravely,
I hope I do as well.
So many, many tributes,
Came pouring in for you.
Donations, cards and letters,
The pile just grew and grew.

You were a very modest man,
Who perhaps would never dream,
Just how many people,
Held you in esteem.

I'm sure you're out there somewhere,
As I write these words tonight,
A man like you could never die,
You've just gone from our sight.
I hope that when the time comes,
To face our final days,
We'll meet again in spirit,
In the place called "Lake of Bays."

APPENDIX 10

REQUIEM

Under the wide and starry sky,
Dig the grave and let me lie.
Glad did I live and gladly die,
And I laid me down with a will.

This is the verse you 'grave for me;
'Here he lies where he longed to be;
Home is the sailor home from the sea,
And the hunter home from the hill.'

By Robert Louis Stevenson

APPENDIX 11

SUMMARY OF MY PERSONAL LIFE

- Born in Toronto, Ontario, Canada - May 29, 1933
- Early education was in Toronto at Oriole Park School
- Moved to Tucson in 1945 for my father's health
- Attended Mansfeld Junior High School in Tucson–1945
- Graduated from Tucson High School in 1951.
- Attended the University of Arizona from 1951-1974
- Married Anthony Kent von Isser (deceased) in Tucson in 1953
- Married Harold John Grieve (deceased) in Tucson in 2008.
- Mother of:
  Josef Kent von Isser (deceased) (Janice)
  Anthony K. von Isser (Elizabeth)
- Grandmother of:
  Tana Jay von Isser
  William Maxwell von Isser
  Josef Alexander von Isser
- Sister of:
  Carol Ella Sinclair
  Murray Malcolm Sinclair (deceased)
- On faculty of University of Arizona from 1977-1997
- Held Commercial Pilot's License
  (Flew across the Sea of Cortez a great deal while working as a bush pilot in Baja)
- Was a certified hypnotherapist
- Traveled broadly—to six of the seven continents (not Antarctica)
- On faculty at the University of Canterbury in Christchurch, New Zealand: 1993-1994
- Active in real estate in Tucson from 1972-1986
- Treasured summers with family at Lake of Bays in Ontario, Canada annually from the age of two months
- Loved the solitude and beauty of our high desert cabin near Arivaca in Southern Arizona, Rancho Escondido
- Adored my nieces and nephews:
  Murray Sinclair (1961)

Stephanie Meigs (1963)
Scott Sinclair (1963)
Ted Sinclair (1965)
Aldine Meister (1968)
Craig Sinclair (1968)
Christopher Sinclair (1979)
Candice Sinclair (1982)
- Godchildren:
  Stephanie Meigs
  Jenny Duffield
  Julia Greenspon
  Jeffrey Grynkewich
  Celia Ann Aldine Romaine

APPENDIX 12

SUMMARY OF MY PROFESSIONAL LIFE

Aldine von Isser, Ph.D.

EARNED DEGREES

Ph.D.	1974	University of Arizona, Special Education and Psychology
M.A.	1969	University of Arizona, Special Education
B.A.	1956	University of Arizona, Elementary Education

PROFESSIONAL EXPERIENCE

1997-Present	Professor Emerita, University of Arizona
1977-1997	Faculty, Department of Special Education, University of Arizona
1975-1977	Research Associate, Department of Special Education (50%), University of Arizona
1974-1977	Research Associate, University of Illinois (50%)
1974-1976	Research Associate, Head Start Program and Project PLUS, Tucson, AZ
1974-1975	Teacher-Educator, Department of Educational Psychology, UA
1969-1974	Project Psychologist, Program Development for Preschool Handicapped Indian Children. Funded to UA by the Bureau of Education for the Handicapped, Washington, D.C.
1974-2000	Certified School Psychologist
1967-1969	Psychoeducational Diagnostician, Tucson Unified School District
1961-1965	Classroom Teacher, Palos Verdes Estates, California

MAJOR PUBLICATION

La Prueba Illinois de Habilidades Psicolinguísticas (SITPA), 1980. Senior Author

This test was written in Spanish for monolingual Spanish-speaking children ages 3 to 9 years to assess learning disabilities. The senior author also trained psychologists in its administration and collected and analyzed statistical data in the major Spanish-speaking countries of the world. This test continues to be used broadly in Latin American countries and Spain.

MEMBERSHIPS

<u>University of Arizona Memberships:</u>

Friends of the University of Arizona Libraries	2005-2007
University of Arizona Graduate Education and	
Research Advancement Board	1997-2002
University Medical Center:	
Arizona Arthritis Center Friends Board	1996-2003
Department of Ophthalmology Advisory Board	1995-2002
University Medical Center Friends Board	1991-2001
President's Club—University of Arizona	

<u>Community Memberships:</u>

Board Memberships

Little Chapel of All Nations	1992-
St. Luke's in the Desert Board of Visitors	1996-2004
St. Philip's in the Hills Church—Vestry	1996-1999

General Memberships:
    Junior League of Tucson Sustainers
    Kappa Kappa Gamma Alumnae Association
    99s International Women Pilots Association
    Arizona Pilots Association
    Council for Exceptional Children
    Arizona Aerospace Foundation
    Pima Air and Space Museum—Education Committee
    Canadian Yachting Club
    Ontario Sailing Club
    UFO (United Flying Octogenarians)

ABOUT THE AUTHOR

Aldine von Isser lives in her home in the Catalina Foothills of Tucson, Arizona. She continues to be involved in her community and thrives on having her family living nearby. Her summers are spent at their cottage, Pelican Point, on Lake of Bays in Ontario, Canada. Her winter retreat, Rancho Escondido, on the high desert of Southern Arizona, continues to attract happy family gatherings as well as afford her time for solitude and reflection–moments she cherishes.

ACKNOWLEDGMENTS

Having been unsuccessful in staving off the debilitating effects of polymyalgia rheumatica, a painful inflammatory disorder often caused by stress with which I was afflicted in 2015 and from which I still suffer, I decided to spend a year at home with hopes that a peaceful life might help it abate. My dear friend, Howard Shenk, insisted that I needed a project to occupy my time and suggested that I write my memoir. I had never thought of doing so but, with over 70 years of diaries, I knew I had ample material to work with. Ample indeed! Never did I dream this little endeavor would become the overwhelming and all-consuming project that it turned out to be. I have both blessed and cursed Howard for his recommendation, but he did provide me with the opportunity to review my life and rekindle so many dormant memories. For this I am eternally grateful.

It would not be possible for me to express adequately the depth of my appreciation to my beloved daughter-in-law Elizabeth von Isser. From the beginning, she was enthusiastic about the idea of writing a memoir and offered to assist in organizing the project as well as in the final assembly of the material, the addition of photographs, and the self-publishing. My son, Tony, was a great help, too, spending many hours assisting Elizabeth and me in amassing hundreds of photographs from which I could choose. Elizabeth has an impressive facility with the computer and has been Johnny-on-the-spot when I have run into problems. She has recovered chapters I had written that I thought I had lost forever. Her acumen and patience are laudable. I merely wrote the memoir. Elizabeth did the work and spent incalculable hours making this publication happen. Thus, the finished product is Elizabeth's creation and I thank her with all my heart for her help, encouragement and wisdom in making decisions—and in making this a lasting legacy for our family. She is a beautiful lady and a remarkable and talented woman – and I love her!

My dear friend Ann Day jumped in from the get-go with an offer to assist with the editing. She has an uncanny command of the English language and punctuation. Ann has been my mentor and support throughout and there aren't words enough to thank her. Ours is not a long friendship but has become one of the closest of my lifetime. We met at one of Elizabeth and Tony's weekly Friday night cocktail parties and our connection was immediate. It took us both by surprise as neither of us is prone to take someone into our hearts as quickly as did she and I. The quality of this memoir is in large part the result of the many hours that Ann put into proofreading and being sure I had my facts straight. I do hope the final result is worthy of her efforts and the love and time she put into it. Ann's husband, Herb Day, is another of my heroes. A skilled photographer, he was able to rejuvenate old photos making them usable in the memoir. I am indeed grateful for his help.

Many thanks go to my friends who undertook the final reading of the manuscript. They were flawless editors. My beloved friend of 44 years, Magda (Misty) Urban, has stood by me through good times and bad, loyally and lovingly. That she was willing to be a reader is icing on the cake. She was my student during her masters and doctoral programs and has a Ph.D. as well as a great deal of editing experience. Not an errant comma gets past Misty! I have seen her develop into an outstanding professional.

Constance Bryden, a precious friend and remarkable woman, is on staff at the Little Chapel of All Nations. She is, in fact, a large part of its heart and soul. Constance is an astute reader and has even done proofreading for prisoners in incarceration facilities who write with hopes of being published. Her attention to detail defies belief. She willingly undertook a final reading and correcting of my manuscript, and I am more than grateful for her help.

An invaluable asset to a lengthy project is a precious friend who has been quietly with me every step of the way with ebullience and a wonderful sense of humor, as well as many scrumptious meals. Such a friend is Laurie Fenske for whom there should be a special star in heaven.

One more person has to be acknowledged. I doubt I could have accomplished this memoir without her in my life. The past few years have been rocky ones for me and Nancy Warren has always been there with encouragement, love and compassion. I "met" Nancy when she contacted me soon after I became a member of the United Flying Octogenarians (UFOs), an international organization of pilots who have been pilot-in-command of an aircraft after their 80th birthdays. She asked me to consider going on the national board (she was the only woman on the board) but I was unable to fulfill the requirement that I would be available via internet at all times. Nonetheless, we established a close relationship through e-mail. At the time of my son Kent's death, she was in touch with me daily lending her wisdom, love and considerable patience. I will forever be grateful for the commitment she made in seeing me through those and other dark days and months. I have never met Nancy and yet she is one of my dearest friends.

And finally I give thanks to my beloved grandchildren for whom this was written and whose enthusiastic anticipation of what was to come inspired me to complete this history even when the going got tough.

PHOTOS: MISCELLANEOUS MEMORIES

Alex's graduation from University of Arizona - May, 2015

Tana with D.J.

Alex, Tana & Max - 2016

Tana & Max's graduation from University of Arizona - May, 2013

Max's graduation from University of Arizona - May, 2013

Alex, Max & Tana - 2010

Tana with Nana – 1990
portrait by Kent

Max & Alex in Aldine's bathtub - 1999

Max, Tana & Alex – sleepover 1999
Aldine slept on the floor

Tana – portrait by Kent

Tana, Aldine & Max - 1991

Aldine's 60th birthday with grandchildren
Max, Alex & Tana - 1993

Tana – portrait by Kent

Tony, Aldine & Kent on Aldine's 80th birthday

Mother beside a portrait of my father in the library
of Little Chapel of All Nations

Aldine & Howard - 1991

Dr. Magda Urban

The *Wanda* – Lake of Bays Steamer

Pelican Point – 2008

Max, Alex, Tony, Elizabeth, Aldine, Tana, Janice & Kent

Aldine with University of
Arizona President Peter Likins

Four generations of Aldines - 1984

Interior of Pelican Bar – Treasure Beach Jamaica

Pelican Point – 2003

Tana, Janice, Kent, Tony, Alex, Elizabeth, Aldine & Max

Anthony Kurt von Isser - 1976

641

Elizabeth & Tony's chocolate
wedding cake

Original member of RBYC - Linda and Bruce Davey, Treacy
and Bob Canavan, Aldine & Tony

Hal & Aldine - Pelican Point - 2016

Aldine in Quebec - 1985

Cousins at dinner – Kent, Scott Sinclair, Tony Jr.
Murray & Craig Sinclair - 1960's

Gravestone of Anthony Kent
von Isser

Kent at Triangle Y Ranch Camp

Kent & Tony with friends – Cañon del Oro

Tony Jr. - 1959

A visit from my paternal grandparents, Bessie &
George Sinclair - 1953

Murray with his bride Ann
McHardy-Smith – 9/12/59

Tony with Hal Grieve on their motorcycles - 1946

643

Murray, Carol & Aldine with Mother - 1940

Made in the USA
San Bernardino, CA
12 March 2020